The Principalship

S I X T H   E D I T I O N

The Principalship

Thelbert L. Drake

William H. Roe

Merrill
Prentice Hall

Upper Saddle River, New Jersey   *Columbus, Ohio*

Library of Congress Cataloging-in-Publication Data
Drake, Thelbert L.
  The principalship/Thelbert L. Drake, William H. Roe.—6th ed.
    p. cm.
  Includes bibliographical references and index.
  ISBN 0-13-094133-6
  1. School principals—United States. I. Roe, William Henry, II. Title.
LB2831.92 .D73 2003
371.2'012—dc21   2001056285

Vice President and Publisher: Jeffery W. Johnston
Executive Editor: Debra A. Stollenwerk
Editorial Assistant: Mary Morrill
Managing Editor: Allyson P. Sharp
Associate Editor: Jessica Crouch
Production Editor: Linda Hillis Bayma
Production Coordination: Clarinda Publication Services
Design Coordinator: Diane C. Lorenzo
Cover Designer: Rod Harris
Production Manager: Pamela D. Bennett
Director of Marketing: Ann Castel Davis
Marketing Manager: Krista Groshong
Marketing Coordinator: Tyra Cooper

This book was set in Palatino by The Clarinda Company. It was printed and bound
by R.R. Donnelley & Sons Company. The cover was printed by R.R. Donnelley &
Sons Company.

Pearson Education Ltd.
Pearson Education Australia Pty. Limited
Pearson Education Singapore Ptd. Ltd.
Pearson Education North Asia Ltd.
Pearson Education Canada, Ltd.
Pearson Educación de Mexico, S.A. de C.V.
Pearson Education—Japan
Pearson Education Malaysia Pte. Ltd.
Pearson Education, *Upper Saddle River, New Jersey*

10 9 8 7 6 5 4 3 2 1
ISBN: 0-13-094133-6

Merrill
Prentice Hall

Preface

The principal of a school today works in a more fluid and expanding context than at any time in history. Information streams in from around the globe and from space, and we can access it at the touch of a keyboard connected to cyberspace. We can chat with faceless colleagues around the world on that same web of communication. The social circumstances for most of the students in our schools are very different from those a few years ago. Pressures are increasing from the business and political communities to produce students who will be useful to the economy. What an array of challenges and opportunities await the principal! Yet the greatest opportunity is answering the question of what is the right thing to do, as well as how to do things the right way. The ground rules that were in effect when schools were formed in similar, unquestioned molds are largely obsolete, leaving the principal to seek new views of leadership.

Although some administrator preparation programs separate courses for the principalship into elementary, secondary, and in some cases middle levels, we contend that the important competencies are common to all levels. We do not wish to reinforce the administration of "things" as opposed to leading a community of learners. We do want to emphasize the principalship as a legitimate career field of its own.

As an educational leader, the principal stimulates and uses input from all people affected by the school and in turn provides them with leadership toward the future. This book describes processes that are workable, responsible, and responsive yet not so rigid or brittle that they shatter under the inevitable stress faced by those who propose to lead. Examples of theories, principles, and practices are intended not to be formulas for success but rather to stimulate the reader to make practical applications appropriate to his or her organization and cultural, social setting.

The overriding message of this book is the simple but often neglected principle that student learning is the supreme reason for the school's existence. The principal's leadership is paramount. Organization and administrative details must be considered to be means, not ends. Yet those details are not to be ignored; therefore, we include many topics and issues faced daily by nearly every principal at every level. The principal works with teachers, students, parents, and the community at large continually to refine and expand a vision of excellence to be achieved. It is from this viewpoint that this book is directed to principals, superintendents, those who want to be principals, and those who prepare prospective principals.

NEW TO THIS EDITION

Topics new to this edition include the questions and issues all schools face regarding the implementation of IDEA 97 for special needs students; collaborative ventures with community agencies to meet mutually identified needs and the challenges of shared authority involved; full-service schools; evaluation as affected by the standards movement and high-stakes testing; and many other topics principals will face from day to day. Case studies have been added dealing with topics such as teacher morale, gay rights, and pressures resulting from mandated testing. The book provides the reader and the instructor a wealth of real challenges for a principal, which can lead to the formation of personal views of what are the right things to do as well as how to do things right.

ACKNOWLEDGMENTS

We wish to acknowledge the efforts of our reviewers: Robert E. Kirschmann, University of Bridgeport; Michael D. Richardson, Georgia Southern University; Nancy H. Stankus, Shippensburg University of Pennsylvania; Clint Taylor, California State University–Los Angeles; and Kathryn S. Whitaker, University of Northern Colorado.

We thank Dr. Mark Smith for contributing to the revision of Chapter 11, "Provision for Special Needs Students." We also thank Dr. Suzanne V. Drake for revising Chapter 12, "A Framework for Evaluation," and Chapter 13, "Evaluation of Individual Performance." We appreciate Dr. Donald S. Kachur's revision of Chapter 14, "Staff Development to Improve Learning." We recognize Nancy Roe Ingram for her contributions to this edition.

Very special thanks are in order for our wives, Suzanne and Vi, who once more managed to put up with us through the highs and lows of producing a work like this. Thank you for being encouragers.

T. L. D.
W. H. R.

Brief Contents

Contents

CHAPTER 13 Evaluation of Individual Performance   317

CHAPTER 18   Business-Related Management of a School   453

CHAPTER 19   Facilities Management   473

Bases for Operation

*S*ocial, political, economic, technological, and legal forces are dramatically influencing what is taught and how it is taught. Relationships with students and teachers within the schools and with individuals, groups, and agencies outside the schools are continuously changing.

If elementary, middle, and secondary school principals are to operate successfully in this dynamic setting, they need a solid foundation that will provide perspective about our changing society. In addition, they will need expertise in creating a community of learners, both staff and students, who can interact with each other and the larger community of which they are a part. Finally, they must work toward forming a responsive and collaborative school culture in a changing and vigorous society. The next seven chapters attempt to provide potential educational leaders with the elements of this important foundational base.

A Social Base for School Operation: Myths, Realities, and Perceptions

*G*lobal economic interdependence and competition, social values that seem to be adrift or at least up for continuous redefinition, and irresponsible acts of violence cause major concerns and too often a tendency to fix blame. The schools are frequently blamed for a situation, seen as the solution to a situation, or used as proving grounds for testing the strength of a legal argument—and occasionally all of these at one time. The principal of a school stands in the middle of this turbulent sea of expectations, blame, proposals, and counterproposals. Schools historically have gone through stages from preparing the young to withstand evil by teaching them to read the Bible, to preparing an informed citizenry for duties essential to a democracy, to being a place where young people from across the globe and from all walks of life are to be educated as contributing citizens of the United States. For many decades, the schools were places where children could learn things that could lead them to a "better life," better than that of their parents. People believed in the schools.

Today people express mixed views and feelings about the schools. Schools are still in the limelight as a solution to the perceived ills of the nation, but in many people's minds, schools are also a contributing reason for the ills. Preparing an informed citizenry should still be voiced as a purpose of schools, but preparing young people so they can help companies to be competitive in the global economy underlies the many calls for reform. The schools have been expected to prepare competitive workers for the economic machinery in an environment of rapidly expanding technology, information, and economic competitors. The schools have been expected to provide opportunities for citizens who in the past may

3

not have had a chance to be contributors, and at the same time have been accused of being used as a sorting device to include or exclude some from participation in the American dream. The schools also have been charged with the responsibility of teaching those children who began life with disabilities in body, mind, environment, or experience.

Mistrust and even confusion are growing among some people within and without the educational community. Can these sentiments be turned around? How did the schools get to this point? Are we in a situation in which "the public lacks a commitment to public education in general, and confidence in its educators in particular?"[1] Are the people within the system losing confidence as well? The questioning of the schools has become so intense that in 1996 Phi Delta Kappa published a book titled *Do We Still Need Public Schools?* The 2000 Gallup poll of the public's attitude toward schools shows a growing lack of confidence in the quality of the schools' work.[2]

THE SCHOOL AND A CHANGING SOCIETY

In 1932, Counts asserted that "only in the rarest of instances does it [the school] wage war on behalf of principle or ideal."[3] His thesis was that schools should exist not just to preserve and maintain the status quo or to pass on accumulated knowledge of the past. Rather, he proposed that teachers should lead the way to the utopian, better life. "We should, however, give to our children a vision of the possibilities which lie ahead and endeavor to enlist their loyalties and enthusiasms in the realization of the vision. Also, our social institutions and our practices, all of them, should be critically examined in the light of such a vision."[4]

Counts's controversial and dramatic statements in *Dare the Schools Build a New Social Order?* touched off a series of lively debates and discussions in professional societies and graduate schools of education throughout the country. The more daring participants were the "changers"; the more conservative, the "maintainers." For more than seventy years, this discussion has ebbed and flowed to the point that there probably is not a thinking educator in this country who has not participated in these debates. Unfortunately, these conversations generated much heat but little action on the part of the schools. Schools are bound to the politi-

---

[1] Roland S. Barth, *Improving Schools from Within* (San Francisco: Jossey-Bass, 1990), 11.
[2] Lowell C. Rose and Alec M. Gallup, "The 32nd Annual Phi Delta Kappa/Gallup Poll of the Public's Attitudes toward the Public Schools," *Phi Delta Kappan* 82 (September 2000): 41–58.
[3] George S. Counts, *Dare the Schools Build a New Social Order?* (New York: Day, 1932), 5. This publication was based on three papers presented by Counts at major educational meetings in February 1932: "Dare Progressive Education Be Progressive?" "Education through Indoctrination," and "Freedom, Culture, Social Planning, and Leadership."
[4] Ibid., 37.

cal entities that control and fund them, which often forces them and their principals into difficult and untenable positions. The changing composition of our communities, divergent values, continuing inequities, and pressures from numerous sources have resulted in many proposed political solutions. The solutions have ranged from withholding funds from the schools that may need them most to shifting the governance of the schools to political offices such as the mayor or governor.

Today we live in an electronic-immersed, hypermedia, hyperturbulent environment, becoming more and more globally interdependent. The dreams of better times for many have become hopes of being able to sustain what they have and not suffer further erosions of their lives. Medved notes that a plague of pessimism grips many people and that our children may suffer prolonged exposure to the dysfunctional elements of our culture.[5] The story has been related of a mother telling her preschooler that Grandma was very ill and needed a great deal of care. The child asked whether the grandmother had HIV because she knew about that.

THE FAITH OF PEOPLE IN EDUCATION

The people of our country have had immense faith in education—and rightly so, for the success of our birth and development as a vibrant democracy could be attributed to an educated, enlightened citizenry. Schools have always been a part of the American way.

Whereas in colonial America religion was a dominant force, as these colonies moved toward independence and statehood, education became a central unifying force of this civilization, the common denominator of life. Something in it stirred the popular pulse. More than three hundred years ago the colonists, on the bleak shore of Massachusetts, in spite of their privations, found the willpower and the means to create the Boston Latin School and Harvard College. Over the years, as early Americans married, built homes, and began taming a primeval land, their children's education was a common concern. From the little they laboriously took from forest and soil, they built their schoolhouses, paid their schoolmasters, and plowed back their savings into coming generations.

It was in America that the voice of authority first proclaimed that education must be provided for all. America was the cradle of the free public school. It was in America that universal education first established itself on a large scale. Here citizens of all sorts were the first to be forbidden to grow up unlettered and uninstructed. Here secondary education, as well as elementary education, was made available to everyone. It was

---

[5] Michael Medved, "Protecting Our Children from a Plague of Pessimism," *Imprimus* 24 (December 1995): 1–7.

in America that free public education was first used as the instrument for creating a constantly broadening middle class, so that all people might eventually be equal participants in the free, competitive, yet cooperative and productive life of the nation. It was in America that an educational ladder was first erected so that all people might ascend, from bottom to top, according to their impulses and talents: ascend, if they might, to positions of the highest leadership in arts and letters; in science, business, industry, and agriculture; in technology; in the professions; and in public affairs. It was in America that education found a new serviceability to humanity by dealing with the realities of everyday life as well as with the gleanings of the scholars of the past. Goethe, a German writer, once said that children are so brilliant that if they fulfilled their early promise, the world would be peopled with geniuses. But it was the unresting American spirit that contrived a system of schools, colleges, and universities designed to make Goethe's observation come true.[6]

The schools served our country well in this regard, for they gave the population the fundamental tools—reading, writing, and arithmetic—necessary for an enlightened citizenry. This was no myth. The public schools did spread literacy and general knowledge throughout the country.

MYTHS

The role of the common school was no myth in regard to helping build America through creating a literate citizenry. However, as our population grew and society became more complicated, and as public and private education became more extensive, a myth probably did develop. We are discovering that some of our fundamental beliefs are fallacious. Because the schools were so important in the building of our country, as society became more complicated—knotted with the problems of urban migration, breakdown of the family, crime, racism, poverty, and unemployment—people turned confidently to the schools and said, "They'll fix it!" Educators with a naive faith that more learning in school solves problems responded, "All we need are more resources and to get all the children for longer periods, and society's problems will be solved." But just more of the same was too simple an answer for the complicated problems. We deluded ourselves by assuming that a basic value system existed that could be a foundation for our teaching, that just sitting together in classrooms and working together in schools—the rich and the poor, the black and the white—would impart to everybody an under-

---

[6] For a more extensive development of this concept, refer to Chapter 1, "Education and the American Way of Life," in Lee M. Thurston and William H. Roe, *State School Administration* (New York: Harper & Row, 1957).

standing of and respect for each other and give each the ability and desire to become a citizen capable of making unique contributions to this great country.

Commager points out that it was most unreasonable to expect the schools alone either to fashion a new society or to solve the problems of national and world affairs. This, says Commager, is not just the schools' but also society's responsibility. The schools cannot and should not function as a surrogate conscience for society, nor should society impose on the schools the task of inculcating standards of conduct that it is itself unprepared to honor or practice.

> To judge by the experience of the past forty years, reliance on the schools to reform society and usher in the millennium by teaching social problems, or world history, has been an almost unmitigated failure. After half a century of exposure to world culture, world history, and world politics—most of it contemporary, of course—Americans turned out to be culturally more alienated and politically more isolationist and chauvinistic than at any time in our history.
>
> It is of course folly to blame these things on the schools. The responsibility is on society itself for requiring the schools to do far more than they could do and deflecting them from doing those things they had done well in the past and were prepared to do well in the present.[7]

Commager seems to be overstating the case by asserting that teaching social studies or world history has been almost a failure. Nonetheless, he makes his point. *We cannot blame the schools for all the failures of society.* The myth was that schools could do anything, and anything they did would be right. This just did not prove to be true! Many people have been disillusioned because they believed so strongly in this myth, or the schools have served as a convenient scapegoat to avoid examining more fundamental causes. It may be more accurate to say that more responsibility has been thrust upon our schools than they should accept, more results have been expected than they could possibly produce, and in too many cases, schools have assumed more than they should. An approach to dispelling this myth is to admit that the schools have been essentially maintainers and reinforcers of existing systems. Is this a cop-out? Were they really established and so broadly supported to build a new social order? Are we asking for "what never was" if we assume they can do so? Will the schools continue to suffer the consequences of unreal expectations, as have the much-touted Japanese schools now viewed as a "failed miracle"?[8]

---

[7] Henry Steele Commager, *The People and Their Schools* (Bloomington, IN: Phi Delta Kappa, 1976), 31.
[8] Gerald W. Bracey, "The Sixth Bracey Report on the Condition of Public Education," *Phi Delta Kappan* 78 (October 1996): 128.

HOW A BROAD-BASED CONCEPT
OF EDUCATION GREW

That this myth grew does not mean we should fault educators for believing so strongly in education. Believing that education could create informed, self-fulfilled citizens, schoolmasters tried relentlessly to enlarge the individual's opportunities through expanding the role of the school. As devoted citizens and educators, they accepted the challenge to correct a wide variety of social problems and, in the process, too often attempted to fill every void created by omissions of the family, church, and society.[9]

This broad concept of education was not developed by chance; to believe this is to do injustice to dedicated educators of the past. If one reviews the history and records of the various educational associations through the years and if one reads their pronouncements, one understands that thousands of teachers had a boundless faith in youth and their education—educators with visions and dreams who enunciated what the good life should be, who planted the seeds, who provided the vision of what education could and should do for a democratic nation. An example of this vision may be seen in the reports issued between 1911 and 1919 by the Commission on Reorganization of Secondary Education.[10] Its key report, *Cardinal Principles of Secondary Education,* completed in 1918, had a significant impact on education and schooling.[11] This report enunciated what the commission considered to be the principal aims of education: (1) health, (2) command of the fundamental processes, (3) worthy home membership, (4) vocation, (5) citizenship, (6) worthy use of leisure, and (7) ethical character.

In the late 1930s and 1940s, some of education's most prestigious and influential organizations conducted studies, followed by a variety of written reports and scholarly publications, expanding on this philosophy. The Educational Policies Commission of the National Educational Association issued the following reports: *The Unique Function of Education in American Democracy* (1937), *Education for All American Youth* (1944), *Education for All American Children* (1948), *Moral and Spiritual Values in Public Schools* (1951), and *Education for All American Youth—A Further Look* (1952). During approximately that same period, the Progressive Education Association was conducting an eight-year study of secondary education, which culminated in 1942 in a five-volume report, known as the

---

[9]   Charles A. Tesconi Jr., "Additive Reform and the Retreat from Purpose," *Educational Studies: A Journal of the Foundations of Education* 15 (1984): 1–10.
[10]   Appointed by the National Education Association and supported by the then U.S. Bureau of Education.
[11]   Department of the Interior, *A Report of the Commission on Reorganization of Secondary Education: Cardinal Principles of Secondary Education,* Bulletin 1918, No. 35 (Washington, DC: Government Printing Office, 1937).

Adventures in Education Series. The study was an attempt to gain greater cooperation between secondary schools and colleges and thereby obtain more flexibility in the curriculum. The general feeling was that the requirements of colleges and universities were causing the high school curriculum to be overly dominated by academics. A quote from *The Story of the Eight-Year Study* captures the philosophy and purpose behind the study:

> The school should be a living organism of which each student is a vital part. It should be a place to which one goes gladly because there he can engage in activities which satisfy his desires, work at the solution of problems which he faces in everyday living, and have opened to him new interests and wider horizons. The whole boy goes to school, therefore, school should stimulate his whole being. It should provide opportunities for the full exercise of his physical, intellectual, emotional and spiritual powers as he strives to achieve recognition and a place of usefulness and honor in adult society.[12]

Is it not interesting to note that over six decades later the concepts of student-centeredness, of authentic curricula, of the whole child—indeed, of the school as a total system—are still to be completely realized in many schools? The one "power" that appears to have been purged from the list is the spiritual dimension, though some argue that culturally derived, secular values replaced the spiritual dimension of yesteryear. Yet today we still read and hear from various political or social pulpits that our spiritual dimension needs to be cultivated and that the schools should be allowed to do their part.[13]

LEGISLATIVE AND JUDICIAL IMPACTS

As the idea of equal education and opportunity for all children was beginning to be accepted, many minority children were being placed in segregated schools. The 1955 Supreme Court decision in the *Brown v. Board of Education* case stated, "No state shall deprive any person of life, liberty or property without due process of law," specifically meaning in this instance that racial segregation in public schools violated the equal protection clause of the Fourteenth Amendment. The Court directed that the situation be corrected with all deliberate speed. As this case was being reviewed and debated, lawmakers and the public became more conscious of the constitutional rights of individuals under the first ten amendments to the U.S. Constitution. A dramatic explosion of legislation

---

[12] Progressive Education Association, *The Story of the Eight-Year Study* (New York: Harper & Row, 1942), 17.
[13] Rachael Kessler, *The Soul of Education* (Alexandria, VA: Association for Supervision and Curriculum Development, 2000).

and litigation followed. It became clear that the U.S. constitutional standards were applicable to state public school matters. In the late 1950s and 1960s, refinements were made in the implementation of the *Brown* decision. In addition, the U.S. Congress, urged on by public opinion, enacted the following landmark legislation:

> *Title VI of the Civil Rights Act of 1964*—This legislation, among other things, bars discrimination on the basis of race, color, or national origin.

> *Elementary and Secondary Education Act of 1965*—This act made federal funds available to local public education for the purpose of serving the educational needs of "culturally deprived" children in both public and nonpublic schools.

> *Emergency School Aid Act of 1972*—The act provided funds to school districts to help eliminate "minority group isolation."

> *Title IX of the Education Amendments of 1972*—These amendments prohibited discrimination on the basis of sex in educational programs or activities receiving federal financial assistance.

> *Education for All Handicapped Children Act of 1975*—Each state must provide a detailed plan for assuring all children with disabilities a free and appropriate public education.

> *Americans with Disabilities Act of 1990* and *Individuals with Disabilities Education Act of 1997*. These are updates of the 1975 act.

Compliance with these acts caused the schools to go through some radical readjustments in organizing for both instruction and administration.

REALITIES

We would be mistaken to assume that the idea of broadening the role of the school was completely accepted, by either the educational community or society at large. Throughout the years, persistent waves of criticism have challenged this viewpoint. Many believed the schools should limit their efforts to basic academic education. A major confrontation regarding these differences of thought was precipitated in October 1957, when the Soviet Union became the first nation to put an object in orbit by launching the basketball-sized *Sputnik*. Looking for a scapegoat for what they considered to be the United States's second-class position in a new space age, American opinion makers concluded that it was the fault of our schools that the Soviets had beaten us in space because schools were devoting too much time to extras and not enough to academics. They asserted that our youths' talent was being wasted, and the result was that we did not have mathematicians, engineers, physicists, and scientists with the skill and know-how necessary for us to be leaders in space exploration.

The unexpected achievement of the Soviets was attributed largely to their educational system. In comparing our two systems, the impression was created that public education in the United States neglected fundamental subjects, that we placed too much emphasis on "life adjustment" problems. These problems, the critics asserted, should be the main concern of the home and nonschool social agencies. A capsulation of the viewpoints on this issue can be found in *The Great Debate: Our Schools in Crises*.[14] In their preface, the authors of *The Great Debate* point out the gravity of the situation, foreshadowing the words in *A Nation at Risk*: "If we fail to educate the present and immediately future generations appropriately and well, we may lose the current conflict with the Soviet powers, and cease to be free to educate and live as we see fit. This is the grim prospect before us."[15]

A considerable portion of the "great debate" of the late 1950s was more emotionally charged than it was reflective. The criticism sent shock waves throughout the educational community. Educators were generally resisting the attacks and denying the charges, while the critics were illuminating and exaggerating errors. Fortunately, balance and perspective began to emerge. A few thoughtful educators, such as James Bryant Conant, through lectures and writings, declared that if issues are fairly presented and freely debated, workable solutions, with merit, could emerge.[16] As a result, through the tremendous interest in education created by this widespread public debate, an unparalleled opportunity arose to make some long-overdue improvements during the 1960s and 1970s. An example of the results is the Elementary and Secondary Education Act of 1965, which gave the federal government unprecedented power and, in effect, made the federal government a champion of equal opportunity in education. This act gave rise to dozens of federal programs that not only flooded the schools with money but also imposed a variety of mandates and regulations. Later, mandates were forthcoming without the funds to implement them, even though the mandates were add-ons to already very full plates for the schools.

TWO DECADES OF REPORTS

1980s

A further spate of criticism began in 1983 when the report *A Nation at Risk* was published by the National Commission on Excellence in Education. This work has been referred to as the "Paper Sputnik" because of

---

[14] Scott C. Winfield, Clyde M. Hill, and Robert W. Burns, *The Great Debate: Our Schools in Crises* (Upper Saddle River, N.J.: Prentice Hall, 1959).

[15] Ibid., iii.

[16] James Bryant Conant was no doubt the most popular and influential spokesperson about education in the late 1950s and early 1960s. He gave hundreds of lectures and wrote several books that were widely read by both educators and laypeople during this period.

the amount of attention that was immediately focused on education following its release. The report opened the door to a series of other national studies and reports. These reports came not from disgruntled or self-styled critics of education but from prestigious organizations such as the National Commission on Excellence in Education, the Carnegie Foundation for the Advancement of Teaching, the National Science Foundation, the Education Commission of the States, and the Twentieth Century Fund, along with a number of well-known professional educators and authors.

With so many reports and studies, and the intensity of the reaction, a situation was created that demanded inquiry and action. As a result, public education became an important part of the national agenda in 1983, 1984, and 1985. Governors and legislators vied with each other to recommend legislative programs to do something about it. By 1985, every state had its own commission, task force, and/or citizens' group in place, studying its schools and recommending various actions. A climate developed that encouraged education reform in both the local community and the nation at large. The broad message was that schools can and should be improved academically, particularly in regard to leadership, management, discipline, teaching, and learning.

As was the case in the *Sputnik* controversy, educators' first reaction was defensive because much of the press and public first considered these reports (compiled in the early 1980s) as attacks on public education. When careful study showed this view was not true, the tone changed. In fact, almost every report reaffirmed that public education is a key element undergirding our society and that it requires—and demands—public support. Therefore, after the first flurry of defensiveness, discussion and study ensued in the educational community, which led to many improvements and plans for fundamental reform. The preponderance of mounting evidence shows that those schools and educators who took the criticism constructively and mounted action campaigns to improve their product gained from the tidal wave of criticism that resulted from *A Nation at Risk*.

1990s

Time seems to speed up as world-changing events occur at a dizzying pace. Pressure from the economic alliances in the European Community and the labor markets of Central and South America and the Pacific Rim countries squeezes out fear and heated arguments for protectionism. Some East European and Middle Eastern countries dissipate into a state of lawlessness; political alliances form along religious and economic lines; technology and materials for mass destruction become the currency for economic survival—all this in the last few seconds of history. The ethnic and racial composition of the schools is changing. The fastest-growing racial group was projected to be Asians and Pacific Islanders, followed by Native Americans, Eskimos, and Aleut peoples.[17] Since then, the Hispanic population has increased and will soon equal the black population. Politicians have called for reform. The National Education Goals Panel—consisting of six governors, four administration appointees, and four members of Congress—formulated six national goals that were adopted in 1990 by the president and fifty governors. The panel hoped that the following goals would have been met by the year 2000:

1. All children in the United States will start school ready to learn.
2. The high school graduation rate will increase to at least 90 percent.
3. American students will leave grades 4, 8, and 12 having demonstrated competency in challenging subject matter including English, mathematics, science, history, and geography, and every school in the United States will ensure that all students learn to use their minds well, so that they may be prepared for responsible citizenship, further learning, and productive employment in our modern economy.
4. U.S. students will be first in the world in science and mathematics achievement.
5. Every adult American will be literate and will possess the knowledge and skills necessary to compete in a global economy and exercise the rights and responsibilities of citizenship.
6. Every school in the United States will be free of drugs and violence and will offer a disciplined environment conducive to learning.

These six goals have precipitated many state-mandated programs, often without resources or with only partial resources to implement them. For example, the local schools found themselves with added responsibilities for early childhood education and after-school programs within the same or nearly the same budget parameters. The Americans with Disabilities Act, which took effect in 1992, and the concept of "inclusion" for students with disabilities continue to stress the human and monetary resources of local schools. Calls from business leaders seem simultaneously to blame and yet look to the schools to win the brain race so this country can be competitive. Is it time for the schools to withdraw, to say no to the ever-expanding expectations put on them?

In October 1992, the National Education Goals Panel issued a second "report card," which cited complacency as a contributor to students

---

[17] U.S. Department of Commerce, *Population Profile of the United States* (Washington, DC: Government Printing Office, July 1995), 13.

and workers not meeting educational and work goals. At one point, the report notes that parents have low expectations in that they are satisfied if their children perform at the sixtieth percentile, while Taiwanese and Japanese parents are not pleased until their children perform at the eightieth percentile. The report also states that schools that failed to teach students basic mathematics skills by the tenth grade had low expectations of students. The question then arises whether the schools are unable to cope with the multiple expectations or simply do not expect enough of themselves and the students. Would an investment in working with parents as colleagues in the educational enterprise result in higher expectations on the part of all concerned?

THE TWENTY-FIRST CENTURY

Attacks on the effectiveness of the public schools have not abated. Pressures from many sources seem to encourage a balkanization of education via vouchers, home schooling, payment by results, digital divides, and privatized contract schools. Special interest groups create enclaves withdrawn from each other, each clamoring for a piece of the funding pie. Accountability has been limited to performance on standardized tests. Yet in spite of all this, as Tanner notes, ". . . it is all the more remarkable that the American people's belief in education has been so far unshakeable and enduring."[18] Even the most astute movie hero would be stymied by today's chaos and complexity. School leaders have a major task of seeing through the mirage of power projected by those who would influence the schools.[19]

DO WE DENY A DREAM?

If educators assert that their only responsibility is academics, they are denying the dreams and visions of so many pioneer educators who dedicated their lives to the crusade against ignorance, poverty, and social injustice, of those who strove so mightily for an educational system with an extended role in self-improvement and social improvement.

If a principal denies these dreams and visions, how can he or she be a true teacher or leader? Those dreams need not be abandoned, but it is time for the educational leader to become more realistic about how they are to be accomplished. This realism can be brought into focus by considering the following points:

[18] Daniel Tanner, "Manufacturing Problems and Selling Solutions," *Phi Delta Kappan* 82 (November 2000): 188.
[19] George A. Goens, "Leadership and Illusion," *School Administrator* 8 (September 2000): 30–35.

- As society has become more complex, schooling (learning in school) and learning, good and bad, outside school affect each other dramatically. Although educators have some control over schooling, they have but nominal control over the extensive learning going on outside the school. Good teachers may hope to guide the total life learning experience, but they actually have little or no control over it. Educators should help the public understand this point, not as an excuse but as a call to collaborative action.

- Many problems are major by-products of our society and the world economic condition. Schools should not shoulder complete responsibility for their assessment or solution, nor should they accept blame for their existence. Schools, however, as one important social institution among many, can and should take an appropriate leadership role and alert the local and state communities to the problems and then work with the broad community to seek solutions. In addition, schools must develop specific procedures for dealing with these problems when they occur in the schools themselves.

- The public school, as an impartial social agency, must be attentive to the wishes of all the people but responsive generally to the majority. Therefore, it cannot hope to please all people, and it will always be subject to criticism. A serious difficulty arises in determining the position of the majority as opposed to those of well-organized, vocal groups.

- The school principal, as administrator of the local school unit, is the one who faces the brunt of criticism on a face-to-face basis. Principals must accept this reality and understand that healthy diversity is part of the American way and is to be expected in a successful democracy. They must know how to deal with criticism gracefully, how to judge and assess it, and particularly how to use criticism to stimulate improvements in the school specifically and in society generally.

- The American public school is rooted in the history of American civilization, and at any given moment, it necessarily operates within the accumulated heritage of the society of which it is a part. When that society changes, when its values undergo a revolution, when technology and transportation shrink the globe in such a way as to make us economically interdependent, it is time for a reexploration and a restatement or possibly a reaffirmation of educational purposes. The roles and functions of the school must be charted for the future, albeit an uncertain and rapidly changing future. The new educational leader must look beyond the school and into society itself to form a vision of an appropriate future. The educators' dreams and visions must be clearly stated to the public, and the resulting conversation can be a collective vision for the greater good of all, giving specific direction for the schools. Educators must rearticulate, in a realistic way, the specific purposes to be served by our public schools. Further, we must indicate how other social agencies can help the school fill the obvious "voids" of society. Unless this is done, the purposes of the public school will remain misunderstood and largely unarticulated—the results of additive reforms occasioned by periodic shifts in public preference.[20]

In truth, then, education finds itself in a real bind: if it acquiesces to the idea that schools can do anything, right away schools become tabbed as failures because of social unrest, ecological disturbances, drug abuse, crime, poverty, family breakdowns, prejudice, hate, racism, and economic hard times.

Many well-meaning and some opportunistic intellectuals and educators have made reputations and much money by attacking the institution of education as a failure. They have blithely accepted and perpetuated the myth that schools can do anything and have used it as the basis for criticizing schools in such vigorous terms that the public, both liberal and conservative, often loses faith in them. The schools too often have served the purpose of being scapegoats for poor decisions in the political and economic sectors of our society. Some people accuse schools of being repressive, authoritarian, inflexible, dull, unequal, unfair, oppressive, and essentially middle class. The more conservative ones see the drugs, sexual activity, violence, lack of discipline, and test scores as symbols of directionlessness and failure.

IT IS A CHANGING WORLD

In addition to the myth about the infallibility of the school as a corrector of social ills, changes in society and education itself have stimulated new pressures, new approaches, and new value systems that create new leadership challenges for the school principal. Among these challenges are the following:

- Culturally diverse and linguistically diverse student populations in a society often accused of racism
- Changing work worlds to information and service industries and increased pressures from the business world to reform education to its own ends

---

[20] Nicholas Appleton, *Cultural Pluralism in Education Theoretical Foundations* (New York: Longman, 1983).

- Life- and property-threatening violence in communities and the schools
- Homeless children, drug- and alcohol-affected babies, and children born to HIV-infected mothers
- Use of test scores to determine funding levels
- Redefinitions of "family" and the resulting impact upon children.
- Parents' choice regarding where their children will attend school
- Community agencies competing for scarce resources rather than collaborating to use available resources more efficiently.
- Court-ordered responsibilities; decisions counter to the community majority

The emergence of the foregoing situations makes us realize that the simple community-power concepts of the past can no longer be unquestioningly accepted. More and more people are recognizing that many of the values and traditions that schools have transmitted are not the values and traditions of all the people. School-community relations programs often face the dilemma of whose set of values they should propound, if any at all.

The school principal must sort out these growing differences and develop new ground rules for leadership behavior. He or she must also come to know all groups, acknowledge their positions on issues, and enter into dialogue with them. The purpose of such knowledge and communications is to form unified support for public policy to achieve quality education for all.[21]

The school must learn to do business with all groups as well as with individuals. One thing is certain: it is the principal who ordinarily comes in closest contact with the groups that have special interests. In most cases, he or she may have to take the most heat and may receive the brunt of direct action from these groups. At the same time, he or she is in a key position to show that the school wishes to, and can, be responsive to all people, particularly if the decision-making apparatus is such that key decisions may be made in the local area or if the school principal is brought into the central administration's efforts to educate everyone.

It is an exciting, ever-changing world for the principal. It is a world in which the only constant is an increasing rate of change. Dare the principal identify himself or herself with such a world and make it real in the school? Can he or she avoid it? Is it not time to take the offensive?[22]

---

[21] Association for Supervision and Curriculum Development, *Preparing Our Schools for the 21st Century,* (Alexandria, VA: Association for Supervision and Curriculum Development, 1999).

[22] Kathy Checkley, "The Contemporary Principal—New Skills for a New Age," *Education Update* 42 (May 2000): 1–8.

Educators, particularly the school principal, have no need to believe they alone should lead the way to the good life for all society. Viewed objectively, this is a most arrogant point of view. On the other hand, in the face of the great problems facing our society, the educator needs to say to people, "The schools are one of the great and important institutions of our nation. Let's work in partnership to identify important goals of our society, and then let's work hand in hand in meeting them."

SUMMARY

The public schools have always been part of the American dream of raising each individual to the highest level of achievement possible. Dedicated schoolmasters through the years furthered the concept of the power of schooling as the "corrector" of the ills of society. Early in this century the notion of complete universal education was encouraged through a series of prominent pronouncements, studies, and reports exemplified by the *Education for All American Youth* series by the Educational Policies Commission.

Now, as our nation has matured and grown, social, political, economic, technological, and environmental forces are dramatically shaping this society, occasionally magnifying its weaknesses. We now see it is a mistaken perception that the schools alone should be held responsible for these weaknesses or bear the brunt of efforts to correct them, for these weaknesses and resultant problems have been created by a society with many diverse peoples and institutions. Children and youth learn so many things outside the school that the schools cannot control. However, as one of the important institutions of this society, schools can and should take shared leadership in alerting communities to these problems and then work cooperatively with the community and its other institutions in finding solutions.

FOR FURTHER THOUGHT

1. Do parents really want their schools to change, or do they want someone else's schools to change?
2. If we accept the point of view that education should get its sense of direction from the kind of social order we desire to create, what core values should we seek to build into our civilization? Should these values change or be redefined continuously?
3. As a principal, which do you think is the proper function of a school: (a) to accept the existing social order but appraise it critically with a view to shaping its future, (b) to accept the social order as it exists and hope it will shape itself, (c) to plan a new social order and

encourage children to accept it, or (d) to forget the social order and concentrate on academics?

4.   Who should control the power to cause or inhibit change in the schools?

5.   Are the changing conditions of our time such as to make it desirable and even necessary that we reconsider the function and purposes of education? Explain.

6.   Review the most recent sociological studies dealing with the status of the family in American life. What is the prognosis regarding the future of the family? How will this affect schools?

7.   List the seven cardinal principles of education. Are these appropriate today? How would you modernize them?

8.   List five to ten areas of conflict in the national and world scene. How do these relate to the task of the school?

9.   In 1990, the National Education Goals Panel issued six national goals. Contrast these goals with those of other national commissions or studies. Will the measurement of these goals actually create a narrower vision of the schools' mission?

10. Review some of the changes in our society's value system in the past two to three decades. Have these changes caused a difference in the way we operate our schools?

11. Will the technology and communication advances tend to create an elitism in the schools and society?

12. Debate or discuss this question: Was the legislation prohibiting discrimination following *Brown v. Board of Education* passed because of educators' influence or in spite of it?

13. Does the "It's not my fault" syndrome affect the schools? How?

$\bullet$ E L E C T E D   R E A D I N G S

Adler, Mortimer J. *The Paideia Proposal.* New York: Macmillan, 1982.

Appleton, Nicholas. *Cultural Pluralism in Education Theoretical Foundations.* New York: Longman, 1983.

Barth, Roland S. *Improving Schools from Within.* San Francisco: Jossey-Bass, 1990.

Commager, Henry Steele. *The People and Their Schools.* Bloomington, IN: Phi Delta Kappa, 1976.

Department of the Interior. *A Report of the Commission on Reorganization of Secondary Education: Cardinal Principles of Secondary Education.* Bulletin 1918, No. 35. Washington, DC: Government Printing Office, 1937.

Counts, George S. *Dare the Schools Build a New Social Order?* New York: Day, 1932.

Educational Policies Commission. *Education for All American Youth.* Washington, DC: National Education Association, 1944.

National Science Board Commission on Precollege Education in Mathematics, Science, and Technology. *Educating Americans for the 21st Century.* 2 vols. Washington, DC: National Science Foundation, 1983.

Ravitch, Diane. *The Troubled Crusade: American Education 1945–80.* New York: Basic Books, 1983.

Tanner, Daniel. "Manufacturing Problems and Selling Solutions." *Phi Delta Kappan* 82 (November 2000): 188–202.

The Principal: The Person and the Profession

A mother demanding to know what the school is going to do about the sexual harassment of her daughter on the school bus; two teachers fidgeting to get attention to report a physically abused child; electronic media personnel pushing into the office to get a sound bite for the six o'clock news regarding the student who attempted suicide—any one of these situations may be part of a principal's Monday morning. These situations are startling, but they actually happened. How are the persons chosen for a principalship prepared for these and other somewhat bizarre situations? By what criteria are they selected? Are there adequate induction processes for the principalship? What do new principals face when they find their name on the door leading to the principal's office?

One can pick up almost any professional journal or daily newspaper and find that principals are the focus of enormous expectations. They are to manage a school so that (to paraphrase Garrison Keillor) all the students are above average, so that the school is safe, sanitary, and scheduled to perfection. If a championship football or basketball team comes along, expectations merely rise. We have seen students' eyes light up when they see us—their friend, advocate, or surrogate parent. We have experienced the strong grip of a father's handshake when he silently acknowledged we had done the right thing for his teenager, and we have shaken the hands of students crossing the stage at graduation when neither they nor we expected them to be there.

A number of commissions, interest groups, and professional organizations have issued reports and recommendations spotlighting the school principal more than at any other time in our educational history. In essentially every report, the need for strong leadership is stressed as necessary to bring our nation's schools to a state of excellence. As the reports were read, digested, and debated, it became apparent that the word *excellence* needed to be more specifically defined. In considering this point, it also became obvious that the school itself, rather than the district, was the basic organizational unit for providing instruction. Examples of outstanding schools are those with a history of high student performance. Identifying these schools and studying them helped ascertain the characteristics that were essential to high performance. Common among these traits was strong leadership at the school level.

The emphasis on the key leadership role of the principal provides an unusual opportunity for the principal to become what he or she claims to have always wanted to be—a strong educational leader. On the other hand, for those who were just paying lip service to being an instructional leader but really gloried in the managerial detail, the times ahead may be difficult. In the past, the duties and the career role of the school principal (whether elementary, junior, middle, or secondary) have been a riddle of considerable proportion. By reading the literature, attending state and national meetings, and discussing the position with incumbents, one gained a mental picture of a professional person being torn apart—on the one hand, by an intense interest and desire to lead in instruction and learning and, on the other hand, by the responsibility "to keep a good school," the latter being the proper administration and management of "things." Black finds that school board members ". . . tend to prize a principal's technical skills, such as designing a block schedule or finding space. . . ."[1] If the board values management skills so highly, then the pressure to perform safely rather than risk change becomes difficult to resist. An eternal struggle seems to take place, and in the end, the strong instructional leadership role is too often set aside because of the immediacy and press of everyday administrative duties.

Studies of the principal's duties have been done many times. Generally, all of them reiterate what is already known: principals spend most of their time on management detail. Many signals that the principal should be an educational leader come from such sources as the National Professional Standards Board for Educational Administration, the American Association of School Administrators, and the literature dealing with leadership in the schools. But between the idea and the reality is this question: Will the powers that be allow the principal the freedom to be an instructional leader, by giving the time and support necessary to do so? Another question: Do the principals themselves have the strength, daring, ability, and inclination to be true instructional leaders?

---

[1] Susan Black, "Finding Time to Lead," *American School Board Journal* 187 (September 2000): 47.

FACTORS CONSPIRING AGAINST
INSTRUCTIONAL LEADERSHIP

Looking back at the development of the principalship, one is somewhat surprised that the principal has had a role conflict because of the emphasis on management. In earlier days, the principal in most cases was selected on the basis of scholarship and recognized teaching ability. Often the principal was addressed as "professor" because of being considered one of the learned members of the community. In fact, it is said the term *principal* was applied because generally this person was considered the best and most talented teacher, or the principal teacher. In most cases, the educational philosophy of the early principal was focused on "book learning." Children who were judged to be slow, disinterested, or in some other way different in attitude, ability, or background fell by the wayside. Nevertheless, some of the same leaders later took prominent roles in more progressive approaches to education, asserting that *all* American youth were entitled to a well-rounded education.

Following World War II, an unusual number of conditions seemed to conspire against the principal's instructional role. A major factor was the unbelievable growth of the school-age population following the war. Baby boomers filling the classrooms to overflowing, combined with the accepted idea that all children had a right to a good basic education, changed the character of school administration. At first, school administrators became preoccupied with building new facilities, hiring teachers, and organizing and managing the burgeoning student population. The school principal's focus became primarily managerial during the 1950s and 1960s. Longevity on the job was common, as was moving into the superintendency. These same principals-turned-superintendents became the role models for and delineated their expectations for the principals who followed them. As a result, the managerial model was perpetuated.

The community also tended to reinforce the managerial viewpoint. Parents and patrons dealt with the principal on managerial concerns and with the teachers on instructional concerns. Community people expected a well-run, orderly, and clean building, and teachers expected the same, along with the resource support to help them teach. The same expectations exist today, but one difference is the view of the principal and others that the principal is now responsible for the instruction and learning outcomes as well as a well-run building. In effect, the principal is considered the personification and communicator of the vision for what should be going on in that school.

Another factor was that not enough emphasis was placed on the principalship as an important professional career in its own right. Too many saw the principalship as merely a stepping-stone to the superintendency and believed that somehow if one's career did not make it that far, then one did not really make it up the ladder of success. Colleges and universities contributed to this idea. In many colleges and universities, the principal preparation program was swallowed up by the overall administrator preparation, which emphasized the superintendency. In fact, in many situations, licensure for building-level administration was something the student picked up on the way to a license for the superintendency. These programs tended to have concentrations on administration and management in contrast to instruction, curriculum, program, and instructional evaluation and improvement.

Pressures from the state and district central offices consciously or unconsciously pushed the principal toward a managerial emphasis via their demands and deadlines for turning in reports, following procedures, and staying out of trouble by reducing risk. When one allows experimentation in program and instructional practice, when not everyone is following the same prescribed procedures in the classrooms, when teachers and specialists make decisions regarding how best to achieve school goals, risk may be involved. It is much more "safe" to maintain a well-kept building, keep supplies on hand and equipment running, and turn reports in on time than to operate primarily in a more ambiguous area.

Superintendents rightly expect the principal to be part of the administrative team. The idea of being a leadership team member is encouraged by principals' and superintendents' associations.

The strength of unions and the increasing militancy of educational associations also pushed the principal toward a more exclusive managerial mode. Administrators were not allowed to be members of these associations. This situation created a labor-management mentality that made it more difficult for the principal to work alongside teachers as colleagues. Collective bargaining often was allowed to enter into the instructional/curricular areas. The principal was caught between loyalty to the central administration and loyalty to the teachers and students in her or his school. It became more difficult to solve problems as a team of colleagues. The attitude of "You do your thing and we do our thing" became more prevalent. All this made it easier for the principal to revert to the exclusively managerial role. Certainly, the managerial role was reinforced by the business community in that the manager held a prestigious place in the corporation and community and was the executive in charge. It is easier to evaluate and account for job activities dealing with things rather than with people. It is easier to evaluate accounting procedures than it is to evaluate activities dealing with ideas, change, and instruction. Unfortunately, this view is still prevalent today.

Regulations from the state and federal governments sometimes put additional demands on the principal's time. An example is the requirement that principals be involved in placement meetings regarding students with disabilities. The focus is on learning, but the time demands can be great. In addition, "the profession has become balkanized,"[2] with special programs or groups committed to this or that approach. It is easy to lose one's focus given the hyper environment of demands.

We do not intend to be pessimistic or devalue the efforts of the professional associations, administrators, universities, board members, and citizens by pointing out the difficulties that the principal may encounter in assuming an instructional leadership role. We are trying to be realistic about what the beginning principal may face as a result of the aforementioned history and pressures that may still be strong in the school and community. Administrators' associations, various state and national policy boards, school board associations, principals' associations, and universities are working to counterbalance the situation by making special efforts to place educational leadership in perspective through their literature, conferences, and preservice and even political activities.

An easy fix suggested by some well-meaning professionals would be to eliminate the managerial elements of the educational programs and leave only the instructional/curricular dimension. Such a deletion of the nitty-gritty would be irresponsible, in our opinion. The principal should have the managerial skills to lead a smooth operation that is well managed and organized.

A SOLUTION

Without question, the administrative-managerial duties need to be performed, and performed well. Schools must operate smoothly and efficiently, with proper resources provided when needed. However, on the basis of observing scores of school systems and talking to hundreds of principals, we feel that it is very difficult to assume that the principal can be a real educational leader and at the same time be held strictly accountable for the often number one priority of actually taking care of general operational and management details. It is refreshing to hear the calls for a reassessment of the principal's role. When realistic restructuring is achieved, organizational changes can be made so that proper management and instructional leadership function in harmony, but the central office will need to establish priorities and procedures so that management is servant to instruction, not vice versa.

Our solution is to have each school employ a services coordinator, who will relieve the principal of certain management details so that the principal has sufficient time to concentrate on the school's instructional

---

[2] Thomas R. Hoerr, "Collegiality: A New Way to Define Instructional Leadership," *Phi Delta Kappan* 77 (January 1996): 380.

aspects. The principal would still be the chief administrator and responsible for the building's orderly operation. With the services coordinator concentrating on management details, the principal could assume the rightful emphasis on being an educational leader. Chapter 8 details the services coordinator role.

Political and economic figures and professional organizations have made it clear that added expectations of the principal are becoming the priority expectations. As the decision-making processes move toward the individual buildings, as instructional means become even more flexible as a result of more freedom from time constraints and advances in instructional technology, the principal can and should become a leader of decision makers—a leader of leaders.[3] The emphasis will be on the learning that takes place, the qualities of life within the school for everyone, the excitement of being part of a group of people who are doing important things.

JOB DESCRIPTION VERSUS REALITY

Reviewing job descriptions for principals throughout the country, one finds the principal's instructional leadership functions descriptively in balance with general administrative duties. The following descriptors or criteria often appear in one form or another in advertisements for principal positions: "maintain open lines of communication with teachers, parents, students, and the public"; "coordinate parent groups"; "a good listener"; "a clear vision for the direction of the school"; "work with a participatory management style." Expectations for the principal's knowledge base are clear in statements such as "knowledge of reform, technology, curriculum and child development." One expectation reflects school-based decisions by stating, "Principal is responsible for the financial solvency of the school." Changing demographics are reflected in one of the criteria from a midwestern school: "Fluency in Spanish and English." In another, a description of the school notes that the student population is 47 percent Hispanic, 40 percent Anglo, 7 percent Native American, 5 percent African American, and 1 percent Asian.

The criteria reviewed emphasize communication, vision, and programmatic knowledge. Conversations with practitioners, however, indicate that reward systems for principals still give top priority to handling management detail, discipline, and evaluation. The aspiring principal needs to recognize that the management of things often becomes the base of credibility necessary to effect the visioning/improvement aspects of the role.

---

[3] National Association of Elementary School Principals, *Principals for the 21st Century* (Alexandria, VA: National Association of Elementary School Principals, 1990), 11.

THE SOCIAL SETTING

The social system or community in which the principal works has a major influence on his or her role behavior. Figure 2.1 depicts some of the forces that have an impact on the principal and in a sense shape his or her role in the school. By the same token, these forces shape the various positions within the school and the expectations of the actors who play those roles.

Each role in a social organization is viewed by those in every other role as having a certain set of expectations regarding the behavior of the incumbent in the role. Teachers have expectations of students and vice versa. Students expect certain behaviors of teachers and the principal, as do parents, cafeteria personnel, custodians, and all those who interact inside and outside the school. Everyone with whom the principal interacts will have expectations regarding the principal's behavior. The idea that the principal is going to focus on students and their learning may be tempered by another realization noted by Daresh: "When a person steps into the principal's office, he or she suddenly finds that the primary group of learners are adults."[4] If improvements are to be made, if there is to be a culture of excellence developed, teachers, parents, staff, and community members at large become the principal's targeted learners, not in lieu of students but to effect improvement in student learning.

New principals can expect problems if they accept the role of principal in a very complex social organization and plunge into their role perception of educational leader when those with whom they must interact view the principal only as a manager of things to support and protect the other actors on the stage. Marshall provides an example of how expectations about the principal's role and behaviors can cripple the principal's intents, actions, and effectiveness. Starting out with the idea of helping teachers by making frequent classroom visits and providing written feedback of observations, affirmations, and specific recommendations, he found himself the object of a grievance and a directive from the superintendent to stick with the approved form and procedure. He felt restricted and began to withdraw to the letter of the law.[5] The social system was in control. The principal's intent was deferred for the moment. Fortunately, that was not the end of the story.

In discussing the principal's role, Prestine notes "a turning of the role of principal 90 degrees from everywhere."[6] This description states

---

[4] John C. Daresh, "Improving Principal Preparation: A Review of Common Strategies," *NASSP Bulletin* 81 (January 1997): 4.
[5] Kim Marshall, "How I Confronted HSPS (Hyperactive Superficial Principal Syndrome) and Began to Deal with the Heart of the Matter," *Phi Delta Kappan* 77 (January 1996): 336–345.
[6] Nona A. Prestine, "Ninety Degrees from Everywhere," in *Reshaping the Principalship: Insights from Transformational Reform Efforts,* ed. Joseph Murphy and Karen S. Lewis (Thousand Oaks, Calif.: Corwin, 1994), 150.

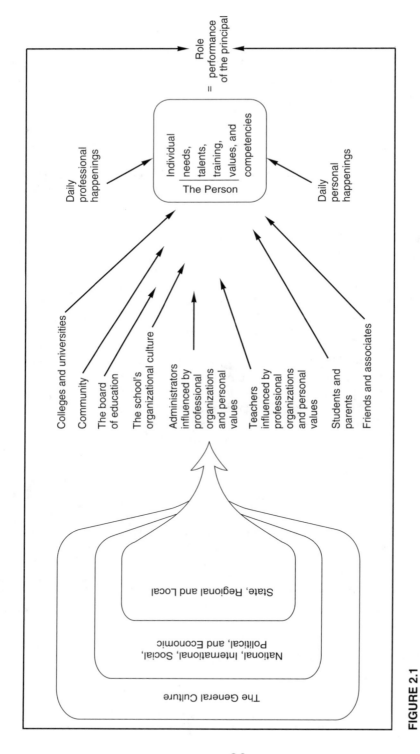

FIGURE 2.1
Influences of the social setting in shaping a principal's role performance

28

well the glass house in which the principal functions. Those glass panels are clear from the perspectives of those looking in, but sometimes they appear clouded when viewed from the inside. The task of clarifying those expectations, ways of doing things here, and the social ties and traditions already in place is a continuous and essential one.

The principal works as part of a complex social system. Systems theory and thinking is shifting toward a multiple dimensional view of human organizations. The school itself is a system within systems. To ignore this fact can only lead to problems for the role player and the school. Razik and Swanson note, "If schooling is to flower in the future, . . . [then] systems thinking is, indeed, a wave of the future."[7] Figure 3.1, in the next chapter, may provide some perspective on the complexity of the school's environment and the influences on it. There is another side of this picture, and that is that the school should be exerting influence on other community entities and viewpoints. Herein lies one of the principal's challenges. While it is true that administrators must be considered the servants of organizational purpose, they also should exert leadership to help shape that purpose within the various communities.

PREPARING THE PRINCIPAL

While the person in a particular position in an organization completely occupies a certain specified role and is shaped through interaction with the various elements of the social system, at the same time, as an individual, that person shapes that role by his or her unique needs, drives, talents, training, and various other capacities. A major question arises as to how we educate this individual so that he or she can perform effectively with minimal role conflict.

As mentioned earlier, one of the reasons that the principalship overemphasized administration and management was that in the past the training programs for principals were oriented in that direction. The influence of national and state professional standards boards and consortia such as the Interstate School Leaders Licensure Consortium (ISLLC) has shifted the language used to describe the preparation of school leaders. Taken from the language of a state standards board and the ISLLC, one principal preparation program states the following outcomes:

1. A school administrator is an educational leader who promotes the success of all students by facilitating the development, articulation, implementation and stewardship of a vision of learning that is shared and supported by the greater school community.

---

[7] Taher A. Razik and Austin D. Swanson, *Fundamental Concepts of Educational Leadership and Management*, Second Edition (Upper Saddle River, NJ: Merrill/Prentice Hall, 2001), 53.

2. A school administrator is an educational leader who promotes the success of all students and staff by advocating, nurturing, and sustaining a school culture and instructional program conducive to student learning and staff professional growth.

3. A school administrator is an educational leader who promotes the success of all students and staff by ensuring management of the organization, operations, and resources for a safe, efficient, and effective learning environment.

4. A school administrator is an educational leader who promotes the success of all students by collaborating with families and community members, responding to diverse community interests and needs, and mobilizing community resources.

5. A school administrator is an educational leader who promotes the success of all students and staff by acting with integrity and fairness and in an ethical manner.

6. A school administrator is an educational leader who promotes the success of all students and staff by understanding, responding to, and influencing the larger political, social, economic, legal, and cultural context.[8]

An additional weakness in the typical program for principals was that the courses were often separated into elementary, secondary, and even middle school, which weakens the power of the principalship as a career field. Further, it helped reinforce the already existing barriers among elementary, middle, and secondary schools. This situation is beginning to change, however.

Calls for changes in administrator preparation programs are heard from inside and outside the profession. A "nontraditional" program at Carnegie-Mellon University rejected the idea that principals are superteachers trained in curriculum and instruction; rather, the program stresses "business acumen, interpersonal skills and leadership talent."[9] Others call for a problem-solving approach to the education of administrators, rooted in practice like the programs preparing individuals for the medical or legal profession.[10] Still others suggest stronger preparation in instruction so that direction and leadership in the business of the school can truly be effected. Principals must be current and skilled in management practices, and their education should be rooted in the reality of the job. It is even more important, particularly given the increased interest in

---

[8] From a leadership preparation program of Indiana Wesleyan University, 2001. The reader also may wish to visit www.ccsso.org/standards.html for additional detail regarding ISLLC standards.

[9] Daniel Gursky, "At University without School of Education, Principals Are Trained Like Business Leaders," *Education Week,* 5 February 1992, 6–7.

[10] Phillip Hallinger and Joseph Murphy, "Developing Leaders for Tomorrow's Schools," *Phi Delta Kappan* 72 (March 1991): 514–520.

site-based decision making, that the principal be able to lead in the day-to-day craft and technologies of the school: instruction and learning.

SPECIALIZED LEARNINGS NECESSARY FOR THE PRINCIPAL

As noted earlier, many influences shape the principalship, including preparation programs. As this text is being written, many states have formed or are forming administrative licensure policy boards to establish licensure requirements that will affect administrator preparation programs. Most of the state-level policy boards will adapt the "domains" developed by the National Policy Board for Educational Administration (NPBEA).

The NPBEA, sponsored by ten professional associations, published a volume in 1993 outlining the knowledge and skill base for practicing principals. The essential domains listed are as follows:

Functional domains
> Leadership, information collection, problem analysis, judgment, organizational oversight, implementation, and delegation

Programmatic domains
> Instruction and the learning environment, curriculum design, student guidance and development, staff development, measurement and evaluation, and resource allocation

Interpersonal domains
> Motivating others, interpersonal sensitivity, oral and nonverbal expression, and written expression

Contextual domains
> Philosophical and cultural values, legal and regulatory applications, policy and political influences, and public relations[11]

The following learnings may provide a foundation of knowledge on which to build inquiry into and reflection on the behaviors and interactions occurring in the everyday operation of the school:

1. The principal should have a broad educational foundation, providing a strong intellectual base on which to develop a well-conceived personal philosophy of education, to give direction to his or her leadership. He or she should take the lead in an interactive community of learners by clearly articulating

---

[11] Scott D. Thompson, *Principals for Our Changing Schools* (Lancaster, PA: Technomic, 1993).

and living his or her beliefs, values, and vision regarding schools.

2. The principal should be thoroughly conversant with findings of psychology concerning the nature, growth, and learning that should underlie teaching methods and curriculum organization. How do students learn, and what implications do their different learning styles have for structuring curriculum, teaching, and experiences?

3. The principal should have a strong sociological background to understand the school and the school community as social systems. In particular, the principal should grasp how the sociology of organizations and a variety of cultures can contribute to his or her understanding of the people in the school's attendance area; the diversity of worldviews; individual needs of community members and families; and the objectives, roles, and functions of community and parent organizations and the resources each can provide the school.

4. The principal should be able to identify not only needs to be met but also the stakeholders and potential collaborators throughout the community who may enrich the services implemented to meet those needs.

5. The principal should be knowledgeable about the strengths and weaknesses of various programs and methods and skilled in effective ways to help the individuals operating them to develop improvements. The principal should learn the knowledge and techniques necessary for the supervision and improvement of instruction and have the skills to learn alongside the teachers in the process of continuous improvement.

6. The principal should understand how best to use auxiliary services such as those provided by curriculum workers, librarians, media specialists, health and counseling personnel, remedial specialists, and available community agencies dealing with related services.

7. Having a closer relationship with teachers and staff than any other administrator, the principal faces a more personal, immediate, and intense problem maintaining and improving morale. In addition, all principals should know the general element of good teacher selection policies and procedures and, above all, the process of inducting new staff into their jobs.

8. In regard to pupil personnel, the principal needs to know the technical procedures of handling admission, attendance, transfer, and accounting; lead in developing effective ways of assessing pupil progress; and establish methods of reporting to parents and accounting to the community at large.

9. The principal must see students as citizens and in so doing must be knowledgeable about techniques for working with students on a large-group basis, for developing realistic student government, social and recreational activities for the students, and civic contributions by the students.

10. The principal should be able to serve as coordinator, mediator, and arbitrator among the various forces that attempt to influence the direction and purpose of education in the school.

11. The principal should have a sound working knowledge of technical areas of the field—for example, school law, finance, budgeting, accounting, and information management as well as the technology to upgrade and support these areas. Without this, the principal will not be able to exercise the best possible leadership in teaching/learning and the management thereof in that the structural support of teaching and learning will be weakened.

ETHICS

We would be remiss to discuss the principal as a person and not to discuss ethics. As noted earlier in this chapter, the Interstate School Leaders and Licensing Consortium's Standard 5 calls for the school administrator to act with integrity and fairness and in an ethical manner. The principal, representing a significant administrative unit within the district, is in a highly visible position of leadership and faces situations day after day that can test moral and professional behavior. As noted in several documents, many day-to-day operational decisions routinely involve subconscious moral bias affecting behavior. Nothing is more shattering to faculty and staff morale than for their leader to be suspect regarding professionalism or integrity. Deviations from the honesty norm can quickly multiply in levels below the administrator, soon corrupting the entire organization. Good advice to the neophyte administrator is to develop for himself or herself a meaningful and ethical code of conduct and wear it as a mantle of personal integrity. It will help the administrator avoid the temptation of questionable action.

Rebore, extrapolating from Hegel's ethical arguments, indicates that ". . . if the decisions of administrators are not prompted by their core values, their decision making will be dislocated from their genuine selves and certainly will be manipulated by circumstances and whims."[12]

---

[12] Ronald W. Rebore, *The Ethics of Educational Leadership* (Upper Saddle River, NJ: Merrill/Prentice Hall, 2001), 74.

At any point in a person's career, it can be helpful to reflect on the relationship between the decisions made and the core beliefs to which one thinks he or she ascribes. If discrepancies appear regularly, the principles driving the decisions need to be examined. Some administrators have stated they cannot be a force for doing good unless they remain in their jobs; thus, serious compromises, not necessarily for the benefit of students or staff, were made so their jobs were secure. The operational principle at work seems to have been to do whatever is necessary to retain the job. Certainly, compromises may need to be made—sometimes at the expense of some basic belief. Yet one can go only so far in this regard. One should not compromise his or her integrity even at the expense of losing the job.

As peers and colleagues accept the principal's personal integrity, it helps and protects the person from innuendo and/or insinuations of improper administrative conduct. It becomes clear to colleagues what the principal stands for and becomes a model for behavior and decision making for others.

The topic of ethics in administration has been deemed important enough that professional associations such as the American Association of School Administrators (AASA), the Association of School Business Officials (ASBO), and principals' associations have developed codes of conduct. Although these codes are well thought out, they are no substitute for the individual carefully developing his or her own moral code as a guideline to determine right or wrong as unique situations occur. Obeying and following the law is not enough, nor is just conforming to the letter and even spirit of school policies.

Unethical behavior can take many forms. Flagrant violations, such as racial discrimination, religious prejudices, unjust treatment of students and employees, failure to honor an agreement or contract, and sexual harassment or physical abuse, may be more easily discerned. More subtle violations of ethical behavior may be favoritism to friends or staff members who curry the principal's favor or various forms of nepotism. The hiring of a spouse or relative solely as a way to attract or retain another person is a questionable practice. Staff or businesspeople who seek to do business with or retain business from the school may wish to give gifts or favors to the administrator. Special gifts may come at holiday times to teachers or administrators with the hope that the gift giver's children will receive special consideration.

An administrator may think it is politically astute or beneficial for the organization to pit one employee against another, setting up "straw men" to rally employees to a cause or course of action. Other actions may be similar but aimed at furthering the administrator's personal or professional advancement in a Machiavellian manner, in which the end justifies the means—examples include the manipulation of policies, people, or procedures to reflect more favorably on self and career accomplishments; self-aggrandizement at the expense of others; and disparagement of a fellow administrator or rival for professional gain.

Everyone wants to be considered loyal. Yet even loyalty may present a problem when one is associated with an employer or organization involved in questionable practices. One can cite many examples that are easy to identify as unethical, but what about the lack of loyalty to a profession, an organization, and/or a colleague whose ideas and ideals can be professionally defended? Is failing to support them unethical? If the colleague is in conflict with an organization that is at best borderline in its practices, is there a moral decision to be made?

Professional and social changes continually confront the administrator and present new problems involving questions of ethics and morality. To give these codes, laws, and policies a solid base from which to operate with some internal security, an administrator needs to personalize his or her own moral standards after prolonged examination of his or her consciously chosen conduct and what that conduct says about what the individual really believes. To examine and refine this process and arrive at a set of ethical standards for oneself requires reading, study, and reflection. Serious discussions with fellow students, professors, colleagues, and students of philosophy and religion are important to the refinement of one's beliefs and values and the resulting standards of conduct. When things get tough, "[y]ou've got to reach deep into your back pocket and get whatever it takes to maintain what you believe and stand for."[13]

A THORNY ISSUE: A CASE STUDY

The Applecraft High School, and the whole school district in general, appeared headed for a major controversy. Elaine Truegood, one of the high school teachers, told the principal that some of the parents had complained to her and to other teachers because they believed the school was honoring gay history month. She said Steve Smart, an English teacher, had placed a gay history month display on the school's main bulletin board and Tom Frank, a math teacher, had posted some statistics about gay teens on his classroom bulletin board. John Short, the principal, ordered the displays removed. Steve Smart protested to the union and the Applecraft Human Relations Club. He asserted that the principal's actions bordered on censorship. He further complained to the superintendent of schools

[13] Jerry Patterson, *The Anguish of Leadership* (Arlington, VA: American Association of School Administrators, 2000), 71.

and alerted the newspaper to the issue. Subsequent newspaper stories inspired a great deal of community controversy, particularly when one story carried the head "Battle Begins When School Forbids Gay History Display."

The school board and the superintendent supported the principal's action at first, but then began to waffle. They were bolstered a bit by an editorial in the newspaper that said in part that the issue was not an appropriate matter for union involvement and that the administrators must have the freedom to decide what materials are acceptable for display in their schools. The editorial went on to support the administration's decision. It further noted that the schools should insist that all students be accepted for who they are and should not give the appearance of advocating one lifestyle over another.

The controversy would not disappear. The union filed a grievance over the issue. The state Antidefamation League then hired a local attorney, threatening what they called a precedent-setting legal case. The attorney met with the school board, asserting, "You can't turn your back and try to pretend that gay students do not exist." He then recited a litany of situations where gay rights were recognized in public schools, citing at least nine states that forbid anti-gay discrimination.

An articulate local parent rose to sum up the viewpoint of the majority of the community. She said, "Gays don't need a display to celebrate their history. Their subculture is a slap in the face to everything that is decent." There seemed to be much support for this statement.

Some Considerations. Should a school be put into a position of either condemning or celebrating lifestyles? Is part of the principal's job to protect students from anti-gay violence and harassment? Does a principal have a right to approve materials posted on school bulletin boards, particularly if most parents and community members find them objectionable? Does observance of gay rights history month fall into the same category as black history month, Hispanic heritage month . . .? What is the ethical issue in this case?

SELECTION OF THE PRINCIPAL

A person beginning the study of school administration may have second thoughts about the principalship as a career after becoming aware of the myriad of conflicting pressures impacting on the principalship. The role will become increasingly complex as the more progressive states and school districts place greater emphasis on the principal and refine their personnel procedures to the point where they can select outstanding educational leaders for the position. Naturally, those school districts that maintain the status quo (and too many do) will fall further behind in the quest for excellence.

The selection of principals, at best, is less than systematic in most situations. Too often the somewhat nebulous words *image* and *fit* may be the most important criteria in the selection procedures of the local marketplace. This approach would place professionalism in a secondary position because *image,* in some cases, might mean physical presence rather than leadership credentials and *fit* might indicate political, cultural, and interpersonal factors. When the latter are the main considerations, the possibilities for strong leadership may be undercut. Even though the best candidate may be selected, the concept of leadership and initiative is often undermined if the new principal feels compelled to limit performance according to long-standing custom and local norms.

Dillon's study of principal selection noted the following criteria relative to the selection of elementary and secondary principals:

Elementary
  1. Leadership
  2. People skills
  3. Communication skills
  4. Clear sense of purpose

Secondary
  1. People skills
  2. Leadership
  3. Communication skills
  4. Character[14]

As noted earlier in this chapter, school district advertisements for principalship positions emphasize communication skills, with the ability to work with diverse groups inside and outside the school. The prospective principal will need to demonstrate these skills to enhance chances for selection. Here two dimensions come together in the selection process: "fitting in" and the interview. The interview is still the most important facet of the selection process because it highlights communication skills. King and Blumer note that candidates skillful in assessing what qualities are being sought can sell themselves into positions that may be a poor fit for them. They caution that ". . . candidates should

---

[14] William D. Dillon, "Public School Principal Selection by Indiana Public School Superintendents" (Ed.D. diss., Ball State University, Muncie, IN, 1995), 125.

judge their job interviews by how successfully they convey who they are and what they value, not by how well they might have been received."[15]

Efforts are being made to recruit and encourage women to prepare for and apply for leadership positions. Their communication skills, interest in continuing in an administrative position, and more years' experience in the classroom may be positive factors for women as school leaders. As a group, the leadership style of women is more interactive, verbal, and inclusive. The involvement of parents and other community persons in schools' operation would seem to require a more interactive, inclusive style of leadership; therefore, the selection process should include at least a hard look at this aspect of the prospective principal's performance.

If the school is to be a place focused on students' learning needs, the prospective principal should be able to demonstrate a commitment to the total student, from the perspective of not only eliminating "glass ceilings" for any group but also enhancing the possibilities for all students. Campbell and Lam sum up their perspective as follows:

> Gender equity must be put on the institutional agenda for the sake of the female and male students we serve, as well as the females and males we work with and employ. Sexism diminishes all our possibilities. If schools are a home to anything, they must be a home to human possibilities. They must be a home for us all.[16]

The potential principal should also be encouraged because of the graying of the principalship. One midwestern city faces the situation where 80 percent of the incumbent principals will be eligible for retirement in the next three years. As more communities tend to rate their schools "excellent" on the basis of the students' academic success rather than the schools' quiet, unobtrusive functioning, more local communities will soon reach that political moment when enough sentiment is built up to demand a change to academic excellence. When that happens, more opportunity will be created for the well-educated candidate with instructional leadership ability because the marginally prepared, management-of-things principal will then quietly fade away.

INDUCTION INTO THE JOB

Fortunately, preparation programs are including real-life experiences via internships and course assignments in the field. The internships vary

---

[15] Matthew King and Irwin Blumer, "A Good Start," *Phi Delta Kappan* 81 (January 2000): 357.

[16] Meg Campbell and Liane Lam, "Gender and Public Education: From Mirrors to Magnifying Lens," in *Gender and Education*, ed. Sarah K. Bilken and Kiane Pollard (Chicago: National Society for the Study of Education, 1993), 220.

from year-long, add-on assignments, to a regular teaching load, to release time with specific assigned duties for a period of time (e.g., one semester). Other programs rely on simulations and case studies to add a reality dimension to the program. Yet that first morning one walks into the office can be a very lonely experience, even though one is surrounded by people, telephone and e-mail messages, piles of paper, and a lengthy to-do list.

Principals' associations, state departments of education, universities, and independent principal centers provide help in the form of conferences, seminars, and conversations with those who have been in the same situation as new principals. School districts may provide mentor programs and workshops, material resources, released time, and moral support.[17]

The new principal (and the experienced one) should take advantage of the opportunities afforded by being an active contributor to the local, regional, state, and national principals' associations. Being a passive participant—that is, reading the journals and newsletters and listening to conference speakers—is better than not participating at all. Being a contributor, a committee member, a presenter, even an organizational "go-fer" will assist the individual on the job, in making contacts with others for ideas or perspective, affirmation or advice, and continuing growth. Also available are development centers or principal centers to assist the principal to assess strengths and weaknesses.[18]

The new principal might be fortunate enough to have a multisource feedback group (360° feedback), in which she or he receives feedback directly from several persons.[19] If not available in a formal way, the neophyte may wish to establish an informal feedback group to assist in the journey through the minefield of the first year.

Taking a position as an assistant principal may provide added dimensions to the induction process; however, the role could be a limiting experience depending on the assignments and the principal in charge. Additional discussion regarding the assistant principalship appears in Chapter 8.

In situations where no planned induction into the job is offered, the individual will have to shoulder the responsibility for making contacts with colleagues and reading the literature. Resources noted earlier can be helpful. Sometimes a new principal is simply given a key to the building and a list of employees. The person is then faced with an early choice: possible stagnation as survival becomes the focus or a carefully chosen path of professional development. The stress associated with doing the

---

[17] Elizabeth McCoy, "The Learning Needs of Principals," *Educational Leadership* 58 (May 2001): 75–78.
[18] A self-assessment tool is available at www.principals.org/training/04.html.
[19] David Giber, Louis L. Carter, and Marshall Goldsmith, *Linkage Inc.'s Best Practices in Leadership Development Handbook* (San Francisco: Jossey-Bass, 2000), 44.

job at the same time one is trying to figure out what the job is can take a toll unless one is prepared. It is helpful, then, to have examined and articulated one's beliefs and values about schools, teachers, students, and learning. Armed with beginning views of what is important, the refinements through reflection will help steer the neophyte through some of the whitewater experiences that are inevitable.

SUMMARY

Principals are the focus of enormous expectations as research and reports have stressed that their educational leadership ability is an important key to bringing U.S. schools to a state of excellence. Very often principals feel as if they face a dilemma as management duties interfere with educational leadership. This concern is real because role expectations of the school and community may often shape the principal's activities, with emphasis on managing people and things. However, a carefully selected principal candidate, properly prepared and motivated, can run a well-managed school and still consider and effect educational leadership as his or her major function.

In recent years, departments of education, professional associations, policy boards, and colleges and universities have engaged in a significant amount of study, research, and field testing in an attempt to identify the characteristics of outstanding schools and the competencies of effective, high-performing principals. A number of state and national centers have been established to help upgrade principal competencies in light of this research. Licensure requirements are changing to reflect these domains or competencies.

FOR FURTHER THOUGHT

1. In general, which is the most important influence in bringing about educational changes: educational leaders and statesmen or changes in the economic, social, and political conditions of the times?
2. To what extent should a school faculty, parents, or students be involved in the selection of a new principal? Develop a plan for the selection process and defend it.
3. Present arguments for and against specialized education for administrators in general versus specialized education for principals. Is it a matter of emphasis?
4. Identify and discuss the specific licensure requirements for the position of principal in your state. Is the emphasis on leadership or administration? How different are the requirements from those for the position of superintendent?

5. Compare the traits of successful and unsuccessful administrators.
6. In your state, what are the resources available for assessing/predicting administrative leadership potential? (For example, are there assessment centers, institutes, district-based development programs . . .?)
7. What are the personal qualities you believe a school principal should have? Can you defend your beliefs on the basis of objective evidence?

SELECTED READINGS

Black, Susan. "Finding Time to Lead." *American School Board Journal* 187 (September 2000): 46–48.

Giber, David, Louis L. Carter, and Marshall Goldsmith. *Linkage Inc.'s Best Practices in Leadership Development Handbook.* San Francisco: Jossey-Bass, 2000.

Gursky, Daniel. "At University without School of Education, Principals Are Trained Like Business Leaders." *Education Week,* 5 February 1992, 6–7.

Hallinger, Phillip, and Joseph Murphy. "Developing Leaders for Tomorrow's Schools." *Phi Delta Kappan* 72 (March 1991): 514–520.

King, Matthew, and Irwin Blumer. "A Good Start." *Phi Delta Kappan* 87 (January 2000): 356–360.

McCoy, Elizabeth. "The Learning Needs of Principals." *Educational Leadership* 58 (May 2001): 75–78.

Rebore, Ronald W. *The Ethics of Educational Leadership.* Upper Saddle River, NJ: Merrill/Prentice Hall, 2001.

CHAPTER 3

The School and Its Communities

*I*ncessant and insistent technological voices are available to students, teachers, parents, and taxpayers, locally and globally, and opinions expressed via various media as well as in cyberspace influence decisions about schools. The idea of the school as an academic island existing apart from the more turbulent community or societal mainland has never been the reality. Certainly, it is not the reality today! The public school is only one of many activities and perceived problems in any community. Education is so complex that it is accomplished through a number of institutions, agencies, and activities, of which the formally organized public school is only one important agency. Collaboration among all agencies of community life is essential to the realization of desirable educational outcomes.

The American public school began as an extension of the home and local community, through a specific delegation of power to each state by a public act of the citizens. Because of this delegation, a partnership was created between the parent and the school, necessitating the active interest and intelligent participation of parents in the education program. From 1642 to today, this partnership concept has been expressed in statutes, judicial decisions, and writings. The partnership is safeguarded by local community control of the education activity through the election of a school board. In some schools, parents of children and other citizens participate, to a limited degree, through formal association; in other schools, they participate more extensively through advisory and/or school-based management councils, adopt-a-school programs, business-school partnership programs, programs providing coworkers and resource persons for classrooms, and similar school-community agencies and organizations.

THE SCHOOL AS PART OF CIVIL GOVERNMENT

From the local and sometimes the state community perspectives, the public school is a part of the civil government, which consists of public works, public health and safety, recreation, social welfare, and education. In addition, making up the community in a less structured way are churches; voluntary cultural, social, recreational, and welfare agencies; and various economic activities. To the people in the community, all these activities are important, although some will appear in stronger focus at different times, depending on the people involved and the problems that confront them. To complicate the community forces even more, none of these institutions or organizations is self-sufficient within the community itself; all are subject to strong regional, state, and national influences. Thus, public education is a part of an intricate complex. There must be collaborative efforts with all because in most cases the school's activities overlap considerably with those of these agencies; the school must be sensitive to all because its well-being as a social institution is dependent on their goodwill. Finally, the school must compete with all of these other agencies for the general support of the public.

The influence of the community on the school and the school on the community is a continuous interactive process. The school's influence on the community is more subtle, long-term, and indirect. The community's influence on the school, however, is far from subtle. Figure 3.1 illustrates the various sources of these mutual influences on the community and public education.

As the agency charged with the responsibility of educating the community's children and youth, the school finds itself subject to the stresses and strains of every organized and unorganized activity within the community. It is under parental and general adult scrutiny at every point, which places the principal and the school staff in a very sensitive position. While some are inclined to resent the community's intrusion on the school, the enlightened principal accepts this interest as natural for an institution as important as the public school. Rather than resent, fight, or disregard it, the successful school administrator will involve the school as fully as practical in community affairs and the community as fully as practical in school affairs. The partnership of the school and the local community is a reality created over the years by custom, legislation, and judicial opinion; it is not just something that ought to be done.

PRINCIPLES

The following principles will provide a firm base on which an administrator may evaluate and plan the school's relationships with its community.

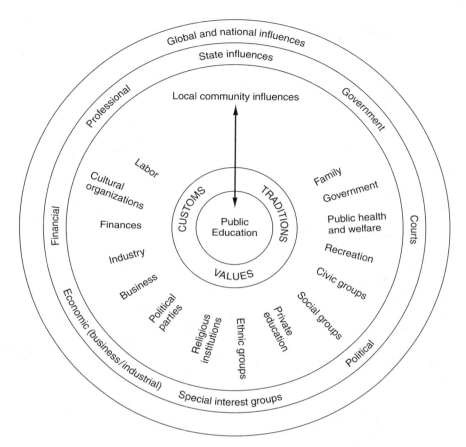

FIGURE 3.1
Influences on public education

First, the process of education extends beyond the walls of the formally organized public school. The influences of outside forces are so important that close cooperation with other community agencies, institutions, and organizations is essential to the development of a sound educational program and to the best utilization of available resources.

Second, the U.S. public school reflects the cultural milieu of which it is a part. It is responsible not only for conserving the useful past but also for preparing the way for progress and change. It must be attentive to the wishes of all the people. Because it must generally operate by consensus, it will always be subject to criticisms, particularly from the extremes of almost any continuum one could identify (economic, religious, humanities, etc.).

Finally, through legal delegation of power, the U.S. public school represents a partnership among the people, the community, and the state; therefore, the school, in a sense, is an extension of the home, the local community, and the state. As such, it requires the active and intelligent participation of parents and patrons in conversations about and direct work in the educational program. In turn, the school must continually inform the people of conditions, purposes, and needs of the educational program.

WHAT IS A COMMUNITY?

In the foregoing discussion of the school and the community, the term *community* has been used in a very broad sense, with city and town governmental limits generally establishing the boundaries of the community. In the twenty-first century, these boundaries are becoming more porous as access to global information, opinions, and viewpoints is so widely available. The concept of community is as elusive as a drop of mercury on a marble tabletop. Sociologists are continually trying to define it in numerous studies that have given us insights into the relationships among people, their group behaviors, and the decision process in communities. *Community* can be defined in scores of ways. Probably almost as many different definitions could be found for *social system* and *institution*. The more one studies the research and writing, the more obvious it becomes that it is almost impossible to define precisely what a community is compared with a social system compared with an institution. The possibility of such diversity of definitions is not meant to confuse but rather to show that a community is not the simplistic phenomenon that many would believe. The precise issue is to alert scholars of education to the complexity of clustering and labeling people, their activities, and their organizations. A vast variety of possibilities exists, depending on one's perspective and purpose.

Communities have been studied from the viewpoints of space, population groupings, shared institutions and values, interactions among local people, power structures, ethnic structures, and social systems.[1] Some authors cite the territorial system view of the community, which serves as a framework in which the "game" of education can take place in a territory bounded by a district but not closed either socially or politically. Much of the literature stresses the concept of the community as a social system. A system contains components, has a definite boundary, receives inputs over which it may or may not have control, and releases outputs into another system(s). Community has been viewed as being made up of several systems, and in turn those social systems may be

---

[1] For a review of these perspectives of community, see Roland F. Warren, *The Community in America*, 2d ed. (Chicago: Rand McNally, 1972), 21–52.

made up of subsystems.[2] Today those systems appear more interdependent, and in the case of schools, they seem more vulnerable to outside influences such as the courts, government agencies, or special interest groups.

Some books on school administration identify the community generally as the governmental unit known as the school district and then consider the interacting units within these boundaries as social systems. When attempting to analyze the individual's role within this system, they often refer to Getzels and Guba's idea that the organizational (nomothetic) and personal (idiographic) dimensions of social behavior interact in such a way as to affect the behaviors of the person in the organization.

A person within a social system (administrator, teacher, or student) makes a decision or performs an act. Based on the Getzels-Guba model, this act or action is conceived as deriving from both the nomothetic and the idiographic dimensions. In other words, one may say that behavior in the school is a function of the role the community and the school expect of the person and his or her personality as defined by a needs disposition.

Although this model has provided a useful way of reflecting on the particular behavior of an administrator, teacher, or student, unless carefully explained it is in itself too simplistic. The assumption is too often made, when considering the normative or nomothetic dimensions, that only one institution—the school—influences the role. Thus, the situation becomes static rather than dynamic. The fact is, for any given person, many institutions of which he or she is a part at that particular time—the church, political party, social clubs, ethnic group, communities, professional organizations—impact role. Influence on behavior is dynamic and ever changing.

The same may be said for the idiographic dimension, which is often seen as a static condition of personality based on past experiences and influences. These influences are very important. However, present-day influences (friends, accidents, unusual experiences, etc.) may change personality and behavior drastically at any given time.[3]

Since these works considering the influences on behavior were written, it has become clear that many communities with which a person interacts affect that person's behavior in the various roles played within those communities. Although we do not intend in this chapter to treat institutions, social systems, and communities in detail and in as disciplined a way as the foregoing studies, we recommend studying these areas as appropriate in the preparation program of every principal.

---

[2] Nicklas Luhmann, *The Differentiation of Society* (New York: Columbia University Press, 1982).

[3] J. W. Getzels, "The Communities of Education," *Teachers College Record* 80 (May 1978): 659–682.

Because *community* implies people, relationships, and shared interests and values and is more personal than the terms *system* and *institution*, we will use *community* as we discuss an analysis of the way people relate to each other in the school. Our definition of *community* in this sense is simple: a group of people conscious of a collective identity through common physical, cognitive, and affective educational relationships. On the basis of this definition, several communities can exist within a broader school community. Each individual within the school community may well represent a variety of different communities, all of which makes the school community a complex network of shared values and expectations.

THE SCHOOL'S COMMUNITY

Each individual school is part of a larger school community known as the school district, which is the governing unit for all of the public schools in the district. The school principal is most immediately concerned with that portion of the community that is part of his or her school. Within the broad school community (the district), he or she shares a limited leadership responsibility with the superintendent of schools, the central office staff, and other school principals. The principal of the neighborhood school becomes the most logical first contact about education for those parents and citizens who live in that neighborhood or attendance area. The boundaries of this more limited community are determined by the general attendance area of the school itself. All citizens living in this attendance area and all persons employed by the school are part of this smaller community. They may be (1) citizens without children in school, (2) parents of children in school, (3) children in school, or (4) teachers and other employees of the school.

For the most part, these smaller school communities have fixed attendance area boundaries; however, with the advent of school choice, home schooling, magnet schools, distance learning, and other required boundary crossings intended to achieve equity of opportunities, the community may be extended and scattered. This dispersion makes it difficult to delineate who makes up the school community and complicates communication; however, it does not eliminate the idea that the school is, or can be, a community.

The changes and complexities of communities, with accompanying changes and complexities of school districts in the last half of the twentieth century, have made it difficult for schools to remain as close and responsive as they were in the eighteenth and nineteenth centuries. The feeling of actually belonging, participating, and being a partner with the school rapidly disappears with mobility and diversity unless something special is done to maintain it. Schools and districts have grown over the years, some by design, some by circumstances. These larger districts have tended to develop into highly bureaucratic organizations. Special efforts are needed to help schools become more responsive. Educational opportunities have been increased by consolidating into larger educational units; however, in planning the educational unit, no one invented or established a realistic, organized way to keep parents and citizens intimately associated with the schools. A person has to go through but one consolidation to feel the lack of community regarding the newly created school district.

A simple answer to bigness and the attendant bureaucratic structures is to put more emphasis on each attendance area, regarding each building as the most important and sensitive unit in the organization. Another dimension is the formation of communities of interest that are enhanced by the advances in communications technology. Persons concerned with a particular school, for instance, can communicate with each other via a number of networks, overcoming the constraints of time and sometimes space that heretofore hindered communication.

Today one can find state building regulations that stress the belief that to provide appropriate curricula and resources, elementary buildings should house no fewer than four hundred; middle schools, six hundred; and high schools, eight hundred. While many questions may be raised regarding the limitations of such beliefs, the trend to consolidate continues, even to the point of having to organize internally to create smaller clusters of teachers and students who can develop a sense of community within.

Proposals have been made to "[r]edesign education for the purpose of re-creating community—community that is ecologically sustainable."[4] This approach would create political entities on a bioregional basis—that is, on an ecosystem base that could be self-sustaining over a long period. New relationships would be fostered among the residents, and education could be based on real life in sustaining the region's long-term self-sufficiency.

Often the phrase "sense of community" is used to describe relationships among people and organizations. The idea is that those relationships are trustful, open, honest, and challenging yet supportive, describing a connectedness or a bond among members. Rubin and Rubin note that the term *community* refers to social integration, "the issues and bonds that link people together."[5] These linkages tie people together affectively and by interest. Etzioni observes that "the individual and the community 'make' one another and that individuals are not able to function effectively without deep links to others, to community."[6]

---

[4] Paul Theobold and Paul Nachtigal, "Culture, Community, and the Promise of Rural Education," *Phi Delta Kappan* 77 (October 1995): 35.
[5] Herbert J. Rubin and Irene S. Rubin, *Community Organizing and Development*, 2d ed. (New York: Macmillan, 1992), 82.
[6] Amitai Etzioni, *A Responsive Society* (San Francisco: Jossey-Bass, 1991), 139.

Sergiovanni sees community members responding to the substance of ideas, which implies that leadership builds a "shared followership . . . not on *who* to follow, but on *what* to follow."[7] A school community, then, is a group of people who share common ideas about schooling, learning, and the purposes of those things.

The implications for school leaders are clear. Persons within the community need to be part of a group working toward the common good, sharing a set of values within the school. The school, as a community entity, needs to be part of a larger group that also has values in common and works toward a mutual good.

For a number of reasons, schools as institutions have exhibited a wide range of interest and effectiveness in operating as a community member, particularly regarding instruction, curriculum, and the use of other resources such as businesses and service agencies. Schools in general have not kept pace with the means and desire for the interconnected operation becoming more prevalent in our economic and, to a lesser degree, our political environments. Is the resistance to interacting with the community at large and parents in particular based on the need to control the educational enterprise?

SCHOOL CONTROL: A CONTROVERSY

Governmental and economic entities seek control of the schools by requiring a certain level of performance on tests, by withholding financial support, or by attempting to influence the public via pundits' "mantras" about the "failure of the public schools." Murphy notes that ". . . the landscape of educational control is being reshaped . . . a new governance algorithm may be emerging—an array of control mechanisms . . . an alternative bundle of ideas about governance. . . ."[8] Researchers from the Center for Educational Policy and Management of the University of Oregon developed a historical review of the phases by which school control was being "wrested from the people."[9] Their major thesis was that local control was first destroyed by the growth of educational professionalism and is under further assault by a "political reformer elite," who see the schools as agents of social and economic change to be manipulated by federal and state legislation.

A number of new players have entered the game. Political figures and business leaders have formed groups intended to influence legisla-

---

[7] Thomas J. Sergiovanni, *Leadership for the Schoolhouse* (San Francisco: Jossey-Bass, 1996), 83.

[8] Joseph Murphy, "Governing America's Schools: The Shifting Playing Field," *Teachers College Record* 102 (February 2000): 79–80.

[9] L. Harmon Zeigler, Harvey J. Tucker, and L. A. Wilson, "How School Control Was Wrested from the People," *Phi Delta Kappan* 58 (March 1977): 534–539. Also see the November 1984 issue of *Phi Delta Kappan*, which has a special section devoted to "The Vanishing Myth of Local Control."

tors and the public to improve the schools by a number of means. Parents have taken matters into their own hands by home schooling their children, a growing phenomenon throughout the country. The idea of parents having a choice regarding which public school their children can attend is also a reality. Nearly 25 percent of students in grades 3–12 were enrolled in public or private schools chosen by their families. Among higher-income families (those with annual income of $50,000 or more), 72 percent opted for some form of choice.[10] Today it is rare to find a political candidate who does not favor some form of school choice for parents.

Bracey notes another sector that has emphasized the negative regarding schools—the media. He points out that the small declines in test scores since the 1970s got a great deal of attention. When scores began to rise, with the 1995 scores showing the largest increase in a decade, these increases were not front-page news and in some cases were not even mentioned.[11] The influentials behind the reports may have something to gain by emphasizing the negative about schools. There are those who decry the schools' effectiveness in producing useful employees and those who use their ideas as a springboard toward total choice of public or private schools. Their motives are sometimes quite transparent. It is a challenge for the educational leader to build a sense of community in a sometimes hostile environment, yet if the ideas about what constitutes good schooling are substantive and workable, the challenge may turn into an opportunity.[12]

TEACHER MORALE A PRINCIPAL'S PROBLEM?
A CASE STUDY

George Goodfellow sat disheartened at his desk. He had just experienced a discouraging conversation with one of his second-year teachers. The young man, Bruce Carver, whom George had considered one of his most promising teachers, had hesitantly come into his office asking for a personal discussion. Bruce very tentatively opened the conversation. "It is satisfying to be an important part of students' lives—teacher, social worker, friend, brother, parent, . . . but it has been so discouraging to hear all the snide remarks against

---

[10] Lawrence Hardy, "Public School Choice," *American School Board Journal* 187 (February 2000): 22–26.
[11] Gerald W. Bracey, "The Fifth Bracey Report on the Condition of Public Education," *Phi Delta Kappan* 77 (October 1995): 153.
[12] The reader may wish to pursue this discussion further by perusing Jack L. Nelson, Kenneth Carlson, and Stuart B. Polansky, *Critical Issues in Education,* 3d ed. (New York: McGraw-Hill, 1996).

public education from talk show hosts that deride public schools. Then during the recent political campaigns, though the politicians say they have the improvement of education as a major priority, their remarks cast public schools in a bad light, and they imply that education needs fixing. The newspapers, TV, and radio repeat these negative comments over and over and seem to be intent on decrying the poor showing of U.S. children on tests compared to those of other countries. Mr. Goodfellow, I'm beginning to feel as if I'm in a second-rate profession! The constant negative atmosphere about public schools is wearing out my desire to be a teacher. Frankly, I'm becoming ashamed that I am a teacher. I need to feel appreciated and feel proud of what I do. I am quitting teaching. I'm tendering my resignation at the end of this school year."

George was rendered almost speechless by this tortured, but obviously well thought through and rehearsed, personal speech. He uttered some inane remarks about how we all get discouraged, but teaching is a time-honored profession. Then he said, "Bruce, please think this over carefully and talk with me again before you really make up your mind."

When the door closed behind young Bruce Carver, George put his hands over his face. Great Scott. This national debate about education is breaking down the morale of teachers. This word service to do good for education was creating an opposite effect. George Goodfellow had been a principal for nine years. He had always prided himself with having a high-spirited staff that worked on common problems and often went well beyond the call of duty to make the school a positive place for students and teachers. He had never worried about the professionalism of his staff, or about their morale, but in the last couple of years, a number of his most supportive and faithful teachers had taken early retirement and had been replaced with younger and, in some cases, more negatively vocal counterparts.

George realized this was a serious situation. He, too, had felt the sting of campaign rhetoric casting the schools as failures in need of fixing. He realized how those kinds of comments could impact young teachers who believed they were devoting their lives to a noble cause that was unappreciated. But what to do?

Some Considerations. What should George Goodfellow do to offset the negative attacks on public schools? One political figure, when discussing the virtues of home schooling, recently stated, "The amateurs are outperforming the professionals." How could or even should George try to offset these kinds of comments? Does he have any obligations to the total school system, or to the profession?

IS THE PROFESSION IN CONTROL?

The professionals, teachers and administrators, at times are accused of neutralizing attempts at improving the feeling of community by their use of jargon, regulations, and a general attitude of "We are the ones who have the expertise to deal with students." This position of keeping others at arm's length does little to foster partnerships with joint ownership in the responsibility to educate individuals or the youth of the nation in general. Perhaps the teachers and administrators view "outside" involvement as an erosion of their legitimate authority.

In dealing with schools, parents too often found themselves in a position of perceived helplessness, frustration, and inferiority. With their special credentials and jargon, the professionals in the various institutions, including the school, had essentially taken over the control of the child. Although this situation has changed, one still sometimes hears the teachers' pleas to be left alone to do their jobs without outside interference.

FEDERAL AND STATE CONTROL

A growing body of evidence indicates that the term *local control* has become more a slogan than a reality because, since 1950, state and federal legislation has eroded local ability to control the schools, almost to the vanishing point. People holding this opinion point to the special federal aid programs following World War II and to the Elementary and Secondary Education Act of 1965, which gave the federal government unprecedented power in education. They also mention civil rights legislation, which made the federal government a champion of equal opportunity in education, enforceable by the punitive action of withholding funds or other law enforcement measures. The civil rights legislation was indeed important in eliminating many injustices to blacks and other minorities, but it changed the public's view of local school boards (i.e., that they had supreme control of the public schools within their districts). Scores of federal programs did provide schools with a great deal of new money. At the same time, these programs established new mandates and many regulations that restricted normal prerogatives of the local community school.

During the Nixon administration, there was growing concern about advancing federalism; therefore, a portion of the federal money began to be funneled through the state departments of education or other appropriate state agencies. This tended to increase the power of states perceptibly, for as they distributed the money, they, too, established regulations as to its use. This process increased even more when the block grants for education passed during the "honeymoon" years of the Reagan administration.

Block grants switched most of the categorical funding by the federal government to what almost amounted to general aid, which was distributed to the states on the basis of their school-age population. Armed with this money and power, and spurred on by the flurry of public concern created by *A Nation at Risk* and other reports, the states began to pass numerous regulations on curriculum, teacher training, textbooks, graduation requirements, competency testing, and so on. Pressure continues from the federal executive branch to increase testing and to tie the results to federal dollars available to schools based upon their performance. Some state legislatures reflect this test/reward or withhold support view of reforming schools. Such "payment by results" programs have resurfaced over the decades. One of the first such programs began in the mid-1800s in Great Britain, where per-pupil aid was provided only if students passed examinations in reading, writing, and mathematics.[13]

Given the diversity of communities across the United States, and given the diversity found within each community, it is important that leaders in those communities work together to take advantage of the opportunities available through state and federal agencies, but when absolutely necessary, they should also work to protect their prerogatives to provide the best education for their particular communities.

REESTABLISHING A NEW LOCALISM AND PARTNERSHIPS

As parents, citizens, politicians, and educational experts began directing attention toward reforming the schools to eliminate the deficiencies noted in the mass of reports, books, and media stories, the first question asked was this: Where can we get the money to have better-trained administrative leadership, better-trained teachers, better facilities, better equipment, and a bigger, better, and longer school year? Is this not always the way one approaches school reform? Yet by trying to use more money to improve the elements of an establishment, as has been tried many times before, one may improve the establishment without necessarily improving *learning*.

The student is really the key element of any school, and the primary purpose of the school is to promote the student's learning. Fortunately, some of the reformers began to focus their attention on the student. Then they realized the obvious: students are not isolated individuals but members of families, peer groups, neighborhoods, and communities. To improve their learning, which is the school's primary goal, one needs to link the experiences in school with the students' lives and hopefully introduce them to positive possibilities beyond their pres-

---

[13] Wade Nelson, "Timequake Alert," *Phi Delta Kappan* 82 (January 2001): 384–389.

ent goals. This linkage means taking into account the variations of relationships and experiences that are meaningful to the student. Improved
services do not necessarily do this, but a spirit of collaboration, support,
and partnership with those who make up the relationships and form the
experiences can create an environment in which learning is valued. Thus,
before much improvement can be made in the school, the partnership
between the school and the community, which has been so severely
eroded by the mutually perceived loss of local control, must be improved
and revitalized.

As pointed out previously, the school-community partnership has
been in existence since 1642 (the Old Deluder Satan Act[14]). But with the
exception of school boards and parents' associations, no nationally
accepted pattern for organizing this relationship has arisen so that it
could give greater strength to the curriculum and to the learning process
without appearing to usurp the teacher's professional prerogatives. A
number of initiatives have provided some success stories regarding service programs that connect youth to communities[15] and agencies that
serve youth and the schools in a more interactive way. Heath and
McLaughlin note that "[s]uccessful organizations . . . empower rather
than infantilize youths."[16] They go on to list some of the characteristics of
the successful organizations:

1. They view youth as resources to be developed, not problems to
   be managed.
2. They focus on activities that yield recognizable products.
3. They vest responsibility for development in the youth themselves.
4. They have roots in the community and draw resources from it.
5. They change as the ecology of the community changes to serve
   the needs that emerge from those changes.[17]

The need for schools to become partners with parents has been recognized for decades. The agriculture-oriented school calendar, which is
very much with us today, is evidence of the need to cooperate with parents and the community.

In 1924, Joseph K. Hart reminded his readers of the need for a
stronger community-school partnership when he wrote:

> Education is not apart from life. . . . The democratic problem in education
> is not primarily a problem of training children, it is a problem of making a

---

[14] We often encounter references to these early acts but seldom read even parts of them.
One source of this and other colonial school laws is Ellwood P. Cubberly, *The History of Education* (Boston: Houghton Mifflin, 1920), 363–366.
[15] See Chapter 10 for a discussion of service learning in the schools.
[16] Shirley B. Heath and Milbrey W. McLaughlin, "Community Organizations as Family,"
Phi Delta Kappan 72 (April 1991): 625.
[17] Ibid., 626–627.

community within which children cannot help growing up to be democratic, intelligent, disciplined to freedom, reverent to the goods of life, and
eager to share in the tasks of the age. A school cannot produce the result;
nothing but a community can do so.[18]

In 1939, when Elsie R. Clapp wrote of her successful experiences in
developing community schools in Kentucky and West Virginia, she
asked, "Where does the school end and life begin?" She then answered,
"There is no distinction between them. A community school is a used
place, a place used freely and informally for all the needs of living and
learning. It is, in effect, the place where living and learning converge."[19]

The W. K. Kellogg Foundation poured millions of dollars into projects furthering the community-school partnership, particularly from the
late 1930s to the middle 1950s. The Mott Foundation of Flint, Michigan,
began financial and philosophical support of the community-school partnership in Flint in the early 1940s and continues to support projects providing leadership for this concept.

Another pressure to be responsive to the community is the rapidly
changing ethnic and racial composition of our population. By 2020, it is
estimated that half the children in this country under eighteen years of
age will be nonwhite.[20] Over four out of five immigrating to this country
come from Asia and Latin America, bringing language challenges in
most instances as well as cultural differences. While these changes can be
enriching to the school, they can be and too often are viewed as obstacles
to doing things "as we've always done them." Schools need to connect
well with all the parents. Schine observed that schools have a challenge
to ". . . recognize they share with the students' families a commitment
to enabling every child to succeed."[21] McCaleb notes that "a new model
of partnership must be created in which parents are seen as a resource
instead of a nuisance."[22] Forming partnerships and collaborative ventures seems to be essential to meeting the diverse needs of students.

In too many instances, it appears that when schools need greater
support, they devise special procedures to involve the parents or the
community, and when the support has served its purpose, the procedure
dies because of lack of effort and concern. This trend has made the public
suspicious of the schools' motives when they ask for support. One thing

---

[18] Joseph K. Hart, *Discovery of Intelligence* (New York: Century, 1924), 382.

[19] Elsie R. Clapp, *Community Schools in Action* (New York: Viking, 1939), 89.

[20] "Children of 2010, Child Trends," U.S. Department of Education in *Principal* 79 (May
2000): 18.

[21] Joan Schine, "Home and School Face Changing Partnership Roles," *Schools in the Middle* 8
(November/December 1998): 20.

[22] Sudia Paloma McCaleb, *Building Communities of Learners* (New York: St. Martins Press
1994), 7.

is certain: in reviewing the stories of successful community-school partnerships, one finds that although the central administration has to have a
policy of endorsing a strong community-school partnership, it is the
school principal who stands in a key leadership position relative to initiating and maintaining activities that strengthen the partnership. The
principal is the first-line contact for both the teachers and the citizens
who make up the immediate community of any particular school. Any
community-school action program needs enthusiastic, innovative ideas
from the principal to get things going and his or her continual input and
support to sustain them.

THE STUDENT COMMUNITY

The Student and School Governance

Seldom does a school district's list of goals or objectives omit a statement
about preparing students to be productive, contributing citizens.
Reviewing the textbooks on curriculum, supervision, and administration
of elementary and secondary schools, one observes a serious concern for
teaching citizenship and providing prototype adult experiences that
show how our democracy works. This well-meaning approach to the
education of children is an example of some of the artificiality that pervades our educational system. We do not need to use make-believe situations, examples, and case studies to align school with life. The student
community is not a make-believe situation. It is a real situation, with all
the ingredients to make it a bona fide democratic community. Students
are not make-believe citizens; they are actual citizens who are part of not
only the school community but also the community at large. In one
sense, it is easy for the student to be the "invisible citizen" because the
parent and the school, both of whom supposedly are acting in the student's best interests, frequently overlook the child's rights as a citizen.

Beyond ignoring real opportunities to develop citizenship perspectives and skills, the schools have been guilty of ignoring students as citizens. Justice Jackson, who delivered the opinion of the Supreme Court in
the "flag-saluting" case, admonished school authorities for disregarding
students' basic rights as citizens:

> The Fourteenth Amendment as now applied to the states, protects the citi-
> zen against the state itself and all of its creatures—Boards of Education not
> excepted. These have, of course, important delicate and highly discre-
> tionary functions, but none that they may not perform within the limits of
> the Bill of Rights. That they are educating the young for citizenship is rea-
> son for scrupulous protection of constitutional freedoms of the individual,

if we are not to strangle the free mind at its source and teach youth to discount important principles of our government as mere platitudes.[23]

This brings us to a very sensitively balanced mode of operation for the school and raises issues in regard to administration-student, teacher-student, and adult-student relationships. Immediately, one can hear the usual questions raised: "Who's in control here, anyway—me or the students?" "Are you going to let the students run the school?" "What are principals and teachers for if they can't tell students how to behave, what to do, and what not to do?"

To allow children to participate fully in their own government is perceived to be a threat to a very basic value system going back to the Middle Ages—a divine right that adults had over the young and the schoolmaster had over students: "Children should be seen and not heard." "Children shall obey the will of the master." "Teacher knows best." "The parent knows best." That school administrators and teachers must have absolute control over students in order not to lose control altogether is a perpetuation of long-standing folklore and a potential source of alienation of the students as well as their parents.

An Institution Responsive to Students

Educators often restrict their consideration of the school to the formal organization that they themselves set up. Too often an institution's response to pressures or turbulence from the outside is to create a more complex system, which in turn appears even more unresponsive to the individual. There is a growing body of research on the student in relation to school environment, the formal and informal student organizations, the student community, the student social system, the social climate of the school and classroom, and the influence of in-school and out-of-school peer groups. In any given student body, the incidents of daily interaction between students may number in the tens of thousands, yet teachers and administrators are inclined to count these interactions as inconsequential unless they themselves are involved. Actually, the social climate of the classroom, the school, and the general community has an important influence on student behavior and student achievement.

Every social system, including a school, is an invented reality. It may be that too often the adult world invents its own reality and that adults impose that reality onto the students and choose to ignore the possibility that their realities are not those of students. A study of the contributions of teacher behavior to the recovery or relapse of students who completed a drug treatment program highlights the point. Many teachers made no differentiation in their responses to students or saw little reason

---

[23] *West Virginia State Board of Education v. Barnette*, 319 U.S. 624, 63 S. Ct. 1178 (1943).

to do so, whereas the students' interpretations of the teachers' behaviors clearly depicted differences in the perceptions of reality.[24]

As our electronic, cyberspace capabilities increase, it may be that each of the users is living in a fragmented community of his or her own design. Interactions may become more and more faceless and less personal. A person's community may be a mosaic of very diverse "tiles" of work, school, home, cyberspace/media, religion, and a few acquaintances who may share some "tile" in the mosaic during the course of a day or week. While such a situation may appear to be problematic, it also provides an opportunity for the school to be one place where many of these somewhat disconnected parts of life can come together with other people to realize a common goal.

Each person, adult or student, has his or her goals, and each group has its goals, some of which are clear and some not so clear. With a student body, when problems come into focus and the students feel repressed, denied, or restrained because the institution is not moving happily toward desired goals or because the students are not respected as an important part of the system, whatever the nature of the problem, the first logical move is to request a change. Employing the traditional concept of following the administrative hierarchy, students go through the various levels of authority to bring about the change. Then, if they have been unsuccessful in their efforts to persuade the "powers that be" to change, they have only three choices: give in, get out, or revolt. Each of these choices creates very special problem areas in schools. If the students give in—do as they are told—it is a submission that can create resentment, frustration, and a developing antagonism. The students may choose to drop out—either psychologically, through apathy or excessive absences, or physically, by actually leaving school. Finally comes the most extreme option of major protests, striking back and revolting because of the rigidity and inflexibility of the system. Many such opinions were put forward relative to the Columbine (1999) or the Santana (2001) high school violence.

Being an accepted member of a community provides the member a feeling of support, purpose, and, to some degree, safety. When sets of expectations about race, disabilities, or allegiances (e.g., gang colors) change the view of whether a person is accepted or valued as a member of the school community, learning, interest, and purpose are affected for students who are on the periphery, or those students are simply tolerated because it is the politically correct thing to do. Schaps et al. note that "the small body of research . . . on schools as communities clearly indicates

---

[24] For an enlightening view of perceptual differences between students and teachers, see Karen S. Boling, "The Effects of Teacher Behavior on Students Who Have Completed Treatment for Alcohol and Drug Dependency" (Ph.D. diss., Ball State University, Muncie, IN, 1992).

that a focus on community provides . . . clear directions for school improvements.[25]

If a system is unresponsive to the people in it, over the years it builds up a larger and larger body of people who become antagonistic or apathetic toward the system. These include not only the students already in school but also a growing number who have left school by either graduating or dropping out. So from both inside and outside, a developing antagonistic force, or at best an uninvolved, apathetic group, is being created that can either destroy the system or force change by sheer power. In either case, the unresponsive institution gradually loses the support it needs as a public institution responsive to the people. It is a form of arrogance for any school to treat the majority of its citizens as if they did not count as part of the school's culture and sense of community.

An Intraschool Community

Much has been made of assessment and accountability of teachers, administrators, and institutions to the public and to the business leaders of the states and nation. Accountability means being appropriately responsive to the needs of the public, which is made up of parents and citizens at large. However, the most intimately affected public is the students themselves. Popular and professional literature and media often decry the effects on youth of watching thousands of hours of television. Sometimes ignored are the effects on students functioning within the school's social culture—of spending 5,500 hours in an intense social community, or culture, as most students do in a K–5 school, or approximately 4,400 hours in a four-year high school. What citizenship learnings are occurring as a result of happenstance in this culture? The student council has been the pro forma establishment way of facing de facto disenfranchisement, but in far too many cases, this organization is operated with "tongue in cheek" by both students and administration. They know that the principal can step in at any time and veto any of the proposals, and there is no simple procedure for appeal or a method by which the principal's decision may be evaluated by an impartial group. The message is clear to the students that their input is not valued, or, at best, it is tolerated in a "test tube" or laboratorylike setting.

If students are to understand that they live in a democratic society that is ruled by laws established by the people, they should become familiar with the democratic process. We are not suggesting here that students govern themselves totally. Rather, we are suggesting that there be well-established policies in every school system that provide guide-

---

[25] Eric Schaps, Victor Battistich, and Daniel Solomon, "School as a Caring Community: A Key to Character Education," in *The Construction of Children's Character*, ed. Alex Molnar (Chicago: University of Chicago Press, 1997), 138.

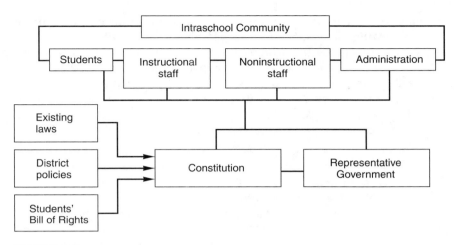

FIGURE 3.2
An intraschool constitutional government

lines for students to participate in their school social system; that a student Bill of Rights be composed that clearly establishes basic rights of all students; that a clear, simple process be established systemwide for review and appeal of decisions handed down by a teacher or a principal; and that each individual school in the school system have some form of self-government that operates within the limits of the district's policies and the student Bill of Rights. This government should provide for realistic student input on decisions relating to the entire school. Some form of government in each school should operate according to a constitution developed by and for the members of that particular school's social system, composed of students, faculty, administration, and nonteaching personnel (see Figure 3.2). If schools are to remain responsive and close to the people, if citizens and students are to remain advocates instead of adversaries of the schools, then the elimination of adversarial situations must be an important goal. The rule by one person, whether teacher or administrator, must be replaced by a government of law, and those who are in the school social system must have meaningful input into the development of that law. A sense of *our* school must pervade the culture.

Creating a Self-Disciplined School Community

The Phi Delta Kappa Commission on Discipline made a comprehensive study of schools with effective student communities, those with little or no disruptive behavior. After a review of programs and qualitative data, the commission concluded that student self-discipline is the key to effective school communities: "Schools with well-disciplined students have developed a sense of community, marked by mutually agreed upon behavioral norms. . . . Student involvement is absolutely essential if students are to value the school and monitor their own behavior. Students must believe the school is their own and not someone else's."[26]

The commission then identified several characteristics that it found were necessary to develop a positive community. Fully developed in Phi Delta Kappa's *Handbook for Developing Schools with Good Discipline*,[27] these characteristics appear here in condensed form:

1. *Creating in students belongingness and responsibility*—These schools recognize the importance of each person in the school community. All students feel needed, important, and worthwhile. Teachers and administrators help students realize that they belong and that the school is worth belonging to.

   Given the increasing diversity in our schools, operating on the assumption that children are ready to participate can lead to serious problems for the students. Focusing on students with limited English proficiency (LEP), Foss and Buckner note several steps schools might take, including establishing student and parent support groups, recruiting teachers with the skills to work with LEP students, and implementing teacher development programs.[28]

2. *Pursuing superordinate school goals*—In these schools, teachers, administrators, and students work together in establishing a set of core values and then translating these values into qualitative statements of purpose. Administrators in these schools promote collective decision making and involve students in identifying problems and suggesting solutions.

3. *Devising symbols of identity and excellence*—These schools create slogans and aphorisms that strengthen and exemplify the values established by the school community. Such slogans tend to serve as constant reminders of the behavior expected and become influential in urging each student to strive for excellence.

4. *Fostering leadership to sustain positive school values*—These schools recognize that leadership is needed to sustain school goals and value systems. They expect the principals and teachers to be leaders in keeping and shaping goals and values. Fur-

[26] William W. Wayson, Thomas J. Lasley, Gary G. DeVoss, and Susan C. Kaeser, "Climates for Excellence: Schools That Foster Self-Discipline," *Phi Delta Kappan* 65 (February 1984): 419–421. This is a brief report of some of the commission's findings. For additional discussion of discipline, see Chapter 16.
[27] William W. Wayson, *Handbook for Developing Schools with Good Discipline* (Bloomington, IN: Phi Delta Kappa, 1982).
[28] For a more complete discussion, see Angela Foss and Kermit Buckner, "The Principles of Compliance," *Schools in the Middle* 9 (February 2000): 34–40.

ther, they create reward systems in which students are recognized as "heroes" when they serve as good models of student citizens who are committed to the behavioral norms of the school.

5. *Creating clear formal and informal rules*—These schools have rules for student behavior that are cooperatively developed, clearly stated, and systematically explained. Schools with effective discipline know that individuals who are not involved in developing the rules have neither a commitment to nor an understanding of them. The following passage describes how the Roy C. Ketcham High School, of Wappingers Falls, New York, developed its rules collectively:

> Our discipline code was developed by a committee of parents, teachers, students, and administrators. After the code was developed, workshops were presented to the parents during an evening meeting, and an entire day of school was spent teaching the discipline code to the students. Each member of the committee worked with twenty-five students, answering questions and explaining rules and regulations. A workshop was also provided for the teaching staff and school monitors. An ongoing review committee, made up of teachers, students, administrators, and parents, functions to keep the discipline code updated and to make sure it is being properly implemented.[29]

The Student and Community Conflict

It is important to realize that a major problem may be that the student is involved in a variety of communities, each perhaps having expectations in regard to the student that compete and conflict with each other and those of the school.

The principal and teacher have difficulty comprehending how serious these conflicts are and how much they will influence the students' behavior in school, for their effects cannot be determined without serious study. These communities may be based on religion, race, peer group, family, or even sexual orientation. They may be mainstream or "alternative." In any event, students bring their perceptions of these communities and where they fit (or do not fit) in them to school each day. They ordinarily face those perceptions alone in an environment known only to each student.

Unconsciously or consciously, when a principal or teacher identifies with a boy or girl, it is that child as part of the school community. So often the principal or teacher does not consider all the other forces impinging on the student that affect his or her actions in school. At the least, those persons interacting with the student should try to identify

---

[29] Wayson, *Handbook*, 43.

the many and possibly conflicting systems of which the student is a part and to understand the potential for seriously conflicting perceptions of the values and expectations facing each student. It is easy to see the relative importance to the student of a community in which the student feels she or he plays a vital part, or at least experiences acceptance, versus one in which she or he is at best tolerated or ignored. Lessons may have been taught at Columbine and Santana high schools.

THE FACULTY COMMUNITY

In any school, teachers form a social system, a formal-informal organization that seems to have a definite personality, a great variety of parts making up the whole, interrelationships that run the gamut from closeness to distance, and wide variations of opinion, from either extreme to neutral. Nonetheless, the challenge of teaching, the complexity of relationships with students, and the great goals of the profession tie the diverse personalities into a workable whole that we call the faculty. Although probably no appropriate description exists for the typical faculty, it truly portrays the definition of an organic system in that it is an interacting entity whose healthy existence depends on effective working relationships among the various parts. To disrupt one element in the system is to create stress, which may in turn result in noticeable effects on the entire system.

To a limited degree, administrators may deal with a teacher as an isolated individual; however, they commit a serious mistake if they believe this should be done in all cases. Each teacher represents himself or herself but also a total faculty, consisting not only of individuals but also of many primary groups that are linked together by a whole series of bridges, which may range from very strong to temporary and weak. A great variety of forces shapes the teacher's thinking and behavior, as illustrated by Figure 3.3.

THE PROFESSIONAL ORGANIZATIONS

Many of the earlier studies of the organization of school faculties were inclined to depict the formal organization only as that sanctioned and controlled by the school administration. This approach usually neglected the professional associations that form a growing area of faculty influence. The number and strength of these associations no longer allow one to consider them as either informal or extralegal organizations. Hundreds of national and regional professional associations exist, and the number of state, intrastate, and local associations is legion. All of these professional groups are conscious that there is power in numbers, and

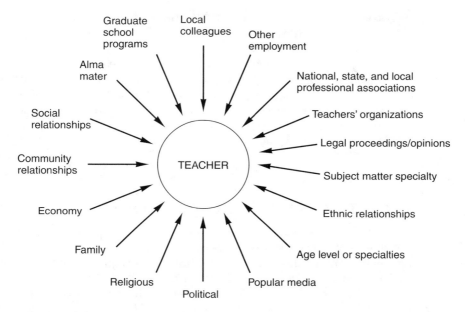

FIGURE 3.3
Some forces that impinge on the teacher

faculty members facing the facts of contemporary life realize that teachers ordinarily will not get the attention and resources they want at the local, state, and national levels, or even a decent hearing about possibilities and needs, unless they speak through organizations. Thus, a typical teacher belongs to local, state, and national educational associations or unions and, in addition, usually a professional organization related to a specialty, such as industrial technology, English, reading, curriculum, or child development. Through these professional organizations, the teacher has a way of communicating with others on, and influencing, the course of events on the state and national scenes as well as in the local school district.

An administrator working with a given faculty member then deals with a many-sided professional individual as well as a person with several personal influences. Disregarding the nonprofessional influence of the community, we see that each teacher is a person influenced by the general educational organization, a specialty educational organization, a local primary education group, and individual professional concerns in the classroom.

The strong development of professional organizations has led to the national movement of professional association negotiations for teachers. The pressures leading to site-based decision making also have contributed to the continually changing process of administering schools. In one sense, teachers have an opportunity to grow and, within limits, control their own destinies; however, not everyone views empowerment as positive. Some view it as a problem in that it appears to weaken the line between being a teacher and being a decision maker like an administrator. The implications for administrators can be quite mixed. Some schools are moving forward and finding the process to be achieving positive results, while others are resisting the idea. There certainly are new demands and expectations within the professional community and on teachers and administrators as they determine how best to serve students.

COLLABORATION AND NETWORKING

The possibilities for collaboration and networking to improve student learning are very great. Linkages between the school and parents, businesses, agencies, universities, and information bases present opportunities for all involved. The term *collaboration* implies that all players contribute to reaching the goal of the partnership, and the schools offer much to their partners. Also implied in the term *collaboration* is the idea of shared decision making. Collaborative ventures need to have input from as many stakeholders as can be identified. The partners' decisions require accurate and complete data; therefore, comprehensive needs assessments can help avoid creating projects that miss the target and/or are not used by the community or the school.[30]

TOWARD A COLLABORATIVE VENTURE

In planning a collaborative venture, avoiding some pitfalls requires an awareness of the culture of the general community, the needs, and potential resources. The principal may visualize a vibrant service to the students and/or the community; however, a number of pieces must fit together to really arrive at a useful service. An example may be a school-based health clinic. Answers to the following questions will be needed before finalizing plans:

1. Who would be the stakeholders in a venture such as a school-based health clinic? Students, parents, teachers, and the potential health service providers would be starting points. Would the religious/faith-based communities have a stake, particularly if counseling regarding pregnancy or the distribution of condoms might be involved? Given the probability that some

---

[30] Nick Caruso, "Lessons Learned in a City-School Social Services Partnership," *Social Work in Education* 22 (April 2000): 108–115.

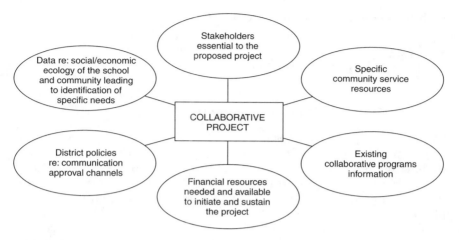

FIGURE 3.4
Development components for planning a collaborative venture

> student might be HIV positive, are agencies of child welfare or even the juvenile court system potential stakeholders?[31]
>
> 2. What district policies exist regarding communication with external agencies relative to exploring collaborative ventures? With whom or through whom would the principal work to assess the willingness of health service providers and funding agencies to develop the idea of a school-based health clinic?
> 3. What resources exist in the community? Would there be a duplication of effort or even a perceived intrusion into another agency's "territory"?
> 4. What existing collaborative ventures are operating success-fully? What was their history and development?
> 5. What specific social and economic data about the community support the needs that are being considered?
> 6. What financial resources are needed to initiate and maintain the collaborative venture? What sources of funding are realisti-cally available?

Figure 3.4 portrays the above components in relation to the project. It is clear that the principal will be sharing decision making and will need to be open to configurations different from the original idea, but still addressing the need, without violating her or his ethical values. Ferrandino calls for principals to ". . . find innovative ways to get involved

---

[31] For additional perspectives of the complexities of interagency collaboration, see Melissa Jonson-Reid, "Understanding Confidentiality in School-Based Interagency Projects," *Social Work in Education* 22 (January 2000): 33–45.

with their communities and to restore the community school to its central place in American life."[32] As our society continues to change, this challenge envisions a continuously changing, proactive school working in a fluid way to meet educational needs.

Student Community Service

Opportunities abound for service to others, to enhance the concept of community. Some examples of venues for student service include health centers, nursing homes, Toys for Tots programs, missions, food drives, and community clean-up projects. Through service programs, the students of any one school can benefit hundreds of people in the community, but, more important, the programs may benefit the students as they find meaning in their school lives. Generation gaps may disappear; socioeconomic chasms may be bridged; indeed, communities may be formed. See Chapter 10 for more discussion about the concept of service learning.

Parents as Partners

At any level of schooling, parents are often the least utilized resource for educating students, and could be one of the most important. Schools have gone through the time when they viewed parents as superfluous to the educational process or as potentially interfering with the professionals trying to educate their children. Now parents are viewed as potential allies in creating a less compartmentalized approach to learning. Since the schools have the students only approximately 13 percent of their lives up to graduation from high school, it makes sense that partnerships be formed with the people who have influence on them a much greater percentage of time.

Providing information to the community at large and to parents in particular is important. McCarthy found that "[a] key component to connecting home and school appears to be the sharing of information."[33] The shared information not only can provide parents with insights regarding ways of helping their children, but also can provide school personnel with ideas to help parents to help their children.

If the schools are not to affirm the already wide discrepancies in educational readiness and aspirations, they need to engage proactively in making differences in the communities they serve. One investment

---

[32] Vincent L. Ferrandino, "Challenges for 21st Century Elementary School Principals," *Phi Delta Kappan* 82 (February 2001): 441.
[33] Sarah J. McCarthy, "Home-School Connections: A Review of the Literature," *Journal of Educational Research* 93 (January/February 2000): 151.

would be to work with the community at large to assist parents in helping preschool children.

School personnel need to be sensitive to making parents and guardians feel safe by using language that communicates to those they are trying to reach, not reverting to our jargon-laden phrases that at best do not communicate clearly and too often alienate. Timing these opportunities for contact is essential, given the number of single parents, grandparents, and others involved in caring for our students.

Schools are becoming more racially, culturally, and linguistically diverse. Care must be taken to avoid labeling. Holman states that even though an established "minority" group lives in a school's attendance area, there may be members of the same ethnic or racial group who have recently moved into the area with very different communication and/or social needs from the established groups.[34]

The view of children coming to school from families consisting of their two biological parents, first marriage (the *Leave It To Beaver* situation of the 1950s and 1960s) is right only about 26 percent of the time. Single-parent families constitute 26 percent; blended families, 21 percent; institutions and foster families, 12 percent. The remaining 15 percent are adoptive, no-parent, or some form of extended families.[35] Such a wide range of types of families dictates a similar range of responses to enlisting parents as partners in educating our youth. Berger provides a number of accommodations that may help schools and parents work together. These include child care, learning centers, parent-to-parent support groups, telephone trees, transportation, library access, summer vacation activities, and many more.[36] The concept of full-service schools provides linkages to community resources for both students and parents.[37] Helping parents view the school as a source of support, assistance, and learning for the whole community will enhance the school's effectiveness in helping all students learn.

School-Business Partnerships

A rich variety of partnership is evident today, ranging from the guest executive doing a one-hour stint in the classroom to businesses "adopting" a school and pouring time and dollar resources into the cooperative improvement of instructional results. A school-business partnership

---

[34] Linda S. Holman, "Working Effectively with Hispanic Immigrant Families," *Phi Delta Kappan* 78 (April 1997): 647–649. The reader may also wish to explore the November 1996 issue of *Education and Urban Society*, which discusses Latino educational experiences from students' and parents' perspectives.

[35] Chandler Barbour and Nita H. Barbour, *Families, Schools and Communities* (Upper Saddle River, NJ: Merrill/Prentice Hall, 1997), 47.

[36] Eugenia Hepworth Berger, *Parents as Partners in Education* (Upper Saddle River, NJ: Merrill/Prentice Hall, 1995), 135–157.

[37] See Chapter 9 for a discussion of the full-service school.

should result in more than the school receiving hand-me-downs, though there are some excellent programs in which businesses give schools excess supplies, from paper to computer disks. Business leaders may be able to provide insights into the needs of business in the coming years, assistance with technical aspects of management, or instruction in special areas not taught by the school's staff.

But there is another aspect of the partnership. Business can gain much from the practitioners in the schools. Computer expertise, language development, cultural insights, people skills, and a host of other benefits may be waiting in the schools for businesses to tap. Summer work programs for teachers not only may sharpen insights that can be taken back to the classrooms but also may provide businesses with needed ideas and perspectives. The results could be networking within the community that will provide "real" education for today's students and tomorrow's inventors, salespersons, and analysts, to name a few. Such partnerships may lead to a clearer vision for the students of the relationship between school work and adult work. They may also reduce the perceptions that schools try to remain aloof, working as closed systems relative to the rest of the community.

Other Configurations

Partnerships may be formed with several entities. For example, a business, university, research institute, and school may form a partnership to use the downtown area as a laboratory for several integrated subjects. One university involved three departments and several school districts to develop visual learning materials in mathematics. A think-tank approach generated ideas and scenarios, media and instructional design specialists created videos, and the materials on laser disks provided classroom teachers with effective teaching tools. Other partnerships, such as commercial media or service agencies, could yield valuable contributions to the education of students and the welfare of citizens in the community.

The school has many resources to offer the community. An exchange of resources across the community enriches all involved. Yet the problem persists of needed additional resources facing the various agencies in the community, including schools. As a consequence, schools and other community agencies spend a good deal of time trying to get more money, in effect competing with each other for these additional financial resources. That approach makes it inordinately difficult, and in practice almost impossible, to do three related things: to confront the possibility that resources will be limited, to examine critically the accepted relationship between problems and solutions, and to figure out possible ways in which agencies can learn to exchange resources in mutually beneficial ways and without finances being a prerequisite for discussion or the basis of exchange. It seems any time something different or extra needs to be done, it cannot be done without more staff, supplies, and equipment, and therefore more money. As agencies see the need for more resources and attempt to get them, most cannot help but feel the sense of competition for funds. They feel alone and beleaguered rather than a part of a mutually supportive community family. The key may be to forget new money and work with fellow human service agencies to establish a network where resources can be bartered. "Let's work together! We can help you in the following ways. How can you help us? Let's exchange in a meaningful, efficient way."

Community, then, is a concept and a process that requires the participants to actively help each other achieve. As a result, a feeling of security, reward, and nurturing may replace some of the negatives found in areas where people have no common purpose, little interaction, a great deal of loneliness, and feelings of hopelessness.

Ⓢ U M M A R Y

The public school is only one source of many activities and problems in any community. The influences of outside forces are so important that cooperation among all institutions and agencies of community life is essential to the realization of desirable educational outcomes. We define *community* as a group of people conscious of a collective identity through physical, cognitive, and affective educational relationships. Thus, individuals represent a variety of different communities. The school community is represented broadly by the overall school district within which there may be many schools (elementary, middle, secondary). Each of these forms a more intimate and specific community made up of citizens, parents, and children dwelling in that school attendance area. The principal is the first line of contact for this immediate community; thus, the principal needs to be an enthusiastic, innovative, and attentive leader to create an effective, viable school community.

As for the students, they are citizens with the same constitutional rights as adults. They, too, are involved in a variety of communities, each of which may have expectations that compete and conflict with each other and those of the school. Both teachers and administrators must be sensitive to this situation. The students need to feel accepted and involved in the larger school community so they will invest in their own learning. Realizing that schools can cause disinvestment in learning, the principal is in a key position to initiate and support efforts to create a community culture focused on learning that contributes to everyone's welfare.

FOR FURTHER THOUGHT

1. Discuss the relationship, if any, between these statements: "Citizen-ship can be taught effectively without providing participatory 'citi-zenship' to immature learners" and "We learn best by doing."
2. If a school is a good school, is a public relations (PR) program needed? Is the PR problem of a school comparable to the PR problem of a local business? Are the terms *school publicity, public relations pro-gram,* and *school communications* synonymous?
3. Should youth and their parents or other caregivers be encouraged to think of educational opportunity as something to be provided by the schools or as something to be mutually achieved? If the latter, what common barriers do the schools construct that discourage mutual-ity?
4. Do the schools with which you are familiar take a proactive stance in affecting the community of which they are a part? What community barriers stop them?
5. Review the extent to which community resources are used in the teaching-learning process of a typical school. Can you propose a plan for increasing school-community interaction in instructional activi-ties?
6. Is it really possible for schools to be an interactive, responsive part of the local community? Should the schools concentrate on making the school part of a global community by installing available technology, hiring teachers with a worldview, and expanding curricula to include international perspectives?
7. Regarding a school with which you are familiar, review the amount of active student participation in making curricular and cocurricular decisions. Is student involvement meaningful? Is there a relationship between the amount of involvement and the students' "feeling" for the school?
8. Design a school organizational structure or chart that represents your philosophy of school-community participation. Which roles would change? What would be the roles of students?
9. What truly collaborative ventures are needed in your school commu-nity to improve learning, involve parents, and/or tap resources out-side the school?

SELECTED READINGS

Barbour, Chandler, and Nita H. Barbour. *Families, Schools and Communities.* Upper Saddle River, NJ: Merrill/Prentice Hall, 1997.

Berger, Eugenia Hepworth. *Parents as Partners in Education.* Upper Saddle River, NJ: Merrill/Prentice Hall, 1995.

Caruso, Nick. "Lessons Learned in a City-School Social Services Partnership." *Social Work in Education* 22 (April 2000): 108–115.

Chance, Paul. "Speaking of Differences." *Phi Delta Kappan* 78 (March 1997): 507.

Etzioni, Amitai. *A Responsive Society.* San Francisco: Jossey-Bass, 1991.

Ferrandino, Vincent L. "Challenges for 21st Century Elementary Principals." *Phi Delta Kappan* 82 (February 2001): 440–442.

Lockwood, Anne T. "Sharing Responsibility." *Focus in Change* (Fall 1991): 3–9.

Maehr, Martin L., and Carol Midgley. *Transforming School Cultures.* Boulder, CO: Westview, 1996.

McCarthy, Sarah J. "Home-School Connections: A Review of the Literature." *Journal of Educational Research* 93 (January–February 2000): 145–153.

Schine, Joan, ed. *Service Learning.* Chicago: National Society for the Study of Education, 1997.

Sergiovanni, Thomas J. *Leadership for the Schoolhouse.* San Francisco: Jossey-Bass, 1996.

Theory, Research, Principles:
A Basis for Action

Serious study of educational administration began with the "best practice" approach. It was a simple formula: ask the "old hands" (the outwardly successful principals or superintendents) what they did to be successful. This approach to the study of school administration, called by some "descriptive," has always been popular and was the essential method of study and training for educational administrators through the 1930s.

In the late 1930s and early 1940s, as the teaching of educational administration became more popular in major U.S. colleges and universities, a few of the professors in the field began to realize that there were few pat answers that could apply to all situations. Our society was changing. Each school organization was a dynamically different system, consisting of different personalities and combinations of different people who were living in different communities with schools administered and operated by different executives with different styles.

Confounding variables were nullifying the pat how-to approach. In the ensuing search for universal verities that could give direction to administrative action, several professors of educational administration—notably Arthur B. Moehlman of the University of Michigan and Paul Mort of Teachers College, Columbia University[1]—advanced the idea that although there are few standard answers, a body of knowledge about our culture exists, essentially derived from the literature of behavioral sciences. Properly distilled, this knowledge could be combined with logically developed purposes of education to form principles to test the wisdom of administrative action. Both men expressed the point of view that

---

[1] Arthur B. Moehlman, *School Administration: Its Development, Principles and Function* (Boston: Houghton Mifflin, 1951); Paul R. Mort and Donald H. Ross, *Principles of School Administration*, 2d ed. (New York: McGraw-Hill, 1957).

principles and the technical aspects of the administrative job are two mutually supporting approaches to studying administration, and they presented their textual material in that mode.

Moehlman's and Mort's books were used by a majority of graduate schools throughout the country. Their principles approach was essentially functional; they did gather, in logical continuity, many concepts of administrative action that had wide popular, professional acceptance, but they included others that were imperfectly organized. However, the roots of the principles were based in the perceived culture and well grounded in the political, social, and economic disciplines.

As the study of educational administration began to thrive and advanced training of principals and superintendents became more important, both the practitioner and the professor realized that a scientific, analytic basis was needed to give direction to administrative action. In the face of a rapidly changing, growing society, the principles appeared to be too value laden and general. However, they were developed from a theoretical base that did point the direction to a new movement in the study of educational administration.

ENTER THE THEORY MOVEMENT

The theory movement in educational administration started in the 1950s. The ground was prepared by professors such as Moehlman and Mort, and the seeds were planted by the Cooperative Program in Educational Administration.[2] It was brought to flower by the National Conference of Professors of Educational Administration.[3] It bore fruit under the leadership of the University Council of Educational Administration.[4] The story of the contributions of various people, representing and working through these organizations, is interesting but too long to be told here. The important point, insofar as school administration is concerned, is that, through emphasis on research, interdisciplinary study (particularly the behavioral sciences), and hard, comparative analysis, the study of educational administration began to move from the folklore and testimonial stage toward a more scientific and disciplined base.[5]

This change does not mean educational administration immediately developed its own researchers and theoreticians. Despite the concentration on theory and the amount of talk and writing about it, one has

---

[2] Hollis A. Moore Jr., *Studies in School Administration: A Report on the CPEA* (Washington, DC: American Association of School Administrators, 1957).

[3] National Conference of Professors of Educational Administration, *Administrative Behavior in Education* (n.p.: Author, 1957).

[4] University Council of Educational Administration, "A Consortium of Universities Having Educational Administration Programs," Arizona State University, Tempe.

[5] Jonathan W. Lathey, "Toward Theory-Based School Leadership," *School Administrator* 41 (April 1984): 24–26.

difficulty singling out early professors of educational administration who can be considered researchers and theoreticians in their own right.[6] However, a major contribution of these professors was that they applied the knowledge, research, and theories of sociology, psychology, political science, business, and the military to the practice of educational administration.

Administrative Theory

Administrative theory may be defined in many ways. Much of the early literature on theory in educational administration is devoted to arguments about its definition. We do not want to join these arguments. We define *theory* thus: systematically organized information and knowledge, with a series of assumptions or hypotheses devised to help analyze, predict, or otherwise explain the specific nature and/or behavior of people and their organization.

Figure 4.1 presents a brief historical review of organization and management theory as contributed generally by behavioral scientists and thinkers over the years. As with many movements, it is dangerous to divide it into specific thrusts and name particular contributors because so many people were involved and so much overlapping occurs. Generally, however, through the years at least the major groupings of ideas seem to emerge relative to the theory of management of people and their organizations, managerial efficiency, organizations as social systems, human relations, problem solving and decision theory, human resources management, and cultural perspectives.

Current thinking of the postmodernists and critical theorists will be challenging the thinking about organizational and management theories. The area below the arrow in Figure 4.1 indicates the contributions that are being developed that will influence thinking about manager/leader behavior in the future.

Managerial Efficiency

The managerial organization-efficiency movement could be described as the movement that attempted to attain organizational goals without concern for the means used or the people involved. If we were to accept that statement at its true value, Machiavelli could be considered the true "father" of the movement. As it is, Frederick W. Taylor is considered the "father of scientific management." Best known for his "time and motion studies," he pioneered in the application of the scientific method to the

---

[6] Daniel E. Griffiths, "Evolution of Research and Theory: A Study of Prominent Researchers," *Education Administration Quarterly* 19 (Summer 1983): 201–221.

Dateline	Management Efficiency	Human Relations	Organization and Social Systems	Problem Solving and Decision Theory
1900	Marshall	Mather	Weber	
1910	Taylor Fayol Gilbreths			
1920	Gantt	Meyer		
1930	Mooney Gulick Urwick	Mayo Whitehead Roethlisberger	Lynd and Lynd Barnard	
1940	Armed Forces Dean	Follett Lewin Lippett	Parsons Warner	Barnard Simon Armed Forces
1950	Van Neumann Dale	Maslow National Training Laboratory Rogers	Hunter Homans Maslow	Tannenbaum Bross RAND Experiments Simon
1960	Koontz Hitch	Bradford Likert Bennis	Merton Simon Getzels Guba Likert	March Cyert Ashby
1970	Drucker	Rokeach Campbell	Blau Weick	Cohen
1980		Schein	Etzioni Baldridge	
1990			Deming	
2000			Senge Nooteboom	

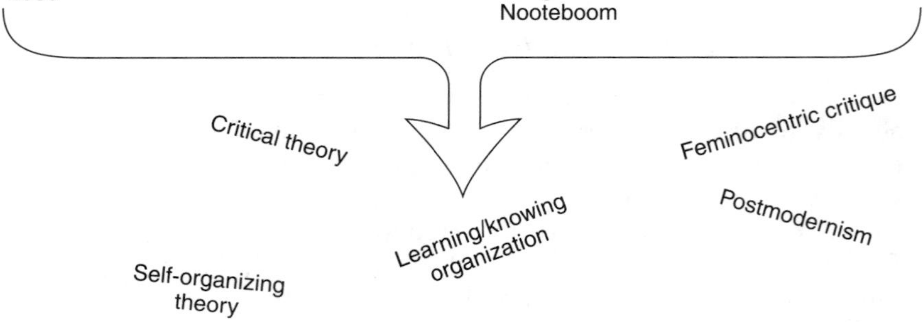

Critical theory

Self-organizing theory

Learning/knowing organization

Feminocentric critique

Postmodernism

FIGURE 4.1
Organization and management theory development

problems of management.[7] His recurring theme was that management was a true science, based on clearly defined principles and laws. Even today Taylor's ideas, revised and adopted by other students in the field, form the basis for much of business's and industry's efficiency control procedures.

Fayol, Gulick, and Urwick analyzed management as a process.[8] Their work eventually resulted in the refinement of such well-known concepts as unity of command, span of control, line and staff, scalar chain, delegation of responsibility, authority, power, and morale. Of course, one should not overlook the identification of the logical functions of the executive under the acronym PODSCORB (planning, organizing, directing, staffing, coordinating, reporting, and budgeting). The armed forces and the U.S. government furthered the rationalization of the formal organization process during and immediately following World War II. During this period, many who later became executives in business, industry, government, and education went through armed forces– and government-sponsored management training programs based on these concepts.

Many authors are inclined to imply that the scientific movement died out in the 1930s and 1940s. However, the movement is still with us—alive and healthy but with the addition of the computer as its basic tool. Its approach has been somewhat diluted by the human relations movement, but traces of Taylor, Fayol, Gulick, and Urwick can be found in the research and theory of business, industry, and government. Practically every school of business administration includes the theory of scientific management in its basic core of knowledge, and systems analysis depends on it for its very existence. In the field of education,[9] it is not too difficult to trace the influence of these early pioneers to management by objectives (MBO), program planning and budgeting systems (PPBS), program evaluation and review techniques (PERT), operations research, critical path planning, and systems analysis, along with many other evaluation and accountability procedures.

Organization and Social Systems

Max Weber, a German sociologist, was one of the early students of organizations.[10] He was concerned with the general unreliability of human

---

[7] Frederick W. Taylor, *Scientific Management* (New York: Harper & Row, 1911).

[8] Henri Fayol, *General and Industrial Management*, trans. Constance Storrs (London: Pitman, 1949); Luther H. Gulick and Lyndall F. Urwick, eds., *Papers on the Science of Administration* (New York: Institute of Public Administration, 1937).

[9] For an interesting account of how the business and industrial efficiency model influenced educational administration, read Raymond E. Callahan, *Education and the Cult of Efficiency* (Chicago: University of Chicago Press, 1962).

[10] Julien Freund, *The Sociology of Max Weber* (New York: Random House, 1968).

judgment and therefore advocated the depersonalized organization. He created a theory of bureaucracy that encouraged large-scale organizations to formalize and systematize their activities to the point of minimizing human error. Talcott Parsons studied Weber's work and early in his career even translated some of his writings.[11] However, Parsons went well beyond Weber by putting people into systems. He developed a theory of social objects that covered a wide range of options. He contended that action is a process occurring between two components of the system, the actor and the situation. He then established five sets of pattern variables as a basis for classifying the action. Although Parsons's work has often been controversial because it lacks a research base, he can be credited with stimulating as much intellectual discourse on the nature of social systems as any other writer or theoretician, if not more.[12]

In a generalized way, one should not overlook the contributions early community studies made to the developing theories on organizations and social systems. These studies provide fascinating descriptions of formal and informal relationships of people in the community, in addition to how power structures developed and how public schools and other public agencies were influenced by community leaders.[13]

Chester Barnard is an example of a businessman (chief executive of New Jersey Bell Telephone) who made a strong contribution to the theory of organization and administration. His classic book, *The Functions of the Executive*, sets forth a number of theories on cooperation and incentives in organization. Barnard believed the formal and informal organizations are intertwined. His central theme is that the vitality of an organization lies in the willingness of individuals to contribute to the cooperative system.[14]

As the human relations movement was coming into its own, it had a decided influence on psychologists and sociologists, and many began to investigate the person in the organization. E. W. Bakke and Chris Argyris proposed the "fusion theory," which states essentially that it is the responsibility of leadership to "fuse" the individual and organization to the point where they both obtain optimum self-actualization.[15]

[11] Max Weber, *The Theory of Social and Economic Organizations,* trans. Talcott Parsons (New York: Free Press, 1974).

[12] Talcott Parsons, *The Structure of Social Action* (New York: McGraw-Hill, 1973); Talcott Parsons and Edward A. Shils, *Toward a General Theory of Action* (Cambridge: Harvard University Press, 1951).

[13] For example, see Robert S. and Helen M. Lynd, *Middletown in Transition* (New York: Harcourt Brace Jovanovich, 1937); William L. Warner et al., *Democracy in Jonesville* (New York: Harper & Row, 1949); Floyd Hunter, *Community Power Structure* (Chapel Hill: University of North Carolina, 1953).

[14] Chester I. Barnard, *The Functions of the Executive* (Cambridge: Harvard University Press, 1938).

[15] E. W. Bakke, *The Fusion Process* (New Haven, CT: Labor and Management Center, Yale University, 1955); Chris Argyris, *Personality and Organization* (New York: Harper & Row, 1957).

A. H. Maslow[16] suggested that the force that causes people to stay and work within an organization is a hierarchy of needs that move, in order of satisfaction, from physiological requirements, to security, to social needs, to esteem, to autonomy, and finally to self-actualization. As needs are met at lower levels, higher-level needs emerge, thus supporting the idea that humans are continuously "wanting" beings. A study of Maslow's theory indicates that, if behavior is to be motivated, this must be done at the level of a need that is currently unsatisfied. Stated differently, a need that is satisfied is no longer a need and therefore is not effective as a motivator in settings with which educational leaders are ordinarily concerned.

Douglas McGregor's Theory X and Theory Y attempted to explain certain motivational factors that are important to an organization's operation.[17] While one is the antithesis of the other, the acceptance of one or the other will certainly affect the way the administrator behaves in an organization.

Theory X postulates that the average human being dislikes work and will avoid it if possible; thus, individuals must be controlled, directed, and implicitly or explicitly threatened so they will work to achieve the organization's goals. Theory Y postulates the opposite, that work is satisfying; therefore, people will direct and control themselves if they are committed to an organization's goals. The best rewards for achieving commitment are self-actualization and ego satisfaction.

J. W. Getzels and E. C. Guba are two social scientists who applied social systems research and theory development to the field of educational administration.[18] Their studies of role and personality as key factors in social power and leadership are quoted widely in textbooks and have made an important contribution to understanding the behavior of the school administrator.

The study and theorizing of organizations as social systems continues at an accelerated pace even today. But in the early 1960s, a new term, *organization development*, began to appear with increasing frequency in the administrative theory literature.[19] Organizational development is a planned, organizationwide effort by the central administration to increase the "esprit de corps" and effectiveness of the organization through particular in-service and development programs that use behavioral science knowledge. Richard Beckhard identifies important elements in operational development that seem to match much of the rationale

---

[16] A. H. Maslow, *Motivation and Personality* (New York: Harper & Row, 1954).
[17] Douglas M. McGregor, *The Human Side of Enterprise* (New York: McGraw-Hill, 1960), 35–57.
[18] J. W. Getzels and Egon C. Guba, "Social Behavior and the Administrative Process," *School Review* 65 (Winter 1957): 423–441.
[19] Ralph B. Kimbrough and Michael Y. Nunnery, *Educational Administration* (New York: Macmillan, 1983).

established by the Educational Leaders Consortium for emphasizing administrative teams:

1. The basic unit for improvement emphasis is the team.
2. Trust and confidence will increase by more communication and collaboration between and across levels of the organization.
3. Decision making must be located at the new information source.
4. The organization's goals must be continually revised and adapted to units and subunits of the organization, and activities and controls must be flexibly adapted to these goals.
5. People affected by change must be allowed to plan and participate throughout the change process.[20]

Readers may recognize in these and in human relations concepts a startling resemblance to the management techniques that made Japanese industry the marvel of latter-twentieth-century productivity. American management experts began to visit Japan in the early 1980s in an attempt to discover the key to Japanese success. Strangely enough, the germ of the idea behind the success was probably imported from the United States during the rehabilitation of Japan following World War II. Simply put, this practice, now often called "Theory Z," embraces the idea that "involved workers are the most effective workers." Therefore, management with participatory, consensual approaches to decision making and operation creates within its workers loyalty to the firm and commitment to the job—all of which increase the productivity of the organization. Total quality management also may be viewed as a by-product of looking at Japanese management. While decisions are data driven, those decisions are made at the point of production, thereby involving the workers, not just supervisors and management.

Human Relations

The human relations movement ushered in a consideration for people and their welfare as an important ingredient in the study of management and organization. Strangely enough, before this movement gained real strength (and unfortunately even today), an employee was too often considered only on the basis of his or her contribution to the organization. The person's personal welfare, along with external and internal motivations, was largely overlooked.

---

[20] See Richard Beckhard, *Organization Development: Strategies and Models* (Reading, MA: Addison-Wesley, 1969); Freemont E. Kast and James Rosenzweig, *Organization and Management: A Systems Approach* (New York: McGraw-Hill, 1974); Wendell L. French and Cecil H. Bell Jr., *Organization Development* (Upper Saddle River, NJ: Prentice Hall, 1973); Robert R. Blake and Jane S. Mouton, *The Managerial Grid* (Houston, TX: Gulf, 1964).

One of the early pioneers in the United States in helping improve the lot of the worker was Lemuel Shattuck, who was instrumental in establishing the American Statistical Society in 1839. Much later William Mather and C. S. Meyers in England made strong contributions in researching working conditions and their relationship to productivity. Mather experimented with reducing the work week, and Meyers directed a number of research studies on worker fatigue and general welfare through the National Institute of Industrial Psychology, established in 1921.[21]

Mary Parker Follett was one of the first to theorize about human relations as a key ingredient in administration and management. She believed that developing and maintaining dynamic and harmonious relationships within an organization were fundamental to that organization's success. Further, she stated that conflict and controversy were normal and that, properly directed, they should be accepted as a "process by which socially valuable differences register themselves for all concerned."[22] Actually, Follett's early writings had little impact on the times, but today they are considered classics by many students in the field.[23]

It was not until the late 1930s that the studies by Elton Mayo, Thomas Whitehead, Fritz Roethlisberger, and others helped conceptualize human relations as an important theory to be considered. As a result of these studies, people became really important in management. Known as the Hawthorne Studies or the Western Electric Experiment, the studies showed the necessity for developing a new, more disciplined approach to motivating workers and dealing with people in the organization.

The major report of the results came out in 1939 in Roethlisberger and William Dickson's *Management and the Worker*.[24] Other books based on the Hawthorne Studies are *Human Problems of an Industrial Civilization, The Industrial Worker*, and *Management and Morale*.

The implications drawn from the Hawthorne Studies were enlarged and promoted by a great variety of researchers and scholars. Several studies on human motivation had strong human relations ties even though they were conducted by social scientists focusing on organizations as social systems.

---

[21] William G. Monahan, *Theoretical Dimensions of Educational Administration* (New York: Macmillan, 1975); Bertram Gross, *The Managing of Organizations* (New York: Macmillan, 1964); William H. Roe, *School Business Management* (New York: McGraw-Hill, 1961), 42–43.

[22] Mary Parker Follett, *Creative Experience* (London: Longman Group, 1924), 300.

[23] Mary Parker Follett, *Dynamic Administration: The Collected Papers of Mary Parker Follett*, ed. Henry C. Metcalf and Lyndall F. Urwick (New York: Harper & Row, 1941).

[24] Fritz J. Roethlisberger and William Dickson, *Management and the Worker* (Cambridge: Harvard University Press, 1939). See also Elton Mayo, *Human Problems of an Industrial Civilization* (New York: Macmillan, 1933); Thomas N. Whitehead, *The Industrial Worker* (Cambridge: Harvard University Press, 1938); Fritz J. Roethlisberger, *Management and Morale* (Cambridge: Harvard University Press, 1939).

In the 1930s, the main thrust of the human relations movement was centered at the University of Iowa, where Kurt Lewin was experimenting with and developing interesting psychological theories on leadership and human behavior. These theories attracted an almost fanatical following of both theorists and practitioners devoted to group dynamics and human relations.

One major development of the movement was the National Training Laboratories established at Bethel, Maine, in 1947. This laboratory's major role was experimentation with human interaction, individually and in groups, along with the development of a technique that could be used to train individuals in group dynamics. The laboratory soon became very popular as a source of training for leaders in business, industry, and education, through T-groups, encounter groups, and various sensitivity-training sessions. Contributors to this movement are too numerous to mention here.[25] It suffices to say that the movement ushered in an important alternative to the traditional notion of authority from the top to the bottom. Its unabashed emphasis was on the importance of people within organizations and their relationships individually and collectively. This focus was expressed both theoretically and operationally through such terms as *shared decision making, group authority, collegiality, democratic leadership, participating leadership, morale, shared authority, group dynamics,* and *group interaction.*

Problem Solving and Decision Theory

Because much of the principal's job entails problem solving and decision making, theory relative to the area is extremely important.[26] The generally recognized steps of problem solving are as follows:

1. Becoming aware of and identifying the problem
2. Defining and limiting the problem in terms of the goals of the enterprise
3. Determining who should be involved in the problem-solving process and how they should be involved
4. Collecting appropriate data specific to the problem
5. Formulating and selecting possible solutions
6. Predicting consequences of possible solutions
7. Identifying a preferred solution, with a rationale for selection, as well as alternative solutions, in priority order
8. Putting the preferred solution into effect

---

[25] Leland Bradford, Jack R. Gibb, and Kenneth Benne, eds., *T-Group Theory and Laboratory Method* (New York: Wiley, 1964).

[26] A *problem* may be simply defined as a state of affairs that creates dissatisfaction in an organization. A *decision* is that planned action taken to resolve that dissatisfaction.

9.   Establishing an evaluative process for determining success[27]

Barnard was one of the first to theorize about the decision-making process.[28] He was most perceptive in his observation that often the executive will create unnecessary problems by attempting to solve a problem or make a decision inappropriately. He proposed that there is a fine art of decision making that consists of (1) not deciding questions not now pertinent, (2) not deciding prematurely, (3) not making decisions that cannot be effectuated, (4) not making decisions others should make, and (5) sometimes deciding not to do anything.

D. J. Bross's contribution to decision-making theory within social systems was to observe that people within organizations and subsystems of organizations are affected in varying degrees (positively and negatively) by a particular decision. One of the administrator's responsibilities in relation to decision making is to identify the various individuals and groups affected by a decision and to analyze the intensity of their feelings on the basis of whether the decision is favorable or unfavorable to them. Appropriately, the effective administrator will stand ready to make necessary adjustments, based on group feelings, when a decision is put into effect.[29]

Herbert A. Simon theorized that decision making is the heart of administration.[30] The task of deciding is truly as important as the task of doing; therefore, principles of organization must be established that ensure correct decision-making processes. Simon also noted that all people in the organization make decisions of one kind or another; thus, there should be horizontal specialization in decision making as well as vertical specialization. He advocated that regular routinized channels be identified for arriving at decisions, regardless of their source in the organizational hierarchy. These would be called *programmed decisions*, and he attempted to develop them as part of a management science.[31]

James G. March proposed a framework for decision making based on standard theories of choice: (1) determine precisely the alternatives,

---

[27] The steps in problem solving have been discussed so widely in the general literature that it is impossible to credit specific authors. Although not clearly identified as such, Frederick Taylor and Henry L. Gantt used these steps as the basis for developing scientific management techniques. Several works in educational administration have advanced theoretical knowledge in this area, including Daniel E. Griffiths's "Administration Is Decision Making" and John K. Hemphill's "Administration as Problem Solving," both chapters in Andrew W. Halpin, ed., *Administrative Theory in Education* (New York: Macmillan, 1967); and Daniel L. Stuffelbeam et al., *Educational Evaluation and Decision Making* (Itasca, IL: Peacock, 1971).

[28] Barnard, *Functions of the Executive*, 194.

[29] Irwin D. J. Bross, *Design for Decision* (New York: Macmillan, 1953).

[30] Herbert A. Simon, *Administrative Behavior* (New York: Macmillan, 1950).

[31] Herbert A. Simon, *The New Science of Management Decisions* (New York: Harper & Row, 1960).

(2) define clearly your value preferences, (3) estimate possible consequences stemming from each alternative, (4) determine the likelihood of occurrences of consequences, and (5) select the alternative that will maximize the desired value.[32]

March and Simon identified problems or breakdowns in the standard decision-making process as creating "conflict."[33] Such a breakdown causes an individual or group to experience difficulty in selecting action alternatives. The study of conflict management is critical to the management field. It is definitely related to decision making and how different goals and purposes will affect organizational decisions—indeed, how those decisions can affect the outside environment.

More recently, rationality as the basis of decision making has been questioned. Wayne Hoy opines, "I believe that non-rational choice is the natural state. Much, if not most, decision making is driven by normative and affective considerations."[34] Given this perspective, it is important that a known set of beliefs and values that shape behavior and subsequently decisions about the school pervade the levels of decision makers.

The Cultural Perspective

The culture and subcultures of an organization have become a focus of researchers and theoreticians since the early 1980s. Observations that each organization, each school was unique in some ways led to a more careful examination of what made them unique. There seemed to be different ways of doing things that were derived from what had worked for the organization's members in solving problems. A sense of "how we do things around here" developed. The members shared certain values and beliefs and centered their practice around them. The staff of each school formed, consciously or unconsciously, ideas they thought were important and believed to be true. Edgar Schein suggests that basic assumptions about the nature of realities, time, space, human nature, activity, and relationships are formed and then lead to values and in turn to the artifacts and behaviors that are observable.[35]

The members of a school may thus believe that some individuals, as a result of their backgrounds, may never be able to perform academically like others of a different background. Therefore, "tracks" are created to accommodate the different performers, and teacher behaviors are adjusted depending on which track they are teaching at the time. The belief may be reinforced in that it seems to work, given the normed test

---

[32] James G. March, "Theories of Choice and Making Decisions," *Society* 30 (November–December 1982).
[33] James G. March and Herbert A. Simon, *Organizations* (New York: Wiley, 1958).
[34] Wayne K. Hoy, "Science and Theory in the Practice of Educational Administration: A Pragmatic Perspective," *Education Administration Quarterly* 32 (August 1996): 374.
[35] Edgar H. Schein, *Organizational Culture and Leadership* (San Francisco: Jossey-Bass, 1985).

scores of the students. In this scenario, would the persons comprising that "culture" be inclined to change it if they felt that their way of doing things works? The obvious answer is no.

The implication is clear that leadership is essential; it is much less clear how best to lead. Several books have been written regarding the idea of the professional culture that redistributes at least some of the authority to teachers.[36] Leadership that keeps the focus on the school's mission may deter decisions being made on the basis of the convenience or biases of the majority. Values, beliefs, and traditional solutions perceived to be good solutions are not easily displaced. The continuing research on and analyses of the cultural perspective of organizational life may prove fruitful for long-lasting changes.

Human Resources Development

Human resources development is "concerned with the forces and processes through which organizational participants are socialized into the organization: how they develop perceptions, values, and beliefs concerning the organization and what influence these inner states have on behavior."[37] Human resources development is the view that as employees become productive, they will tend to be more satisfied rather than less satisfied. The grounding in research might go back to the questions Mayo was asking in the 1930s, but the thinking regarding culture and climate has refined the focus on the individual's filter system of beliefs and values, which is partly formed through experience.

Although much of the work has focused on adult workers or teachers in schools, it may be useful to think about students in a similar vein. What forces are at work in the development of the students' filter systems through which they process experience and information about the school and the society it represents? Would serious thought about the students' views of effectively solving their problems in the organization lead to different ways of dealing with them?

Critical Theory

Critical theorists look at schools as one entity in a much larger context of social, political, and power relationships. If the leader of a school views her or his role as one that connects with other power in the larger social context, the boundaries of the leader's role are expanded beyond improved management to include ideas and values. Critical theorists

---

[36] See, e.g., Ann Lieberman, ed., *Building a Professional Culture in Schools* (New York: Teachers College Press, 1988).

[37] Robert G. Owens, *Organizational Behavior in Schools* (Upper Saddle River, NJ: Prentice Hall, 1991), 166.

view current organizations as the causes of problems in organizations and society at large.

Postmodernism

Postmodernism is based on the ideas of deconstructionism, which questions the existence of organizations as we know them. Deconstructionists see their goal as eliminating organizations that have caused or that perpetuate repression or alienation of certain segments of society. They see schools as serving the needs of some at the expense of others, to the economic benefit of those well served.

Margaret Grogan suggests that ". . . post modernism provides us with concepts . . . [that] include discourse, subjectivity, power, knowledge and resistance." She explains that "[w]e are molded by or subjectified by a discourse in the sense that we make meaning of our experiences according to the dominant values and beliefs expressed within the discourse."[38] The postmodern or deconstructionist view, then, is one of uncertainty, and what is right results from the interactions between people or the outcomes of the discourse. We have witnessed the meaning of words being changed by being questioned or redefined via the media or political figures. It is possible under this view that morality or what is right to do is defined by poll, or by majority vote, or by political or economic power.

Feminocentric theories also question organizations' purposes and processes from the perspective that organizations are male dominated and thus serve male purposes, function in an authoritarian context, and operate as machines, with a focus on the bottom line as a measure of success. Generally, this approach seeks to feminize organizations in the sense of becoming more egalitarian and relational. Taher Razik and Austin Swanson describe female leaders as "more likely to feel themselves at the center of things instead of viewing themselves 'at the top.'"[39] Such a view is consistent with the idea that the principal's role is 90 degrees from everywhere (see Chapter 2).

A LEARNING/KNOWING ORGANIZATION

Some observers and theorists have viewed successfully surviving organizations as learning/knowing entities. C. W. Choo notes a cycle of sense

---

[38] Margaret Grogan, "Laying the Groundwork for a Reconception of the Superintendency from the Feminist Postmodern Perspectives," *Educational Administration Quarterly* 36 (February 2000): 127.

[39] Razik, Taher A. and Austin D. Swanson, *Fundamental Concepts of Educational Leadership*, 2d ed. (Upper Saddle River, NJ: Merrill/Prentice Hall, 2001).

making, decision making, and knowledge creating in successful organizations.[40] The knowledge created may include how to go about the work of the school differently and more effectively. Bart Nooteboom observes that there is ". . . no single, universal best form of governance."[41] While inertia and a deeply rooted culture may be difficult to overcome, a school that is continuously learning will question what learning is important and how it is best effected.

It is important to raise questions continuously about the bases for the ways schools go about their work, but it is equally important to offer alternatives if we perceive flaws in the rationale for why we do what we do. If schools really are being used as a sorting mechanism for society, if they are really being shaped to become only suppliers of workers for the economic sector, the principal has a golden opportunity not only to resist some views of the school's purposes but also to help shape other views that may be more useful to both individuals and society. The opportunities for leadership contributions are almost limitless.[42]

RESEARCH AND THEORY AS THEY RELATE TO THE PRINCIPAL

In the development and attendant inquiry regarding the aforementioned theories, a large body of research has accumulated, particularly in the behavioral sciences. This research can be as good a source of direction for the principal as the theory itself, if not better. However, the principal must be prepared to interpret and apply the results in his or her own setting. If the research is industry based, the results may be much different when applied to a school situation or an educational problem. When considering the application of industrial- and business-focused theory and research to the school, one must be very conscious of the differences between the school as an organization and the business, industrial, or military organizations. In attempting to fit schools into the organizational framework of business and industry, one fails to account for what is special about educational organizations.

Actually, no organization is exactly like the public school. William Greenfield notes that schools differ from other organizations, given "the uniquely moral character of schools; a highly educated, autonomous

---

[40] C. W. Choo, *The Knowing Organization* (Oxford: Oxford University Press, 1998).
[41] Bart Nooteboom, *Learning and Innovation in Organizations and Economies* (Oxford: Oxford University Press, 2000), 167.
[42] Cerylle A. Moffett, "Sustaining Change: The Answers Are Blowing in the Wind," *Educational Leadership* 57 (April 2000): 35–39.

workforce; and regular and unpredictable threats to organizational stability."[43] The fact that critical decisions about learning are made by teachers who are somewhat independent of those above them in the organizational hierarchy, and who are in a sense separate from their colleagues,
makes the school unique. Little imagination is required to give examples
of unpredictable threats to stability, given regular school board elections
and the issues that drive the success or failure of the candidates. Probably the most distinguishing characteristic is the perceived moral character of schools. Students are vulnerable and required to be in school, and
the community and parents in particular entrust their children to the
schools for proper education, care, and safety. It becomes clear that the
principal cannot operate solely from hierarchical, positional power and
expect to provide the kind of leadership essential to an effective school.

THEORY: A GUIDE TO ACTION?

The preceding brief review of the development of organization and management theory should not give the impression that there is a solid body
of theory that principals can apply in the operation of their schools. Such
is not the case. Rather, what have been described are developing theories
that warrant study and consideration by the practitioner.

The theory movement attempts to make the study of educational
administration more scientific and disciplined, but contrary to expectations, what has not emerged is a universal theory, or set of theories, that
could provide overall direction to administrative action. Too often it
became an "in" concept, associated with everything that had been studied over the years. Gradually, however, educational administration theorists became disappointed; they were at a loss when an advocated theory
did not stand up in replication studies and when clear relationships to
educational practice did not materialize. It took time to learn that theory
is not necessarily fact.

Wayne Hoy and Cecil Miskel help provide a perspective of theory
building when they state, "The fact that our knowledge may be flawed
or incomplete should not cause discouragement; it simply underscores
the tentative nature of knowledge."[44] But what has this got to do with the
school principal? If there is not a universal theory to provide a basis for
action, what is the use of theory at all? Although theory admittedly may
have been oversold and misunderstood, it still can be very useful for the
administrator.

[43] William D. Greenfield, "Toward a Theory of School Administration: The Centrality of
Leadership," *Educational Administration Quarterly* 31 (February 1995): 61.
[44] Wayne K. Hoy and Cecil G. Miskel, *Educational Administration: Theory, Research and Practice,* 5th ed. (New York: McGraw-Hill, 1996), 22.

While theory may be thought to explain behaviors or organizational phenomena, it may also serve as a safeguard to quick and simplistic answers. Robert Owens reminds us that "[s]ystems theory . . . puts us on guard against the strong tendency to ascribe phenomena to a single causative factor."[45] One must fully realize that one is dealing with theory, not fact, and therefore be ready to adjust actions accordingly.

Theoretical conceptualizations are good when they have relevance and applicability to what administrators do. One may often discuss and describe theories of administration but fail to comprehend their particular application to problems encountered by the principal. We often assume that the application is obvious, but more likely the practitioner disregards it. Learning how to apply and utilize theories is much more difficult than learning the theories themselves. Principals use theory continuously whether or not they are aware of it. Their behaviors are rooted in their own explanations (right or wrong) of what makes things work like they do. Knowledge of other ways of explaining phenomena may expand the practitioner's way of thinking and thus increase her or his range of responses to situations.

SHOULD A PRINCIPAL HAVE PRINCIPLES?

We think there is a place for principles for principals. Like practically everything else in our world, principles can become outdated, and they may have a cultural bias, but if one recognizes these points and adjusts accordingly, principles can provide a consistent framework for action.

While the values of our society are ever changing, some value concepts are generally agreed on in our society at a given time, and these can form the basis for a set of principles. Logical purposes and procedures, based on educational philosophy and legal precedent, can form the framework for a set of principles. Similarly, some practices have been so thoroughly tested that they can be recognized and adopted as principles.

In addition, we believe that as principals become students of their art and craft, they can develop their own personal administrative principles, based on their experience, values, style, and knowledge of the field. These principles provide principals and schools with a consistency of action. Outstanding principals, then, are ones who are students of people, of organization and leadership, and who, through a broad knowledge of education and its related fields, through comprehension of the theory and research, and through an understanding of their own values, skills, and experiences, develop a set of principles for themselves that provides guidelines for action.

---

[45] Robert G. Owens, *Organizational Behavior in Education*, 6th ed. (Boston: Allyn and Bacon, 1998), 42.

PRINCIPLES, FOR EXAMPLE

The following illustrate principles we believe can be accepted logically as a guide to administrative action. Analyzing each principle, one can see, in varying degrees, the influences of culture, political and educational philosophy, educational practice, legal opinion, and theory and research. We believe that these principles encompass enough universality, at this time in our culture, that they can have specific application to practice. We agree that they can become outdated as our society changes, for principles, like policies, must adapt to a changing culture; however, this does not decrease their value for here and now.

1. There can be no invisible citizens. A child of four is just as much a citizen as a man or woman of thirty or ninety-three. Certainly, the student in school is of an age where we should be particularly scrupulous to protect constitutional freedoms. Care must be taken that we do not unconsciously teach youth to discount important principles of our government as mere platitudes because of the way we teach or treat them.

2. The process of education extends beyond the walls of the formally organized classroom. Important learning takes place within the school community as well as within the classroom itself, and the school staff must make every effort to cooperate with the school community to make this learning positive, effective, and productive.

3. The influences of forces outside the school are so important that close cooperation with other agencies, institutions, and organizations is essential to the development of a sound educational program.

4. The American public school reflects the cultural milieu of which it is a part but is also responsible to seek to improve the community where needed. It is responsible not only for conserving the useful past but also for preparing the way for progress and change. A public institution, especially, must be attentive to the wishes of all people. However, because an institution such as a school cannot hope to please all people, it and its leaders will always be subject to criticisms.

5. The goals, objectives, and roles of the school must be effectively communicated to the various social systems of which it is a part. Those with responsibility must stand ready to work with these social systems to revise and adapt these goals, objectives, and roles to changing times.

6. Those affected by administrative action should be involved in the development of policy relative to action taken. Involvement will depend on the sophistication/maturity of the staff/students and on varying circumstances.

7. All schools should have written policies to guide their activities. These policies should be in a state of continuous development and revision. Instead of operating on a visceral base, from conflict to conflict, the administrative leader must be sensitive to changes in the social system that might require new or revised policy.

8. The chief administrator and staff are responsible (in varying degrees) to and for all social systems and power elements that are a part of the institution.

⑤ U M M A R Y

The study of educational administration has moved in the last half century from the how-to, folklore, and testimonial stages to a more scientific, theory-oriented, and disciplined base through emphases on interdisciplinary study, behavioral research, and hard comparative analysis. The scientific theoretical approach to the study of educational administration has made a major contribution to the field and significantly changed for the better both the preparation program for administrators and the way they behave. Newer theoretical approaches suggest a more connected, interactive role for the leader, one that includes shaping the purposes of education.

However, placing so much emphasis on theory that the importance of principles of administration is downplayed would be a mistake. Principles should provide a solid base for an individual's administrative behavior. As principals become students of their art and craft, they can develop their own personal principles. We believe the outstanding principal is a student of people, organization, and leadership who, through comprehension of theory and research as well as of society's and his or her own values, knowledge, skills, and experience, can develop a set of principles for herself or himself that will provide consistent guidelines for administrative action.

⑥ OR FURTHER THOUGHT

1. Some of the luster of the Hawthorne Studies has been tarnished by the so-called Hawthorne effect. What is the Hawthorne effect? Could it be developed into a theory or principle that might be important to the administrator? Discuss.

2. What is the difference between theories of administration and principles of administration? Is it possible that the failure to define these terms operationally creates confusion in our study of administration?

3. Develop a rationale to present to community business leaders that there is no organization quite like the public school.
4. What are the dangers of believing in certain principles of administration based on your individual value system?
5. Compare and contrast the administrative philosophies of Machiavelli and Mary Parker Follett.
6. Debate: The concept of "shared decision making" is based on sound research findings.
7. What responses might be effective to those who would "deconstruct" the school because it serves economic or power broker purposes?
8. If the school does actually serve those purposes, what specific curricular or organizational changes would you make?

ⓢELECTED READINGS

Argyris, Chris. *Reasoning, Learning and Action: Individual and Organizational.* San Francisco: Jossey-Bass, 1982.

Barnard, Chester I. *The Functions of the Executive.* Cambridge: Harvard University Press, 1938.

English, Fenwick W. *Theory in Educational Administration.* New York: HarperCollins College Publishers, 1994.

Griffiths, Daniel E. "Evolution of Research and Theory: A Study of Prominent Researchers." *Educational Administration Quarterly* 19 (Summer 1983): 201–221.

Grogan, Margaret. "Laying the Groundwork for a Reconception of the Superintendency from the Feminist Postmodern Perspectives." *Educational Administration Quarterly* 36 (February 2000): 117–142.

Hoy, Wayne K., and Cecil G. Miskel. *Educational Administration: Theory, Research and Practice,* 5th ed. New York: McGraw-Hill, 1996.

Lieberman, Ann, ed. *Building a Professional Culture in Schools.* New York: Teachers College Press, 1988.

March, James G. "Theories of Choice and Making Decisions." *Society* 20 (November–December 1982): 29–40.

Moehlman, Arthur B. *School Administration: Its Development, Principles and Function.* Boston: Houghton Mifflin, 1951.

Mort, Paul R., and Donald H. Ross. *Principles of School Administration,* 2d ed. New York: McGraw-Hill, 1957.

Nooteboom, Bart. *Learning and Innovations in Organizations.* Oxford: Oxford University Press, 2000.

Owens, Robert G. *Organizational Behavior in Schools,* 6th ed. Boston: Allyn and Bacon, 1998.

Razik, Taher, A. and Austin D. Swanson. *Fundamental Concepts of Educational Leadership*, 2d ed. Upper Saddle River, NJ: Merrill/Prentice Hall, 2001.

Schein, Edgar H. *Organizational Culture and Leadership*. San Francisco: Jossey-Bass, 1985.

Senge, Peter M. *The Fifth Discipline: The Art and Practice of the Learning Organization*. New York: Doubleday, 1990.

CHAPTER 5

Organization

$\mathcal{I}$n the United States, education is a state function, not a
national function as it is in most countries. This philosophy—
accepted by the men who shaped our Constitution, embedded in the
constitutions of the states, and reinforced by court decisions—has
resulted in a nation with fifty different state school systems. Still further
differences arise because the legislatures of practically all states have delegated much of the operation of schools to the local communities.

While all systems are not exactly alike, all have much in common.
All school districts have a top administrative officer, usually known as
the superintendent; all school districts have some type of board of education or local administrative board; all schools have principals, directors, or head teachers; all public school systems have some federal funding as well as state and local funds. All states have recognizable
patterns of local school organization and school curricula, all work
under certain minimum standards, and all attempt to provide a minimum of twelve years of schooling. These similarities exist because of
legal constraints and because board members and educators have
observed the developments and inventions of the systems around them
and have adapted or used in their own systems their neighbors' good
ideas.

WHAT IS AN ORGANIZATION?

The organizational structure of a school is its framework or platform
for operation. It may also be an artifact of the underlying beliefs of the
decision makers about how an organization should work. It is important
for students of administration to take a special look at organization.
According to Caplow, "an organization is a social system that has an

unequivocal collective identity, an exact roster of members, a program of activity, and procedures for replacing members."[1]

Hall provides a brief developmental history of definitions of organizations that reinforces the idea of organizations having boundaries and consisting of social relationships and coordinated activities to achieve goals. He then defines an organization:

> An organization is a collectivity with a relatively identifiable boundary, a normative order, ranks of authority, communications systems, and membership coordinating systems; this collectivity exists on a relatively continuous basis in an environment and engages in activities that are usually related to a set of goals; the activities have outcomes for organizational members, the organization itself, and for society.[2]

The idea of boundaries in organizations has been questioned by Ashkenus et al., who note that a boundaryless organization may be more able to change when needed.[3] Boundaries are identified among hierarchical levels, interunit divisions, and internal versus external organizations.

Throughout the definitions in the literature, the structuring, controlling, and establishing of functional relationships are found in one form or another. Developing organization, then, is the process of systematically establishing proper relationships that move the group toward accomplishing its work. When a school administrative unit has been properly organized, means are at hand for getting things done, routines have been established for doing them, responsibility for seeing that they are done has been fixed upon competent shoulders, and processes have been established so that decisions are made by the person or persons most likely to develop accepted and effective solutions. In an effective organization, things get done, and done well, within an appropriate time frame. In an ineffective organization, the unimportant things may tend to get done, and the important ones may tend to be slurred over and neglected; the decision-making process may be carried out in a halting and often irresolute fashion; and eventually the constituted authorities may be bypassed and decisions made in obscurity by a power system that has taken over without an appropriate assignment of responsibility.

Too often the organizational structure of today's school system follows a pattern of topsy-turvy growth somewhat like the construction of the proverbial old New England farmhouse—that is, without any general plan. Occasionally, mandates from whatever source have elicited temporary fixes or add-ons that have operated at the periphery of the

---

[1] Theodore Caplow, *Principles of Organization* (New York: Harcourt Brace Jovanovich, 1964), 1.

[2] Richard H. Hall, *Organizations, Structures, Processes and Outcomes* (Upper Saddle River, NJ: Prentice Hall, 1991), 32.

[3] Ron Ashkenus, Dave Ulaich, Todd Jick, and Steve Kerr, *The Boundaryless Organization* (San Francisco: Jossey-Bass, 1995).

school structure. Symptoms are treated rather than causes. A danger of continuing this approach of organizational tinkering is that the focus of the organization can be lost or even replaced by the peripheral activities. The real organization becomes a response unit rather than a focused, proactive entity.

VIEWS OF ORGANIZATIONS

Organizations have been viewed as machines, brains, organisms, and social cultures. Other descriptive terms applied to organizations include *rational bureaucracies, organized anarchies, closed* or *open systems, loosely coupled, collegial,* and *political.* Students of business, industrial, and military organizations and how people behave in them have tried to fit schools into the nomenclature. Theories developed in nonschool settings often influenced how organizational theorists looked at schools.

There is no institution or agency identical to the public schools. Therefore, if one attempts to force all schools into theoretical organizational patterns that were established for conventional industrial models, one fails because the schools' distinctive qualities and characteristics are not easily accommodated. Important aspects are too often overlooked or disregarded. Further, a typical mistake is to study the schools as if they were closed systems, not recognizing the very complicated "openness" of public schools, including both ends of the social spectrum.[4]

Another confusing aspect is to have researchers analyze a school as a single social system and overlook that it is part of a greater system, involving one or more communities, the county, the state, and, to a limited extent, the federal government. This criticism does not mean that we should disregard the theory and research of the behavioral scientists. Their methods and results help us examine schools from a variety of angles and better understand their nature. However, we should use their work as a starting point and then focus on the distinctive qualities and characteristics of the school.

Allison makes an excellent point in this regard when he asserts that educators have relied too heavily on using specific behavioral science nomenclature and theories when studying the organization of schools. As a result, they have crafted such "a bewildering array of images that claim to represent the nature of the school organization that too often it

---

[4] See Chapter 3. Because of the public school's legal relationship to the community, county, and state and its actual organizational pattern, it is impossible, legally, for a public school to be a closed system. Furthermore, schools have little or no control over their "input" in terms of types, abilities, attitudes, environments, economic status, and other factors regarding students.

has created confusion rather than clarification."[5] He calls for judicious use of the insights that behaviorists may offer rather than an uncritical acceptance and application of their substance.

A Mechanical or Machine View

The Weberian bureaucracy is a persistent, mechanistic organization, in which there is a hierarchical pyramid of top-down authority, written rules and regulations, assumed rational behavior, specialization, and authority based on hierarchical positions. The machine organization behaves as if it is a closed system in that it chooses when and how it will interact with its environment. Such a view of the organization is somewhat limiting to a school that has little control of its "raw material" and that is subject to external forces such as state legislatures and court rulings, which can change the rules abruptly. The worker's role in a machine organization is somewhat like an interchangeable part with a set of specific, preassigned tasks to perform in a predetermined way. When applied to the schools, teachers would be easily interchangeable and expected to teach preassigned curricula in a prescribed manner.

Rowan cites curriculum alignment as an example of the ineffectiveness of a mechanical organization. He points out that regardless of whether a teacher makes the mandated changes, there are neither rewards nor punishments.[6] Hence, the machine "breaks down."

The mechanical view assumes that the hierarchy knows best and can prescribe the best way to do each of the jobs required, whether it is sweeping the floor or dealing with diverse students or selecting materials for implementing a complex curriculum. Shades of Taylor's scientific management approach are clearly at work in the machine organization.

The Organic Organization

The organic view of organizations sees the parts of the organization as interdependent and the organization as a whole interacting with persons, agencies, and other institutions external to the organization. In the 1980s, the organic organization view was applied to schools. Given that the organic view sees the organization interacting with its environment and dealing with diverse inputs, teachers were given autonomy to meet the needs facing them.[7] Teachers are regarded in a decision-making role, in

---

[5] Derek J. Allison, "Toward an Improved Understanding of the Organizational Nature of Schools," *Educational Administration* 19 (Fall 1983): 16.
[6] Brian Rowan, "The Organizational Design of Schools," in *Images of Schools,* ed. Samuel B. Bacharach and Bryan Mundell (Thousand Oaks, CA: Corwin, 1995), 18.
[7] Samuel B. Bacharach and Bryan Mundell, eds., *Images of Schools* (Thousand Oaks, CA: Corwin, 1995), 23.

that they are continuously coping with uncertainties. Such a view is similar to the professional organization, in which the professionals hold much decision power. Hoy and Miskel discuss the professional bureaucracy, which relies on the standardization of skills to coordinate the organizational efforts.[8] Authority is grounded in expertise rather than in hierarchical positions.

The increasing collaborative ventures between schools and community agencies, services, and expertise signal that the organic view of schools as organizations is growing. Johnson and Fauske note that ". . . effective organizations are those that create bridges and buffers between themselves and the environment."[9] Interaction with the environment has become essential to meeting the needs of the students and the community.

The Learning or Brain Organization

The learning organization operates systemically and learns to re-form and renew itself as needed. There is little redundancy in parts of the organization (e.g., each department does not need a media specialist of its own) in that activities, somewhat like those in the brain, are carried out in separate parts, but the whole organization thinks congruently. Internal boundaries are permeable. Issues are addressed rather than avoided or hidden, as might occur in the political, machinelike organization. (See the discussion in The Adaptive, Future-Oriented Organization, page 118.)

The implications of the learning organization for principals are far reaching. As problems are faced and solutions created, jobs within the school change, contentions for power are greatly reduced, and restructuring comes from within rather than being resisted because of rigid job descriptions or power positions. Since the school's population changes each year with new first-year students and since new technologies are continuously becoming available, the school might reorganize itself and its resources at least annually to meet the challenges. "Leaders of schools, like leaders of businesses and hospitals, want their organization to be flexible and responsive, able to change in accord with changing circumstances. The ideal organization is characterized as 'self renewing' or as a 'learning organization.'"[10]

[8] Wayne K. Hoy and Cecil G. Miskel, *Educational Administration: Theory, Research and Practice*, 5th ed. (New York: McGraw-Hill, 1996), 71–75.
[9] Bob L. Johnson Jr. and Janice R. Fauske, "Principals and the Political Economy of Environmental Enactment," *Educational Administration Quarterly* 36 (April 2000): 159.
[10] Ron Brandt, *Powerful Learning* (Alexandria, VA: Association for Supervision and Curriculum Development, 1998), 49.

Organizations as Cultures

Writings over the last few years have emphasized that every organization has a culture; it may be peculiar to itself, but it may also be grounded in the history and tradition of other organizations and environments of the past.[11] An analysis of that culture helps one understand why people behave the way they do. People in the organization create its present culture, but they have been influenced by people and traditions of the past. Understanding the dynamic forces that govern how culture evolves and changes can be the key to organizational improvement.

What is culture? Deal states that "culture enjoys as many definitions as there are people who study it. . . . Kluckhohn noted 164 definitions."[12] Schein defines culture as "the set of shared, taken-for-granted implicit assumptions that a group holds and determines how it perceives, thinks about, and reacts to its various environments."[13] Sergiovanni writes that culture "refers to the values and rituals that provide people with continuity, tradition, identity, meaning, and significance as well as to the norm systems that provide direction and that structure their lives."[14] Obviously, many more definitions could be cited, but the idea is clear that culture can be pervasive with an organization, it can be controlling, and it can provide meaning to the enterprise.

The person who proposes to lead cannot ignore studying the culture of the group(s) forming the people dimension of the organization. An examination is necessary of what is important, of what meanings stories, ceremonies, and rituals have for the people in the organization. If a firmly established culture is present, it can serve as a formidable barrier to change. On the other hand, a culture that values excellence, new ideas, and learning can be a stimulating, exciting experience for a leader.

DESIGNING AN ORGANIZATIONAL STRUCTURE

Organizational structure establishes human and material relationships consistent with the objectives and resources of the organization, and it harmonizes activities through strategically placed executive officers who can facilitate administrative details. The organizational setup should take into account the benefits of specialization, the limitations of functional status authority, the problems of communication, the need for stimula-

---

[11] W. G. Dyer Jr. *Culture in Organizations: A Case Study Analysis,* Working Paper 1279–82 (Cambridge, MA: Sloan School of Management, MIT, 1982).

[12] Terrence E. Deal, "Symbols and Symbolic Activity," in *Images of Schools,* ed. Bacharach and Mundell, 111.

[13] Edgar H. Schein, "Culture: The Missing Concept in Organizational Studies," *Administrative Science Quarterly* 41 (June 1996): 236.

[14] Thomas J. Sergiovanni, *Leadership for the Schoolhouse* (San Francisco: Jossey-Bass 1996), 20.

tion and leadership, and evaluation. Above all, it should provide proper balance so that personal relations are harmonious and satisfying.

A pattern of organization establishes the bounds of action of particular individuals and groups; it outlines the way they work and provides them with a base or framework within which to work. Some attention should be given to avoid creating the impression that each unit or subgroup is to make its decisions independently. The structure can cause serious problems as a result. "Often problems come because people focus on their own decision and ignore how those decisions affect others."[15] Rather than focusing on problems facing the total organization, defending the turf of subunits becomes the focus. Such a situation leads at best to maintaining the status quo, and at worst to creating a dysfunctional organization.

We must emphasize that although organizational structure is a pencil-and-paper affair, its actual operation is a matter of human relationships. A pattern of operation is in reality but a basic theory of personal relationships within an organization. Thus, because they deal with people, both organization and operation must be flexible and adaptable, not rigid, for the formal structure has little meaning unless it enhances the behavior of the participants. Dysfunctional structures must be changed ". . . so that reform can proceed unencumbered by such factors as low trust, competing priorities, turf issues and a lack of clear, sustained focus."[16] These points are most important in a school system. Any school organization that institutionalizes its working relationships, rigidly stratifies its personnel, and develops a stolid hierarchical form of control without allowing the full reservoir of the participants' abilities to be used (students included) will fail to reach its full potential. By the same token, because public school systems belong to the citizenry at large, they must be sensitive and responsive to the public need and to wide variations in the clients to be served.

Begin with the Goals and Objectives

In designing an organizational structure, one logically starts with the goals and objectives of the enterprise. Schools now have imposed standards and competencies, which can cause some dissonance between the schools and those who would hold them accountable. (See the discussions in Chapters 12 and 16.) A question arises regarding whose goals to achieve. How should the organization restructure to meet the required

---

[15] Bert Frydman, Iva Wilson, and JoAnne Wyer, *The Power of Collaborative Leadership: Lessons for the Learning Organization* (Boston: Butterworth Heinemann, 2000), 7.
[16] Cerylie A. Moffett, "Sustaining Change: The Answers Are Blowing in the Wind," *Educational Leadership* 57 (April 2000): 35.

standards? What principal leadership is necessary to resolve what may appear to be conflicting goals?

Prescribing a precise formula appropriate for all school districts is impossible. Many conditions within a state or local community affect the character of the organizational structure: (1) custom, tradition, and local culture; (2) constitutional provisions; (3) the degree to which statutes define the authority and responsibility of school districts or schools within the districts; (4) the way courts have interpreted the U.S. Constitution, state constitutions, and federal and state statutes; (5) the number, competencies, and abilities of personnel; (6) the finances available for operation; (7) the educational needs in the state and community; (8) the importance of education to the people of the community; and (9) the backgrounds and abilities of the children to be educated. Some of these conditions may be altered, but American education, because of its closeness to the people, demands an organization flexible and adaptable enough to fit local conditions.

Examine Beliefs and Values

To paraphrase an old saying, our structure and procedures often speak louder than our words. As noted earlier in this chapter, what we really believe and value will shape how we behave. What is important to us will dictate our actions. Granted, many structures are inherited, have been in place a long time, and in some way reflect the values of the people in them. At least the members seem to have resigned themselves to doing nothing about it, a choice that itself expresses a belief. The leader who wishes to see improvement, who is willing to try to make a positive difference, must understand her or his own values and priorities. It is one thing to parrot what is expected during an interview to get the job (or on a test in a graduate class), but it is quite another to put into practice the beliefs that all students can learn, that teachers can become effective decision makers and change agents, and that everyone is a valued learner in the school. After reflecting on one's own beliefs and value priorities, one should examine the organization and procedures to try to determine what underlying values are operating that make it what it is. Then it is time to begin to develop a cooperative strategy for change.

Consider Principles of Organization

The following principles are suggested as guides to developing proper organizational structure for schools:

1. The basic objective of the school is to facilitate positive learning; thus, the value of all organizational forms, agents, agen-

cies, and practices should be determined by their contribution to the achievement of this objective.

2. The plan of organization should facilitate the learning process and stimulate the best in instructional activities.

3. The organization should provide for the division of the total work into related parts that will ensure the most effective use of the services of available personnel. These divisions should not be viewed as permanent fixtures, nor should they create fiefdoms to be defended.

4. The organization should attract and retain the most competent personnel by providing, insofar as is possible, conditions under which they can do their best work.

5. The school should be so organized that unity and teamwork are emphasized through the effective coordination of the efforts of all educational units and agencies toward fulfillment of the objectives of education.

6. The organizational structure should be as simple as possible, with the need to coordinate the work of the school.

7. Each unit in the structure should have a clear understanding of its mission and the responsibilities of the individuals comprising the unit.

8. An individual should clearly understand to whom he or she is responsible for the performance of particular functions.[17] Moreover, final authority should be clearly vested. Whenever authority is vested in a group, the group should have one person who is responsible for the execution of group decisions.

9. The number of persons directly responsible to an individual should not be greater than can be coordinated effectively. Activities should be grouped into the smallest feasible number of units without creating an inflexible administrative hierarchy.

10. The organization of the school should reflect the complete service offering in the school. It should be possible to identify easily the various activities both individually and in relation to broader areas.

11. All personnel within the school, including students, should feel that they belong to an identifiable group and have a definite home base at any given time. Administrative units within the school should have compatible groupings so that subgroups within the units have real group identity for the responsibilities at hand.

---

[17] An oft-repeated administrative principle is that a person should be responsible to only one administrative officer. It has usually been compared with the biblical quotation "A man cannot serve two masters." There is no reason that a person cannot serve several administrators so long as it is clear to whom one is responsible for a particular function and clearly specified, open lines of communication prevail between those to whom he or she is responsible. See Chapter 8 for further discussion of this principle.

12. Although the organization must have a basic stability, it should also have a built-in flexibility, with sensitivity to problems and to problem solving. That flexibility should lead to an openness for the need to change so that it can adjust easily and adapt itself to the future.

Examine Principles of Operation of a School Organization

An organization itself is sterile and lifeless until it is in operation. Thus, operational principles, such as those enumerated here, are as important to success as is the organizational structure itself.

1. A school cannot exceed effectively the restrictions placed on it by the popular understanding of its function. The organization needs to "get its message out" continually to the community.
2. The importance of education demands that the school not be viewed as a player in partisan politics.
3. The educational process is so complex that it can be carried out only through a number of institutions, agencies, and activities. Cooperation, coordination, and collaboration with educational and social agencies are essential activities of any school.
4. An effective organization will emphasize and constantly use in proper balance the constituent elements of administrative activities: (a) planning, (b) organizing, (c) staffing, (d) leadership, (e) communication/interpretation, and (f) evaluation and appraisal.
5. Persons affected by policies, both within and outside the organizational structure, should have a part in shaping those policies. The level of democratic action at any time depends on the competence and conscience of the individual involved.
6. The aim of administration is to facilitate learning and the instructional process. Administrative personnel should provide leadership in improving learning and should see that the members of the staff have the necessary time, sufficient materials, and proper working conditions to perform their functions.
7. The organization should be structured so that the participants (teachers, administrators, students, etc.) can learn and share their knowledge in order to improve the school's overall effectiveness.
8. To achieve excellence, staff members must be allowed to avail themselves of opportunities to make significant contributions locally, nationally, and internationally. A school's standing in the community will be measured by the kind of job it does and by the achievements of its personnel as they work individually and cooperatively.

9. A school organization should have enough flexibility and adaptability to handle newly developing needs or to initiate programs/techniques to improve its effectiveness. Its structure, policies, and programs should be subject to continuous evaluation. However, there should be sufficient continuity of organization and program to provide the necessary feeling of security for both the staff and the public at large.

10. A major purpose of the school is to help preserve the benefits of our present culture and pass on the accumulated knowledge of the past. At the same time, it has a basic responsibility to exert leadership in the overall improvement of our society. This task requires a certain amount of risk taking and courage in propounding causes that may not always be the most popular.

11. Goals and objectives of the school organization should be jointly developed by the constituent elements of that organization, and processes established for their periodic review and revision. Administrative and supervisory personnel are responsible for keeping all members of that organization continuously aware of these goals and objectives.

12. The school organization should have easy access channels for communication and feedback so that each subunit of the organization may formally react to its relationships with other subunits and the central administration. Decisions should be made from the perspective of the total organization, not just separate parts.

MAJOR ADMINISTRATIVE DIVISIONS
OF SCHOOL SYSTEMS

The organization of a school system is actually a translation of its purposes, principles, and activities into a structural administrative plan; thus, it is realistically developed by identifying its goals, listing all the work that is being done and should be accomplished, and then grouping these activities into related areas. How definitive the grouping is or how many categories are accepted as major areas of work makes the difference in the pattern.

Probably the classic model of school organization today is one in which the school district is divided administratively into three major areas according to function: (1) instruction, (2) educational services, and (3) business management. *Instruction* deals with the teaching process itself in each local school and includes the certified personnel who teach and the consultants and specialists who help with the specific teaching function. *Educational services* are provided by people trained in the field of education who assist the teachers directly through specialized professional services. These include library and media utilization, guidance and counseling, physical and psychological services, child accounting and attendance, visiting teacher services, and research. *Business management* is that phase of the organization that serves the other two functions in a facilitating and supporting role. It may be simply defined as that part of school administration dealing with the management of finances, facilities, and similar noneducational services necessary for the operation of a school system.

In the past, there was great diversity in the organization of these functions. Today one may study schools throughout the nation and find almost every conceivable type of organization, including those with multiple and dual executives and top-heavy, highly departmentalized structures. Because learning is the key activity of the school system, with all other activities serving an auxiliary or facilitating role, educational administrative theorists advocate a type of control under the leadership of a professional educator, who serves as the chief executive to the board of education. This encourages the making of instructional decisions at the top operational level. Figure 5.1 illustrates an organizational pattern of this type in its simplest functional sense.

Studying the historical development of this type of organization in our schools and observing that the unit type of executive, with its perfect pyramid, is a relatively recent development in today's schools, we would assume that this type of organization is a modern device. Actually, it is not; the concept it represents is very ancient. One may cite examples from the Old Testament (Exodus 18:14–22), the ancient Chinese Empire under the Ts'in and Han dynasties, the Roman Republic, the Venetian State, the Prussian Civil Service under Frederick William I, the U.S. military structure, and industrial and business organizational patterns.[18] Although generally popularized by Weber and Parsons in the early 1940s, neither the pyramid type of organization nor the complicated line-and-staff organization is a modern invention.[19]

THE PERSON IN THE MIDDLE

The principal of the local elementary, middle, or secondary school is in the middle of the administrative hierarchy. As titular head of the school building unit, he or she is the person who, with the teachers, is the closest communications link with parents and citizens in the school's attendance area. At the same time, the principal's office is represented as the

---

[18] Caplow, *Principles of Organization,* 50–56.
[19] Max Weber, *The Theory of Social and Economic Organization,* trans. Talcott Parsons (New York: Free Press, 1947).

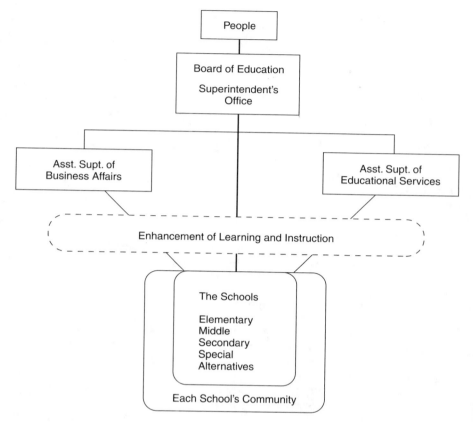

FIGURE 5.1
A line-and-staff organization along functional lines to emphasize that the administration, staff, and community must work as a team to improve the instructional process

switchboard, or closest local communicating link, to the central administration. Despite this, in too many cases organizational structure and operational procedures make the principal a school building manager who is responsible for maintaining the day-by-day routine but little else (see Figure 5.2). Principals are often bypassed by local pressure groups when they attempt to influence school activities or policy. Principals are not included by teachers when they decide on issues for negotiations. Too often principals are not significantly involved by the central administration in developing major policy decisions and operational procedures that affect the operation of their schools.

An example of bypassing the principal is illustrated in the following case:

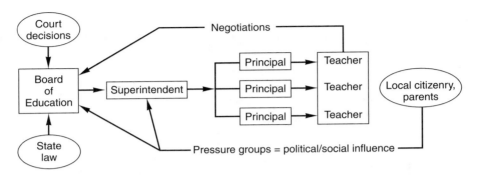

FIGURE 5.2
Bypassing the principal

One of the many presentations at an evening open house at the high school was centered on the benefits of the family life discussion course. A film was presented, and students outlined some of the discussions held concerning problems they felt were important to them. Concerns about sex and potential pregnancy and/or diseases were discussed freely. The course is an elective, and students present signed parent approval cards before registering for the course.

Within days after the open house, several local citizens, only a few of whom had children in the course, had formed a pressure group to have the course removed from the offerings. They went directly to media available to them and personally contacted board members and conservative ministers in the community. They then presented their case at a board meeting, with several of those whom they had contacted in attendance.

Everyone at the building level was bypassed until the issue came up at the board meeting. The only role open to the principal, teachers, and students was a reactive one. In this instance, they made excellent presentations at a subsequent board meeting.

ADAPTING THE ORGANIZATION TO MEET CURRENT NEEDS

Local schools have attempted to overcome some locked-in organizational and operational structures through special devices such as parent-teacher associations, local parent and attendance area advisory boards, and parent task forces. With passing years, it has become obvious that such groups have less and less influence on significant matters. As their recommendations have been lost because of the inflexibility of bureaucracy, they have become less enthusiastic and less effective—in many cases, dying a slow and agonizing death.

Rather than students, teachers, and parents trying to adapt to the organization that exists, perhaps more significantly the organizational structure of the schools needs to be radically changed to adapt to meet the needs facing them every day. The schools belong to the people. They require public support if they are to continue. To maintain the supportive parent-citizen's advocate role (as contrasted to the adversary role), organizational structures must be developed that keep the parent-citizen in close communication with the school and allow the individual school to be responsive to student as well as parent-citizen concerns and desires. This assertion is not new.

A report by the New York State Fleischmann Committee highlights rather dramatically how traditional organizational structure and operational procedures were unable to cope with the developing society in the 1960s and 1970s. This report, entitled *High Schools in Crisis*, was reviewed by the American Association of Colleges for Teacher Education:

> *At the heart of these crises, the report says, are the high schools' massive size, monolithic structure, and authoritarian lines.* . . . According to the chief author, Dr. Alan E. Guskin of Community Resources Limited, "The more potent issues in high schools are the crises in the organizational structure of the school."
>
> The report called for *a drastic altering of the organizational and educational structures of our high schools* so that "students will learn, within such settings, how to cope with their future in order that they may gain a sense of the potential of a democratic society, that they may understand their own equality as humans and thereby gain a sense of determining their own lives, and that they may understand their own role as potential change agents of society."[20]

Passow analyzed the reports of eight national commissions and panels that had studied education in detail from 1972 to 1976. These reports examined the nature and causes of the problems of educating youth and detailed shortcomings of the school. The common theme running through these reports was the need for a significant restructuring of education.

> The reports proposed reforming the schools by integrating the learning resources of school and community, by making available a wide variety of educational options and program alternatives to attain educational objectives, by involving the school in providing valid and meaningful work experiences for all, and the school's shedding some of its primary and ancillary functions.[21]

If one follows the reports of weaknesses in education from the 1950s through the 1990s (which in each decade seemed to build to a crisis) and then reviews the literature at the beginning of the twenty-first century, it is interesting (but disheartening) to observe that the themes

---

[20] *Concern: AACTE Newsletter for Teacher Educators* (November 1971).
[21] A. Harry Passow, "The Future of High Schools," *Teachers College Record* 79 (September 1977): 28–29.

are uncomfortably familiar and the problems uncomfortably similar. Obviously, the solutions of the past have been neither adequate nor lasting. Why have the seemingly endemic problems of schooling been so difficult to correct? Americans have been serious in their desire to improve their schools. When the occasion demanded, they generally came up with the finances to support them. What, then, is the problem? The answer seems to be the "quick-fix" approach. The typical response to the crisis has been to appoint more commissions and committees, pass new legislation, provide more finances with new mandates, establish new standards, and inaugurate new testing requirements. The real solution is more basic, and much more complicated. There is no serious way to improve our schools without revamping the structure. The structure of the school itself serves as a powerful force to maintain the status quo of the classroom.[22]

Though some changes in school structure have occurred through the years, they have been insignificant in relation to those in the U.S. living pattern: communications, values, careers, family, needs, and technology. Leonard, in his article "The Great School Reform Hoax," makes the point that we have essentially the same structure as we had in 1884, when less than 5 percent of America's sixteen-year-olds went to school. It is terribly inadequate now, when well over 90 percent of our sixteen-year-olds—a culturally, emotionally, and intellectually diverse group—are in school. Without a thorough restructuring of schools, any reform is a "hoax," he asserts. The reformers in this space age are offering the nation an educational horse and buggy. "They would improve the buggy, keep the passengers in it longer and pay the driver more . . . but it would still be a horse and buggy."[23] Boyer, asserting that the schools have become disturbingly bureaucratic, proposes a reorganization that would place greater responsibility at the building level, where the real action takes place.[24] Goodlad recommends that we improve schools "not by discarding schools we have but redesigning them piece by piece."[25] He, too, believes that the organization should be structured so that in each school the decision-making authority is close to parents, teachers, and principals.

Sizer notes that, in many assessments of the reforms needed, the word *restructuring* appears, implying a shift in power. "Consistent among virtually all of these restructuring efforts is the assumption that

[22] Theodore R. Sizer, *Horace's Compromise: The Dilemma of the American High School* (Boston: Houghton Mifflin, 1984).
[23] George Leonard, "The Great School Reform Hoax," *Esquire* 101 (April 1984): 50.
[24] Ernest Boyer, *High School—A Report on Secondary Educators in America* (New York: Harper & Row, 1983), 363.
[25] John I. Goodlad, "A Study of Schooling: Some Implications for School Improvement," *Phi Delta Kappan* 64 (April 1983): 555. See also David T. Kearns and Denis P. Doyle, *Winning the Brain Race* (New York: Kampmann, 1988).

top-down hierarchical control has to yield."[26] The organization will reflect decision making at an operational level, namely, at the building and classroom levels. In a school like Horace's, a shift from teaching content to teaching students will take place. Teachers will take more general responsibility for students' education and will expect much from them in a nonthreatening way. Students will be seen as the producers of learning. Such views should positively change the structure of the school.

Schools are not alone in seeing the need to restructure by placing emphasis and responsibility for innovation and improvements at the operational or "customer" levels. Manufacturing (e.g., Saturn and Toyota automobiles) has been shifting toward team problem solving, as have service organizations such as hospitals. Hospitals are finding that they are becoming more effective in delivering services and gaining the public's confidence by inverting the traditional hierarchical pyramid and listening to the "customers" and the persons performing services. The founder of the Wal-Mart stores became a multimillionaire by emphasizing this philosophy in the management of the stores.[27] The analogies for educational organizations are obvious. Education needs to identify clearly the "producers" and the "customers" and create responsive structures to meet demands and exert leadership in the field. If schools are focused on learning as the "product," are not the students the "producers"? Are not the members of the community the "customers"? Who, then, are the professionals in the school?

SCHOOLS NEED CLOSER LIAISON WITH GRASS ROOTS

Regardless of the degree of efficiency of the central administration, a dynamic democratic organization cannot be maintained without active and intelligent participation at levels where results can be observed. A dynamic, participatory democracy requires that each citizen see that his or her ideas, wishes, and efforts have an impact on public agencies and institutions at their unit level. At the same time, these units should have strength enough to have an impact on larger units, and so on, up to the central government.

The nucleus of people at this basic participating unit naturally should be determined by some type of community relatedness. A community whose boundaries are determined by the legal units of a megalopolis, or a sprawling school district, is just too large to maintain an intimate participatory spirit. The complicated organizational structure of a

---

[26] Theodore R. Sizer, *Horace's School: Redesigning the American High School* (Boston: Houghton Mifflin, 1992), 12.
[27] The reader may wish to read *Made in America: My Story* (New York: Doubleday, 1992), Sam Walton's autobiography.

typical school district and its relationship with regional, state, and federal educational agencies tend to create a bureaucracy that is difficult for the layperson, and sometimes even the average educator, to understand. Carpenter reminds us that "much of educational research involves single-variable studies in schools so complex, that to change anything, one must change many things."[28] Complex organizational changes need to be made in school government so that each school within a school district may establish a closer liaison with parents' and citizens' groups in the local attendance area. This liaison must go beyond the usual "know your school" week, citizens' committee, PTA, or advisory group.

Although such school-community efforts are laudatory and for the most part have been serious attempts to involve the citizenry in the school, it has been made clear to the adults that the institution is master and important decision making is still the prerogative of the district. School districts should be reorganized internally so that each school within the district has maximal self-determination and parents and citizens within the attendance area have a reasonable impact on the decision-making process. Only through such radical legal change in school district structure can true local citizen advocacy and partnership be maintained.

The healthy school organization ". . . is characterized by open and trusting relationships among teachers and a strong academic emphasis by teachers, students and parents."[29] Similar trusting and open relations between the principal and the district offices will encourage community support.

Owens noted that ". . . organizations tend to atrophy over time becoming obsessed with maintaining themselves, . . . and seeking to shore up traditional practices."[30] An organization in atrophy is unhealthy. The principal can help the school by helping stakeholders, including community members, develop problem-solving attitudes and actually move toward real solutions. To do this, the principal will find it important to work closely with the "grass roots" of the school and community.

IS DECENTRALIZATION THE ANSWER?

The local community school is the bulwark of a democratic society. Schools can be brought closer to the people by decentralizing them, but such efforts will not succeed unless governance is actually passed down

---

[28] Wade A. Carpenter, "Ten Years of Silver Bullets," *Phi Delta Kappan* 81 (January 2000): 385.
[29] Joseph W. Licata and Gerald W. Harper, "Organizational Health and Robust School Vision," *Educational Administration Quarterly* 37 (February 2001): 10.
[30] Robert G. Owens, *Organizational Behavior in Education* (Boston: Allyn and Bacon, 1998), 303.

and principals and teachers are ready and capable of handling the move. Otherwise, it is likely that another bureaucratic level will be added above the individual school. Figure 5.3 depicts one district's structure to involve the community as well as to create learning-focused, more responsive groupings of schools within the larger district.

Decentralization, to be effective, must be a way of thinking. "Decentralization itself is the evolution of authority. . . . [T]he schools make the decisions on key matters that affect them."[31] Decentralization will affect the roles of central office personnel in that the central office will be viewed as more of a service center as opposed to a control center. Parsley, in his account of this transformation toward a support function, states, "The district office continued to do those things it can do most efficiently, notably strategic planning, curriculum coordination, transportation, legal services, accountability and research, payroll, and food services, while emphasizing new and expanded roles at the building level."[32] He also describes the changes in roles at both the central office and the building levels.

The change in structure is somewhat like the total quality management (TQM) ideal, in which the central office views the building level as its "customer" and satisfactory service to that customer is an important goal. Bosting agrees, noting the following as a critical part of the total quality approach: "The organization must focus, first and foremost, on its suppliers and customers."[33] A note of caution to those who would like to have a "turnkey" system to install: Each organization needs to develop its own meanings and relationships because the TQM approach develops from within and is a new way of thinking about what we do in schools.

Effective decentralization would also require a participating faculty team with the skills, understanding, and willingness to work together to define goals, design curriculum, and plan instructional procedures. For teachers to be part of such a team, they would have to be willing to work above and beyond the normal call of duty and would have to change some of the unions' hard-line limitations on meetings and other time restrictions. For an administrator to work with such a team would require a special kind of person, one with unusual leadership skills.

We are convinced that decentralization is an answer. The move to humanize and personalize instruction for students is an important educational adaptation for our changing society. With this move must come stronger parent and citizen involvement in schools, both for the education of children and as a resource for any adult's own personal growth.

---

[31] Daniel J. Brown, *Decentralization* (Newbury Park, CA: Corwin, 1991), 21.
[32] James F. Parsley, "Reshaping Student Learning," *School Administrator* 48 (September 1991): 13.
[33] John Jay Bonstingl, "The Quality Revolution in Education," *Educational Leadership* 50, no. 3 (November 1992): 6.

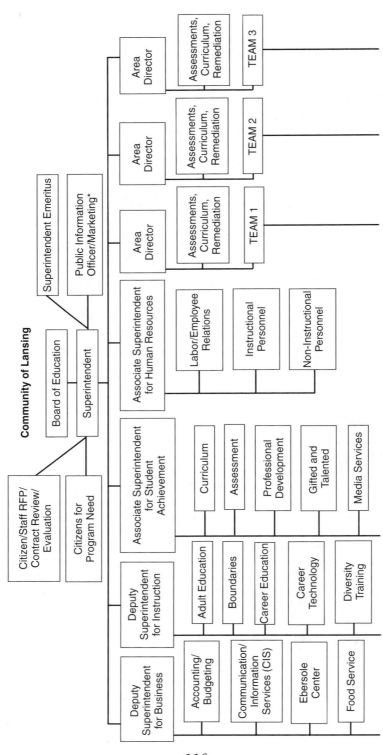

Community of Lansing

- Board of Education
- Superintendent Emeritus
- Public Information Officer/Marketing*
- Superintendent
- Citizen/Staff RFP/Contract Review/Evaluation
- Citizens for Program Need

Area Director
- Assessments, Curriculum, Remediation — TEAM 1

Area Director
- Assessments, Curriculum, Remediation — TEAM 2

Area Director
- Assessments, Curriculum, Remediation — TEAM 3

Associate Superintendent for Human Resources
- Labor/Employee Relations
- Instructional Personnel
- Non-Instructional Personnel

Associate Superintendent for Student Achievement
- Curriculum
- Assessment
- Professional Development
- Gifted and Talented
- Media Services

Deputy Superintendent for Instruction
- Adult Education
- Boundaries
- Career Education
- Career Technology
- Diversity Training

Deputy Superintendent for Business
- Accounting/Budgeting
- Communication/Information Services (CIS)
- Ebersole Center
- Food Service

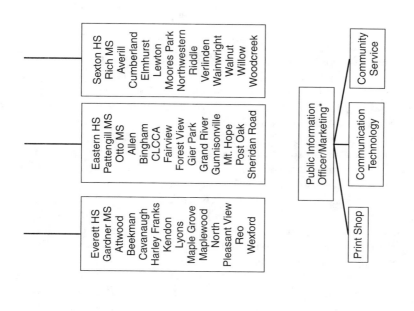

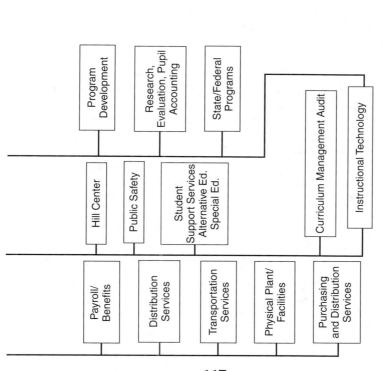

FIGURE 5.3

A structure for learning-focused, responsive schools—Lansing, Michigan

From the Lansing, Michigan Public Schools

Involvement, support, and advocacy cannot be created by impersonal bureaucracies. They are created by responsive, understandable organizational structures that provide opportunities for citizens, the customers, to have a reasonable impact on the decision-making process. Site-based shared decision making, seen as a legacy of the reform movement, may alleviate this situation.[34]

The organizational model in Figure 5.4 depicts an attempt to restructure an overall organization, to break the usual pattern of centralization that has been viewed as universally sacrosanct. This model proposes that each local school within a given school district be provided with a maximum amount of self-determination for its own direction. The school district board would still be responsible for overall direction of the school district and retain basic authority and responsibility through minimum standards, broad basic policy, and leadership. However, it would consciously create enabling policy in which each school unit, operating through an advisory board of representative citizens within its attendance area, has the responsibility to recommend policy and direction appropriate to its local needs. This approach means each school would have a central budget that, once approved by the district board, would allow it to operate within that budget for the year. It means long-range program planning would be encouraged and the central board would make reasonable long-term commitments to each individual school. It would mean the principal, faculty, students, and parents of each school could develop their own operational procedures and programs and establish their own codes, so long as they complied with minimum standards of the district and state and federal laws and regulations. It means a faculty would be required to make a stronger commitment to a particular school as an overall personnel policy of the district. Hopefully, through careful deployment of central administrative staff to the existing schools, it would mean the elimination of excessive superstructures, which are developing in the central offices of school districts throughout the nation.

The involvement of people—lots of people—is important, though not necessarily a quick fix. Involvement and participation are crucial to this model. We think they are the key to a responsive school and a dynamic democracy.

THE ADAPTIVE, FUTURE-ORIENTED ORGANIZATION

As Tushman and O'Reilly note, "Structural and cultural inertia can hold the organization hostage to its past."[35] Schools have a very long history

---

[34] John H. Holloway, "The Promise and Pitfalls of Site-Based Management," *Educational Leadership* 57 (April 2000): 81.
[35] Michael L. Tushman and Charles A. O'Reilly III, *Winning through Innovation* (Boston: Harvard Business School Press, 1997), 29.

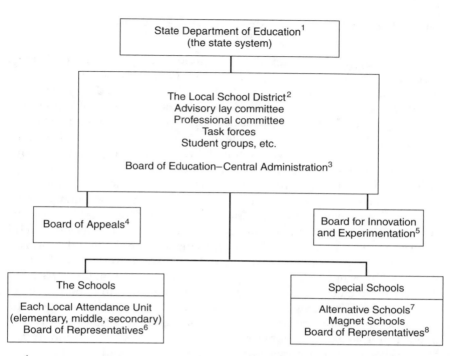

[1] The State Department of Education exerts direction and leadership according to the state constitution, legislation, and recommendations from state lay-professional groups.

[2] The local school district is enlarged to include complete metropolitan areas (urban and suburban) and strong larger rural areas.

[3] The Board of Education, responsible for overall legislation of the school district, retains basic authority and responsibility through minimum standards, broad basic policy, and leadership; however, it consciously creates *enabling* policy whereby each school unit has authority with responsibility to determine specific policy and direction appropriate to the local needs.

[4] Proposed is a six-member board appointed by the Board of Education and composed of students, teachers, and Board members. This board reviews and rules on cases of conflict and overlap. (A new professional position may emerge in connection with the activities of this board and recent court actions. This would be an appeals administrator to handle procedural duties in connection with problems arising out of due-process situations, etc.)

[5] This board reviews, evaluates, and approves radical deviations from basic patterns. It, too, would have six members appointed by the Board, representing students, teachers, and Board members.

[6] There would be a Board of Representatives for each local school attendance unit. It is recommended that this board be a nine-member board consisting of two students, two teachers, four lay citizens (each elected by their constituency), and the school principal, who acts as executive officer by virtue of his or her office. This board's responsibility is to develop and endorse school policy and advise on operational procedures in the school.

[7] Alternative and magnet schools are open for attendance by any appropriate student in the school district. Such schools are characterized by being innovative and experimental, deviating rather radically from the conventional school by concentrating on open special and self-directive approaches to learning.

[8] Same as item 6.

FIGURE 5.4

An adaptive, responsive organizational structure with a local advisory board for each attendance unit

of a relatively rigid structure that can hinder changes to a more flexible, responsive, future-oriented organization. Given the societal and economic changes that are occurring, the standards imposed by the professions and states, and the demands for alternative forms of school, the closed system (a traditional bureaucracy) is no longer adequate. These demands call for a responsive, flexible organization focused on outcomes. After studying superintendents' reactions to external pressures for reform and strategy, Wills and Peterson conclude, "Unless a set of clearly defined outcomes for strategic change is provided, differing interpretations, comfort issues, local political interests, or more 'manageable' strategies may lead to a detour around improvement efforts."[36] Serious consideration of structural change may not occur, and changes may tend to be cosmetic, with no shifts in power to make or implement decisions.

The learning organization or future-oriented organization described by Senge is ". . . an organization that is continually expanding its capacity to create its future."[37] For any organization to remain static in a continuously changing environment seriously impairs its viability. The organization must learn in order to adapt. Leithwood notes that collective learning views an organization as a mind that is ". . . found in patterns of behavior that range from 'intelligent' to 'stupid.'"[38] The principal's role becomes less that of a manager of things and more that of an interpreter, a leader of learning, and a facilitator of the change process. In most cases, the principal faces an obligation to initiate structural and collaborative change. "If schools are to be viewed as effective, then school leaders should be ready to change, to restructure the ways their schools operate . . . and to plan strategically for the future."[39]

The successful, adaptive organization that will meet yet unknown challenges will focus on the customer success function, assembling critical customer process resources on demand.[40] Since student learning needs change over time and societal needs also change, schools must be organized to be flexible and to change processes more quickly than they have in the past. Continuous analysis of student learning requires organizational flexibility to meet those needs. A structure locked in for years may not be able to respond in time. Successful schools in the future may

---

[36] Frances G. Wills and Kent D. Peterson, "External Pressures for Reform and Strategy Formation at the District Level: Superintendents' Interpretations of State Demands," *Educational Evaluation and Policy Analysis* 14, no. 3 (Fall 1992): 259.

[37] Peter M. Senge, *The Fifth Discipline: The Art and Practice of the Learning Organization* (New York: Doubleday, 1990), 14.

[38] Kenneth Leithwood (ed.), *Understanding Schools as Intelligent Systems* (Stamford, CT: JAI Press, 2000), 101.

[39] Jeannie Pritchett Johnson, Martha Livingston, Robert A. Schwartz, and John R. Slate, "What Makes a Good Elementary School? A Critical Examination," *Journal of Educational Research* 93 (July/August 2000): 346.

[40] For a discussion of this view, see Terrence T. Burton, *The Future-Focused Organization* (Upper Saddle River, NJ: Prentice Hall, 1995).

be organized very differently from each other in that they are responding to different needs, to different "customers" and "clients," and may be at different aspiration levels.

⑤UMMARY

Organizational structure deals with the overall arrangement of an enterprise. It establishes human and material relationships consistent with client needs, school objectives, and resources and harmonizes its activities through strategically placed leaders.

Organizations and the way they work together spell success or failure in spite of anything a principal can do. The classical model of school organization today divides administration into three major categories or functions: instruction, educational services, and business management.

One serious way we can improve schools is by revamping their structures. Structures need to be developed that keep citizens in close communication with schools and allow individual schools to be more responsive to students and parents. Greater decentralization can bring schools closer to the people so that the schools can make decisions that will immediately affect the local area and provide the opportunity for their "customers" to have a reasonable impact on the decision-making process.

Given the diversity within and between schools, it seems logical that schools may become much more varied in structure than they are today.

ⒻOR FURTHER THOUGHT

1. Discuss the problem of people versus functions in organizing.
2. How might the composition of boards of education affect the growth and development of schools? Should the principal be involved in influencing who should serve on the board of education?
3. What aspects of education do you think should be under the control of (a) the local community, (b) the state, and (c) the federal government?
4. Is there a point at which an elementary school, middle school, or high school can become too large? Present arguments, research evidence, and authoritative opinion to support your position.
5. Why is it not uncommon to find the principal bypassed when groups wish to influence the schools? What implications does this have for the role of the principal?
6. Should the principal ever be found as an advocate for parents and pupils versus the board? Discuss.

7. Develop some enabling policies that a district board of education could adopt to give a local school greater autonomy and the school community greater self-determination.

8. Collect some organization charts from different school districts in your state. Are the schools and instruction highlighted, or is central administration emphasized? What values do the charts seem to convey?

9. Develop what you consider to be the ideal school organizational structure.

10. Compare a school district's organizational structure with that of several larger industries in your state. What are the similarities and differences?

SELECTED READINGS

Bacharach, Samuel B., and Bryan Mundell, eds. *Images of Schools.* Thousand Oaks, CA: Corwin, 1995.

Bosting, John Jay. "The Quality Revolution in Education." *Educational Leadership* 50, no. 3 (November 1992): 4–9.

Brown, Daniel J. *Decentralization.* Newbury Park, CA: Corwin, 1991.

Caplow, Theodore. *Principles of Organization.* New York: Harcourt Brace Jovanovich, 1964.

Hall, Richard H. *Organizations, Structures, Processes and Outcomes.* Upper Saddle River, NJ: Prentice Hall, 1991.

Hoy, Wayne K., and Cecil G. Miskel. *Educational Administration: Theory, Research and Practice,* 5th ed. New York: McGraw-Hill, 1996.

Johnson, Bob L., Jr., and Janice R. Fauske. "Principals and the Political Economy of Environmental Enactment." *Educational Administration Quarterly* 36 (April 2000): 159–185.

Leithwood, Kenneth, ed. *Understanding Schools as Intelligent Systems.* Stamford, CT: JAI Press, 2000.

Mintzbery, Henry. *Power in and around Organizations.* Upper Saddle River, NJ: Prentice Hall, 1983.

Schein, Edgar H. "Coming to a New Awareness of Organizational Culture." *Sloan Management Review* 25 (Winter 1984): 3–16.

Sizer, Theodore R. *Horace's School: Redesigning the American High School.* Boston: Houghton Mifflin, 1992.

Tushman, Michael L., and Charles A. O'Reilly III. *Winning through Innovation.* Boston: Harvard Business School Press, 1997.

Wills, Frances G., and Kent D. Peterson. "External Pressures for Reform and Strategy Formation at the District Level: Superintendents' Interpretations of State Demands." *Educational Evaluation and Policy Analysis* 14, no. 3 (Fall 1992): 241–260.

Leadership

rincipals are expected to be leaders. The question is not whether the principal must behave as a leader but rather *how* the principal can be an effective leader. One cannot escape the expectations of the teachers, community, students, or board of education members—the principal should make a positive difference.

Opportunities to exert leadership are abundant. The shift toward teacher empowerment; site-based decision making; rapidly developing technology in the workplace, home, and school; increased pressure on the tax dollar; rising demands from the business or political communities for tangible "results" of schooling—all these demand leadership. Leadership is required on behalf of those youth who may be devalued by virtue of economics, language, or disabilities but who still may have the potential for great contributions to our world. Leadership is required on behalf of those gifted and talented students who may never realize their potential because they are "bored" into dropping out or content to live with mediocrity for a variety of reasons, including peer pressure.

The old patterns of principal behavior will not be sufficient to meet the new opportunities for leadership. No longer can the principal spend a major amount of time on efficiently organized "administration" to indicate that his or her role is being competently fulfilled. In fact, an attempt to do so may provide evidence to the contrary. This is not to say that the administrative details are unimportant. To ignore them would be to undermine many of the other gains the leader hopes for. But they must be ordered and addressed in a hierarchy of importance in a manner that does not detract the principal from higher priorities. Otherwise, schools may come to be described as Kotter describes most U.S. corporations, namely, "overmanaged and underled."[1] He goes on to point out that

---

[1] John P. Kotter, "What Leaders Really Do," *Harvard Business Review* 68 (May–June 1990): 103.

strong leadership with weak management is as bad as the opposite. And so it is in schools; a balance of strength in both dimensions is essential.

The principal of today and of the future must increasingly be willing to prepare for wise, critical participation in a society characterized by conflict, chronic change, increasing interdependency, and often a culture resistant to personal responsibility. New technologies to obtain, analyze, and communicate information are arising daily. Given the past performance of schools in adopting or adapting to trends of the future, the principal who is dutifully carrying out board policies and central administration directives, and who limits his or her efforts to these tasks, likely will find himself or herself as captain of a vessel no longer serviceable for duty in the twenty-first century. Therefore, a vision of what should be, and what can be, is essential. Without it, changes one makes are merely reactive.

Robinson believes that the difference between management and leadership is the distinction that "often lies between doing a job and considering whether the job needs to be done."[2] In this case, he associates the term *management* only with administrative detail. Buhler indicates that managers tend to rely on their legitimate authority, whereas leaders lead by example.[3] The leader helps envision goals and set standards, and communicates in such a way that all associated directly or indirectly know where the school is going and what it means to the community.

VIEWS OF LEADERSHIP

Leadership as a Set of Traits

The concept of leadership has been examined over centuries, with volumes written analyzing the qualities of recognized leaders. The focus on persons such as Charlemagne, Churchill, Gandhi, Napoleon, and even Hitler traditionally has been intended to find traits that made them the leaders they were. Hundreds of studies have tried to identify specific qualities or characteristics that distinguish leaders from nonleaders. Many of the traits studied seem to be inborn attributes, such as physical characteristics or intelligence, and some are acquired skills, such as impeccable social behavior or dynamic public speaking. However, for the most part, these studies have failed to yield any truly discriminating traits or sets of traits.

In leadership studies spanning over a quarter of a century, Stodgill asserts that leadership characteristics by themselves hold little significance for purposes of either prediction or diagnosis of leadership. He

---

[2] James A. Robinson, "Leadership Not According to Machiavelli," *National Forum* 63 (Fall 1983): 48.
[3] Patricia Buhler, "Leaders vs. Managers," *Supervision* 56 (May 1995): 24.

does not discount traits entirely, as do many researchers, but believes that collectively these characteristics appear to interact, to generate "personality dynamics advantageous to the person seeking the responsibilities of leadership."[4] He classifies these traits in three categories: (1) self-oriented traits that include intelligence, physical, social, and personality characteristics; (2) task-related characteristics, such as achievement, enterprise, and drive for responsibility; and (3) social characteristics such as cooperativeness, prestige, diplomacy, and sociability.

Considerations of Charisma

A common image of the leader is the charismatic person who attracts followership by the strength of her or his personality. Trust, respect, and even affection for the person can develop into effective charismatic leadership. Fisher provides an interesting discussion of charismatic power, suggesting that charisma can be developed. Certain factors contribute to charisma, such as "sincerity, appearance, goodness, confidence, wisdom, courage, thoughtfulness, kindness, control . . . but the principal conditions for charisma are distance, style and perceived self-confidence."[5]

The principal should determine the proper distance he or she will need to maintain, and that acceptable distance is affected by the culture of which the school is a part. But it will be of even greater concern to ascertain the degree of effectiveness the charismatic base is achieving, for it has been noted that leadership based on charisma is expendable. Often the charismatic leader can be effective during a time of organizational crisis. Once the crisis is past, to continue effectiveness the leader must eventually move toward the power base of expertise. Fisher takes the position that "the leader who combines charismatic power with expert and legitimate power, adding a carefully measured portion of reward power and little or no coercive power, achieves maximum effectiveness."[6] Drucker sees the charismatic approach as counter to the laws of probability and as such would have limited usefulness.[7]

Analysis of Leadership Behavior

Lewin and others conducted studies on leadership in 1939 that attracted a great deal of attention. In one study, three groups of nine- to twelve-year-old boys were to complete a carpentry assignment. Each group was "led" by adults who acted in leadership styles labeled democratic (gets

---

[4] R. M. Stodgill, *Handbook of Leadership* (New York: Free Press, 1974), 82.

[5] James L. Fisher, *Power of the Presidency* (New York: Macmillan, 1984), 43.

[6] Ibid., 40.

[7] John E. Flaherty, *Peter Drucker: Shaping the Managerial Mind* (San Francisco: Jossey-Bass, 1999): 272.

TABLE 6.1
Results of leadership styles

Leadership Style	Leader Leaves	Leader Returns	Task Completion
Laissez-faire	Boys leave	Empty room	Incomplete
Autocratic	Pandemonium	Order restored; work continues	Completed
Democratic	Work continues	Work continues	Completed

commitment from group members to do specific tasks and helps with suggestions as needed), autocratic (arbitrarily assigns tasks on a continuing basis), or laissez-faire (brings in instructions and drawings and remains completely passive).[8] The results are illustrated in Table 6.1.

Leadership behavior can vary greatly along an autocratic-democratic continuum. As simple as they were, studies of this nature did encourage a great deal of further research and contributed to the understanding of group and individual reactions to certain styles of leadership.

Additional Studies

Bowers and Seashore offer an excellent summary of the correspondence of leadership concepts of different investigators from 1950 to 1964.[9] They conclude that the research up to that point identified four dimensions of leadership: (1) support, (2) interaction facilitation, (3) goal emphasis, and (4) work facilitation. Others have identified systems and person orientations as leader behavior factors. If one merges the illustrations of leadership theories, a congruence of opinion clearly surfaces about the two dimensions with which the leader must concern himself or herself. These are centered on the needs, goals, and performance of people and the needs, goals, and performance of organizations.

A useful series of studies for the school administrator is the Ohio State Leadership Studies, commencing in 1945.[10] A major contribution of these studies is the development of the Leadership Behavior Description Questionnaire (LBDQ). This questionnaire generally abandoned the notion of leadership as a trait and attempted to concentrate instead on an

---

[8] A complete discussion of these early studies may be found in Ralph White and Ronald Lippitt, "Leader Behavior and Member Reaction in Three Social Settings," in *Group Dynamics: Research and Theory*, ed. Dorwin Cartwright and Alvin Zander (Evanston, IL: Row, Peterson, 1953), 585–611.

[9] David G. Bowers and Stanley E. Seashore, "Predicting Organizational Effectiveness with a Four-Factor Theory of Leadership," *Administrative Science Quarterly* 2 (September 1966): 248.

[10] Initiated and directed by Carroll L. Shartle and reported in Andrew W. Halpin, *Theory and Research in Administration* (New York: Macmillan, 1966).

analysis of leaders' behavior. The LBDQ has been used in numerous studies to analyze the leadership behavior of school administrators. Two major dimensions of leadership behavior that have consistently emerged through use of the LBDQ are *initiating structure* and *consideration*. These were first identified by Halpin and Winer through factor analysis.[11] Other investigators have consistently substantiated their findings.

These studies were the first to emphasize the importance of both task direction and consideration of individual needs in assessing leadership behavior. Task direction is exemplified by *initiating structure,* a type of behavior that clarifies the relationship of the staff within the organization and what is expected of them. It implies a well-planned, coordinated operation with clearly identified goals and standards of performance and with procedures established to encourage maximum achievement. *Consideration* refers to a relationship with the staff that implies friendship, cooperation, teamwork, rapport, and approachability. The leader is thoughtful of the staff, essentially treating them as equals.

At approximately the time of the Ohio State Leadership Studies, the University of Michigan conducted research on leadership styles. In the Prudential Study, Likert identified high-producing supervisors as (1) being employee oriented; (2) spending more time on the job, with a major portion of their time devoted to general and specific supervision of employees; (3) receiving general supervision from their supervisors; and (4) liking the authority and responsibility of their job.[12] Continuing his research on leadership and reviewing hundreds of other research studies, Likert found that it is likely production will improve and/or remain high if a system is associated with leadership processes based on teamwork, trust, and participatory decision making.[13]

Sergiovanni, Metzcus, and Burden studied the relationship between teachers' needs orientations (based on Herzberg's hygiene-motivation theory[14]) and their perceptions of the ideal principal. They concluded that "teachers, regardless of needs orientations, see the ideal principal as being both systems and persons oriented." They further identified two "qualities" of leadership style that they called "optimizing" and "controlling."[15] Again, they found that teachers, regardless of orientation,

---

[11] Ibid., 88.

[12] Rensis Likert, in *Productivity, Supervision and Morale in an Office Situation,* ed. D. Katz, N. Macoby, and N. Morse (Ann Arbor: University of Michigan Survey Research Center, 1950).

[13] Rensis Likert, "Management Styles and the Human Component," *Management Review* 2 (October 1977): 23.

[14] For a further explanation of job satisfiers and dissatisfiers, see Frederick Herzberg, Bernard Mausner, R. O. Peterson, and Dora F. Capwell, *Job Attitudes: Review of Research and Opinion* (Pittsburgh: Psychological Service of Pittsburgh, 1957).

[15] Thomas J. Sergiovanni, Richard Metzcus, and Larry Burden, "Toward a Particularistic Approach to Leadership Style: Some Findings," *American Education Research Journal* 6 (January 1969): 73, 77.

FIGURE 6.1
Leadership dimension grids

generally responded favorably to the optimizing style of leadership rather than to the controlling style.

Current research indicates that the effective leader will optimize or facilitate the meeting of the needs and the achievement of the goals of both the organization (school) and the people who comprise it. A number of students of leadership have illustrated these dimensions on a grid that ordinarily puts relationships on one side and task performance on the other.[16] Figure 6.1 notes some of the terms used to label personal dimensions on the left and organizational dimensions on the bottom. These studies are useful in identifying the leader's emphases and potential effectiveness in certain situations, as noted in the following discussion of Fiedler's work.

The Situational Approach to Studying Leadership

The situational approach to studying leadership acknowledges that various types of situations determine the type or style of leadership that is effective. Situational variables that become special areas of study in situational research are the organizational climate, the task or type of assignment performed by the group, and the degree of formal authority or power. A large amount of research was conducted in these areas during the 1960s and early 1970s. Fiedler and his associates utilized much of this research in their development of the contingency model of leadership.[17] The contingency theory holds that the group's effectiveness is contingent on the interaction between two variables: (1) the motivational system of

---

[16] Words used as descriptors of the dimensions have been taken from the works of Robert Blake and Jane Mouton, Jacob Getzels and Egon Guba, and W. Reddin. Several other writers have used these terms or similar ones to describe the leadership dimensions.

[17] F. E. Fiedler and M. M. Chemers, *Leadership and Effective Management* (Glenview, IL: Scott, Foresman, 1974).

the leader—his or her style in relating to the group—and (2) the favorableness of the group situation—the degree to which the situation allows the leader to control the group. Leaders with given styles will perform better in situations favorable to their style. The leadership situation includes three components, listed in order of importance: (1) leader-member relations—the degree to which group members support, respect, and like the group leader; (2) task structure—the degree to which group tasks are spelled out; and (3) position power—the power vested by the organization in the leader's position or the degree to which the position enables the leader to get the group to accept his or her leadership.

Fiedler classified leaders as either task oriented or human relations oriented, as determined by the leader's score on a personality measure called the Least Preferred Co-Worker Scale (LPC). He then tested his theory on the findings of over eight hundred studies completed between 1951 and 1963. Analyses of the studies indicated (1) low LPC or task-motivated leaders were most effective in high-control or low-control situations and (2) high LPC or human relations–motivated leaders were most effective in situations of moderate control.

While Fiedler's work is controversial (he implied that the leader's style of management is incapable of being changed), others, following up on his research, have critically examined leadership methods and have maintained that leaders can and should alter their style of leadership in concrete situations to better fit their style to the demands of the situation. In fact, not to do so would tend to lead to failure.

Hersey and Blanchard suggest that the leader should adjust behavior to the maturity level of the group.[18] They use the term *maturity* relative to the group's skill and willingness to set high goals and take the responsibility for achieving those goals. If the group is immature in terms of skills, the leader must direct how things are to be done—a high task and low relationship orientation. A leader who misjudges the group as immature or who needs to be controlling and directive will tend to maintain or force a group into behaving immaturely. This approach to management has been referred to as *management for infancy.*

On the other hand, a leader may assess the situation to require little direction and foist on the group members more responsibility than they can assume. In either case, the subsequent effectiveness is going to be lower than it need be. The leader may assume that everyone in the group is at the same maturity level, an assumption not likely to be correct. If the leader follows the model, allowances need to be made on an individual basis.

---

[18] Paul Hersey and Kenneth H. Blanchard, *Management of Organizational Behavior,* 5th ed. (Upper Saddle River, NJ: Prentice Hall, 1988).

Leadership as a Consensus Process

In discussing the nature of leadership, Wynn and Guditis review three broad categories of leadership, identified by Katz and Kahn: (1) an attribute of position, (2) characteristics of a person, and (3) category of behavior.[19] Although each of these views of leadership may have some merit, to date none of them has been fruitful in identifying the way to exert leadership. However, studying leadership as a function of responsibility of a person or persons most qualified in a given context may have promise.

Wynn and Guditis look at leadership as a consensus process. They define *consensus* as "agreement to implement management decisions on the part of all members of the 'thinking together' group."[20] When the members of a group feel that they understand others' positions and that others understand theirs, but that all will support the position of the group, then consensus is reached. Voting then has no place in the process, since voting is a win-or-lose procedure. The process of reaching consensus is as important as the consensus.

CONSIDERATIONS OF POWER

Much of the literature on leadership centers on power or control. Without control, little progress is made, but hierarchical control can evolve into rigid authoritarianism, and centralized, diffused control can degenerate into chaos. Thus a dilemma! When analyzing the principal's legitimate power base, one will be all the more concerned to discover that this base is really quite small when compared with the usual concept of an administrator's power. As a result, a typical principal might be very jealous of the power that seems to be left in the role and guard it with fervor.

Power Base

Does power imply being invulnerable? Does one lose power by becoming vulnerable to those who are followers? Can a leader be a fellow learner alongside followers and still maintain leadership power? What do we mean by power?

French and Raven list five bases of power:

1. *Reward power*—ability to reward
2. *Coercive power*—ability to threaten or punish

---

[19] Richard Wynn and Charles W. Guditis, *Team Management: Leadership by Consensus* (Columbus, OH: Merrill, 1984).
[20] Ibid., 29–30.

3. *Legitimate power*—power or authority that the organization assigns to the leadership position along with internalized values of staff members that give the leader authority to influence them

4. *Referent power*—a person's feelings or desire to identify with the person possessing power

5. *Expert power*—the extent that subordinates attribute expertise and knowledge to the leader[21]

Considering today's school and the professional staff, none of these sources provides a full measure of power. Reward power is blunted by collective bargaining. Few schools have merit increases. The salary scale agreed on at the bargaining table applies to all (good, bad, or medium) of like experience and education. Reward by praise and special recognition has been the main source of this power in schools. The implementation of career ladders, monetary rewards for performance, and other plans recognizing excellence holds promise.

Coercive power is lessened by tenure and grievance committees. True, the principal has responsibility for rating teachers, but usually this affects only the very poor teacher. Few teachers are concerned with threats of punishment, although they do respond favorably to positive professional overtures to help them improve their teaching.

Legitimate power is blunted by the general professional role of the teacher. We pointed out in Chapter 5 that the school organization is different from any other organization in that the school's main function is carried out in the classroom by the teacher, who is the chief executive of that classroom. Few teachers stand in awe of the legitimate power of the principal. The teacher is a professional equal who may know more about his or her subject and how to teach it than the principal. The teacher is "monarch in the classroom castle."

Given the adversarial relationships established in collective bargaining procedures, referent power can operate in just the opposite direction. Many teachers do not wish to identify with the administrator possessing legitimate power, particularly the autocratic or bureaucratic administrator.

Expert power holds great promise, though the principal needs to realize that the expertise he or she exerts will be that of assisting others to grow, removing barriers, creating opportunities, and bringing resources to bear on challenges. Expert power will help the principal in his or her leadership role and will work best in schools of today and tomorrow. A review of research shows that schools that rate the principal

---

[21] J. R. P. French and B. H. Raven, "The Basis of Social Power," in *Studies in Social Power*, ed. D. Cartwright (Ann Arbor: University of Michigan, Institute of Social Research, 1959). See also Amitai Etzioni, *A Comparative Analysis of Complex Organizations* (New York: Free Press, 1961), for his concept of power sources.

as having and using expert power received high scores for teacher morale, teacher satisfaction, and teacher performance. Conversely, it has been noted that principals in less than effective schools may emphasize human relations, but without substantive expertise.

Sharing Power

One point of view is that power exists in a fixed quantity, that it is limited: if one person gains power, then someone else in the organization has to lose it. Over the years, research has indicated that this belief is not true, that in fact power is both expansible and reciprocal and has synergistic qualities.

The principal can foster the acceptance of responsibility by sharing authority, or empowering those responsible to do the job. If the principal fully shares his or her power with the teachers, community, and students and has the expertise to develop a true team spirit within the school, the resulting support will increase the principal's power. The combined forces can provide a strong base for accomplishing the school's goals. Examples of such achievements can be found in some areas where school-based decision making is practiced. Principals make themselves vulnerable, but at the same time, they gain power overall.

Participation in Decision Making

Encouraging participation and sharing power do not mean a faculty needs to get together every time a decision is made. This in itself would be poor leadership! It means that procedures are established that provide the faculty with opportunities to have appropriate input on decisions that may be important to them. The following list may serve as a guide to the principal on faculty participation in decision making:

1. The faculty can agree on policies that will give the principal all the direction necessary to make various types of decisions on his or her own.
2. Some decisions affect only certain faculty members or certain departments. Only faculty affected should ordinarily be involved. In other words, do not involve the history faculty if it is exclusively a problem impacting the physical education department.
3. Some decisions may be more appropriately handled by having a department head, chairperson, or spokesperson for a group provide feedback to the principal to help him or her with the decision.

4. Some decisions may be handled by memoranda to faculty, asking anyone with strong feelings about the decision to contact the principal. Establish a time limit for contact.

5. Some decisions may require only the involvement of recognized experts on the faculty.

6. Faculty may not be interested in being involved in some decisions.

7. Some projects, particularly those related to curriculum changes or teaching procedures, will require deep involvement by faculty if the project is to be properly implemented and supported. Principals should make participation a planned educational process on decisions of this type.

8. The faculty must understand that some decisions must be made exclusively by the administrator.

9. Some decisions must be made immediately, and the administrator must be brave enough to do so. Crises happen; action is essential.

10. On some decisions, the faculty may procrastinate. The principal must have enough courage to make a final decision when closure is necessary.

11. Most faculty members do not want to be involved in decisions not affecting them, such as the technicalities of tasks remotely related to the classroom or the teacher's welfare. In fact, to involve the teachers in decisions about which they are indifferent may be counterproductive.

Participatory Leadership

The ideas of participatory leadership and shared power often conjure up images of a lumbering, slow-moving organization, with nothing ever really getting done because everyone has to have a say on everything. This has not been the case in adaptations of what has been called *Japanese management*. In most instances, production has been greater and morale higher. It is important to remember that research has shown that what has been called *initiating structure* is a major dimension of leadership. Teachers have identified it as a requirement for leadership in almost every major research study in which they have been involved.

Again, initiating structure is a type of leader behavior that clarifies relationships within the organization. It conveys the idea of a well-planned, coordinated operation that has clearly identified goals and standards of performance, with procedures established to encourage maximum achievement.

Nothing here is contrary to shared power or participatory leadership. One of the first things a principal should do is work with the faculty and central administration to clarify the structure of relationships.

He or she should research legislation, board policies, and central administration directives that may be basic requirements for structure and then involve the faculty as fully as possible in filling in the gaps. The following cautions should be observed when working with faculty in this process:

1. Do not neglect to identify clearly basic requirements from higher echelons of administration; good or bad, they are requirements. They must be included. If they need to be changed, let that be a separate battle. Do not disrupt process by allowing too much arguing over them.

2. Let your preferences be known about how you believe things should be structured to fit in with your administrative style, and be willing to debate the issues. Identify to the faculty those processes and actions that are so important to you that you do not want a vote on them; explain to them why, and provide an opportunity for them to react. In short, stand for something.

3. Develop a plan setting out procedure and process for establishing your initiating structure so that there is sufficient time for participation of faculty but also an understood system of closure on the issue. It is a leader's responsibility to see that discussion and involvement are brought to a logical conclusion in a reasonable time so that the work of the school can go forward.

4. Identify ahead of time those issues that are appropriate for faculty to vote on and those that are nonvotable administrative prerogatives.

5. Do not be tempted to use participation as a manipulative device, which would tend more toward infancy management than toward professional growth and development.

Tirozzi describes the enlightened principal as one who " . . . strives to create a continual sense of urgency . . . especially as related to . . . low expectations for students, poor achievement . . .," and many other critical issues.[22] This part of the leadership role requires not only expertise in the craft and technologies of the school, but also the collaborative building of a vision of excellence with the staff and the larger community.

TRANSFORMATIONAL LEADERSHIP

The transformational leader is " . . . one who gets others to sacrifice their own interests for the good of the group . . . [to] engage others to

---

[22] Gerald N. Tirozzi, "The Artistry of Leadership," *Phi Delta Kappan* 82 (February 2001): 438–439.

raise one another to higher levels of motivation and morality."[23] In addition, the transformational leader raises followers' levels of consciousness about the values of specific ourcomes and raises their needs to higher order needs.[24] Frazier sees the transformational leader guiding " . . . the organization through the adoption of the new paradigm to where it becomes self-sustaining and people accept and practice the change willingly."[25] The implication is that the manager manages within a paradigm, but the leader leads between, or from one paradigm to the other, forming a common commitment to a vision and providing the means (concepts, skills, resources) to realize it. The tranformational leader helps others to think "outside the box" and to see expanded challenges and opportunities and commit themselves to meeting those challenges.

THE UPWARD LOOK

The reader is familiar with the type of administrator who relies entirely on the legal resources or status of position for power and control. Various behaviors are typical of this orientation: carefully checking for compliance with written regulations and "how to" directives, focusing on the letter of the law rather than the spirit of it, and putting off decisions on any unusual situation. The principal can easily find himself or herself in such a situation; indeed, it may be "comfortable" to behave that way.

The classic bureaucratic model immediately comes to mind, in which administrators act solely on the basis of written rules and regulations from above. If a unique situation occurs outside specified authority, the administrator forwards it upward for decision. He or she tries to understand the thinking of those above so that his or her own actions will conform to their norms. The teachers and students are not the major concern in this model unless they are a priority of the upper echelon.

It has been noted that all too often principals have had little or no effect on school climate in the typical urban district. The explanation of these research findings is that these principals are selected in the "image of the school district." Many had been reared as teachers, as vice principals, and in other positions in the same district. They were prepared to behave in a rational, predictable, and uniform manner acceptable to the district, and the longer they were in the system, the more they perpetuated existing tradition and acted as the central administration expected

---

[23] Richard L. Henderson, James B. Huffman, Chris A. Caram, and Robert L. Kennedy, "Transformational Leadership: The Impact on Organizational Health and School Improvement," *AASA Professor* 23 (Spring 2000): 7.
[24] Fred C. Lunenburg and Allan C. Ornstein, *Educational Administration,* 3rd ed. (Belmont, CA: Wadsworth/Thomson Learning, 2000), 150–151.
[25] Andy Frazier, *Quality Transformation in Education* (Boca Raton, FL: St. Lucie Press, 1997), 33.

them to act. (In other words, they were good apprentices.) Such principals serve only as supporters of the central system, rather than as leaders, and thus their schools approach homeostasis.

Fortunately, some principals make for outstanding exceptions; and, as they note, even though they sometimes had a price to pay, they also reaped rewards.

IMAGES OF THE LEADER

Leadership continues to be studied but more recently in ways using metaphors to convey richer images. We have used the terms *visionary, steward, facilitator,* and *learner* to discuss some images of leaders. *Hero, captain of the ship,* and or similar expressions describing the top of a tall power pyramid may be useful in some situations where the "followers" have a wide range of purposes and/or are immature in some ways.

Leaders, however, like schools, do not operate alone or apart from an organizational culture. Unless one has the happy experience to plan a new school, hire and induct new faculty, and grow a new culture, the principal must operate in a culture already in place with firmly entrenched beliefs, values, and traditions.

LEADERSHIP IN A CULTURAL CONTEXT

Each school district and school building—indeed, every organization that has been in operation for some time—has its own culture. Leadership thus occurs in a cultural context.

Organizations themselves appear to have cultures, not independent of the larger culture and its changes, but nevertheless different from other organizations affected by the same culture. Those differences may appear to be profound when closely examined, but when viewed from farther away, they may simply seem somewhat different, like figures in a large, coherent tapestry.

As noted in Chapter 5, organizational culture is composed of beliefs, values, and a set of norms about how one behaves and how things are done in this place. It results in traditions, symbols, rituals, and a set of group norms about how people should respond to certain situations, whether those situations are opportunities, problems, or challenges to the existence of the school itself. The process of making meaning out of what is happening is a cultural process. As Williams notes, "[C]ulture can be identified as the idea or habit patterns that forms the basis for action."[26]

---

[26] Ray Williams, "Systemic Change and Staff Development," in *Systemic Change: Touchstones for the Future School,* ed. Patrick Jelnick (Palatine, IL: IRI/Skylight, 1995), 235.

Burlingame, in reviewing essays on leadership and organizational culture, makes three additional points: (1) schools may be viewed as artifacts of past culture as well as creators of future culture, (2) much conflict persists in schools and about schools, and (3) technical solutions to administrative problems are limited.[27]

Vaill's studies of high-performing systems identified the leader's role in "purposing"—that is, the "proposings which have to do with the establishment, clarification, and modification of purposes."[28] In the high-performing system, Vaill indicates that what a leader stands for, and what he or she communicates, becomes very important. One who proposes to lead in a school setting finds himself or herself at once an interpreter and advocate of a culture and a subculture, each to the other.

If a principal is to make significant, lasting change in a school or even preserve a school's quest for excellence in a changing environment, culture building and in some instances maintenance are essential. The leader is challenged to address the very core of beliefs about the school and how the participants respond to various stimuli. Accurately identifying present beliefs and common solutions (suspending problem students, dropping field trips if a problem occurs, etc.) is essential, but equally important is the principal's recognition of her or his own values and beliefs. Inconsistent behavior that can be perceived as directionless reactions cannot build or maintain an organizational culture. The principal's day-to-day actions need to be consistent with a set of values and beliefs about what the school is about. Articulating those values needs to be done at every opportunity via writing, speaking, and conversing informally. The principal who preaches that the school should be a learning community but does not engage visibly in her or his own learning or provide for the teachers' learning is only paying lip service to the value of learning.

Sergiovanni broadens the scope of leadership to a wider community, which increases the potential influence group. While complexity increases as the entity becomes larger, the role of the leader remains the same. The emphasis becomes "building a shared followership . . . not on *who* to follow, but on *what* to follow."[29] The implication is clear—a leadership of ideas is necessary to shape the organizational culture. Some of the considerations noted earlier—traits, charisma, behaviors alone—may be useful in some situations at least for a time, but long-term changes arise from a collective acceptance of shared solutions and responsibilities. These in turn directly affect students' motivation and learning.[30]

---

[27] Martin Burlingame, "Theory into Practice: Educational Administration and the Cultural Perspective," in *Leadership and Organizational Culture*, ed. Thomas J. Sergiovanni and John Corbally (Urbana: University of Illinois Press, 1984), 304.

[28] Peter B. Vaill, "The Purposing of High-Performing Systems," in *Leadership and Organizational Culture*, 91.

[29] Thomas J. Sergiovanni, *Leadership for the Schoolhouse* (San Francisco: Jossey-Bass, 1996), 83.

[30] See Martin L. Maehr and Carol Midgley, *Transforming School Cultures* (Boulder, CO: Westview, 1996).

THE LEADER AS A VISIONARY

The visionary is not a mystical person somehow connected to intelligences or powers beyond our knowing. The practical visionary is one who can clearly articulate what ought to be, what is, and what should be changed to make progress from *is* to *ought*. The person who can only articulate a set of descriptors of what ought to be is like the person who accurately predicts rain but cannot envision the need to build an ark.

More important is that the person who would be a leader has a clear idea or image of what she or he believes is excellent instruction and an excellent school. The idea that the principal needs to develop his/her personal image of what is good, what is ideal, and what is worth working toward is not a new one, but it is still often not accepted even by the principals themselves. The reader is encouraged to sit down in a quiet place and list those conceptions or principles he or she believes constitute a personal vision of an excellent school.

Barth lists the following points as composing his personal vision of a school:

1. The school is a community of learners.
2. The school is characterized by collegiality.
3. Risk-taking is valued.
4. People have chosen to work at the school.
5. There is respect for differences.
6. The school is a place where the question "Why?" is appropriate and welcomed.
7. Regard is given for humor.
8. Everyone gets a chance to be a leader.
9. There is a condition of low anxiety and high standards.[31]

Developing a personal picture of excellence is essential if the principal is to be able to articulate goals and direction and behave in ways consistent with his or her vision.

The visionary leader can be effective by helping others chart a path toward what should be rather than handing them a map. True, the leader must have a map in mind, but to simply lay out a plan to get from A to B does little to develop those who must travel the path and as a result somewhat impoverishes both the travelers and the leader.

THE LEADER AS MINISTER OR STEWARD

If one accepts the responsibility for a group or an organization's welfare, then a moral obligation forms. Sergiovanni sees the school as a potential

---

[31] Roland Barth, *Improving Schools from Within* (San Francisco: Jossey-Bass, 1990), 161–172.

community in which moral covenants are forged as visions are shared and brought together. Leadership then would include a moral obligation to meet the needs of the institution, to serve as a steward guarding and protecting the school's purposes, caring for the school for the parents, students, and community.[32]

THE LEADER AS POTTER AND/OR POET

Cultures of schools can be shaped even from relatively shapeless entities. Hart and Bredeson describe principals as potters working with the ingredients of values, symbols, rituals, ceremonies, myths, and routines to shape a school's culture.[33] As noted earlier, a culture is reflected in shared values and shared meanings. Hart and Bredeson see this point entailing a poet's role, in which meanings and values are sustained by language, through words, mottoes, and stories.[34] The power of the organizational stories, the metaphors used, and the meanings that result is strong. The principal has the potential to create powerful images and meanings that can make important differences to all who come in contact with the school.

THE LEADER AS LEARNER

Earlier we noted that the position of principal had at one time been viewed as head teacher or principal teacher. In the context of a school becoming a community of learners, the principal might well be viewed as the lead learner with a group of learners made up of youth and adults in a wide context. Ash and Persall refer to the principal in this mode as the chief learning officer (CLO), who learns alongside the staff in solving problems.[35] Such an image conveys an obligation to seek and create knowledge that makes a difference to colleagues traveling a similar path. Given the rapidly expanding infosphere accessible via developing technology, the image forms in our minds of interactive worldwide learning nodes in which teachers interact with teachers, and students with experts, as easily as conversations with colleagues occur today.

---

[32] Sergiovanni, *Leadership for the Schoolhouse*, 84.
[33] Ann Weaver Hart and Paul V. Bredeson, *The Principalship* (New York: McGraw-Hill, 1996), 140.
[34] Ibid.
[35] Ruth C. Ash and J. Maurice Persall, "The Principal as Chief Learning Officer: Developing Teacher Leaders," *NASSP Bulletin* 84 (May 2000): 15–22.

THE PRINCIPAL AS LEADER

The principal must be a positive leadership force. It must be realized, however, that leadership does not come from the power base of old. We face an ever-changing world in educational administration; our processes must be geared to a changing society and a changing educational organization. We need definitions of leadership and administrative processes that are appropriate to education in its present and future contexts.

Leadership is a complex, dynamic, interactive process. Studies reveal that leadership effectiveness depends on how we define leadership, the criteria we use to evaluate it, the kind of organization within which the leader operates, the type of staff, their proficiency, the tasks they have, the situations they face, and the culture in the school itself and in which the school exists. Leadership holds exciting possibilities to foster change in people's views of themselves, their work, and the continuously improving results of their collective efforts.

A word of caution: Although many approaches to leadership have in some circumstances proven to be positive, no one approach or style is a panacea. Also, positive results may be subject to the observer, and positive results may not be viewed the same over time. The leader needs to be armed with an arsenal of leadership approaches to draw from as conditions change. He or she should then possess a sensitivity to identify accurately the shifts requiring leader behavior changes.

We believe that leadership opportunities are still as great as ever and more exciting than ever; therefore, the definition of educational leadership should be comprehensive enough to recognize the growing competency of teachers and the tremendous power of a group of professionals and students learning and growing in a stimulating environment.

LEADERSHIP DEFINED

We define *leadership* as a deliberate process that results in the following outcomes for all in the school community:

1. Working collaboratively toward an ever-expanding vision of excellence in the achievement of organizational and personal/professional goals and objectives.
2. Creating a threat-free environment for growth so that the creative talents and skills of each person are maximized.
3. Encouraging and building working relationships that are individually and organizationally satisfying, unifying, and strengthening in the realization of mutually determined goals and objectives. Such relationships result in effective group problem solving.

4. Optimizing available human and material resources.

With this definition, leadership is where you find it. Leadership may erupt from a student, teacher, staff member, parent, board member, or other person associated with the school. The leadership task for the principal is to nurture, develop, and reinforce leadership wherever it is found to further the shared purposes of the school.

⑤ U M M A R Y

Leadership is complex. Traits, charisma, attitudes, behaviors, position, and several combinations of these have been studied. Without people and without purpose, *leadership* is clearly a hollow term—it cannot exist apart from a social setting. Furthermore, leadership does not result from an applied formula or decrees from on high. Parks and Worner note four essentials of leadership: (1) leaders know what they want to accomplish, (2) leaders know how to get support and assistance, (3) leaders exert the energy needed, and (4) leaders know the limits of what is possible.[36]

In short, leadership does not just happen. It is a planned process of interaction in a social setting in which goals that are mutually satisfying to the school organization and to the individuals in the school are established and means are developed to achieve them. The following list summarizes the points made earlier regarding the exercise of leadership, but it is not intended as a formula for the same:

1. Know your own beliefs, values, and biases regarding schools, students, teachers, and community.
2. Clearly articulate a vision of excellence, achievement, and community.
3. Develop and maintain an environment of growth for each individual in the school—pupils, staff, and, yes, the principal, too.
4. Optimize the environment to satisfy the needs of both the organization and the people.
5. Develop leadership among the staff and pupils so that the school becomes a community of leaders.
6. Look in more than one direction for a leadership base.
7. Share authority and responsibility with those whom you propose to lead.
8. Recognize and accept the limitations of those with whom you share responsibility.

[36] David Parks and Wayne Worner, "Four Essentials of Leadership," in *Principal,* ed. National Association of Elementary School Principals (Alexandria, VA: National Association of Elementary School Principals, 1992).

9. Realize that one of the most effective leadership bases is that of professional competence. The principal must be able to "produce" in the area accepted by those who are led and be perceived as a proper source of professional authority.
10. Be prepared to rock the boat.

To be effective, the principal will need to lead from a stronger base than just status position or the controlling of and accounting for resources. He or she should be able to make significant programmatic contributions to the achievement of the school's purposes, craft, and technologies and will need to share, not abdicate, his or her authority.

The opportunities for exerting leadership in a school are almost innumerable and are, in a sense, the measure of the principal's responsibility to lead. The greater the opportunity, the greater the responsibility.

FOR FURTHER THOUGHT

1. In your own words, define *educational leadership*; then give some examples of effective leadership acts.
2. What are the risks in accepting the limitations of those with whom one shares responsibility? How can one reduce the risk and at the same time provide for the participants' real growth?
3. Do all informal leaders make effective formal leaders? Explain.
4. Have you ever observed a sharp rise or fall in the morale of a faculty? If so, what factors do you think caused such a marked change? In the case of a fall in morale, what behavior on the part of the principal might have alleviated the problem?
5. If you were the principal of a school where a faculty was content to let you run the school as you wished, would you try to involve them, or would you be happy to run the school without interference? Why?
6. Is a climate that allows mistakes compatible with evaluation and accountability?
7. What metaphors would you use to describe your school? What differences are there between those metaphors and the ones you would prefer a school to be?
8. How would operating as the chief learning officer change your view of the principalship?

SELECTED READINGS

Barth, Roland. *Improving Schools from Within.* San Francisco: Jossey-Bass, 1990.

Buhler, Patricia. "Leaders vs. Managers." *Supervision* 56 (May 1995): 24.

English, Fenwick W. *Theory in Administration.* New York: HarperCollins, 1994.

Fiedler, F. E., and M. M. Chemers. *Leadership and Effective Management*. Glenview, IL: Scott, Foresman, 1974.

Fisher, James L. *Power of the Presidency*. New York: Macmillan, 1984.

Hersey, Paul, and Kenneth H. Blanchard. *Management of Organizational Behavior*, 5th ed. Upper Saddle River, NJ: Prentice Hall, 1988.

Kotter, John P. "What Leaders Really Do." *Harvard Business Review* 68 (May–June 1990): 103–109.

Maehr, Martin L., and Carol Midgley. *Transforming School Cultures*. Boulder, CO: Westview, 1996.

Sergiovanni, T. J. *Leadership for the Schoolhouse*. San Francisco: Jossey-Bass, 1996.

Tirozzi, Gerald N. "The Artistry of Leadership," *Phi Delta Kappan* 82 (February 2001): 434–439.

C H A P T E R   7

Legislation and the Courts: A Sound Base of Authority

S chools are not exempted from today's litigiously turbulent environment. While much of the litigation has been and still is over who controls decisions about the education of children, other agendas enter the fray concerning social issues and values as well as perceived cases of negligence or wrongful behavior.[1] The principal has the responsibility to lead and administer in an institution operating in a society whose values are changing constantly, dependent on which attorneys are able to define or redefine what they are. Constituents represent extremes of conservatism and radicalism, and advances in knowledge and technology are made so rapidly that old ideas and principles are often perceived as obsolete.

The principal soon discovers that very little is really constant and the search for firm ground on which to stand to make a decision is difficult. One major source of strength for the principal is the legal basis of educational operation. But even here problems arise if we assume that the law is inflexible and therefore not influenced by social pressures. Nonetheless, the law as we know it here and now should guide our mode of operation. At the same time, by observing some of the changing interpretations the courts have given these laws, we can draw reasonable conclusions about the directions in which society is going.

Before the 1970s, school authorities assumed virtually unrestricted control over students, supported by the common law principle of *in loco parentis*. As long as teachers and administrators acted in a reasonable manner, they were accorded wide discretion, enjoying the same rights as parents in controlling their children. But during the late 1960s and the

---

[1] William D. Valente and Christine M Valente, *Law in the Schools*, 5th ed. (Upper Saddle River, NJ: Merrill/Prentice Hall, 2001), 4.

early to late 1970s, the Supreme Court extended a plethora of constitutional rights to public school students. To school administrators and indeed to the lower courts, the message from the Supreme Court seemed to emphasize the rights of students over school administrators' control of students. However, Supreme Court decisions during the late 1980s have indicated the Court's willingness to give school administrators more control over students and the curriculum. This certainly does not mean that school administrators can begin to ignore the rights of students, inasmuch as recent studies indicate that the number of lawsuits filed against school districts and school administrators remains very high.[2]

A KNOWLEDGE OF SCHOOL LAW IS IMPORTANT

Courses in school law are often dismissed with the statement "Let's not try to make an attorney out of the school administrator or teacher." Certainly, that should not be the intent of such courses. Rather, the purpose should be to acquaint teachers and administrators with some of the legal fundamentals affecting their positions and the education profession. A thorough working knowledge of the court cases relative to education, the state school code, and local board policy will help school administrators establish and maintain strong leadership roles as school administrators. (An index of court cases appears in the Appendix.)

This point has been reinforced by the U.S. Supreme Court in *Wood v. Strickland*. The Court held that administrators and school board members are not immune from liability for damages if they knew, or reasonably should have known, that the action officially taken would violate the constitutional rights of the students affected or if the action was taken with malicious intention to cause a deprivation of constitutional rights.[3]

A good administrator understands state regulations and directives as well as local school policy. Logically, the professional educator might even be more expert in law affecting schools than the average lawyer. This does not mean that the school principal should serve as a pseudo-lawyer. Rather, it suggests that school law is particularized and that the school administrator must have a professional knowledge of school laws to make decisions that normally affect education. Employing an attorney on school law should not be necessary unless some question of technical interpretation arises, a legal document has to be prepared, or legal action must be initiated. On the other hand, although a lot of law relates specifically to education, a much greater body of law concerns the operation of

---

[2] Michael Imber and Gary Thompson, "Developing a Typology of Litigation in Education and Determining the Frequency of Each Category," *Educational Administration Quarterly* 27 (1991): 225. See also Perry Zirkel, "The 'Explosion' in Education Litigation: An Update," *Education Law Reporter* 114 (1997): 341.
[3] *Wood v. Strickland,* 420 U.S. 308 (1985).

government generally and affects education because education is a part of government. Here, too, the services of an attorney are necessary.

McKinney and Drake examined the role of the school attorney in the context of providing legal advice that results in official school policy.[4] They found that school lawyers are heavily involved in the policy-making process. Lawyers exert a great deal of influence, particularly in the policy areas of teacher dismissal, teacher discipline, student discipline, religion in the schools, and special education. McKinney and Drake note that there is a danger "in expanding the role of school attorneys to the level of school administrators and school board members."[5] It is essential that school personnel know enough school law to exercise their professional educational judgment.

RELIGION AND THE PUBLIC SCHOOLS

The relationship between religion and the public schools has been a perennial controversial issue in the United States. The religion clauses of the First Amendment of the U.S. Constitution provide that "Congress shall make no law respecting an establishment of religion or prohibiting the free exercise thereof." The apparently straightforward clauses have been the cause of considerable confusion, controversy, and litigation in education for decades. James Madison, who along with Thomas Jefferson is generally acknowledged to have authored the First Amendment, predicted the continuing controversy over the meaning and application of the First Amendment when he said, "It may not be easy, in every possible case, to trace the line of separation, between the rights of the religious and the civil authority, with such distinctiveness, as to avoid all collisions and doubts or unessential points."[6] John Adams noted that the First Amendment would mean the "Congress will never meddle in religion."[7] Thomas Jefferson coined the metaphor "wall of separation between church and state" to express his lifelong view of the proper relationship between church and state.

Indeed, members of the Supreme Court who have interpreted the meaning of the First Amendment repeatedly and frequently recognized the difficulty in balancing the establishment and free exercise clauses of the First Amendment. In the landmark establishment clause decision, *Everson v. Board of Education*, the Court analyzed and incorporated the

---

[4] Joseph R. McKinney and Thelbert L. Drake, "The School Attorney and Local Educational Policy-Making," *Education Law Reporter* 93 (1994): 471.

[5] Ibid., 480.

[6] Adrienne Koch, *Madison's Advice to My Country* (Princeton, NJ: Princeton University Press, 1966), 43.

[7] Kern Alexander and David M. Alexander, *American Public School Law*, 3d ed. (St. Paul, MN: West, 1992), 113.

history of the First Amendment into its opinion.[8] In *Everson*, parents were reimbursed for bus fares paid to send their children to parochial schools. The Court upheld public funding of transportation for parochial school students, finding the transportation program analogous to providing public safety services such as police and fire protection. Although four justices dissented in *Everson*, all nine justices seemed to embrace Thomas Jefferson's notion of separation between church and state. The "wall of separation" concept became firmly established as a cornerstone for subsequent First Amendment analysis.

Since *Everson*, the U.S. Supreme Court has adhered to one constitutional principle consistently with respect to separation of church and state. The Court has maintained that neutrality is what is required of states. The state must confine itself to secular objectives and neither advance nor impede religious activity.[9] The Supreme Court has firmly attached itself to the idea of governmental neutrality as the central theme for regulating church-state relations.[10]

In 1971, the Supreme Court developed a three-criteria test to determine state neutrality in *Lemon v. Kurtzman*.[11] It has relied on this test in almost every case involving the relationship between government and religion in education since 1971. The three criteria articulated by *Lemon* are as follows:

1. The statute must have a secular legislative purpose.
2. Its principal effect must be one that neither advances nor inhibits religion.
3. The statute must not foster "an excessive government entanglement with religion."

This test is commonly referred to as the *Lemon test* or the tripartite test.

Questions regarding prayer and Bible reading in the public schools have generated a great deal of controversy and litigation for the past four decades. On the last decision day of 1961, the Supreme Court in *Engel v. Vitale* ruled that the regents' prayer prescribed by the school authorities of the state of New York could not constitutionally be made a part of the state's education program.[12] The prayer read, "Almighty God, we acknowledge our dependence on Thee, and we beg Thy blessings upon us, our parents, teacher, and our Country."[13] The Court ruled that the state-sponsored prayer violated the establishment clause of the First Amendment.

---

[8] 330 U.S. 1 (1947).
[9] *Roemer v. Maryland Public Works Board*, 426 U.S. 7836 (1974).
[10] See, e.g., *Wallace v. Jaffree*, 472 U.S. 38 (1985); *Corporation of Presiding Bishop of Church of Jesus Christ of Latter-Day Saints v. Amos*, 483 U.S. 327 (1987).
[11] 403 U.S. 602 (1971).
[12] 370 U.S. 421 (1962).
[13] Ibid., 425.

In 1963, the Supreme Court extended its position on school-sponsored prayer in the companion cases of *School District of Abingdon Township v. Schempp* and *Murray v. Curlett.*[14] These cases challenged Pennsylvania and Maryland statutes that allowed prayers and Bible reading at the opening of each school day. Children were excused from the exercise upon parental request. However, the Court ruled that the religious practices and the statutes regarding them violated the establishment clause. At the time of the Court's 1963 decision, thirty-seven states allowed such exercises; thirteen mandated them.[15]

Reaction to the school prayer decisions since the 1960s has been strong, and some legislatures have passed legislation that variously authorizes silent prayer, meditation, volunteer prayer, or moments of silence during the public school day. In fact, twenty years after the *Engel* and *Schempp* decisions, nearly half of the states had enacted laws permitting a moment of silence, including prayer, in their public schools.[16]

The Supreme Court rendered a decision in 1985 dealing with the issue of state-imposed silent meditation or voluntary prayer. In *Wallace v. Jaffree,* a majority held that an Alabama statute authorizing a one-minute period of silence in public schools for meditation or voluntary prayer was unconstitutional because it violated the establishment clause of the First Amendment.[17] Justice John Paul Stevens, writing for the majority, emphasized that the legislative purpose in passing the statute was improper because it constituted a state effort to endorse religion. The Court devoted much of its decision to an inquiry into the intent of the statute. If the intent is to promote religious purposes, as the Court found in *Wallace,* or to emphasize voluntary prayer over meditation, then the Court will find an establishment clause violation.

The Court left open the possibility that statutes permitting a moment of silence, meditation, or prayer might be constitutional. Justice O'Connor, in her concurring opinion, rejected the *Lemon* test as applied and suggested her own test to determine whether the statute's purpose is valid. She states, "[W]hether the government's purpose is to endorse religion . . . , the crucial question is whether the state has conveyed or attempted to convey the message that children should use the moment of silence for prayer."[18]

The Eleventh Circuit Court of Appeals said in 1997 that public schools may begin each day with a state-mandated moment of silence.[19] The Supreme Court upheld a Georgia law that required students to begin

---

[14]   374 U.S. 203 (1963).
[15]   Thomas Hunt, "Moral Education and Public Schools: A Tale of Tempest," *Religion and Public Education* 13 (Spring 1986): 25–36.
[16]   See Justice O'Connor's dissent in *Wallace v. Jaffree,* 472 U.S. 38, 70–71 (1985).
[17]   472 U.S. 38 (1985).
[18]   Ibid., 73.
[19]   *Bown v. Gwinnett County School District,* 112 F.3d 1464 (11th Cir. 1997).

each day with a one-minute silent reflection on the anticipated activities of the day.

Another volatile issue involving school prayer has been prayer at graduation ceremonies. In a ratification of strict church-state separation, the Supreme Court ruled in a 5–4 1992 decision, *Lee v. Weisman,* that benedictions and invocations by clergy at public school graduation ceremonies violate the establishment clause of the First Amendment.[20] The Court did not address the issue of whether student-led programs at graduation exercises are likewise unconstitutional.

The federal appellate courts have split in their decisions on whether voluntary, student-led prayer at graduation ceremonies is constitutional. The Fifth Circuit Court of Appeals held that student-organized and student-led nonsectarian invocations at their graduation were permissible.[21] However, the Ninth Circuit Court of Appeals disagreed with the Fifth Circuit and found the practice of allowing members of the senior class to vote on whether they wanted prayers delivered at graduation and on which student would give the prayer violated the establishment clause.[22] In 1989, the Eleventh Circuit Court of Appeals ruled that pregame invocations at public school athletic events violate the First Amendment.[23] The Supreme Court refused to review the decision. Likewise, prayers led by a girls' basketball coach after games and before practices were found to violate the establishment clause.[24]

The controversy continued with *Santa Fe v. Doe,* regarding a school policy that allowed student-led prayer at an athletic event. The U.S. Supreme Court decision on June 19, 2000, " . . . rejects students deciding to offer prayer at school events."[25] The implications of the decision, even related to graduation ceremonies, are still in question.[26]

Individual Voluntary Prayer

School administrators should be aware that no court has ever declared it impermissible for a student to utter a voluntary private prayer at school. To the contrary, in *Wallace,* Justice O'Connor said, "Nothing in the United States Constitution as interpreted by this court . . . prohibits public school students from voluntarily praying at any time before, during, or after the school day."[27] *Chandler v. James* provides further clarification.

---

[20] 505 U.S. 577, 112 S. Ct. 1249 (1992).

[21] *Jones v. Clear Creek Independent School District,* 977 F.2d 963 (5th Cir. 1992).

[22] *Harris v. Joint School District,* 41 F.3d 447 (9th Cir. 1994).

[23] *Jager v. Douglas County School District,* 862 F.2d 824 (11th Cir. 1989).

[24] *Doe v. Duncanville Independent School District,* 994 F.2d 160 (5th Cir. 1993).

[25] David Schimmel, "Court Outlaws School-Sponsored Student Prayer: An Analysis of Santa Fe v. Doe," *West's Education Law Reporter* 150 (March 1, 2001): 1.

[26] T. C. Mattocks, "Reactions for Santa Fe v. Doe: Is Student Prayer at Graduation Still an Option?" *West's Education Law Reporter* 150 (March 15, 2001): 333–344.

[27] *Wallace v. Jaffree,* 67.

"School officials cannot censor religion from student speech, and also cannot actively supervise or participate in student-led religious speech."[28]

Additionally, the Supreme Court has not precluded the study of religion or the Bible in the public schools. In *School District of Abingdon Township v. Schempp*, the Court explained, "It certainly may be said that the Bible is worthy of study for its literary and historic qualities. Nothing we have said here indicates that such study of the Bible or of religion, when presented objectively as a part of a secular program of education, may not be consistent with the First Amendment."[29] Thus, public schools may use the Bible or other religious literature as a means to study history, government, sociology, culture, civilization, or ethics but not as a means to promote religion. Educators must be sensitive and careful not to use the Bible or studies about religion as a way of proselytizing and instead teach classes in an objective manner.[30]

Released Time and Community Service

The question of *released* or *dismissed time* during regular school hours for religious ceremony or instruction comes up with some frequency in every school. Two important Supreme Court decisions address the issue of public school accommodations regarding student released time for religious instruction. In 1948, in *McCollum v. Board of Education*, the Court invalidated a public school program that excused students from secular subjects to attend regular religious instruction classes, at their parents' request, in the public school facility.[31] Students who did not participate continued to study secular subjects. The Court struck down the practice as a violation of the establishment clause because the program aided religion.

In *Zorach v. Clauson*, a Supreme Court case decided by a 6–3 vote a mere four years after *McCollum*, the Court upheld the dismissal of students from school during the school day to permit them to pursue religious instruction off school premises.[32] The Court distinguished *Zorach* from *McCollum* on the basis of where the religious instruction took place. In *Zorach*, religious instruction did not occur on public school property, and the Court upheld the practice. Another release time issue surfaced in 1981 before the Tenth Circuit Court of Appeals. The court invalidated a

[28] *Chandler v. James*, 180 F.3d 1254 (11th Cir. 1999).
[29] *School District of Abingdon Township v. Schempp*, 225.
[30] See *Hall v. Board of School Commissioners*, 656 F.2d 999 (5th Cir. 1981), modified, 707 F.2d 464 (1983).
[31] 333 U.S. 203 (1948).
[32] 343 U.S. 306 (1952).

Utah state policy that allowed public school credit for religion courses taken at parochial schools during "release time."[33]

The practice of mandating community service for high school students as a prerequisite for graduation has swept across the country. Maryland actually requires community service for high school graduation. The practice has broad support from teachers, administrators, students, and school board members. As one might expect, the practice has been challenged in court several times on various grounds. However, every court that has heard a challenge to the practice has upheld the legality of community service as a requirement for graduation.[34]

Equal Access Act and Voluntary Student Religious Meetings

Congress adopted the Equal Access Act in 1984. This act makes it unlawful for public secondary schools that receive federal financial assistance and that have created a "limited open forum" to deny equal access or fair opportunity to, or discriminate against, any "student-initiated" non-curriculum-related groups on the basis of the religious, political, or philosophical content of their speech.[35] A "limited open forum" exists, according to the act, and the equal access requirements are triggered whenever a public school "grants an offering to or opportunity for one or more non-curriculum-related student groups to meet on school premises during noninstructional time."[36]

For the first time, in *Board of Education of Westside Community Schools v. Mergens,* the Supreme Court ruled on the legality and constitutionality of student-initiated voluntary religious activities on public school premises.[37] School authorities refused to grant official recognition to a Bible study group that had been meeting on school premises after school. A student, Bridget Mergens, claimed that the high school officials discriminated against the religious group in not providing a faculty sponsor. A faculty sponsor was necessary under school rules for full school recognition, which accordingly provided for access to the school newspaper, school facility, bulletin board, public address system, and annual Club Fair. By an 8–1 vote, the Supreme Court held that the Equal Access Act did not violate the establishment clause. Second, the Court held that the school had violated the student's rights under the Equal Access Act.

The Court's interpretation of the Equal Access Act is very significant to school administrators because the Court analyzed and defined the meaning of "limited open forum." Once a public school creates a lim-

---

[33] *Lanner v. Wimmer,* 662 F.2d 1349 (10th Cir. 1981).
[34] See *Steirer v. Bethlehem Area School District,* 987 F.2d 989 (3d Cir.), cert. denied, 510 U.S. 824 (1993); *Immediato v. Rye Neck School District,* 73 F.3d 454 (2d Cir. 1996).
[35] 20 U.S.C. § 4071.
[36] 20 U.S.C. § 4071(b).
[37] USLW 4720, 110 S. Ct. 2356 (1990).

ited open forum, school administrators cannot discriminate against students who want to conduct a meeting within that school on the basis of religious, political, philosophical, or other content of the speech at such meetings.

The Court concluded that a limited open forum is created when a school permits one or more non-curriculum-related student groups to meet. A non-curriculum-related student group, according to the majority in *Mergens,* is any student group that does not directly relate to the body of courses offered by the school. Justice O'Connor then set forth five characteristics of student groups. A student group directly relates to a school's curriculum (1) if the subject matter of the group is actually taught in a regularly offered course or (2) will soon be taught in a regularly offered course; (3) if the subject matter of the group concerns the body of courses as a whole; (4) if participation in the group is required for a particular course; or (5) if participation in the group results in academic credit. Any group meeting at least one of these characteristics will not trigger the act's requirements. Therefore, the act will depend on the school's individual curriculum.

The Ninth Circuit found that a non-curriculum-related religious club for students could meet during the school lunch period during which no classes met and other student clubs were allowed to meet.[38] The school argued that the Equal Access Act did not apply because the act defines noninstructional time as time set aside by the school before actual classroom instruction begins or after classroom instruction ends. The school further argued that its lunchtime was not before or after the school day. The Court disagreed, reasoning that the act was to be interpreted broadly; noninstructional time was that time when no classroom instruction was taking place and other student groups were allowed to meet.

TORT LIABILITY

Tort law provides students and their parents, and in some instances, school employees, an opportunity to obtain compensation and other relief for injuries or harm they have sustained in school. A *tort* is a civil wrong, also known as a private wrong, not involving a breach of contract, for which damages may be recovered in a court of law.[39]

The law of torts can be traced to English common law. Like common law, the law of torts in this country consists of fifty separate lines or bodies of state tort law. Although states borrow freely from each other's

---

[38] *Ceniceros v. Board of Trustees,* 66 F.3d 1535 (9th Cir. 1995).
[39] See, generally, Page Keeton, Daniel Dobbs, Robert Keeton, and David Owen, *Prosser and Keeton on Torts,* 5th ed. (St. Paul, MN: West, 1984).

case law, it is noteworthy that each state's body of tort law is different. Most states have passed various legislation, known as *tort claims acts,* that must be complied with as a prerequisite to recovery by anyone claiming an injury as a result of governmental negligence.[40]

Three theories of redress or categories of tort actions provide the framework for constructing a comprehensive basis of liability for tortious acts: (1) negligence, (2) intentional torts, and (3) strict liability.

Negligence

The most prevalent tort with which school districts and school personnel become involved is negligence.[41] *Negligence* is conduct falling below an established standard that results in injury.[42] Generally speaking, the standard by which an educator's conduct is judged is defined as that of the reasonably prudent teacher. The skills and knowledge expected of a qualified teacher or school administrator are factors considered in establishing the hypothetical reasonably prudent teacher. The reasonably prudent teacher standard constitutes a higher degree of care than the usual standard of care of the reasonably prudent person (noneducator). Courts consider the standard of care owed to students to be flexible, and it varies according to such factors as the student's age, intelligence, and experience and the environment and circumstances under which an injury took place. The standard of care required of school administrators by courts increases with the immaturity, lack of mental capacity, or inexperience of students.[43] The principal of an elementary school, for example, will look at the activities in the cafeteria somewhat differently than a high school principal, though both need to be conscious of potential problems.

Intentional Torts

A second category of torts involves intentional torts. *Intentional torts* include assault, battery, trespass, and false imprisonment. The most frequently litigated intentional torts relating to educators have historically been assault and battery.[44]

A subcategory of intentional torts is the *tort of defamation,* which encompasses libel and slander actions. It is a hybrid subcategory of intentional torts because at common law an individual may be liable for a defamatory statement, whether made intentionally or negligently. *Defamation* is generally defined as an injury to a person's character, fame,

---

[40] See, e.g., *Indiana Code* §§ 34-4-16.5 et seq.

[41] Imber and Thompson, "Developing a Typology," 225.

[42] See *Smith v. Archbishop of St. Louis,* 632 S.W.2d. 516, 521, 522 (Mo. 1982).

[43] See, e.g., *Barbin v. State of Louisiana,* 506 So. 2d. 888 (La. App. 1987); *Rodriguez v. Board of Education,* 480 N.Y.S.2d 901 (1984).

[44] Imber and Thompson, "Developing a Typology," 227.

or reputation by a false, malicious statement. Alexander and Alexander note that educators are particularly susceptible to charges of defamation because "of the sensitivity of personal information that they come into contact with each day."[45] Principals face additional complex problems because they communicate information concerning teacher evaluation and performance "to other administrators or to school board members."[46]

Various defenses are available to principals who are sued for defamation. In many states, the defense of truth, which is a complete defense in cases involving defamation, is guaranteed by state constitutions. Other defenses, such as absolute or qualified privilege, may also be available to school administrators. Educators have used extensively the qualified privilege, which excuses defamatory speech; it extends to communications between parties sharing an interest or duty, including school personnel. Therefore, courts will not assess liability if communication was made in good faith, without malice, in answer to an official inquiry, or in the performance of a legitimate educational duty.[47]

Strict Liability

The third tort area is *strict liability*. An injured person may maintain an action against a defendant who has created an ultrahazardous or unusual danger. It need not be established that the injury was intentionally or negligently caused. Strict liability has had only marginal application to public school law; nevertheless, allegations against school personnel for creating hazards relating to laboratory experiments, vocational education, athletic equipment, and playground equipment have appeared in education-related cases.

Adequate Supervision

The most prevalent tort action involving public schools and school administrators is based on liability arising from allegations of negligent acts. Negligence, it must be emphasized, necessarily involves a foreseeable risk, a threatened danger of injury, and conduct unreasonable in proportion to the danger.[48] The classic elements of a cause of action for negligence are these:

1. A duty on the part of the actor to protect others
2. A failure on the part of the actor to exercise an appropriate standard of care

---

[45] Alexander and Alexander, *American Public School Law,* 502.
[46] Ibid., 502.
[47] See *Rich v. Kentucky County Day Inc.,* 793 S.W.2d 832 (Ky. App. 1990); *Desselle v. Guillary,* 407 So. 2d 74 (La. App. 1982).
[48] Keeton et al., *Prosser and Keeton on Law of Torts,* 288.

3. A causal connection between the act and the resultant injury, usually referred to as *proximate cause*
4. Actual loss or damage to the injured party as a result of the injury

School administrators have a duty to care for students in their charge. However, for liability to be proven, the educator's act or failure to act must be shown to have a close causal connection to the student's injury. Liability may be mitigated or extinguished if it can be demonstrated that the cause of the injury was an intervening or superseding act or if responsibility for the injury can be transferred to a more culpable party.

The courts have repeatedly indicated that they do not intend to place an undue burden on teachers and administrators while they supervise the safety of students. In fact, the generally accepted judicial rule is that the law does not require schools to act as ensurers of their students' safety, nor does it subject them to liability for accidental harm that could not have been avoided by the exercise of reasonable care.[49]

The extent of reasonable supervision required by courts for the care and supervision of students' safety will depend on the age and physical and psychological condition of the students involved as well as the type of activity and conditions under which the activity took place. Courts are more likely to find teachers and administrators liable for inadequate supervision if the occurrence leading to a student's injury is foreseeable and the accident could have been avoided if school personnel had taken appropriate steps. Courts examine the facts of each individual case, searching for factors that tend to suggest that a reasonable person would have foreseen the accident's occurrence. Two major indicators of foreseeability are unreasonably dangerous conditions or situations and past behavior patterns of students, such as known violent propensities. Given these factors, liability is more likely to be found if a teacher leaves a classroom or a principal does not direct and call for appropriate supervision.

Educators run a serious risk of being held liable for inadequate or incompetent instruction and teaching that leads to student injury. The greatest risk of liability in connection with negligent instruction seems to arise with respect to physical education, shop, laboratory classes, and coaching activities.[50] The level of the appropriate standard of care will vary with the degree of danger associated with the activity. School principals may be found liable for failing to exercise reasonable care in supervising the development, planning, and administration of the school's programs.[51]

[49] See Valente and Valente, *Law in the Schools*, pp. 98–117.
[50] Imber and Thompson, "Developing a Typology," 243.
[51] See *L v. Independent School District No. 314*, 289 N.W.2d 112 (Minn. 1979).

Although courts have been more or less sympathetic to the difficult roles of teachers and administrators, they have held them generally responsible for injuries sustained in many school-related activities. School administrators have a duty to maintain school buildings, school grounds, and equipment in proper condition.[52] Schools owe a duty of care regarding field trips and other school-sponsored activities, taking special precautions when such outings or activities entail unusual activities or unfamiliar places.

When schools provide transportation to and from school, liability may be found for negligent operation of the bus, inadequate supervision of students on the bus, negligent supervision of students at bus stops, and unsafe equipment.[53] Schools also may be liable for the off-campus injuries of a student who leaves school without school or parental permission if the leaving was a result of negligent supervision.[54]

A Safe Environment

Providing a safe school environment free from violence is a major responsibility of school administrators. A California constitutional provision enacted by a vote of the people of California in 1982 gives students and teachers an "inalienable right to attend schools which are safe, secure and peaceful."[55] While other states have not enacted such sweeping protections, it is clear that school authorities have a duty to ensure the safety of students and teachers against injuries from both insiders and third parties. If assaults on students or teachers are reasonably foreseeable, then school administrators should take appropriate precautions, including warning students, teachers, and parents and increasing safety measures such as police patrols. School administrators must take allegations of sexual harassment very seriously and take steps to prevent it and investigate all claims.

School administrators who must defend against allegations of negligence have several traditional defenses available to them. *Contributory negligence* is the defense used most often. School personnel raising this defense must show that the injury resulted from the injured person's own neglect or failure to exercise the required degree of care necessary to ensure safety. Courts recognize that the applicable standard of care expected of children varies from case to case and will be fixed by the jury considering the unique circumstances of the case.[56]

---

[52] See, e.g., *Scott v. Board of Education of City of New York,* 597 N.Y.2d 385 (App. Div. 1993); *Bauer v. Minidoka School District No. 331,* 778 P.2d 336 (1989).

[53] See, generally, 34 A.L.R.3d (1990 Supp.).

[54] See *Hoyem v. Manhattan Beach City School District,* 585 P.2d 851, 22 Cal. 3d 508 (1978); *Gary v. Menche,* 626 So. 2d 901 (La. App. 1993).

[55] California Constitution, art. I, sec. 28(c).

[56] For contrasts in outcomes, see Perry A. Zirkel, "Safe Promises," *Phi Delta Kappan* 81 (April 2000): 635–636.

Tolerance for Zero Tolerance? Zero tolerance for drug possession, distribution, or use; zero tolerance for fighting; zero tolerance for gang-related symbols or activity—all sound good to the community entrusting their children to a school. High standards of behavior are implied as well as school being a safe place. Yet we have all heard or read accounts of the North Carolina eleven-year-old who was suspended for bringing a homegrown pepper to class, the girl who was suspended for having a nail clipper, or the boy who was trying to defend himself and was suspended for fighting. Granted, the zero tolerance policy in the last instance seemed to be responsible for reducing fights in the school from nearly two hundred in one year to fewer than five. By clearly stating and rigidly enforcing a zero tolerance policy, do we risk teaching everyone that intolerance of and the resulting consequences of "undesired" behavior are appropriate? Even in a zero tolerance policy, the "rule of reason" must prevail. The school should not place itself in a situation where it not only risks litigation but also deserves ridicule for the way it tries to create a safe environment.

Governmental Immunity?

Historically, school districts were protected from liability by the old common law doctrine that the state is sovereign and cannot be sued without its consent.[57] Educators, riding on the tail of this common law cloak, seldom were held liable for carelessness or questionable supervisory practices. However, in more than half of the states today, the doctrine of governmental immunity for torts has been eliminated or substantially eroded by legislative or judicial actions.[58] Likewise, educators' protection against personal liability has been lost or substantially curtailed in many states. The doctrine of immunity has been criticized for often leaving injured parties without any means for compensation for losses caused by the state.

While the courts may have sharply limited the doctrine of immunity for teachers and administrators, a growing number of states have enacted *save harmless,* or indemnification, legislation. Such statutes require school districts to pay the legal expenses or damage claims assessed against employees. The cardinal rule of all save harmless statutes is that educators will be indemnified for monetary losses as long as the tortious acts occurred within the scope of their employment.

On January 19, 2001, the U.S. Department of Education issued new guidelines regarding the school's liability in sexual harassment cases. Included is the guideline that " . . . a school should recognize and

---

[57] Derived from English law: "The King can do no wrong."
[58] Valente, *Education Law: Public and Private,* Vol. 2. (St. Paul, MN: West, 1985), 224.

effectively respond to sexual harassment of students in its programs as a condition of receiving federal assistance."[59]

Constitutional Torts

A constitutional tort is separate from a common law tort. While the law of common law torts can be traced to England, the genesis of the constitutional tort is found in the Civil Rights Act of 1871, codified as Title 42 of the United States Code. Congress passed the legislation during Reconstruction to protect the rights of African Americans.[60]

Many injured parties seek redress in federal court under 42 U.S.C. § 1983 (Section 1983) against school districts and school personnel. This cause of action is commonly called a *constitutional tort*. Section 1983 of the Civil Rights Act of 1871 provides for liability if a person acting under the color of state law violates another individual's civil rights.

In a Section 1983 action against a school governing body, a plaintiff must prove he or she has suffered a deprivation of a constitutional right through the act of a school official or employee who was directly implementing a policy or custom of the school board. Second, the plaintiff must show that the school official or employee knowingly, willfully, or at least recklessly caused the constitutional deprivation by his or her action or failure to act.

Before 1975, school board members, school administrators, and teachers were considered immune from liability for constitutional torts. In *Wood v. Strickland,* a student discipline case, the Supreme Court reduced this protection to a "good faith" qualified immunity. The divided Court held that a public school educator could be liable for damages if "he knew or reasonably should have known that the action he took within his sphere of official responsibility would violate the constitutional rights of the student affected."[61]

The Supreme Court has interpreted the good faith standard to mean that school authorities will not be found liable in their individual capacities under Section 1983 unless they personally violate clearly established constitutional rights of individuals.[62] Neither compensatory nor punitive damages are recoverable under Section 1983 unless the constitutional deprivation resulted in actual harm.

An increasing number of student-initiated Section 1983 actions have been brought against schools over the past several years. Many of the cases involve allegations of sexual misconduct and violence inflicted on students.

---

[59] For the U.S. Department of Education guidelines on sexual harassment, see www.ed.gov/ocr/shguide.

[60] Alexander and Alexander, *American Public School Law,* 488.

[61] *Wood v. Strickland,* 332.

[62] *Harlow v. Fitzgerald,* 457 U.S. 800 (1982).

CORPORAL PUNISHMENT

Corporal punishment is often a major controversial issue. More and more school districts are prohibiting (or placing restrictive controls on) corporal punishment through written school policy. At least twenty-five states have banned corporal punishment in the public schools.[63] In the other states, under the doctrine of *in loco parentis,* school authorities have the right to administer disciplinary corporal punishment in the same manner and to the same extent as parents. Generally speaking, under *in loco parentis,* educators may use physical force that is reasonable under the circumstances but may not use force that goes beyond that reasonably necessary to effect a legitimate educational purpose.[64] In *Daily v. Board of Education of Morrill County School Dist. No. 62-0063,* a teacher had struck and restrained a student for disruptive behavior. The state's student discipline act did permit teachers and administrators to use physical contact to preserve order and control but not corporal punishment, which was in violation of state law.[65]

The use of corporal punishment in America as a method of discipline in its schools can be traced to the colonial period. The U.S. Supreme Court upheld the use of corporal punishment by a 5–4 vote in *Ingraham v. Wright* in 1977.[66] It rejected the plaintiff's claim that the Eighth Amendment ban on cruel and unusual punishment applies to disciplinary corporal punishment of public school children. The Court indicated that teachers and administrators are properly constrained from using excessive force because educators are subject to civil and criminal liability if they exceed the use of moderate corporal punishment.

The Supreme Court also held in *Ingraham* that the due process clause of the Fourteenth Amendment does not require procedural safeguards, including notice and a hearing, before employing corporal punishment, since the practice is authorized and limited by the common law.

The principal and the teacher should understand that they must abide by the regulations of their school district and the laws of their state. Failure to do so constitutes insubordination. Educators who use excessive corporal punishment or act without authority open the door to civil and criminal charges of assault and battery and child abuse.

SCHOOL DISCIPLINE

The judiciary uniformly recognizes the right and duty of school boards and school authorities to maintain order and control in the classroom

---

[63] John Dayton, "Corporal Punishment in Public Schools: The Legal and Political Battle Continues," *Education Law Reporter* 89 (1994): 729.
[64] See William Prosser, *The Law of Torts,* 4th ed. (St. Paul, MN: West, 1971), 137.
[65] 588 N.W.2d 873 (Neb. 1999).
[66] 430 U.S. 651 (1977).

and public schools. School boards are accorded wide discretion in making and enforcing rules that govern school operations. The particular rule must have a reasonable relation to the educational process and must not be discriminatory in operation toward a student or a class of students or violate students' constitutional rights. School principals are given the primary responsibility of carrying out disciplinary rules and preventing interference with the educational process at their schools.

Suspension and expulsion constitute two of the most drastic disciplinary actions available to school authorities. During the 1960s, courts began to recognize that students had a right to procedural due process in connection with school suspensions and expulsions.[67] The Fourteenth Amendment to the Constitution prohibits states from depriving "any person of life, liberty, or property without due process of law."

In 1975, the Supreme Court took up the question of what constitutional standards would apply to disciplinary action taken by school officials. In *Goss v. Lopez,* the Court asserted that students have constitutional rights that they do not "shed . . . at the schoolhouse door" and that suspension from school without due process violates both liberty and property interests possessed by public school students.[68] The Court specifically found that "due process requires, in connection with a suspension of ten days or less, that the student be given oral or written notice of the charges against him and, if he denies them, an explanation of the evidence the authorities have and an opportunity to present his side of the story."[69] The Court added that there need be no delay between giving notice and holding the hearing. Thus, it concluded that even a short-term suspension of ten days or less would deprive a student of two protected constitutional interests. It noted that for suspensions exceeding ten days more formal requirements would be in order. Special education students require additional consideration, as noted in this chapter and Chapter 11.

Following the *Goss* decision, state legislatures passed laws respecting short-term suspensions and expulsions. States have established elaborate procedural schemes to be used for expulsions. It is critical that principals learn their respective state's set of expulsion procedures and local policies and procedures and adhere to them meticulously. In the event the principal perceives a discrepancy between state and local procedures, clarification should be made immediately.

Some schools impose academic sanctions on students for misconduct or truancy. This practice has been the subject of litigation. Academic sanctions may conflict with a state's compulsory attendance laws. They may also be viewed as arbitrary and unrelated to disciplinary purposes. Yet other challenges have been based on substantive and procedural due

---

[67] *Dixon v. Alabama State Board of Education,* 294 F.2d 150 (5th Cir.), cert. denied, 368 U.S. 930 (1961).
[68] 419 U.S. 565 (1975).
[69] Ibid., 581.

process claims.[70] From an educational point of view, it is somewhat questionable to "reward" students through suspension or expulsion with the very situation they may have wanted—namely, not to be in school.

Academic sanctions for student misconduct must be directly related to the student's academic performance. An Indiana appellate court held that a rule requiring a 4 percent grade reduction for every day missed on account of a suspension for consuming alcohol during school hours was a violation of the student's substantive due process right.[71] The court reasoned that a student's grades should be reflective of academic performance, which includes such factors as test scores, class participation, and class attendance. Reducing grades for the consumption of alcohol was not rationally related to and did not reflect academic performance. In furtherance of this holding, the court noted that while 4 percent of Smith's grade was determined for each day she missed, a similar percentage was not determined for other students.

CONFIDENTIALITY OF SCHOOL RECORDS AND STUDENT PRIVACY

Consideration of the school's counseling activities and concern for the welfare and best interest of children and youth under its care lead to the whole question of the student's school records, their character, and how private and public they actually are. With the advancement of the computer and capacity to gather, store, and immediately retrieve massive amounts of personal data, the potential conflict between concerns for the individual's privacy and the school's need for information becomes a difficult issue, particularly as to data protection, confidentiality, and accessibility.

In 1974, Congress passed the Family Educational Rights and Privacy Act (FERPA), also known as the Buckley Amendment, which provides protection for the privacy interests of students and their parents in connection with school records.[72] FERPA gives students and their parents a right of access to the student's education records. Students are given the same rights as parents under the act upon reaching age eighteen. Requests for files by parents must be honored within forty-five days, and those making the request have the right to make copies of the file, at their own expense. If an eligible student or parent wishes to amend a record because it is inaccurate or misleading, the act provides a process for such challenges.[73]

---

[70] *Katzman v. Cumberland Valley School District,* 479 A.2d 671 (Pa. Cmwealth. 1984).
[71] *Smith v. School City of Hobart,* 811 F. Supp. 391 (N.D. Ind. 1993).
[72] 20 U.S.C. §§ 1232 et seq.
[73] 34 C.F.R. § 99.11.

A parent or student has a right to a hearing if school officials do not amend the file upon the parent's initial request. The hearing may be conducted by a school district employee who does not have an interest in the proceeding. The hearing officer must render a written decision explaining his or her findings and conclusions. Complaints alleging violations of FERPA may be filed with the U.S. Department of Education. Violators of the act may lose federal funding.

FERPA also prohibits the release of any personally identifiable information without the express written consent of the parent or eligible student except to certain specified government agencies and officials. However, FERPA does not prohibit disclosure to the public of general information concerning students, such as a student's name, address, telephone number, date and place of birth, field of study, degrees, awards received, and participation in school activities. In addition, schoolwide information regarding student achievement, graduation rates, and so forth can be disclosed to the public without parental consent as long as the information does not personally identify students.

States have also enacted public access/privacy legislation dealing with state agencies, including public schools, that collect and maintain personal information systems. Principals should consult those laws as well as FERPA before disseminating student record information.

The principal must take care in all instances to ascertain correctly who the parent, guardian, or other eligible person(s) is regarding the request and/or release of information. In a society of multiple family patterns, this may be no easy task.

LEGAL LIMITS ON SCHOOL SEARCHES

To discourage the use and sale of drugs in and around the school, and generally to improve school security, many schools have initiated searches of student lockers and even students themselves, used specially trained dogs to sniff out drugs, and authorized the use of metal detectors to ferret out guns and other weapons.[74] The question is, How closely must the school administrator follow the search-and-seizure limits established for law enforcement officials under the Fourth Amendment?

On January 15, 1985, the Supreme Court, in *New Jersey v. T.L.O.*, rendered its first decision on a search-and-seizure issue involving the public schools.[75] The Court held that the Fourth Amendment applies to searches and seizures conducted by school authorities but that the probable cause

---

[74] Eugene Bjorklun, "Using Metal Detectors in the Public Schools: Some Legal Issues," *Education Law Reporter* 111 (1996): 1.
[75] 469 U.S. 325 (1985).

standard (applicable to law enforcement officials) is not required of public school officials. Instead, the constitutional requirement for public schools is that the search must be reasonable. In other words, school officials must have *reasonable*, rather than *probable*, cause to justify a search of a student. The Court ruled that reasonableness is to be determined by a "twofold inquiry: first, whether the . . . action was justified at its inception and second whether the search as actually conducted was reasonably related in scope to the circumstances which justified the interference in the first place."[76] The Court also found that the search warrant requirement of the Fourth Amendment did not apply to school authorities.

The *T.L.O.* standard requires teachers and administrators to act in a reasonable manner considering all the circumstances that led up to the search and caused the educator to continue the search. The Court said a warrantless search is permissible if the official "has reasonable grounds to believe that a student possesses evidence of illegal activity or activity that would interfere with school discipline and order."[77] It pointed out in reaching its conclusion that it was balancing a student's interest in privacy with the equally legitimate need to maintain an environment in which learning could take place.

During the summer of 1995, the Supreme Court ruled that public schools can require drug tests for athletes, whether or not they are suspected drug users, maintaining that privacy rights sometimes must yield to the fight against drugs.[78] Justice Scalia wrote the majority opinion for the divided 6–3 Court, stating that random drug tests did not violate student athletes' right to privacy. The Court said that the U.S. Constitution allowed an Oregon school district to bar a teenager from his school football team for refusing to take a drug test.

Generally, courts have upheld the warrantless search of lockers without a student's permission. Courts have differentiated between locker searches and student searches, holding that the locker is school property and a student's expectation of privacy is lessened. Although school officials' authority to inspect lockers is broad, the courts have been reluctant to allow school administrators to single out lockers for search purposes without reasonable suspicion that specific illicit materials will be found in the locker.

Some school districts have used dogs to discover students hiding drugs on their persons and in their lockers and cars. The federal judiciary has uniformly allowed the use of dogs to sniff students' lockers and cars based on general information of drug use by students. The Seventh Circuit Court of Appeals did observe that searches of students' pockets and purses were searches within the Fourth Amendment, but the alert by the

---

[76] Ibid., 742.
[77] Ibid., 743.
[78] *Veronica School District 47J v. Acton*, 515 U.S. 646, 115 S. Ct. 2386 (1995).

trained dog constituted reasonable cause to believe the student was con-
cealing narcotics.[79] However, the Fifth Circuit specifically held that
schools may use dogs to sniff a student only when they have individualized, reasonable suspicion that the student possesses contraband.[80]

In one instance, school officials had searched lockers on the basis of
information from police and had found a gun and a knife. The student
was subsequently arrested. The courts upheld the school's interest in
safety. Locker searches remain problematic, but in *In re: Patrick Y,* it was
noted that a locker search is not an intrusion of the person.[81]

With respect to strip searches, because of their intrusiveness, courts
have required probable cause and substantial evidence. As a general rule,
in determining the permissible extent of a search, courts balance the
severity of the alleged misconduct with the student's age, sex, and record
in school.[82]

CENSORSHIP: SCHOOL AND THE STUDENT

When reviewing the problems of censorship as it relates to schools, it
becomes obvious, but ironic, that we are looking at two issues. On the
one hand, we have the problem of local citizens attempting to prevent
administrators and teachers from having certain books in their library or
using certain teaching materials in their classes. On the other hand, we
have an attempt by teachers and administrators to restrict the issuance of
student newspapers or publications because they disapprove of the content.

School Censorship

Major educational problems often result from conflicts arising over curriculum decisions. Curriculum decision makers operate in a broad social
and cultural environment that imposes many constraints. The curriculum of a school reflects the consensus of pressures and interests brought
to bear on the school by parents and organized groups.

Virtually every court that has commented on the matter has
acknowledged a grant of broad discretion to school authorities in matters
relating to the method of teaching, decisions regarding the curriculum,
and the selection of books for use in the public schools.[83] However,

---

[79] *Doe v. Renfrow,* 635 F.2d 582 (7th Cir. 1980), cert. denied, 451 U.S. 1022 (1981).
[80] *Horton v. Goose Creek Independent School District,* 490 F.2d 524 (5th Cir. 1982), cert. denied,
463 U.S. 1207, 103 S. Ct. 3536 (1983).
[81] *In re: D.E.M.,* 727 A.2d 570 (Pa. Super. 1999); *In re: Patrick Y.,* 746 A.2d 405 (Md. App.
2000).
[82] See Jacqueline Stefkovich, "Strip Searching after *Williams:* Reactions to the Concern for
School Safety?" *Education Law Reporter* (1994): 1107.
[83] *Epperson v. Arkansas,* 393 U.S. 97 (1968).

school officials' discretion is not completely unfettered by constitutional considerations of the rights of students and teachers.

The removal of educational material from the curriculum and the censorship of library books present recurrent problems for school administrators. The Supreme Court addressed the issue of library censorship in *Board of Education, Island Trees Union Free School District No. 16 v. Pico.*[84] In this case, the school board ordered the principal of the high school to remove nine books from the school library. Justice Brennan, writing for a 5–4 majority, found that, if the removal of books from a school library is motivated by an intent to suppress or deny access to ideas with which school board members disagree, then the removal is unconstitutional. However, the Court ruled that a school board could remove books if prompted by the "pervasive vulgarity of the book" or its "educational unsuitability," "bad taste," or "irrelevance or inappropriateness for the pupils' age and grade level."[85]

The Eleventh Circuit used the *Hazelwood School District v. Kuhlmeier* decision (discussed below), which granted school administrators increased control over school-sponsored activities, to uphold a school board's decision to ban a humanities textbook from the curriculum. The textbook contained English translations of *Lysistratra* and *The Miller's Tale*. Parents objected to these selections because of their sexual explicitness. The court noted that *Hazelwood* established a "lenient test for regulation of expression which may be fairly characterized as part of the school curriculum." Such regulation is permissible "if it is reasonably related to legitimate pedagogical concerns."[86]

Another controversial area with respect to the public school curriculum is the alleged use of textbooks and materials that promote secular humanism or offend religious beliefs and values. The Sixth Circuit Court of Appeals reversed a Tennessee federal district court's judgment that ordered several children excused from a reading program because parents objected on religious grounds to the use of the Holt, Rinehart, and Winston basic reading series.[87] The court noted that mere exposure to religiously objectionable material does not constitute an unconstitutional burden on students under the free exercise clause. In an Eleventh Circuit case, parents claimed that history, social studies, and home economics books used by an Alabama public school district violated the establishment clause by advancing the religion of secular humanism.[88] The trial court had concluded that secular humanism was a religion and that forty-four textbooks on the Alabama list of approved books violated

---

[84] 457 U.S. 853 (1982).
[85] Ibid.
[86] *Virgil v. School Board of Columbia County, Florida,* 862 F.2d 1517, 1521 (11th Cir. 1989).
[87] *Mozert v. Hawkins County Board of Education,* 827 F.2d 1058, 1072–1073 (6th Cir. 1987), cert. denied, 484 U.S. 1066 (1988).
[88] *Smith v. Board of School Commissioners of Mobile County,* 827 F.2d 684 (11th Cir. 1987).

the establishment clause. In reversing the trial court, the appellate court held that the banned textbooks had a nonreligious purpose and did not endorse secular humanism or any religion. The court agreed with the public school position that the books promoted such values as independent thought, self-respect, tolerance of diverse views, and self-reliance.

The heightened concern with violations of the establishment clause present in elementary schools due to the tender years of their students is counterbalanced to a great degree by the broad discretion that a school board has to select its public school curriculum. With this in mind, the Seventh Circuit held that a school reading program that arguably taught ideas counter to the tenets of Christianity by using books containing stories of witches, goblins, fantasies, and myths was nevertheless promoting the legitimate secular goals of literacy and creativity.[89] The court concluded that in using such a reading curriculum the school was not promoting anything reasonably like a coherent, identifiable religion or that, at the very least, any religion asserted as a violation by the plaintiffs was too amorphous to be seriously considered under the establishment clause.

The Student as a Responsible Citizen: Free Speech and Free Press

The hallmark of civil liberties in the United States is the First Amendment. The First Amendment states that "Congress shall make no law respecting an establishment of religion, or prohibiting the free exercise thereof, or abridging the freedom of speech or of the press; or the right of the people peaceably to assemble; and to petition the Government for a redress of grievances."

The major issue that arises for school administrators is defining the limits of student expression that are entitled to constitutional protection under the First Amendment. To what extent are school officials permitted to impose limits on student expression? Before the 1970s, school authorities assumed virtually unrestricted control over students via the common law principle of *in loco parentis*. The privilege doctrine pertaining to control of student expression changed in the landmark case *Tinker v. Des Moines Independent Community School District*.[90] In a statement that has been cited often in subsequent student expression cases, Justice Fortas seemed to capture the philosophy that would guide student expression jurisprudence for nearly two decades: "First Amendment rights, applied in light of the special characteristics of the school environment, are available to teachers and students. It can hardly be argued that either students

---

[89] *Fleischfresser v. Directors of School District 200,* 15 F.2d 680 (7th Cir. 1994).
[90] 393 U.S. 503 (1969).

or teachers shed their constitutional rights to freedom of speech or expression at the schoolhouse gate."[91]

In *Tinker,* the Court considered whether high school students had the right to wear black armbands in school as a protest against the Vietnam War. In reversing the school official's suspension of the students who wore the armbands, the Court concluded that school authorities may not discipline students for exercising their free speech rights unless these authorities can establish that there were facts that reasonably led them to forecast substantial disruption of or material interference with school activities or unless they can prove that the activity did in fact materially and substantially disrupt the school. The Court also held that student expression could be regulated if the speech "collided with the rights of others."[92] The Court emphasized that unpopular views that might cause discomfort among faculty and students could not be curtailed simply to avoid an unpleasant situation.

Decisions of the Supreme Court during the late 1980s indicate the Court's willingness to give educators more control over students and tend to deemphasize students' right of free expression. The Court ruled that while students are entitled to First Amendment protection in the educational setting, this protection is not coextensive with that of adults. The Court explained in *Bethel School District v. Fraser* that public schools have the responsibility to "inculcate the habits and manners of civility as values in themselves" and the mission to transmit "the shared values of a civilized social order."[93] The Court ruled that school authorities may determine what manner of speech in the classroom or school assembly is inappropriate. Speech that is vulgar or offensive can be punished and prohibited in school-sponsored educational activities.

The issues of the extent of First Amendment protection accorded to student newspapers and concomitantly the permissible degree of control that school authorities may exercise over student publications have been the subject of considerable litigation. The landmark Supreme Court decision *Hazelwood School District v. Kuhlmeier* erased much of the uncertainty as to the constitutional rights of students with respect to student publications.[94] The Court granted school administrators broad editorial control over curricular publications, thus substantially restricting student freedom of the press in school-sponsored publications. It held that school authorities may "exercise control over the style and content of student speech in school-sponsored expressive activities so long as their actions are reasonably related to legitimate pedagogical concerns."[95]

---

[91] Ibid., 736.3.
[92] Ibid., 740.
[93] 478 U.S. 675 (1986).
[94] 484 U.S. 260 (1988).
[95] Ibid.

However, the Supreme Court decision in *Hazelwood* does not permit school administrators to censor student publications that are not school sponsored, such as unofficial underground newspapers. The *Tinker* doctrine applies to underground newspapers; thus, school officials must show that the newspaper materially disrupted school activities before punishing students for distributing the newspaper.[96]

The federal courts are divided on the issue of whether school officials may condition the distribution of non-school-sponsored student publications on approval by school officials. School authorities can establish reasonable regulations with respect to the time, place, and manner of distribution of non-school-sponsored student publications. Of course, school administrators are free to establish rules and discipline students who publish and distribute obscene or libelous material on school premises.

OTHER LEGAL RESPONSIBILITIES TOWARD STUDENTS' FIRST AMENDMENT RIGHTS

Regulation of Dress and Personal Appearance

The controversy over the regulation of dress and personal appearance of pupils has been long and somewhat tiresome. Although this controversy has not been as vehement in the 1990s as it was in the preceding thirty years, enough cases have appeared in the courts and newspapers to make interesting reading and to provide a note of caution to the new principal because, unfortunately, in many of these cases the school administration is made to look arbitrary and reactionary.

In general, courts have upheld dress code regulations that prohibit immodest or excessively tight skirts and pants and any dress that would create a distraction from the educational function. In addition, clothes that are dirty, contain vulgar language, and disrupt the educational process may be prohibited. Generally, less justification is required to sustain a dress regulation than to sustain a hair regulation. The dress code must bear some rational relationship to the orderly conduct of the school.

It is essential that the school demonstrate that the wearing of an article of clothing is disruptive. Wearing a Confederate flag T-shirt or quietly displaying a Confederate flag to a small group discussing the Civil War was not considered disruptive, given the school's history of little or no violence and none as a result of the clothing or flag.[97] Even tattoos are in question, especially if they are viewed as "gang-related" symbols. Where a student had a tattoo of a cross between the thumb and the

---

[96] See *Bystrom v. Fridley High School,* 822 F.2d 747 (8th Cir. 1986).
[97] *Denno v. School Board of Volusia County,* 182 F.3d 780 (11th Cir. 1999).

forefinger, the school lost its case that such a display was gang related and disruptive.[98]

A state appellate court upheld a school corporation's ban on boys wearing earrings to school, saying the dress-code rule was consistent with community standards and helped promote educational goals.[99] The appeals court said that the dress code was a factor in improving students' attitudes toward school and that this change in attitude had led to improvements in school attendance, dropout rates, and academic performance. It noted that it is reasonable that a community's schools be permitted, within constitutional strictures, to reflect its values, and it is a valid educational function to instill discipline and create a positive educational environment by means of a reasonable, consistently applied dress code. Courts have also upheld dress codes that are aimed at deterring gang activity.[100]

The federal circuit courts are divided as to a student's constitutional right to choose his or her hairstyle. Five circuits have upheld hair length regulations; four circuits have rejected them. Typical of the legal reasoning employed by those courts striking down hair regulations is this passage from *Arnold v. Carpenter:* "the right to wear one's hair at any length or in any desired manner is an ingredient of personal freedom protected by the United States Constitution." To limit or curtail that right, the state bears a "substantial burden of justification."[101] The Supreme Court has not issued an opinion on hairstyle or dress regulations for public school students.

Flag Salute and Pledge of Allegiance

On June 14, 1943, a day to pay tribute to the American flag—Flag Day—the Supreme Court ruled that a state could not command students, who were required to attend school by a compulsory education law, to salute the American flag or participate in the Pledge of Allegiance. In this landmark case, *West Virginia State Board of Education v. Barnette,* the Court held that a flag salute regulation infringed on the free exercise of speech guaranteed by the First Amendment.[102]

Since *Barnette,* the courts have consistently ruled that school officials may not force students to participate in Pledge of Allegiance exercises. However, the Seventh Circuit upheld a statute mandating that the Pledge of Allegiance be recited every school day. The court noted that the statute did not force every student to stand and recite the pledge.[103]

---

[98] *Stevenson v. Davenport Community School District*, 110 F.3d 1303 (8th Cir. 1997).
[99] *Hines v. Caston School Corp.*, 651 N.E.2d 330 (Ind. App. 1995).
[100] See *Jeglin v. San Jacinto Unified School District*, 827 F. Supp. 1459 (Cal. 1993).
[101] 459 F.2d 939, 941 (1972).
[102] 319 U.S. 624 (1943).
[103] *Sherman v. Community Consolidated School District*, 8 F.3d 1160 (7th Cir. 1993).

Married Students and Pregnancy

A very common source of litigation in earlier years was the expulsion of a student or the withholding of a diploma because of marriage or pregnancy. While some people seem to have an implicit desire to punish the girl who has "transgressed" (like Hester Prynne in Hawthorne's *The Scarlet Letter*), court decisions and legislation have caused schools to reassess their attitudes, policies, and practices regarding married students and pregnancy.

Courts have held that married students cannot be prevented from attending school or participating in interscholastic sports and other school-related activities. To justify such a rule, courts have held that the school must demonstrate some compelling interest in restricting married students from such activities. A state appeals court ruled that a school district and athletic association regulation prohibiting married high school students from participating in athletic and extracurricular activities denied the students equal protection of the law under the Fourteenth Amendment.[104] However, courts have upheld state statutes that allow married students to choose to be exempt from compulsory attendance laws.[105]

School administrators also have less regulatory control than in the past with respect to pregnant students. The regulation implementing Title IX of the Education Amendments of 1972 prohibits the exclusion of pregnant students or students who have had an abortion. Separate schools or educational programs for pregnant students are permissible, but participation must be voluntary for the student.[106]

SEX DISCRIMINATION IN PHYSICAL EDUCATION AND INTERSCHOLASTIC ATHLETIC COMPETITION

Title IX of the Education Amendments of 1972 provides that no person shall on the basis of sex be excluded from participation in, denied the benefits of, or subjected to discrimination under any educational program or activity receiving federal financial assistance.[107] Title IX generally prohibits excluding a male or female from a class solely because of sex or offering separate courses for boys and girls. However, sex education classes may be taught separately, and physical education instructors may classify students by physical ability and separate males and females for participation in contact sports.[108]

---

[104] *Indiana High School Athletic Association v. Raillce,* 329 N.E.2d 66 (Ind. App. 1975).
[105] See, e.g., *In re Rogers,* 234 N.Y.S.2d 172 (1962).
[106] 20 U.S.C. § 1681.
[107] Ibid.
[108] 34 C.F.R. Part 106.

With respect to interscholastic sports participation, Title IX allows schools to establish separate teams when team selection is based on competitive skill or the activity is a contact sport. Courts generally hold that contact sports must be open equally to both sexes where only one team is supported by the school.[109] Courts have held that when a comparable girls' team is available, requests by females to be permitted to try out for a place on the boys' team may be constitutionally denied.[110] However, the Court of Appeals for the Ninth Circuit held that a rule prohibiting boys from playing on girls' volleyball teams does not deny the boys equal protection even where there are not separate boys' volleyball teams.[111]

Regarding the issue of participation by both sexes in contact sports, the courts are split on whether girls have the right to play on boys' teams. However, girls have won a substantial number of victories regarding the right to try out for boys' teams in competitive contact sports.[112]

COMPETENCY TESTING

Legislatures and state departments of education have emphasized schools' accountability to show progress in student learning. Standards have been adopted, high-stakes testing for graduation is in place in many states, and pressures continue to test every child in grades three through eight to show educational progress.

Many of these testing schemes for students have come under legal attack. The grounds for legally challenging competency tests have been numerous. One legal challenge is based on evidence that the testing programs create racially discriminatory effects because of the testing instruments used. These discriminatory effects give rise to Fourteenth Amendment equal protection actions. Schools have had difficulties in validating the tests and demonstrating that the tests are aligned with the curriculum.[113] In other words, the issue becomes whether minimum competency tests accurately reflect what students are taught in school.

The issue of withholding a diploma from a student based on the results of a competency test was litigated in a well-known Florida case. In *Debra P. v. Turlington,* the plaintiffs challenged the use of competency tests for determining eligibility for a high school diploma.[114] The Court of Appeals for the Fifth Circuit found that the state had violated students' due process rights by providing only one year's notice that successful

---

[109] See *O'Connor v. Board of Education,* 645 F.2d 578 (7th Cir. 1981).
[110] *Ruman v. Eskew,* 333 N.E.2d 138 (Ind. App. 1975).
[111] *Clark v. Arizona Interscholastic Association,* 886 F.2d 1191 (9th Cir. 1989).
[112] See, e.g., *Stephanie v. Nebraska School Activities Association,* 684 F. Supp. 626 (D. Neb. 1988); *Force v. Pierre City School District,* 570 F. Supp. 1020 (W.D. Mo. 1983); *Yellow Springs v. Ohio Athletic Association,* 647 F.2d 651 (6th Cir. 1981).
[113] *Debra P. v. Turlington,* 644 F.2d 397 (5th Cir. 1981).
[114] Ibid.

completion of the test was a condition of receiving a high school diploma. The circuit court also required that the state prove "curricular validity" for its test (i.e., the test must cover what students are actually taught in school). The court remanded the case to the trial court to determine the test's instructional validity and examine the possibility of an equal protection clause violation because of the disproportionate number of African-American students who failed the exam. The federal district court found that the competency exam had curricular validity and concluded that there were no remaining effects of de jure segregation that caused the disproportionate number of black students to fail the test.

The federal Office of Special Education Programs (OSEP) has responded to a number of complaints regarding competency exams and students with disabilities. It points out that establishing proficiency standards for a high school diploma is a state function. In a memorandum on the subject, OSEP stated:

> However, while it is appropriate for States to set standards for the receipt of a high school diploma, including the use of proficiency examinations, . . . a student who meets the standards established by the State for a high school diploma cannot be denied a diploma on the basis of his or her disability. To ensure that students with disabilities do not experience discrimination, federal law requires the provision of appropriate test accommodations, such as extended time or alternative formats, for students who require these accommodations because of their disabilities.[115]

RIGHTS OF STUDENTS WITH DISABILITIES

Two federal statutes, the Individuals with Disabilities Education Act (IDEA), formerly known as the Education for All Handicapped Children Act (EAHCA), and Section 504 of the Rehabilitation Act of 1973, combine to form the basis of extensive substantive and procedural rights that afford children with disabilities a right to a free appropriate public education.[116] Section 504 is a general anti-discrimination statute (it provides no public money to schools) and should be viewed as an overlapping complementary statute to the IDEA.

The IDEA requires that all children with disabilities between the ages of three and twenty-one who need special education are to be identified, located, and evaluated. It requires that children with disabilities be provided an education in the least restrictive environment. The act also mandates that education is to be individualized and appropriate. The U.S. Supreme Court has defined an appropriate education under the

---

[115] Letter to Anonymous, 25 IDELR 632, 633 (OSEP 1996).
[116] IDEA, 20 U.S.C. §§ 1400 et seq.; Section 504, 29 U.S.C. § 794.

IDEA as providing a basic floor of opportunity to children with disabilities that consists of access to specialized instruction and related services individually designed to provide education benefits to students with disabilities.[117]

The substantive due process right to a free appropriate public education is undergirded by the comprehensive procedural rights, rules, and requirements mandated by the IDEA. At the core of procedural due process is notice and a right to a hearing. The IDEA requires written notice before a school "(1) proposes to initiate or change, or (2) refuses to initiate or change the identification, evaluation, or educational placement of the child or the provision of an appropriate public education."[118] A basic underlying theme of the IDEA is that parents should be involved in the education of their child as one means of protecting the child's rights.

Hearings may be requested by either the school district or the parent and must be conducted by an impartial hearing officer at a time and place convenient to the parent.[119] According to the IDEA, during the pendency of any administrative or judicial proceeding, unless the school and the parent agree otherwise, the child shall remain in his or her current educational placement.[120]

One of the most controversial issues related to special education is discipline. Educators must determine whether a causal relationship exists between the misconduct of a student with a disability and his or her disability before imposing long-term suspension or expulsion.[121] A student with a disability may be expelled when the misconduct is not related to the disability. However, a complete cessation of educational services is not permissible under the 1997 amendments to the IDEA.[122]

The Supreme Court held that under the IDEA a suspension exceeding ten days constitutes a change of placement for a student with a disability. During the pendency of expulsion proceedings, a student must be kept in his or her then current educational placement (unless a parent agrees otherwise).[123] However, school personnel may order a change to an appropriate alternative education setting for not more than forty-five days if the child brings a weapon to school or to a school function or if the child possesses, uses, or sells illegal drugs.[124]

A great deal of discussion has focused on the educational concept of "inclusion," which, legally speaking, translates into a discussion of the least restrictive environment mandate of the IDEA. The IDEA requires

---

[117] *Board of Education of Hendrick Hudson School District v. Rowley,* 458 U.S. 176 (1982).

[118] 20 U.S.C. §1415(b)(1)(c).

[119] 20 U.S.C. § 1415(b)(1).

[120] 20 U.S.C. § 1415(e)(3).

[121] See *Stuart v. Nappi,* 443 F. Supp. 1235 (D. Conn. 1978); *Doe v. Koger,* 480 F. Supp. 225 (D.C. Ind. 1979).

[122] See *S-1 v. Turlington,* 635 F.2d 342 (5th Cir.), cert. denied, 454 U.S. 1230 (1981).

[123] *Honig v. Doe,* 484 U.S. 305 (1988).

[124] 20 U.S.C. § 1400, Section 615(k)(2)(a).

school districts to offer children with disabilities an appropriate education in the least restrictive environment, which means the "regular" classroom whenever possible.

Seven recent U.S. court of appeals decisions have addressed the issue of the least restrictive environment within the meaning of the IDEA. The First, Second, Third, Fifth, Sixth, Ninth, and Eleventh Circuits have decided inclusion cases, each crafting its own approach or standard to decide least restrictive environment issues. However, common factors and themes may be gleaned from the cases. Courts have analyzed inclusion cases using four factors: (1) the educational benefits of full-time placement in a general education classroom, (2) the extent to which nonacademic needs would be met in a general education placement, (3) the student's effect on the teacher and other students in the classroom, and (4) the costs to educate the child in a general education classroom.[125]

Finally, the worldwide health problem of acquired immunodeficiency syndrome (AIDS) has visited the public schools. Several cases involving students who have tested HIV positive or who have AIDS have arisen in the context of the public schools. The judiciary has generally ruled that students with AIDS have a disability and must be permitted to attend public schools if their attendance does not pose a health risk to the school community.[126]

ⓈUMMARY

Statutes, school codes, school policy, and the interpretation of these by the courts are a firm source of authority on which every school administrator can rely. Of course, the laws cannot specify the what, where, and why of every possible condition; therefore, principals must have a wide range of implied powers to make reasonable use of legislated expressed powers. Because they lack specificity, implied powers are sources of much litigation, but they allow those activities that one might reasonably expect to be necessary to carry out the spirit and letter of the law. On the other hand, they allow progress, growth, and experimentation for the dynamic and imaginative administrator. Expressed powers are those powers specifically listed in legislation authorizing action.

Certainly, one cannot disagree with the philosophy that a school should serve as a model democratic institution, reflecting the goals of our democratic society, where an individual's worth and rights are paramount and where children learn to be sensitive, productive citizens.

---

[125] See *Sacramento City Unified School District v. Rachel H.*, 14 F.3d 1398 (9th Cir. 1994); *Oberti v. Board of Education*, 995 F.2d 1204 (3d Cir. 1993).

[126] See *Doe v. Bolton*, 694 F. Supp. 440 (N.D. Ill. 1988); *School Board of Nassau County v. Arline*, 480 U.S. 273 (1987).

Upon review of the litigation regarding the governing of children in school, schools appear often to be restrictive. A great deal of suppression of a student's rights may take place under the guise of proper order and operation of the school. Too many school authorities assume that the discipline of the school will break down unless children recognize that the teacher is the master, whose rule is absolute. Uniformity rather than individuality is the major order of the day in many schools.

We often think of our courts as conservative stabilizing elements in our society; however, to observe the changes in the interpretation of our laws as they relate to the rights of the individual, which are guaranteed in both our federal and our state constitutions, is to observe the upholding of the basic rights of people. These same cases, however, create concern about the impact of our schools because it appears that schools lag behind in their administration of justice to the individual. There is no litigation concerning a school having gone too far in upholding rights of the individual—it is always just the opposite. Case after case reveals a record of schools being quite arbitrary in the suppression of unpopular and minority viewpoints. It becomes even more a matter of concern when one recognizes that most students and parents who experience such suppression never litigate; they are simply silenced by the plenary power that school authorities exercise over their lives. Fortunately, these cases are the minority.

FOR FURTHER THOUGHT

1. Is there a distinct dividing line between educational opinion and legal opinion? Illustrate.
2. Is it true that every administrative action must be taken within a specific legal framework? Give some examples.
3. Why do practices that are begun under the authority of *implied* powers often become *expressed* powers and laws?
4. How should elementary and secondary school principals participate in the development of laws affecting education?
5. Debate: Schools have generally lagged behind in their upholding of the rights of the individual.
6. Review a summary of all the educational legislation passed in your state in the last two years. What effect has this legislation had on school curriculum? On teaching personnel? On school services?
7. What do you think is the best way for principals and law officers to work together on cases in which students may be involved in breaking the law? What cooperative preventive measures might be taken?
8. Is it possible for a school principal to be overly concerned about the legal implication of school activities? Discuss.

9. Debate: In a widely diverse community, the principal should be on the side of inaction rather than risk action that may be contested.
10. Review the court cases in your state over the last five years that have dealt with "education" and the "schools." What areas seem to be the most subject to litigation?

SELECTED READINGS

Alexander, Kern, and David M. Alexander. *American Public School Law*, 3d ed. St. Paul, MN: West, 1992.

Delon, Floyd G. *Legal Issues in Dismissal of Teachers for Personal Conduct*. Topeka, KS: National Organization of Legal Problems of Education, 1983.

Deskbook Encyclopedia of American School Law. Burnsville, MN: Oakstone Legal and Publishing, 2000.

Hunt, Thomas. "Moral Education and Public Schools: A Tale of Tempest." *Religion and Public Education* 13 (Spring 1986): 25–36.

Hyman, Irwin A. *Reading, Writing and the Hickory Stick*. Lexington, MA: Lexington Books, 1990.

Imber, Michael, and Gary Thompson. "Developing a Typology of Litigation in Education and Determining the Frequency of Each Category." *Educational Administration Quarterly* 27 (1991): 225–244.

Keeton, Page, Daniel Dobbs, Robert Keeton, and David Owen. *Prosser and Keeton on Torts*, 5th ed. St. Paul, MN: West, 1984.

Valente, William D., and Christine M. Valente. *Law in the Schools*, 5th ed. Upper Saddle River, NJ: Merrill/Prentice Hall, 2001.

Yell, Mitchell L. *The Law and Special Education*. Upper Saddle River, NJ: Merrill/Prentice Hall, 1998.

Improving Learning

*T*he emphasis of this book has been on improving learning. Its overriding philosophy is the very simple but often neglected principle that the students' learning is the supreme reason for the school's existence. Teaching, curriculum, materials, facilities, organization, and administration must then be considered as means, not ends.

The increasing tendency to hold principals responsible for the students' learning stresses the centrality of educational leadership in the principal's role. The school is composed of many people; it serves a wider community than those within its walls during school hours. The scope of learning should not be viewed as being confined to the building or the hours of the school day. To do so would limit the potential for learning for all associated with the school. To view learning as taking place continuously, in school and outside school, will expand the scope of educational leadership beyond the school's walls and will positively affect the learning that occurs within the school.

CHAPTER 8

The Principal's Major Task

*T*he principal's major task is to exercise leadership in order to make a positive difference in student learning and to improve the quality of life of each individual within the school. The principal makes this task a priority. Making a positive difference is not an easy task in the best of situations and an almost overwhelming one in districts suffering from poverty of vision and hope as well as monetary resources.

The expectations of the principal have steadily expanded to "gargantuan proportions," including visionary leadership, operations management, daily details, community leadership, and commitments without end.[1] It is easy to lose perspective as the demands become louder and more frequent.

It is also important how the incumbent views the role of principal. Rutherford notes that approximately 22 percent of principals are "initiators"—that is, persons who will do what it takes to get the job done.[2] That leaves 78 percent as persons who are either managers (33 percent) or responders (45 percent). Responders, according to Rutherford, accept the circumstances in which they find themselves as limiters to action and reasons not to act. A person facing the task identified in the first paragraph of this chapter must be an initiator, a collaborative, supportive, visionary leader. To look for direction from above, to see circumstances as constraints and not challenges, to view improvement as someone else's job is to abdicate the role of principal as we see it.

The principal is one who helps "grow a vision" for the school, assists staff to grow continuously and keep refining what is meant by excellence, provides means to get things done, remains deeply involved in improving instruction in the school, and sees that managerial details

---

[1] Michael A. Copland, "The Myth of the Superprincipal," *Phi Delta Kappan* 82 (March 2001): 530.
[2] William L. Rutherford, "The Principal Spectrum Runs from Initiators to Responders," *Executive Educator* 12 (May 1990): 22.

are done well. If one thing appears to be a serious hindrance to carrying out all these tasks, it is the time allowed each of us per day.

Calls are made for restructuring so that principals can return to the role of the principal teacher. This is not to say that, in addition to the many tasks already expected of the principal, he or she should now assume responsibility for teaching a class for part of each day. Rather, improving teaching and learning should be the focus of his or her time. In a few districts, principals are being asked to assume teaching duties or leadership in two or more buildings. Unless the circumstances are very unusual, such a practice almost ensures that the principal primarily will serve most "administrivial" functions and the educational/instructional improvement functions will be reduced to mandated activities and minimal time.

Improving education and learning has been interpreted to mean many things to many people. To those who wish to spend time on accounting and acquisition functions, it means that having a smoothly running accounting system for all funds, supplies, and equipment and getting teachers the things they want improve the educational program. To those who operate on a troubleshooter level, ready for all comers, it means that devoting time to "protecting" teachers from outside troubles allows them to teach and hence improves learning. These things do contribute to the educational enterprise. But should the principal concentrate on these at the expense of more direct involvement with learning improvement?

Much administration unquestionably consists of organizing and managing things, some of which are detailed, repetitive, and even mundane. This observation does not mean that these tasks are not important, for it is by efficiently accomplishing these tasks that a case for administrative credibility can be made. If monies are not properly accounted for, if nonteaching technical and production work is not provided for the teachers, or if the maintenance and safety features of the building are not attended to, then educational leadership activities, however well planned, will lose their impact. Such impact will be lost initially because of the administrative credibility gap. Innovations must have effective resource support if any stabilizing effect is hoped for. Even if the support is merely a well-thought-out scheduling of space, the lack of such support can create a barrier, or at least an excuse for not pushing ahead with the logical next steps in the plan. The question is not whether careful attention should be paid to this aspect of administration; the question is, Should the principal first be held responsible for the accomplishment of these management tasks if he or she is primarily expected to exert educational leadership? A study of an influential group of parents responds with a resounding "No!"

Local PTA presidents, state Congress of Parents and Teachers board members, and parent council presidents chose the following functions as high priority for the principal:

1. Initiating improvements in teaching techniques and methods
2. Making certain that curricula fit the needs of students
3. Directing teachers to motivate students to learn at their optimal levels
4. Affording teachers the opportunity to individualize programs
5. Directing teachers to coordinate and articulate the subject matter taught on each grade level

The least important items were cited as follows:

1. Becoming involved in community affairs
2. Scheduling school maintenance
3. Scheduling the activities of the school
4. Maintaining school records
5. Performing other administrative duties assigned by the superintendent[3]

Parents' groups, it seems, may be viewed as advocates for the idea that the principal should focus primarily on educational improvement as opposed to administrative detail.

USING TIME PRODUCTIVELY

Time Use

Ethnographic studies of principals on the job describe how they spend their time. Critics have cautioned that knowing how time is spent is not establishing either cause-effect relationships or qualitative differences in the use of time. Nevertheless, some of the studies do give us a base for reference; general questions can be raised, and further study of the principals' time spent on each task can be designed.

Morris and colleagues documented the work lives of sixteen urban principals.[4] They state that a principal's day consisted of fifty to one hundred separate events and up to four hundred interactions. Eighty percent of the time was spent on face-to-face interchanges with staff, pupils, and others; 8 percent on telephone conversations; and 12 percent at the desk. An interesting note is that the principal initiated the contacts approximately 66 percent of the time. Over 75 percent of the contacts were unscheduled. Contrast this with the business executive, who spends 10 percent of his or her time in unscheduled contacts.

Levin notes in an observational study in Philadelphia that principals were spending "80 percent of their time doing two things: discipline

---

[3] A study sponsored by the Indiana Congress of Parents and Teachers.
[4] Van Cleve Morris, Robert L. Crowson, Emanuel Hurwiz Jr., and Cynthia Porter-Gehrie, *The Urban Principal: Discretionary Decision-Making in a Large Educational Organization* (Chicago: University of Illinois Press, 1981).

and compliance."[5] In such a setting, it is no wonder that little may be accomplished toward changing what is happening in classrooms. This is not to say that people are not working hard; it merely points out that the time may be used up on nonproductive or even counterproductive activities. MacKay and Ralston pointedly cautioned, "Don't pat yourself on the back for doing things well that do not deserve your time."[6]

Change is essential if the amount of time allocated is to be commensurate with the importance of educational leadership activities. A beginning step would be to *develop a priority list of activities.* How should time be spent to exert educational leadership? Should more time be spent supervising in the cafeteria? Designing extracurricular activities? Observing in the classrooms? Supporting instruction? Growing a positive vision for the school? Seeking alternative technologies and methods for continuous improvement?

A second step is simply to *record how one spends time.* The log may be divided into any time intervals deemed appropriate, but they should be small enough to allow one to see separate activities. An hour or a half hour is usually too large a unit because too many activities can occur and be lost or inaccurately recorded. Fifteen-minute intervals may be most useful. Activities recorded for a "typical" week may suffice, as a beginning.

Included in the record should be the nature of the activity, the person(s) involved, and the results of the activity. The last is useful for determining "dead end" or aimless activity. The list of priorities can then be compared with the activities logged. If there are discrepancies between the lists, an accounting of what interfered needs to be made.

Did crises interfere? Were those crises clustered in one or two areas, such as discipline or a particular department or grade level? Or were they associated with a few individuals? Were clerical duties getting in the way, duties that might better be someone else's task? Were there interruptions that could have been handled by someone else or at a different time? Did the principal interrupt others who were doing tasks that, if accomplished efficiently, would free the principal's time? How many activities led nowhere? How many activities were repetitive (either daily or weekly)? Could someone else be taught to do these tasks just as well? Imagine that the principal spends an hour a day in the cafeteria and the school year is 180 days; it is unlikely that the board realizes it hired the person to spend 4.5 weeks supervising the cafeteria (assuming a forty-hour week). In fact, we suspect that few principals are aware of their time expenditure in that way.

---

[5] Ron Brandt, "On Building Learning Communities: A Conversation with Hank Levin," *Educational Leadership* 50 (September 1992): 20.
[6] Louise L. MacKay and Elizabeth Welch Ralston, *Creating Better Schools: What Authentic Principals Do* (Thousand Oaks, CA: Corwin Press, 1999): 81.

Eliminating poor filing systems, software or hardware that does not fit needs, telephone interruptions, or poor office procedures can prove helpful. Other time wasters, such as a hostile work environment, frequent staff turnover, or the pressure to deal with too many things at once, may be harder to solve. One of the more difficult problems is a central office that demands instant responses or instant presence at meetings when a little planning could have avoided the problem, especially when the topic is one that could have been handled by the central office without involving principals, or at least all principals. The investment of time to resolve some of these points may pay good dividends in the long term.

The principal may save time by clustering similar activities, doing one thing at a time, and buffering himself or herself from messages that are not important or do not require an immediate response. An effective secretary is obviously a must.

Time can be freed up to do the important things in other ways, too. To carry out some of the suggestions in the following section, time must be invested in training, educating, and developing and in convincing people that certain tasks are better done by someone else.

Preventing Means from Becoming Ends

Too often carrying out necessary management and support tasks leads to the distortion of the goals of the principal's job. The management tasks become the main goal, and learning improvement is worked in wherever there is time or, as noted later, assigned to an assistant. Such behavior on the part of the administrator reinforces those who work with him or her in giving priority to secondary goals; hence, running a tight ship or keeping school becomes the distortion of the goal of educating children. Again, the management system, or means, becomes the end. The profession must protect the role of educational leadership from becoming a secondary goal. The person incumbent in such a position must be given the means to maintain his or her focus on educational leadership and should not allow the support tasks to be unattended or less effectively done.

Obviously, the size of the school is a factor that influences the balance of support tasks and leadership tasks. A small elementary school of eleven teachers and two hundred fifty pupils will not demand the same amount of support tasks as a middle school of six hundred and a staff of twenty-six or a high school of two thousand and a staff of one hundred. In several communities, the small school is the order of the day, by design, tradition, or both. It is possible that the principal can be expected to carry out both sets of tasks equally well. Practice would indicate that over a period of time this may not be the case, in that one set of tasks tends eventually to dominate, and, of course, it is that set with which the principal feels most comfortable or for which central administrators hold him or her primarily responsible.

In the larger schools, particularly in larger systems, day-to-day support tasks demand priority so that the institution works smoothly. Traditionally, the principal has overseen this function. What provisions can be made so that the primary responsibility of educational leadership is not displaced by "management" and "clerking" functions?

Is an Assistant Principal the Answer?

Size may not be the sole determinant regarding the hiring of an assistant principal. If a school needs to concentrate on staff development, achievement, program changes, behavior, combinations of these, or other areas, temporary help may be appropriate until changes are effected. But once these are in place, one must make sure that such additional resources do not become permanent fixtures. A clear understanding of the purpose and length of time that the additional resources will be needed must be worked out prior to their allocation. Adding positions is not so important as setting priorities.

If a permanent assistant, associate, or coprincipal is to be added to the school, the functions to be linked with the position need to be carefully analyzed. Marshall notes a range of duties assigned to assistant principals, the most common in order of frequency being student discipline, evaluation of teachers, attendance, school policies, special arrangements, and the master schedule.[7]

Part of the rationale for an assistant principal position is that the experience that can be gained by the person so appointed is valuable to his or her preparation for a principalship. This kind of training experience may very well be the reason it is necessary to write about means becoming ends. Is it really necessary for a person who holds, or is working for, an advanced degree or certificate to spend several years dealing with the support tasks to learn how best to effect instructional/learning improvement and exert transformational leadership? Such a thesis is questionable. Should not the selection process for prospective principals be centered on such behaviors as exhibiting an orientation toward people, optimizing, motivating, innovating? It is somewhat encouraging to note a shift in assignments toward instructional matters, yet one cannot but wonder what the shift frees the principal to do about improving learning that she or he was not able to do before.

We examined data for differences in time use according to the number of assistant principals working in schools. There was very little difference in the way the principals spent their time, whether with no assistants or with one or two. These and other data highlight the need to keep

---

[7] Catherine Marshall, *The Assistant Principal* (Newbury Park, CA: Corwin, 1992), 5.

the role of educational leader uppermost when developing job descriptions for assistant principals or other administrative team members. The use of a principal's time should change as a result of an assistant's appointment, and the change should be toward a greater proportion of time being spent directly on improving learning and developing the culture of the school.

Principals have a teaching role in relation to assistant principals. The assistant principal should be encouraged to develop a professional reading agenda; participate in conferences and seminars; know everyone's job description; respect everyone; and maintain a positive, energetic image.[8]

Some situations may warrant the sharing of instructional supervision and curriculum development responsibilities with assistants and associates. Such action necessitates clear communication with the central office, with the teachers, and especially with the person assigned, regarding the scope of the authority inherent in the position and the specific expectations of the principal regarding the role outcomes.

A Coprincipalship?

A coprincipalship or principalship team may allow instructional leadership to remain preeminent. Responsibilities may be divided so that one may concentrate on curriculum development, the other on classroom instruction and staff development or a variety of other tasks. One coprincipalship of three persons divides responsibilities among them, while some are shared team responsibilities. A partial list of the separated responsibilities follows:

> Principal A—technology, transportation, curriculum development, equipment . . .
>
> Principal B—food service, student activities, state reports . . .
>
> Principal C—staff development, building and grounds, program development . . .
>
> Team responsibilities—mission, goals, budget, hiring, appraisal, academics, behavior . . .

Using their own team as a model, they form teacher teams to assist with various tasks and/or decisions. Decision making is shifted from individuals to specific teams.[9]

---

[8] John C. Daresh, "Making the Most of It," *Principal Leadership* 1 (January 2001): 72; Randy Johnson, "Other Duties as Assigned: Four Rules for Surviving the Assistant Principalship," *NASSP Bulletin* 84 (January 2000): 86.

[9] John Trout, Parke Smith, and Steve Bloomfield, "The Co-principalship: When Three Are Better than One," *Principal* 80 (January 2001): 47–48.

Given a team dedicated to improving learning and leading in educational matters, the coprincipalship may provide interactive support between two or more professionals as well as emphasizing the purposes of the school. A variation on the theme might be a principal team formed by two or more principals from different buildings who draw on each other's strengths and provide leadership in those areas in both buildings. The idea fosters growth and strong decision making, and the collegial model may generate a number of positive spin-offs as teachers and other colleagues see the results.

Differentiated Deployment of Resources

The principal can no longer try to be all things to all people all of the time. New views on deploying resources need to be sought and new patterns implemented. Additional effort needs to be made to staff schools adequately so that they can function as places of inquiry, innovation, and improvement rather than just barely "keep school." One would be hard-pressed to find any retail or service agency that deals with large numbers of people with less than 15 to 20 percent supervisory/administrative support personnel; but schools, with one of the highest concentrations of relatively unpredictable people in one place, usually have 7 percent supervisory/administrative support personnel at the building level. Marlowe reports that " . . . the average number of people employed per executive, administrator or manager in the manufacturing sector was 5.8 in 1999 . . . in the communications industry—3.6, . . . in the elementary schools . . . 12.8.[10]

The Services Coordinator

The first edition of this text proposed the establishment of a position(s) in each school district or in each large school that might be given the title of services coordinator. Other titles have been proposed such as building manager and executive assistant. Kennedy sees that " . . . it is time to divide the principalship into two positions—instructional leader and building manager."[11] Given the inclination of the lay public, including school board members, to assume the word *manager* carries more weight than the term *leader,* we would worry about the labels causing a problem with the expectations of who is to "call the shots." We welcome the idea of needing more management help so the principal can focus on improving learning.

---

[10] John Marlowe, "Mythbusters," *American School Board Journal* 187 (July 2000): 42.
[11] Carole Kennedy, "Splitting the Principalship," *Principal* 80 (March 2001): 60.

A services coordinator might be assigned responsibility for supporting services in two or more smaller schools, and larger schools might require a full-time coordinator, or even assistants to the coordinator.

The services coordinator would work as a team member with the principal and the faculty, providing the best possible system of support services in all areas. This individual would not necessarily be required to be a certified teacher, but he or she would certainly be more effective if conversant with the educator's point of view regarding the day-to-day operation of the school.

The coordinator role would be regarded as a career-type position, but it should not be viewed as a "dead end" by the system or the incumbent. The purposes of such a position would be to

- Free the principal for learning improvement activities,
- Develop more effective and efficient means of providing supporting services,
- Assist in operational planning, and
- Provide needed day-to-day operational services to the instructional staff.

The roles of the principal and the coordinator would mesh in long-range planning and day-to-day operation, as portrayed in Table 8.1. The persons assigned to the coordinator position would be held directly responsible by the central administration for supporting the management services necessary for the effective operation of each school within the district. They would be accountable to the central administration for the proper operation of these services according to a coordinated, districtwide plan and at the same time would be accountable to the principal to see that the school is receiving the services efficiently. In the larger school or the site-managed school, the services coordinator would report to the principal only. In smaller schools, the coordinator would be accountable to the central office administrator for those services, procedures, and reports dealing with the business functions of the schools. Salary considerations would be under the central office; however, the principal's recommendations as to work effectiveness should have a major influence on the decision.

The services coordinator would be accountable to the principal for facilitating the instructional program. Any apparently unresolvable conflicts between the principal and the services coordinator could be resolved by any of the next higher positions, making it clear that the business stream is a service to instruction. Clearly delineated areas of responsibility would minimize misunderstandings. The organizational chart could look like Figure 8.1. Variations on this would depend on how many schools could be serviced.

TABLE 8.1
Possible tasks of the principal and the services coordinator

Principal	Services Coordinator
Instruction	*Instruction*
Objectives development	Data gathering and reporting
Staff development	(development of needed systems)
Program evaluation—development and interpretation with staff, students, and community	Maintenance of media/computer equipment
Media and technology applications	
Curriculum	*Curriculum*
Development/innovation	Materials acquisition and accounting
Research	
Materials development and research	Materials production
Students	*Students*
Direct involvement	Data gathering/analysis
Monitoring progress/achievement/behavior	Reporting to central office
	Scheduling activities
Faculty	*Faculty*
Selection	Local school responsibility for records and reporting
Assignment	
Development	Communication of personnel information to faculty
*Community Site Advisory Board**	*Community Site Advisory Board**
Planning and executing two-way communications programs	Materials production
Involvement in community affairs tangential to educational concerns	Scheduling and arranging school/community activity
Finances	*Finances*
Planning with central staff	Accounting for all income and expenditures
Preparing budget with coordinator/advisory board	Operating cost system
Approving internal projects	Preparing budget with principal
Assisting in finding outside resources	
Space	*Space*
Establishing programmatic priorities	Scheduling/utilization
Planning new and renovated space	Maintenance/operation
	Clearinghouse operations

*May include teachers and specialists as well as community members.

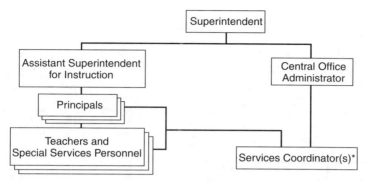

*One services coordinator might serve several small schools.

FIGURE 8.1
Organizational chart showing use of a services coordinator

The individual school or system could decide how best to communicate needs and receive services from the coordinator. His or her function would be strictly a staff function and would not have line authority over any professional staff in the individual buildings.

The major responsibility for educational decision making should lie with the principal; he or she should be relieved from being held accountable by the central administration for supporting services and management detail. The strategy of employing a coordinator returns to the principal the role of educator so that he or she no longer is swamped with demands not directly related to the learning of children or is able to use those demands as excuses for not being directly involved.

One Cannot Serve Two Masters? If a position such as the services coordinator is staffed, an outdated objection might be proffered that the services coordinator cannot be responsible to both the principal and a central office administrator. As we mentioned before, practice will show that this not only can be done well but also in many cases can result in improved services to the unit concerned. Specialists such as reading, speech, and social work personnel are responsible to the principals of the buildings they serve as well as to a director of special services. Clearly understood objectives, procedures, and channels of communication will alleviate problems, should they arise. Over the last few years, the matrix management model has proven successful in the business world. Task teams come and go, and reporting responsibilities change from task to task. One person may report to several others regarding certain aspects of his or her work. Carefully planned divisions of responsibility should fix the priorities on instruction and learning. Central administration staff should see themselves more in the role of providing service to that function, working through the building principal.

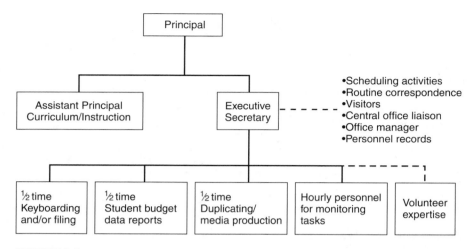

FIGURE 8.2

Organizational chart for small school employing an executive secretary and part-time personnel

Other Possibilities

The principal must not be forced to choose between being a manager-procurer-scheduler and an educational leader. Yet forces continue to push toward making that choice. Again, the "ends" serving the "means" problem comes to the forefront, in that the person responsible for improving learning in the school may be boxed into serving the central office support system. If the principal is to spend the majority of the time improving learning and working with classroom teachers and specialists, another person(s) must be assigned responsibility for performing management details.

The positive aspects of hiring permanent part-time help to do specific tasks are being documented by business at an increasing rate. Scheduling, gathering and analyzing data, completing report forms, ordering and maintaining materials, answering routine correspondence, conducting and maintaining inventories, and performing many other functions may best be done by persons trained in these specific tasks. A highly efficient administrative assistant or executive secretary could head a services team of full-time and/or part-time people. Figure 8.2 suggests how this might work for a small school. Certified or licensed personnel are not needed for many of these functions.

In some school settings, an army of competent, committed volunteers can do many routine functions, such as collecting lunch money, taking attendance, or reporting, receiving, and directing visitors, if they are freed from the telephone. Often retired persons enjoy doing these things for a school and are usually responsible and reliable.

All of the foregoing suggestions are made to direct and reallocate the principal's time to a set of activities to improve instruction. There is another set of considerations, however.

Keeping Personal-Time Priorities in Order

A most insistent set of voices demands that time be spent on administrative detail. These voices are so loud that principals often do spend most of their time on these details rather than on the main function of the school.

A study of principals' estimates of how they spend their time versus how they would like to spend their time proves interesting.[12] The study included discrepancies between actual and desirable times as well as those tasks considered to be important or relatively unimportant.

The first phase of the study identified fourteen tasks; 80 percent of the principals identified three of these tasks as being highly important: (1) evaluating teachers, (2) developing curriculum, and (3) dealing with teacher concerns. It is interesting that many of the respondents did not rate any of the tasks as being unimportant or of low priority. Four tasks, however, were rated as being of low priority by one-third or more of the principals: (1) contract management, (2) supervision of noncertified employees, (3) special education concerns (conferences, IEPs, etc.), and (4) extracurricular activities. It should be noted that special education concerns were rated as being of low priority by almost half of the principals in smaller schools, rural schools, and schools having specialists in charge of those activities.

Table 8.2 indicates the percentages of time spent on fourteen tasks. As a group, the respondents spent 3.63 percent of their time on special education activities, compared with 10.85 percent on extracurricular activities. Figure 8.3 compares the reported actual percentages of time spent and the percentages of time deemed desirable by the respondents. The principals did not see as desirable spending an average of one day per week on any single task. The greatest percentage of time desired (13.45 percent) was on teacher evaluation. The respondents saw as desirable spending approximately one-half day per week on their high-priority items.

A serious discrepancy still remains between the amount of time principals spend doing important tasks and the time they think they should spend on them. Gaziel added the dimension of high-performing versus average-performing schools to the desired and actual uses of principal time. The contrast was highest in the percentages of time spent in office management, instructional management, and planning/acting for school improvement. The principals at high-performing schools (H)

---

[12] This study was conducted by T. L. Drake.

TABLE 8.2
Percentage of time spent on fourteen tasks

Task	Percentage
Preparing reports—e.g., attendance, budget, etc.	6.85
Written communications	8.43
Telephone	5.95
Teacher concerns—problem solving, social, program, etc.	9.65
Student supervision/counseling	10.55
Discipline—referrals, parent conferences	8.13
Extracurricular activities	10.85
Meetings—staff/central office	6.20
Supervision of noncertified employees	4.55
Contract management	3.75
Curriculum development/supervision	7.95
Teacher evaluation	9.55
Special education conferences, staff	3.63
Professional growth—conferences, reading	4.05

spent 22.4 percent of their time in office management versus 34.2 percent by the principals at average-performing schools (A). Instructional management consumed 13.4 percent (H) versus 9.4 percent (A). Planning and acting for school improvement accounted for 7.1 percent (H) and 3.9 percent (A).[13] Observing these data, we may conclude that principals tend to do those things they want to do or, put another way, that principals have time to do those things they put first.

Occasionally in the development of a school, the principal needs to devote considerable time to student behavior, discipline, and attendance. These activities should not become the main role; rather, the principal should help set up strategies to assist all concerned in resolving the current problems and prevent similar ones in the future. The focus of solving these or similar problems should be on improving learning and learning opportunities. This emphasis should be clearly articulated.

The following points may stimulate the reader's thought regarding means to free time for instructional leadership through the management-by-exception principle:

1. What details are required of principals by the central office that could be changed? A group of principals in the school system

---

[13] Haim Gaziel, "Managerial Work Patterns of Principals at High- and Average-Performing Israeli Elementary Schools," *Elementary School Journal* 96 (November 1995): 184–185.

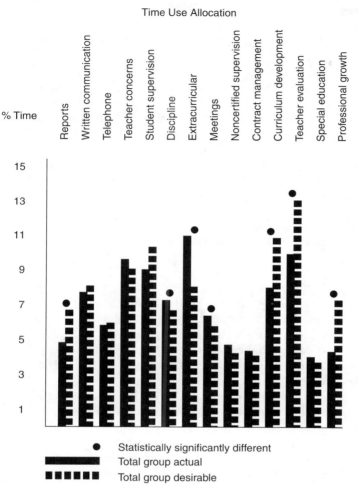

FIGURE 8.3
Actual and desired time use

may wish to prepare a staff study that would identify the possible changes and how they might be made, along with a plan that shows what should be done with the time gained. Some areas that might be examined are noted here:

a. Many meetings concerned with details and reports are called, requesting the presence of the principal; both central office and the individual school would be better served if the assistant principal, a faculty member, or a secretary could attend. Everyone likes to have the chief at the meeting, but obviously it is not reasonable to have a principal spend most of her or his time this way.

  b. When reports are required, correspondence and telephone calls often are directed to the principal, who then is required to relay instructions and provide personal direction to the staff. This consumes time.

  c. The principal is often required to sign (or often insists on signing) all reports and correspondence that are sent from the school. There is no real reason that this needs to be done if the school has an involved staff and if procedures, policies, and quality assurance procedures are established to give them proper direction.

2. Learn to delegate authority and responsibility to the staff. Delegation can be the key to maximizing the contribution and output of the school's employees. Theodore Roosevelt once said, "The best executive is the one who has sense enough to pick good men to do what he wants done and then the self-restraint to keep from meddling with them while they are doing it." In short, do not micromanage.

   There is a real art to the process of delegation. If one ensures that a person fully comprehends and is given instruction relative to the details of the assignment, receives the proper resources and authority to complete it, and then is given credit for a job well done, one can very soon develop a confident staff with the competency to carry on business, to the point that only matters of exception or special concern need to be referred to the principal.

   The principal might say, "But I don't have an assistant." Secretarial and clerical personnel can be as effective as educationally trained persons in handling most noninstructional reports and detail, and often more thorough in many aspects.

3. Gain the confidence of the central office in relation to your reporting procedures and the delegation thereof. This normally can be done as follows:

  a. Learn the expectations of central office personnel in relation to reports and management detail. Convince them that your data are accurate and usable.

  b. Develop carefully written procedures relative to each report and/or management detail.

  c. Make specific assignments to staff.

  d. Provide for the proper training of the person assigned the task.

  e. Establish a checklist of action control processes for the person assigned.

  f. Develop a calendar control process for supervision and evaluation. Conduct periodic checks during slack periods, such as summer or vacations.

4. Introduce staff to the various personnel in the central administrative office dealing with their assignments in order to encourage direct contact and confidence in the delegation process. The typical central administration consists of ten or more divisions or units (personnel, plant, payroll, etc.). The administrator for each of these units appropriately believes that his or her work is most important and invariably wants to deal directly with the "boss" of the school, that is, the principal, thinking this is the best way to get things done. This viewpoint can be changed so long as these administrators can be assured details important to them are being properly handled. Often, as relationships are developed, the requesting unit will help in training the staff member to handle the details exactly as they wish.

To accomplish whatever set of tasks is chosen, the principal will be dealing with many variables. The number of variables will change from building to building and from time to time in any one building. Since options arise wherever changing variables exist, alternatives can and should be developed. The principal needs to optimize the human and material resources available, including those of his or her own personal behavior.

RESOURCE VARIABLES

People

The most important of all the resources is human. People—students, staff, parents, patrons, and "outsiders"—are the essence of a school. This fact alone provides the principal with an almost endless variety of alternatives. The principal who feels "locked in" or in some way prohibited from initiating and implementing worthwhile changes is kidding himself or herself. The hundreds of interactions that occur between the principal and others within and outside the school provide a fertile field for planting ideas, values, and visions. The school is a system, and as such, a change in one part causes changes elsewhere in the system. If changes are made in one of the people variables, the other people are affected, as are time, information, program, and so on.

A simple listing will illustrate the variety of people variables with whom principals can work in developing the culture of the school:

- Students
- Classroom staff
- Specialized staff (counseling, health, etc.)
- Central office staff (information services, budget, data analysis, etc.)

- Community resource persons (artists, musicians, civic planners, volunteers, senior citizens, etc.)
- Professional consultants (state department of education, universities, organizations, private resource persons, etc.)
- Interns, externs, work-study learners, and other trainees

A decision to use community resource persons will raise a host of questions that, when answered, will affect the use of time, space, and possibly materials and money. (See Chapter 3.) For example, will community persons be relegated to the role of guest speaker, or will they become true resources, working alongside the faculty? Will they work with faculty independently, with students, or with both? Will they assist faculty in helping interpret the school's effect on out-of-school time? Several schools have found the interaction between senior citizens and students to be beneficial for both. Business-school collaboration has also proved to be mutually beneficial.

Obviously, changes will occur if community people begin to work in the schools. If having more adults available simply means the students are doing more of the same kinds of activities that have not proven successful in the past (e.g., more drills, more seat work, more problems), then there may not be a qualitative improvement in the lives of either students or teachers.

How will specialized staff be utilized? Should their services be directed to referred student clients only? Should they serve a dual role, consulting with teachers and providing direct services to students? Are their opinions to be used only when sought, or should their inputs be formally planned in decisions about students?

Time

The use of time is one of the cost items over which the principal has the most control. Smith urges " . . . administrators to view the allocation and management of time as one of their most important and powerful functions."[14] The principal's management of personal time has been discussed. The time of students, teachers, specialists, and others is the resource under consideration. The principal may wish to help teachers focus on the amount of noninstructional time they use. In one district setting, teachers were observed for use of instructional time and noninstructional time. Teachers classified as "productive" used only 14 percent of their time as noninstructional, while others used as much as 30 percent.[15] Of course, the principal will need to examine influences such as special

---

[14] BetsAnn Smith, "Quantity Matters: Annual Instructional Time in an Urban School System," *Educational Administration Quarterly* 36 (December 2000): 653.
[15] Ibid., 662.

days, celebrations, all-school programs, and so on, which may detract significantly from instructional time.

State laws and regulations usually fix a minimum school day and school year. Teacher contracts often state maximums in terms of time. States, accrediting agencies, and institutions of higher education set minimum times students must spend to meet graduation or admission standards. Yet, within these parameters, the principal and staff have many alternatives available to them. To improve learning, teachers and staff need to find the time to interact, to work together on finding solutions.

More details are given in Chapter 9, but for now let us say that time can be used in a number of ways to accomplish goals or meet requirements. Several schools are experimenting with four- and four-and-a-half-day weeks. Doubling planning time, increasing the length of the school day, and creating "saved" time for half-day work sessions are all possibilities.[16]

Time needs to be viewed as being much more elastic than it often is treated. The use of time in the school day should be considered an expenditure item for the pupil as well as for the faculty. Is the school giving the student his or her time's worth? If one listens closely to the real messages behind the usual static, the students seriously question whether their time is being spent wisely. The principal may find it useful to study the expenditure of the students' time, in addition to that of the faculty.

Is it possible that the options available to students for the expenditure of their time contribute to their change in attitude toward school as they progress through the grades? Helping teachers use time productively can improve a number of statistics from test scores to discipline problems. In a study of student engagement with the tasks at hand, Yair found that lecturing secured student engagement less than 50 percent of the time, while working in groups, completing laboratories, and giving presentations secured 70 percent engagement. Yet lectures comprised almost three-fourths of the instructional menu.[17] Time can be spent, or time can be invested if used to realize the greatest learning returns possible.

What is the quality of the time spent in school for all personnel? Should not the principal be helping teachers and pupils spend their time more productively? If the principal needs to spend more time on the task of improving learning, one of the best investments would be to assist others in spending their time on more productive, and therefore more rewarding, learning activities as opposed to repetitive seat work or homework or work that seems disconnected to needs or reality.

---

[16] Alan Burke, "Time . . . Time . . . How Can We Find More Time?" *WAMSLE Newsletter* 5 (Winter 1992): 2.
[17] Gad Yair, "Not Just about Time: Instructional Practices and Productive Time in School," *Educational Administration Quarterly* 36 (October 2000): 503.

Information

The principal is continuously faced with the need for information. It is important to determine what information is necessary and for which individuals or groups of individuals: budget, costs, community resources, and so on. Different formats will be required for each "audience" or set of users.

Information is usually thought of as a necessary ingredient in making decisions. But it is also important in making friends. A good example is relationships with the press. How many "one-sided" news stories or "misinformed" reports might have been offset or avoided completely if a sense of sharing information with the reporter had been fostered instead of reinforcing the closed-system image? Does the education editor of the local paper know the principal personally? Is information gathered, analyzed, and written in easily digested form for quick distribution? Is information volunteered (with proper central office clearance, if required) on locally "hot" issues?

The planned sharing of information with various community/parent patron groups is an opportunity not only to gain support in attitudes but also to discover and tap resources. Clearly stated facts in lay language (as opposed to pedajargon)—in short, well-prepared pieces distributed at "rap sessions" in the community—could go far to dispel the negative feelings generated by the appearance of hiding information. In working with a site advisory board, the principal who is inclined to keep information "close to the vest" may find stronger support from well-informed members.

Almost equally important is eliminating the generation and recording of superfluous data. Principals need to be alert to the all-too-common practice of different offices gathering the same data on different forms. This situation arises both internally and from central administrative offices. Certainly, time spent duplicating information is not time spent optimizing resources. Relational databases can be helpful in this regard.

Another dimension of the information resource is the information received. The principal will do well not only to listen and read widely from a variety of sources but also to ascertain the accuracy and completeness of the information received. Good decisions and leadership cannot be based on poor, inadequate, or narrowly conceived information.

Programs and Materials

An almost endless variety of combinations of programs and materials is available, as is obvious at any display area at almost any education convention. The principal's concern should be to effect the right matches between these combinations and the people who use them, both faculty and students. The principal should ascertain the consistency of these matches with the goals and objectives of the school. For example, an objective may be to individualize instruction according to needs, interests, and individual learning rates. The principal should be alert to the possibility that many "individualizing" programs are merely focusing on individualizing the rate at which students deal with the material to be learned. Still others may be highly structured "scripts" for teachers, designed to ensure that all the children participating are doing so at approximately the same rate.

A great variety of on-line sources is available to enrich the school's offerings, but the variance in quality is quite wide. Compact disk stacks and the Internet are available to supplement traditional resources. The principal cannot make, or at least should not make, decisions about these matters in isolation. Others must be involved.

Money

Too often the lack of money is blamed for the lack of innovative teaching-learning situations. It is true that more money can make a good program better by providing more alternatives to the users. Yet many of the variations previously mentioned do not require more money; they may merely demand the reordering of priorities. The individual school should be given as much budgetary independence as possible. This policy does not reduce accountability; rather, it increases the principal's accountability to use funds wisely toward the improvement of the specific learning situations in the school.

The idea of reallocation of resources within buildings is not new, but with the growing crunch of costs and tax limitations, the practice will become more common. The responsibility for reallocation of resources among departments, services, materials centers, and various offices should rest with the principal. To optimize available resources, the principal should involve (as much as is practical in terms of their time and interest) those affected by the decisions.

The principal will also be expected to be involved in the decision-making process for district-level reallocations. He or she should be well prepared with facts, probably beyond those data required by the central office, to support claims for reallocated funds.

Other possibilities for increasing flexibility include the independent school or district foundation and many sources of grant funds from the state and private foundations. (See Chapter 18 for additional discussion.)

Space

The utilization of available space is often controlled by tradition. The principal may wish to explore the effective use of walls, plants, outdoor areas, and community space resources, such as parks, the arboretum, the craft center, and businesses. Creatively using existing floor space is important. Of course, safety regulations should be observed, but hallways, stages, and other underutilized areas could add to the flexibility of the school program. It may be that space resources can be found throughout the community for a variety of learning and service activities.

Optimizing Resources

Regardless of the amount of resources at hand or the galaxy of problems to be solved, certain variables or options are available to the principal—to bend, shape, expand, or cut. These include people, time, information, programs, materials and equipment, money, and space. Granted, each has limits, but how they are used is critical to the continuous improvement of learning. If leadership occurs, change results. Given the nature of a school, change in the variables is inevitable.

The principal optimizes the utilization of available resources to improve the teaching-learning situations within the school. Two guides are suggested to enhance the optimization process: (1) eliminate the compartmentalization and segmentation of the school, the community, and even the lives of the students; and (2) view the selection of alternative solutions to problems as a process involving those people affected by the decisions. There will be pressures from parents, students, teachers, and others to try to use the principal to foist off onto the school their special interest solutions. Obviously, the principal must be sensitive to these often honest attempts to improve the situation but at the same time resistant to being used improperly.

Even though the chief concern is the goal of improved learning, the principal is as concerned about the people aspects of the problem as about the nonpeople aspects of the problem. Figures 8.4 and 8.5 partially illustrate the differences. The principal should not ignore budget restric-

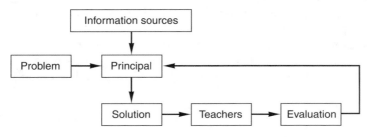

FIGURE 8.4
Principal-centered process

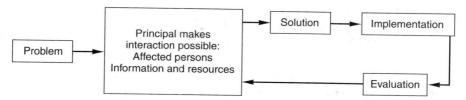

FIGURE 8.5
Problem-/people-centered process

tions, time problems, policies, and so forth. To do so is to act irresponsibly. But such things are neither the essence of his or her job nor a cudgel with which to reinforce his or her position. These, too, should be viewed as aids to reaching the optimum solution. In some instances, effecting change in the nonpeople aspects of the problem may be the best solution, but those strategies may be merely devices to avoid facing the real problem.

Regardless of the shape of the organizational chart, we find the principal working with people. The important consideration is the emphasis of the work with them and the quality of the time spent. If the management of things (attendance, accounting, supplies, reports, etc.) is the usual bill of fare rather than the improvement of the learning of individuals and groups of individuals, it is not hard to see why the image of the principal is diminished to a clerklike role.

Throughout this chapter, the educational leadership role has been emphasized, with direct involvement with staff and students. The principal should be concerned about administrative detail and support roles. Periodic reviews of routine tasks are needed to avoid the trap of "If it isn't broken, don't fix it." Every task can be improved, and every person can improve her or his work.

S U M M A R Y

The major function of the principal is to exert leadership to make a positive difference in student learning and to improve the quality of life of each individual within the school. This task is done by articulating and developing a shared vision, empowering (and developing) a community of learners and leaders, and creatively providing the resources to implement the vision. The community, faculty, and students must regard the principal as being primarily accountable for achieving these functions. To accomplish them effectively, the principal must be free to direct time and energy to those tasks rather than having time and energy drained away because of being held responsible primarily for business and management.

A services coordinator, responsible to the central administration through the business stream of the organization, might be employed and held accountable for supporting services and accounting functions of the school. The staffing of a position such as a services coordinator is not suggested as the only solution, but we do believe that unless some restructuring occurs, the "business" functions may nudge out educational improvement.

Given the studies of effective versus noneffective schools and the leader behavior literature, clearly the principal cannot effectively carry out the major task of educational improvement by emphasizing an excellent job of attending to administrative detail. What else is needed? The following behaviors appear to be contributors:

1. Have a well-developed vision of what intellectual, emotional, and social maturities are and which learning experiences and environments contribute to these forms of maturity. Know specifically what outcomes are expected, and articulate those to all.
2. With staff and, when appropriate, students, cooperatively develop a plan of specific steps, going from a realistic assessment of the current condition of the school to the ideas and outcomes desired.
3. Articulate those ideas and plans to students, teachers, colleagues, and the community.
4. Provide direct help and support to teachers in improving learning, making them more successful in their jobs, and nurturing their professional growth.
5. Be prepared to "rock the boat" and face the consequences thereof.
6. Closely monitor the learning achievement of students.
7. As teachers and students mature in their respective tasks, shift supervisory behavior toward that of delegation of responsibility, collegial learning, and support.

The principal can make a significant difference. In fact, the principal cannot avoid making a difference, one way or the other. The absence of the aforementioned behaviors can mean a regressive situation—directionless and sometimes counterproductive. In other words, failure to carry out the major task of educational improvement and growth may be viewed as a form of negligence.

Roles can be redefined. Interaction patterns can be changed. Options can be identified, alternatives can be developed, and, we hope, restriction of the principal's role to just keeping school can become a thing of the past.

Focusing on leadership and being freed to provide it certainly have implications for the competencies needed by a person proposing to be a principal. But it is time—indeed, long past time—that we make the move.

FOR FURTHER THOUGHT

1. If the purpose of the school is student learning, should the leader of the school be held responsible for that?
2. If a school uses community resource persons in addition to the regular teaching staff, other than certification and salary what distinguishes the professional staff from the community resource persons?
3. How would you defend to a superintendent or a school board member the idea that the principal should not be the primary contact for every situation?
4. Why is it that occasionally a teachers' group will suggest that the position of the principal could be eliminated with no loss to the quality of the educational program?
5. If a good administrative secretary could do many of the things the principal does, why does she or he not do them?
6. Successfully attending to detail can enhance the principal's claim to expert leadership. What safeguards can be set up to keep attention to detail from becoming the main task?
7. Conduct a survey of principals regarding how they spend their time versus how they would like to spend their time.
8. How can a principal maintain the image and/or reputation of a leader and at the same time become a learner alongside the teachers and students? Are these positions incompatible?

SELECTED READINGS

Brandt, Ron. "On Building Learning Communities: A Conversation with Hank Levin." *Educational Leadership* 50 (September 1992): 19–23.

Copland, Michael A. "The Myth of the Superprincipal." *Phi Delta Kappan* 82 (March 2001): 528–533.

Daresh, John C. "Making the Most of It," *Principal Leadership* 1 (January 2001): 72.

MacKay, Louise L., and Elizabeth Welch Ralston. *Creating Better Schools: What Authentic Principals Do* (Thousand Oaks, CA: Corwin Press, 1999).

Marshall, Catherine. *The Assistant Principal.* Newbury Park, CA: Corwin, 1992.

Smith, BetsAnn. "Quantity Matters: Annual Instructional Time in an Urban School System." *Educational Administration Quarterly* 36 (December 2000): 652–682.

Creating Appropriate Structures to Improve Learning

*E*ach of the over fourteen thousand school districts has the opportunity to create its own unique approach to providing education. Such a situation would suggest broad and varied educational opportunities for children. Actually, the basic organizational and instructional patterns of schools throughout the United States are startlingly similar, particularly at the secondary level, and the options, while there, are seldom exercised to the extent one might expect. Many pressures cause the similarities. Some are financing patterns, concerns of professional associations, political pressures, and more recently the standards movement supported by business/political individuals and groups.[1]

SIMILARITIES ARE UNIVERSAL

There may be diversity in a relative sense when U.S. schools are compared with European or Pacific Rim schools; however, considered nationally, variations are minor. In general, the similarities are so universal that certain aspects of organization, structure, teaching procedures, and learning processes apply to most schools throughout the United States:

1. Classes are for the most part graded rather than nongraded.
2. Students are taught each subject by a single teacher rather than by a team or series of teachers.

---

[1] See Chapter 12 for a discussion of the standards movement and assessment programs.

3. Class periods are of a uniform duration, such as forty to sixty minutes, during which one subject is studied separately from other subjects.
4. The school year consists of approximately 180 days.
5. Formal schooling is held fall, winter, and spring, with special or remedial classes during summer months.
6. Secondary academic subjects are given an equal amount of time throughout the semester, no matter what the subject.
7. The academic courses in the school curriculum are essentially the same.
8. The student is expected to complete at least twelve years of school before graduation.
9. All classes begin at the beginning of the semester and end at the end of the semester.
10. The formal school day starts at a certain time for all students and finishes at a certain time for all students.
11. An evaluation system (usually with letter grading) is provided for pupils and compares them with the group rather than themselves.
12. Most schools have some semblance of a college preparatory, vocational education, and general education track system for students.
13. The school building and the classroom are where formal education takes place.
14. Schools have a superintendent, a principal, and a teacher hierarchy.
15. All schools have a board of education and are part of a state system.

One could go on with a score of other similarities.

Observing these patterns throughout the country, we could conclude that there are indisputable laws of learning and unimpeachable, noncontroversial teaching principles that force the aforementioned characteristics on our schools. Such is not the case; in fact, in many instances what is known about learning is inconsistent with patterns that have become so popular. The conclusion emerges that custom, tradition, and the demands of managerial simplicity have had more impact on the way schools are organized than anything else. In a sense, a voluntary bureaucracy has emerged throughout the nation, reinforced by custom, accrediting bodies, university entrance requirements, and federal and state influences. Throughout the United States, students are impounded into similar types of highly structured school systems. They are fit into a college preparatory, general studies, or tech-prep curriculum. If they cannot adapt to that system and rebel through overt or covert behavior, and if they are in a school system with enough resources, enough concern, and enough leadership, a special program will be provided for them.

Although a limited number of school systems do provide a broad, flexible program, it is clear that a child must be declared a failure, have an unusual problem, or exhibit a special disability before he or she will become eligible for most of these special programs or be provided some type of alternative school. One must wonder whether the problem(s) being addressed was the effect the system had on the student rather than something inherent within the student.

The pattern of showing national concern after people have become problems is unfortunate. It is time for more school systems to incorporate diversity, flexibility, and a variety of options and learning places into the school and into the community so that all students can find learning strategies that suit them best and can move forward successfully in terms of their unique talents and interests.

GRADE ORGANIZATION AND GROUPING PATTERNS

Practical economics and tradition influenced the various ways of organizing grades in schools in the United States. Following the Civil War, the trend was for children to start school in an eight-year elementary school, beginning at age five or six and continuing to age thirteen or fourteen. A few of the better or more affluent students would then go to secondary education in a four-year high school, from ages fourteen to eighteen.[2] This organization, known as the 8-4 plan, is the basis for most types of grade organizations that attempt to take into account the particular schooling needs of different age groups of children and youth within a particular school district.

Today the four-year high school is the most common. With the rapid growth of the junior high school in the 1920s and the middle school in the 1960s and with a middle school resurgence in the late 1980s, a great variety of organizational patterns is evident in the elementary and middle grades. While many middle schools may have been created to justify the facilities at the high school—that is, to move the ninth grade back into the high school so enrollments appear appropriate—others have been formed specifically to meet the needs of the early adolescent.

A remarkable shift has occurred from the 7–9 school to the 6–8 school. Over six thousand more middle schools emerged from 1970 to 1990. In 1970, there were approximately four times the number of junior high schools as there were middle schools. Today there are more than twice as many middle schools as junior high schools.

---

[2] The four-year high school was probably influenced by the first public high school in the United States, which was established in Boston in 1821 as the English Classical School and then renamed the Boston English High School in 1824. This school originally began as a three-year school and soon adopted the four-year pattern. Half a century of trial and error followed in other states, with three-, four-, and five-year high schools, but after the Civil War, the four-year program emerged as the most popular.

An analysis further reveals a decided transition in the organization of the intermediate grades. Obviously, the middle school movement and the continued experimentation with grade levels in the junior high school made this a highly dynamic situation, for organizational patterns vary greatly throughout the intermediate grades.

At the turn of the twentieth century, educators recommended a smoother transition from elementary school to high school on the basis of the adolescent's physiological, social, and intellectual needs rather than on the basis of research into the effectiveness of various grade organization or grouping schemes. Today's educators are making similar recommendations—this time for the middle school—in the belief that today's adolescents experience the onset of puberty earlier than did their parents. Once again, however, the immediate reason for establishing middle schools was probably to relieve crowded conditions in other schools. Others suggest that the middle school movement is getting an unexpected push from declining enrollments and fiscal austerity. The middle school provides an easy place to put children when faced with the task of closing some elementary schools and even high schools.

MIDDLE-LEVEL EDUCATION

The dynamics of grade organization within schools paralleled the vast changes going on in our country following the turn of the twentieth century. The population was growing dramatically as a result of both an increasing birth rate and immigration. The West was expanding, and urbanization and industrialization were taking place. As a result, there were pressures to establish an educational system that could better relate to the realistic needs of a changing society, "Americanize" immigrants, and help promote societal reforms.[3] The strengthening of the four-year high school appeared to be the answer. The 8-4 type of organization was the pattern then, but with more high schools coming into existence and more and more children going on into high school, a need to ease the transition from elementary to high school soon became apparent. Thus was born the junior high school movement.

McEwin cites additional factors influencing the acceptance of the junior high school: reports of national education committees recommending this reorganization; the dropout problem; the child study and mental testing movements, which drew attention to individual differences; changing societal needs; and the feeling that needed educational

---

[3] The reader may wish to study the effects of the child labor movement and to compare the growth of public education with social reforms.

reforms were almost impossible to achieve in the traditional 8-4 pattern but might be accomplished in a new educational unit.[4]

The growth of this new administrative unit (grades 7–9), known as the junior high school, was very rapid. In 1920, there were fewer than four hundred junior high schools, but fifty years later more than seven thousand were in place. For the first time in history, early adolescents were attending schools especially designed for them.

MIDDLE SCHOOL MOVEMENT

The middle school movement was proposed in the early 1960s because of the evident gap between theory and practice. The purported purpose of the junior high school was to provide a transitional program for early adolescents that would meet their educational and developmental needs. In truth, however, the junior high school was, for the most part, just a scaled-down version of the senior high school, with complex departmentalization, rigid scheduling, poor articulation, interscholastic sports, and developmentally questionable social events. It lacked exploratory activities and trained, committed personnel. The middle school movement offered a second chance to develop a realistic program based on the characteristics of ten- to fourteen-year-olds. As in the 1920s, it was thought that by dropping the ninth grade from this unit and starting out with a clean slate, it would be easier to create the necessary reforms.

The middle school is presently the most popular organization for middle-level education, with grades 6 through 8 the most common configuration. From 1988 to 1994, the number of middle schools increased from 9,086 to 11,792, an increase of nearly 30 percent in six years.[5]

The greatest benefit of the middle school seems to be in student attitude and school atmosphere. Research on the developmental needs of adolescents in this age group does indicate that the quality of the program is more important than grade organization. The following are among the ingredients that promote that quality:

1. Developmental counseling programs
2. Scheduling that encourages programs based on students' needs and interests
3. Opportunities for students to progress at their own rates
4. A variety of exploratory opportunities
5. Planned social experiences for that specific age group

---

[4] C. Kenneth McEwin, "Schools for Early Adolescents," *Theory into Practice* 22 (Spring 1983): 119–125.

[5] National Center for Education Statistics, *In the Middle* (Washington, DC: U.S. Department of Education, 2000), 57–61.

6. An emphasis on health and wellness that takes into account the physical and emotional changes experienced by early adolescents

7. A teaching staff trained especially for teaching early adolescents[6]

A renewed interest in middle schools is evident in recent literature. The topics include curricula, alcohol abuse prevention programs, balanced calendars, multiage teaming, and many others.

GROUPING

The concept of grouping within a grade level appeared when critics of graded classrooms challenged the idea that all children should be placed in one grade according to their ages. They charged that this approach was too regimented for students. The use of cross-grade grouping, in-grade grouping, and nongraded grouping appears to be a growing practice, the premise being that it creates greater flexibility and increased efficiency in teaching-learning situations.

Teachers generally believe that grouping students by ability improves instructional effectiveness, makes teaching all levels of students easier, results in fewer discipline problems, and is fairer to the students.

Ability grouping per se has been the topic of a massive amount of research since 1922 at both the elementary and the secondary levels.[7] Even though the majority of teachers believe that ability grouping improves the effectiveness of instruction, it has been found to be generally ineffective in improving academic achievement.[8]

Studies reviewed suggest the practice has deleterious effects on teacher expectations and instructional practices (especially for students in the lower ability group), student perceptions of self and others, and the academic performance of lower-ability students. It interferes with opportunities for students to learn from—and learn to accept—peers of different socioeconomic backgrounds and may perpetuate the notions of superior- and inferior-class citizens.[9]

---

[6] McEwin, "Schools for Early Adolescents," 123–124.
[7] For a review of earlier studies, see Walter Borg, *Ability Grouping in the Public Schools*, 2d ed. (Madison, WI: Dunbar Educational Research Service, 1966); and Warren Findley and Miriam Bryan, *The Impact of Ability Grouping on School Achievement, Affective Development, Ethnic Separation* (ED 048-382, JM 000.502) (Washington, DC: U.S. Office of Education, 1970).
[8] Susan J. Rosenholtz and Carl Simpson, "The Formation of Ability Conceptions: Developmental Trend or Social Construction?" *Review of Educational Research* 54 (Spring 1984): 31–63.
[9] Marjorie Wuthrick, "Blue Jays Win! Crows Go Down in Defeat," *Phi Delta Kappan* (March 1990): 553–556.

The results of research on the subject have been highly inconclusive and therefore generally ineffective. The literature has addressed the process of "untracking" or "detracking." If indeed ability grouping in various forms shows no overall positive usefulness regarding achievement, social development, and expectations for achievement, then alternatives must be found. In a Council of Chief State Schools Officers publication, some of the commonalities of the culture of detracking were listed:

- Recognition that tracking is supported by powerful norms . . .
- Willingness to broaden the reform agenda so that changes in the tracking structure become one of a comprehensive set of changes . . .
- Engagement in a process of inquiry and experimentation . . .
- Alternatives in teachers' roles and responsibilities . . .
- Persistence . . . sustained by risk-taking leaders who are clearly focused on scholarship and democratic values.[10]

Clearly, the principal's leadership skills will be challenged. To move an organization from having a potentially negative impact on students to having a more positive effect is central to the principal's role. Restructuring to recognize the potential of all students may mean a comprehensive revamping of curricula, time, and instructional processes and assessments. A worthy challenge indeed!

Wheelock notes that parents are key players in the untracking process.[11] Developing a program to inform and involve via attending classes, plus designing a phase-in program until all staff are well prepared for heterogeneous classes, may help parents become supporters instead of hecklers.

The general feeling is that some grouping, judiciously planned for specific learning situations with appropriate instructional adaptations, may be beneficial to student learning so long as it involves a minor portion of the student's schooling. "Appropriate adaptations" do not mean simply "dumbing down" the material.

MULTIAGE GROUPING/TEAMING

Several schools have moved to multiage grouping within grade spans of two to three years, e.g., primary grades 1–3, upper grades 4–5, and even the middle school grades. Individual and schoolwide success stories are being told in which true learning communities are forming, individuals who were labeled as failing are "catching up," and smoother continuous

---

[10] Jeannie Oakes, "Reflections on Detracking Schools," *Turning Points* 2 (March 1992): 1.
[11] Anne Wheelock, "The Case for Untracking," *Educational Leadership* 50 (October 1992): 9.

progress is evident. An elementary school in Illinois has changed from a few multiage classes in 1996 to ninety multiage classes in 2001. Opportunities for team learning and student-to-student assistance seem greater in familylike groups than in groups formed only by chronological age. The stigma of the slower developing student is reduced, and the chances for some younger students to advance more quickly than in a traditional age-based setting are improved.

UNFORTUNATE OVEREMPHASIS

Perhaps it is unfortunate that so much concern and study were spent on how students should be grouped and classes organized for the education of our youth. A great deal of strong discussion and preoccupation regarding the assignment of students within grades according to age groups has been generated. In many cases, it has caused educators and the public at large to overlook the possibility that a class or grade system of organization might have been wrong in the first place. One could hazard the hypothesis that overemphasis on preschool through grade 12 and the assignment of students to these grades according to age have done more to retard proper learning than perhaps any other factor in school administration.

As far back as 1913, Dr. Frederic Burk, president of the San Francisco State Normal School, wrote a strong indictment of the traditional class system:

> The class system has been modeled upon the military system. It is constructed upon the assumption that a group of minds can be marshaled and controlled in growth in exactly the same manner that a military officer marshals and directs the bodily movements of a company of soldiers. In solid unbreakable phalanx the class is supposed to move through the grades, keeping in locked step. This locked step is set by the "average" pupil—an algebraic myth born of inanimate figures and addled pedagogy.
>
> V. The class system does permanent violence to all types of pupils. (1) It does injury to the rapid and quick-thinking pupils, because these must shackle their stride to keep pace with the rate of the mythical average. They do so, usually at the price of interest in their work. Their energy is directed into illegitimate activities with the result that in the intermediate grades a large portion of them fall into the class of uninterested, inattentive, rebellious, and unmanageable pupils.
>
> (2) The class system does a greater injury to the large number who make progress slower than the rate of the mythical average pupil. Necessarily they are carried off their feet by the momentum of the mass. They struggle along, with greater or less pretense, but eventually they are discovered and put back into the next lower class. . . . By setting the pace of a mathematical average, education for nearly one half the class is made

impossible. They are foredoomed to failure before they begin. . . . This policy is, of course, as inhuman as it is stupid.

Could any system be more stupid in its assumptions, more impossible in its conditions, and more juggernautic in its operation? Every one of its premises is palpably false, every one of its requirements is impossible, and every one of its effects is inefficient and brutal. Nevertheless, this system has endured and has been endured for centuries.[12]

Ninety years later the schools are still wrestling with the issue.

Possibly the most succinct statement about the controversy is this oft-quoted verse: "Best organization? Let fools contest. Whatever works best is best." Unfortunately, the concentration for the most part has been on the grouping of students for the best administrative organization or for the convenience of instruction (or instructors?) rather than on the needs of the individual student. The question that needs to be faced honestly is, Best for whom? In all cases, grades, classes, constant schedules, fixed classrooms, assessment practices, and textbooks were constant structures that could not seem to be eliminated when attempts were made to focus on the individual.

EARLY TEACHING-LEARNING STRATEGIES

Looking back over the past decades of educational development, one can observe constant attempts to focus on the individual child. Research in child development and theoretical and scientific contributions in educational psychology, sociology, and philosophy, particularly in the early 1920s, were clear indicators that each child is an individual and that learning cannot be neatly categorized. Research also affirmed that children do not learn at the same rate and in the same way. Taking cues from these studies from the 1920s on, cutting-edge educational thinkers and practitioners developed a great variety of new, organized teaching plans. These new plans attempted to adapt the new principles. Some tried to solve the problem of individual differences through double promotion or informal homogeneous ability grouping, that is, grouping by age or grades, such as the Cambridge three-track curriculum and the Pueblo Plan. Others tried more formal ability grouping, by intelligence and achievement, as in the Detroit XYZ Plan and the Santa Barbara Plan. Some, like the city schools of St. Louis, tried to provide flexibility by establishing quarter grades to shorten the time units and minimize the failures. Some tried special coaching (Batavia Plan) for children whose rate of learning was too slow or who were handicapped by illness.[13] The

---

[12] Frederic Burk, *Remedy for Lock-Step Schooling* (Department of Education, State of California, 1913). In using the term *class system,* he was referring to assignment of children to grades or heterogeneous assignment of pupils to classes within grades.
[13] Arthur B. Moehlman, *School Administration* (Boston: Houghton Mifflin, 1951), 276–279.

Dalton Plan, the Winnetka Plan, and the Montessori Schools tried to organize their complete school so as to emphasize individual differences in learning but with specially organized social activities.[14] The early John Dewey School asserted that adequate learning could be realized only by close cooperation among children, teachers, and parents, and, by the way it was operated, it tried to make this American partnership a reality.[15]

In addition to the more famous plans and schools, a large number of other schools throughout the years tried to organize special teaching approaches or methods—for example, the project method, unit method, activity program, contract plan, child-centered school, ability grouping, homogeneous grouping, independent study, experience curriculum, common learning, core curriculum, and life adjustment programs.

Most of these early special plans and programs were related to elementary education because it was easier to establish new approaches at this level. Elementary education was almost exclusively responsive to the local community and its school district, but secondary education was restricted seriously by controls regarding state and regional accrediting, college requirements, and the state department of education. In 1932, however, the Progressive Education Association contributed immeasurably to changes in secondary education through the Eight-Year Study, conducted by its Commission on the Relation of Schools and Colleges.[16] The belief at that time was that colleges and universities were forcing secondary schools into a restrictive curriculum pattern because of their insistence on too many academic course requirements for college entrance.

The study, generally approved by colleges and universities in 1932, established an effective cooperating relationship between them and thirty secondary schools for the eight-year period of the study. It permitted and encouraged the participating schools to radically reconstruct their secondary curriculum to serve more nearly the needs of youth, regardless of whether they were going to college. The commission and the schools held the following beliefs:

1. Success in the liberal arts college does not necessarily depend on the study of certain subjects for a certain period in high school.
2. There are many different kinds of experiences by which students can prepare themselves for successful work in college.
3. Relations more satisfactory to both school and college could be developed and established on a permanent basis.

---

[14] Helen Parkhurst, *Education on the Dalton Plan* (New York: Dutton, 1922).
[15] Katherine C. Mayhew and Anna C. Edwards, *The Dewey School* (East Norwalk, CT: Appleton-Century-Crofts, 1936).
[16] Progressive Education Association, *The Story of the Eight-Year Study* (New York: Harper & Row, 1942).

4. Ways should be found by which schools and college teachers can work together in mutual regard and understanding.

A careful examination of the findings can leave no doubt as to the conclusions that must be drawn. First, the graduates of the thirty schools reviewed were not at a disadvantage in terms of their college work. Second, departures from the prescribed pattern of subjects and units did not lessen the students' readiness for the responsibilities of college. Third, students from the participating schools that made the most fundamental curriculum revisions achieved distinctly higher standing in college than did students of equal ability with whom they were compared.[17]

The overall effect of these new approaches to teaching and learning certainly did much to break the lock-step of the traditional school, broaden the curriculum, and encourage a remarkable increase in special services, such as audiovisual materials, library, curriculum materials, guidance, work experience, school lunch, transportation, school health, and recreation.

Looking back over these early years of educational development, it is clear that the most radical changes in program and outlook took place in elementary schools and involved more concentration on the individual child. At the secondary level, the changes have been essentially in broadening services and offering more courses rather than altering the teaching processes. The middle school and the junior high school have reaped some benefits from both levels, but recent changes can be characterized as being student centered as far as developmental and learning styles are concerned.

Reflecting on these movements historically, one can trace development and emphasis starting in the 1920s, through the leadership of John Dewey, Frederic Burk, William Kilpatrick, Carleton Washburne, George Counts, and many others who could be classed as part of the progressive education and life adjustment movement. This movement began to fall into disrepute in the late 1940s and early 1950s. With *Sputnik* came a strong swing back to traditional teaching and schooling, along with an emphasis on the "basics." At this point, most of the special organizational attempts to consider and take care of individual differences were eliminated and forgotten. Then, in the 1960s and 1970s, the pendulum began to swing back to the progressive mode when major problems of the cities began to be felt. With these problems came the realization that schools were not really geared, in action or philosophy, to meet the needs of certain minorities and culturally different children; thus, a new movement developed that encouraged new approaches to teaching and learning and even suggested some alternative forms of schooling that would

---

[17] Ibid., 116–117.

be radically different from the normal public school.[18] Unfortunately, this new movement failed for the most part to build on the strengths, and learn from the weaknesses, of the past. This is a serious problem in the education profession: we tend to ignore the results of previous attempts to deal with the same or similar problems.

THE EMPHASIS ON CHANGE AND INNOVATION

While social forces pressed for new thinking in regard to education, action by the federal government, through the U.S. Office of Education, was instrumental in popularizing the emphasis on innovation and change. *Brown v. Board of Education* in 1954 seemed to jump-start the movement and was followed by several pieces of implementing legislation. The landmark Elementary and Secondary Education Act of 1965 especially recognized inequalities in U.S. education and provided special funds to correct these inequities where there were concentrations of poor people. Head Start, Upward Bound, and Follow Through had similar objectives. Title III programs in particular stimulated new thinking and a turnabout attitude in regard to traditional approaches that were not working. New and appealing schemes for teaching and learning began to spring up, and in the early 1970s, change-oriented educators were advocating new approaches, incorporating such terminology as *team teaching, open education, integrated day, alternative education, differentiated staffing, independent study,* and *experimental schools.*

A general criticism of this period could be that in too many cases there was innovation and change just for the sake of change. Characteristically, the educational reform attempts were rediscovered many times over again by the young and uninformed because there was so little knowledge of similar experiences and programs developed in the 1920–1960 period and no serious attempt to learn from successes and failures of past experiments. Despite these negative generalizations, the period did develop some exciting new approaches and created an environment more conducive to change.

WHAT ARE THE RESULTS?

As one reviews various experiments, special programs, and the organization of "different" teaching methods, one gets the impression that education over the past century has been an ever-changing, dynamic, exciting adventure, led by innovative thinkers. This has been true on the "edges,"

---

[18] R. Freeman Butts, *Public Education in the United States—From Revolution to Reform* (New York: Holt, Rinehart & Winston, 1978).

but somehow the positive teaching-learning approaches that should have resulted from these pioneer projects have been generally elusive. Not enough of either the spirit or the methods seem to have penetrated to the core of the education profession. In spite of the pioneer efforts and current departures from tradition,

- we do not teach as well as we know how, now;
- we have not generally developed school environments that provide the best kinds of learning situations;
- we still teach the textbook and subject matter instead of the child;
- we structure for groups instead of individuals;
- we still operate schools as if all teachers are the same and all children learn the same things at the same rate in the same way;
- we still teach as if the school is the only place a child can learn; and
- we still teach as if children can learn only from adults, and certified adults at that.

The thoughtful educator knows that many areas in our schools need improvement. What are our excuses for not incorporating the successes of some of those methods that we know would bring about improvements? Is it finances? Is it overcrowding? Is it lack of properly trained teachers? Is it lack of time? Is it lack of will? Is it lack of leadership? Is it lack of dedication? Is it comfortable to remain the way we are? And in what ways do the organization and structure of our school systems discourage change?

Creative people always see a better way of doing things, and schooling is no exception. The following sections describe several alternatives to the traditional school that have developed or are in process.

ALTERNATIVE SCHOOLING

Rapid Growth of Alternatives

The growth of alternative schools in the early 1970s represented a protest against the organizational and curricular inflexibility of the traditional public school. We have always had protest schools in the United States. These have been generally represented by the private schools, which are a recognized part of our total educational system and have educated over the past few years 13 percent of our school-age children. The alternative school movement of the 1970s, however, was not part of that pattern; rather, it appeared to run parallel to and correspond with the general social upheaval of the times. The movement encompassed both private and public education, and it forced school officials to realize that our school systems should be more flexible and responsive if they are to survive.

What Is the Alternative School?

As in many cases in the field of education, it is almost impossible to provide a definition for alternative schools on which everyone will agree; however, the following are general characteristics common to most alternative schools:

1. The alternative school is smaller and less structured than the traditional, regular school.
2. It has a distinct, identifiable administrative unit, with its own personnel and program, with enough separateness from the regular school to sustain a distinct climate and ethos; further, a special effort is made to create in both students and teachers a strong sense of special affiliation to that unit.
3. It is geared to strong teacher-student interaction in all phases of operation.
4. Students and staff enter the alternative school as a matter of choice rather than assignment.
5. The teaching-learning program is designed to meet the particular needs, interests, and desires of that particular student group, and it is different from the regular school teaching-learning program.
6. The staff has enough autonomy so that it can develop its own vision of schooling.
7. The alternative school does not generally limit itself to cognitive and academic goals; it is essentially student centered, and its aim is all-around student development.

Alternative schools emphasize a spirit of freedom—freedom of individuals to learn and grow, follow their natural curiosity, and do what they feel is necessary to meet their needs. Essentially, these schools deemphasize the usual structure, organization, and formality of the regular schools and stress flexibility and openness. They pride themselves on responsiveness to human need and an ability to reform and reshape themselves to meet the challenge of the times.

Both public and nonpublic alternative schools have been established at all levels—nursery, primary, elementary, secondary, and college. They have been called counterschools, cool schools, schools without walls, experimental schools, free schools, street academies, independent schools, and charter schools as well as their more conventional name, alternative schools. Thousands of such schools were established in the early 1970s. The attrition rate was high as schools opened and closed or were changed into more traditional schools or became "regularized" in one way or the other. At first, the alternative schools appeared as a movement counter to and in competition with the regular school, with many groups establishing their own schools with private funds and private energy. Soon these groups, several representing minorities, developed into political forces demanding to be heard. Thus, the story of the alternative schools merging as a part of the regular school establishment makes an interesting case study of subdominant power groups taking on the established dominants, and winning.

Becoming Part of the Establishment

Although many of these alternative schools were established to protest against the public school system, it is interesting to note how soon many were actually sponsored and even supported by the public school system. These became special schools within a particular school district or within a particular school itself. Often alternative schools started as a way of preventing dropouts, or they sprang up in ghettos and inner cities where the public school system decided to turn a portion of education over to minority groups to satisfy their demands for immediate action in reforming the educational system.

The California continuation school is often given credit for stimulating alternative forms of public secondary education. California attacked the dropout problem in 1965 by enacting legislation ordering all school districts to establish and maintain alternative continuation schools. These schools took many forms. There was the "open campus," to accommodate working students; the alternative learning center for small groups of students with disabilities; the street academy for any dropout who walked in the door; the vocational career development center for both young adults and sixteen- to eighteen-year-olds; and the formal continuation teaching of vocational and academic subjects for dropouts and potential dropouts.

The California Commission for the Reform of Intermediate and Secondary Education (RISE Commission) indicated the need for full-scale reform of the California schools to "make the schools more effective, more enjoyable and more conducive to a continued interest in learning."[19] Through the commission's support, the Alternative School Act was passed by the California legislature; it encouraged and authorized the governing board of any school district to establish and maintain alternative schools.[20] It became obvious that simply tweaking programs or doing more of what was already unsuccessful does not solve the problems being addressed.

---

[19] *Report of the California Commission for Reform of Intermediate and Secondary Education* (Sacramento: California State Department of Education, 1975).
[20] The bill became effective on 30 April 1977. The program still exists, although it has been altered by legislation over the years.

The Modern Alternative School Movement

The rambunctious alternative school movement of the early 1970s settled down into an optional school movement of the mid-1980s and 1990s. Philosophically, the idea that there should be greater flexibility and a variety of learning options for each student has been generally accepted even though it has not yet been generally implemented. Currently, state legislatures have encouraged the development of alternative schools that will better prepare the students of the twenty-first century.

Alternative schools are continuing to increase in number and grow in size, even though many of them have rigid enrollment limits. They do have a rather precarious and fragile existence because they depend so much on dedicated, aggressive leadership; a special, concentrated interest; and special funding. They are not, however, the fly-by-night structures some have claimed.

In Raywid's survey of alternative schools, approximately half of the schools responding were at least six years old. Her findings show surprising durability for these schools as well as continued growth for the alternative school movement in general.[21] In contrast to many special programs that started up with the incentive of federal funding and then faded out with the disappearance of federal funds, alternative schools have been effective and popular enough to attract a significant amount of local and private funding.

In the 1970s, alternatives served approximately one million children in the United States, which was roughly 2 percent of the elementary and secondary enrollment. These schools were found in every size school district; however, they were more likely to be found in the larger districts, with twice as many being in secondary education.[22] A 1995 directory of alternative schools in one state of fewer than three hundred school districts lists eighty-six alternative programs.

All evidence indicates the optional school movement is continuing in popularity. It is not as radical and unique because it is no longer on the fringe, but it has become an important phase in the planning of many school districts, and its significance is definitely having an impact on the mainstream of educational thinking so that formats such as charter schools are seen as viable means to address both problems and opportunities.

Charter Schools

Charter schools have been described as " . . . the liveliest reform in American education." Manno et al. define a charter school as " . . . an

---

[21] Mary Anne Raywid, *The Current Status of Schools of Choice in Public Education* (Hempstead, NY: Hofstra University, 1982), 97.
[22] National Association of Secondary School Principals, *A Decade of Alternative Schools and What of the Future* (Reston, VA: Author, October 1978).

independent public school of choice, freed from rules but accountable for results."[23] It carries with it hope and great expectations, including the key to true educational reform.

The idea had spread from two states in 1993 to thirty six states and over 1,700 schools by 2000. Many plans have already been approved by legislatures, and they encompass a variety of funding patterns, eligible sponsors and autonomy and a range of compliance with education laws and regulations. The schools tend to employ a number of instructional approaches, many of which are regularly used in the traditional public schools. A number of the charter schools are using a back-to-basics approach that results in achievement growth as measured by standardized achievement tests.

Several charter schools involve parents in home-based instruction. The regular public schools would do well to adapt this idea and initiate more involvement with parents as instructional colleagues. Given the Internet, communitywide computer networking, and voice mail devices, this task is becoming more realistic. As noted in Chapter 3, the schools need to address the several barriers to parent involvement. It may be a worthwhile investment, as many charter and private schools have discovered.

In reviewing California's legislation regarding charter schools, Hart and Burr caution that charter schools may develop the same maladies that other innovations have encountered. "[C]harter schools sometimes . . . focus on governance issues and get mired in political struggles. . . . Charter schools need to stay focused on issues of curriculum, instruction and assessment."[24] Such an observation is one that a principal of any school should reflect upon to see if any action might be needed to refocus the energy of the school community.

The role of the principal of a charter school differs considerably from that of a principal of a traditional school. The principal of a charter school ordinarily operates autonomously in regard to personnel, budget, and even curriculum decisions. Often the charter school operates more days than the traditional 180- to 185-day calendar. Marketing the school is an important part of the charter school principal's role. Holding visitation days, conducting orientations, speaking to various groups about the mission of the school, preparing materials for distribution, and arranging media-visible activities are just part of the marketing of a charter school. Maintaining funding demands time and energy beyond the traditional school role.

Home Schooling

A quietly but quickly growing number of students are being taught at home. It is estimated that over one million students are being home

---

[23] Bruno V. Manno, Chester E. Finn Jr., and Gregg Vanourek, "Beyond the Schoolhouse Door: How Charter Schools Are Transforming U.S. Public Education," *Phi Delta Kappan* 81 (June 2000): 736.

[24] Gary K. Hart and Sue Burr, "The Story of California's Charter School Legislation," *Phi Delta Kappan* 78 (September 1996): 90.

schooled. As large as that number seems, " . . . it is only a shadow of what it will be 20 years from now."[25] Generally, parents home school their children for the first few years and then send them to private or public schools for at least the last six years. Home-schooled students have achieved well in some cases, and many have qualified for admission into fine colleges and universities.

Occasionally, a concern is raised about the socialization and social skills of home-schooled students. Home-schooled students tend to interact with persons of different age and maturity levels in the course of their school day or year, and as a result, they learn to get along with a variety of individuals, possibly to a greater extent than those in age-based classrooms. Home-schooled students are not limited to persons in their age group or interest group. Medlin points out that home-schooled students " . . . have good self esteem and are likely to display fewer behavior problems than do other children . . . and may be more socially mature and have better leadership skills."[26]

Home-schooled students have been requesting a variety of services from and in public schools, ranging from participation in one class (e. g., art, technology, chemistry) to participation on sports teams. The latter has caused some serious dilemmas for some schools in that to exclude the home-schooled student might exclude an excellent athlete. For example, there were at least two home-schooled students playing on National Collegiate Athletic Association Division 1 teams in 2001. On the other hand, do they really represent the high school if they are not enrolled full-time in the school?

Maintaining a focus on the welfare of the individual is important, but knowledge of state and local regulations is essential as well. It would be helpful to review district policies regarding placement, testing, partial participation, resulting budget implications, attendance, and other pertinent areas. Special considerations regarding the home-schooled student afford one more opportunity to engage the larger community and to reinforce bridges under construction to the community.[27]

What Can We Learn from Alternative Schools?

In summary, alternative schools have begun to institutionalize diversity and appear to be well-established components of certain school districts throughout the country. Their success has, in a sense, caused some of the pioneers in the movement to believe that their very acceptance has taken some of the spontaneity and spunk from the movement. Further, their

---

[25] Michael P. Farris and Scott A. Woodruff, "The Future of Home Schooling," *Peabody Journal of Education* 75 (2000): 254.
[26] Richard G. Medlin, "Home Schooling and the Question of Socialization," *Peabody Journal of Education* 75 (2000): 119.
[27] See the discussion on the virtual high school in Chapter 10.

success has caused a large number of school districts to use the alternative school as a way, though perhaps a questionable one, to handle special situations such as the following: (1) establishing special programs and schools for the least desirable students (dumping), (2) using alternative or magnet schools to meet the legal requirements for an adequate racial mix (desegregation), and (3) establishing alternative or magnet schools for the specially talented and gifted (skimming).[28]

In spite of this trend, it seems apparent that the philosophies and processes the alternative school represents could play a crucial role in improving the future structure of schools in the United States, for alternative schools have provided instances of impressive success. They have been particularly effective in improving student (1) attitudes, (2) productivity, (3) self-concept and self-esteem, (4) attendance, (5) behavior, and (6) academic success. Furthermore, they stimulate interest, increase the will to learn, and cause a decrease in the dropout rate.[29]

What has made these schools so generally successful? A review of their redeeming features should help the principal as an instructional leader in his or her school. (A goal might be to re-create the "goodness" of the following features in your own school.) For one thing, the alternative school has great flexibility and adaptability, offering students more diversified learning activities, such as independent study, community service, field trips, experiential and action learning, and intervisitation. It responds more explicitly to particular problems and to students' special needs. It has a small staff, and the student-teacher ratios tend to be very favorable—approximately eighteen students per teacher. The fact that both students and teachers choose to be in the school is a pervasive feature. Schools stress the importance of student-teacher interaction, more than any other single feature. Teachers are more than content specialists; they share freely in a great number of tasks and work with students in many ways. A great deal of control resides within the school, with the feeling that the principal and teachers make up a teaching team under informal governance arrangements. The role of the principal or director is more consistent with our idealized notion of an educational leader. The best schools report the highest autonomy levels, similar to the charter schools discussed earlier. The manageable smallness of the school increases its intimacy. Teachers seem to be the central key to school improvement. Their attitude toward each other is that of a group of friends and professional colleagues. The teachers are more likely to view students as members of the family and do not expect to give up on a student because he or she fails or resists assistance. The school lacks the central authority atmosphere—the more independent the school, the more

---

[28] Elizabeth Sendor, "The Residential Magnet School Attracts North Carolina's Best and Brightest," *American School Board Journal* (April 1984): 38–39.
[29] Mary Anne Raywid, "Synthesis of Research on Schools of Choice," *Educational Leadership* 41 (April 1984): 70–78.

often students share in a significant part of decisions. Students trust teachers and do not view them as wardens or disciplinarians. A major emphasis in alternative schools is on human relations and interaction. There is usually a multiage grade level of learning, with frequent peer teaching and peer tutoring. Last, teacher and student reflection about the school appears to be a continuing feature of life within alternative schools, which probably encourages effort to search for ways to improve.

Small Units within Large Schools

The concept of smaller "schools" within a large school began experimentally during the booming school enrollment period following World War II. As schools grew in size throughout the country because of the rapid growth in population and population shifts, there came an increasing concern and awareness that some of the intimacy, individual contacts, and personal interaction among students, teachers, and administrators was being lost. As a result, particularly in larger cities, a number of plans were advanced that divided the large school administratively, organizationally, and even instructionally into a number of smaller units.

The basic purpose of such plans was to establish more or less self-sufficient operating units within the larger whole that should give the individual pupils opportunities for full participation, individual attention, satisfactory interpersonal relationships, a sense of belonging, and an opportunity to participate in the full variety of learning activities that is characteristic of the small neighborhood school. Other names for organizations established for this purpose are the unit school plan, the little school plan, the house school plan, and clusters. McPartland and Jordan support smaller units because they " . . . can decrease anonymity, raise student achievement, and improve attendance and school climate."[30]

Typically, these operating units were established with three hundred to six hundred pupils. They were assigned their own administrators, counselors, and basic faculty and were housed in a specific wing or location of the building. Students assigned to the "little school" or "unit" took their basic courses together and worked and played together in all of their regular activities. Only where it was necessary to have special classes and unusual or advanced programs was the student scheduled on a schoolwide basis. At the same time, major facilities such as the library, auditorium, and gymnasium could be shared by several units.

Figure 9.1 shows one way to structure secondary schools into smaller units. Variations on this theme extend upward into university-type settings, where the smaller units are identified with living units, dormitories, or combinations of living units. In the other direction, mid-

---

[30] James M. McPartland and Will J. Jordan, "Restructuring for Reform: The Talent Development Model," *Principal Leadership* 1 (February 2001): 28.

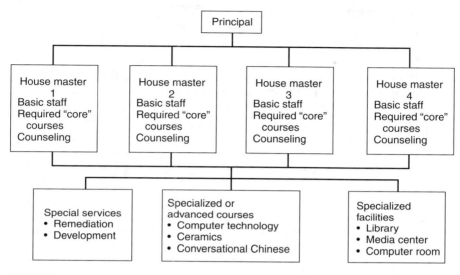

FIGURE 9.1
Illustration of a school-within-a-school organization

dle schools are often large enough to be concerned with creating workable, "family-like" units within a larger setting.

Smaller, teacher-led interdisciplinary units may alleviate the alienation ascribed to large, impersonal organizations. Decisions regarding the composition of the student body in the units are basic. Shall the units be just another way to track students, to sort them into achievement levels? Oxley sees the smaller units as an opportunity to expand student choice, but choice that could reduce opportunities for some students.[31] She advocates that the units be formed heterogeneously. As noted earlier regarding tracking, such a practice might reduce the possibility of select teachers being assigned to select units.

SCHEDULING

Time is the student's major investment, and in one sense, it is a trust fund wholly controlled by people other than the investor. Scheduling the expenditure of the student's time is an important responsibility, one that should focus on the student's learning rather than on factors that appear to be tied to bureaucratic convenience. Everyone is familiar with the traditional secondary schedules of classes of forty-five to fifty-five minutes,

---

[31] Diana Oxley, "Organizing Schools into Smaller Units: Alternatives to Homogeneous Grouping," *Phi Delta Kappan* 75 (March 1994): 522.

five days per week. There have been several changes in this approach in response to the demand to create better learning opportunities.

At the secondary level, the modular schedule was an attempt to develop flexibility in the teaching-learning pattern and to break the straitjacket of the forty- to sixty-minute class period, which is scheduled day after day, week after week, month after month throughout the school year. The flexible schedule was usually built on short modules of time, usually ten to fifteen minutes. Thus, each day or week, a schedule can be built so that a varying number of modules can be allocated to different subjects and pupil activities, depending on the learning needs of the pupils and the time needed for presentation and preparation of the subject.

The primary purpose of the flexible schedule was to individualize and personalize learning, freeing learners to concentrate on those areas of need and interest, freeing them from time cells of passive knowledge intake. As such, it became a tool to open up the teacher's day and the pupil's day, giving both an opportunity for personal relationships, which are essential to good education.

Though various forms of the flexible schedule operate in schools today, the complexity of maintaining it, the problems with educating the public, and other factors have eroded enthusiasm for it, and teachers and administrators continue to search for a better use of the time available.

Block Scheduling

The fifty-minute period five times per week seldom allows teachers or students to involve themselves in an in-depth project or to refine a product (e.g., electronic research reports, multimedia presentations, writing, art). The block schedule offers a chance to devote more time to in-depth work and follow through on jobs begun; a popular block of ninety minutes seems to address the need. Teachers can—indeed, they must—vary instructional techniques over this ninety-minute period. There are several variations on the block schedule. One of the most frequently used is the Block 8, which simply schedules four major periods per day, every other day. A student schedule might look like the following:

Red Day	**White Day**
French	English 2
Health/P.E.	Biology
History	Computer Lab/Study
Math/Science	Art

It is obvious that one does not decide in May to move from a traditional schedule to a block schedule the following August. Faculty planning, community support efforts, and student preparation will take lead time of two to three years. Bringing the community into a supportive position is very important once the school board has supported the idea. Teacher involvement early in the planning process can offset serious problems. A series of meetings to ascertain concerns, questions, and staff development needs may be a starting point. Staff development over one to two years may help generate many ideas to take advantage of the expanded time and to anticipate actions needed to use the resources that can become available with the expanded time. Simply retabbing the yellowed pages of notes into 50 percent longer units will not do.

Students will need to be prepared for the block schedule so they can plan for completing their work on an every-other-day basis, using technology for extended periods of time, and taking advantage of new ways of learning. A change to block scheduling should result from addressing the need for the change and gaining wide acceptance from parents and students. Often high school juniors and seniors do not like the idea, since their experience has been ten to eleven years of traditional schedules. One study notes that " . . . parents supported block scheduling only to the extent they believed it would increase academic achievement."[32] Transfer students may need special orientations if they have not experienced the block schedule. Electives and accreditation are important considerations if the school seeks to accommodate a wide range of opportunities.[33]

Parallel Block Scheduling

At the elementary level, parallel block scheduling has provided an opportunity to develop the synergy of team problem solving, more time on task, more individual attention, and decision making at the classroom level. Principals and teachers who have tried it caution that team members must want to be involved and must accept that they may find more children in their classes. Time will not be available for team meetings while the children are present. The rewards seem to outweigh the inconveniences in that achievement appears to improve, teachers gain respect for each other as professionals, and discipline problems are reduced.[34] Figure 9.2 illustrates a parallel block schedule for a team of four second-grade teachers and seventy-five students. The extension room time is when "pull-out" programs may have access to the students. The teachers

---

[32] John R. Slate and Craig H. Jones, "Student Perceptions on Block Scheduling," *High School Journal* 83 (February/March 2000): 63.

[33] Several books are available to help guide the principal in designing a block schedule. An example is Thomas L. Shortt and Yvonne V. Thayer, *The Complete Handbook of Block Scheduling* (Bloomington, IN, Technos Press, 1999).

[34] Robert L. Canady, "Parallel Block Scheduling: A Better Way to Organize a School," *Principal* (January 1990): 34–36.

	8:40–9:40	9:40–10:40	10:40–11:40	Lunch 11:40–12:10 P.M.	12:10–12:40	12:40–1:15	1:15–1:50	1:50–2:25	Organization and dismissal 2:25–2:30 P.M.
A 1,5	Directed Reading (DRG) 5	LA 1,5	DRG 1		Specials Prep	Math 1	Math 5	Science / Social Studies / Health	
B 3,4	DRG 3	DRG 4	LA 3,4		Math 4	Specials Prep	Math 3	Science / Social Studies / Health	
C 2,6	LA 2,6	DRG 2	DRG 6		Math 2	Math 6	Specials Prep	Science / Social Studies / Health	
Extension	1 / 4	3 / 6	5 / 2		3 / 6	5 / 2	1 / 4	Prep	

FIGURE 9.2
A sample parallel block schedule for second grade

are able to work with one group while the rest of the class (approximately half) is in extension activities. The principal has the task of working with special teachers to schedule pull-outs during extension time. The principal also needs to find space that facilitates the program. Although the program can be done in four regular-sized classrooms, it would be better if the extension room could accommodate a variety of enrichment centers as well as space for group activities.

A word of caution regarding the parallel block scheduling, in addition to other types of scheduling: It would be easy to separate the groups and then provide no review of individual progress, so that a student could become locked into a particular level for the year. Such an arrangement could be rationalized by pointing out that the students would have to learn to work with a new group in the extension room, which might create a potential for disruption. Obviously, the trade-offs will have to be weighed in terms of student progress.

REALITY-ORIENTED LEARNING

Structuring learning opportunities around real-life situations and problems is not a new idea, but for schools to make conscious efforts to do so may border on being newsworthy. Vocational programs traditionally have tried to deal with reality, though often with yesterday's problems and technologies. Current efforts in technical preparation programs attempt to incorporate the "academic" subjects into an application mainstream and hold promise that more able students will be attracted to them.

Teachers have noted success in creating "economic communities" at the elementary level. Students manage banks, stores, community councils, and so forth, which provides opportunities for a number of disciplines to be integrated into the operation of the classroom community. Outside consultants from the community help the students with structures, decisions, and accounting within the classroom. Such an approach easily leads to a variety of projects and learning opportunities that integrate the disciplines rather than compartmentalizing them into thirty minutes of this and twenty minutes of that.

Seldom in the real-life work world are tasks so compartmentalized. Seldom are problems presented to a corporation in such a way that one person must deal with them separate from coworkers. Most problems are solved cooperatively or by already organized teams. One of the few enterprises that isolates people in the problem-solving process is a school where teachers are "alone," and even students are isolated in dealing with the work presented to them.

As practiced by some schools, a student-centered approach to learning addresses the integration of subjects and, where appropriate, cooperative efforts at problem solving. The following are some basic assumptions about the approach:

1. Not all children learn best in the same way.
2. Not all children are interested in the same thing at the same time.
3. Learning is unbounded and requires interaction with ideas and materials.
4. Learning is continuous and connected to personal experience.
5. Learning is social—children teach each other.
6. Learning is transcendent.
7. Children learn better when they can influence their learning environments.
8. Children should have some say in developing the alternatives available to them.
9. Learning is a natural outcome of children's exploratory behavior.

Such an approach means that the learning environment provides an opportunity for these assumptions to be tested and developed. Any classroom can be conducted informally. Although the careful arrangement of physical space can be very helpful, even a wall-less classroom is not essential.

At its best, this approach to education is carefully structured to ensure student mastery of the fundamentals. The principal has a crucial role to play, not only in helping teachers and pupils to implement student-centered, reality-oriented learning but also in making certain that the implementation helps fulfill the school's educational goals.

THE BALANCED CALENDAR SCHOOL YEAR

The terms *year-round school* and *balanced calendar school year* are not interchangeable. The year-round school was being advocated in the late 1960s because, along with other benefits, it would allow greater utilization of educational facilities and equipment, thus reducing the need for new construction. Because of the leveling off and even decline in school enrollments, the pressure from this front has waned. As a result, a portion of the strength of the year-round school movement has been lost. On the other hand, the balanced calendar school year seems to be gaining interest.

The balanced calendar school year usually consists of the same number of school days for both teachers and students as in traditional school years, e.g., 180–185 days. The year-round school often had an expanded year of 200 days or more. The balanced calendar school year spreads the 180 days (or whatever the legal number of days would be) over the twelve month period with breaks between quarters.

Figure 9.3 shows one school's balanced calendar teachers' schedule. The first day of school is July 26 and the last day for the teachers is June 15. One week during each three-week break period (see days labeled B) was devoted to Extended Learning Opportunity Programs (ELOPs), which allowed students to do remedial work or engage in enrichment opportunities. Teachers participate on a volunteer basis and are paid extra for the ELOP.

Teacher contracts are the same as for other teachers in the district in terms of number of days required, and the same salary scale applies. In the example shown in Figure 9.3, the principal's contract is for 203 days. A study of the school found that the teachers took advantage of the three-week breaks to work out curricular improvements and develop a variety of instructional approaches.[35] The principal notes a change in the mobility of families from 34 percent to 18 percent since the new calendar was adopted. Given that the school's population is 55 percent Title I eligible, the reduction in mobility is noteworthy.

It is unfortunate that invariably the decision to do something instructionally good may be discarded because it is contrary to custom, it is difficult to accommodate within the existing structure, or the culture of the school opposes it. Universal acceptance of a year-round concept might be one of the ways of breaking up the inflexible school structure, which seems to be so resistant to improvements in schooling.

THE FOUR-DAY WEEK

Several schools have experimented with the four-day week. In some instances, weather considerations and energy use were major factors in the decision to move to such a schedule. Savings might be realized in maintenance and custodial personnel. Reasons similar to those supporting the block schedule could encourage the four-day week in that the students would be expected to be in school longer per day, which would allow for greater concentration of effort on the projects at hand. Transportation savings could also be realized, especially in districts covering large geographic areas.

Ⓢ U M M A R Y

A myriad of organizational plans are designed to break down the inflexible character of the school structure and improve learning. Tools to effect

---

[35] Delwyn L. Harnish and Najmuddin Shaik, *An Evaluation of Southern View Elementary School's Year-Round Program* (1999): 35.

July

Sun	Mon	Tue	Wed	Thu	Fri	Sat
						1
2	NS	NS	NS	NS	NS	8
9	NS	NS	NS	NS	NS	15
16	NS	NS	NS	NS	NS	22
23	AT	AT	FD	27	28	29
30	31					

August

Sun	Mon	Tue	Wed	Thu	Fri	Sat
	1	2	3	4	5	
6	7	8	9	10	11	12
13	14	15	16	17	18	19
20	21	22	23	24	25	26
27	28	29	30	31		

September

Sun	Mon	Tue	Wed	Thu	Fri	Sat
					1	2
3	X	5	6	7	8	9
10	11	12	13	14	15	16
17	18	19	20	FQ	PT	23
24	SI	B	B	B	B	30

October

Sun	Mon	Tue	Wed	Thu	Fri	Sat
1	B	B	B	B	B	7
8	B	B	B	B	B	14
15	16	17	18	19	20	21
22	23	24	25	26	27	28
29	30	1/2 WS				

November

Sun	Mon	Tue	Wed	Thu	Fri	Sat
			1	2	3	4
5	6	7	8	9	X	11
12	13	14	15	16	17	18
19	20	21	22	X	X	25
26	27	28	29	30		

December

Sun	Mon	Tue	Wed	Thu	Fri	Sat
					1	2
3	4	5	6	7	8	9
10	11	12	13	14	MY	16
17	18	19	SQ	B	B	23
24	B	B	B	B	B	30
31						

January

Sun	Mon	Tue	Wed	Thu	Fri	Sat
	B	B	B	B	B	6
7	8	9	10	11	12	13
14	X	16	17	18	19	20
21	22	23	24	25	26	27
28	29	30	31			

February

Sun	Mon	Tue	Wed	Thu	Fri	Sat
				1	2	3
4	5	6	7	8	9	10
11	X	13	14	15	16	17
18	WS	20	21	22	23	24
25	26	27	28			

March

Sun	Mon	Tue	Wed	Thu	Fri	Sat
					1	2
						3
4	X	6	7	8	9	10
11	12	13	14	15	TQ	17
18	19	20	21	22	23	24
25	B	B	B	B	B	31

April

Sun	Mon	Tue	Wed	Thu	Fri	Sat
1	B	B	B	B	B	7
8	B	B	B	B	B	14
15	B	17	18	19	20	21
22	23	24	25	26	27	28
29	30					

May

Sun	Mon	Tue	Wed	Thu	Fri	Sat
		1	2	3	4	5
6	7	8	9	10	11	12
13	14	15	16	17	18	19
20	21	22	23	24	25	26
27	X	29	30	31		

June

Sun	Mon	Tue	Wed	Thu	Fri	Sat
					1	2
3	4	5	6	7	LD	9
10	E	E	E	E	E	16
17	NS	NS	NS	NS	NS	23
24	NS	NS	NS	NS	NS	30

NS = No school

WS or AT = Teacher workshops

FD = First day

B = Break

PT = Parent Teacher conferences

X = Holidays observed

FQ, SQ, TQ = End of quarters

LD = Last day

SI = Special workshop

MY = Midyear

E = Days reserved if needed as a result of emergencies, e.g., snow days.

FIGURE 9.3

A sample balanced calendar for one school year

234

such plans include modular scheduling, interage grouping, cooperative learning, and a host of others. The means for providing for individual interests and needs are not lacking. Alternatives are available to break away from the patterns reinforced by custom, tradition, and the demands of managerial simplicity. Focusing on individual human beings, each of whom has his or her own needs and potential contributions, forces us to seek structures that are flexible instead of rigid, that enhance learning rather than stifling it, that can change and thereby strengthen themselves rather than breaking under the stress of pressure from the outside.

Some of the options available to provide flexibility may be established only by action of the board of education and the superintendent of schools. Others may be planned and initiated by the faculty-administration team in an individual school. Still others may be forced on schools by political/economic forces mandating change. As principal, will you have enough leadership ability and creativity to structure a school so that teaching and learning are improved?

FOR FURTHER THOUGHT

1. Is developing alternatives for learners compatible with efficient organization? Why?
2. Debate: Ability grouping results in the development of undemocratic attitudes.
3. The focus of organization for instruction is on learners. What, if any, consideration of faculty and staff should enter into decisions regarding organization for instruction?
4. Are specialized high schools such as tech prep, fine arts, or college preparatory a threat to equality of educational opportunity?
5. Some critics of our schools charge that too many electives are offered and students are permitted to take too many courses without gaining any depth of knowledge. What is your reaction to this charge, especially as it relates to the emphasis on standards and testing?
6. What does research show about relative achievement in long or short periods? Is this adequate information on which to base a decision regarding block scheduling or a four-day week for a school?
7. What schools in your area have balanced calendar school years? What have been the results regarding student achievement, behavioral changes, or community reactions?
8. Alternative schools have been particularly successful because a special team spirit seems to be engendered as students, teachers, and administrators work together to make their school work. Review some of the special characteristics of the alternative school, as presented in the early portion of this chapter. Could these characteristics

be made a part of a regular school? Could a principal do this on his or her own?

9. What are the provisions for student enrollment and funding in charter schools in your state? How have charter schools affected the rest of public education in your area?

10. How would you organize a school to improve learning? Be specific about some of the special features you would include.

11. What are the provisions for home-schooled students in your state? What accommodations does your school make for them? Do these accommodations appear to be made for the greatest benefit of the students involved, or partly or mostly to protect the school's interests?

ⓢELECTED READINGS

Boyer, Ernest. *High School: A Report on Secondary Education in America.* Princeton, NJ: Carnegie Foundation for Advancement of Teaching, 1983.

Buechler, Mark. *Charter Schools: Legislation and Results after Four Years.* Bloomington: Indiana Education Policy Center, 1996.

Eisner, Elliot W. *Cognition and Curriculum: A Basis for Deciding What to Teach.* New York: Longman, 1983.

Manno, Bruno V., Chester E. Finn Jr., and Gregg Vanourek. "Beyond the Schoolhouse Door: How Charter Schools Are Transforming U.S. Public Education." *Phi Delta Kappan* 81 (June 2000): 736–744.

Medlin, Richard G. "Home Schooling and the Question of Socialization." *Peabody Journal of Education* 75 (2000): 107–123.

Oakes, Jeannie. "Reflections on Detracking Schools." *Turning Points* 2 (March 1992): 1.

Premack, Eric. "Charter Schools: A Status Report." *School Business Affairs* 62 (December 1996): 10–15.

Restructuring for the Individual Learner

ducators have a multitude of ways to individualize the teaching-learning process. Easier access to powerful and fast hardware and software, satellite or direct-line interactive television for distance learning, the Web, multimedia presentation software, and other on-line communication devices provide excellent opportunities for personalizing learning. New developments in scheduling time and teacher teams such as those noted in Chapter 9 can also enhance education. Continuous improvement management models, such as total quality management (TQM), emphasize teaming. Each person and team becomes a quality control center. An atmosphere of possibilities and opportunities is created in which individuals have a say, can exercise control, and feel as if they can make a difference. Collaboration with external resources has similarly stimulated renewal in schools.

The idea of one teacher, one classroom with four walls, and twenty to thirty students still pervades the structure and practice of the school and the general thinking of the public. If changes or reforms do not in some way conform to this traditional pattern, they become a challenge to implement.

The principal's major personnel responsibility is to help develop a staff and a teaching-learning environment that can most effectively and efficiently help the student learn how to become a productive, self-sufficient individual. This simple statement means different approaches to teaching, and learning will become an accepted outcome of informed practice as teachers and learners begin to focus on the business of learning as a continually dynamic process of involvement of everyone within the process.

A STAFFING CONCEPT

Student learning is the major reason schools exist. To carry out this educational task requires people (the school staff) who utilize time (the school day and its daily schedule), space (the school building, with its classrooms and laboratories, and the extended community), programs and materials (books, computer software, media, and other work and learning materials), information (data, organized and analyzed to clarify decisions), and money.

In the early days, the U.S. schooling process became systematized by having a school with classrooms and a teacher in each classroom who was given the responsibility of teaching children certain quantities of subject matter during a regularly scheduled time period. The great majority of American adults have been schooled according to this pattern, and it is their idea of good schooling, whether they enjoyed it or not, or were actually educated as a result. Teacher training institutions have reinforced this pattern, if not consciously, then by extending the rigid time/space compartmentalization in their own classes and professorial assignments. Also, the teaching profession itself has reinforced the idea by the stands taken during collective bargaining on the basis of a perceived good teacher-pupil ratio or a time/scheduling allocation. Thus, the education system in the United States was for years essentially static as far as the teacher-student organization was concerned. The teacher and the classroom, with twenty to thirty students, had become a self-reinforcing system, with the teacher's professional responsibilities and authority being built almost completely on this limited role. The majority of proposed staffing alternatives were often merely variations of the same theme, based on the assumption of a teacher with a set number of pupils.

The traditional teaching pattern typically dominated the thinking of those considering the question, Which type of education is best for the learner? The question really became, Which type of education is best for the learner based on the system with which we are familiar and, as a result, comfortable?

One can break away from this static, structured role by concentrating on the learner, his or her learning needs, and his or her optimum learning style. For the moment, one must forget teacher-pupil ratio and the teacher's role in front of a classroom and consider the teacher strictly as a professional resource who, working with other teachers, internal and community resource people, and auxiliary personnel, plans and uses time, space, and materials so that each student can learn at his or her optimum.

Conceptualizing the education process in this manner, one may then end up with the traditional teacher in the traditional classroom; however, this learning situation probably will be one of many alternative learning situations for the student. Contrary to many opinions, such an approach does not "downgrade" the teacher. Rather, it places him or her in a more respected professional role. It recognizes that learning is a function of the learner and that the teachers are the professionals who engineer and set the tone of the entire learning process by

- Contributing directly to institutional and classroom learning goals,
- Diagnosing the learning needs and style of each student with other professionals,[1]
- Cooperatively prescribing programs and various types of teaching-learning situations,
- Arranging for and implementing the prescriptions, and
- Evaluating the results.

Following this approach, the collective teachers' judgments are utilized in regard to the way each student learns best, and then personnel and material resources are appropriately deployed to meet the unique needs of the learner.

Most school systems of any size have all or most of the resources to carry out these five basic tasks; however, few have organized them into functioning operational units that continuously follow the student through the total pattern. At the same time, teachers themselves agree that an individually centered approach is an intelligent way of creating a productive and satisfying learning situation for the student, but operationally they appear to be afraid to move too far from the safety of their traditional environment—the classroom and the group. Parents and the community also feel comfortable with the traditional arrangements.

It appears that a different concept of the instructional staff of the school will need to be accepted before much that is significant can be done to improve the learning process. It will need to be a concept that focuses on instructional teams working together to create the best learning environment possible. On these teams, licensed teachers would be key persons, but there would also be technicians, aides, consultants, counselors, psychological examiners, administrative support persons, and so on. Whether they would team teach, with hierarchical titles and complicated differentiated salary schedules, is beside the point as far as instruction is concerned. The important point is that all possible learning resources would be focused on the learning efforts of the student, whether he or she is in the traditional classroom or in some other appropriate learning environment.

---

[1] Current pressures from politicians, and businesspeople to meet certain standards as measured by standardized tests may impede this function. See Chapter 12 for a more detailed discussion.

A number of systematic efforts to use the staff and structure the program so that more emphasis is focused on the individual learner rather than the classroom have reemerged. Many of these so-called movements are not so much new ideas as currently focal ones. They are often adjusted from plans tried many times through the years. (Note the Lancaster Plan, used in 1806, and the National Society for the Study of Education 1925 yearbook, entitled *Adapting the Schools to Individual Differences*.) There should be no limitation on thinking about ways to differentiate instruction. As Pettig points out, "To say there is a single, perfect pattern of differentiated instruction is a contradiction in terms."[2] This chapter will explore several of the often-recurring themes and some uses of newer technologies aimed at improving the learning of students.

PARAPROFESSIONALS AND INSTRUCTIONAL AIDES

The first major experiment with the use of teacher aides and paraprofessionals was initiated in a partnership project, partially financed by the Fund for the Advancement of Education, between the public schools of Bay City, Michigan, and Central Michigan University. This project captured the imagination of both educators and laypeople and led the way for hundreds of other teacher aide projects, which were funded by a great variety of sources, particularly by the federal government through the U.S. Office of Education. It was first hailed by educational leaders as a "panacea for all the ills and problems of education." However, the teachers' unions began to fear that it was an economy move that could undercut the teaching profession, and they dragged their heels before endorsing the program. The American Association of Colleges of Teacher Education implied that the employment of paraprofessionals was delayed because the profession itself spent too much time arguing over process and techniques rather than outcomes. The association identified the following opposing positions in the controversy:[3]

> *Position A:* The stature and security of the classroom teacher must not be threatened by variations of pay or establishing variations in teacher ranks. The ushering in of subprofessionals to invade teachers' roles or limit their career advancement looms as a menace to the organized interests of the teaching profession.
> *Position B:* It is wasteful to employ professional talent for the performance of so many semiprofessional and subprofessional duties. If dentists find technicians to be valuable aides and if plumbers can employ helpers to

---

[2] Kim L. Pettig, "On the Road to Differentiated Practice," *Educational Leadership* 58 (September 2000): 14.
[3] American Association of Colleges of Teacher Education, *Educational Personnel for Urban Schools: What Differentiated Staffing Can Do* (Washington, DC: Author, 1972), 3.

good advantage, why cannot teachers increase their level of professional productivity through the use of auxiliary personnel?

Although we are as concerned as anyone over economy moves that would undercut the teaching profession, we find it difficult to see how any gain can be made either professionally or educationally by a "holding the line" attitude. A teacher aide can perform many tasks for the teacher that are not strictly professional in nature. Evidence points to the fact that greater professionalism actually exists when the teacher has help from a variety of assistants. Of course, the professional teacher's duties must be carefully defined to differentiate what is best done by the teacher and what should be done by the aides, who play supportive roles by doing the things the professionals do not need to do.

The use of paraprofessionals has become a viable and integral part of education. They appear to be used throughout all areas of the United States. Teachers and principals both rate the use of teacher aides as valuable in improving instructional services. Within individual school districts, the use of teacher aides has generally been limited only because of budgetary constraints, not because of educational theory or practice or individual teacher opposition. The concept of inclusion has expanded the need for classroom aides.

Most discount stores are better staffed to realize the goals of the organization than are schools. As noted in Chapter 17, the school office could become more effective by using aides to cover routine tasks that do not require a high degree of professional judgment or skill. That is also true of the classroom. Aides can be used for technology assistance, small-group projects, materials procurement, special topics expertise, community liaison assistance, and a variety of other tasks for which the full-time professional staff of the school has little time or sometimes not the expertise.

Of course, the identification, orientation, training, and assimilation of auxiliary staff into the school system comprise a long-term process requiring careful faculty-staff planning, but they are more worthy of the teacher's time than some of the routines presently being performed.

STAFFING PATTERNS

The one teacher, one class pattern of staffing has been the predominant staffing pattern for centuries and will continue to be for the foreseeable future. Variations have been tried and continue to be developed to meet the needs of students better, particularly given the explosion of information and access to that information.

Differentiated Staffing

Differentiated staffing was implemented seriously in the 1960s and 1970s; however, most of the programs have disappeared as originally started. In the schools that did have formalized differentiated staffing plans, one can still see vestiges that are improvements over the traditional pattern: (1) deploying staff more judiciously, (2) utilizing input from the teachers to make decisions about curriculum and support services, (3) making good use of paraprofessionals and community resource people, (4) employing teachers in leadership roles, and (5) incorporating more teaming of faculty.

Teaching Teams

A number of variations can occur in which two or more teachers combine efforts to teach students. Teams may form across discipline lines. In one middle school setting, science, social studies, and English teachers formed a team. The instructors became aware of each other's intents and decided to complement each other's objectives by focusing on a science assignment and working with students in English and social studies to help with language skills on the science project. It was easy to switch later to a history project and so on.

Teams may find a number of instructional patterns to enhance learning. Ordinarily, a single pattern for team teaching for all teams will not optimize the human or material resources. Individual teacher strengths need to be enhanced. Also, the process emphasizing continuous improvement will play out differently for one team than for another.

A variety of patterns can be implemented in which teachers see students for enrichment and additional help, see large groups and then small groups, specialize in a few disciplines and then all reinforce the concepts, or simply plan together and then evaluate the results. The results for students and the developmental outcomes for teachers and other team members can be positive. The principal will find that flexibility in time, space, materials, and technology is essential to success. The idea that a whole school should be teaming the same way may defeat the intended outcomes. Flexible envelopes of time and space for each team are important.

The principal can be helpful by providing leadership in the teams' efforts to evaluate the process and results. A variety of quantitative and qualitative techniques may yield sufficient information to assist the teams' decisions. The team members can become their own quality control managers as they develop skill in generating relevant statistics about what is occurring as a result of their efforts.

Team Decision Making

If we have learned anything from Deming's work with Japanese companies,[4] it is that team efforts often reap greater long-term benefits in productivity than would a group of individuals working independently. Site-based decision making forms a team of teacher decision makers at the building level. Team decisions can be tailored to the learning needs of the students, with the idea that these decisions will produce better results than those handed down from administrators far removed from the situation. Opportunities exist to refine further the decision making at the closest operational level by creating teams or allowing them to form within grade levels, departments, or disciplines or across discipline lines.

The following are implications for the principal regarding teaming and team decision making:

- The principal must be committed to supporting the team as it seeks solutions to problems.
- Team opportunities may require quite some time before members form a true working group; thus, forming teams by administrative fiat or convenience may be counterproductive.
- Communication needs to be open and threatfree. The idea is that a group of people are seeking to optimize resources and methods to enhance student learning. Blame is not the focus—solutions are.
- Support should be provided so that team members can tap into the experiences of others who have tried similar solutions or even ideas totally new to the team. A number of techniques ranging from teleconferencing to visits may be helpful.
- The team members should expect that there will be continuous refinement or even new directions as the proposed solutions are implemented. A one-time decision providing an etched-in-stone solution will result in simply substituting one rigidity for another.
- The principal will need to be patient as teams mature in decision making.
- The principal will need to be prepared to accept the risk of imperfect results.

The Quality Circle Approach

The quality circle is a formal decision-making process used in business and industry and in some schools to identify problems, determine possible solutions, and formulate recommendations to the administrators. The

---

[4] W. Edwards Deming has been credited with the increase in production and quality of Japanese industry following World War II. His fourteen points associated with total quality management (TQM) have recently been scrutinized regarding their applicability to education. The reader may wish to read the November 1992 issue of *Educational Leadership*, which has TQM as its theme.

principal's role is similar to that encompassed by the seven points just noted. It is important that central administration be supportive of the process over time; otherwise, the development of recommendations could deteriorate into a guessing game of "What will they accept?"

The quality circle is usually cross-disciplinary, sometimes including support staff, and it should have a leader trained in the process. It is not a *Robert's Rules of Order* type of meeting but rather a formal process in which everyone has input and an opportunity to seek and give clarification and move on toward solutions.

ENHANCING PERSONALIZED LEARNING

Individualized instruction has been a particularly successful teaching process throughout the centuries. Socrates, Comenius, Pestalozzi, Montessori, Dewey, and many other teacher-philosophers have advocated it. An excellent teacher on one end of a log and the student on the other end is often cited as the best example of schooling.

A number of individualized learning systems have been developed. A few well-known ones are (1) the Westinghouse Learning Corporation's Planning for Learning in Accordance with Needs (PLAN); (2) Individually Prescribed Instruction (IPI) and Adaptive Environments for Learning (AEL), developed by the Learning Research and Development Center of the University of Pittsburgh; (3) the Durrell Pupil-Team Learning Concept, developed by Durrell; (4) Bloom's Mastery Learning Plan; and (5) the Individually Guided Education (IGE) program, developed by Herbert Klausmeier. The last was widely used, particularly in the Wisconsin area, and adapted into different plans by J. Lloyd Trump and the Kettering Foundation. Yet nearly all of these are systems of instruction. As noted by Cresswell and Rasmussen, "[T]raditionally, schools have been places of teaching rather than places of learning."[5] Obviously, this view needs to be changed to schools as places for learning for all involved, but particularly the students.

MASTERY LEARNING

Bloom devised a form of individualized learning (generally known as Bloom's Mastery Learning Plan) based on mastery learning.[6] Schools intending to use Bloom's approach to mastery learning require a great

---

[5] Robert A. Cresswell and Patty Rasmussen, "Developing a Structure for Personalizing the High School," *NASSP Bulletin* 80 (December 1996): 27.
[6] Benjamin S. Bloom, *Human Characteristics and School Learning* (New York: McGraw-Hill, 1976).

deal of flexibility, planning time, and expertise. In regard to flexibility, they need the following specific items:

- *Flexibility of time*—Bloom's theory is that any normal person can learn almost anything, given the right amount of time.
- *Flexibility in grouping*—Students may do individualized study or may be grouped according to need and purpose. Grouping can change with each subject and unit.
- *Flexibility in space*—A variety of spaces are needed to accommodate large-group, small-group, and individual instruction.
- *Flexibility in equipment and materials*—A wide variety of teaching resources are needed, ranging from televisions and computers to simple print material, to accomplish the learning tasks.
- *Flexibility in staffing*—The staff should represent a variety of skills in both subject matter and teaching styles. Volunteers, paraprofessionals, and even students might handle certain jobs, but other jobs might need highly trained specialists.

Mastery learning challenges the basic tenets of the traditional school organization and structure, such as the use of time and space, and teacher-pupil roles in the classroom. It has stimulated the special programming of units of learning on television, with computers, and in print. A number of schools have used basic elements of Bloom's Mastery Learning Plan to raise the level of achievement of their schools.[7] One administrator was given the Leadership for Learning Award by the American Association of School Administrators when he reformed the schools in his entire school district in conformance with Bloom's Mastery Learning Plan.[8]

Mastery learning research has been questioned by those who point out that we have no long-term results regarding the retention of facts learned in the short term.

TECHNOLOGY, CYBERSPACE, AND STRUCTURE

The current population of students has been referred to as the *netgeneration*. Coupled with the ever-expanding *infosphere,* as Berenfield labels the growing interdependence and accessibility of information,[9] schools need to become enrichment and access centers to learners. Layton observes

---

[7] Stephen E. Rubin and William G. Spady, "Achieving Excellence through Outcome-Based Instructional Delivery," *Educational Leadership* 41 (May 1984): 37–45. This is the story of Center School in New Canaan, Connecticut, which has raised achievement by grouping students according to skills they are ready to learn and by teaching for mastery.
[8] Jonathan W. Lathey, "Towards Theory-Based School Leadership," *School Administrator* 41 (April 1984): 24–26.
[9] Boris Berenfield, "Linking Students to the Infosphere," *T.H.E. Journal* 24 (April 1996): 77.

that "digital children are more independent, more intellectually open, more tolerant, and more adventurous than most 20th century children."[10] If this is the case, then are digital children more vulnerable? Do the schools accrue some responsibility to create safeguards? In so doing, is there a risk of guarding to the point of diminishing the very characteristics needed for students to explore beyond the present?

No subject area is missing from the electronically accessed, ever-expanding storehouse of information. For instance, if one hears a ten- to twenty-second report on a national newscast and wishes to know more about it, one can access the network's Web site for more details. Rich deposits of historical data are available on-line as well as in each school's media center. (Do not throw out those old tapes, records, and movies.) Students can learn in the virtual mode and via telesharing as easily as with what were known as traditional materials (e.g., texts, references, radio, TV). A stack of references on CDs accessible from all classrooms can be the beginning of students doing research and preparing multimedia reports using the virtual library.

Given the rich infosphere surrounding all of us, the learning potential is nearly limitless. Obviously, funding, space, and expertise are practical limitations faced by any school, but prioritization of resources can help expand access for students and teachers. Courseware, computers, and access to other learners worldwide are not incompatible with current school structures of staffing or time. As access and learner sophistication increase, some of the structures may need to be reexamined so that adjustments can be made. An example might be the time changes mentioned in the previous chapter.

Reil and Fulton suggest that technology can be used by the larger community to educate the next generation. They point out possibilities such as on-line mentoring, science investigations, electronic field trips, interactions with students across the globe as learning circles, and even cyberfair exhibits.[11] While these possibilities of global classrooms are exciting, there can be a goal displacement problem inherent in merely accessing and gathering data. Bushweller questions " . . . what may be lost to the multi-tasking individual who substitutes gathering more information for synthesizing, reflecting and focusing. . . ."[12] Leadership and professional development implications are obvious. Reflection on the purposes and the results of technology use is essential.

---

[10] Thomas G. Layton, "Why Tomorrow's Schools Must Learn to Let Go of the Past," *Electronic School* (September 2000): 23.
[11] Margaret Reil and Kathleen Fulton, "The Role of Technology in Supporting Learning Communities," *Phi Delta Kappan 82* (March 2001): 519–523.
[12] Keven Bushweller, "Lessons from the Analog World," *Electronic School* (September 2000): 25.

Multimedia and Learning

Today's students are accustomed to sound bites, remote control choices, and quick input regarding their interests. Individual or group projects, sometimes linked with students in another grade or school in Europe or Asia, can bring the excitement of quick access to multimedia information, and preparing the presentation in multimedia format with a potentially wide audience can be a stimulating, real-life experience. Agnew et al. remind planners that "[t]he essence of multimedia, however, is interactivity rather than just multiple media."[13] The students are constructing their own knowledge and creating presentations for multiple audiences. The writing skills involved are not seen as "how many pages for the term paper" but rather as a functional way to communicate to real audiences. Students with disabilities have an opportunity to create and to learn via a medium that may open avenues of contribution heretofore unavailable to them.

Teachers and Technology

Teacher education programs incorporate technology into preservice and often graduate programs. Still, many teachers may need help in reaching a comfort level with technology, the Internet, or multimedia. Thompson et al. suggest the following for teachers who are helping students access and use the available technologies for learning:

- Provide professional development in a nonthreatening environment where even "dumb" questions can be asked safely.
- Provide sufficient on-computer time to gain proficiency.
- Provide year-round assistance.[14]

Schools need to protect their investments in hardware, software, and maintenance. They sell the taxpayers and the students short if they do not prepare the teachers to use this technology to full advantage.

The Virtual High School

Several states are investing in what are called virtual high schools. These "schools" provide courses on-line to students who may need additional work to finish high school, who may wish to take courses their school is unable to offer, or who wish to explore advanced placement courses.

---

[13] Palmer W. Agnew, Anne S. Kellerman, and Jeanine M. Meyer, *Multimedia in the Classroom* (Boston: Allyn & Bacon, 1996), 8.

[14] William A. Thompson, James P. Denk, Richard A. Giffin, and Nancy P. Moreno, "Maximize Your Investment in Technology with Professional Development and Support for Teachers," *School Business Affairs* 66 (February 2000): 16.

Concerns have been raised that the virtual high school may further widen the digital divide. Approximately 58 percent of U.S. households had a computer in 2000.[15] Unless support is provided to greatly increase this percentage, many students have access only in the school, at a friend's house, in the public library, or at an Internet kiosk in a large shopping mall.

The virtual high school could provide home schoolers an enriched curriculum for preparation to enter a public school or go on to higher education. The school leader can seize the opportunities available to further options for the individual learner.

Practicalities and Policies

Using technology may require budget shifts and often additional resources, such as more personnel, professional development, and space. Cooley notes that in most instances additional personnel will be needed to fully utilize available technology.[16] The creative principal and staff may find a number of ways to augment personnel via collaboration with community resources, universities, local media personnel, and so on. Internal assignment shifts may also provide the support for an innovation environment to flourish.

Parents, community members, and staff may have concerns about students surfing in the infosphere and encountering materials ranging from excellent, to questionable, to simply bad. The principal should help develop policies that ensure proper use and allay such concerns. Software is available to assist in blocking access to objectionable material, but its use should be just part of the policy picture. Sanchez[17] lists the following areas that access policy statements should deal with:

Contacts with objectionable or questionable materials or persons

Objectionable behavior or destructive behavior

Violation of access and privacy rights

Without a set of policy guidelines, the school can be vulnerable to attacks from concerned citizens and parents at either end of the religious or political spectrum.

---

[15] U.S. Department of Education, "Table 45-1 Percentage of Students in Grades 1–12 Who Had Potential Access to a Computer," *The Condition of Education 2000*, Washington, DC: National Center for Educational Statistics, USDE, 161.

[16] Van E. Cooley, "Technology: Building Success through Teacher Empowerment," *Educational Horizons* 75 (Winter 1997): 77.

[17] Robert Sanchez, "Students on the Internet: Can You Ensure Appropriate Access?" *School Administrator* 53 (April 1996): 18–22.

Technology and Staffing

The school that sees itself as a learning and contributing station within a larger context of data and information will find a number of ways to provide learning opportunities to students. The teacher, technical assistant, or tutor becomes a resource person to the learner as the student interacts with the technological tools to gain, synthesize, or present information. Task differentiation is possible. Telecollaboration across states or oceans is possible, too, as is within-school networking. The teacher's role may shift from assigning to managing inquiry. Linkages with community partners may yield not only reality-based learning but also stronger support from the community. Indeed, the idea of differentiated staffing may be passé in that the exception to the rule may become the traditional classroom using lecture, chalk, and an overhead projector as the predominant technologies. Individualized or small-group inquiry may become the rule rather than the exception. Integrated or thematic projects will require staffing patterns that facilitate communication among teachers as well as electronic communications. The principal will need to seek information-based, computer-literate, hypermedia-oriented staff as opportunities to add or replace teachers arise.

One wonders what would happen if we were able to forget the existing culture, traditional structure, and organization of our present school system. What type of educational system and programs would we devise today if we made the best use of what we really know about learning and technology through such approaches as matching teaching to learning styles, interactive television, and computer communications? We expect our schools would be quite different, limited only by the creativity and imagination of all learners, adults and students.[18]

SERVICE LEARNING

Positively and visibly linking the school to the community is a win-win situation, and when students feel they are involved in reality and making individual contributions, the results can be exciting. Couple the foregoing with quality analyses and reflection on what is occurring as the students participate in carefully planned service learning, and a stimulating learning environment will expand within and outside the school. Service learning is a planned, coordinated program of student involvement in experiences that meet real needs, and through such experiences, students may gain skills, insights, and a sense of their responsibilities toward others.

---

[18] The reader can find additional information in M. D. Roblyer and Jack Edwards, *Integrating Educational Technology into Teaching*, 2nd ed. (Upper Saddle River, NJ: Merrill/Prentice Hall, 2000).

Service learning is not a new idea.[19] Nor is it pervasive throughout middle and high schools. Yet it is a topic of serious consideration as schools contemplate curricular reform and the need to enrich the concept of community. Students often feel disengaged from the "real world" in school settings, but active involvement in seeking real answers to real problems and/or helping fellow students or adults by sharing insights and knowldge may help them see themselves as citizens today, not waiting for some time in the future.[20]

The implications for the principal are obvious. Service learning in visible contexts in the community can be viewed as controversial (e.g., exploitation of students, simply another charity, not related to passing nationally normed tests, etc.) and disconnected from traditional academic subjects. Developing commitments and understandings among teachers, school officials, and community leaders is critical to a successful program. Service learning may hold the potential for true reform and even stronger communities. Several teachers, students, and communities have seen positive results. The idea provides a means for students to be contributing citizens while at the same time reflecting on the society of which they are a part. Could this approach be the nub of really creating a new social order, a caring group of young citizens, a transforming experience for a school?[21]

SCHOOL TO WORK: WORK-BASED LEARNING

Opportunities for in-school learning in the world of work have existed for many decades. With the School to Work Act of 1994, greater emphasis has been placed on preparing youth to enter the work world and on providing school and work experiences to assist in the transition. Hamilton and Hamilton define work-based learning as that occurring in locations in which the primary activity is producing goods and services.[22] Though not truly work based, many related exploratory experiences can occur in school, ranging from electronic field trips to simulated job tasks.

The school-to-work or school-to-career movement is not without its opponents. Questions or objections range from beliefs that the programs

[19] For a brief history and review of research on the effectiveness of service learning, see Richard J. Draft, "Service Learning: An Introduction to Its Theory, Practice and Effects," *Education and Urban Society* 28 (February 1996): 131–159.
[20] For a review of the service learning movement and current successful programs, see James C. Kielsmeier, "A Time to Serve, A Time to Learn," *Phi Delta Kappan* 81 (May 2000): 652–657.
[21] The reader may wish to visit www.UMN.edu/~serve to access research on service learning and even program evaluation forms. Other sites are www.learningInDeed.org and www.cng.gov.
[22] Stephen F. Hamilton and Mary Agnes Hamilton, "When Is Learning Work-Based?" *Phi Delta Kappan* 78 (May 1997): 678.

interfere with teaching required material, to fears that vocational teachers' jobs will be threatened. However, some view the movement as a real opportunity to revitalize secondary instruction and curriculum as well as motivate students otherwise not motivated in the traditional school.[23]

Combining the school and the work/career sector so that students have the opportunity to ground learning in reality without being limited academically or exploited in the workplace will require thoughtful leadership. School-to-work has the risk of becoming another tracking system. Another concern is when to begin such a program. Is the sophomore year too late? Learning, work habits, and responsibility are formed early. If the students (and parents) view school as not being "real world" and the "real world" is somewhat of a mystery to the students, the reasons for doing diligent work, showing up on time, and finishing the job well may not be relevant. Hopefully, linking learning to reality can be an area in which the school leads rather than having programs imposed from the state or provided by the business sector.

THE FULL-SERVICE SCHOOL

A growing idea is collaboration between a number of community agencies and the school to deliver services to students and families in the school setting or closely related to the school. This idea led to the full-service school. "Full service schools attempt to integrate programs such as health care, mental health services, parent education, or after school care into the schoolwide change process."[24] The concept has been implemented to some degree in elementary, middle, and high schools. The planning process is extremely important to avoid unnecessary conflict and potential alienation of groups that may assure that the service and facilities at best are underutilized. As noted earlier in Chapter 3, collaboration projects can raise many issues such as religious objections, confidentiality while sharing information,[25] and fears of coming to a school for assistance.

The principal has the opportunity to expand possibilities for students but at the same time must share authority with the planning groups and other agency directors and boards and must obtain increased input from a variety of sources. Such a situation may be viewed as an

---

[23] The reader may wish to review Barbara Gomez, "Service Learning and School-to-Work Strategies," *Education and Urban Society* 28 (February 1996): 160–166; and Susan Goldberger and Richard Kazis, "Revitalizing High Schools," *Phi Delta Kappan* 77 (April 1996): 547–554.

[24] Laura S. Abrams and Jewelle Taylor Gibbs, "Planning for School Change: School-Community Collaboration in a Full-Service Elementary School," *Urban Education* 35 (March 2000): 80.

[25] Melissa Jonson-Reid, "Understanding Confidentiality in School-Based Interagency Projects," *Social Work in Education* 22 (January 2000): 33–44.

erosion of power but actually can be an expansion of the principal's sphere of influence.

LEARNING AND TEACHING STYLES

In considering staffing to improve learning, one cannot disregard the growing amount of research on learning and teaching styles. Learning style diagnosis in particular has been credited as being the foundation of a truly modern approach to education, providing educators with a powerful tool to motivate students.

The administrator who reviews the research in the field of learning styles might contemplate with growing trepidation the difficulties in trying to match learning and teaching styles. With eighty or more different models of teaching styles and as many or more identified learning styles, the task could indeed be mind-boggling. In considering this provocative but potentially valuable field, probably the best advice is to maintain a sense of practicality, combined with a spirit of inquiry and imagination.[26]

The situation is not really as complicated as one might fear. The literature has already shown that individuals do not need to be locked into either one type of learning style or one type of teaching style. Assessing learning styles provides today's principal and teacher with new directions to take toward developing a more personalized form of instruction. The most versatile teacher is the one who can develop a varied repertoire of teaching styles; thus, such a teacher has at hand many applications that can offer students multiple learning patterns. At the same time, students can be encouraged to become curious and learn more about how they learn best. After becoming better informed about their own particular learning styles, they can experiment with different learning situations and perhaps put learning on an objective plane; this approach might counteract some of the issues of low self-image that haunt the slow learner today.

S UM M A R Y

Research cites the following as characteristics of effective schools: successful instruction; positive leadership; an orderly, safe learning environment; clear goals; expectations for high student achievement; and a well-designed evaluation process. Basic to all of this, however, is the faculty team, which is responsible for "on-line" implementation and which creates the climate necessary for student improvement.

---

[26] See Howard Gardner, "Reflections on Multiple Intelligences, Myths and Messages," *Phi Delta Kappan* 77 (November 1995): 200–209.

Teamwork is a major ingredient in any attempt at instructional improvement. We know we cannot win without teamwork in football or basketball, but we seldom think about it with teachers in a school. The principle is the same! The principal has the responsibility of developing a staff that thinks and acts like a team—a team that looks at every student in the school and thinks, "It isn't just that student in my class who is important; it is the welfare of that student in our total school, with all the faculty. And beyond that, the student's welfare in his or her total learning life. That student is our total faculty team's responsibility. What can we do together to make his or her total schooling more productive?"

Newer, successful configurations expand the team concept beyond the school's faculty and staff to include professionals providing services via collaborative efforts. No longer can the school try to be an island; rather, it is a dynamic partner in the larger community.

It is so easy for deadly monotony to settle in on students, which often happens when school life becomes compartmentalized, when each schoolroom is a teacher's little secluded world, and when students come to be acted upon by the teacher in his or her own particular way. A principal's greatest task in staffing is that of selecting teachers who are intellectually flexible and who will make good team members. Then the principal must structure the school operation so that the faculty will develop and maintain the collaborative team concept and will understand that schoolrooms are not separate compartments but rather parts of a unified whole that provides educational opportunities for all.

FOR FURTHER THOUGHT

1. Do you agree that the principal should retain veto power over teachers' decisions as to the way they should teach? Discuss.
2. How would you expect the duties of the principal of a small high school to differ from those of the principal of a large high school in regard to developing a positive teaching-learning environment?
3. How might your school utilize the offerings in a virtual high school?
4. What "safeguards" can the principal set up to avoid having attention to detail become his or her main task, especially when successfully caring for detail can enhance his or her credibility?
5. What central office expertise would be helpful in maintaining currency in developing a technologically competent school?
6. What is your vision of the future of education as far as technology is concerned? Do you think the organization and structure of schools hamper its development as a teaching-learning tool? Discuss.
7. Can you anticipate what serious concerns teachers and parents in your community would have about implementing a service learning

program? Outline how you would respond to a group of concerned conservative citizens.

8. Are typical teacher education programs stimulating or hindering more creative approaches to teaching and learning in our schools? Discuss.

9. We have conducted follow-up research on various innovative and experimental school programs during the revisions of this book. A high rate of attrition has occurred in these programs nationally. An overwhelming number of programs, were begun with a great enthusiasm and were generally successful have disappeared, and the schools are now operating essentially as they did before the programs were started. Why? Do you have some ideas about this situation? Can you see any relationship between the innovation's lack of longevity and the culture of the organization? The answer would make a great research study!

ⓈELECTED READINGS

Abrams, Laura S., and Jewelle Taylor Gibbs. "Planning for School Change: School-Community Collaboration in a Full-Service Elementary School." *Urban Education* 35 (March 2000): 79–103.

Berenfield, Boris. "Linking Students to the Infosphere." *T.H.E. Journal* 24 (April 1996): 77.

Brown, Daniel. *Decentralization.* Newbury Park, CA: Corwin, 1991.

Cooley, Van E. "Technology: Building Success through Teacher Empowerment." *Educational Horizons* 75 (Winter 1997): 77.

Kessler, Robert. "Shared Decision Making Works." *Educational Leadership* 50 (September 1992): 36–38.

Kielsmeier, James C. "A Time to Serve, A Time to Learn." *Phi Delta Kappan* 81 (May 2000): 652–657.

Reil, Margaret, and Kathleen Fulton. "The Role of Technology in Supporting Learning Communities." *Phi Delta Kappan* 82 (March 2001): 519–523.

Schine, Joan, ed. *Service Learning.* Chicago: National Society for the Study of Education, 1997.

Provision for Special Needs Students

*I*ndividuals who differ from what is perceived as "normal" in our society commonly encounter a number of hurtful questions. Why am I different? Why did this happen? What are the causes? What is my value to society? Could this "difference" have been prevented? These individuals often experience alienation. This alienation takes different forms, such as being segregated, ignored, rejected, or treated in special ways that emphasize the differences. Among schoolchildren, rejection has been associated with such diverse factors as intelligence, achievement, skill, personality characteristics, physical appearance and disabilities, language proficiency, socioeconomic level, and race.

Another reaction to children who are different is to pigeonhole them by applying labels. Such terms as *learning disabled, mildly/moderately handicapped, multiply handicapped, exceptional, emotionally handicapped,* and *special needs* have been used. *Special needs* refers to those children who have physical, social, psychological, or environmental characteristics that impact student instruction or programming. Programs purportedly designed for the majority of children do not afford students with special needs opportunities for optimum adjustment and progress; therefore, specifically targeted instruction may be required.

Society, through its agency, the school, identifies additional special needs. The actions and reactions of persons in the school constitute judgments as to the social value of certain characteristics of individuals within the school. Such judgments can, and too often do, create and maintain handicaps for these individuals. Most schools place such a high value on academic achievement that a child with the slightest limitation

---

Mark Smith, Ed.D., Indiana Wesleyan University, contributed to the revision of this chapter.

in this area is quick to be noticed and devalued. From a different per-spective, imagine students placing a high value on a particular style of clothes. A child whose parents cannot afford such clothes would be more noticeable and more apt to be handicapped. Although this is not the accepted norm when one thinks of handicap, socioeconomic variables are influencers in the process of deciding if one is handicapped.

Two terms, *disability* and *handicap,* frequently are used interchange-ably. It is almost assumed that they are inseparable, that a disability can-not exist without a resulting handicap. Yet each one of us is disabled, probably in several ways, but since our disability is not viewed as impor-tant and since we do not call attention to ourselves as a result of our dis-ability, we usually avoid devaluation. That is, we do not develop a hand-icap. For example, a child who lacks the sense of smell has an objectively measurable disability, but others will not notice it and society does not particularly devalue it. Thus, the child will not have a handicap unless he or she later decides to become a chef or a "nose" for a perfume com-pany. In short, most handicaps are societally imposed.

IMPORTANCE OF THE PRINCIPAL'S ROLE

The principal is regarded by the community, the board of education, the central administration, and the teachers as the person responsible for exercising leadership in his or her attendance center. He or she is the allocator or withholder of resources and information that can make a dif-ference. The principal is the one who can encourage or discourage, free or inhibit, exercise positive leadership or drag his or her heels. The prin-cipal reinforces or dispels attitudes that can create and/or reinforce handicaps. Even if the principal attempts to avoid directly facing the issue of persons with disabilities, the status quo, which may create hand-icaps, is reinforced. As Goor et al. state, "The principal establishes the overall climate and influences instructional practices; in fact the key pre-dictor of a program is the principal's attitude toward it."[1]

The principal must operate within a framework already established by laws and individual school district policies. The principal can exert influence in the development of local policy and work with the staff in the implementation of policies so that individual children experience the greatest good and the least harm.

It is the principal who is in a position to aid the staff in breaking down the handicapping process that is occurring in the minisociety of the school, or at least to intervene at appropriate points in the process.

---

[1] Mark B. Goor, John O. Schwenn, and Lynn Boyer, "Preparing Principals for Leadership in Special Education," *Intervention* 32 (January 1997): 133. See also the February 2000 issue of *NASSP Bulletin,* which is devoted to the principal's role related to students with disabilities.

Therefore, as the larger society questions why many more children are considered "different," "exceptional," or "handicapped" in school than are so identified before or after the school years, the accountability buck begins to come to rest in the hand of the leader of the minisociety that is creating and maintaining the handicaps. Since the attendance area community holds the principal responsible for the learning environment in the school, there is scarcely anyone to whom the principal can pass the buck.

Implications for Principal Preparation

Preservice preparation or professional development for principals is important for effective leadership for inclusive schools. Inclusive schools are those schools in which students with disabilities are viewed as full participating citizens, the same as all other students. In fact, it would be wise for school leaders to each year include staff development in this area to avoid legal concerns. Serious efforts to include students with a wide range of disabilities in the least restrictive environment require changes in personnel assignments, new views of the learning potentials of the disabled, responsibility shifts to the "regular" classroom teacher, and new relationships between that teacher and special education personnel.[2] To effect such changes, resulting in positive learning for all, the principal's leadership is essential.

Serious questions, some generated out of fear, will be posed: Who should be included or excluded? Will students with serious behavior problems be included? Are pull-outs permissible?[3] The leader needs to have responses to such questions, and these responses need to go beyond the fact that the changes are mandated. Professional development that devotes sufficient time initially and continues over time is important if the principal is to serve as a positive leader for an inclusive school.[4]

What Can the Principal Do?

The principal should be primarily concerned with the quality of education for each child in the school; therefore, the focus is on human interactions and the instructional program that serves as the framework for

[2] For additional discussion, see E. Pearman, M. Huang, and C. Mellblom, "Educating All Students in School: Attitudes and Beliefs about Inclusion," *Education Training and Mental Retardation* 27 (1992): 176–182; and F. Wilczenski, "Measuring Attitudes toward Inclusive Education," *Psychology in the Schools* 29 (1992): 306–312.
[3] James McLesky and Nancy Waldron, "Responses to Questions Teachers and Administrators Frequently Ask about Inclusive School Programs," *Phi Delta Kappan* 78 (October 1996): 150–156.
[4] Doris E. Speicher, "The Use of Professional Development in Establishing an Inclusion Program in Indiana Public Schools" (Ph.D. diss., Ball State University, Muncie, IN, 1995), 224–225.

these interactions. The principal can take the following steps to enhance opportunities for the student with disabilities:

1. Demonstrate to participants that all children are valuable regardless of evident disabilities. Value of human life is the utmost quality to be embraced and incorporated into policy.
2. Clarify a personal understanding of handicapping conditions and why the school should make provisions to ensure that students with disabilities are as free from such conditions as possible.
3. Examine along with the staff beliefs about the learning potential of all students, the locus of responsibility for learning, and the range of learners that can be accommodated.
4. Become thoroughly familiar with the controlling laws and regulations, and ensure their implementation at the building level.
5. Analyze the instructional program in terms of "excluding" practices and materials, and identify where school personnel can intervene in the handicapping process.
6. Examine the organizational structure for the delivery of instruction to determine possible rearrangements of staff and resources to provide for a greater range of individual differences. This is particularly important given the inclusion concept.
7. Establish working cooperation with local, regional, and state special education personnel, with an eye toward developing resources for the instructional staff.
8. Institute a staff development program, including preservice when appropriate.
9. With the staff, develop learning alternatives for students and a wider range of instructional techniques.
10. Conduct an inventory of facilities to determine whether architectural barriers exist for some students, and improve the use of interior and exterior spaces to avoid emphasis on disabilities.

CLARIFYING UNDERSTANDING

To reduce successfully the probability and possibility that one's school creates and perpetuates handicaps, the principal should understand the process of handicapping. To give a perspective, some views of disabilities and handicaps follow.

A *disability* may be thought of as an impairment or dysfunction that is objectively measurable in terms of performance in a particular society. Children with a physical disability are limited in physical ability and may be limited in the kind of activities in which they can participate. Their parents, other adults, and their peers may treat them differently. They may feel they are different, and they may also feel they are less worthy. That is, they *do* have a disability, and they *may* have a handicap.

Some limitations on behavior are not disabilities but socially imposed handicaps. For example, in our culture a female was for years disqualified from jobs that were well within her capacities. Race, sex, and religion have been disqualifiers from entry into certain social groups. A *handicap* might be thought of as an arbitrarily imposed, relative position in a particular society.

A disability stimulates certain expectations for behavior. It is difficult to escape from these stereotypes, particularly for those having more noticeable disabilities. Such expectations may be used to assign persons with disabilities to certain social roles. To a great extent, others' expectations will shape the disabled person's self-concept and will determine what he or she can do and how he or she will behave.

Mention also should be made of the relationship between a disability and an emotional handicap. A disability does not require a psychological maladjustment. If an emotional handicap exists in a person with a disability, it does not stem directly from the disability but has been mediated by social variables. A full discussion of this topic is beyond the scope of this text, but an explanation of this process and an example, both drawn from the comprehensive and very interesting work by Meyerson,[5] should be instructive.

The mediation between a disability and psychological behavior occurs as follows: (1) a person lacks a tool that is required for behavior in his or her culture and knows that he or she lacks it, (2) other individuals perceive that the person lacks an important tool and devaluate him or her for the lack, and (3) the person accepts the judgment of others that he or she is less worthy and devalues himself or herself. The 1-2-3 sequence is a unit. If step 1 or 2 does not occur, step 3 does not occur. If step 3 does not occur, there is no emotional handicap.

The handicapping process may be illustrated as follows:

1. Some students come to school from families who speak non-standard English when conducting their business outside the home, while using a language other than English among themselves within the home.
2. The dominant group devalues these families and students, believing their lack of English language facility indicates low intelligence, mistrust, low worthiness, or even laziness.

---

[5] Lee Meyerson, "Somatopsychology of Physical Disability," in *Psychology of Exceptional Children and Youth,* 2d ed., ed. William W. Cruickshank (Upper Saddle River, NJ: Prentice Hall, 1963), 1–52.

3. The families and students recognize such perceptions through the different ways they are treated, suspicion, newspaper stories addressing "the problem," debates in the state about making English the official language, opportunities for employment, and so forth. The families accept the idea that they have some deficiencies and convey to their children that they must do well in school or face the same devaluation.

4. The students have the idea reinforced in school when others avoid them, they get special assignments the teachers "think they can handle," and they are subjected to similar behaviors.

5. The students devalue themselves and as a result are handicapped, not because they cannot do the work or speak the way others do but because others have convinced them that they are less worthy.

It is clear that there is a process, a series of steps, that can create and perpetuate a handicap. Thus, persons with handicaps are often those who are victimized by other persons. External characteristics (e.g., cerebral palsy, obesity, a different skin color, ill-kept or cheap clothing, language usage) and labels that reinforce differences convey sets of misinformation, fears, and expectations. These sets are translated into almost inescapable expectations about how "those students" will perform, and the phenomenon of the self-fulfilling prophecy reinforces the preconceived fears. The fact that certain characteristics and/or behaviors are present does not mean that the student's whole set of abilities, values, needs, aspirations, and ability to learn is also so different that he or she does not belong or cannot profit from being in a "regular" classroom. Each of us has different relative strengths and weaknesses. The fact that a child's language pattern may be different, as is the case with some children, does not mean that the child is innately low in verbal ability or that he or she cannot or does not wish to communicate effectively. The child will not wish to communicate with someone who "puts down" his or her language pattern as inferior, however. Such devaluation behavior on the part of the teacher, the school's grading system, and/or other reward systems will constitute an arbitrarily imposed relative position in the school society—hence the potential establishment of a handicap.

A student enrolled in an academically oriented high school, which sends 80 percent of its graduates on to college, may be "handicapped" by certain teachers and students if he or she performs poorly academically or has little interest in college.

A child with a motor disability that impedes negotiating stairs or that simply slows progress down long corridors can also experience such devaluation. The many exclusions from activities and the "special treatment" received call attention to the disability and increase the chances that a handicap will develop. Although special treatments must be effected, special treatments can also accentuate differences and thereby perpetuate handicaps. Thus, in providing special programs, a principal should weigh all possible alternatives and select those that will minimize the likelihood that they will make the child's difference more obvious.

Even given the Americans with Disabilities Act (ADA), the Individuals with Disabilities Education Act (IDEA), and Section 504 of the Rehabilitation Act of 1973, many attitudes and practices transcend the "letter of the law" and can result in not-so-subtle hostility or, at best, benign neglect of those pupils and/or parents who seek proper education for their children.

The following list summarizes the discussion thus far:

1. A disability or a handicap must be thought of in relation to a particular society.
2. A handicap is imposed on a human being by other human beings.
3. A disability stimulates expectations regarding the behavior of the disabled person.
4. There is an identifiable sequence of steps in creating an imposed handicap.

PRACTICALITIES FOR THE PRINCIPAL: AN OVERVIEW

In the educational ferment of the past few years, perhaps no other identifiable element of public education has experienced changes as far-reaching and significant as educational programming for students with disabilities. Perhaps the foremost change has been the articulation and establishment of the right to education for all children with disabilities in the least restrictive environment in the public schools. As has been true in much of the history of American public education, the forces and influences producing this and other changes came from outside the education profession.

Parents, advocacy groups, and persons with disabilities have provided the major impetus to the instigation of change. However, during the 1970s, professional educators of students with disabilities evidenced strength and a voice for the profession through the Council for Exceptional Children. They provided informational and other resources, in cooperation with the nonprofessional advocacy groups, and were successful in asserting education as a basic right for the people with disabilities.

Before 1970, only a handful of states mandated special education for people with disabilities. Some states operated limited programs, under permissive legislation, and many states had no statutory language of any consequence on this issue. For years, parents and advocacy groups had attempted to obtain increased educational services for people with disabilities via lobbying in the state legislatures, but this proved a slow, uncertain, and disappointing approach except in those states with well-organized and well-funded lobbying machinery. With the civil rights movement of the 1960s, advocates noted the success of other minorities in claiming certain fundamental rights before the federal courts, and so, using this model, parents and advocacy groups began litigation in federal courts, asserting the violation of basic constitutional guarantees. Most cases were class action suits articulating specific complaints and invoking such constitutional bases as the right to due process and freedom from discriminatory treatment. By 1976, more than forty cases of this fundamental nature were heard, and in no case did the plaintiffs lose. Also, in no case did the defendants (usually local and state boards of education, administrators of public schools and institutions, and sometimes professional practitioners, such as school psychologists) appeal the verdict or findings of the courts.

Concurrent with the activity in the federal courts, legislative activity in Congress began to lay groundwork affirming the inclusion of people with disabilities under all civil rights guarantees derived from the Constitution. Section 504 of the Rehabilitation Act of 1973 addressed the right to education for individuals with disabilities, although it was not until 1977 that the Department of Health, Education, and Welfare promulgated the regulations to implement the legislation. In 1975, Congress passed the Education for All Handicapped Children Act, PL 94-142, which included provisions for funding. Again, not until August 1977 were the final regulations regarding PL 94-142 published. These two major pieces of legislation represented a "new order" for the organization and administration of educational programs for persons with disabilities, with the primary responsibility for implementation resting on the public school systems of the nation.

In 1990, the IDEA (PL 101-476) and the ADA were signed into law. States immediately revised their regulations to be in compliance. Certain language differences addressed the previous discussion. In the IDEA, all references to "handicapped children" were changed to "children with disabilities," thus beginning to make the distinction between the terms. Many refinements emerged, as did additional responsibilities for the schools, such as providing a statement of needed transition services for a student before the student leaves the school, recommending that students with severe disabilities be educated with their nondisabled peers, and requiring early identification (ages 0 to 2) of children with disabilities.

In 1997, IDEA 97 was passed, which included a series of amendments to IDEA 90. IDEA 97 was passed to take care of two major issues:

1. The challenges of developing and implementing effective individualized education plans (IEPs)
2. The challenges of effectively assessing the achievement of short- and long-term goals

IDEA 97 added new requirements for principals and teachers:

1. Understand how the child's disability affects the child's involvement and progress in the general curriculum.
2. Write "measurable" goals for each child.
3. Provide a listing of related services that will lead to meeting the measurable goals.
4. Project when goals will be met and suggest modifications.
5. Provide a statement of how goals will be measured and progress will be made.[6]

The new law places responsibility upon the provider to measure, make progress, and update. Perhaps the most agonizing part of the new IEP is the voluminous amount of paperwork required for all involved. A practical suggestion for the principal would be to insist that the special education coordinator or teacher develop a system of "simplicity" to ensure compliance and document progress.

The ADA affects the principal's planning for personnel accommodations as well as providing for students with disabilities. The ADA went into effect on January 26, 1992, with sweeping implications for school leaders. The reader is encouraged to update his or her knowledge of the changes that have been made in his or her state and their implications for practice.

The following are major elements of IDEA and ADA legislation that have an impact on program organization and operation:

- Represents a federal commitment to ensure that *all* children with disabilities are provided with a *free and appropriate public education*
- Incorporates *full due process* rights for children and parents in the referral, evaluation, and placement procedures
- Requires an *individualized education plan* for each child with a disability
- Requires *regular review* of the plan of each child with a disability
- Requires placement of children with disabilities in the *least restrictive alternative*. The Regular Education Initiative (inclusion) seeks that all students with disabilities be educated with their nondisabled peers.

---

[6] Dixie F. Huefner, "The Risks and Opportunities of the IEP Requirements under IDEA '97," *Journal of Special Education* 33 (Winter 2000): 195–196.

- Requires that *testing and evaluation* materials and procedures used to evaluate and place children with disabilities be selected and administered so as not to be racially and culturally discriminatory
- Extends *program scope* into what have been traditionally viewed as pre- and post-school-age groups and includes a number of disabilities such as autism and traumatic brain injury
- Requires *cooperation* among local, state, and federal levels to assure compliance with the law
- Requires *measurable objectives,* which are reviewed for progress and rewritten for the next steps of progression in the student

Even a casual perusal of these items reveals concepts that, though not new to education in every instance, had not been implemented in practice on a national scale. Many administrators have viewed the IDEA regulations as excessively detailed, requiring excessive documentation and record keeping, laden with parental prerogatives in educational decision making, and limiting to administrative discretion or professional judgment. On the other hand, parents and advocates for students with disabilities have viewed the regulations as minimal guarantees that are long overdue and necessary to correct injustices and poor practices of the past. Naturally, differences of opinion regarding the meaning and intent of various segments of the regulations have resulted in administrative and judicial tests and interpretations at the local, state, and federal levels, with clarifications slowly emerging. Specific topics addressed in the courts will be shared in a later section, but no major deletion or revision of the federal act has transpired as a result of such interpretation. Thus, it would seem prudent for school administrators to master the content of the law; to recognize the implications for program planning, organization, and operation; and then to mobilize resources required to carry out a quality educational program for people with disabilities. Elaboration on the implications of the aforementioned major elements is now offered, but the reader must apply each with recognition of the acceptable legal variations in state and local practice.

A Free and Appropriate Public Education for Children with Disabilities

While the basic policy statements and procedures regarding implementation of these mandates will be formulated at the board and central administrative level, the fulfillment of the mandate will occur at the classroom level. This means that the principal should be prepared to work cooperatively in developing delivery systems of special services for pupils with disabilities in the building. In the past, when the dominant mode of special education was the full-time self-contained special class, not all buildings housed such pupils, but "inclusion" and parental pre-rogative clauses in the IDEA now eliminate this likelihood. While full-time self-contained classes are not eliminated by the mandate, the clear intent of the law is that as many disabled pupils as possible be served in regular classrooms and in contact with nondisabled peers. It appears that the "appropriate" education concept will be most nearly satisfied when it can be demonstrated that a flexible educational delivery system for pupils with disabilities is functional within a building. Providing instruc-tional space for special itinerant or resource personnel, facilitating com-munication between such personnel and regular classroom teachers, coordinating time schedules for pupils and the various instructional or supportive staff members serving them, and being directly involved in determining the educational plan are all tasks that require the principal's planning, implementation, and monitoring.

Perhaps more fundamentally, the federal mandate to serve all chil-dren with disabilities eliminates the option of local boards of education and administrators at all levels to arbitrarily exclude such children from school enrollment and access to education. Even when no state statutes or official local policies addressed this question, it was not unusual to find building principals exercising judgment as to a disabled child's admissibility to school based only on the child's physical appearance and the principal's private interpretation of implications for education. It was precisely such practices that led to the enactment of the federal legisla-tion guaranteeing the right to education for all children with disabilities. The principal is now obligated to accept all children being presented for enrollment and, in the case of visible and more severe disabilities, to communicate immediately to parents the steps that the school and par-ents cooperatively must follow to assure that an appropriate educational plan will ensue. The principal will then initiate the process as a first step to mobilizing the service system.

The lack of financial resources, facilities, staff, or existing program cannot be invoked by the schools as an excuse for not providing an appropriate program, for placing students on waiting lists, or for other-wise delaying the evaluation and placement process. In recent years, courts have affirmed that the law requires the school to provide educa-tional opportunities even if additional costs are incurred, as suggested in the 1999 Supreme Court ruling in *Cedar Rapids Community School District v. Garret F.*[7] In addition to the foregoing implications, it is required that the public schools show positive efforts to identify and locate all children with disabilities, including those from birth through age 2, within the school district. These efforts have sometimes been organized as specific systemwide programs. The focus of search activities is usually a public information effort, seeking to reach every home in the community, and

---

[7] 526 U.S. 66, 119 S. Ct. 992 (1999).

may include newspaper publicity, radio and TV spot announcements, billboards, posters, and talks before community groups. The principal may be asked to disseminate flyers to the homes of all pupils in the building and to schedule opportunities for speakers before the PTA or PTO.

Full Due Process Rights for Children and Parents in the Referral, Evaluation, and Placement Procedures

Perhaps the most challenging regulations pertain to the full due process rights for children and parents as they apply to the referral, evaluation, and placement procedures. Undoubtedly, these regulations, in addition to relevant state and local regulations, will be incorporated by the board and central administration into a single set of operational procedures for the local program of special education for children with disabilities. It is also probable that in most school systems a central office administrator will have responsibility for the overall functioning of the special education program, including monitoring to assure compliance with the federal, state, and local regulations. Depending on the size of the school system or a cooperative of several school districts, there may even be a cadre of supervisors whose duties include the monitoring of special aspects of the referral, evaluation, and placement procedures. Nevertheless, the actual processing of pupils through the entire set of steps takes place most frequently at the building level and requires that the principal be aware, informed, and ready to participate in any way that will facilitate the processing in a legally correct manner. Some of the newest concerns are proper notification of the parent, selection of a meeting site in close proximity to the parent, and full parental input into any plan.

The importance of the regulations cannot be overemphasized because they demand rigorous attention to procedures that have often in the past been handled in an informal, loosely structured manner. Because certain rights of parents and children are so clearly defined, the school system becomes very vulnerable to complaint procedures available to parents if they believe any such rights have been violated. On occasion, parents have the assistance of advocacy groups during the process. Though the legally required steps to referral, evaluation, and placement are detailed, time-consuming, and therefore costly, it would seem prudent to make a commitment to their implementation as a part of standard operating procedure rather than seeking shortcuts that are potential sources of litigation. In this respect, the principal must know the detailed steps of the entire procedure, communicate them to his or her professional staff, solicit their commitment and cooperation, and monitor those that may be specifically a responsibility of his or her staff or own office.

Principals and regular classroom teachers must be aware that the due process considerations become effective at the moment a pupil is suspected of educational problems that may require behavioral evaluation beyond the observations that the classroom teacher makes of all pupils assigned to the room. Before any diagnostic staff or instructional specialist personnel may pursue data collection pertinent to determining the nature and significance of the problem, the child's parent must be informed of the suspected problem by written notice and must give informed consent in writing for preplacement evaluation. The notice must include a full explanation of all the procedural safeguards available to parents under the federal regulations. The notice must be written in language understandable to the general public or in the native language of the parent, unless it is clearly not feasible to do so, in which case it must be translated orally or by another mode of communication. These initiating tasks for pupil referral will usually rest with the principal and his or her staff, although even this cursory look may indicate a need to request assistance for communication in unusual cases or to invite the presence of a consultative diagnostic staff member to help explain the assessment procedures, instruments, or tests appropriate for preplacement evaluation.

A promising practice that appears to offer benefits to pupils in educational difficulty, while reducing the need for premature parental contact and the actual numbers of referrals necessary, is a prereferral system at the building level. Essentially, such a system involves the establishment of a building-based child study team, with variable membership, but usually including the principal, classroom teacher, and as many auxiliary school personnel as are available in the building, to study information on children about whom the teachers have educational concerns. Auxiliary personnel may include the remedial reading teacher, special education resource room teacher, school nurse, counselor, physician, mental health professional, advocate, and the like. By making informal classroom observations, gathering samples of classroom work, and examining available health or developmental information, all of which may be available and legally gathered for all children, the child study team can confer, make suggestions for instructional variations to the teacher, and exhaust standard options for addressing the learning problems of students. The collective judgment of the child study team will resolve the problems of many children without invoking the due process safeguards of the IDEA (PL 101-476) or will provide a solid basis for requesting a parent conference for those children clearly requiring referral and further evaluation.

Once parental approval has been obtained in writing, responsibility for scheduling the evaluative process usually resides at the central administration level. However, the evaluation itself will probably be carried out in the building, and the principal will need to arrange for appropriate space(s) in which this may be done, coordinate time schedules, and communicate with the teacher in the event that the pupil assessment is carried out in sessions on different days or by a variety of diagnostic team members.

After the relevant diagnostic data have been assembled, a second conference must be scheduled to include the parent and child (if deemed appropriate), all personnel participating in the evaluation, the child's teacher, an administrator of special education representing the superintendent's office, and other individuals at the discretion of the parent or the school system. While the principal is not mandated to participate by the act and in many school systems will not have responsibility for convening the conference, he or she may be assigned the role of the administrator acting as the superintendent's designee. In most instances, principals will be invited, probably have to schedule space, and in most cases wish to participate inasmuch as the findings of the evaluative process will be shared and an individualized education plan formulated for the child. If the principal cannot attend, a briefing is recommended, which makes the principal aware of any associated problems so that he or she can work to resolve those concerns.

Aside from input the principal may wish to offer at the conference, there is a need to be aware of the educational plan developed for the child and to be ready to cooperate in the implementation of the plan. It is important to note that the child's placement in special education, or the need for related services, may not be predetermined by any professional staff member connected with the case and must take place within the case conference, with final written approval by the parent before implementation may occur.

If the parent disagrees with the recommendations of the case conference or the findings of the evaluative procedures, or if the parent agrees to placement and later has a change of mind, and the differences of opinion cannot be resolved with the professionals acting for the school, the parent has the right to request a hearing before an impartial hearing officer.

The specific elements of parental rights are as follows:

- The right to receive written and timely notice of the place and time of the hearing
- The right to have the hearing as close to the parent's home as possible
- The right to review all information and records the school has compiled on the child
- The right to obtain an independent evaluation at the expense of the school
- The right to be represented by counsel
- The right to bring witnesses
- The right to present evidence
- The right to cross-examine witnesses

- The right to receive a complete written report of the hearing proceedings and findings
- The right to appeal the decision

There is little doubt that these rights represent an unprecedented legal intrusion into educational procedures previously assumed to be matters of policy to be determined by state or local boards of education or by administrative regulation. The potential impact of these rights on the principal seems self-evident, and it may be significant to the extent that parents invoke such procedures. Generally, the arrangement of a hearing will be the responsibility of the central administration level, with counsel from the board's attorney. However, the principal can expect to provide assistance in preparing the school's case and should be ready to testify at the hearing, with the recognition that cross-examination is a likely part of such testimony.

We have by no means exhausted the many nuances of due process rights in this brief review, but the considerations raised are primary ones that relate to the fundamental steps of referral, evaluation, and placement of pupils in programs of special education and services, as is the parent's right to participate in decision making in each step. Although even these may seem imposing and legally excessive to educators, it would seem prudent to have the entire professional staff aware of them and to implement operating procedures taking them into account. Once the school system has made the necessary adaptations in procedure, the likelihood of parents invoking the complaint procedures should be considerably diminished. Over a period of years, the schools have an opportunity to generate a record of credibility with the community in such issues so that most parent concerns can be resolved on the basis of communication, mutual trust, and respect.

Figure 11.1 provides a generic checklist of procedures specified or implied in federal law and regulations. The details of state and local variances in such areas as appeal routes, the process for changing a previously agreed-on placement, and so on must be checked.

A great majority of parents will accept the school's evaluation and educational plan for their children. A few exceptions might arise in which the parents, though full of good intentions, react irrationally and emotionally to the news that their child may need special help. They can refuse special placement and programming and in some instances seriously affect their child's welfare. At this point, the school is faced with a problem. We believe that the principal or other administrators would be under a moral obligation to initiate further hearings on the child's behalf. Hopefully, the school would not need to press charges under child neglect laws or other appropriate laws. Such a situation will, and possibly should, occur if regulations continue to be overloaded in favor of one "side" or the other with a possible negative effect on the student.

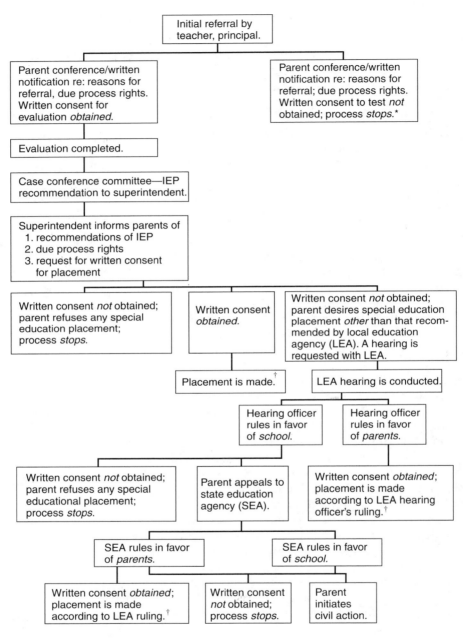

Initial referral by teacher, principal.

Parent conference/written notification re: reasons for referral, due process rights. Written consent for evaluation *obtained*.

Parent conference/written notification re: reasons for referral; due process rights. Written consent to test *not* obtained; process *stops*.*

Evaluation completed.

Case conference committee—IEP recommendation to superintendent.

Superintendent informs parents of
1. recommendations of IEP
2. due process rights
3. request for written consent for placement

Written consent *not* obtained; parent refuses any special education placement; process *stops*.

Written consent *obtained*.

Written consent *not* obtained; parent desires special education placement *other* than that recommended by local education agency (LEA). A hearing is requested with LEA.

Placement is made.[†]

LEA hearing is conducted.

Hearing officer rules in favor of *school*.

Hearing officer rules in favor of *parents*.

Written consent *not* obtained; parent refuses any special educational placement; process *stops*.

Parent appeals to state education agency (SEA).

Written consent *obtained*; placement is made according to LEA hearing officer's ruling.[†]

SEA rules in favor of *parents*.

SEA rules in favor of *school*.

Written consent *obtained*; placement is made according to LEA ruling.[†]

Written consent *not* obtained; process *stops*.

Parent initiates civil action.

* State statutory language may permit the school to instigate further action to facilitate proper placement.

† The principal should be aware that parents may request a change in placement at a later date.

FIGURE 11.1
Generic checklist of procedures specified or implied in federal law and regulations

The opposite side of the coin may present problems when parents insist their child should have special placement. The process can be initiated and completed with no indication of need. Again, the school leadership has to act in the student's best interest even though additional hearings are imminent. Mediation is possible if both parties agree to it. The IDEA 97 provides guidance for the mediation process. States are obligated to bear the costs associated with the mediation process.[8]

An Individualized Education Plan for Every Student with a Disability

The concept of providing educational opportunities and experiences for individual learners according to their unique abilities and needs is not new to education. It has generally been recognized as the educational ideal toward which teachers should strive in organizing for instruction, even though the public schools have traditionally been organized on a mass production model, with the individual being first identified as a member of a group employing age- or grade-level designations. Concerns over the needs of the individual versus the realities of group instruction and management have occupied a central position in educational philosophy and practice over many generations, but the language of the legislation takes this question out of the realm of speculation and debate for the education of students with disabilities.

The federal mandate requires an IEP for each identified student before special services or placement may occur. This plan must be formulated in an individual case conference, which will include the parent and child, if appropriate, and the educational personnel previously mentioned. The conference must generate a written plan that is agreed on by the participants and attested to by the signature of each. The IEP must include the following items:

- The student's present levels of educational performance in academic and nonacademic areas, specifying the effect of the disability on the student's performance
- Annual *measurable* goals that describe what the student can be expected to accomplish within twelve months
- Short-term instructional objectives designed to meet each annual goal
- The specific special education placement and the related services to be provided, including the length, frequency, and type of services and the modifications to be made to the general education program, if applicable

---

[8] Steve Baldridge and David Doty, *Mediation under the New IDEA: Room to Be Reasonable* (Horsham, PA: LRP Publishers, 1998), 3.

- The extent to which the student will be able to participate in the general education program, including noninstructional, nonacademic, and extracurricular activities for which the student is eligible
- The projected dates for initiation of services and anticipated duration of services
- Objective criteria and evaluation procedures and a schedule for determining, at least annually, whether the short-term instructional objectives are being achieved
- The projected school year and semester in which the student will be reevaluated
- A statement of necessary transition services for the student beginning no later than age fourteen or the freshman year of high school, whichever comes first, including, when appropriate, a statement of the interagency responsibilities or linkages, or both, before the student leaves the school setting

For students in early childhood special education programs, objectives for parents to implement in the home may be included.

The case conference to consider the foregoing must meet for as long as necessary to reach agreement, or it may be reconvened at another session if time constraints so dictate and if the time deadline (see your state guidelines) of forty days between referral and the preplacement conference is not violated. The principal has direct responsibilities at the conference, and developing the ultimate content of the IEP and allocating resources are part of those responsibilities. Resource allocation includes such considerations as personnel needed to work with the student in the regular classroom(s), transportation, provisions for safety during emergencies, training of personnel working with the student and documenting case conference procedures, and information regarding the least restrictive environment. The question of district and personal liability is ever present in the decision-making process.[9]

Annual Review of Each Student's Educational Plan

One may assert that regular review of educational progress has long been practiced in U.S. schools, as manifested in the issuance of periodic report cards to parents and administration of systemwide achievement tests at selected grade levels. Nevertheless, the regular review of the plan for a student with disabilities involves more than reducing complex learning and behavior to marks on a report card or obtaining norm-based achievement scores. The review refers specifically to the IEP and

---

[9] For a discussion of one case and references to several others, see Perry A. Zirkel, "Another Withering Decision," *Phi Delta Kappan* 78 (October 1996): 171–172.

represents an evaluation of its contents. The review process requires a conference to include the parent, the child if appropriate, all instructional personnel in contact with the child, and any supportive or diagnostic staff deemed necessary to a thorough review. The primary objective data to be compiled in advance of this conference will in most instances be quantitative and relate to the criterion measures of goals and objectives stated in the IEP. If the objectives are written in behavioral and therefore measurable or observable terms, the major basis for judging the adequacy and appropriateness of the student's educational plan can be more readily attained. However, this conference must also allow for observations and considerations that may be more subjective in nature. Certainly, the principal may wish to offer input on items that relate to least restrictive environment or readiness for assignment to another setting within the school.

Once a student has had an IEP that has been implemented through an academic year and evaluative data have been gathered, the annual case review can serve as the conference during which the next academic year's IEP can be generated. Measurable accountability is a special area of concern as IDEA 97 is implemented. School personnel are required to show measurement of goals. A common problem of past IEPs was the writing of goals without true measurement and accountability. The new law removes that possibility. Recent court rulings are upholding the IDEA 97 stipulations of measurement and accountability that in the past may not have happened. Progress must be assessed and new goals established to ensure additional learning occurs.

The principal should be aware, too, that even though most IEPs will be based on the academic year and will prove adequate for that time period, the parent or teachers associated with the child have the right to, and may request, a review of the child's progress and program at any time during the year.

Inclusion as the Least Restrictive Alternative

The consideration of least restrictive environment in the educational placement of children with disabilities represents a marked departure from past practice in the provision of special education. The traditional practice of serving most children in full-time self-contained classes underwent considerable challenge and resistance from parents and advocacy groups prior to the passage of PL 94-142. This influence undoubtedly has shaped PL 101-476 provisions regarding the concept of least restrictive alternative. *Inclusion* is the term used to describe the process of ensuring that special education students are included in the regular classroom. Daniels and Garner capture this best: "The phrase 'full membership' captures the meaning of inclusive education."[10]

---

[10] Harry Daniels and Philip Gardner, *Inclusive Education* (London: Kogan Page, 1999), 13.

This concept presumes that the regular classroom, undifferentiated on the basis of the personal characteristics of the pupils assigned, is the most normal school environment and one where the student with a disability would be if the student had no disabilities. Implementation of this concept necessitates that schools greatly expand the range of delivery systems by which children with disabilities can be served.

Figure 11.2 indicates a continuum of theoretically desirable/undesirable combinations of educational services provided to students with disabilities. Any continuum entails many shadings, and Figure 11.2 is no exception. The alternatives that may be developed can fall in between many of these environments and types of personnel, but the intent is that the principal see the potential combinations. The principal and staff need to supply the realities on which the decisions about the best combination of services for each student are based.

In effect, it is presumed that the regular classroom and the full-time special classroom represent polar extremes of a continuum, with the regular classroom being the optimal environment for children and the full-time special classroom or special school the least desirable. Remember that, in the case conference to develop the IEP, it is necessary to address the question of the extent to which the child's special needs can be served with minimal movement or time away from the classes he or she would attend if he or she had no disabilities. Also, IDEA 97 requires that a regular education teacher be present to discuss the student's IEP. The rationale is that the lack of a regular education teacher suggests that only a restrictive environment is being discussed.

Principals involved in any degree with students with disabilities realize that information given to the regular education teachers and a readiness on the principal's part to play a strong supportive role are essential to successful efforts. Informing the staff requires more than a note in the end-of-year bulletin in June to the effect that students are to be integrated or reintegrated in regular classes the following September. The school is required to provide both staff development experiences to implement the idea and time to incorporate cooperative relationships that may ensue from the presence of a newly defined delivery system and new professional special education staff. The clarification of roles and lines of communication among regular, special, supportive, and administrative staff may need continued attention over a long period of time.

The supportive role alluded to earlier may be manifested by the need of the principal to act as a facilitating third party in smoothing the course of staff relationships until, hopefully, both regular classroom and special education or supportive staff have developed trust and mutual professional respect. In this instance, as in so many other educational situations, the need to practice and reinforce positive human relationships and continued communication efforts cannot be overemphasized. Prag-

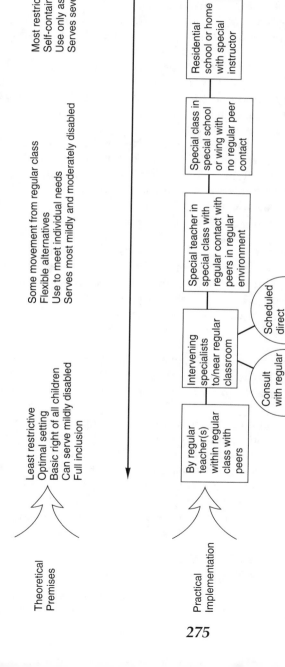

Theoretical Premises

Least restrictive
Optimal setting
Basic right of all children
Can serve mildly disabled
Full inclusion

Some movement from regular class
Flexible alternatives
Use to meet individual needs
Serves most mildly and moderately disabled

Most restrictive
Self-contained settings
Use only as necessary
Serves severely disabled

Practical Implementation

By regular teacher(s) within regular class with peers

Intervening specialists to/near regular classroom

- Consult with regular classroom teacher
- Scheduled direct service to children

Special teacher in special class with regular contact with peers in regular environment

Special class in special school or wing with no regular peer contact

Residential school or home with special instructor

Institutional care/training

FIGURE 11.2

Theoretical and practical continua for the implementation of educational services, illustrating the concept of the least restrictive environment

matically, these considerations must also extend to the parents and to the children whose welfare must be the primary common interest of all the adults involved.

The principal may also need to be an advocate for additional support such as aides, consultants, or in-class special education teachers. Beyond personnel, technologies are available that can support the achievement of students with disabilities. Computers, speech synthesizers, and a variety of software can enhance the opportunities for a student to learn, communicate, and become a contributor.[11] The continuous search for dollars may include external possibilities such as foundations, the state, or corporations. Parents of students with disabilities may also need assistance to seek funds so they can be full partners with the schools in educating their children.

Certain responses can be rationally anticipated. Parents of children with moderate, severe, profound, or multiple disabilities will generally be aware of the nature of their child's needs before the age of school admission, and they are often fairly realistic regarding educational options, goals, and aspirations. Most of these parents will understand that physical management, fire, and other safety considerations; possible limited communication skills of the child; the level at which learning experiences may have to be structured; and numerous other factors may render the concept of least restrictive alternative difficult to implement at all levels. For aspects of the child's growth, development, and sometimes simple survival, a self-contained setting may be necessary and acceptable, from both the school's and the parent's point of view, and should not be ruled out, at least for some activities. In short, there may be situations in which a student would be served better in settings outside the regular classroom.[12]

On the other hand, students who are disabled as a result of attention deficit disorder (ADD), learning disabilities (LD), undiagnosed sensory defects, or special health problems are often unrecognized until the nature of the problem is manifested by lack of progress in school. In these cases, the school becomes the "bearer of bad tidings" to the parents and therefore the object of maladaptive psychological responses from some parents, who may then demand unreasonable, or even nonexistent, educational solutions to their child's need (e.g., insisting that all of the identified needs be resolved within the regular classroom or, quite the opposite, requesting special placement). One caution should be noted in these areas; many school districts have found ADD and LD easy areas to overdiagnose. Critics have suggested this is done because of the easy

[11] Janet Barry and B. J. Wise, "Fueling Inclusion through Technology," *School Administrator* 53 (April 1996): 24–27.
[12] Richard W. Smelter, Bradley Rasch, and Gary J. Yudewitz, "Think of Inclusion for All Special Needs Students? Better Think Again," *Phi Delta Kappan* 76 (September 1994): 35–38.

revenue stream for the district. Whether or not this can be proven, the principal has the responsibility to thoroughly review such decisions so that the child has every opportunity to succeed in the regular classroom. A label, just for dollars, placed on a problem student is an ethical violation of the greatest nature in the profession. A challenge is placed on each principal to understand and protect the student. If diagnosis is required, here, again, the human relations and communication skills of the principal and the entire case conference team may be put to the test in attempting to develop an IEP that will give maximum priority to the child's needs and be less concerned with the parents' psychological needs. Indeed, the generalizations cited here should be treated cautiously, but they may provide some general perspective for the principal's operational frame of reference.

Assessing Performance of Children with Disabilities

Tests and evaluation instruments for students with disabilities must be selected and administered so as not to be racially or culturally discriminatory. This policy and the local response to it will probably be developed at the school board level and monitored through an office of the central administration. The principal must be aware of the federal and state requirements and associated policies and procedures and should communicate these to the building faculty before possible violations occur.

Since most group and individual tests in the field today are subject to criticism, it would seem wise to allow only the use of assessment approaches stated in board policy or those permitted to professional diagnostic staff. The general rule governing evaluation of children for services permits the use of testing or evaluative tools without parental approval so long as such assessment is made of all pupils in a classroom or at designated age or grade levels by official board policy. The use of any diagnostic approaches or instruments used only with selected students, and not covered by general policy, requires parental consent in the framework of the due process guarantees discussed earlier. So, while the content and implementation of a testing program may rest outside the principal's direct responsibility, the need to be informed and monitor the activity of the building staff in this area will be a tangential responsibility of that office. This is particularly true as the school makes appropriate accommodations for state-mandated tests, especially high-stakes tests related to graduation.[13]

---

[13] For additional issues regarding accommodations in testing, see Daniel Koretz and Laura Hamilton, "Assessments of Students with Disabilities in Kentucky: Inclusion, Student Performance and Validity," *Educational Evaluation and Policy Analysis* 22 (Fall 2000): 255–272.

Cooperation among Local, State, and Federal Levels Assures Compliance

The burden of proof regarding compliance with mandates rests with the local education agency (LEA), and a commitment to rigorous documentation is fundamental to such proof. The LEA is required to have a legally correct set of records to which one may refer in case of parental questions or disgruntlement that may lead to a hearing or litigation. Further, a detailed record of professional activity is necessary, which may be important in the long-range planning, management, and evaluation of the educational program for pupils with disabilities.

Monitoring for compliance with the requirements of PL 101-146 varies in practice from state to state. Some states have initiated LEA on-site visitations by state education agency (SEA) audit teams for program monitoring. Some states schedule regular visits on a rotating one-, two-, or three-year pattern, and others make on-site visits on a spot-check basis or as a follow-up to those LEAs generating complaints from parents and advocacy groups. Federal fiscal and program audit teams also make scheduled or unannounced visitations to select states on an apparently random basis to check for both state and local compliance.

Implications of the foregoing will probably vary for principals from one building to the next, depending on the extent to which numbers of students may be involved in special education and the nature of the special education services delivered in the building. Certainly, all principals will need to stock certain standard forms, such as referral forms for parents or classroom teachers, and they should maintain a file of written communications to the parents. Also, though it may seem excessively cautious, a log should be kept of phone conversations, initiated by either the principal or the parent, pertinent to a referred student or a student receiving special education services. In addition, principals should make certain that their responsibilities, in the total process of referral, evaluation, placement, and review of individual pupils with disabilities, are well defined and that a complete file of documentation through these steps is maintained for each pupil served in the building. Only in this manner can principals be prepared to assume appropriate accountability that may relate to individual pupil progress, program audits, or parent-initiated complaint procedures leading to hearings or litigation.

LITIGATION, INTERPRETATIONS, AND CLARIFICATION

With legislation as comprehensive in scope as PL 101-476, one might expect that many questions requiring interpretation of specific elements of the regulations would be raised, and, of course, such has been the case. The number of individual issues and concerns raised defies listing in detail, but in general they have revolved around semantic and/or conceptual problems, such as the definition of "free appropriate education," the application of the least restrictive environment principle, the nature of nondiscriminatory testing, the extent of "related services" required, criteria for the classification of students with disabilities, and implementation of due process procedures. Questions have been generated by both parents and schools in the quest for clarification and common understanding.

Since the IDEA provides for resolution of differences at several administrative levels, many interpretations have been made, at local and state levels, to the satisfaction of the parties concerned. As administrative decisions, they obviously are applicable only to the specific issue addressed and the locale in which the questions were raised; as such, they represent nonjudicial opinion, with no binding force on similar cases in other jurisdictions. A great many cases, of course, have been appealed beyond the administrative steps and have been taken to the civil courts for adjudication.

Classification of cases is difficult and somewhat arbitrary because some questions encompass a number of issues. Suits for inclusion come primarily from parents who believe that appropriate special education and related services are not being provided for their children with severe disabilities. Other parents seek exclusion from special education services or placement, believing that their children who are already in school as regular students should not be labeled by placing them in special programs for children with disabilities. In terms of administrative ramifications for the schools, it is necessary to examine more specific issues, those that have yielded judicial opinion.

Since the foundation principle of PL 94-142 and PL 101-476 is the mandate that all students with disabilities receive a "free and appropriate public education," it is not surprising that this language has generated numerous questions. The extent to which education for children with disabilities is free to parents has been affirmed in the courts and includes the costs for independent evaluation of students by nonschool professionals, an extended academic school year for severely retarded pupils, twelve-month residential school placements, and out-of-state placement if no appropriate program exists within the state. Also included are catheterization and other support services if such services are necessary for the child to benefit from special education.

What some parents will request as "free" is, of course, closely related to what they perceive as "appropriate" education for their child. A number of federal district courts have affirmed that appropriate education for youth with disabilities incorporates the least restrictive environment concept. The courts have upheld parents' requests to have children reassigned (from neighboring school districts to the district of residence or from special residential schools to local public schools) based on that principle. On the other hand, federal district courts in Indiana, Iowa, and Virginia have affirmed that the concept of "appropriate" need not meet a criterion of "most ideal," "best possible," or "maximal program," which many parents have asserted is a right under the appropriateness concept.

Interestingly, the first Supreme Court decision on PL 94-142 dealt with this issue in 1982, when the Court ruled 6 to 3 that public schools are not required to provide sign language interpreters for deaf students. In *Howley v. Board of Education of Hendrick Hudson Central School District,* the Court overturned a lower court ruling that fourth grader Amy Howley, of New York State, was entitled to a deaf interpreter, under PL 94-142 requiring that students with disabilities receive a "free appropriate education." The Supreme Court majority ruled that the requirements of the law were met if the school district complied with PL 94-142 procedures and showed that an IEP was developed, by means "reasonably calculated" to ensure that individuals received educational benefits. In the majority opinion, Justice Rehnquist stated that PL 94-142 "generates no additional requirement that the services provided be sufficient to maximize each child's potential commensurate with the opportunity provided other children." He added that the act was intended "more to open the door of public education to handicapped children than to guarantee any particular level of education once inside."[14] The decision may have been influenced in part by the fact that Amy Howley had been showing normal progress, as evidenced by passing grades and regular grade promotions before the request for an interpreter. The request for such assistance was based on the belief that the increasing workload of succeeding grades would necessitate resources beyond those inherent in the child herself. While the *Howley* opinion is undoubtedly a landmark decision, the Court did not really clarify the criteria for determining "appropriateness" and in fact injected the concepts of "adequacy" and "equal opportunity" into education for children with disabilities, terms that are likely to prove as elusive and controversial as the original question of "appropriateness." Decision makers, and at times the courts, wrestle with these definitions today. With the passage of IDEA 97, experts wonder if the courts will be forced to change their interpretation of *Howley.* IDEA 97 includes the statement about measurable annual goals associated with progress in the general curriculum. Huefner suggests that "if the current IEP langauage more clearly expects measurable progress, it may force the courts to review the child's IEP more carefully for results."[15] The courts to this point have upheld the *Howley* ruling, but they may change soon.

---

[14] As reported in *Programs for the Handicapped: Clearinghouse on the Handicapped,* no. 4 (Washington, DC: U.S. Department of Education, Office of Special Education and Rehabilitative Services, July–August 1982), 1.
[15] Heufner, "The Risks and Opportunities," 195–196.

One concern of school officials has been the extent to which they might be liable for damages if charged with negligence or failure to comply with aspects of PL 94-142. A definitive answer by the Supreme Court was given to this question in 1982, when the Court let stand a lower court ruling that held that PL 94-142 could not be used as a basis to sue for monetary damages. In the case, *Special School District of St. Louis County v. Miener,* the parents of Terry Miener sued the school district for $525,000, alleging failure to provide her with an adequate education, having placed her in a state hospital program. The parents, however, had also sued under Section 504 of the Rehabilitation Act of 1973, the civil rights act assuring freedom from discrimination in education because of a disabling condition. The Supreme Court let stand the lower court ruling, which held that violation of freedom from discrimination was a legal basis for an individual suit seeking monetary damages. On appeal, the ruling of the federal district court was upheld by the U.S. Court of Appeals for the Eighth Circuit and then by the Supreme Court, as noted here. The appeals court held that Section 504 allowed such private lawsuits because administrative remedies (as per PL 94-142) were not always sufficient to vindicate an individual's rights.[16] So it appears that the schools are free from suit for monetary damages for alleged neglect or other failures under PL 94-142 but that Section 504 is available to plaintiffs if they believe their grievance is addressed under the civil rights guarantees of that statute.

The issue of applying discipline policies to students with disabilities has received considerable attention owing to the fact that some categories of disability, such as emotionally disturbed or mentally retarded, will, by definition, include students exhibiting behavioral deviations that require monitoring and management. At the same time, the law clearly spells out the due process steps for making changes in educational placement for identified students with disabilities. The chief question is the extent disruptive and/or destructive behavior in students with disabilities must be tolerated and how suspension or expulsion policies apply to such students.

A number of such cases have been heard in federal district courts and courts of appeal, and, without citing specific cases, general consensus has held that suspension and expulsion policies may be invoked, but only while observing the procedural safeguards of PL 94-142 and PL 101-476, which view these steps as a change of educational placement.[17] This approach requires, primarily, the convening of a case conference to consider the merits of a change in educational placement; the conference

---

[16] As reported in *Nation's Schools Report* 8 (25 October 1982).
[17] Donald G. Turner, *Legal Issues in the Education of the Handicapped* (Bloomington, IN: Phi Delta Kappa, 1983), 26–27.

must include the parent and, when appropriate, the student. A key distinction noted in several court cases is whether the disruptive behavior had a causal relationship to the disability; this needs to be determined before applying the standard exclusion policies. For example, if a physically disabled student in a wheelchair is apprehended for selling illegal substances on school grounds and such behavior has no relationship to the disability, as determined in a case conference, then the school's policy on suspension or expulsion can be implemented, just as in the case of any nondisabled student. On the other hand, if profanity or insubordination is exhibited by a seriously emotionally disturbed student and the case conference determines that the behavior is related to the disability, the school's expulsion policies could not be invoked. Instead, changes in the IEP, including change in placement, could be considered and implemented, so long as the free and appropriate public education principles are preserved. Today administrators are even more concerned that disruptive students be in a controlled environment. Again, with the extreme violence that has occurred in a few schools, many experts expect the courts to review this area in the future and give schools latitude in dealing with extreme cases.

Before a determination of relationship between misbehavior and disability, a short-term emergency suspension of perhaps three days would likely be upheld in most courts, but anything longer should definitely call for implementation of the procedural safeguards. Since expulsion must certainly be viewed as a change in placement, the principal or other responsible administrator should take care to assure that all requirements are duly observed. Expulsion would necessitate the determination of some form of alternative educational service or placement.[18]

The foregoing discussions on interpretations have by no means been exhaustive; they do illustrate issues that have been the subject of litigation. No doubt clarification of these and other issues will continue, as questions and concerns are brought before the courts. A perusal of legal interpretations regarding special education may indeed seem intimidating to school administrators, but one should remember that the overwhelming majority of differences of opinion among parents, citizens, and the school are resolved at the local level, without litigation. On the other hand, school officials, and especially the building principal, can function more confidently if they are knowledgeable of the law and observe it in principle and practice. In this respect, the admonitions and suggestions for program implementation offered earlier seem particularly relevant. The principal, especially, is in a key position to mediate many of the initial concerns of parents and defuse many problems before they become time-consuming and potentially costly—that is, if the hearing process or litigation is pursued.

---

[18] Ibid.

SUMMARY OF IMPLICATIONS

It will be obvious to principals that practically everything about the federal acts has implications for the utilization of time, and ultimately personnel, whether professional, paraprofessional, or clerical. The principal will be challenged to prioritize time use to supervise or monitor new activities within the building and will be a direct participant in case conferencing, telephone communications, and other responsibilities that may emerge as programs develop. Principals must also provide for the participation of both special and regular education teachers in IEP conferencing and case reviews. These required activities may take significant periods of time, depending on how many children are served in the building.

The necessity for documentation (noted in an earlier discussion) also has implications for the use of professional staff time, and administrators cannot expect to impose these added tasks on existing role definitions, which include a full instructional day, without the risk of creating serious morale problems. Adding tasks may also violate working conditions agreed on in bargained contracts with the instructional staff. Principals must be alert to such developing needs and ready to communicate them to the central administration, along with requests for the human and materials resources required if a quality program is to ensue.

Again, the principal is in a pivotal role in the process of personal and professional growth that has challenged all educators to maintain maximum adaptability throughout a continuing era of rapid social change.

OTHER SPECIAL NEEDS STUDENTS: THE GIFTED AND TALENTED

Thus far we have focused primarily on those exceptional students who have disabilities and for whom the school environment presents some kind of problems. The definition of *exceptional* offered at the beginning of the chapter is equally applicable to the student who has superior intellectual abilities or special talents that far surpass those of the average or normal student. Nevertheless, the schools have been much slower in developing differentiated learning opportunities that nurture and enhance the academic performance and talent productivity of such students.

The neglect of this group nationwide was brought to the fore by the *Marland Report to the Congress* in 1971,[19] which reported that of all U.S.

---

[19] See S. P. Marland, *Education of Gifted and Talented.* Vol. 1, *Report to the Congress of the United States by the U.S. Commissioner of Education* (Washington, DC: U.S. Department of Health, Education, and Welfare, August 1971).

schools included in a 1969–70 survey, 57.5 percent reported no gifted pupils. Marland notes that other research showed 54.6 percent of high-ability students working below their ability levels, a majority below expectancy based on measured potential. One statewide study found that 3.4 percent of all school dropouts had IQs of 120 or higher, with this total representing 17.6 percent of the gifted school population and twice as many gifted girls as boys dropping out.[20] Renzulli and Park state that dropout gifted students cited failing in school (49%), getting a job (40.7%), or being unable to keep up with the homework (38.1%) as reasons they dropped out. Socioeconomic level seemed to affect gifted students in that over 48 percent of the gifted dropouts were from the lowest quartile of the socioeconomic sector.[21]

Political fortunes for programs for the gifted and talented have fluctuated widely, but by the end of the 1980s, most districts had made provision for and received funds for special programs for the academically able.[22] Approximately 30 states have mandatory identification of gifted and talented students, and 26 states have mandatory programming. At the high school level, only 35 percent have a consultant or coordinator associated with gifted and talented programs.[23]

The principal and teachers will face a number of questions regarding special programs for the gifted and talented, ranging from gender questions to equity, social development elitism, and special facilities, materials, and equipment questions. Strides are being made regarding gifted and talented females, yet further inquiry into providing supportive environments is needed. Questions remain concerning identification of the gifted and talented among lower-income families who have not been able to provide enriched environments for their children.

Early identification programs occasionally miss students who are not able for a variety of reasons to participate in after-school programs or who have different language facility. At least one separate program has been found to generate feelings of isolation, segregation, or seclusion among half the students.[24] The principal's awareness of such possibilities is important to safeguard against potentially negative social results.

Suffice it to say that the experiences of gifted and talented children in the public school often have not been as satisfying or as rewarding as they should have been, with both the children and society the poorer for it.

---

[20] Ibid.

[21] Joseph S. Renzulli and Sunghee Park, "Gifted Dropouts: The Who and Why," *Gifted Child Quarterly* 44 (Fall 2000): 265–266.

[22] For an interesting review of a gifted program in operation since 1922, see Suzanne Gold, "Sixty Years of Programming for the Gifted in Cleveland," *Phi Delta Kappan* 65 (March 1984): 497–499.

[23] Rachael Sytsma, "Gifted and Talented Programs in America's High Schools: A Preliminary Survey Report" (Storrs, CT: National Research Center for the Gifted and Talented, Spring 2000). Available at www.sp.uconn.edu/~nrcgt.

[24] Julie Alexander, "Long Term Effects of an Early Intervention Program for Gifted and Talented Students" (Ph.D diss., Ball State University, Muncie, IN, July 1995), 76.

As in the other areas of exceptionality, the principal, as instructional leader, shoulders the major tasks of day-to-day operation of programs for the gifted and talented. Ideally, all principals, as a part of the district administrative team, would be included in planning and organizational decision making when programs are being initiated. If this is not feasible, the steps and decisions of the planning process should be communicated to the principal as they unfold and as implications for the principal's role become evident. Some fundamental administrative considerations to program initiation and implementation are outlined here:

Step 1: Development of Program Rationale
   A. Conceptualization—Make a general statement of purpose for the program with a justifying rationale.
   B. Authorization—Verify legal bases including local school board approval and consistency with relevant state or federal regulations.
   C. Long-Range Goals—Expand on and refine general statements consistent with the concept (item A).
   D. Definitions and Identifications—Make consistent with items A, B, and C, regarding who is to be served. What are the criteria for student qualification? What systematic identification efforts are to be employed? The National Research Center for the Gifted and Talented may be of assistance in the above steps.[25]

Step II: Organizational/Curricular Planning
   A. Professional Staff Involvement—Generate awareness, staff input and acceptance, and cooperation of administrative, instructional, and support staff.
   B. Specific Program Objectives—Refine long-range goals into curricular specifics.
   C. Organizational/Curricular Alternatives—Explore models for delivery of differentiated pupil learning.
   D. Program Supervision—Define roles and responsibilities for program management, monitoring, other administrative tasks.
   E. Instructional Staff—Identify teacher characteristics, selection, orientation, and in-service; community human resources integration.
   F. Evaluation—Establish data-gathering procedures, pre/post-measures, and so forth.
   G. Funding—Define sources, accountability, limits, and so on.

---

[25] The National Research Center for the Gifted and Talented is located at the University of Connecticut, Joseph S. Renzulli, Director. The Website is www.sp.uconn.edu/~nrcgt. See also J. S. Renzulli, "What Makes Giftedness? Re-examining a Definition," in R. Diessner and S. Simmons (eds.), *Notable Selections in Educational Psychology* (Guilford, CT: Dushkin/McGraw-Hill, 2000), 373–384.

H. Public Information—Disseminate information to community for awareness, support, cooperation.

Step III: Instructional Implementation
A. Instructional Space—Identify in-school and between-school resources, community facilities and resources.
B. Grouping Options/Individual Plans—Consider individualizing learning experiences and common learning.
C. Instructional Materials—Use in-school resources and community contributions.
D. Strategies, Approaches, Techniques—Consider pacing the learning, determining how and when various organizational/curricular options are exercised.

Since the steps and tasks outlined here are premised on a school district's systemwide commitment to serving the gifted and talented, it would seem to be expedient to clarify in advance those tasks that are exclusively the principal's and those that may be alternating (or consensual) with central office personnel or instructional and support staff. However, in some instances, a specific school or selected schools within a district may be identified as locations for delivering gifted/talented education, in which case all of the steps and tasks outlined may have direct implications for the principal(s) involved. It is also possible that in the absence of definitive school district commitment and policy, the building principal, as instructional leader, may determine that the gifted/talented pupils in his or her school deserve differentiated learning opportunities and will exercise leadership to bring this about. In this latter instance, the same steps and tasks will need consideration and may remain entirely at the building level, with, of course, concomitant responsibilities and accountability assumed by the principal and his or her staff. Several universities have centers devoted to the study of teaching gifted and talented students. The principal may wish to explore those available and accessible to the school.

ANALYSIS OF THE INSTRUCTIONAL PROGRAM

Unfortunately, many opportunities exist to reinforce the idea that human variance is a negative thing, even variance toward genius. Although most persons involved in the instructional program will give strong verbal support to the idea that differences must be provided for, facilities, materials, and practices may be implying something else. Because of this dichotomy between verbal assent and actual practice, the principal might find the following assumptions and questions helpful in looking at the instructional program and in further developing his or her own sets of assumptions and questions:

Some Assumptions

1. Because of the wide variances in human beings, an instructional program of truly individualized instruction would best provide for the special needs student.
2. To deal effectively with a wide range of differences, the regular teacher will need to extend his or her conversance with instructional competencies needed for meeting a wide range of human variance.
3. Close liaison between special and regular education teachers is not only desirable but also essential.
4. Individualization is not possible without definitive knowledge of where each child is in terms of the competency in question or without a continuing assessment of each child's progress.

Some Questions

1. Are the materials available to the teachers distributed in quantities that assume all the children in a given classroom are at the same level of competency? What additional resources are readily available, on a practical basis, to each teacher?
2. Does the way the children spend their time on designated activities encourage compartmentalization of "subjects"? Do all the children in a class have X number of minutes for reading, Y minutes for arithmetic? Does this approach assume that all children get the same amount of learning by spending the same amount of time on a given topic?
3. What diagnostic techniques are used by the teacher for individual students? What instructional provisions are made as a result of the use of these techniques?
4. What opportunities are afforded children to interact with persons outside their own class or age group?
5. What opportunities do students have to interact with adults in nonschool roles?
6. What specific objectives do teachers have for individuals in their classes? What measures do teachers use to determine whether the objectives have been met?
7. Are students with disabilities "excused" from performance objectives?
8. What provisions are made for exceptionally talented students to extend themselves, or are they limited to doing more of the same until others catch up?
9. What is the nature of the referrals of teachers to get special help for children?
10. What specific provisions are now being made for the students with disabilities? Do such provisions tend to identify a group

and fix that group identification in the perceptions of teachers, students, and community?

11. What instructional strategies are employed in support of the fact that children learn as well or better from other children as they do from adults?

12. What effect does the alignment of professional standards, curriculum, instruction, and assessment have on the students at either end of the achievement continuum?

DEVELOPING COOPERATIVE RESOURCE BASES

As the allocator of resources in a given school, the principal has at least two tasks in providing for exceptional students: (1) continuously assessing the use of resources, including time, and (2) developing new resources. In the first instance, the principal must keep in mind not only physical inventories of materials and supplies but also human resources of skills and time. Often the students' time is overlooked as a valuable resource. It would be appropriate, particularly in considering exceptionalities, to assess the use of students' time. This might be done most effectively as a cooperative study by the teacher, the principal, and observers knowledgeable about the behavior of exceptional children.

The principal is faced with the problem of maximizing task and people dimensions while at the same time integrating the two for both sides of the artificial dichotomy of special education and regular education. (This dilemma is somewhat like the problem of putting together four blocks of red, blue, green, and white sides so that they all appear to be alike: when all seems right on one or two sides, they are completely out of line on another.) A promising tack for the principal is to increase the interaction of the more child-oriented teachers with their counterparts in special education. This approach is particularly helpful when teachers identify a current instructional problem as one that will provide worthwhile learning experiences for exceptional children.

Not only should the principal be very familiar with existing and probable legislation dealing with exceptional children, but also he or she should have a face-to-face working relationship with local and, as much as possible, regional and university special resource persons. Such a relationship should provide the school with direct service to children, inservice education for teachers, resources for materials, assistance in planning, and continual updating about many aspects of providing for exceptional children. The principal should also experiment with different staffing patterns that have been found effective in similar situations, such as teaming, with one member of the team being trained in special education; use of a resource teacher; and in-service/preservice education teams.

SUMMARY

If provision is made for each student, the result is education for all, and the labels "special education" and "education of the exceptional child" are redundant. Until such time as our society does not include or exclude on the basis of variance from the norm, the principal needs to be sensitive about the curricular and instructional provisions for all, development of resource bases, and continuing staff development. Time spent on providing for each student is at the center of the principal's major task. It would seem appropriate that an individualized educational plan should be prepared for each child, not just those fitting under some legal provision or for whom extra funding might be obtained.

The principal can exert much influence on the educational attitude of a school toward eliminating school-imposed handicaps by exposing them for what they really are. We believe that it is imperative that he or she make every effort to do so.

FOR FURTHER THOUGHT

1. Why is the principal a key person in influencing the educational attitude of a school toward providing for the exceptional student?
2. Is it conceivable that a family name can serve as a handicap to a child? How can such an occurrence be minimized?
3. A group of parents of "normal" children are aroused about the large expenditures of funds for a very few children, draining away dollars from their children. Outline your public response to this group.
4. How can others' expectations shape a disabled person's self-concept, both negatively and positively, and help shape what that person can do?
5. Debate the resolution that it takes unequal spending to provide equal opportunity.
6. Does the concept of inclusion restrict the alternatives for the exceptionally able student?
7. Should every child be entitled to a personalized educational plan?
8. What new staffing patterns are being used to accommodate the regular education initiative (inclusion)?
9. Given the concept of inclusion, what liability may school personnel incur regarding medically fragile children in the classroom? What guidelines does your state provide practitioners for these situations? What litigation has occurred regarding the medically fragile student in classrooms?
10. What impact will the IDEA 97 statement "measurable goals that show progress upon assessment" have upon the school system?
11. Debate the issue of granting individual students rights vs. ensuring corporate student protection.

⑤ELECTED READINGS

Baldridge, Steve, and David Doty. *Mediation under the New IDEA: Room to Be Reasonable.* Horsham, PA: LRP Publishers, 1998.

Barkhoff, Alison N. *Serving Medically Fragile Students: The Supreme Court Prepares for a Review.* Horsham, PA: LRP Publishers, 1998.

Barry, Janet, and B. J. Wise. "Fueling Inclusion through Technology." *School Administrator* 53 (April 1996): 24–27.

Farr, Beverly, and Elsie Trumbull. *Assessment Alternatives for Diverse Classrooms.* Norwood, MA: Christopher-Gordon, 1997.

Ferguson, Dianne. "The Real Challenge of Inclusion." *Phi Delta Kappan* 77 (December 1995): 281–291.

Gardner, Howard. *Frames of Mind: The Theory of Multiple Intelligences.* New York: Basic Books, 1993.

McLesky, James, and Nancy L. Waldron. "Responses to Questions Teachers and Administrators Frequently Ask about Inclusive School Programs." *Phi Delta Kappan* 78 (October 1996): 150–156.

A Framework for Evaluation

$\mathcal{E}$ valuation is an essential ingredient of leadership. Few would disagree with that statement, but from that point forward, concerns and disagreements are legion, with some positions based on experience and fact and others on misinformation, local lore, or perceptions of political necessity. The principal is often expected to fulfill the evaluation expectations of the school board, central administration, organized groups, and/or allegedly aggrieved individuals. To these expectations, add the pressure for school reform from state and national leaders who react to public outcries for accountability at all levels. Imbedded in the accountability pressures is high-stakes testing, which often becomes a major factor in decisions about students' promotion or graduation and about rewards or punishments for the school. Evaluation will continue to be a source of pressures, concern, and debate for this decade. Yet all would agree that evaluation is essential to the continual improvement of the quality of life of each individual within the school, including students and teachers.

This and the following chapter give the principal a frame of reference for the evaluation process and some insights regarding the initiation and implementation of the process. Just as a consistently successful coach must translate his or her philosophy about how the game should be played into game plans and specific offenses and defenses, so the school leader must have a framework in which the components of the evaluation program are consistent with a set of beliefs about education and individual performance. It is not within the scope of these chapters to make the reader an expert evaluator; however, several references are cited in the following two chapters that will be helpful in developing the evaluation concepts and skills necessary for a school principal.

This chapter was revised by Suzanne V. Drake, Ph.D.

The two chapters are organized as follows: this chapter establishes a framework for evaluation and discusses making decisions, determining what is to be evaluated, generating data, analyzing data, valuing, and setting guidelines. Chapter 13 treats the evaluation of results based upon assessments of individual student performance by teachers, other school personnel, and the principal.

The primary purpose of evaluation in education is to help the educational process better meet the client's needs. Evaluation does not stop at the point of inspecting to see whether something occurred. Rather, it is a *continual process* that should constantly emphasize improving effectiveness in reaching the school's goals and objectives.

The people seeking evaluation results often want to know whether the program, process, or job performance is meeting the goals set. If indeed the thing being evaluated is intended to serve the client, merely checking to see whether the program/work met the goals may not yield the view of reality hoped for because the goals may have been set by persons who thought they knew what was good for the client or by persons with a vested interest in the program's "success." The evaluation process is linked with decision making, for improvement cannot result from evaluation unless implied changes are implemented. These changes may be developing and using selected instructional skills; or reordering priorities, purposes, and/or resources; or dropping or adopting alternative means to accomplish specific objectives. At this point, the school fulfills the concept of accountability in that it goes beyond a description of what *is* and develops new, supplemental, or corrective actions.

Although the meanings of terms often used interchangeably do overlap, there are subtle differences between words such as *evaluation* and *assessment*. *Evaluation* is the reflective process of gathering data through formal and informal means and then making decisions for action. *Assessment* is a systematic process of determining the extent to which objectives are achieved. It is important to use multiple sources of data to provide sufficient information for making appropriate judgments. A carefully designed framework supplies the crucial structure for the evaluation plan.

Evaluation is a way of showing concern for students, faculty, staff, and even the community itself. It should not be a fearsome, oppressive checking to see whether goals have been efficiently met and, if not, the basis for an inquisition. Rather, the evaluation process should be thought of as the clarification of purpose, generation of data, and analysis thereof into meaningful information to determine the next steps in improving current practice. The principal will have opportunities to offer leadership to a variety of stakeholders to question, modify, and change some of the current perceptions, practices, and trends in place or being proposed.

EVALUATION IS DECISION ORIENTED

Evaluation implies that judgments will be made. Central to the making of judgments is the "valuing" part of evaluation. Ordinarily, these judgments are best made by those who must implement corrective or supplemental action decisions. Seldom is any evaluation effective as a unilateral, solo effort, whether the soloist is a principal, a parent, or even a legislator. The judgments made usually will focus on the teaching-learning process and the supporting environment of that process.

Figure 12.1 depicts the steps used to make decisions based on information resulting from the evaluation. Evaluation is a process that seldom provides an instant "good" or "bad." The individual who inserts a coin into a device to measure blood pressure does not know whether the numbers indicate a better or worse situation unless he or she can put them into a context. The same is true of the evaluation process: the data are meaningless until analyzed in the proper context. Even then, in the decision process values may be operating that make the outcome quite different from that expected or even desired by an observer.

STANDARDS MOVEMENT

The current debate about national, state, and local standards may evoke images of the past as educators remember minimum standards for functional literacy and accountability for basic competencies of students. Bracey warns that during that era the minimum often became the curriculum for most children, including those who did not always attain these competencies in spite of repeated testing.[1]

The current movement is about much higher standards, driven by the goals of competing with other countries in the global economy, guaranteeing equal opportunity for all students to learn, and preparing students for success in the twenty-first century. Policy makers and leaders

---

[1] Gerald W. Bracey, "A Critical Look at Standards and Assessments," *Principal* 73 (January 1994): 6–10.

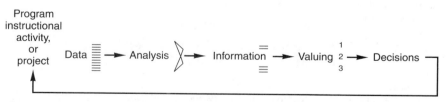

FIGURE 12.1
Steps in using evaluation to make decisions

often mandate that content standards be developed to specify learning outcomes and then direct teachers and administrators to determine how best to attain these outcomes for all children. *Content standards* denote what should be learned in various subject areas. *Performance standards* define levels of learning that are considered satisfactory where students demonstrate how well they can apply what they know. Thus, very general, open statements allow much flexibility and preserve local control of the curriculum. But this in turn can create problems with a concept of "one assessment fits all," since the actual content for instruction can vary widely among schools and classrooms. On the other hand, very strictly defined standards and proficiencies may be more closely tied to a standardized assessment instrument but erode local control as well as dictate the curriculum to be taught. Teaching to the test often becomes the obvious result, and this type of accountability system then provides a vehicle for rewards and punishments in the schools.[2]

After much debate and much voluntary experimentation by many of the states, national and state leaders are proposing a system of standards and assessments that would be initiated at the state level in accordance with the national policy. Through the Goals 2000 legislation and the reauthorization of the Elementary and Secondary Education Act, much national attention has been given to educational reform. As a result of the amendments to the Individuals with Disabilities Education Act (IDEA) enacted in 1997, many students with disabilities are now included in large-scale assessments, with recommendations for appropriate accommodations and modifications moving closer to ensuring that all students perform at high standards.[3] Currently, national, state, and local committees are attempting to sort out how this mandate will be operationalized for students with special needs. (See Chapter 11 for additional information regarding special needs students.) Some critics argue that a standards-driven curriculum could ignore the resource-poor schools and promote a lack of support for change. Much has been written about resistance to education standards based upon issues of local control of the schools, expansion of educational opportunity and success for all, and competing values of the common good versus ranking and sorting students to preserve distinctions of winners and losers in the system.[4] Some important questions for principals and teachers to consider include the following:

- What are the essential knowledges and skills that all students must have?

---

[2] W. James Popham, "Teaching to the Test?" *Educational Leadership* 58 (March 2001): 16–20.
[3] Stephanie Wood-Garnett and Cynthia L. Warger, "Requirement for Accountability," *Principal Leadership* 1 (January 2001): 26–31.
[4] David F. LaBaree, "Resisting Educational Standards," *Phi Delta Kappan* 82 (September 2000): 28–33.

- How can content standards emphasize critical thinking and problem solving rather than rote learning of isolated facts?
- What is the most appropriate way to evaluate student learning?
- What use will be made of the results from standards-driven assessments?
- What is the federal role in promoting school improvement?
- How well does the idea of national or state standards provide for diversity?

"If curriculum frameworks and learning standards are to make a difference in classroom practice and lead to improvements in student learning, we must give serious consideration to how they can be implemented practically and efficiently."[5]

SO WHAT IS TO BE EVALUATED?

An evaluation should zero in on the results of a program, project, or instructional activity. The relationship between what the program is attempting to accomplish and what the results are is the focus. The starting point is ordinarily the goals and objectives of the program or activity. Ideally, the goals and objectives of the program, project, or instructional activity are clearly specified at the beginning of the program. Such a situation appears to ease the evaluator's task. Thompson issues a call for collaboration around a common set of standards so that students, parents, and teachers have a widely shared understanding of common educational goals.[6]

In some subject areas such as mathematics, the national standards have been carefully developed by professionals in the field with input from teachers, researchers, content specialists, and parents. Forty-nine of the states have already developed or are in the process of developing educational standards, while Iowa chose to allow local districts in the state to develop their own local standards.[7] In many cases, national standards for content areas have been translated into state proficiencies with expected outcomes and often standardized assessments.

In some subject areas, there is little common agreement on the content standards or the instructional objectives. In the likely event that specific objectives are not stated, the evaluator must decide whether to assist those responsible for the activity in clarifying and stating goals and objectives in definitive terms. Given the realities of the constant press on school leaders from all quarters, the decision may be a pragmatic "yes."

---

[5] Thomas R. Guskey, "Making Standards Work," *School Administrator* (October 1999): 44.
[6] Scott Thompson, "The Authentic Standards Movement and Its Evil Twin," *Phi Delta Kappan* 82 (January 2001): 358–362.
[7] John Merrow, "Undermining Standards," *Phi Delta Kappan* 82 (May 2001): 652–659.

The principal's role in this regard is crucial. He or she should be continually aiding faculty and staff to develop, review, and revise clear objectives. Timing may force the evaluation of an existing program before staff have had time to review or rewrite their program objectives. If this is the case, already the evaluation process has a valuable finding and a recommendation—namely, objectives need to be developed. The evaluation really cannot proceed much further without them if the intent is to determine whether the program successfully met its objectives.

How can the evaluator aid in identifying program objectives and study their alignment with state standards? An analysis of all program documents and appropriate materials is a beginning. The evaluator should be alert to the consistency or inconsistency among materials used in the program or between the materials and stated program objectives. For example, it is not uncommon to find faculties stating their goal as being the individualization of instruction so that pupils can learn according to their needs and interests and at their own rates. But the program and materials may be designed to individualize only the learners' rates and not their needs and interests. An example would be learning activity packages or software programs that everyone must complete but at different rates. It may be helpful to have the faculty prioritize the objectives so that the evaluation can focus on the most important of these and thereby be manageable and practical.

The evaluator will wish to look at more than student learning objectives if he or she is working in an ordinary situation in which there are many audiences. Student learning objectives alone can be misleading and may not provide the kind of decision information needed at some other level. The principal is cautioned not to use techniques focusing on selected microcomponents of the school to determine the effectiveness of the total program.

IDENTIFYING STANDARDS, GOALS, AND OBJECTIVES

Generally, *goals* are defined as long-range, broad aims of an institution or program. *Objectives* are short-range aims, with specific time frames, and are ordinarily related to the broadly stated goals in that they specify steps toward achieving the goals. Goals may be the strategic aims, and objectives the tactical steps toward achieving those aims.

State goals for learning that described expectations for student learning were forerunners of state learning standards. Clear and specific *standards* communicate to students, teachers, administrators, and parents more precise statements of student learning and provide a basis to evaluate student progress toward meeting these expectations. Standards can provide a framework upon which to build. Learning goals are broad statements of knowledge and skills that organize the content of each learning area. Learning standards identify specific statements of knowledge and skills within a stated goal. Learning *benchmarks* are progress indicators for gauging students' achievement of each standard, forming the basis for measuring student achievement. Local schools set student learning *objectives*, which are designed to meet or exceed the state goals. The principal has a key role in leading faculty to compare their local objectives to the state standards and make modifications when deemed necessary.

One can become hopelessly bogged down in the quagmire of terms and definitions. One criticism is that highly specified performance objectives tend to focus on trivia, to the point that important educational outcomes are ignored. Another criticism is that performance objectives seem to degrade all their instructional intentions into narrow terms. Yet defensible objectives are important guides for programs and people as well as for evaluators. Statements of instructional objectives should be specific enough to provide focus for both teaching and assessing learning without limiting the teacher's flexibility in selecting teaching strategies and materials.

Learning objectives should convey to a reader or observer precisely what outcomes are expected and how one will know whether a stated standard has been reached. This provides a useful guide for instruction and sets the stage for assessment. Also, the objectives should describe the context within which the instruction or program is to take place. Given the emphasis on performance assessments, the objectives should specify expected demonstrations of the learning that should be the outcomes of the instruction or program, including intellectual, affective, and performance skills.

Administrators and teachers have a long history of developing or modifying objectives. In the past, these objectives often focused on the teaching aspects. For example, examine the following objectives:

To teach history so that the students will appreciate its impact on today's society

To teach poetry so that the students will learn to like it

To develop understanding of the basic principles of geometry

To conduct class so that the pupils behave better

It quickly becomes obvious that if the evaluator is to determine whether the program or activity has succeeded, some way must be developed to assess the students' appreciation, liking, understanding, or behaving. An effective way to check an objective when reading or writing it is to ask, "What evidence is there to substantiate attainment of this objective?" If there is no clearly indicated evidence in the objective, it should be rewritten, or additional subcategories of objectives should be written. For example, the last of the illustrated objectives could be rewritten to include examples of better behavior, such as "To organize work so that the pupils are out of their seats fewer times per day than they are now" or "To provide learning opportunities in which students are interested so that fewer interpersonal clashes occur between pupils per day than is the case now." In some situations, these may be very appropriate objectives; in others, they could lead to rigid, stultifying classroom conditions. Again, the evaluator should be careful not to base evaluation on one piece of information.

Currently, instructional objectives direct attention to the students and to the types of performance students are expected to demonstrate. These learning outcomes clarify the specific types of student learning to be assessed and convey intent to students, parents, and other stakeholders. Instructional objectives should begin with verbs such as *name, define, compare, explain,* and *construct,* which imply activity on the part of the student.[8]

Carefully prepared objectives for any enterprise are important for those engaged in the activity as well as for someone trying to determine whether the activity is achieving its intent. Even though the objectives are all praiseworthy, there comes a time when priorities factor in. Thus, it is the principal's role not only to help develop clear objectives but also to assist faculty and staff in prioritizing objectives. Just as the time, energy, and even the emotion expended by faculty in preparing specific objectives are cost items that the principal must take into account, so is the prioritizing of objectives. Principals can encourage teachers to prepare objectives cooperatively by grade level, department, or common interest, providing for input, ownership, and access. A trend toward grade-level clusters for learning benchmarks that may be broader than those found at specific grade levels allows flexibility in the structure and the amount of time needed to achieve the standards. It is necessary to document incremental steps in the progress.

In our earlier discussions of vision and visioning (Chapter 6), we described the processes of arriving at a vision. One of those is mentioned by Barth in his list of ways to develop a vision by buying a vision.[9] He rightly points out that such an approach for a school perpetuates the dependency training to which we have been so often subjected. Buying a set of objectives, or limiting an instructor or a program to a set of objectives—whether many or few, well written or not—may be putting oneself into a dependent, although maybe self-satisfied, mode. In a sense, the stakeholders can use the objectives as a set of blinders and be com-

---

[8] For further information, see Norman E. Gronlund, *How to Write and Use Instructional Objectives,* 6th ed. (Upper Saddle River, NJ: Merrill/Prentice Hall, 2000).
[9] Roland S. Barth, "Coming to a Vision," in *Reflections 1992* (Cambridge, MA: International Network of Principals Center, 1992), 76.

pletely satisfied that all is well when all specified criteria/standards are met. If the people of a school are in the process of "growing" a vision, then it seems unlikely that a program or activity will keep the same set of objectives for a long period of time. It may be that over time one piece of information that is needed is how the objectives have changed, matured, indeed grown as the definition of excellent performance has expanded.

Should not a concern for students influence every decision made? Maher suggests the new standards must be phased in more responsibly with realistic time lines, appropriate resources, safety nets, and the essential support needed to be successful.[10]

A note of caution: One can write objectives that will be easily measured. Such an approach, on the surface, can make everyone happy. What is happening is that only that which is easy to measure becomes valued. There may be situations in which individualized programs are reduced to a series of objectives that deal only with surface behaviors or learnings, while underlying attitudes, motivations, and attributes more difficult to measure are avoided. Conversely, one might find it easy to hide behind the idea that some of the more important things are not easily measured, and therefore it may be best not to measure anything, particularly in a standardized way. This sort of avoidance should not be tolerated.

GENERATING DATA

Data may be generated by observation, testing, questionnaires, opinionnaires, rating instruments, self-evaluation, mechanical recording (audio or video) analysis, or historical records of achievement, behaviors, program results, and so forth. A beginning point in determining what data should be generated is to ask how each set of data is to be recorded, stored, and analyzed. As part of this beginning process, another question must be asked: How does each data set relate to each other set and to the intended outcomes of the program or activity? Generating data is easy. Generating appropriate data from several sources and placing them in the proper context so as to yield useful information take careful thought.

Stufflebeam, in his discussion of unresolved ethical issues in evaluation, points out the problems associated with the fact that "the subfields of student evaluation, program evaluation, and personnel evaluation are not well integrated."[11] As a result, if a program is judged to be good, it may be accepted without examination as to whether the instruction (and instructors) and the learning outcomes are also good. The reverse may

---

[10] Robert E. Maher, "Let's Not Forget the Children," *Principal Leadership* 1 (January 2001): 7.
[11] Daniel L. Stufflebeam, "Professional Standards and Ethics for Evaluators," in *Evaluation and Education: At Quarter Century*, ed. Milbrey W. McLaughlin and D. C. Phillips (Chicago: National Society for the Study of Education, 1991), 275.

also occur even though the context may indicate that the instruction has been outstanding. The person responsible for using the report of the evaluation should be conscious of the very loose, if not absent, linkages between the subfields of evaluation and not commit errors of oversight or make false assumptions about unevaluated subfields.

A process of curriculum benchmarking is a form of curriculum auditing that helps to answer questions about success or need for improvement. Using documents, interviews, surveys, observations, and other tools, the evaluator seeks data that will best inform the stakeholders such as school boards, administrators, teachers, students, and the public.[12] Queen discusses long-term and short-term methods of evaluation for curriculum and instruction. Basic attributes for evaluation of educational programs from the American National Standards Institute (ANSI) include feasibility, propriety, and accuracy.[13]

Selecting the Most Appropriate Data

In very few instances are educational situations or selected facets of those situations either all good or all bad, completely unquestionable or totally unacceptable. The evaluation process inherently has many possibilities of relative effectiveness or ineffectiveness, appropriateness or inappropriateness. The important consideration for the principal is the relationship of the data generated to the outcomes of the program or to the evaluated activity. Almost every program or project has both positive and negative features. The evaluator should be concerned with generating data that may yield information regarding both strengths and weaknesses.

On occasion, controversy rages regarding the usefulness of subjective data versus objective data. Many learning outcomes cannot be adequately measured by traditional paper-and-pencil assessments. To assess these types of learning, teachers may have to depend more heavily on observation, anecdotal records, and portfolios of student work. Very different student performances and exhibits can reflect attainment of the same standard. Teachers can develop their abilities to be fair and consistent evaluators of diverse student performance.[14] Portfolios that may be very useful in formative evaluation within the classroom may present problems that must be addressed on a statewide level.

Since teaching, learning, and assessment are now seen as critically interrelated, principals may offer guidance in alignment of curriculum

---

[12] Richard W. Shelly, "Curriculum Benchmarking: A Tool for School Improvement," *NASSP Bulletin* 84 (April 2000): 40–46.
[13] J. Allen Queen, *Curriculum Practice in the Elementary and Middle School* (Upper Saddle River, NJ: Merrill/Prentice Hall, 1999), 281–302.
[14] C. Taylor, "Assessment for Measurement or Standards: The Peril and Promise of Large-Scale Assessment Reform," *American Educational Research Journal* 31 (Summer 1994): 243.

and assessment. In a standards-driven environment, there will be a need to match the assessments with content standards and classroom instruction. A range of performance tasks should have reference to a set of accepted content standards that reflect a consensus about what knowledge and skills a student must acquire in a given subject area.[15] Moving standards from a written document filed in the office or a teacher's desk drawer into classroom practice and action takes time, effort, and resources. Useful evaluation is labor intensive, complex, and subtle, especially if it provides information useful to improve the process of teaching and learning.[16]

Multiple Sources of Data

Some evaluation questions are very limited in time and scope, but most are complex. Data ordinarily need to be generated from more than one source. To seek data from only one source can create a distorted picture, even though several kinds of data are collected. "Standardized test scores provide just one small snapshot—and anyone can look bad in one picture."[17] Few programs or projects or instructional activities affect only one group or one kind of student. An experimental program in teaching journalism in the high school, for example, may appear to be excellent if information is sought from only the students or only the teachers. There may be many other groups that should provide information input to the evaluation. Administrative problems may arise with scheduling facilities or teachers' or pupils' time. If it is a field-based program, serious accountability, safety, or even insurance problems may arise. A shift in pupil-teacher load may be necessary. Per-pupil expenditures may be much more. Parents may have concerns. The local press may react. In short, the principal should identify key groups affected and gather usable data from them. One method of collecting feedback from multiple sources is called the *360-degree model*, using feedback from a full-circle evaluation of needs and interests. Input from multiple sources, obtained through questionnaires, inventories, surveys, interviews, and other instruments, keeps communication open and involvement high.[18] We are not suggesting that each time a question comes up a full-scale data-gathering effort should be mounted, but it is important to seek input from key sources if subsequent decisions are to be effective. Kean suggests

---

[15] Beverly P. Farr and Elsie Trumbull, *Assessment Alternatives for Diverse Classrooms* (Norwood, MA: Christopher-Gordon, 1997), 25.

[16] Elliot W. Eisner, "What Does It Mean to Say a School Is Doing Well?" *Phi Delta Kappan* 82 (January 2001): 367–372.

[17] William Henderson, "When They Say You're Last," *Principal* 73 (January 1994): 28.

[18] Karen M. Dyer, "The Power of 360-Degree Feedback," *Educational Leadership* 58 (February 2001): 35–39.

that the school administrator answer the following questions in selecting various types of data:

1. What information does each stakeholder need?
2. How is the stakeholder going to use this information?
3. Does the stakeholder value and trust the information?[19]

Action Research Generates Useful Data

Generation of data at the classroom level may be most useful. There has been a renewed interest in teacher-initiated action research within classroom settings. A classroom teacher may identify a persistent problem or question for study, often in cooperation with a colleague or mentor. The principal has a key role in encouraging teachers to engage in classroom studies by securing adequate resources and supporting these efforts. Administrative support could take the form of assisting teachers to make contacts with research specialists in university settings or in professional organizations, or with available personnel within the school district. Providing funds to secure mini-grants for faculty to attend workshops and for teacher-researchers to report their findings at professional meetings may be a worthwhile investment for professional development as well as generating useful data for classroom practice.[20]

Timing of Generating and Gathering Data

The evaluator needs to be sensitive to the effect that *time* has on all situations. Everything that occurs at a given time does not necessarily relate to the success or lack of success of a particular program or activity. For instance, a person could statistically establish a high direct correlation between a rise in ice cream sales and a drop in children's retention of academic facts. There is no causal relationship between the two; rather, it is the onset of warm weather and summer vacations that affects both. Unfortunately, this type of misinterpretation of data occurs much more often than it should.

Data available over a period of time about the same program or instructional behaviors may reflect different contexts for any or all participants. In fact, if some projects or activities are successful, the context will be changed from the start to the completion of the project. For example, if a school has significantly increased parents' involvement in improving the learning of their children at home, then the contexts of both home and school have been changed. The data should be interpreted from that

---

[19] Michael Kean, "Multiple Measures," *School Administrator* 53 (December 1996): 15.

[20] James F. Baumann and Ann M. Duffy, "Teacher-Researcher Methodology: Themes, Variations, and Possibilities," *Reading Teacher* 54 (March 2001): 608–615.

perspective. The evaluator may wish to gather data about pupil achievement, attitudes, and behaviors, in addition to counting the number of parents involved at some level. Then a careful look needs to be taken at the appropriateness of expectations now that a new base of operation has been established.

Although over a period of time the same measures may actually be yielding different scores, the evaluator should be cognizant of the fact that different things may be being measured. Hence, a comparability problem exists. Goldstein reminds us that changes in approximately linear trends will not continue unless acted on by some external force. He also cautions the evaluator not to succumb to the "parallel times fallacy, as exemplified in the legendary tale about the number of storks and the changes in the Swedish birth rate."[21]

Data-Gathering Means

Within the scope of this chapter, we cannot detail the instrumentation process; rather, we aim to provide the principal with some general considerations, definitions, and references regarding the instruments that are used in evaluation.

General Considerations. When selecting or developing an instrument, the evaluator should consider its validity, reliability, comparability, and practicality. These are defined as follows:

- *Validity*—The instrument measures what it is intended to measure.
- *Reliability*—The instrument is consistently valid.
- *Comparability*—The instrument is valid and reliable when administered to different groups; that is, it measures the same thing for different groups.
- *Practicality*—The investment of time, money, and expertise should be such that the returns to the school decision-making process are worth the expenditures.

Quality or Quantity? Qualitative or Quantitative? As noted earlier, it is sometimes perceived to be easier and/or safer to limit evaluation efforts to those things that can be quantified. After all, it is hard to argue with the numbers. Qualitative evaluation and research, however, are drawing more and more attention. One of the assumptions regarding much qualitative or artistic evaluation is that the observer is the primary instrument in generating "data." This causes much concern from some

---

[21] Harvey Goldstein, "Measuring Changes in Educational Attainment over Time: Problems and Possibilities," *Journal of Educational Measurement* 20 (Winter 1983): 376.

quarters in that they seek comfort in data that are somehow viewed as free from judgment. The act, result, or set of predetermined criteria is either there or not there. No one is making judgments, and, therefore, one feels safe. To limit evaluation to such a bleak set of data may lead to intellectual or at least performance starvation. A framework for evaluation should combine both qualitative and quantitative assessment data.

Commercial or Local Instruments? Obviously, the answer to the question of whether to use commercial or local instruments is "It depends." It depends on the need for generalizability versus specificity, on the availability of the prepackaged instruments, on their applicability to the local situation, on costs, on the expertise of available persons to develop instruments, and on a host of other factors. If supporting evidence is needed to make comparisons to some sort of norms, decisions must be made regarding (1) what set of norms, (2) the availability of norms, and (3) the practicality of generating local norms. Norm-referenced measures for purposes of educational evaluation often lack congruence between what the test measures and what is stressed in a local curriculum. A combination of prepackaged and teacher-made instruments may be most appropriate and complementary.

Also available to schools are the national and state results of the National Assessment of Educational Progress. School districts can piggyback on the state's assessment program to obtain comparable district-level results. Additional data are available to the principal from scores on college entry examinations as well as other competitive examinations for scholarships or recognitions. The principal will wish to examine the data in the proper context and with appropriate personnel from the district level. Assistance may also be provided by state departments of education and state universities.

A Locally Designed Questionnaire? The principal and/or evaluator must consider several steps regarding the construction of a questionnaire. The first step, frequently passed over lightly, is carefully and very specifically defining what is to be measured and how the resulting information will be used in making decisions about the educational program. It might be best not to develop an instrument until these points are clearly distinguished.

A second concern is deciding how the respondents will indicate their answers. Should they respond on a scale from one to five, answer yes or no, or check one column out of several specifically named columns? Should the items be open-ended for essaylike responses?

After the questionnaire is written, it should be field-tested on a sample population before general distribution. Obviously, the group selected for the field trial should be as nearly representative of the total group of respondents as possible. There should be provision for documented feedback as the respondents attempt to complete the question-naire. Feedback can be sought by asking respondents to write comments in the margins or by encouraging them to "think out loud" as they encounter each item.

Examination of the results should give insights into construction, semantic, or ambiguity problems. If everyone responds to certain items exactly the same way, the evaluator might question the need for the item in that it does not seem to differentiate between respondents. The respondents should be given the opportunity to suggest missing parts.

Carefully planning and executing the steps of (1) defining what should be measured, (2) scaling, (3) writing items, and (4) field testing are important. The final revision should then provide information with which the decision maker will feel more comfortable.[22]

RATING AND OBSERVATION INSTRUMENTS

A common device to generate data is the observation or rating instru-ment. Rating instruments have been maligned as devices by which pre-determined biases can be quantified. Observation instruments have not escaped the criticism of being misused or designed from biased view-points. Certainly, instances of abuse occur, but there are many defenders of rating/observation scales. The principal or evaluator must view the numerical results as points on a continuum of judgment. Those points are arrived at through each rater's filter system; thus, the "scores" them-selves are neither sacred nor absolute.

USE OF OUTSIDE EVALUATORS

If outside evaluators are used, their roles must be defined and clearly understood before the evaluation process begins. Such clarification is important to offset misunderstandings on the part of faculty, administra-tion, students, the community, and other potential users of the evalua-tion. There appear to be two camps of evaluators when it comes to view-ing their roles. One group wishes to gather, analyze, and present data to the consumers in a way that is as free of the evaluator's values as possi-ble. Another group wants to take valuing responsibility—to write up the results as "good" or "bad" and often to recommend action. Occasionally, not having a clear understanding about everyone's roles can result in not only losing the impact of the main plot but also seriously injuring the directors and producers.

---

[22] For additional information, see James F. McNamara, *Surveys and Experiments in Education Research* (Lancaster, PA: Technomic, 1994).

Another area of needed clarity is the responsibility factor. To whom is the outside evaluator responsible—those persons implementing the educational activity being evaluated or decision makers outside the activity? Who owns the data and information generated? To whom are the evaluators to report, and in what format? If an unanticipated demand for their findings arises from some quarter, to whom shall outside evaluators turn for clearance?

The caution here is not that outside evaluators are suspect and therefore to be avoided. Carefully developed prior agreements should be made, and these agreements should be made known to those involved in the evaluation.

When schools struggle with the many aspects involved in evaluation, the collective group may define new directions, evaluate progress, and carefully examine the curriculum and teaching strategies for school-wide change that would not be possible with entirely external assessment. Evaluation within the local schools can create a dynamic process of staff development and school development.[23]

ANALYSIS OF DATA

Deciding on the method of analyzing the data is not a last step. It is done concurrently with determining exactly what is to be measured and with selecting or developing instruments to gather the data. It is not to be left to the end so that the evaluator is faced with the problem of having data and wondering what to do with it.

In assessing achievement, growth, or other kinds of change, the evaluator is faced with the following set of questions, among others:

1. Do I want to compare one group with itself over a period of time?
2. Do I want to compare one group with another group?
3. How are those groups alike or different?
4. Do I want to describe merely the present status of a group?
5. What external factors other than program or instructional activities may be affecting the data (e.g., a rapid population shift or an emotionally laden controversial issue in the community, the effect of the program or activity itself)?

If two or more groups will be compared, obviously the groups should be as alike as possible or not statistically different at the beginning of the program. Matching each possible variable is impossible. Vari-

---

[23] Linda Darling-Hammond and Jacqueline Ancess, "Authentic Assessment and School Development," in *Performance-Based Student Assessment,* ed. Joan Baron and Dennie Wolf (Chicago: University of Chicago Press, 1996), 53.

ous techniques are available to the evaluator to solve this problem partially and to determine how alike the groups really are. (See Selected Readings at the end of this chapter.)

Comparing "Gains"

Cautions are raised in comparing units of change, or "gain scores." An example might use the gain scores of two groups of ninth-grade students running the mile. Assume that the criterion for effectiveness is how much improvement in time has been made. The data are to be gathered by measuring the times for each group at the beginning of the semester and at the end of the semester. The gains in time will then be determined and the two groups compared. For the sake of the example, assume that one group ran an eight-minute mile at the beginning of the semester and a six-minute mile at the end of the semester. The other group's times were six minutes and four and one-half minutes. Clearly, the first group had the greater gain, that is, two minutes as compared with one and one-half minutes. However, as is obvious to any jogger, it can be reasonably argued that the second group had the greater gain, even though the "gain score" might not be as large. It is much more difficult, and requires more training and conditioning, to match the second group's "gain" than to match the first group's gain. Which group deserves the higher grades, if that is a consideration? Or which coach deserves the merit increase?

Of course, another set of questions might be raised. Of what value is increased speed? What overall effect might the increased speed have on general physical fitness or the lack of gain on self-image?

The foregoing discussion appears to be more straightforward than it is. Gain scores are generally derived from measures less than 100 percent reliable; hence, the gain score is even more unreliable. Accurate comparisons of test scores to determine progress made should be based on the scores of the same student groups across test dates rather than the scores of a sample of the same grade level of students from test date to test date. Also, variables such as transfer and dropout rates should be taken into account.[24]

Value-Added Indicators

With a growing demand to hold schools accountable for their performance, few educators are entirely satisfied with the performance indicators currently in use. For several reasons, the average test score may be highly misleading in determining how successful a school, a program, or

---

[24] "NASSP Board Takes Stands on Key Issues for Principals," *NewsLeader* 48 (April 2001): 3. See also www.principals.org, which provides additional cautions concerning uses and abuses of gain scores.

an individual's performance is at a given time or in comparing gains made over time. Attention has been given to developing "value-added" indicators, which measure school performance and the effect of policies and inputs but isolate statistically the contributions to student achievement from other sources such as family and neighborhood characteristics.[25]

Using Norms

If a group's scores are to be compared with some norms, the appropriateness of the norms must be examined. The group used to develop the norms should be similar in many ways to the group being compared with the norms. The recency of the norms should be checked. The conditions under which the data were gathered should be similar.

The measurement phenomenon of regression to the mean should also be considered. For example, imagine any group that widely deviates, either above or below, from the mean for similar groups in a given skill. If they are measured in this skill a second time, shortly after the first time, their scores will tend to regress to the mean. That is, those who scored very low the first time will tend to score higher the second time. Those who scored very high the first time will tend to score lower the second time. Suppose a group of students is selected for the reason that their reading scores are very low. The mean on their first test may show that they are four years below grade level. If nothing different is done and within two weeks they are tested again, the mean will tend to show an increase.

To illustrate further, if a child has two unusually tall parents, his or her height will tend to be closer to the mean than that of the parents because there is not a perfect correlation between height of parents and height of children. If a special treatment in reading instruction had been given to the group of children who were four years below grade level, we could not state that the rise in their scores was attributable to the treatment. It could merely be the function of measurement and the tendency of regression to the mean. The principal should be aware of these tendencies in reviewing data and designing new evaluation programs.

Norm-referenced tests, although reliable and valid, are not without a variety of problems, and the evaluator should be cognizant of these. One problem noted earlier concerns the reflection of norm-referenced tests on what is or is not being taught in the school's curriculum. Learnings that one may deem most important may be omitted on the norm-referenced test. Occasionally, the principal may need to illuminate this

[25] Robert H. Meyer, "Value-Added Indicators of School Performance," in *Improving America's Schools*, ed. Eric A. Hanushek and Dale W. Jorgenson (Washington, DC: National Academy Press, 1996), 197–223.

point to parents and teachers concerned about test performance and encourage study of the match between test items and actual content taught.

An alternative to predetermined norm-referenced tests is criterion-referenced (C-R) tests. These tests are usually teacher made, with the attendant weaknesses. Criterion-referenced tests are costly to construct and require sophisticated measurement technology. Of course, commercial prepackaged C-R tests are available, often provided by textbook publishers. The principal should approach these cautiously. If carefully selected, they do tend to match the curricular emphases of the school's programs and be more sensitive to change in performance, but not without limiting the view of success to only those specific skills measured.

Newer forms of performance-based assessments are viewed as an integral part of daily classroom instruction and are often aligned with specific objectives, state-mandated proficiencies, and national standards. Special emphasis on connections to real-world applications and needs of individual students provides for new perspectives in the role assessments play in the instructional process related to curriculum goals. In the following chapter, procedures including standardized, informal, and performance-based assessments are discussed.

INFORMATION CONSIDERATIONS

Evaluation is based on information. It is important to consider what is meant by the term *information* as opposed to *data*. *Information* is data structured in a way that it can be used in decision making within a context. *Data* merely reflect the status of a variable or set of variables within a situation.

For example, the fact that absenteeism rises sharply, at an almost predictable rate, from April 1 to the end of the school year, in three or four schools in a particular section of a city, is not really information in itself. Nor is the fact particularly revealing that 20 percent of the schools' enrollments are children in families that work in certain agricultural regions during crop planting and harvesting times. Another fact about attendance in these schools is that there is a relatively low rate of student attrition; that is, when a student enrolls in one of these schools, she or he usually completes the eighth grade. A search to find out whether and how these data are related is necessary, and many other data will need to be collected before the picture is clear. Once this is done, the investigator can form a piece of information that will be helpful in making some decisions.

Very few situations can be evaluated by using one piece of information, particularly in education, where the human variables are almost limitless, not to mention the social, political, and economic factors. Any program results from several factors, and the same program will have several outcomes. Therefore, a single piece of information will fall far short of really evaluating a program.

By the same token, to look at just one outcome may bias the results to the point of making decisions about the program with a piece of information that points in the opposite direction from all the other pieces of information. For example, consider a device a teacher used to teach some middle-grade students the multiplication tables. Several audiotapes were made with multiplication table drills and answers on them. The first ten minutes of class each morning were spent with the tape recorder, the drill tapes, and class responses to the tapes. If one piece of information was used to evaluate the program, decisions might be made to expand it to other areas, publicize it to other teachers, or at least continue it with future classes. If the only question asked was "Did the students learn their multiplication tables?" the answer would be an unqualified yes. However, other interesting data emerged: the number of times the tape recorder was used for other purposes decreased, and tardiness for that particular room increased alarmingly.

The evaluator is then faced with another reality: all the data about a program or project cannot be collected and analyzed. The evaluator should see that a hierarchy of the importance of certain outcomes is established, including criteria for what counts in data analysis. The principal should be involved in this process with teachers as they evaluate their efforts and with outside evaluators as they work in the school. If a decision will be made regarding the tape-recorder technique for drill in the multiplication tables, the ordering of one set of outcomes in relation to another set is necessary.

VALUING

The crux of evaluation is the valuing. After all the analyses and resulting information are in, those responsible for making decisions about what happens next must go through an ordering process, a filtering, which will eventually make some things more important than others. It is true that valuing has already taken place after determining which data were collected by whom, using which techniques and analyses; but the process now culminates in the judging process.

Figure 12.2 represents the judging process that takes place. As implied in the figure, one type of comparison may not be sufficient to make judgments about a specific program. To provide resources confidently to a program that appears to be better than any similar program in surrounding schools may be extremely naive and in fact irresponsible if based on one comparison. On the other hand, to discontinue a program

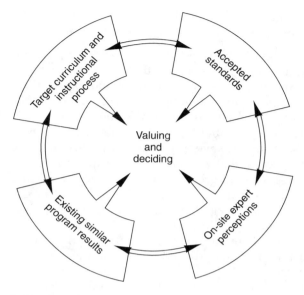

FIGURE 12.2
The judging/valuing process

because it does not meet some standards of excellence may be equally naive and irresponsible.

CONSIDERATIONS FOR PRESENTING EVALUATION RESULTS

Planning for this step is not to be left to the end of the evaluation process. Planning for presentation should occur concurrently with the other steps so that relevant data are collected and the information produced is meaningful to the recipients.

A question that should be answered at nearly each step of planning an evaluation is, *Who* needs to know *what*, relative to what kinds of *decisions?* As this question is resolved, the ways the data should be collected and stored will emerge. The various kinds of reports that may be necessary will also become evident. There is no indication that one form of reporting is best under all conditions or in all circumstances.

The evaluation design, collection of the data, and treatment of the data may be beyond question, but there is one sensitive step to take: presenting the results to the intended, and often unintended, audiences. Seldom is there a single audience; therefore, seldom does one type of presentation suffice. The complexity of the evaluation process would dictate against a smorgasbord approach to reporting the results. Whether à la carte or a complete meal, the report should be prepared for the specific consumer. The following points may serve as guides for the evaluator:

1. The impact of the evaluation on the people and the program must be a consideration. The mere fact that a program is being evaluated stirs up different sets of emotions and expectations in the people implementing the program as well as in external observers, who may wonder why the evaluation was necessary in the first place. The potential for the Hawthorne effect revisited is rather high in that several persons have now become participants in a process that will change their expectations.

2. No audience, even a small group of teachers, will identically interpret and utilize the data presented. The pitfalls of misinterpretation should be anticipated, and the presentation, written or oral, should guard against misuses.

3. The sophistication of the audience's understanding of data analysis, even raw data, will dictate the amount and type of audience preparation needed. If the presentation includes differences between sets of scores but only a few of the differences are statistically significant, the presenter should ask certain questions: Do the readers or listeners know the meaning of "statistically significant"? If not, will they understand after a brief explanation? Will the picture be confused by showing all differences?

4. The information, written or oral, will remain in one form or another for quite a long period of time and will likely be related to new information presented at a later date.

5. The limits of applying the findings, and of generalizing from the findings, must be dealt with carefully.

The principal should not overlook the possibility of retaining the services of a professional writer to prepare reports for general consumption. This should increase clarity, diminish jargon, and possibly even raise some pertinent questions for further study.

A well-planned evaluation can lose much positive impact by careless handling of the results. Whatever form the presentation takes, the "consumer's" misusing or overgeneralizing from the information should be minimized. This is not to suggest that information be withheld but rather that only information pertinent to the audience's needs be presented, and then with the limitations of its application clearly defined.

GENERAL GUIDELINES

The evaluator will wish to keep the following tips in mind as she or he reviews past evaluations and plans the evaluation processes that relate to the programs being assessed and to the audiences interested in the evaluation:

1. Those persons involved in the educational activity being evaluated should be involved as meaningfully as feasible in the design of the evaluation.
2. In designing an evaluation program, one should include a listing of possible outcomes that could result from the evaluation.
3. Evaluation of data and analyses should be planned prior to the beginning of a program, project, or targeted instructional activity.
4. One single piece of data or information will seldom provide a sufficient base for evaluation, nor will data from a single source ordinarily be sufficient.
5. Programs, processes of data generation, treatments, and types of data or instruments are not always strictly good or bad. There are continua of relative degrees of appropriateness in nearly all cases.
6. Possible/probable influences external to the evaluated educational activity should be examined and considered in the valuing process.
7. Planning an evaluation should include identifying the audiences that will receive the results and specifying how those results will be presented.

SUMMARY

Evaluation is a continual process focused on improving the effectiveness of people within the organization in achieving the organization's goals. In the case of schools, that goal is the positive learning of students in all areas of knowledge and behavior. Evaluation shows concern for students and employees as well as demonstrating a concern for effectively carrying out the school's mission for the communities it serves. Evaluation that does not result in decisions probably is nonfunctional or even dysfunctional.

The total evaluation process based upon a workable framework and the use of the results derived from the process must be phased in responsibly with realistic time frames, appropriate resources, and the essential support needed to be successfully implemented.

The active involvement of a number of persons in an evaluation effort can serve the organization well if all are well informed about the purposes, processes, and analyses of the data generated. Sharing evaluation results is a sensitive process requiring consideration of the audience and the implications the recipients may draw from the results. Evaluation should encourage not accusatory finger-pointing but rather ways to improve programs or jobs already being well done.

ⒻOR FURTHER THOUGHT

1. How can the principal become an advocate for the evaluation process?
2. Who should design the evaluation process for the middle school mathematics program? Who should not be involved in providing data?
3. Programs evaluated by an internally designed evaluation process can be "doomed to succeed." Discuss how this outcome can be avoided.
4. Evaluations are essential, but at what point might they be overdone?
5. Under what circumstances would the use of student input be essential to an evaluation? Parent input? Outside professional evaluators?
6. Give some examples of the statement "Figures do not lie, but often statistics do."
7. What are the values and dangers in the comparison of the scores of students in one school with those of students in other schools? Other states? Other nations?
8. Debate the advantages of and problems with the standards movement at the local, state, and national levels.
9. How does the role of the federal and/or state government in school accountability affect your role in school improvement?
10. Develop a statement of your basic philosophy for establishing a framework for evaluation. How would you respond to this topic in an interview for a position as school principal?

ⓈELECTED READINGS

Baumann, James F., and Ann M. Duffy. "Teacher-Researcher Methodology: Themes, Variations, and Possibilities." *Reading Teacher* 54 (March 2001): 608–615.

Bracey, Gerald W. "A Critical Look at Standards and Assessments." *Principal* 73 (January 1994): 6–10.

Charles, C. M. *Introduction to Educational Research*, 3d ed. New York: Longman, 1998.

Dyer, Karen M. "The Power of 360-Degree Feedback." *Educational Leadership* 58 (February 2000): 35–39.

Farr, Beverly P., and Elsie Trumbull. *Assessment Alternatives for Diverse Classrooms.* Norwood, MA: Christopher-Gordon, 1997.

Glatthorn, Allan A., Don Bragau, Karen Dawkins, and John Parker. *Performance Assessment and Standards-Based Curricula: The Achievement Cycle.* Larchmont, NY: Eye on Education, 1998.

Goldstein, Harvey. "Measuring Changes in Educational Attainment over Time: Problems and Possibilities." *Journal of Educational Measurement* 20 (Winter 1983): 369–377.

Gronlund, Norman E. *How to Write and Use Instructional Objectives,* 6th ed. Upper Saddle River, NJ: Merrill/Prentice Hall, 2000.

Guskey, Thomas R., and Jane M. Bailey. *Developing Grading and Reporting Systems for Student Learning.* Thousand Oaks, CA: Corwin, 2000.

Jackson, Anthony W., and Gayle A. Davis. *Turning Points 2000 (Educating Adolescents in the 21st Century).* New York: Teachers College Press, 2000 (Chapter 3: "Curriculum and Assessment to Improve Teaching and Learning").

Joint Committee on Standards for Educational Evaluation. *The Program Evaluation Standards: How to Assess Evaluations of Educational Programs.* Thousand Oaks, CA: Sage, 1994.

LaBaree, David F. "Resisting Educational Standards." *Phi Delta Kappan* 82 (September 2000): 28–33.

Madaus, George F. "The Influence of Testing on the Curriculum." In Margaret J. Early and Kenneth J. Rehage, eds., *Issues in Curriculum.* Part II, Ninety-Eighth Yearbook of the National Society for the Study of Education, 73–111. Chicago: University of Chicago Press, 1999.

McLaughlin, Milbrey W., and D. C. Phillips, eds. *Evaluation and Education: At Quarter Century.* Chicago: University of Chicago Press, 1991.

Merrow, John. "Undermining Standards." *Phi Delta Kappan* 82 (May 2001): 652–659.

Shelly, Richard W. "Curriculum Benchmarking: A Tool for School Improvement." *NASSP Bulletin* 84 (April 2000): 40–46.

Thompson, Scott. "The Authentic Standards Movement and Its Evil Twin." *Phi Delta Kappan* 82 (January 2001): 358–362.

Tomlinson, Carol A. "Reconcilable Differences? Standards-Based Teaching and Differentiation." *Educational Leadership* 58 (September 2000): 6–11.

Worthen, Blaine R., W. R. Borg, and K. R. White. *Measurement and Evaluation in the Schools.* New York: Longman, 1993.

CHAPTER 13

Evaluation of Individual Performance

*E*valuation is a challenging and often frustrating topic for study because it concerns not only measures of knowledge and demonstration of proficiencies but also the anxieties and consequences of interpreting and using this information at all levels. The evaluation of individual performance continues to be an area of concern for those evaluating and those whose performance is being evaluated.

A variety of terms regarding evaluation are used in the literature and in educational settings, among them *performance assessment, authentic assessment, alternative assessment, portfolio assessment,* and several variations. Currently, significant changes are occurring in evaluation of individual performance for all persons involved in the school setting. Principals have a unique opportunity to offer leadership in making a difference in the selection, development, and use of alternative means of assessment as well as in addressing uses and abuses of traditional forms of assessment.

Many opportunities are available to explore ways to improve the interpretation and use of traditional standardized tests and to improve the construction and development of teacher-made tests. There is even a greater need to understand authentic assessment and to develop, administer, and interpret alternative assessments in relation to the program goals. The overarching goal is to see assessment as an integral part of improvement of instruction and learning. Curriculum-based assessments affect choices of instructional strategies and materials used in the classroom. The process of evaluation can be a lever for change in the total school environment.

This chapter was revised by Suzanne V. Drake, Ph.D.

Evaluation occurs continually. In a school setting, students evaluate each other and their teachers; parents evaluate the maintenance of the building; teachers evaluate the principal; and so on. These informal, subjective evaluations are not always helpful, and sometimes they are irrational and can be harmful. Formal, data-based evaluations are needed for substance and adherence to objectivity. No planned program of evaluation is going to change the informal, subjective, and almost unconscious evaluation process; however, misconceptions may be alleviated through a carefully designed and executed evaluation of individual performance.

Developing, maintaining, and documenting quality learning environments and experiences for students are essential. The principal shares the responsibility for the evaluation of individuals and groups of individuals. It is only through the behavior of individuals and the interactions among them that the purposes of the school, or of any organization, are achieved. It is mandatory that the results of these behaviors be evaluated in terms of the achievement of the school's purposes.

In this chapter, critical issues are addressed relating to evaluation of individual performance within the school setting. This includes teachers, other staff members, the principal, and individual students. Using the framework for evaluation discussed in Chapter 12, the principal has a key role in setting the climate for a continuous process of evaluation, promoting opportunities for growth for all individuals involved.

EVALUATION OF TEACHING

Many problems are associated with the evaluation of one human being by another human being. Indeed, this may be the crux of the problem—namely, that evaluation is perceived as deciding a person's worth; then his or her relative worthiness becomes a matter of official record. Often the arguments are used that one cannot properly assess the teaching act and that no proven relationship exists between many personal characteristics and good teaching. It would appear to be appropriate, then, to reduce the emphasis on the person by focusing on the results of his or her work.

The calls for national assessment of student achievement add to the din about the schools' failures, the need to shore up education, and the need for standards and restructuring. Within this noise lie truth, fact, and misconception. McDonald asserts, "A national examination—even elegantly realized in regional variations and alternative formats—may well drive schools toward mindless accountability."[1] Merrow believes that high-stakes tests on which decisions about retention and graduation are

---

[1] Joseph P. McDonald, "Mistaking the Periphery for the Center," *Education Week*, May 1992, 36.

based may "choke the life out of many excellent schools" and drive gifted teachers from the classroom as pressure for accountability overwhelms common sense.[2] On the other hand, amazingly adaptable people can simply jump through the hoops and go on about their business, or they might even begin to believe that jumping through the hoops *is* their business.

As if the emotional overtones and the questionable state of the art of measurement science and qualitative assessment were not enough, the negotiated contracts and the positions taken by organizations have added to the difficulties of the evaluator. Yet a review of teacher organization resolutions reveals an acceptance of the evaluation of teaching as part of improving instruction. In fact, some state teacher associations call for the dismissal of the incompetent teacher.

The stipulation by most contracts that the evaluator must not be part of the bargaining unit does not negate the fact that teachers look to the principal as a resource for improving teaching performance. On the other hand, some school boards and administrators, and occasionally the popular media, seem to interpret state- or nationally mandated evaluation as limited to determining which teacher goes and which one stays. The principal once again is in the middle but has a unique opportunity to provide guidance. Evaluation should be approached cautiously, due to the complexity of the teaching-learning situation.

A model for evaluating teaching is provided in Figure 13.1. An assumption made regarding this model is that specific, measurable objectives or observable outcomes have been determined and that valid means of measurement are available. Another assumption, which should be examined if an evaluator applies this model, is that those outcomes

---

[2] John Merrow, "Undermining Standards," *Phi Delta Kappan* 82 (May 2001): 653.

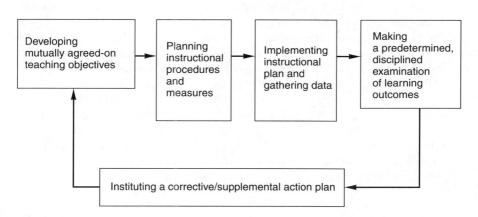

FIGURE 13.1
Teacher evaluation model

are in fact the important ones and inclusive enough to represent the total impact of the teaching-learning situation being considered.

Two other approaches to evaluating teachers are via the instructional acts performed by the teacher and the personal indicators of a successful teacher. In the first instance, definite relationships are assumed to have been established between certain types of teaching behaviors and learning. Serious considerations have been raised regarding the judging of a teacher's skill simply by watching him or her teach. Yet behavior is manageable in that it is at least observable. Some cautions regarding observations of teaching performance are noted later in this chapter.

At least one danger is present in limiting evaluation to determining the presence or degree of specific behaviors: it is possible to limit one's considerations to only those behaviors that are easily identifiable and/or measurable. To do so limits the concept of the teaching act or art to only the "safe" areas, those areas with which the evaluator feels comfortable. This approach can lead down the same well-traveled road used by some researchers: if it cannot be measured, it is not worth researching. Many important considerations can be discounted or avoided by applying this belief simplistically.

On the other hand, the evaluator can be trapped into dealing with the inferences that certain qualities (ethical behavior, concern for students, inquiry orientation) are good teaching behaviors and are associated with positive student learning. In isolation, these qualities may have no effect or even a negative effect on outcomes. Observable input variables and outcomes are meaningless unless they are set into a relatively complete context. "What makes excellent teachers recognizable may be a combination of competence (professional knowledge), skillful relationships (interpersonal knowledge), and character (intrapersonal knowledge)."[3] Professional knowledge includes competence in subject matter, curriculum, and pedegogy. Interpersonal relationships with students, colleagues, administrators, and local communities are essential. Intrapersonal knowledge involves ethics, attitudes, beliefs, and sensibilities.[4] The evaluation of an individual's performance must be carefully planned and implemented. It is also clear that no one approach will be sufficient, but neither will unrelated bits and pieces form a clear picture.

Not only is it the professional obligation of the principal to evaluate faculty and staff, but also it is each teacher's responsibility to evaluate his or her own performance. There should be a congruence of concern between principal and teacher regarding the effectiveness of the teacher's behavior as it relates to student learning and behavior. (See Chapter 14 for a discussion of staff development.)

---

[3] Vivienne Collinson, "Redefining Teacher Excellence," *Theory into Practice* 38 (Winter 1999): 10.
[4] Ibid., 4–11.

The Evaluation Process Must Be Consistent with the School's Philosophy

It is easy to lose sight of the philosophy of the school when teachers' performance is under consideration. A common philosophy is that people are different from each other and provisions should be made accordingly. Attitudes and behaviors exhibited at one level of the organization will tend to be reflected at the next lower level. Therefore, it is not unreasonable to expect that, if the evaluation of teachers reflects no consideration of human variability, the teacher's evaluation of pupils could be affected accordingly.

Another example of a school's philosophical commitment is the idea that each student should grow to realize his or her potential. While much semantic quibbling can occur regarding such a statement, clearly its intent is that no individual should be denied the opportunity to develop his or her strengths. Such a philosophy holds implications for the teacher evaluation process in that the evaluation process should identify strengths as well as weaknesses, and it should result in determining ways to capitalize on those strengths.

The Evaluation Process Must Encourage Growth

To avoid deterioration to the role of inspector, the principal can plan the evaluation program so that each individual will be encouraged to study and develop skills that may exist now in the embryo stage or not at all. To do so implies the ability to grow on the part of the faculty, which results in improved teaching. The teacher who is growing professionally will tend to be able to lead students toward self-fulfillment more effectively than one who is not growing. Such an approach is consistent with the idea of maximizing the meeting of both the individual's needs and the institution's goals.

A further indication that individual growth may result from the evaluative process might be achieved if that process itself is developed on a cooperative basis. If the process is to have real meaning to the person being evaluated, he or she should invest in the development of the process.

If the focus of evaluation is on the growth of individuals, it is not intended to narrow performance into greater conformity. The emphasis will really be on the many options that can be developed rather than uniform behavior.

The Purposes of the Evaluation Should Be Developed Cooperatively

A clear understanding of the purposes of the evaluation is necessary to reduce the tensions or threats that could result. The teacher can more readily identify with the goals of the school if he or she helps develop the goals and is involved in the process of assessing contributions toward achieving those goals. One is reminded of the marksman who never missed the center of the bull's-eye. Upon observation, it was discovered that he merely aimed at an unmissable object, found the hole where the bullet had hit, and then drew the concentric circles of the target around the hole. By involving the teacher throughout the evaluation process, the teacher will not feel that a target was drawn around the evaluator's findings.

The outcome of the evaluations is affected by the purpose of the evaluations. All parties involved need to understand whether the purpose involves merit pay, professional development, progress toward tenure, retention, or other ratings in order to secure full cooperation and fairness.

Clarify Criteria for Assessing Performance Prior to Evaluation

It is generally accepted that evaluation must be related to objectives concerned with the learning of the students. It follows that the criteria for assessment must be related to what happens to and with students, and how these conditions affect the academic and social behavior of students. As with the purposes of the evaluation, the assessment criteria are best developed cooperatively, between the evaluators and the evaluated. This is not to say that there are no prior givens. The expectations of the community, the board of education, and the parents are important inputs. These are important considerations for the principal and the teacher as they relate the performance criteria to the purposes of the school.

Evaluation Should Be Continual and from Multiple Sources

Evaluation should not be thought of as consisting of a flurry of half-hour, or even half-day, visits twice per year, mostly clustered in the spring semester. Professional growth does not flourish according to a visitation schedule. The overall evaluation plan must be continual throughout the calendar year, and there should be continuity from year to year.

Using a variety of performance measures and providing some teacher choice about which measurements to use can improve the evaluation process for teachers and principals. Rather than relying only on visits or observations by the principal, teachers may elect to include multiple sources of data, including parent surveys, student surveys, achievement data, professional activities, action research results, and other performance indicators.[5] The principal still has the responsibility

---

[5] Kenneth D. Peterson, Christine Wahlquist, Kathie Bone, Jackie Thompson, and Kaye Chatterton, "Using More Data Sources to Evaluate Teachers," *Educational Leadership* 58 (February 2001): 40–43.

for important decisions based on the total evaluation, but teachers may take a more active role in gathering and presenting data for the ongoing, continuing evaluation process.

The Results of Each Stage of the Evaluation Should Be Recorded and Reported

If the parts of the evaluation process have value to the point where an expenditure of time and effort is made, it is important enough to record the results. Board policies, law, and/or negotiated contracts may influence this process, and the principal should be familiar with each of these guides. Also, if the real purpose of teacher evaluation is to improve students' learning, the teacher must have feedback throughout the process. Evaluation is not the filling out of a sterile checklist but rather part of a learning process itself. Feedback also should be continual, not embodied in an accumulated list of strengths and weaknesses to be revealed at a witching hour in the spring, prior to contract time.

MEANS OF EVALUATING STAFF

As noted earlier, various levels of the organization and community receive and utilize the results of evaluation procedures. This particular section is concerned with the building-level professional staff as they seek to improve instruction.

Studying What Is

It is important to have some background information, including what database has already been established, prior to developing an evaluation system. The principal has many data already available. While some of it may need to be reorganized for study, most schools will have data concerning individual faculty, achievement of students, and previous evaluations. Often annual reports or outside survey team reports (e.g., accrediting agency reports, long-range planning surveys) are available.

Studying the Faculty

The principal will wish to study the faculty as a whole to see what groupings or patterns may exist. Data are available in placement folders, personnel files, transcripts, and previous evaluation reports. Hopefully, much of the data is stored in a computer file and is retrievable in a variety of formats. As the data are sorted into meaningful information, the principal will find not only a base from which to develop an evaluation process but also probably many questions for further investigation.

The following are examples of questions that may help the principal develop pertinent information about the faculty as a whole.

The Total Faculty

1. What are the age and experience ranges of the teachers? Does this information show a curve skewed to one side or the other? Are there hiring or reassignment implications?
2. Where do the faculty live in relation to the school and the attendance area the school serves? Is there an obvious reason for this pattern, if one exists? What implications does this pattern have in terms of community interaction and impact?
3. What teacher education institutions are represented on the staff? Is there a balance of input from this point of view?
4. What is the tenure pattern of teachers within this school? Is the turnover rate typical for the district? For the region? Is the turnover balanced in terms of age groups, disciplines, and educational backgrounds?

Individuals

1. What special strengths (in preparation or experience) does this person have? What potential for future development of expertise?
2. What do previous evaluators regard as this individual's strengths? Are previous evaluations consistent?
3. Are any outside interests evident that could contribute to the program of the school? Technology expertise? Drama? Group leadership activities?
4. What has been this person's professional growth pattern? Planned program of study? Summer courses? What types of courses? In what fields?
5. Are there any outside influences that might hinder professional activities or growth or interfere with job performance?
6. What additional professional contributions have been made? Organizational work in local, state, or national organizations? Research? Articles published?
7. Does this person exhibit interest in accepting responsibility? What leadership activities has she or he done?

During the course of gathering data, the principal will wish to be alert to various groupings of persons. These groups may emerge as he or she analyzes the faculty by age, institutions, grade level, subject matter, and so on. Such information may be helpful in organizing for instruction.

Studying Achievement Patterns

Many data are available regarding student achievement patterns in classrooms and in schools. Some propose that student learning must be the *touchstone* by which successful teaching may be gauged. Although some efforts have been less than useful in this area, an evaluation of achievement patterns may enable teachers to inquire productively into the effects of their teaching on student learning. "A close linkage between artifacts that demonstrate student learning and analyses that show how that learning grows out of specific actions and decisions is critical to judging teaching effects."[6] It is important for teachers to evaluate themselves in relation to their students' successes, which may provide powerful avenues for continual professional development.

The achievement of students may be viewed along at least six strands: standardized test scores; teacher grades; behavior anecdotes; feedback from internal/external studies; relationships with others; and contributions such as artwork, volunteer work in and out of school, clubs, class offices, and the like. The following list of questions will aid the reader to develop questions pertinent to his or her own school.

Standardized Test Scores
1. What is the testing pattern, using what tests? What kinds of learning do the tests probe?
2. What are the ranges of growth between one testing time and another, for each specific area? Are these data consistent from one year to the next?
3. Are the ranges of growth we have mentioned consistent with the intervals at which the tests are given?
4. Does an analysis of growth by teacher and by subject area indicate any significant variations from the typical or average growth increment for that area? What obvious factors contribute to any variation? Is the variation consistent from one year to the next?
5. What norms are typical for these tests in schools similar to yours?

Alternative Assessments
1. What other means are used to document the progress of students' learning? Are there a variety of performance assessments? Are portfolios developed? Are rubrics developed for evaluating results?
2. In what ways are the alternative assessments used by the teachers? By the students?
3. What is the relationship between the assessments and specific curricular goals? State proficiencies? National standards?
4. Are the alternative assessments used consistently throughout the school?

---

[6] Linda Darling-Hammond, "Standards for Assessing Teaching Effectiveness Are Key," *Phi Delta Kappan* 79 (February 1998): 471.

5. What is the content of teacher-made tests? How do the teacher-made tests relate to the standardized tests and to the overall curricular goals?

Teacher Grades

1. Does the individual teacher's distribution of grades approximate a normal distribution curve? Is that appropriate?
2. Are the distributions of grades relatively consistent throughout the faculty? Within departments? Within grade-level groups?
3. Is there consistency between the grades given in classes in certain subject areas and the performance of those same students on achievement tests?

Behavior

1. Are the anecdotal comments of the teachers about student behavior consistent? Do the comments really distinguish among students, or do they say the same things as if taken from a "phrase book" or catalog of comments?
2. Do school records show any pattern of behavior problems that are apparently concentrated in one grade, class, subject, and so on?
3. Do certain classes have behavior problems and also low achievement scores?

Follow-Up

1. Using a sample, or the total population, what grades by subject do the students receive at the next higher level? Is the distribution typical of the schools they are attending?
2. How do the students feel about their preparation?
3. Do studies of the various assessments, including standardized and state-required tests, give an integrated picture of student achievement, or do they yield data related only partially to the stated school goals?
4. What follow-up is attempted with those students not attending a next higher level of formal education?

Relationships with Others

1. What interaction patterns exist across age groups, racial groups, and socioeconomic levels?
2. What evidence is available regarding out-of-school interactions? Are there patterns of interaction between the community at large and certain groups of students?

Student Contributions

1. What sorts of contributions do the students make to the school and to the community? Is there any indication of volunteering for these contributions?

2. Do the contributions appear to come from just one or a few groupings of students (e.g., socioeconomic group, grade, subject matter)?

3. From what sources do the opportunities to make contributions come?

Though clearly not exhaustive, this list illustrates many of the questions the principal should answer systematically in preparing to design, or help design, an evaluation of the results of the school's efforts. With information gained from answering such questions, a base can be developed to relate the evaluation of teaching-learning acts to student achievement and to the school's goals.

OBSERVATION OF THE TEACHING-LEARNING SITUATION

A multitude of evaluation forms, scales, and other observation instruments is available, but many of these devices are not really designed as purely observational. They are expected to serve a dual purpose: recording data about the teaching-learning situation that is being observed and placing value on those observations.

Classroom observation has a long tradition that is generously sprinkled with examples and magnified rumors of misuse, abuse, and general ineffectiveness. Reaction has taken many forms, from well-rehearsed show lessons to restrictive sections of negotiated contracts. Much of this sort of reaction can be avoided or alleviated by delineating the part that the classroom observation is to play in the process of improving instruction. (This idea is later expanded under the heading "Analysis of Data and Information.") In addition, limiting observation to those techniques designed in cooperation with the teacher will aid in keeping this facet of evaluation in the "improve" camp rather than the "prove" camp. Judgments made about the data generated should be made by both the observer and the observed whenever possible.[7]

The principal is aware that the presence of any outside observer does affect the class and teacher being observed. It may be helpful to discuss this effect with the staff involved, before observing, so that mutual understanding is developed as well as means employed to minimize this effect.

Some school reform efforts expand the role of teachers to include mentoring and peer coaching as they become team leaders, department heads, and members of personnel committees, breaking down isolated

---

[7] The reader may wish to study views of observation by reading Carolyn M. Evertson and Judith L. Green, "Observation as Inquiry and Method," in *Handbook of Research on Teaching*, 3d, ed. Merlin C. Wittrock (New York: Macmillan, 1986), 162–213.

role distinctions and promoting collaboration in interdisciplinary teams. A study of teachers' perceptions of their roles as leaders and as team members confirmed previous conclusions that all teachers do not perceive the same situation in the same way.[8] Through additional study of the expanding role of teachers as leaders and as decision makers, insights may be gained into the complexity of the teaching-learning process and new opportunities developed to support the highest-quality schools in the twenty-first century.

Formalized Observation Techniques

Observation devices are available for recording selected behavior of teachers and students and interactions between them. They range from relatively narrow, often simplistic devices to horrendously complex, costly processes requiring several trained observers.

The current status of negotiated contracts may preclude the use of many of these complex instruments. Regardless of contract language, the faculty should be involved in the decision to use, and the selection of, the observation instrument(s).

The reader is cautioned not to adopt any techniques without carefully determining how the data will be gathered, analyzed, and used. Before selecting an observation technique, the following points should be considered:

1. Does the technique require extensive observer training? Much suspicion can be cast upon the results because of the adequacy or inadequacy of the observers' training.

2. An observation technique should be employed only if it really shows differences in behavior and not just a recording of impressive behavior.

3. An observation technique should not be used as a single source of data on which to base the evaluation of a teacher's performance.

4. Data should be generated about important behaviors and should be recorded in such a way that it can be analyzed by persons other than the recorder.

5. What are defensible connections between observable teacher behavior and actual measures of students' achievement?

6. Many "unobserved" factors may enhance mediocre performance or negate outstanding performance. For example, attitudes conveyed by body posture, tone of voice, and selection of words with negative or positive connotations can all contribute

---

[8] Sharon Conley and Donna E. Muncey, "Teachers Talk about Teaming and Leadership in Their Work," *Theory into Practice* 38 (Winter 1999): 46–55.

to the effectiveness or ineffectiveness of a specific, observable, recordable behavior.

These limitations are not intended to discourage the reader from using observation techniques but rather to give perspective on their appropriate use.

Locally Developed Observation Procedures

A disciplined approach to observing can lead to noting behaviors or situations not usually observed. For example, it might be decided cooperatively between the teacher and principal to count the number of praise versus censure statements directed toward individuals in the class, so that a frequency chart could be established showing this information for a certain period of time. The teacher might discover that a large percentage of his or her praise statements were directed toward two students and an equally large percentage of censure statements were directed toward one student. Gathering these data two or more times over a period of two weeks or even two months might be very instructive for the teacher. The principal, supervisor, department head, or trained observer may use many such counting procedures to help the teacher evaluate his or her performance. Some suggestions include these:

1. How much time does the teacher spend speaking versus listening to students?
2. How many times does the teacher give directions to the whole group as opposed to individuals or small groups?
3. How many times does the teacher interrupt working with a student or students to correct the behavior of another student?
4. How much time does the teacher spend lecturing versus questioning?
5. How many questions are the recall-facts type, and how many questions are designed to elicit responses requiring the application of knowledge and other higher-level thinking skills?
6. Are there gender differences in questioning, prompts, and teacher responses to males and females in the class?
7. What is the "wait time" following teacher questions before expected student responses?
8. With which students does the teacher interact verbally? Nonverbally? How often? Who is overlooked?
9. Which students are on task, and for how long?

And the list can go on and on with specific questions generated by the teacher or the evaluator. Audio- and videotaped recordings of specific time segments may prove valuable to both teachers and principals for analysis and discussion.

The principal should attempt in all instances to relate his or her observations of teacher performance to student behavior and the results of teaching. The purpose of an observation should be to formulate an accurate description of the classroom situation. We question the accuracy of a description if it is based on an isolated, "posed snapshot" sort of observation, once or twice per year. The description should be as free as possible from value placed on the data. Only as the data are compared with the specific objectives the teacher had set does that description become part of the evaluation process. If the evaluation process is to be useful to the teacher in improving competencies, he or she should be involved in planning that process by clarifying instructional objectives, indicating which data might be helpful, and aiding in establishing criteria to interpret the results of the observations.

RATING PROCEDURES

Ratings for administrative accountability purposes might be conceived as points along a continuum of process evaluation for instructional improvement purposes, as illustrated by Figure 13.2. The number of times necessary to rate an individual's performance for administrative accountability purposes will probably be dictated by local policies.

Before You Rate

The rating process has pitfalls. Several studies have shown that there is little or no correlation between various raters' judgments about the same

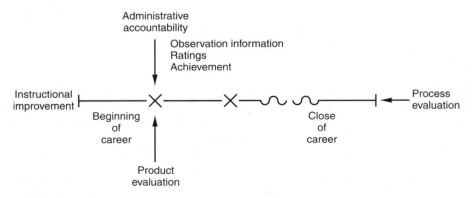

FIGURE 13.2
Rating for accountability as an integral part of rating for instructional improvement

teaching-learning situation. Part of this problem is caused by the limitations of the real measuring devices—the individual raters.

We have on more than one occasion distributed a twelve-item rating form to a graduate class in supervision. With very few exceptions, all participants were experienced teachers, some holding supervisory or administrative responsibilities. A film was shown of a teacher introducing a unit of study. The rating form provided for five points on a continuum, from "excellent" to "needs improvement." Each time, the ratings of the group for each item ranged over four of the five points, and occasionally over all five. The range was present even regarding the appropriate dress of the teacher.

The rater's lack of self-knowledge limits the accuracy of rating. Raters tend to overlook defects like their own, and they tend to rate those persons they like higher than those they do not like. A history of outstanding incidents can positively or negatively affect the rating of a current teaching-learning situation.

Rating forms have been in use for a long time, and there seem to be enough of them to boggle the mind of the evaluator. They range from simple environmental checklists to heavily value-oriented scales.[9] Although recording observations on predetermined items helps the evaluator cover items that are important to him or her and also provides an instant record of the evaluation, several cautions should be noted regarding the use of such forms.

Too often these forms emphasize personal characteristics and physical environment. While both are real factors, they tend to deemphasize the learning of the students as the prime consideration. Also, a teacher could score very high in many of the areas (e.g., punctuality, record keeping, poise, good grooming, personal fitness), and the students would still be achieving very little. The opposite is also possible.

This discussion is not intended to discount these areas or devalue the use of rating forms but rather to give a perspective in the selection and use of forms. Scores on rating forms tend to be indices of compatibility between rater and rated. This may also apply to the items selected for rating, in that the rater will tend to select those items or rating forms that emphasize those items with which the rater feels most comfortable.

Rating scales may be judged as measuring devices according to the following qualities:

1. *Objectivity*—The data yielded are not a function of the rater and are reproducible.

---

[9] The reader might be interested in knowing that a sixteen-point diagnostic rating scale was developed and used by T. L. Torgenson in 1930. The scale included items on types of criticism, individualization, on-task behavior, behavior control, and remedial instruction. It was used for self-evaluation and supervisor evaluation, with follow-up confirming observations. How far have we come in over seventy years?

2. *Reliability*—The same values will result under the same conditions.
3. *Sensitivity*—The data will show as fine distinctions as are typically made regarding the behavior selected for rating.
4. *Validity*—The results recorded are an accurate reflection of what was intended to be measured.
5. *Utility*—The effects on improvement should be in balance with the expenditures of time and personnel commitment.

The use of numerical ratings (e.g., 1 to 5) without further description can cause misinterpretation later, in the event the data are used in dismissal proceedings. Rund provides the following example:[10]

Professional image displayed	5
Punctuality	3
Attendance	4
Professional advancement	5
Teaching effectiveness	2
Discipline	1

Key: 5 = excellent; 1 = poor

While the individual rated in this example dresses well and is taking night classes toward a master's degree, there are some serious problems in the classroom. This is not apparent to an outside hearing officer if an average of the six values is taken. The resulting average of 3.3 might convey an above-average rating. It is important to emphasize those areas that are most important versus those that are peripheral to teaching effectiveness.

While planning the rating process, the evaluator may wish to consider the following point: "teacher evaluation that is educationally sound should . . . (1) be based on learner growth as the criterion for teacher success; (2) provide specific, usable information to teachers about their strengths and weaknesses; (3) provide clear differentiation between more effective and less effective teachers; and (4) be flexible enough to assess reliably a wide range of individual teaching styles."[11]

Involve Those Being Rated

If the purpose of rating is primarily to improve instruction, then it is important to involve those being rated in selecting and/or developing the items to be rated and the criteria to be applied. This may be spelled

---

[10] Robert W. Rund, "Seven Evaluation Syndromes to Avoid," *Indiana Elementary Principal* (Fall 1978): 5.
[11] William G. Webster, *Learner-Centered Principalship* (Westport, CT: Praeger, 1994), 204.

out by the negotiated contract. The principal will find the following steps helpful in implementing this facet of individual performance evaluation:

1. Clearly state the purposes of the evaluation as related to policies and contractual agreements.
2. Delineate the procedures to be employed and the criteria to be applied.
3. Wherever feasible, develop the items with the staff.
4. Plan cooperatively to assess the evaluation. Clarify the channels.
5. Throughout the process, emphasize the diagnostic usefulness of the evaluation.
6. Assist the staff in using the information for self-evaluation.

SELF-EVALUATION

One of the principal's goals for an evaluation program could be to help those being evaluated to become skilled self-evaluators. Developing the ability to reflect on what has occurred in the teaching situation and to analyze the various outcomes can lead to more effective instruction. Experienced teachers may profit most from self-evaluation techniques. They should be encouraged to develop their own structures for self-evaluation but may profit from examining existing instruments available or developing new ones individually and in personnel committees.

For beginning or relatively inexperienced teachers, Drake suggests the following set of questions for initiating a self-study report based on an analysis of an audio- or videotaped lesson. This process has proven useful to both preservice and in-service teachers.

1. What are some of my personal idiosyncrasies? What can I do about them?
2. What happens to my voice? Is it different in different situations?
3. How did the students respond initially to the lesson? What did I do to motivate or set the climate for learning?
4. Did I meet my specific objectives for this lesson?
5. What can I say about the interaction between myself and the students? The students with each other?
6. How did I feel during my own observation? What did I like or dislike?
7. What are the most important things I can learn through self-evaluation techniques such as analysis of tape-recorded lessons?

8. Where should I improve to become the kind of teacher I want
    to be? Where could I receive assistance?[12]

The principal may have as a goal that each teacher will assess her
or his own performance so the effectiveness of instruction is increased.
Indeed, it is reasonable to expect that teachers are interested in self-
assessment. The principal can encourage this interest by creating threat-
free vehicles through which the teacher may assess his or her work. A
plan can be worked out cooperatively to obtain feedback from students
and even from colleagues. Some schools have found peer viewing of
videotaped lessons to be effective. Having the observers share ideas with
the teacher and the teacher explain the techniques used has proven to be
an effective two-way improvement process. The teacher may wish to
develop a checklist for his or her own observation of the students to try
to determine his or her effect on the classes. A self-evaluation checklist of
the teacher's feelings about individual performance might include the
following areas of concern:

- Relationships with students in regard to their behavior, sensitiv-
  ity to their needs, and inclusion of their interests
- Use of a variety of materials, technologies, other media, and
  instructional aids
- Relevance, involvement, and interaction with students regard-
  ing topics studied
- Initiative and responsibility of students for their own learning
- Effectiveness of evaluation of students' work
- Relationships between students
- Relationships with colleagues
- Evidences of self-improvement and professional development

The inclusion of self-evaluations in the total evaluation process may
be helpful to both the principal and the teacher. Koehler points out that
self-evaluations could help the supervisor understand the teaching style
and why the teacher employed certain instructional techniques.[13] Including self-evaluation results in the total process would be a natural point of
departure in any observation preconference.

A staff member may find it helpful to use the school's rating instrument as a self-evaluation device, by having the teacher and the principal
each complete the form independently and then comparing their findings in a conference. It could provide an opportunity for a productive
discussion between the staff member and the supervisor in which they
compare perceptions and identify strengths plus areas for improvement.

---

[12] Suzanne V. Drake, "Self-Evaluation Techniques to Improve Teaching," *Illinois School
Research and Development* 24 (Fall 1987): 8.
[13] Michael Koehler, "Self-Assessment in the Evaluation Process," *NASSP Bulletin* 74 (September 1990): 40–44.

Recently, administrators have embraced the idea of using portfolios as a tool for evaluating teachers. "When individuals maintain performance portfolios which document their efforts and achievements in their work, they learn to assess their own progress because it requires them to reflect on their work as they collect information."[14]

Teachers can showcase what they have accomplished, presenting achievements in a concrete form. Murphy shares steps to be initiated and supported by the principal as she points out special provisions needed in terms of time, materials, space, and procedures.[15]

Cushman suggests that educators presenting portfolio evidence of learning and growth could include feedback from colleagues, holding each other accountable and providing a more authentic way to measure performance against established goals and standards.[16] Portfolios provide another tangible tool for reflection and future goal setting. Regardless of the self-evaluation approach used, opportunities should be available for the open discussion of the results with colleagues and/or supervisors.

STUDENT INPUT IN THE EVALUATION PROCESS

Student evaluation of the teaching-learning situation has caused much emotional reaction. The arguments against it need not all be repeated here, except to point out that they generally center around a person's reaction to another person's judging personal worth. This may well be the key to redirecting the focus toward the more neutral turf of the learning environment and learning outcomes rather than the teacher. Certainly in no instance should an evaluation consist of just student input.

Given students' time investment, it seems logical that their opinions would be helpful in the evaluation for improvement of instruction. Yet student input must be used cautiously, and it is used best as direct feedback to the teacher. Consistent feedback over a period of time will tend to identify strengths and weaknesses, but to get the true picture, one must get below the surface. Stories abound about the popular teacher, the one who nearly always is nominated for "teacher of the year" or to whom the yearbook is dedicated. But a few years later, when students recall teachers whose instruction has been helpful to them, the name of the popular teacher may not surface. In short, charisma carries a great deal of weight, although not in the long run.

---

[14] Carole H. Murphy, "Steps to Successful Portfolios for Principals," *National Forum of Educational Administration and Supervision Journal* 14 (1997–98): 32.
[15] Ibid., 32–38.
[16] Kathleen Cushman, "Educators Making Portfolios," *Phi Delta Kappan* 60 (June 1999): 744–750.

Can younger children really make judgments about teaching? Several writers apparently feel they can and should. For an interesting instrument for this purpose, see Hughes and Ubben's book.[17] Can older students really make judgments that are helpful to the teacher and the evaluator? Kleiner notes that the following factors appear to increase student ratings: nonthreatening environment, less rigorous objectives or testing, and entertaining classes.[18] He adds that challenging and imaginative teaching may damage the evaluations. It would appear that teachers can make the most productive use of student feedback in a self-evaluation mode. A second viewpoint, to confirm or question some of the conclusions the teacher may have drawn, is also valuable.

When considering merit pay or tenure, student input should be treated as only one piece of the picture, given the several facets of a professional's contributions.

ANALYSIS OF DATA AND INFORMATION

The analysis of the data begins as soon as the evaluation process unfolds, when decisions are made regarding goals, processes, and what data are relevant to the outcomes of those goals and processes. Subjective judgments are made about what is important to evaluate. Once gathered, the data are then analyzed.

Making a value judgment on the data and information gained by the use of observation techniques, rating scales, and self-evaluation is a very important step in the whole process. At this point, directions for positive change may be determined. Here, too, the persons being evaluated must play an active part. A supervisory practice employed to involve the persons being evaluated is clinical supervision, with an emphasis on identifying and interpreting patterns in the teaching-learning acts. Cogan distinguishes between general supervision and clinical supervision: "General supervision subsumes supervisory operations that take place principally outside the classroom . . . activities like writing and revision of curriculums . . . units and materials of instruction. . . . In contrast, clinical supervision is focused upon the improvement of the teacher's classroom instruction."[19] Sergiovanni defines supervision as a system of help for teachers as they achieve goals that they consider important.[20] Principals can provide assistance, support, and reinforcement as the process unfolds. He stresses that greater

---

[17] Larry W. Hughes and Gerald C. Ubben, *The Elementary Principal's Handbook* (Newton, MA: Allyn & Bacon, 1984), 238–241.

[18] Brian Kleiner, "Viewpoint: Student Evaluation of Teaching," *Journal of European Industrial Training* 13 (1989): 16–17.

[19] Morris L. Cogan, *Clinical Supervision* (Boston: Houghton Mifflin, 1973), 9.

[20] Thomas J. Sergiovanni, *The Principalship: A Reflective Practice Perspective*, 2d ed. (Boston: Allyn & Bacon, 1991), 316.

satisfaction for teachers comes from the accomplishment of worthwhile and challenging tasks in a pleasant and supportive atmosphere.

A major outcome of analyzing the data and information with the teacher(s) is that the teacher becomes more adept at self-evaluation of his or her performance. If the principal works in the classroom directly with the faculty, he or she will be assisting them by demonstrating how to develop questions or hypotheses about their performance, how to generate data relevant to these questions, and what means to use to analyze the data. If the school is very large and/or departmentalized, the principal may find it more productive to work with department heads or level coordinators in a clinical fashion, thus not only meeting his or her own responsibilities effectively but also enhancing the department heads' effectiveness in improving instruction within their own departments.

The following points are essential to the effective analysis of teaching-learning acts:

1. The emphasis must be understood by both supervisor and teacher(s) to be on developing the strengths of the teacher(s) as they relate to student outcomes in academics and behavior. Obviously, weaknesses will occasionally prohibit student learning to the point where the weaknesses must be dealt with immediately, but these should be viewed as exceptions.
2. Data should be so recorded that both teachers and supervisors can analyze them separately as well as together, patterns of behavior can be identified, and the data can be reviewed later if necessary.
3. The interaction between the supervisors and the teachers should be relatively threat-free and should not focus on the value of the job performance except as it pertains to the students' behavior and learning.
4. The principal should clearly articulate achievement and behavior expectations.
5. The principal needs to be sensitive to systemic problems of the organization that hinder growth.

Current organizational patterns that put faculty into "teams" hold much promise for an enriched clinical approach to improving instruction. Some schools have experienced a renewal of professional interest and growth by employing variations of the quality circle approaches found in industry. (See Chapter 10 for further information on team decision-making.)

SUSPENSION AND/OR DISMISSAL

When one considers evaluation and accountability of personnel, the enlightened approach for the principal is to see the process as a positive one. The process should be considered a diagnostic tool to assess strengths and weaknesses of the school and individuals working in the school. It should provide clues and means to correct the weaknesses and buttress the strengths.

Unfortunately, a time may come in every school when the only legitimate recourse in correcting a weakness is to dismiss an employee. If necessary, dismissal should be done as simply, fairly, and effectively as possible, without attendant public controversy, which can do so much to harm a teacher professionally or shake the confidence of the public in the school. Analyzing the hundreds of court cases that have resulted from suspensions, dismissals, and attempted dismissals, one discovers that controversy and the resultant lawsuit often occurred because of lack of proper procedures by the board of education generally and school administrators specifically. Procedural deficiencies fall within three broad headings:

1. The school district did not have written guidelines that would give teaching personnel direction as to dress, speech, general behavior, and appropriate teaching conduct.
2. The school district and its administrators did not maintain detailed, written records of an anecdotal nature delineating questionable behavior, teaching deficiencies, and procedures used to attempt to correct those deficiencies.
3. The school district did not have an established, written administrative procedure for suspension and dismissal of personnel that adhered to local contractual agreements regarding dismissal, state statutes regarding dismissal, and/or nationally accepted "fundamentally fair" procedures that recognize the constitutional rights of individuals.

Written Guidelines

Thousands of school districts operate throughout the United States, representing a full spectrum of possible viewpoints, from ultraconservative to ultraliberal. Each district has a basic right to establish its own rules and regulations regarding the behavior of its personnel so long as it operates within the law and the state and federal constitutions. If there are basic norms of conduct, dress, or general behavior, and especially if there are accepted teaching and student discipline and relationship modes, these should be specifically spelled out and made available to teachers in the system.[21]

---

[21] We believe that such guidelines for conduct should be developed jointly by teachers, administrators, board members, and citizens. However, the point of this discussion is that no matter how they are developed, they should be written as specific policy of the district and made available to each teacher. See *Lucia v. Duggan*, 303 F. Supp. 112 (D. Mass 1969), for further discussion on this point.

Teachers cannot be dismissed for exercising their constitutional rights, but dismissal can occur if professionals fail to meet the high standards and expectations of their profession.[22] These high standards and expectations can be those generally held by the profession itself or specifically held by the district in which the teacher works.

The major reasons for which discharges and suspensions are allowed are incompetency, insubordination, immorality, and "good cause." Of course, these terms are so general that a school board is obligated to define what it actually means when using them, preferably in written form and made available to all who could be affected. If a personal action is taken, the board should specify what the defendant did as examples of action or lack of action to trigger the board's proceedings.

Flygare has made the point that policies or regulations covering classroom conduct and general teacher behavior are very important in a court's decision relative to a school district's dismissal rights. He further declares that a teacher has a greater chance of winning the suit if the "guidelines are vague and overly broad."[23] Lest one be lulled into a sense of false security by the absence of guidelines, Flygare reviews an interesting case in the Tenth Circuit Court of Appeals that held "that even in the absence of guidelines teachers could be discharged for employing unconventional teaching methods particularly when more competent teachers are available in the labor market: *Adams v. Campbell City School District* 511 U.S. 1242 (1975)."[24]

Detailed, Written Anecdotal Records

The time is long gone when a teacher can be dismissed because of generalized negative observations of a principal. Records of a teacher's deficiencies must be specific, detailed, and collected over a long enough span of time so that the deficiencies cannot be classed as incidental behavior. In serious situations, the supervisor should have observations verified by a responsible second party. Further, the supervisor should have available as a matter of record a description of efforts to apprise the teacher of deficiencies and suggested methods for correcting said deficiencies.[25] Information of this type is considered privileged. So long as it is not indiscriminately broadcast and is released only to those who have a right to receive such information, the administrator need have no fear of charges of libel.

---

[22] *Pickering v. Board of Education*, 291 U.S. 563 (1968); *Keyishian v. Board of Regents*, 385 U.S. 589 (1967).

[23] Thomas Flygare, *The Legal Rights of Teachers* (Bloomington, IN: Phi Delta Kappa Foundation, 1976), 11.

[24] Ibid.

[25] *Bott v. Board of Education*, 392 N.Y.S.2d 274 (N.Y. 1977).

An illustration from a court case in Illinois helps emphasize this point. A school administrator made statements before the board of education to the effect that a certain teacher left the classroom unattended, lacked ability as a teacher, and did poorly in certain courses at a teachers' college. The teacher brought suit for damages, alleging that the statements were untrue and that, since they formed the basis for her discharge, they were defamatory in nature.

The court did not agree. So long as the administrator (1) had made the remarks in the line of duty, (2) to persons having the right to receive such information, and (3) without malice or harm intended, his communication was conditionally privileged (*McLoughlin v. Tilendis*, 253 N.E.2d 85 [Ill. 1969]).[26]

Sendor describes a case in Maine (*Wytrwal v. Saco School Board* 70 F. 3d 165 [U.S. App. 1995]) in which the school board decided not to renew the contract of an employee who had been a vocal critic of the district's administrators.[27] As litigation proceeded, it became more and more essential for the administrators to be able to show that they had carefully considered and documented the reasons for their decision and that they could clearly articulate these reasons. The decision to deny a continuing contract was based on written comments by the principal and the assistant principal about the teacher's trouble in managing her students, her problems working with colleagues and supervisors, and her considerable number of absences from the classroom. The courts accepted the administrators' testimony about the teacher's job performance, and the key point of documented evidence was proof that the administration would have made the same personnel decision whether or not the employee had spoken out.

Established, Written Administrative Procedures

Specific procedures for suspension or dismissal are usually described in a local bargaining contract, state legislation, and/or state department of education regulations. Case law also provides guidance. Beyond this, of course, are the basic constitutional rights of any individual. These are generally referred to as due process rights given to every citizen by the Fifth and Fourteenth Amendments to the U.S. Constitution. The courts, through their interpretations of these rights, have defined citizens' rights and the circumstances under which these rights may be restricted and at the same time guarantee to each citizen an opportunity to refute any attempts by government to deprive him or her of substantive rights. A

---

[26] National Association of Secondary School Principals, *A Legal Memorandum* (Reston, VA: Author, April 1974), 5.

[27] Benjamin Sendor, "When a Gadfly Gets under Your Skin," *American School Board Journal* 183 (April 1996): 22–25.

school district should use these as the base, but beyond this it is desirable to detail more specific procedures appropriate to the local situation to give the administrator clear direction in suspension and dismissal cases.

Redfern provides a four-phase process regarding teacher dismissal: (1) early diagnosis, (2) performance-improvement plan, (3) notification of corrective action, and (4) implementation of termination.[28] The teacher should be given specific direction regarding performance improvement, and time to improve, and should be monitored throughout the process. Of course, careful documentation is essential. If the improvement required does not materialize, corrective action must be taken. Redfern indicates that this action consists of four parts: (1) notification of still existing deficiencies, (2) detail of these deficiencies, (3) assistance available to the teacher, and (4) a deadline for deficiencies to be corrected.

Throughout the process, documentation of efforts to provide help to the individual is required. A definite plan for providing assistance to all faculty members, such as a clinical supervision procedure, can be useful. The plan should be one that can be explained to a layperson, making it evident that the plan does provide direct assistance and supervision to the teachers. If corrective action fails, the defendant should be given (1) notice of the reasons for the proposed termination, (2) a hearing at which he or she can question "accusers," (3) time to prepare and present arguments, (4) a hearing before an impartial decision maker, and (5) a statement of the reasons for the decision and the evidence on which the decision was based. Any action following the hearing must meet the procedural and substantive guarantees set out in the school board's administrative code for all discharge proceedings.

Pratt lists points for reflection regarding the legal and ethical issues in teacher dismissal. He encourages principals that "by taking actions that respect the dignity and worth of another human being, the decision is likely to withstand legal challenge and assure that the interests of school and students are best served."[29]

Beating the Rap

In the meeting halls of administrators' conventions or in teachers' lounges, one hears story after story of the flagrantly incompetent teacher who "beat the rap" when the school district tried to fire the person. The personal and professional good name of a teacher is a precious thing to that individual. Our system of government recognizes this and has made

---

[28] George B. Redfern, "Dismissing Unsatisfactory Teachers: A Four-Phase Process," *ERS Spectrum* 1 (Summer 1983): 17–20.
[29] Frank Pratt, "The Ethical Principal and Teacher Nonretention," *Journal of Personnel Evaluation in Education* 10 (March 1996): 35.

every effort to see that one's good name will not be carelessly or capriciously smeared through unfounded accusations. If the truth were known, we would see that in most cases incompetent teachers beat the rap because of poorly designed personnel processes or the ineffectiveness of evaluation procedures and/or administrative practices.

Dealing with Pressures

Under the best possible conditions, the process of evaluation can put great pressure on faculty, students, and administrators to achieve the rewards and to avoid the punishments related to all levels of accountability. Some are asking if the expectations are too high, unrealistic in some settings, and incompatible with many of the goals of school reform. "Must standards and improved test scores come at the expense of teacher creativity, critical thinking skills, interdisciplinary instruction and a student centered approach?"[30]

How will the principal deal with the pressures from within and from outside the school? The following case illustrates the point and provides an opportunity to identify and prepare to deal with the intense pressures on all involved. While exploring this case, the reader may consider the following questions:

1. What evidence of agreement between teacher and principal can be found?
2. Is it proper to separate the evaluation of the teacher's performance from the teacher as a "whole person"?
3. What current policies in accountability and educational reform may contribute to these teacher behaviors?
4. Can evaluation become a vital tool in planning professional development and curriculum reform?
5. What ethical issues does this principal face?
6. What are the decisions the principal faces, and how should he or she proceed?

MISS PINKSTON: A CASE STUDY[31]

The twenty-four teachers of the Brandon Elementary School (K–6) are evaluated annually by the supervising principal, Mr. Burke. Individual conferences follow classroom observations with discus-

---

[30] Samuel R. Lewbel and K. Michael Hibbard, "Are Standards and True Learning Compatible?" *Principal Leadership* 1 (January 2001): 16.
[31] This case was written by Suzanne V. Drake, Ph.D.

sion and the signing of forms by both teacher and principal. Of special concern are those teachers now completing their third year of successful performance and therefore being considered for tenure recommendations.

Miss Pinkston taught first grade in this school system the preceding two years, and her classroom performance ratings are good, based on Mr. Burke's biannual observations. Miss Pinkston is single and lives alone in an apartment near the school. She has few friends among the staff members or known friends outside the school. At lunchtime, Miss Pinkston carries her tray back to her own classroom, closes the door, and eats alone. She never seems to take a coffee break during free periods.

Mr. Burke expresses concern for her lack of communication or exchange of professional ideas with other staff members and seeks her out for involvement on committees. He also suggests to her that some lively discussions at the faculty lunch table are challenging and interesting. On one occasion, Miss Pinkston did venture out at lunchtime. Once she came into the small, crowded faculty lunchroom and found the table already filled. The group squeezed in closer to provide room for another chair and welcomed the new arrival. Upon being seated, Miss Pinkston placed her unchilled can of tuna fish and a can opener on the table and proceeded to grind away. The pungent odor of warm tuna fish clouded the corner of the room as she devoured the whole can of tuna. One by one, the other faculty members hurriedly finished their lunches and departed, soon leaving Miss Pinkston seated alone in the lounge.

Her evaluation of the first-grade students assigned to her has resulted in many pleased parents who have experienced glowing conferences and outstanding grades on report cards at each marking period. For the past two years only the principal and some second-grade teachers have been aware of the telephone calls from parents expressing concern about their children suddenly experiencing difficulties in the second grade and receiving sharp drops in report card evaluations.

Of special interest to the principal are the end-of-level tests published by the basal reader company and administered by all teachers at the completion of each reading level. Composite scores for small instructional reading groups within each room are recorded and turned in to the principal's office before filling book requests for subsequent instructional materials. As these test summaries are filed in the office, it becomes apparent that Miss Pinkston's groups score consistently high. Almost without exception, every child achieves nearly perfect scores.

This year Miss Pinkston has been selected to work with a small group of at-risk first graders. Only fifteen children designated by their kindergarten teachers as least ready for formal reading were chosen for this one classroom, with extended prereading activities recommended.

It is past midyear, and six small-group reading reports have already been submitted by Miss Pinkston. Mr. Burke notes that these at-risk students have completed the same number of levels as her previous groups and with a majority of perfect scores.

To gather additional information, Mr. Burke calls Miss Pinkston's room and requests a conference to go over the actual assessments just completed. He explains his special interest in this transition group and hopes to involve her in decisions about future curriculum revision and alternative assessments of student performance.

Upon examining the test booklets, he sees evidence of numerous erasures on all booklets. On many items with three choices for answers, three answers had been marked at some time. It is doubtful that the neat, complete erasures were done entirely by first graders, since there are no evidences of tearing, wrinkling, or roughing of the paper but only the indented lines from concentrated pressure of first-grade, soft-lead pencils.

Mr. Burke is faced with several important decisions. He must first determine what is the most appropriate action to solve the immediate problem. Next, he must consider how this situation affects the recommendations for Miss Pinkston's tenure. The forms are due in the superintendent's office next week.

Kohn suggests that principals and other administrators should never boast about high or rising scores, which serve only to legitimize the tests as desirable ends rather than the important learnings that may not be measured on tests. He suggests that principals should absorb as much pressure as possible without passing it on to teachers and students, and then as professionals work to change a system that may be inappropriate.[32]

EVALUATION OF NONTEACHING STAFF

The principal has a role in understanding the contributions and evaluating the performance of a wide variety of support staff who are vital to the mission of the school. Nonteaching professional staff such as school counselors, social workers, psychologists, nurses, athletic directors, and

---

[32] Alfie Kohn, "Fighting the Tests: Turning Frustration into Action," *Young Children* 56 (March 2001): 19–24.

others have carefully defined roles and functions related to their specialized training and licensure. It is important to have a locally defined job description for each, based upon identified school needs. This position description can then be translated into specific goals and objectives in a document that is periodically reviewed and modified. The goals and objectives are jointly evaluated through a variety of tools such as checklists, rating scales, portfolios of accomplishments, and feedback from multiple stakeholders. One example for evaluation of school counselors may be adapted to other staff roles.[33] Since many of the nonteaching staff serve more than one school building, it may be beneficial to use a full-circle evaluation plan such as the 360-degree feedback process[34] described in Chapter 12.

Additional nonteaching staff include maintenance/custodial staff, cafeteria workers, office and clerical personnel, and others that make important contributions to the overall success of the school. (See Chapters 17 and 19 for a discussion of suggested evaluation procedures.)

EVALUATION OF THE PRINCIPAL'S PERFORMANCE

In too many instances, principals have reported that their evaluations are superficial, nonexistent (in a formal sense), or based on informal feedback to the superintendent and/or board members. The principal may do well to seek an evaluation process that provides useful information on which appropriate changes can be based. These changes should be aimed at moving the school toward realizing its goals. Such a process not only would be helpful in terms of the development of the principal but also might offset some of the problems that could arise from informal feedback about principal performance. Most important, an effective evaluation process will strengthen the person who is a key to successful schools.

The most common evaluation process is some adaptation of management by objectives. The person to whom the principal reports confers with the principal, and they set mutual goals for the year. Ordinarily, means to measure goal achievement are laid out, and at a predetermined point in the year, an evaluation conference is held to review progress toward those goals. While this procedure is sound, the quality of the process may vary considerably, and the results may range from superficial to very helpful. The principal may wish to add some dimensions to his or her evaluation to serve as more specific indicators of direction.

---

[33] Jeannine R. Studer and Judith A. Sommers, "The Professional School Counselor and Accountability," *NASSP Bulletin* 84 (April 2000): 93–99.
[34] Karen M. Dyer, "The Power of 360-Degree Feedback," *Educational Leadership* 58 (February 2001): 35–39.

Instructional leadership is a key expectation regarding the principalship; therefore, the total evaluation should include this leadership dimension. Jones believes that the leaders of the district need to define instructional leadership activities, suggesting visibility and accessibility to staff as a good start.[35] He also notes behaviors such as classroom observations, evaluation reports written by the principal, the relationship of the number of formative visits to the number of summative reports, and in-service workshops, as well as teacher feedback regarding the principal's instructional leadership. Some states have principal leadership academies that have developed guidelines for the evaluation of principals' work. Principals' associations also provide guidelines to help district leaders develop appropriate evaluation processes. The National Associations of Secondary School Principal (NASSP) offers several assessment and development programs that assist principals in establishing or revising a personal plan for career advancement. Tirozzi discusses standards for principals with specific skill sets to handle issues involved in the standards of the Interstate School Leaders Licensure Consortium (ISLLC).[36] He suggests Websites to assist twenty-first century school administrators in building skills to become effective leaders.

Since many district-mandated evaluation systems do not facilitate the professional growth of principals, new dimensions are being explored. Abbott describes a peer assessment venture through teams composed of two to four principals working together.[37] The principals were encouraged to identify one or more areas that they wanted to improve during the school year. Then they selected exemplary principals who had special expertise in these skill areas to work with during the year. Preassessment conferences were held to establish growth expectations and means of support. Methods for assessing growth included working portfolios, observations, self-reflection journals, peer coaching, and conferences. Participants reported that as an outgrowth of experiencing new learning they became better leaders. As they relinquished the traditional district evaluations and became risk takers willing to share knowledge about their craft, they learned firsthand that administrators cannot lead where they are afraid to go.

The principal might wish to include data regarding student perceptions of the principal's effectiveness. Do the students view him or her as aloof, bound to the office, not really known as a person? As the enforcer? Are they able to articulate what the principal stands for, what his or her

---

[35] R. Robert Jones, "How Do You Evaluate Instructional Leadership?" *School Administrator* 48 (February 1991): 39.

[36] Gerald N. Tirozzi, "The Artistry of Leadership," *Phi Delta Kappan* 82 (February 2001): 434–439. For further information, see www.ccsso.org/standrds.html and www.principals.org/training/04.html.

[37] James E. Abbott, "Sharing Craft Knowledge: The Soul of Principal Peer Assessment," *T.H.E. Journal* 24 (November 1996): 97–100.

expectations of the students are, what their feelings about his or her fairness are? Obviously, the list should grow considerably, according to the individual school situation. A similar set of questions might be of interest: those regarding the parents' and patrons' perceptions of the principal's performance.

If evaluation is used as a tool for growth, the principal certainly should benefit from having a well-designed evaluation of performance by the superintendent, as well as complementary assessments by peer teams.

EVALUATION OF STUDENT PROGRESS

Persons attempting to make a valid evaluation of student progress face many pitfalls. One is that of evaluating the student rather than the student's work or progress. The problem is obvious and, as mentioned earlier in this chapter, applies to evaluating the work of any human being. Other obstacles may be the inappropriateness or narrowness of evaluation instruments, the interpretation of results, the reporting procedures, or, as will be discussed, the lack of relationship between the evaluation and the program objectives. Mandated standards and proficiencies further complicate the picture.

Two often unrelated purposes are ever present in the school setting: (1) gathering information about student achievement to facilitate instruction and (2) using relative measures of students, schools, districts, states, and countries for comparisons and accountability. Bonstingl proposes a move from the old paradigm of teaching and testing to a new paradigm of continual learning and improvement.[38] Perhaps principals should encourage teachers to give more attention to what happens between assessments. McTighe shares the following basic guidelines:

> Establish clear performance targets.
>
> Strive for authenticity in products and performances.
>
> Publicize criteria and performance standards.
>
> Provide models of excellence.
>
> Teach strategies explicitly.
>
> Use ongoing assessments for feedback and adjustment.
>
> Document and celebrate progress.[39]

---

[38] John Jay Bonstingl, "Are the Stakes Too High?" *Principal Leadership* 1 (January 2001): 8–14.
[39] Jay McTighe, "What Happens between Assessments?" *Educational Leadership* 54 (December 1996/January 1997): 7–11.

CONSIDERATIONS FOR STUDENT EVALUATION

While providing a balance between formative assessments, which assist teachers in providing for individual student progress, and summative assessments, used for comparisons, accountability, and important decisions affecting students lives, those who are implementing the total evaluation process must weight the values derived from the various components of student evaluation.

Evaluation Should Assist the Student

The principal can help the faculty develop the concept of using the evaluation of students' work to assist them in making continuous progress. A mere recording of the relative goodness of a student's work is not a sufficient evaluation.

Whenever feasible, students should know the criteria by which their work and performance will be evaluated. Little will be gained, and often much lost, if the evaluative process is viewed as a mystical rite performed by the faculty to put individuals into rank order. Students should be encouraged to reflect on their own progress toward specific goals and to identify strengths and needs.

Evaluation Should Provide a Record of the Student's Growth for Longitudinal Study

Most recording of evaluation is a mark derived from many inputs, such as teacher tests, standardized tests, performance assessments, observations, and general interaction between teacher and student. It is appropriate to raise the question of whether these measures have value as evidence of student growth and whether they provide sufficient data for longitudinal study. If each evaluator had the same objectives, used the same measuring devices, and applied the same criteria, then the record would be an excellent device for study. The type of information found in many student "grade" records would serve only to support statements about the relative consistency of the student's academic performance in a particular school.

Evaluation Should Be a Diagnostic Tool for the Faculty

The evaluation of student performance, both short and long term, is valuable to the student if the objectives are being met. If properly designed, the evaluative devices should yield information that would help determine the adequacy of the methods and materials used. On the short-range basis, evaluation can provide a means by which individual-ization can become a reality.

Faculty face the challenge of providing a positive learning environ-ment for a highly diverse student population. Various fields that deal with the education of exceptional children have led to many applications for education in general. Skills and interest in educational diagnosis pro-vide a deeper understanding of the scope and depth of evaluation, with appropriate programs for all students.[40] Principals can initiate and sup-port opportunities for professional development as faculty, both individ-ually and in teams, update their abilities to develop, interpret, and use tools of evaluation and available data in their classrooms.

Evaluation is viewed as a continual process to improve the teaching-learning situation. Whether student evaluation or teacher eval-uation, the information generated is one part of a larger picture.

Evaluation Should Provide a Means of Communicating with Parents and the Community

Parents insist on evaluation and reports of the results. The evaluation program must yield information that is relevant to the student's develop-ment and relevant to the parents' frame of reference.

Marshall, the principal of an inner-city elementary school, describes the challenges of helping all children meet rigorous standards and achieving excellence.[41] Principals are challenged to aid teachers in devel-oping a new generation of assessments that will drive a process of con-tinuous improvement through frequent, detailed, and honest feedback to students and their parents. Progress in learning is celebrated, and areas for improvement become a team focus.

Local schools and districts continue to revise reporting systems to improve the alignment among standards, benchmarks of achievement, and various adaptations of letter grades and descriptors. Although the efforts of committees to change report cards often meet with resistance from faculty, students, and parents, the principal can continue to encour-age the study and use of improvements through incremental steps. Greater attention can be given to informing the community of evaluation results through carefully prepared statements set in appropriate contexts with interpretation by professionals.

---

[40] James J. Gallagher, "Accountability for Gifted Students," *Phi Delta Kappan* 79 (June 1998): 739–742.
[41] Kim Marshall, "No One Ever Said It Would Be Easy," *Phi Delta Kappan* 78 (December 1996): 307–308.

TOOLS FOR EVALUATING STUDENT LEARNING

Students' progress should be evaluated in relation to their own goals and capabilities. In addition, students' work should be evaluated in relation to the standards and objectives of the educational programs in which they participate. Carefully stated criteria should be developed to give meaning to the data generated in the evaluation process. Data indicating that a student is able to use grammar skills in a way comparable to the way an "average" sixth-grade student would be able to use them are not particularly informative in and of themselves. But if this is a reasonable performance criterion for this student in the learning situation, they become meaningful. The principal has the responsibility to develop with the faculty specific objectives that meet or exceed the standards for the various learning units or subunits in the school programs. But beyond that, the principal must help them relate the evaluation process directly to these objectives. Each of the tools described next should be designed with program objectives in mind.

Observational data can provide one basis for evaluating pupil progress. Some simple counting devices may be employed. For example, how often does a student volunteer answers? How often does he or she initiate interaction with his or her peers? How often is he or she on task versus off task? In addition, work samples over time can be very useful when collected in a working portfolio.

The principal can assist the faculty in developing expertise in this area by using resources available from curriculum specialists, supervisors, or consultants specializing in these skills. Interviews, both structured and unstructured, often yield important insights regarding the students' development.

Teacher-made tests are useful and effective diagnostic tools if properly constructed. In-service programs designed to develop skills in test construction and measurement could be valuable. "The professional support and training of teachers is emerging as the pivotal factor for determining the success of the assessment reform process."[42]

Standardized tests should be viewed as but one means of getting the whole picture of a student's development. Care should be taken to inform the faculty and the public of the limitations of standardized tests and of the various problems inherent in interpreting the results of such tests.

Testing students to measure learning has long been an accepted practice in American education. During the last two decades, critics have pointed out cultural biases in tests, pressure to teach to the test, the narrowing of the curriculum, and an overemphasis on lower levels of think-

---

[42] Michael B. Kane and Vidhi Khattri, "Assessment Reform (A Work in Progress)," *Phi Delta Kappan* 77 (September 1995): 31.

ing. D'Agostino points out that in spite of the time and resources used, achievement testing has never fulfilled the goal to improve schools.[43]

The exclusive use of *norm-referenced tests* really indicates that the school's goals are circumscribed by the items on the test. This might make interesting copy if the teachers were to teach to the test and thereby prove they had met all the school's goals. Of course, if a large population were to answer all those test items successfully, the test publisher would tend to throw out the items. The principal may wish to develop norms for his or her own school, with norms developed for the system. While it is not within the scope of this book to review the intricacies of testing and measurement, we believe the principal must have the skills and understandings basic to this area.[44]

Severe limitations are inherent in many of the *criterion-referenced tests* accompanying technology packages and textbooks (e.g., reading-level tests associated with basal texts). The principal must be able to work with the faculty to clarify the purposes of these assessments and aid them in appropriately interpreting the results. The principal also must be aware of the varied perceptions of teachers, parents, and students regarding the total program of evaluation of student learning.

Performance-based assessment provides the faculty with excellent opportunities to review program objectives as well as to review their effectiveness in individualizing instruction. An important distinction is that this approach focuses attention on the individual student's progress relating to growth and demonstrated proficiencies rather than comparing his or her achievement with that of other students. "[P]erformance assessment is aimed at moving away from testing practices that require students to select the single correct answer from an array of four or five distractors to a practice that requires students to create evidence through performance that will enable assessors to make valid judgments about 'what they know and can do' in situations that matter."[45] Through a variety of assessments with carefully developed scoring rubrics, the teacher receives specific information about each student's progress that can be directly used in reporting to parents.

There are time demands with this process, but the faculty may find the time well spent. The teacher who uses performance-based assessment will have to be committed to the idea; that is, the principal cannot proclaim it as the thing to do and expect it to be effective. One of the

---

[43] Jerome V. D'Agostino, "Achievement Testing in American Schools" in *American Education: Yesterday, Today and Tomorrow,* Part II, Ninety-Ninth Yearbook of the National Society for the Study of Education, ed. Thomas L. Good (Chicago: University of Chicago Press, 2000), 313–337. This source is especially useful for those interested in a concise summary of the development and pitfalls of achievement testing over the past 150 years.

[44] W. James Popham, *Modern Educational Meansurement: Practical Guidelines for Educational Leaders,* 3d ed. (Needham Heights, MA: Allyn & Bacon, 2000).

[45] Elliot W. Eisner, "The Uses and Limits of Performance Assessment," *Phi Delta Kappan* 80 (May 1999): 659.

greatest problems with alternative assessment is that the types of behaviors most easily identified and measured are often not the most important. There is a tendency to stop short of an effective assessment program. The specific assessments should not be designed for showing only short-term success. They should have functional validity; that is, they should measure more complex learning on a long-term basis with application to other situations both inside and outside the classroom.

Several dilemmas involving the nature and usefulness of performance assessment are not easily solved but provide points for the principal and faculty to consider.[46] Pearson et al. describe how performance assessments are referenced to standards rather than norms and students' work is rated according to how well it reflects the standards.

Portfolio assessment is one popular example of the performance-based process that may involve both teacher and student as they cooperatively select the "product" that will be included in the portfolio. Work samples and reflections collected over a period of time provide a means of evaluating progress as well as reporting to parents. A strong case can be made for developing portfolios for each student. The portfolios could contain samples of work over a period of time for student, parents, and teachers to review. Portfolios need not be restricted to print samples. Using media including audio- and videotape, samples become components of an electronic portfolio in which student performance and reflections can be scanned and stored for a variety of purposes.

Portfolios can have a direct influence on teachers' beliefs and classroom practices. They serve as tools for both teachers and students to document evidence of learning and progress. Not only do portfolios provide contexts whereby teachers can learn more about the individual growth of their students, but also they provide opportunities for students to gain insights about their own growth not evident in traditional tests. Kieffer and Faust propose multiple purposes and complementary uses for portfolios.[47]

This method is becoming more widely used as a means to provide evidence of actual competence. It is also effective in working directly with secondary students regarding their development in several skills. Samples of work provide the teacher with tangible means to establish a baseline of performance for a student with evidence of demonstrated learning in relation to expected outcomes. Digital portfolio software can be used to create a multimedia collection of student work and to connect that work to performance standards.[48]

---

[46] P. David Pearson, Lizanne DeStefano, and Georgia E. Garcia, "Ten Dilemmas of Performance Assessment," in *Assessing Reading 1: Theory and Practice,* ed. Colin Harrison and Terry Salinger (New York: Routledge, 1998), 21–49.
[47] Ronald D. Kieffer and Mark A. Faust, "Portfolio Purposes: Teachers Exploring the Relationship between Evaluation and Learning," *Assessing Writing* 3 (1996): 149–172.
[48] David Niguidula, "Picturing Performance with Digital Portfolios," *Educational Leadership* 55 (November 1997): 26–29.

REPORTING RESULTS

The principal must relate the reporting procedures to the total evaluation framework and process. Several means of communicating with parents regarding the progress of their child are possible: "grade" cards, checklists, narrative descriptions, parent-teacher conferences, telephone conferences, and any combination of these.

Many educators use a grading system as a means of sorting and ranking students according to class performance, which sets up tensions among students and between students and teachers. Labeling students with "grades" may encourage teachers to focus on negative behaviors and lead to a search for evidence to defend giving lower grades. These results may cause students to become discouraged, or even humiliated. "Students are not the only victims of the competitive grading system. . . . It hurts teachers as well by skewing their values and ultimately robbing them of the satisfaction inherent in promoting student learning."[49] Krumboltz and Yeh also point out that, if all students are viewed as capable of success, the teacher may be encouraged to seek evidence of strength and growth by using a variety of ways for students to demonstrate competencies and attainment of established standards.

Regardless of which means of assessment are used, the principal should plan so that each step is carefully monitored. Faculty should be given time to prepare the reports. If parent-teacher conferences are used, in-service education dealing with ways of organizing data and presenting them to parents might be very helpful. If narrative descriptions or portfolios are used, analysis of appropriate reporting techniques could be quite valuable. Performance assessment works best when it is phased in gradually and the scoring procedures and usefulness can be demonstrated to students, teachers, and parents.[50] Yeagley proposes using one of several software tools available for integrating and analyzing school data. These tools will assist with the integration of information from a variety of sources the identification of patterns of student learning, and the tracking of goal progress. The programs create graphs or tables, which can help principals communicate with stakeholders.[51]

As when reporting the results of any evaluation, the audience must be considered. In the case of parents, they tend to want to hear whether their child is performing at grade level or better. A word of caution regarding the reporting of grade equivalences: A third grader who scores a grade equivalent of 6.0 in mathematics cannot be expected to do all of the sixth-grade work the average sixth grader would. The reverse is true

[49] John Krumboltz and Christine Yeh, "Competitive Grading Sabotages Good Teaching," *Phi Delta Kappan* 78 (December 1996): 324.

[50] David Bartz, Suzanne Anderson-Robinson, and Larry Hillman, "Performance Assessment: Make Them Show What They Know," *Principal* 73 (January 1994): 11–14.

[51] Raymond Yeagley, "Data in Your Hands," *School Administrator* 58 (April 2001): 12–15.

of a score slightly below grade level but well within the normal range. Additional complications arise in that the compression of scores is much greater in the lower grades than in the upper grades or secondary levels; thus, at one stage, one grade below is much more a departure from "average" than at another stage. Also, the reporting of progress should be in a form that has real meaning to the consumer, be it the student, the parent, or the school. As with the total evaluation program, the reporting process should be designed to help the student and not be considered apart from the student.

EVALUATION IS SENSITIVE

The evaluation of a student's work is a sensitive area from the student's point of view as well as from that of the parents and faculty. One problem that the principal should help the faculty deal with is the potential of any evaluation program to cause goal displacement for the student. It is equally important to work with parents in this regard. If the student sees the "grade," the "score," or some other value symbol resulting from evaluation as the main goal, as perceived by parents and teachers, it can easily become the main goal. The means of assessment, rather than the proposed objectives of that student's education, can become the end.

Wesson points out that reported test scores have typically had a high correlation to the socioeconomic characteristics of parents, including occupation, level of education, family income, and location of the school, which he calls the "Volvo Effect." He suggests it is time to reexamine our faith in standardized testing and look for more valid indicators of intelligence and knowledge that are of significant educational, personal, and social value.[52]

Parents want their children to do well. They want the evaluation program to tell them how well their children are doing. A responsibility of the principal and faculty is to help the parents focus on the developmental progress of each child rather than his or her relative position on a scale, one that might be quite unfair and even meaningless. Parents are rightly concerned about whether the evaluation process is fair. They are also concerned about what the results of the process mean for their child's future.

The principal and faculty must be alert to the fact that the results of evaluation become a permanent record that can provide a basis for predetermining the student's performance.

---

[52] Kenneth A. Wesson, "The 'Volvo Effect'—Questioning Standardized Tests," *Young Children* 56 (March 2001): 16–18.

SUMMARY

Evaluation is a complex process requiring knowledge, skill, and wisdom. One must be able to recognize effective behaviors that indicate a particular role (e.g., teacher, student, principal) is being carried out well in relation to the school's purpose. The principal should be informed about all local district policies as well as state regulations and accepted personnel evaluation standards. At the same time, a narrow focus on certain behaviors or outcomes (e.g., achievement test scores) may ignore the impact the process or results have on the individuals or many other important factors related to success.

A wide variety of individual assessment tools is now available to document student performance on significant tasks in real situations. Evaluation of student learning can focus educators on the essential goals of education: to help students learn and teachers teach. Making judgments about individual progress toward selected goals can also address accountability and total program evaluation.

Sensitivity to how outcomes are received is important. The evaluation process is best perceived as a means toward growth and improvement and related to the achievement of the school's purposes. Viewing evaluation from this perspective sets a positive tone that creates possibilities.

FOR FURTHER THOUGHT

1. How is shared authority compatible with the evaluation process?
2. How does the standards movement affect the evaluation of teachers and principals?
3. Is a climate that allows experimentation and mistakes compatible with an evaluation program and accountability?
4. List ways in which the reliability of the data and information gathered for evaluating teachers' performance can be increased.
5. Propose a plan to deal with the situation described in the case study of Miss Pinkston.
   Compose an original case study based upon personal educational experiences.
6. Is the idea of self-evaluation for principals incompatible with the idea of a bargaining unit for principals?
7. Are the concepts of building and maintaining self-esteem and holding high performance expectations incompatible? Will not the latter concept, if maintained throughout the school years, result in a greater incidence of failure?

8. Develop a speech to defend the school's student evaluation program, including high-stakes testing, as a sufficient basis for denying promotion or graduation.
9. What steps can be taken to avoid having meaningless evaluative statements recorded in "open" personnel and student files?
10. Identify the major problems in implementing performance-based assessment. How would you address these concerns?
11. Do most of the ways used to evaluate schools by state departments of education and other accrediting agencies tend to encourage uniformity or individuality? Which should be encouraged?

SELECTED READINGS

Baron, Joan B., and Dennie P. Wolf, eds. *Performance-Based Student Assessment: Challenges and Possibilities.* Chicago: University of Chicago Press, 1996.

Bonstingl, John Jay. "Are the Stakes Too High?" *Principal Leadership* 1 (January 2001): 8–14.

Borich, G. D. *Observation Skills for Effective Teaching,* 3d ed. Upper Saddle River, NJ: Merrill/Prentice Hall, 1999.

Burke, Kay. *How to Assess Authentic Learning,* 3d ed. Englewood Cliffs, NJ: Prentice Hall, 1999.

Collinson, Vivienne. "Redefining Teacher Excellence." *Theory into Practice* 38 (Winter 1999): 4–11.

D'Agostino, Jerome V. "Achievement Testing in American Schools." In Thomas L. Good, ed., *American Education: Yesterday, Today, and Tomorrow.* Part II, Ninety-Ninth Yearbook of the National Society for the Study of Education, 313–337. Chicago: University of Chicago Press, 2000.

Darling-Hammond, Linda, and Beverly Falk. "Using Standards and Assessments to Support Student Learning." *Phi Delta Kappan* 79 (November 1997): 190–199.

Farr, Beverly, and Elsie Trumbull. *Assessment Alternatives for Diverse Classrooms.* Norwood, MA: Christopher-Gordon, 1997.

Gronlund, Norman E. *Assessment of Student Achievement,* 6th ed. Needham Heights, MA: Allyn & Bacon, 1998.

Hebert, Elizabeth A. "Lessons Learned about Student Portfolios." *Phi Delta Kappan* 79 (April 1998): 583–585.

Kohn, Alfie. "Fighting the Tests: Turning Frustration into Action." *Young Children* 56 (March 2001): 19–24.

Koretz, Daniel, and Laura Hamilton. "Assessment of Students with Disabilities in Kentucky: Inclusion, Student Performance, and Validity." *Educational Evaluation and Policy Analysis* 22 (Fall 2000): 255–272.

Linn, Robert L., and Norman E. Gronlund. *Measurement and Assessment in Teaching,* 8th ed. Upper Saddle River, NJ: Merrill/Prentice Hall, 2000.

Nitko, Anthony J. *Educational Assessment of Students*, 3d ed. Upper Saddle River, NJ: Merrill/Prentice Hall, 2001.

Oosterhof, Albert. *Developing and Using Classroom Assessments*, 2d ed. Upper Saddle River, NJ: Merrill/Prentice Hall, 1999.

Popham, W. James. *Modern Educational Measurement: Practical Guidelines for Educational Leaders*, 3d ed. Needham Heights, MA: Allyn & Bacon, 2000.

Pratt, Frank. "The Ethical Principal and Teacher Nonretention." *Journal of Personnel Evaluation in Education* 10 (March 1996): 29–36.

Sergiovanni, Thomas J. *The Principalship: A Reflective Practice Perspective*, 4th ed. Needham Heights MA: Allyn & Bacon, 2001.

Ubben, Gerald, Larry Hughes, and Cynthia Norris. *The Principal, Creative Leadership for Effective Schools*, 4th ed. Needham Heights, MA: Allyn & Bacon, 2001.

Waintroob, Andrea R. "Remediating and Dismissing the Incompetent Teacher." *School Administrator* 52 (May 1995): 20–24.

Wiggins, Grant. "Designing Authentic Assessments." *Educational Leadership* 54 (December 1996/January 1997): 18–25.

Staff Development
to Improve Learning

*G*iven the rapid changes in technology, the standards movement, and assessment, and the increasing pressure for
accountability, as well as the changing role of teachers and administrators, continuous staff development is an essential cornerstone to any
school improvement. Staff development is not simply offering a "sit and
get" or "one-time only" workshop at the beginning of the school year. It
is not just bringing in a speaker to talk about a topic and then expecting
teachers to immediately incorporate it into their practice. It is not just hiring a substitute so a teacher can visit some exemplary program. Each of
these activities may be part of a good staff development program, but to
be effective over time, a staff development program consists of more
than just these activities. It involves the integration of learning outside of
the classroom and school with what takes place inside the classroom and
school.

A closer examination of what makes an effective, comprehensive
staff development program makes clear that one crucial element is the
vocal and visible commitment and support from the principal to staff
development. The role of the principal in staff development is significantly expanding and now includes articulating beliefs and expectations
and implementing practices and procedures that foster a culture of collaboration and teacher learning.[1] In addition, the priincipal serves as a
coach to assist all staff to augment their knowledge and skills.

The principal is faced with the challenge of (1) selecting professional and talented people; (2) nurturing a learning community that will
inspire and release these talents; (3) promoting staff development experiences and projects that will ultimately impact student achievement;

This chapter was revised by Donald S. Kachur, Ed.D.
[1] Rick DuFour, "In the Right Context," *Journal of Staff Development* 22 (Winter 2001): 14.

(4) encouraging teachers to be reflective about their creativity in solving educational problems; (5) creating relevant opportunities for the staff to work together; and (6) supporting with enthusiasm, personal attention, and additional resources those teachers who collaborate with one another to develop and implement ideas to raise student performance.

Staff development consists of the entire range of activities and efforts of the school that contribute to the personal and professional growth of all employees so that they can perform better and with greater satisfaction. It also includes the efforts of the school to foster collaboration and commitment among staff members to achieve a compelling vision for the school.

Effective staff development starts with a well-organized personnel management system, which ultimately tailors recruitment, selection, and placement to each school within the system so that the principals and teachers are involved in the building of their own school team. It then follows up with supervisory practices, personnel policies, and developmental opportunities that should align with the goals of each school.

ANALYSIS OF DEVELOPMENTAL NEEDS: AN OVERVIEW

Whether principals try to staff a school with a new faculty or, as is more often the case, find themselves the only new addition to their respective staff, they need to acquire an understanding of the staff as a whole. Obtaining an overview of the faculty may begin by examining the following characteristics:

1. *Educational status*—What degrees do the faculty hold? What majors/certifications? What proportion of the faculty was educated at the same institution? What evidence indicates current professional growth? What kinds of in-service or staff development efforts have been provided in the last five years? What were the results? What needs data or decision-making processes were used to select those in-service experiences?

2. *Experiential background*—How long has each individual been teaching in the current level and field? Has it been in the same school/system? Does the faculty consist mostly of persons who have stayed in the community, or are they from outside the community? If the faculty comes from outside the community, what types of schools and systems did they experience? What evaluation records of past performance are available, and what patterns do they show? What job experiences have persons had outside education? What leadership activities do they demonstrate in the community? In the school?

3. *Communications about needs*—In a relatively open environment, people will communicate their needs in a variety of ways. The principal needs to be sensitive to replies to the often-asked question "How are things going?" as well as to responses on evaluations of staff development efforts, needs assessments, requests for support, and supervisory conferences.

4. *Degree of cooperation*—What opportunities are available for staff to work together across subject and grade levels? How is problem solving conducted? What idea sharing takes place? How is time used? What opportunities are provided for sharing solutions?

5. *Resources*—What resources have been tapped to provide staff development opportunities? Federal, state, and/or local education agencies? Professional associations? Businesses? Community agencies? Foundations?

6. *Data availability and analyses*—What do the data show from various evaluations of student performance? What patterns of needs emerge, and what alignment needs exist between perceived needs and data indicators?

Information derived from the above data will help identify certain strengths and weaknesses that may provide clear implications for personnel selection criteria as attrition or expansion occurs. The data may also help the principal make better use of certain faculty members' skills and interests through reassignment. Obviously, a beginning analysis, as mentioned, is just that—a beginning.

Other important inputs are necessary before the needs picture can be considered complete. The analysis must be comprehensive and continuous to be effective. Other inputs should include classroom observations, self-assessments, peer assessment reports, student and parent feedback, research findings, and evaluation of individual teachers' goal plans. Also, student achievement data must be generated, analyzed and interpreted, and this responsibility should be shared with the teachers and staff. Like any information system, data need to be current, or today's decisions that affect the future will be made on the basis of outdated information. The information should be updated at least annually, and it should be in a readily available, easily interpreted form.

SELECTION OF STAFF

Part of the staff development picture is the selection of replacements or additions to the staff. As in any system, a change in one part affects the others. The social/professional system of the staff is no exception, for every time a staff member leaves or one is hired, the total impact of the school is altered. This important personnel function of the principal is one of the most challenging. In some cases, the selection of teachers is removed from the principal's domain, although the principal should ordinarily influence the final decision. While this function may not be the exclusive prerogative of the principal, neither should it be completely removed from the principal's responsibility. The principal and faculty should have input into the selection process based on the total staff profile, the specific competencies needed, and the long-range plans for school improvement or renewal. The interview selection process should also be shared on a carefully planned basis with the principal, the faculty with whom the person is to work, and appropriate personnel in the central office.

Foolproof, predictive data for the selection of staff are nonexistent; therefore, choosing staff is probably one of the most frustrating tasks the principal faces. Yet the principal can turn to several sources for indicators of success. Records of past performance, found in the placement files or obtained through direct inquiry to the candidate's former colleagues, can indicate the relative success of an individual. In most instances, it is wise to follow up written evaluations with telephone or face-to-face inquiries, particularly when the written recommendations are nebulous or appear to leave out important information. Rarely are sets of placement credentials found to be really negative; therefore, such documents must be scrutinized carefully and critically.

Within the set of credentials will be evaluative reports of student teaching and other types of clinical teaching experiences. Consideration should be given to the type of school(s) in which the applicant taught, the length of teaching, the level(s), and, if available, the training institution's rating policies. One should be careful not to screen out those candidates coming from institutions whose rating scale provides only for "pass" or "fail," "successful" or "unsuccessful." This is particularly true when receiving credentials from institutions awarding A's to nearly all student teachers and reserving B's for those who were weak. The principal should also check the certification status of the candidate as to level, subject, and any reported deficiencies.

In the case of both student teachers and experienced teachers, an on-site visitation, when feasible, may provide the principal valuable insights regarding the candidate. Appropriate clearances from the candidate and his or her superiors should be obtained ahead of time. A videotaped lesson can provide the principal with some idea of the person's "best" teaching.

Additional aids to completing an accurate composite of the candidate's qualifications include structured interviews, scores on standardized tests (e.g., National Teachers Examination), scores on institutional or state competency examinations, grade point averages in content subjects, and other information of record.

Principals value the characteristics of "enthusiasm" and "communication" highest when interviewing prospective teachers. Place and Drake report the results of a study of Illinois and Ohio principals that documented these characteristics as the most important in considering candidates.[2] The researchers asked which criteria were used to determine the presence of enthusiasm and communication. Not surprisingly, principals reported no common criterion or even set of criteria used. The most frequently noted indicators of enthusiasm were "body language and movements," "animated conversation," and "voice." These three indicators accounted for 56 of the 162 responses regarding enthusiasm. The characteristic "communication" was determined by the principals' using "quality of answers," "written evidence," and "grammar" as the most frequently mentioned indicators. Those indicators represent about one-third of the responses. It is clear that there is a very wide range of judgment regarding what constitutes two of the primary selection characteristics. Such a wide range suggests implications for principals' staff development as well as for prospective candidates.

Whether the teacher is new to the district or a potential transfer, it is imperative that the principal view the selection of staff as a proactive role and not a passive situation. The principal should be involved in the cooperative development of the vacancy announcement, at least to include those competencies and expectations unique to the community and school program. Likewise, faculty should be involved to the extent that they, too, will assume responsibility for the new faculty member's success.

FACULTY PROFILE IMPLICATIONS
FOR STAFF DEVELOPMENT

From 1942 to 1972, U.S. school administrators faced unprecedented enrollment increases, and because of this continued need for additional teachers, it was very difficult to maintain an adequate professional staff. The concerns in those years were to develop greater maturity and experience in the staff and provide in-service education to supplement preservice training that was generally of "short-cut," emergency quality. The in-service sessions were too often temporary "quick fixes" just to maintain minimal competencies among staffs.

During the mid-1970s and early 1980s, an oversupply of teachers flooded nearly all fields except the sciences, mathematics, industrial technologies, and special education. The oversupply of certifiable persons,

---

[2] William Place and Thelbert L. Drake, "The Priorities of Elementary and Secondary Principals for the Criteria Used in the Teacher Selection Process," *Journal of School Leadership* 4 (January 1994): 87–93.

drops in school enrollments, opportunities opening up to both genders in business, and the ever-widening gap between teacher salaries and other salaries contributed to a steep decline in teacher education enrollments. Many teacher preparation institutions graduated fewer than half the number of teacher candidates they did in the 1970s. Today America is witnessing a reversal in teacher supply and demand as pupil enrollment growth, retirement incentives, and policies such as class-size reduction are creating a fast-growing demand for teachers again. There are concerns about a teacher shortage as it appears that the numbers entering teaching as a profession are not growing as fast as the job demands warrant.

The average age of the teaching staff in many communities, particularly the medium-sized urban areas in regions of stable population, is in the mid- to upper forties. Exceptions are in the growing Sunbelt regions and sections of the large urban areas where working conditions are perceived to be less desirable. This adds up to bimodal staffs in some schools in that there might be a staff composed of a large number of teachers very new to the profession and another large mass of highly experienced, educated staff approaching retirement. Such wide ranges of experience from newer teachers to those who have been teaching for quite some time create differing needs for professional development. The situation produces a need for rethinking the old concepts of in-service education.

Many bemoan the "graying of the teaching profession." However, a faculty does not need to be young to be dynamic. In fact, a mature faculty offers many advantages. The more mature teachers tend to be increasingly involved in professional organizations, professionally committed, and politically active. They also profess stronger ties to the community. They potentially have greater insights into the behavior of the young and often are the ones to whom students turn for counsel. The highly experienced teachers can provide the stability that can reduce many discipline problems. They also are in the best position to become leaders in the process of developing school improvement plans and strategies aimed at improved student achievement.

IN-SERVICE EDUCATION VERSUS STAFF DEVELOPMENT

Terms often found connected with teacher growth and development and used interchangeably are *in-service education, staff development,* and *professional development.* The term *in-service education* elicits a variety of responses, for a variety of reasons. Many of the negative responses may stem from past experiences in which the planned in-service activity had little or no relationship to the needs of those attending the program. For many, in-service means "one-shot" training whereby teachers passively receive knowledge from an expert on a given topic. Traditional in-service training can be frustrating if it is (1) not linked to the needs of the participants, (2) not related to the school's/system's goals, (3) not designed with the input of its participants, (4) something done to a group, and (5) not related to moving individuals closer to realizing their own personal and professional goals.

In-Service Training/Education

In-service training/education may be useful to help teachers and staff become aware of new developments, regulations, required procedures, or continuing refinements regarding legal or risk issues. Examples of the latter might be offering teachers and staff workshops on administering cardiopulmonary resuscitation (CPR) or dealing with blood-borne pathogens. Other in-service examples might include presentations on implementation of the school's crisis management plan and operation of the new security system.

In-service sessions are generally stand-alone events or happenings narrowly targeted and of benefit to all alike. They may or may not be part of a larger staff development program.

Staff/Professional Development

The terms *staff development* and *professional development* are even more difficult to define. Different sources have varied definitions for the two terms.[3] Regardless of how they are defined, teachers, principals, and other educators need to engage in continuous learning of job-related knowledge and skills throughout their careers.

A key word in staff or professional development, however it is defined, is *planned*. An effective staff development program is an outgrowth of perceived needs. Obviously, the person(s) who perceived these needs can be anywhere on the organization chart, but unless those persons who are going to be the primary recipients of the staff development also perceive these needs, the success of the staff development program is on shaky ground.

Staff development should not be regarded as merely formal, planned programs for a number of grade-level subjects or faculty, or even for a total building or a systemwide faculty. To regard it as such is to compartmentalize the experiences, as if they had little or nothing to do with helping students learn. Staff development should take place as an

[3] Laura Robb, *Redefining Staff Development: A Collaborative Model for Teachers and Administrators* (Westport, CT: Heinemann, 2000), 14; Dennis Sparks and Joan Richardson, *What Is Staff Development Anyway?* (Oxford, OH: National Staff Development Council, 1997), 3.

integral part of the day-to-day operation of the school. The planning of the staff development program should be influenced directly by the school improvement goals or renewal goals of the school or system, by student achievement results, and by the teacher evaluation program.

Each school has unique characteristics and needs, as does each individual in that school. Principals must be alert to these differences as they help plan staff development programs and/or react to proposals for programs. Principals cannot leave the planning and implementation of staff development programs to another office or agency, although they will find such help valuable. Staff development is as much a faculty responsibility as it is the principal's responsibility.

AWARENESS OF STAFF DEVELOPMENT TRENDS

Staff development is undergoing constant change as a result of research on what makes such development effective. The principal who serves as a leader when it comes to staff development must be aware of the trends, resources, and opportunities that abound for educators. A leading association that has spearheaded many changes toward a more contemporary view of effective staff development is the National Staff Development Council. Created in 1969, this association has been instrumental in providing educators with the tools and knowledge they need to implement quality professional development programs that support high levels of learning for all students.[4]

Standards now abound in education. There are curriculum standards for student learning, standards for teaching, and standards for instructional leadership. In addition, there are standards for staff development. The National Staff Development Council has established national standards aimed at giving schools, districts, and states direction in what constitutes quality staff development for all educators. These standards are developed for elementary, middle, and high school levels. They help inform decision makers about the selection of content, learning processes, and organizational structures to support effective staff development.[5]

A more recent emphasis in staff development is to identify linkages between professional development programs and student outcomes. This focus appears to be of paramount concern to legislators and other policy makers who make funding decisions about education. Sometimes

[4] The National Staff Development Council can be accessed on the Web at www.nsdc.org or by calling 800/727-7288.
[5] *Standards for Staff Development*, Elementary School ed./Middle School ed./High School ed. (Oxford, OH: National Staff Development Council, 1995).

referred to as learner-centered professional development[6] or results-based staff development[7] the notion is that teacher learning should have a connection to student learning. When considering this view of staff development, the following questions serve as a guide:

- What are the student outcomes desired?
- What kind of knowledge and teaching skills do teachers need to reach the desired outcomes?
- What kinds of staff development will enable teachers to help students realize the desired outcomes?

The emphasis on outcomes places a focus on measurable improvements in student achievement as a result of the staff development activities.

The contemporary view of high-quality staff development is that it is long term, is aligned with district and school goals, and actively engages teachers in learning and applying new skills and knowledge. To help schools better design and operate professional development activities, the U.S. Department of Education (ED) provides a toolkit.[8] Developed by ED, along with the federally funded North Central Regional Educational Laboratory (NCREL) and Mid-Continental Regional Educational Laboratory (McREL), this toolkit draws upon the lessons learned by ED's outstanding Model Professional Development Program award winners. This user-friendly toolkit takes the principal through the process of designing, implementing, evaluating, and improving professional development.

In the new view of staff development, teachers are engaged in job-embedded learning every day in the classroom and school. Their learning is embedded in the assignments and work they do every day in the classroom as they try to better understand their own performance in relation to their students' performance.[9] This means that teachers must be provided opportunities to meet with others in their grade levels and/or subjects and with the faculty as a whole. They need to learn about and share common instructional strategies to ensure greater consistency of high-quality instruction. They need to be involved in such activities as

[6] Willis D. Hawley and Linda Valli, "Learner-Centered Professional Development." *Research Bulletin* (Phi Delta Kappa International) No. 27 (August 2000) 7.
[7] Joellen Killion, *What Works in the Middle: Results-Based Staff Development* (Oxford, OH: National Staff Development Council, 2000).
[8] North Central Regional Educational Laboratory, *Professional Development: Learning from the Best. A Toolkit for Schools and Districts Based on the National Awards Program for Model Professional Development.* Accessible by contacting www.ncrel.org/pd.toolkit.htm.
[9] National Partnership for Excellence and Accountability in Teaching, *Revisioning Professional Development: What Learner-Centered Professional Development Looks Like.* (Oxford, OH: National School Development Council, 1999), 2.

peer coaching, action research, study groups, and curriculum develop-ment. Teachers must have opportunities to see new strategies demon-strated, practice them, use new teaching and learning strategies on a reg-ular and appropriate basis, and see the effects of newly learned behaviors.[10]

Technology has become a major focus of staff development. To attain a goal of preparing teachers for the effective use of technology, a well-planned staff development program is crucial. The principal must be instrumental in helping promote the meaningful technology integra-tion that helps empower teachers to enhance student achievement, rein-forces established curriculum goals and objectives, and provides both teachers and students with the ability to use powerful new tools to sup-port teaching and learning.[11] Like any other staff development process, professional development for technology needs to be connected to stu-dent learning, provide hands-on experiences, be ongoing, have curricu-lum applications, and have support for on-the-job use.

The National Board Certified Teachers program of the National Board for Professional Teaching Standards (NBPTS) opens new avenues for staff development. NBPTS certification is a way for the teaching pro-fession to define and recognize highly accomplished practice. To be certi-fied by the board, a teacher has to demonstrate in a variety of settings the ability to make sound professional judgments about students' best inter-ests and to act effectively on those judgments. The principal might have board-certified teachers in the building who can be asked to work with other teachers in professional growth activities. A good portion of all teachers' learning is acquired with colleagues in their schools.[12]

Research on effective staff development is changing the face of what once were regarded as traditional practices. Table 14.1 illustrates how the contemporary view of staff development has evolved from the traditional view.

OPPORTUNITIES FOR DEVELOPMENT ACTIVITIES

There are numerous advantages for school improvement when individ-ual teachers and administrators attend courses, workshops, or confer-ences as their primary means of staff development. However, while these particular developmental activities are valuable and represent one

---

[10] Willis D. Hawley and Linda Valli. "Learner-Centered Professional Development." *Research Bulletin,* (Phi Delta Kappa International) No. 27 (August 2000): 8.

[11] The Pathways to School Improvement Internet site (www.ncrel.org/pathways.htm) includes a recent Critical Issue document, *Providing Professional Development for Effective Technology Use.*

[12] The National Board Certified Teachers program of the National Board for Professional Teaching Standards can be accessed on the Web at www.nbpts.org/nbct_program.html.

TABLE 14.1
Traditional and Contemporary Views of Staff Development

Traditional View	Contemporary View
Focus on district needs	Focus on school-based improvement and personal professional needs
Focus on subject (curriculum)	Focus on student learning outcomes
Disconnect between professional development and school improvement	Connection between professional development and school improvement
Separate from supervisory process	Integrated with supervisory process
Determined by central office	Planning/input from principal/teachers
Fragmented, hit-and-miss experiences	Planned, long-range experiences
One- or two-day events	Ongoing and integrative process
One-size-fits-all training	Personal professional development plans
Pull-out-from-the-classroom in-service	Job-embedded professional development
Expert delivered/lectured	Interactive, hands-on activities and problem solving tasks
Large-group activities	Small-group and individual activities
Passive exposure to ideas	Reflection on practices
Training	Training, practice, and feedback
Little or no follow-up	Intensive coaching/support
Participant satisfaction	Return on investment (impact on student achievement)
Expense	Investment

dimension of a comprehensive staff development program, they are not the only means by which staff development helps organizations achieve their collective goals.

Many other opportunities, some of which are less formal, ongoing, job related, or job embedded, equally represent developmental experiences that can have wide impact for teachers and staff. The following list represents a beginning for the reader's own expanding list:

- Teaching college or university courses
- Presentations by fellow teachers, administrators, community resource persons, experts in selected fields, and so on

- On-line instruction (e.g., delivered via the Web; CD–ROMs; delivered via intranet)
- Telecommunications conferences with other practitioners and/or experts in selected practices
- Use of information networks, bulletin boards, and computer conversations available in state and national databases
- Mentoring arrangements
- Peer coaching and analyses of teaching incidents
- Shadowing another teacher or professional in the field
- Peer observations
- Teacher position exchanges
- Visits to programs and projects of interest within the school or system or to other schools or agencies both nationally and internationally
- Study or support groups/cadres
- Fact-finding and data-interpreting teams
- Action research and experimental projects
- Reflection log or journal
- Planned faculty retreats
- Curriculum committee work
- Specialized committee work (e.g., facilities provision for students with disabilities, inclusion)
- Schoolwide committee project leadership
- Supervising a student teacher or teacher education candidate in clinical supervision
- Involvement with local, regional, state, or national teacher centers
- Development of proposals for outside funding
- Reviewer of university teacher preparation programs
- Reviewer on external or internal school or school district review teams
- Participation in business, school, or community partnerships directly related to student achievement or school improvement plans
- Reading of journals, educational magazines, books
- Video or audio recordings
- Publishing educational articles, columns, chapters, or books

This list is but the start of the many opportunities a faculty and principal have for initiating meaningful developmental experiences. Educational travel, summer institutes, degree programs, and the like can also prove invaluable.

Principals should think not only of teachers when developing in-service programs but of themselves as well. According to a report by the National Staff Development Council, "[s]trengthening the skills and knowledge of the nation's 100,000 principals is likely to have more immediate payoff in raising student performance than any other area of school improvement."[13] In addition, ancillary staff such as school psychologists, social workers, speech therapists, counselors, and the like, as well as noncertified staff such as clerks, secretaries, aides, custodians, and food and service personnel, can profit by in-service experiences designed with their help.

THE UNIVERSITY'S ROLE IN STAFF/PROFESSIONAL DEVELOPMENT

Collaborative partnerships between schools and universities, in existence for several decades, have traditionally supported staff development activities that benefit both schools and higher education. Universities have developed response systems to meet a great variety of staff development needs. For example, under an ideal relationship, a given school system could assess the special professional requirements of its faculty. Following the needs assessment, it could contact a nearby higher education institution, through the college of education or the office of continuing education, to get help in establishing a workshop, seminar, or course that would satisfy the faculty's needs.

Telecommunications linkages as well as on-line course offerings now available through many universities provide other possibilities for interactive programming and problem solving. If a school faces a particular problem, a team composed of the teachers and administrators might decide they would like to work formally on this problem in a disciplined way. They could contact a university and plan a workshop so that the professional resources of the university would be made available to the team in finding solutions to the problem. In some states, a number of higher education institutions have pooled resources through collaborative alliances or partnerships to help local schools solve their problems. As an example, some universities sponsor councils or centers composed of a number of school districts. These types of coalitions provide broader-based opportunities for staff development activities for faculty and staff alike.

PROFESSIONAL DEVELOPMENT SCHOOLS AND CENTERS/ACADEMIES

Other opportunities are available to those planning staff/professional development programs. One example is professional development

---

[13] Dennis Sparks and Stephanie Hirsch. *Learning to Lead, Leading to Learn* (Oxford, OH: National Staff Development Council, 2000), 1.

schools (PDSs). A PDS can be an elementary, middle, or high school, found in an urban, rural, or suburban area, that works in partnership with a university or other PDS sites. One major goal of a PDS is to create a learning environment that mixes the best of theory, research, and practice. Undergraduate and graduate classes are taught on-site for both preservice and certified educators in PDS sites. Many PDS sites have a relationship with The Holmes Partnership, a network of universities, schools, community agencies, and national professional organizations working in partnership to create high-quality professional development.[14]

Some districts have teacher centers or academies that offer development work. These sites are designed to provide educators access to information and resources related to proven instructional and curricular practices that promote overall school improvement. The centers and academies are sponsored by school systems themselves, professional organizations, state departments of education, universities, and special grants from foundations and corporations. They offer possibilities that may include training sessions, on-line education, mentoring, action research on topics of interest, and networking.

PRINCIPALS' CENTERS AND ACADEMIES

Every principal needs to continue to grow personally and professionally. Principals must set the "model" for professional development. Just like teachers, their own professional development must be planned, long term, embedded in their jobs, focused on student achievement, and supportive of reflective practice and must include opportunities to work, discuss, and solve problems with colleagues.

Principals' centers and academies are among choices that can provide practicing and aspiring principals opportunities to meet together in settings to explore and reflect on current school and leadership topics. Their programs are varied and may meet the unique needs of principals through conferences, forums, study groups, workshops, seminars, institutes, and grants to pursue projects of one's own design. There are national, statewide, and regional centers or academies, and some within cities. The point is that they all offer principals an opportunity to renew, reflect, and receive support from colleagues. These centers and academies may be sponsored by state funds, membership dues, or combinations of foundation and corporation funds, dues, and gifts. Many of the centers are connected with the International Network of Principals' Centers sponsored by the Harvard Graduate School of Education, where

---

[14] The Holmes Partnership can be accessed on the Web at www.holmespartnership.org or by calling 614/688-3592.

members are linked with educators throughout the world to determine best practices in instruction and school leadership.[15]

SUPERVISION AND STAFF DEVELOPMENT

Some question may arise about whether supervision is a part of the staff development process because the word *supervision* evokes a variety of meanings. It can mean general overseeing and control, management, administration, evaluation, accountability, or any and all of the activities in which the principal is engaged when "running" the school.

Because of the variations in the meaning of *supervision*, we will use the more descriptive term *supervision of instruction* when discussing supervision as part of staff development. Used with this specificity, it has a deeper meaning: the process through which the principal attempts to work with teachers in a positive way to achieve the major goal of the school, which is superior teaching and learning. The principal's role in supervision of instruction is to include those leadership activities in which the principal engages cooperatively with teachers and other staff members to improve teaching and learning in the school. When instructional supervision is used in this way, it is inextricably tied in with leadership and staff/professional development in a learning environment.

Even with this more specific and definitive use, we recognize that there are contradictions and conflicts inherent in the process of instructional supervision. Consider, for instance, the following questions:

1. Can the principal separate supervision from evaluation?
2. Must the principal in the instructional supervision role take the stance that he or she is more knowledgeable about teaching and learning on all subjects than the teacher who is a specialist?
3. How does the principal deal with supervision and the supervisor (consultant) from central administration?
4. Does the principal have the time to accept major responsibility for instructional supervision?

SUPERVISION AND INSTRUCTION

Supervision of instruction goes beyond inspection. The role of the principal in a supervisory relationship with staff is one of teaching; providing support, guidance, and resources; and fostering cooperative problem

---

[15] The International Network of Principals' Centers can be accessed on the Web at www.gseweb.harvard.edu/principals/about/international.htm or by calling the Principals' Center hotline at 617/495-9812.

solving to achieve the major instructional goals of the school. From this perspective, it is impossible to separate supervision from evaluation.

Supervisory evaluation is formative and cooperative. Its goal is to enable the teacher or any other staff member to accomplish the tasks at hand more effectively. The principal's supervisory role is one of human resources supervision, based on the idea that a teacher or staff member will be a more satisfied, motivated person if she or he is continually growing and has a sense of accomplishment.

If supervision of instruction is to succeed, it must be considered as a process separate from summative evaluation, even though they are both important responsibilities of the principal. The supervision process in the old days may have meant inspection and evaluation, example, telling how and what, and then inspecting to see whether it was being done. Today working with teachers as knowledgeable and professional educators makes us realize that much more can be gained by professional stimulation and cooperation than by force and coercion; in fact, the latter can often be counterproductive.

Instructional supervision, then, must be as threat-free as possible. As designated leader of the school, the principal accepts responsibility for encouraging and increasing activities that will help the teacher improve teaching and learning in the classroom. In this sense, the principal acts as a motivator, initiator, and change agent. Rather than telling the teacher what to do, the principal and teacher discuss, as colleagues and peers, how to improve teaching and learning. They brainstorm and exchange ideas, discuss alternatives, and generate data about areas of interest and concern. The principal may identify and offer other resources as necessary, but avoids whenever possible any implications of judgment or criticism based on his or her organizational position in the administrative hierarchy. At the same time, the principal must act decisively in any situation in which students are being harmed academically or in any other way.

The following guidelines may enhance the effectiveness of supervision of instruction:

1. The teacher can openly share concerns with the principal when there is free communication, and each can react and disagree without fear of hurt feelings or reprisal.
2. A genuine feeling prevails that the teacher and principal are solving problems as professional colleagues, as fellow learners.
3. There is realization that expertise is a function of knowledge and experience and that the administrative position does not in and of itself make the principal an expert.
4. The teacher recognizes that the principal values his or her worth as a person and is concerned about both personal and professional growth.

5. The teacher's professional competence is recognized by the helpfulness of feedback and the supportive way it is given.

6. The infinite variability in human beings, which makes rigid, universal applications in teaching and learning questionable, is acknowledged. Teaching can be risk taking, and failure in some experiment or new venture is not a sign of incompetence.

7. The teacher feels professional freedom in that he or she may experiment with teaching procedures and seek help in many different directions without being made to feel inadequate.

8. There is an understanding that teaching is both rational and emotional and that discussions of feelings and interpersonal relations may be as important as talking about the teaching process itself.

9. The developmental aspects of supervision should be seen as part of a normal growth process, not as correcting deficiencies.

10. The development of threat-free collegiality among teachers is viewed as an opportunity for individual growth.

THE PRINCIPAL AS AN EXPERT

It is a serious mistake to assume that because the principal is administratively responsible for instructional supervision, he or she is, and must be, the expert in any and all fields represented in the school. Along with providing motivation and support as a professional colleague to improve teaching and learning, the principal's supervisory function is to develop instructional teamwork. If a school is to be something more than a group of isolated, disconnected classes, the faculty needs to go through the process of identifying schoolwide goals, and then each teacher must be committed to accepting responsibility for linking individual subject-matter goals with those of the entire school. The principal then can help each teacher coordinate teaching with the goals of the school, realizing that his or her teaching is part of a cooperative enterprise.

It is true that principals can gain much support through the expertise they exhibit, but the expertise should include broader technical, human, and conceptual skills, such as the following:

- Expertise in motivating teachers to improve, to be creative, productive teachers who are part of a unified working faculty
- Expertise in being able to place the school in perspective with the local, state, and national educational enterprise
- Expertise in marshaling a great variety of resources and technology that can help the teaching-learning situation
- Expertise in working with the community and central administration to gain the necessary support for the teachers and the school

- Expertise in working with students to mold them into an effective, productive learning community

SUPERVISION: THE PRINCIPAL AND THE CENTRAL OFFICE

Given the trend toward focusing on the school as the key decision-making unit for change, the principal may find it useful to use subject or grade-level expertise available in the central office staff. Call it restructuring, decentralization, or school-based management, relationships between the building level and the central office are undergoing change as the concept of building-level decision making matures. Once seen as the place from where mandates were handed down, the central office staff today is viewed as part of the support team for the building levels in their school improvement efforts.

The overwhelming majority of supervisors have been staff rather than administrative personnel. Principals, on the other hand, are by board direction the administrators of their respective buildings and are responsible to the superintendent and the board for all activities (including instructional supervision) carried on in the buildings to which they are assigned. Thus, it is the principal's responsibility to use central administration supervisors as a resource for the school faculty, individually and collectively. They are part of the team, but they usually neither control nor administer, and they work through the principal's office. They should work alongside the principal and with the faculty to develop internal policies, practices, and procedures so that all possible resources can be used to the fullest advantage. The expertise of the principal should be evident in the exercise of his or her ability to utilize central administration supervisors as part of the school improvement team effort.

EVALUATION OF STAFF DEVELOPMENT

A focus of staff development evaluation today is to determine the effects of staff development on students, educators, schools, and school systems. Evaluation of professional development is going beyond just measuring the satisfaction of teachers who experience various staff development activities. The emphasis is shifting to assessing actual changes in teaching and student learning. The extent to which staff development has influenced student achievement provides the real picture of the value and impact of staff development.

Though a comprehensive staff development program is constituted of many kinds and levels of activities, it is nevertheless a program. The principles noted about evaluation in Chapters 12 and 13 apply. Since a comprehensive evaluation program has so many dimensions, it serves a number of functions. A program to entice disaffected teachers to stay in the system may get the job done—to the detriment of the system.

SUMMARY

In a community of learners, the principal's role as a model learner is reflected clearly in the staff/professional development program, from planning to evaluation. Given the rapid changes occurring in schools and society, continuous learning is essential. Planning a continuous staff development program affords an exciting opportunity for professionals to grow and increase their skills in improving learning for all in the school.

The principal plays a key role in promoting effective staff development. In particular, the principal should

- Demonstrate commitment to continuous learning.
- Create a school climate supportive of professional development.
- Involve teachers in the identification of what they need to learn and the staff development processes to be used.
- Make suggestions, provide feedback, model, and praise.
- Provide opportunities for staff to exchange ideas with one another and with those outside of the school/system.
- Work toward helping with the bridging from teacher learning through staff development activities to student learning.

FOR FURTHER THOUGHT

1. What is your own vision of an effective staff development program for your school, and what can you personally do to work toward that vision?
2. Give some examples of how staff development needs might differ between new teachers and very experienced teachers and how those needs might best be addressed through staff development.
3. Secure a copy of the staff development standards developed by the National Staff Development Council, and analyze how well your school/system meets those standards.
4. Secure the listing of the U.S. Department of Education's Model Professional Development Program award winners, and review the content and processes of those programs that demonstrated an impact on student learning.
5. Explore principal centers or academies that might be available in your area, and consider attending a professional development offering at that site.

6. Review your school improvement plan, technology plan, and any other planning documents of your school, and analyze how well your staff development program aligns with those plans.
7. Using the points of view of some of the experts in the field, determine the fine distinctions among *staff development, professional development* (as we are beginning to understand it), and *in-service education* (as we used to know it).
8. Examine evaluation forms of staff development sessions. Do they provide data appropriate to decisions about the effectiveness of the learning in relation to the objectives of the school? What improvements would you make?
9. Some contend the purposes of administration, supervision, and evaluation are such that the principal can never be a part of the "team" in working with teachers to improve teaching and learning. Discuss.

SELECTED READINGS

Bailey, Gerald, and Dan Lumley. *Staff Development in Technology.* Bloomington, IN: National Education Service, 1997.

Glickman, C. D., S. P. Gordon, and J. M. Ross-Gordon. *Supervision of Instruction: A Developmental Approach,* 4th ed. Needham Heights, MA: Allyn & Bacon, 1998.

Guskey, Thomas R. *Evaluating Professional Development.* Thousand Oaks, CA: Corwin, 1999.

Hawley, W. D., and L. Valli. The Essentials of Effective Professional Development: A New Consensus. In G. Sykes and L. Darling-Hammond, (eds.) *Handbook of Teaching and Policy.* New York: Teachers College Press, 1999.

Joyce, Bruce, and Beverly Showers. *Student Achievement through Staff Development: Fundamentals of School Renewal,* 2d ed. New York: Longman, 1995.

Koehler, Mike, and Connie Kalback. *Administrator's Staff Development Activities Kit: Ready-to-Use Techniques and Materials for Training, Supervision and Evaluation.* Center for Applied Research. Columbus, OH: Prentice Hall, 2000.

Loucks-Horsley, Susan, Peter Hewson, Nancy Love, Katherine Stiles, Susan Mumme, Cary Sneider, and Karen Worth. *Designing Professional Development for Teachers of Science and Mathematics.* Thousand Oaks, CA: Corwin, 1998.

Senge, Peter, Nelda Cambran-McCabe, Nelda Lucas, Timothy Smith, Bryan Dutton, and Janis Kleiner. *Schools That Learn.* New York: Doubleday/Currency Publishing, 2000.

Sparks, Dennis, and Stephanie Hirsh. *A New Vision for Staff Development.* Alexandria, VA: ASCD, 1997.

Speck, Marsha, and Caroll Knipe. *Why Can't We Get It Right? A New Look at Professional Development Programs and Practices.* Thousand Oaks, CA: Corwin, 2000.

Zepeda, Sally. *Staff Development Practices That Promote Leadership in Learning Communities.* Larchmont, NY: Eye on Education, 1999.

Special Problems and Issues

*T*he principal is continually dealing with problems and issues that emanate from our society in general. Many of these issues never seem to "just go away." They are always with us to some degree or other. For many, there appear to be *no* absolute solutions. However, if we cannot entirely eliminate the problems, we can use approaches, strategies, and attitudes to eliminate much of the trauma (to both the school and the student) accompanying them.

An important part of the preparation program for a prospective principal is to help him or her understand the perennial problems facing each school and learn how to work with students, faculty, and the community in dealing with them in a way appropriate to that particular school community.

Problem solving is considered one of the principal's most effective and important abilities. In fact, most principals cited as exemplary are rated high in ability in this area. Problem-solving methods used by many effective principals are identified as basically intuitive; however, much of this so-called intuition has an experiential and educational base. Two specific approaches toward problem solving emerge when studying their methods: one emphasizes process; the other, personal qualities.

The principals who tend to use principles and steps of problem solving when confronted with a problem list the following steps as part of their process:

1. Investigate and diagnose the factors that seem to be the cause of the problem.

2. Identify and assess the various alternative means of resolving the problem; look creatively for that third or fourth or fifth alternative.
3. Meet with a variety of people, particularly those who are to be affected by the problem or its resolution.
4. Use mediation, counterproposals, and compromise in the approach to problem solving.
5. Select a proposed resolution of the problem only after considerable analysis and thought.
6. Plan carefully and thoughtfully the implementation of the proposed solution.

A number of principals emphasize the importance of several personal qualities in problem solving:

• Being a good listener
• Not becoming defensive or emotional
• Being able to take pressure or tension
• Staying "cool"
• Being fair and reasonable but firm
• Showing stick-to-itiveness

Over the years, a number of problems have persisted, such as violence, discipline, gender bias, child abuse, substance abuse, children home alone, and teen motherhood. In addition, hate crimes, gang activity, and infectious diseases present more challenges to the principal.

These topics are discussed in the following two chapters. It is not possible to draw neat, clean lines between what might be considered a school problem and what might be labeled a societal problem. Certainly, the schools and society at large could share responsibility for these problems' existence as well as contributions toward solutions. Nonetheless, it may be seen that many of the problems in the school are a by-product more of society than of the way a particular school operates.

Society-Related Problems

*T*he pervasive societal problems are not found just in the schools, nor are they by-products of the schools. We believe schools make a serious mistake in shouldering *complete* responsibility for either the assessment or the solution of these problems and in accepting blame for their existence. However, as an important social institution, the school can and should take appropriate leadership in alerting the community to the problem and should work as a cooperative team member with the broader community in seeking solutions. In addition, the school can develop specific procedures for dealing with these problems when they emerge in the school itself. This chapter focuses on violence, child abuse, substance abuse, teen pregnancy, occult practices, and sexually transmitted diseases.

VIOLENCE IN SOCIETY

Schools are one of the safest places to be in our society. That having been stated, schools are places of violence for school personnel. In large cities, school employees are targets of assault at a rate second only to that of corrections personnel.[1] An example occurred when a mother of a second grader walked into the classroom and hit the teacher in the head to "teach her a lesson about punishing children." In a survey of principals, 58 percent of the principals had experienced false accusations; 71 percent, verbal threats; 50 percent, shouting and profanity; and 15 percent, an invasion of their personal space.[2]

These incidents occurred in school but may be only a carryover from a society filled with frustrations, needs for power, and perhaps

---

[1] Marilyn Elias, "Making Jobs Safe," *USA Today*, 8 August 1996, 20.
[2] Charles M. Jaksec, "Research Past Due on Parent Aggression against Middle School Administrators," *In the Middle* 9 (February 2000): 43.

growing desensitivity to the harming or taking of life. Whether the appeal of joining a gang or the pressure to do so is rooted in gangs' pushing the ideas of power, respect, and a code of honor to death or whether there exists a vacuum of security and meaningfulness, the facts are that individual and gang violence is spreading cancerlike across the country. Katz describes the overwhelming urge to steal and the sensual attraction of crime, including "the strange joy of killing."[3]

A study of the opinions of several hundred middle and high school students in a midwestern city indicates a consistent approval of violence in domestic and peer relationships, including illegal acts. Violence begets violence, and the results of the study may be a grim affirmation of that. Over 8 percent of the teens surveyed approve of hitting one's girlfriend if she embarrassed him. Almost 15 percent approve of the girl hitting her boyfriend if he embarrassed her. One-third of the students approved of carrying knives in school, and one-third approved of parents hitting a teenager who talked back to the parents.[4]

In early 1996, the country was shown scenes of the beating of illegal immigrants. On September 11, 2001 the reality of violence and vulnerability was expanded. The children and teens watching these tapes being played over and over on newscasts have learned lessons. What they learned may be played out in society in general and in school hallways or grounds in particular.

In 1984, then Chief Justice Warren Burger stated, "Crime in this country is probably the worst in the civilized world."[5] While the statement shocks, it may provide a perspective on how well schools are doing rather than the opposite. Yet there is much to do, as evidenced by the number of prisons being built.

Every school principal has an important stake in the issue of violence for at least two important reasons. First, the principal's leadership is necessary to help the public understand the nature of this national problem; the solution to crime in the school does not lie solely within the schools. These are social problems, with roots deep below the surface, in the very foundation and structure of our society. Second, the central conclusion of all the studies we read on the subject seems to be that the principal's leadership is one of the strongest factors in reducing school vandalism and violence.

The researchers who conducted the *Youth Survey on Approval of Violence in Peer and Domestic Relations* recommend educational programs to intervene in students' approval of violence, particularly focusing on

---

[3] Jack Katz, *Seductions of Crime: Moral and Sensual Attractions in Doing Evil* (New York: Basic Books, 1988).

[4] *Youth Survey on Approval of Violence in Peer and Domestic Relations* (Muncie, IN: Ball State University, Social Science Research Center and Department of Criminal Justice and Criminology, 1991).

[5] Statement made on CBS, 20 June 1984.

rationalizations for violence (e.g., self-defense). These programs would give attention to gender roles and alternative nonviolent means of conflict resolution. In addition, exposure to adults opposed to violence and to nonviolent approaches to child rearing were recommended.[6]

The principal can exert leadership in a variety of ways:

- Reviewing and/or establishing uniform disciplinary practices known by students, teachers, parents, and school board members. These practices would be included in a written code of responsibilities developed by a group of persons (including students) representative of the school and community served.
- Involving as many adults in the school as possible.
- Meeting problems early and openly.
- Visiting in the community and enlisting the help of neighbors to monitor the school area for unusual or destructive behavior.
- Planning with custodial and maintenance staff regarding opportunities they may have to help instill pride in the facilities (such as conducting building tours), effect rapid repairs and cleaning, and suggest procedures and materials to alleviate potential problems.
- Establishing a liaison with police officials to agree on when police should be called and how such incidents will be handled for the proper protection of all.
- Developing a plan to keep weapons out of school. Some schools have found electronic devices necessary on a spot-check basis.
- Providing in-service education to faculty and staff on how to deal with fights, violent parents, unknown intruders, and even organized gang activity.

Again, the principal exerts leadership by articulating standards and expectations, providing assistance and information, and bringing people together in a problem-solving situation.

GANGS, HATE GROUPS, AND VIOLENCE

Symbols of gang members communicating with each other are evident on the walls of garages, retaining walls, buildings, and even schools. The "colors" are worn with pride, and the nonverbal displays of identification and greetings may precede exchanges of bragging about great times with drugs and other destructive activities. Unusual displays of affluence in cars, cash, or clothes appear. The first reaction is that the situation described here is set in a large city on the coast. Actually, it can be anywhere in the Midwest or South and in relatively small communities.

---

[6] *Youth Survey on Approval of Violence*, 1991.

A gang has been defined as a group that has identifiable marks, symbols, or signs and that claims territory and engages in antisocial behavior. Riley cites the California Council on Criminal Justice Task Force's criteria, which must be met before a group is classified as a street gang:

- The organization must have a name.
- The organization must claim territory or turf.
- The members must continually "hang out" with each other.
- They must distinguish themselves from other groups.
- The organization must be involved in criminal activity.[7]

Some of the reasons noted for joining gangs include the need to be accepted, the need to belong, the need to be secure, and the way to get what one wants using the resources available. Implications for school leaders are clear. The reduction of alienating acts and environments, the creation of a variety of ways to belong and achieve status, and a total community effort to demonstrate realistic routes to achieve real goals of respect and material things seem to be essential for addressing the appeal that only gangs seem to offer youth. Actively seeking parent involvement via information and support programs may appear to be the proverbial drop in the bucket, but it may save lives.

Another important preventive measure is knowing the individual students well. Knowing students well helps not only relative to the gang problems but in many other areas as well. Changes in behavior, dress, attitude, and friends can be recognized quickly, and help may be provided in time to divert the student's turning to gang activity. Teachers should encourage students to discuss the influence of gangs on their lives.[8]

Being willing to recognize that there is gang activity in the area and even in the school is a positive step toward dealing with the problem. A 1992 graduate survey of middle and high school principals in a medium-sized city yielded a surprising unwillingness to recognize gang activity in or around the schools, yet gang graffiti and colors were photographed even on school property as well as on buildings around the schools.

Larson suggests the following steps to confront the problem: use respect; provide relevant programs; express zero tolerance for weapons, drugs, and violence; open school doors to adults for parent/citizen

---

[7] Kevin W. Riley, *Street Gangs and the Schools: A Blueprint for Intervention*. (Bloomington, IN: Phi Delta Kappa, 1991), 11–12. See also A. P. Goldstein, *Delinquent Gangs: A Psychological Perspective* (Champaign, IL: Research Press, 1991); *My Bloody Life: The Making of a Latin King* (Chicago: Chicago Review Press, 2000).
[8] Michele Wagner, Carla Knudsen, and Victoria Harper, "The Evil Joker," *Educational Leadership* 57 (January 2000): 47–52.

safety committees; keep records (preferably video) of incidents; regulate attire; welcome police; support teachers; and take control.[9]

Metal detectors may be a deterrent to the presence of weapons. If the need to control weapons is clear, then the detectors should be installed permanently and used regularly. There is expense involved; however, Gilbert points out an often overlooked expense—defending new safety measures in lawsuits.[10] Involvement of the community prior to installing and using devices and searches will alleviate the reaction problem.[11]

Hate crime has resurfaced as a concern for schools. Hate group membership has grown dramatically over the last few years. There are nearly five hundred hate groups known in the United States, some of which are branches of or merged with European groups.[12] Hate groups' Website messages are increasing rapidly and are easily accessible by school-age children. Hate group targets include persons of "different" religious faiths or races, or even those expressing global political ideologies. Bodinger–de Uriarte notes that schools, along with "churches . . . cemeteries and camps . . . are where hate crimes occur."[13] She adds that often hate crimes begin in minor ways—taunting, name calling, and minor harassments—but too often end in serious injury or death or the destruction of valued property. Again, the principal can exert leadership by helping colleagues become sensitive to what is going on around them and deal with potential problems early.[14]

VIOLENCE TO SELF: SUICIDE

The principal, counselors, staff, and community leaders had to decide quickly whether to hold a memorial for the student who had taken his own life last night. The crisis team had been alerted, and a number of counselors were available for students. Then the class officers came to the principal to request a memorial service for the school.

Youth suicide is not a new phenomenon, but it is a growing one. Among children five to fourteen years of age, suicide is the fifth leading cause of death. The phenomenon increases through the high school years to

---

[9] Rick Larson, "Get Past Denial, Then Tackle Your Gang Problem," *School Administrator* 53 (February 1996): 30–31.

[10] Christopher B. Gilbert, "How to Keep Your Schools Safe and Secure," *School Business Affairs* 62 (November 1996): 6.

[11] See Lawrence F. Rossow and Jacqueline A. Stefkovitch, *Search and Seizure in the Public Schools*, 2d ed. (Topeka, KS: National Organization for Legal Problems in Education, 1995).

[12] Mark Potok, "The Year in Hate," *National Forum* 80 (Spring 2000): 32–36.

[13] Cristina Bodinger-de Uriarte, "The Rise of Hate Crime on School Campuses," *Research Bulletin* (Phi Delta Kappa) (December 1991): 2.

[14] The reader may wish to read *Hate Crime: A Sourcebook for Schools Confronting Bigotry, Harassment, Vandalism and Violence* (n.p.: Southwest Regional Laboratory, n.d.).

become the third leading cause of death. About 60 percent of high school students have reported suicidal ideation, and 14 percent have made some attempt to commit suicide.[15] Suicide ideation does not seem to be related to poverty, inner city, or similar stereotypes. "In a town with a median household income of $65,970 (in 1999), 12.2 percent of the students did attempt suicide, 23 percent considered it, and one in four made a plan.[16] Suicide may appear to be a viable alternative for the youth who faces multiple problems, sees no solutions, and watches suicides on film or in TV dramas or listens to news accounts of the suicides of famous persons. A death of a fellow student may cause the adolescent to consider death as a way to cope. The school staff needs to be alert to warning signs and take them seriously when several symptoms begin to appear. The Suicide Prevention Center in Dayton, Ohio, cites the following warning signs:

- Talk about death or suicide
- Feelings of helplessness or hopelessness
- Drop in grades
- Schoolwork reflecting death-oriented themes
- Withdrawal from friends and usual activities
- Hostility and irritability
- Changes in eating or sleeping habits
- Crying, moodiness, depression
- Recklessness
- Use of drugs or alcohol
- Inability to concentrate
- Giving away favorite possessions
- Suffering recent loss through death, divorce, moving
- Previous suicide attempts[17]

An intense interest in religious beliefs and life after death also may alert those around the person that suicide is being contemplated.

The principal is in a key position to communicate to parents and teachers about detecting early warning signs and to identify appropriate resources for help when stress signals are apparent. The following tips may be helpful:

- Train the staff to recognize warning signs.
- Plan carefully for new students.
- Make teachers and counselors available to troubled students.
- Recognize the special needs of students.

---

[15] Martha M. McCarthy and L. Dean Webb, "Legal Principles in Preventing and Responding to School Violence," *NASSP Bulletin* 84 (March 2000): 43.

[16] Andy Levinsky, "On the Line," *Principal Leadership* 1 (January 2001): 68–69.

[17] The reader may wish to contact the American Foundation for Suicide Prevention, 120 Wall St., New York, NY 10005, or visit afsp.org, or visit www.surgeongeneral.gov for *Youth Violence: A Report of the Surgeon General.*

- Establish communications with parents.
- Help parents assist small children in learning about school in advance.
- Recommend physical examinations for children showing signs of stress.
- Take your community's economic pulse for its effect on children.
- Begin antidrug, antialcohol, and antismoking programs early.
- Assess the school's emotional climate.

School systems across the country have initiated programs for professionals who work with youth, to help them recognize and react appropriately to the signals children send. At times in suicide situations, schools face a lawsuit charging failure to prevent the suicide as a result of not preparing staff, not having a prevention program in place, or not making parents aware of the symptoms. "Although courts thus far have been reluctant to impose liability on school districts for student suicides, . . . as our knowledge of the risk factors and warning signs for suicide expand, the potential for school district liability will also increase."[18]

Crisis teams are helpful in dealing with deaths of students or faculty. A well-conceived plan for a variety of situations can make the difference between simply reacting to the crisis and controlling it. Questions such as these need to be answered ahead of time:

- What counseling resources are available?
- Who will deal with media? With the police?
- Under what circumstances should a memorial be held at the school?
- Shall students be excused to attend services?
- Should any school events be canceled or postponed?
- What kind of expressions of sympathy are appropriate?
- How quickly should the school return to business as usual?
- What segments of the community should be involved in dealing with student reactions?

The principal may be the person most often shouldering the responsibility of managing the crisis of a death in the school and guiding the activities of the crisis team. Yet teachers and staff may be left out of the mainstream of the crisis control process if care is not taken to consider them. Dunne-Maxim and Underwood point out that staff members can experience grief and common survivor reactions and at the same time carry the burden of being role models and helping others cope.[19] The crisis plan should include all people to help them learn appropriate

---

[18] McCarthy and Webb, 2000.
[19] Karen Dunne-Maxim and Maureen Underwood, "Keeping Afloat in Suicide's Wake," *School Administrator* 48 (May/June 1991): 21.

verbal responses, talk about their own reactions, and provide for linkages with the crisis team for their own help as well as for that of the students.[20]

THE OCCULT AND CHILDREN IN SCHOOL

The last few years have seen a decline in overt cult activity, particularly in the occult practices of Satan worship. Communications from chiefs of police and investigators note an increase in young people becoming more involved in the WICCA movement. The movement is described as a polytheistic, pagan religion with a reverence for the natural world. Websites associated with WICCA cite witchcraft, magic, spells, clothes, and jewelry available for "practicing" WICCA ceremonies. There may be a variety of reasons for students' involvement in cultlike practices, including the seeking of power as a result of low self-esteem, a feeling of helplessness, or even the forced participation in ceremonies by parents involved in the practices. While evidences of the occult observed in students' behavior or possessions may only be the result of curiosity or a fascination with the movement, a continued involvement of the student in displaying symbols, reading the literature of the occult, and progressively changing in physical appearance and behavior is cause for serious concern.

A review of writings regarding the occult produced the following list of observable indicators of potential problems:

- Student artwork and writings
- Literature possessed and read (such as the satanic Bible)
- Preoccupation with death
- Paraphernalia/jewelry worn
- Denouncing conventional religion
- Police reports on vandalism of churches, cemeteries
- Self-mutilation such as symbols scratched into the skin
- Preferring being alone; becoming secretive
- Teenage or younger child suicides[21]

In addition, the following indicators were identified by a questionnaire to principals in one state:

- Graffiti on school property
- Evidence of animal sacrifice

---

[20] Elaine Winter, "School Bereavement," *Educational Leadership* 57 (March 2000): 80–85.
[21] The reader may wish to read D. K. Cursan, "Why Troubled Teenagers Might Turn to Satanism," *American School Board Journal* 176 (1989): 12–14, 39; A. Moriarity and D. Story, "Psychological Dynamics of Adolescent Satanism," *Journal of Mental Health Counseling* 12 (1990): 186–198; and B. Wheeler, S. Wood, and R. Hatch, "Assessment and Intervention with Adolescents Involved in Satanism," *Social Work* 33 (1988): 547–550.

- Student confessions
- Style of dress

Several of these indicators are the same as or similar to those associated with alcohol and the so-called drug culture and/or organized gangs. Each of them has communication codes and symbols, and so do many practitioners of the occult. The symbols often portray the opposite of well-known symbols of Christianity (e.g., the cross, the sacrificial lamb) where a broken cross is displayed upside-down within a circle or a symbol drawn or displayed as a hand signal. Occasionally, groups or movements adopt a symbol similar to or the same as that used in occult practices. One should not jump to hasty conclusions about the group or movement. Fine and Victor caution that "Satanic tourism" or legend trips can mislead officials into making forays into the occult attractive to teenagers.[22] Too much attention to these "beyond trips" on the part of school personnel may even enhance the status of the student in his or her own estimation rather than causing concerns about continuing to explore such activities.

The principal will find it helpful to make contact with law enforcement agencies who deal with the problem. Often larger law enforcement agencies have a person who specializes in investigating or helping people cope with incidents that may be associated with occult practices. Information can be shared with the school or other agencies to better serve the clients involved. As with other abuses affecting children, the principal will wish to help the staff become knowledgeable about recognizing possible involvement in occult practices and sensitive to the effects such practices may have on students of all ages. Counselors in particular should have background information to discuss the issues with students and colleagues. Very few schools are prepared to cope with the potential problem.

School leaders may find the following tips helpful in preparation for the occurrence of occult practices affecting students:

- Become informed of indicators of cultlike practices.
- Help staff, particularly counselors, become knowledgeable about effective practices in providing direction to students.
- Develop linkages with other agencies facing similar situations.
- Develop a formal plan to deal with the problems that may occur.
- Review policies/procedures to avoid becoming embroiled in freedom of religion issues, since Satanism, WICCA, and others are considered to be religions.

---

[22] Gary Alan Fine and Jeffrey Victor, "Satanic Tourism," *Phi Delta Kappan* 76 (September 1994): 70–72.

CHILD ABUSE

Concern about child abuse is not new to popular media or to professional literature. The first child protective case was recorded in 1874. Literature focusing on this problem has been accumulating rapidly, particularly since Kempe et al.'s 1962 paper "The Battered Child Syndrome."[23] The statistics are alarming: the problem appears to be widely distributed, and the consequences are long term. The following discussion is not an appeal that the school take over a neglected area in family or societal responsibility. It presents the facts about the situation and suggests that school personnel assume their places alongside others in exercising moral and legal responsibilities.

Dispelling Myths and Stereotypes

What are the facts regarding the distribution and incidence of child abuse? It is impossible to categorize the abuser according to skin color, ethnic heritage, religious preference, or home. Helge states that low income is a significant factor in that the child in a low-income family is four times more likely to be abused than a child in a higher-income family.[24] Yet one cannot stereotype the abuser because abuse crosses all socioeconomic levels. Child abusers have two characteristics in common: they hurt children, and they need help.[25]

The term *child* often is misleading. The literature on child abuse usually refers to a child as being between birth and age eighteen. The estimated figures are astronomical, but based on actual cases, it is estimated that 50 percent of all abused children are over six years of age, and about 20 percent are teenagers. Child abuse is an area of concern for educators at every level. As the school's responsibility is extended downward to include younger children, the percentage of cases the school sees rises. Though not presently documented, the number of cases investigated or officially reported may be merely the tip of the iceberg. Aside from the many unnoticed situations, some are ignored and avoided by persons not wishing to "become involved," others are incorrectly reported, and still others are carefully concealed by the abusers.

Who abuses children? Two-thirds of the child abusers are parents of the children, and the remaining one-third are nearly always family members or people with access to the home. Abusing parents ordinarily were themselves abused or neglected, physically or emotionally, as children.

---

[23] C. Henry Kempe, F. N. Silverman, B. F. Steele, et al., "The Battered Child Syndrome," *Journal of the American Medical Association* 181 (7 July 1962): 105–112.
[24] Doris Helge, *Child Sexual Abuse in America: A Report of a National Study* (Bellingham: Rural Development Institute, Western Washington University, 1992), 13.
[25] For additional information, contact the National Committee for the Prevention of Child Abuse, 332 South Michigan Avenue, Chicago, IL 60604.

The implications of this for school personnel are clear. Helping correct a problem of child abuse is not just solving the problem at hand but also possibly aiding in preventing occurrences in the next generation. Another message can be heard: What positive role can the school play in providing for children an emotional environment rich in love, tolerance, and example?

Abusing parents can be helped, as can abused children. The school must enter into an active partnership with other community agencies to make homes safe for children.

The incidence of sex crimes, another concern, is high and widely distributed. In most cases, the offender is known to the victim, possibly a relative or close friend of the family. Incestuous relationships occur with far more frequency than often suspected. Sexual abuse appears to be on the rise, or at least increased awareness is causing a more hostile environment for offenders, and abuse is reported more frequently. One of the authors was aware of two pregnancies resulting from incest, in a two-year period, in a first- to eighth-grade school. Monohan states that "typically, sexual abuse began from five to nine years of age."[26] Frequently, the mother of the teenager will not report such a relationship, even though she may be aware of it.

Having an awareness of some risk factors may help teachers and administrators be sensitive to potential problems. Indicators include frequent moves, evidence of physical abuse, fewer than two friends in school, alcohol abuse in the home, and a mother in poor mental health.[27]

Legal Responsibilities of School Personnel

The moral obligations are clear but often easily avoidable because, if a problem is everybody's business, it can be easily left to the next person, thus becoming nobody's business. All states have passed legislation outlining mandatory reporting of suspected physical injury inflicted by other than accidental means, maltreatment, sexual molestation, cruel punishment, or deprivation of food, clothing, or shelter. Anyone can report cases of child abuse, but the law *requires* medical personnel, school principals, teachers, social workers, clergymen, and police officers to report such cases. Those who report suspected abuse in good faith are granted immunity from civil or criminal liability. It should be noted that one need not have "proof"; it is only necessary to have reason to believe a case of child abuse exists to file a report.

---

[26] Kathleen Monohan, "Crocodile Talk: Attributes of Incestuously Abused and Nonabused Sisters," *Child Abuse and Neglect: The International Journal* 21 (January 1997): 22.
[27] Jillian Fleming, Paul Mullen, and Gabriele Bammer, "A Study of Potential Risk Factors for Sexual Abuse in Children," *Child Abuse and Neglect: The International Journal* 21 (January 1997): 53.

An important partnership link can be effected if school personnel can give support to the abused child and his or her siblings. The support might take several forms but would include providing an environment of acceptance, opportunity for successes, recognition of those successes, and continued observation of the situation for any recurring negative symptoms.

Recognition of Child Abuse by School Personnel

The principal will wish to alert faculty and staff to some of the common signs of abuse and neglect of children. It cannot be assumed that teachers know how to discharge their responsibilities as required, in either recognizing suspected abuse/neglect cases or reporting them. Most teachers feel comfortable in reporting suspected cases of child abuse; only about 15 percent do not feel comfortable about reporting. Fear of retribution is most commonly mentioned as a reason not to report. Fears commonly expressed include the staff members' concern for their personal safety and for that of the student. Mandatory attendance at school may be an abused child's first regular contact with the outside world, so the first professionals to see an abused child may be elementary school teachers.

Child abuse is a familial problem; therefore, recognition of child abuse in a school-age child may lead to detection of abuse in younger siblings—possibly enabling these younger siblings to survive to reach school age.

Principals can assist children by alerting teachers and staff to the signs of abuse and/or neglect. Most states provide detailed lists of symptoms, and there are physicians and social agency personnel available to conduct staff development sessions to assist school personnel in recognizing potentially serious problems.

Some physical characteristics of abused children include injuries or wounds in various stages of healing; perpetually dirty fingernails, nose, eyes, or ears; and unexplained tenderness in unusual areas of the body. Children will seldom admit to abuse, particularly if a parent is involved. The children are often passive and fearful.

Staff development discussions should also give attention to characteristics of abusing parents, who often have no emotional response if questions are asked about abuse, have unreasonable expectations about child behavior, and express a belief in physical force to obtain compliance.

Where to Turn

Figure 15.1 suggests a procedure for reporting *suspected* child abuse. Several sources of help are available to the schools. These agencies and ser-

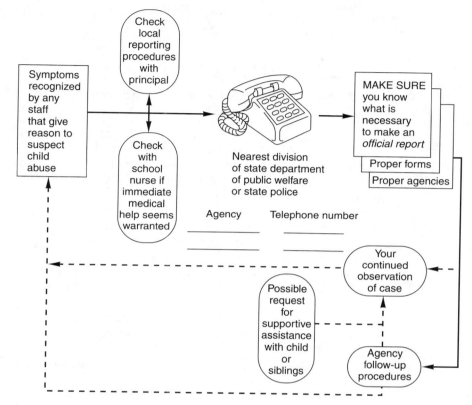

FIGURE 15.1
The steps in reporting a suspected case of child abuse

vices have different names from state to state but are ordinarily easily identified once the task is begun. Listings under the headings of county, city, or state welfare agencies may include the following names:

Children and Family Services

Child Welfare Department, Child Protective Services Registry of Child Abuses

Society for the Prevention of Cruelty to Children

Children's Division of the American Humane Association

These headings are merely representative of the services available.[28] Greater communication between local services as well as with the public

---

[28] Several films are available through local or state child protection agencies, in addition to commercial firms. Most state agencies offer schools literature, flyers, posters, and other teaching aids. Video programs are often shown on PBS and commercial stations. The National Education Association provides a training kit for educators.

is perhaps necessary. As a community leader, the principal can exert influence to effect increased communication.

Suggestions for Implementation

The following guidelines will be helpful to the principal who is considering a proper role in meeting the problem of child abuse:

1. Learn to recognize signs and symptoms of child abuse in pupils.
2. Know enough general background about the phenomenon to feel comfortable explaining it to school personnel and local officials.
3. Alert the staff to the clusters of indicators of child abuse. As noted earlier, various sources of help are available for educating professionals. Often specially targeted projects have developed programs and have speakers available for this purpose.
4. Know what community and state resources are available for investigation, follow-up, and treatment of child abuse and how to report to them.
5. Learn and help the school staff learn the legal responsibilities and local policies governing the implementation of those responsibilities.
6. Develop definite communication channels for all staff to report suspected cases of child abuse.
7. Proper, current reporting forms should be available in the school office. The end result of these communications should be correct reference and reporting of the case to appropriate agencies. Too often oversights in the reporting procedure result in no further investigation.

Conclusion

Prevention of further injuries to children is unquestionably right. Yet taking steps to do so has been avoided by many professionals for many reasons, including lack of follow-up cooperation and sanctions imposed by the community. Schools often report difficulties after reports have been made with the proper agency (or agencies) in that for a variety of reasons there was little or no follow-up, and in some instances the children suffered even more. Teachers have been reluctant to report, though legally required to do so, because of fear for the children as well as for their own safety. The most effective programs have not been reporting but rather prevention programs alerting children to what is acceptable and what is not. The principal's leadership in supporting such programs and establishing effective liaisons with agencies is important to all. The effort expended is well worth it if one child can be spared further injury and if a next generation can be saved as a result.

SUBSTANCE ABUSE

A national debate rages over the use of marijuana, the fact that the major supply sources are in the United States, and the legalization of its use for medical purposes. These discussions are not lost on the young. Ironically, concerned adults do not see that their use of tobacco and ingestion of alcohol, coffee, and other chemicals in effect make them part of a drug society.

The leadership of the principal and staff in reinforcing the efforts of other societal units is important, and may be necessary, to jolt others from their "hope it will go away" attitude toward this pesky problem, which "other" people seem to have. It is not the school's place to accept the sole responsibility for "educating" youth about drug abuse, in either the correction or the prevention mode. It is more appropriate that the school actively seek to do its part and clearly communicate this to other agencies and the public in general, and that it help enlist assistance in presenting a united effort to deal with the problems.

Establishing Perspectives

It is often painfully clear to the pupils, if not to the faculty, that those attempting to provide drug education sometimes are much less sophisticated about drug abuse than the pupils. To teach, or to guide learning, one must begin where the learner is. In this unusual circumstance, the pupils are sometimes sharply divided between those who are quite knowledgeable through their own use of illicit drugs and those who are quite naive—as naive as the teachers. Hence, it is extremely difficult to teach the drugwise student and the naive student without missing both or without creating a fascinating world that must be enjoyable to be shared with those more knowledgeable.

Perhaps the most effective program against drug abuse is that which enhances the self-concept of students and helps them build a sound basis on which to make decisions about their own behavior. The school's staff needs to know the effects of drugs on youth, but to tell whether behavior for one student is abnormal, the staff person must know that student as a unique human being. Otherwise, there is no known baseline of behavior from which to note departures, much less meet the needs prompting the behavior.

An amazing number of youth have used or at least experimented with drugs or alcohol. Alcohol is the substance used most frequently by school-age youth, yet students generally do not recognize it as a drug. A unit in health or a short series of lectures on alcohol abuse does not seem effective. Gordes reports that "[s]chool-based programs closely linked to other community activities have been shown to reduce drinking in pre-adolescents, whereas programs that rely strictly on education have not been shown to have any long-term effect in delaying adolescent alcohol use."[29] Statistics from community agencies dealing with substance abuse clients show a remarkable parallel between the percentages of adult users and users under eighteen years of age.

A major concern faces the schools—children born to and raised by drug abusers. As many as 350,000 drug-damaged children may be born each year.[30] Schools have instituted training programs for teachers to be more effective with children prenatally exposed to drugs. More structured classrooms appear to be more effective with children addicted to drugs; providing a predictable environment is helpful; teaching social skills is important, as is the learning of language through motor skills.[31] If only 10 percent of the students in a school were affected by drugs prior to birth, we are dealing with the same as one to three classrooms of those children in most schools. In the urban high school of two thousand, for example, as many as four hundred students may be so affected, and as many as seven hundred may be living in a family in which one or more members suffers from drug/alcohol abuse.

At the Midwestern Educational Research Association (MWERA) 1991 conference, Thompson et al. presented the somewhat startling finding of a very high correlation between students who work part-time and substance use. For example, over 70 percent of the students who had frequently driven a vehicle while under the influence of alcohol were students who worked during the school year. Similar high percentages were noted for marijuana and cocaine use among those who worked. The researchers make the point that the study does not encourage students not to work but rather suggests careful monitoring of their behaviors to help them use their earnings in more constructive ways.[32]

The implications for schools may be to (1) assist parents and employers in reducing the drug opportunities in the work environment and (2) help students see positive opportunities for using their purchasing power. An analysis of the results of many programs yielded the discouraging finding that they had little effect on attitudes, and in some instances, usage increased after the programs. It may be instructive to

[29] Enoch Gordis, "Research on Alcohol Problems," National Forum 79 (Fall 1999): 26.

[30] Janet Meyer and John Morris, "Don't Give Up on Me—I Can Learn," Principal 74 (September 1994): 36.

[31] Linda Delapenha, "New Challenges for Changing Times," School Safety (Winter 1992): 11–13.

[32] Jay C. Thompson Jr., Christina M. Rice, Van E. Cooley, and C. Van Nelson, "Should Students Work?" (research paper presented at the MWERA annual conference, October 1991).

examine the messages being conveyed via some of the programs that are designed to solve or alleviate the problems. Thompson et al. perceive three weaknesses: (1) the goals of the programs are nonspecific, (2) these programs attempt to prevent by changing attitudes, and (3) they attempt to prevent by promoting responsible drinking or decision making. They point out that attitudes do not really change behaviors. Regarding the third weakness, they ask whether the schools are really saying usage is acceptable.

Developing Policies

Every school system should have policies relating to the possession and use of drugs on school property. The beginning point for the principal is the legal basis for action, and then the board of education's specific policies must be administered.

After determining goals, specific policies and procedures need to be developed. Sample policies are available from state departments of education, principals' associations, and other school districts. These policies and procedures should be specific and widely understood by all school personnel.

Emergency Procedures

Procedures should be developed to cover both physical and disruptive emergencies. Such procedures or regulations should be officially approved, and all personnel concerned should be notified, including parents, students, teachers, administrators, and the community.

Physical Emergencies. Physical emergencies arise during any of the following situations:

- If the student has been rendered unconscious
- If a student verbally or by his or her actions threatens harm to himself or herself or others
- If a student exhibits abnormal coordination so as to injure himself or herself or others

Suggested Procedures for School Staff. The roles of school personnel should include the following:

- *All personnel*—The student at no time should be left unattended. If the use of controlled or narcotic drugs is suspected, be prepared, if warranted by the specific circumstances of the emergency, to advise the school principal or medical authorities. No statement of any type should be released by staff members to the news media.

- *Teacher*—Immediately involve the school nurse, providing all pertinent information. Be prepared to discuss facts and impressions, carefully distinguishing between the two, assuming an inquiry will be held at a later time. Keep a written record of the incident.
- *School nurse*—Take appropriate steps to notify the student's parents or inform the building administrator, who should do so. If a critical health situation is involved, consult the family physician and/or school physician. Attempt to determine whether drug use is an isolated instance or part of a pattern. If controlled or narcotic drugs are involved, be prepared to provide pertinent facts to the appropriate school official if circumstances so indicate. Keep appropriate records.
- *School physician*—Treat for any medical emergency. Attempt to determine whether drug use is an isolated instance or part of a pattern, and whether the matter is a behavioral or health problem. Report the circumstances to appropriate school officials. If controlled or narcotic drugs are involved, follow the reporting procedures required by statute.
- *School principal*—In an emergency, be sure parents are immediately notified of the circumstances. The superintendent of schools or designated officer should be alerted and kept fully informed. Arrange for whatever conferences may be needed. Maintain necessary records.

Disruptive Emergencies. Occasionally, a student may disrupt a school function or activity by acutely abnormal or bizarre behavior. While no uniform set of procedures can be applied to all situations, the following observations should be kept in mind:

- Such behavior may be emotionally, organically, or chemically induced, and immediate differentiation may be impossible.
- Immediate assessment of real danger to the student, other students, staff, and property must be made.
- If time permits, consultation with and/or assistance from pupil services personnel or other personnel who may already know the individual student or have specialized skills in this area may avoid unpleasant and unnecessary complications.
- If the crisis persists and no reason can be determined for the obvious and sudden personality change, the parent and/or doctor should be called immediately.
- In most instances, a referral to pupil services will be indicated to determine the most appropriate long-range plan for the child.
- Punitive disciplinary measures are usually contraindicated in these situations.

The principal must prepare to take leadership in the event of emergencies and should see that all the staff knows the basic policies of the school regarding the use and abuse of drugs. Furthermore, the staff should be knowledgeable about some of the perceived pressures and values that create a climate for experimentation with drugs. The staff will need to know not to "hassle," touch, or threaten the student if he or she appears to be influenced by drugs.

Dealing with drug abuse is a human-to-human process that demands quality, not quantity, of interaction. Moralizing is not effective. Meeting human needs *is* effective. Creating a social environment where there is a rejection of use but acceptance of the user may help reduce abuse.

TEENAGE PREGNANCY AND SEX EDUCATION

Many statewide and local programs, reduced sexual activity, and the use of contraceptives have resulted in a drop in teenage pregnancy (ages fifteen to nineteen) to a record low.[33] As noted in Chapter 3, collaborative projects and/or full-service schools have made some important differences as a result of services being more readily available to teenage mothers. Day-care centers and clinics in middle and high schools are becoming more common so that students and their children can receive proper care. Whether the mothers tried to get pregnant to express frustrations with their environments, wanted someone to love or to love them, or simply thought conception could not happen, the fact remains they are mothers. Too often they do not know how to care for the child physically or developmentally in terms of language and experience. The school day-care center and clinic can provide assistance and direction to help both the baby and the mother.

Boys and girls often are left to face adult feelings without adequate knowledge, maturity, or experience to place them in perspective or understand the consequences of experimentation. There has been general failure to appreciate the problems of developing adolescents within our contemporary society. Our society presents a broad range of moral codes, most of which seem to conflict. Books, magazines, television, movie characters, and even the Internet inspire free sexual behavior, which inevitably conveys mixed, confused, and inaccurate messages to the young about what they should or should not do.

Over half of all students are estimated to experience sex before they finish high school. Further, some teens become pregnant on purpose to have someone to love or gain recognition from those who are significant

---

[33] See the 2001 report entitled *Births: Final Data for 1999,* from the National Center for Health Statistics, Washington DC.

to them. The idea that these pregnancies result primarily from teenage classmates having sex is incorrect. A 1996 study indicated that most fathers were four to seven years older than the teen mothers.[34]

The problem is not related to racial or ethnic groups as much as to groups with low educational and job expectations. The implications for the school seem clear. If the people in the school are effective in raising their own expectations, as well as the students' perceptions of their achievements, current and future, the chance of reducing some of the propensities for teen pregnancies also increases.

Pregnancy is not the only physical consequence. The incidence of sexually transmitted diseases is increasing, particularly in children. Another risk is that of raising the potential for child abuse, given the mother's probable lack of knowledge regarding nurturing, developmental activities, and normal infant behavior. Beyond that, reactions to the frustrations attendant to child care by the immature mother may put the infant at risk. Children of teenagers have a higher risk of physical problems than do children of older parents, thus compounding the situation.

Another risk is extending the poverty cycle. The majority of teenage mothers tend to come from a low-expectation group; without some intervention, they will remain there, along with their children.

Because we are talking about school-age youth, the schools are deeply involved with the problem, and they should be. Sex education courses have not solved the problem, and, in addition, what has ensued in so many instances is community reaction that creates bitter conflict rather than joined forces to focus on the problem in a united, flexible way. Sex is an educational issue. It is also a moral, religious, family, medical, social, and personal issue. It is impossible to reach consensus on sex issues in our pluralistic, changing society. We are wrong to expect to find one set of acceptable sex behaviors for all adolescents at all times and then to instill in them these behavior patterns by having them sit in a class, listening to a lecture.

Like drugs, crime, poverty, and discrimination, sexual behavior is a social issue that must be dealt with on a wide base. Educators, no matter how good their intentions, should not assume they can solve this problem on their own—they cannot. The problem is so visible to them, however, that they should take the initiative in helping all segments of their community realize the extent of the problem and then propose working hand in hand to find proper resolution of the problem. The question is, What do we seek to resolve? Do we want to simply eliminate unwanted pregnancy by providing contraceptive knowledge and accessibility? Do we seek to eliminate sexually transmitted disease by offering treatment or methods of prevention? Do we wish we could eliminate all problems

---

[34] See Mike Males, "The Ages of Fathers in California Adolescent Births, 1993," *American Journal of Public Health* 18 (April 1996): 564.

by preaching and teaching nonmarital sexual continence? Should we look for underlying causes and help young people deal with their sexuality responsibly? A logical response may be "All of the above, and more!" Whatever the response, all responsible people and agencies in the community—the churches, the family, social agencies, and the school—must join forces to face the problem.

Dealing with Pregnancy in the School

The day is long past when the school can ignore teenage pregnancy. The school needs to examine curricular offerings to see whether sex and sexuality are placed in the proper context in course offerings and whether the topics are being dealt with effectively. Are courses available to the teenage parent that will provide marketable career skills? Are efforts being made to move teenage parents who need jobs into ones that will give them experience, income, and a degree of confidence?

The following principles can guide the principal in dealing with this issue:

1. Every student in the United States has a right to and a need for education that will help prepare for a career, family life, and citizenship.
2. The public school should not attempt on its own to establish a policy on a social issue that divides the larger society. The school must take responsibility to alert and educate the community regarding the teen pregnancy issue, and it should involve the community as completely as possible in any policy decision. However, community pressure should not be an excuse for denying constitutional rights to a student because she is pregnant.
3. The public school should be considered an agency that develops policies, programs, and attitudes that open futures, not close them. The fact that students are different from the norm or that something unusual happens to them is no reason to exclude them; it is all the more reason to give them some special help and attention.
4. The school should not attempt to provide all services to the pregnant student. The education function and the needs of students are so complex that they must be accomplished through a number of institutions, agencies, and activities. Strong cooperation and coordinated working relationships with other education and social agencies are essential in the solution of most problems in the school.

CHILDREN ON THEIR OWN

Children who must care for themselves for part of the day outside of school, latchkey children, are not necessarily just from single-parent homes, though the topics are often related. In a greater percentage of families, both spouses now work outside the home. Given our society's mobility, the husband may be from Maine and the wife from Colorado, and they may be living on the West Coast. As a result, the traditional support/care persons (e.g., grandparents, aunts, uncles) may be hundreds of miles away. Furthermore, the couple may not know their neighbors in their apartment complex (which may have an annual turnover rate of 25 percent or more).

In an elementary school of five hundred, it would be reasonable to expect that fifty to seventy-five children would sometimes be in a self-care situation before and after school hours. Obviously, the figures vary considerably from school to school, but in almost any school, a surprising number of children fend for themselves for some period of the day.

Several communities have responded to this need by setting up telephone answering services responsive to calls from children. Many of the services operated by volunteers are available from midafternoon until about 6 P.M. Depending on available funding and volunteers, the services may include simple checks on arrivals at home, safety tips, and responses to calls for help as a result of injuries or other emergencies.

Volunteer teachers may meet with children and youth in central locations (e.g., housing area recreation rooms, churches) and provide tutorial work, homework assignments, and other instruction. Questions of policy regarding the school-age day-care concept include the following: (1) Will there be multiple sources of service? (2) If so, should there be coordination and/or quality control? By which agency? (3) What sources of funds are appropriate? (4) Will the services be available seven days a week? Twenty-four hours a day? (5) What should the criteria for admission be? (6) What curricular activities are appropriate? (7) Should only selected schools provide the services? (8) Should there be licensing of personnel? (9) What responsibilities accrue to the principals for the day-care operations?

Prevalent in society today is the single-parent family, as a result of death or divorce, never-married women who have children, and single persons who have adopted children. Approximately 50 percent of children eighteen years of age or older are in or have experienced being in a single-parent home. Single parents perceive that school personnel do not see their situation as "normal" and think the children's problems result from their status. The accuracy of the perceptions may be questioned, but the reality of the perceptions needs to be addressed.

Even if not required by law or regulation to do so, the principal may find it useful to gather data to predict the single-parent population living in the school's attendance area so that faculty may be informed and the school can make helpful adjustments. Discussions should be held with teachers regarding children's reactions to the single-parent home and their special needs. Appropriate responses by the school staff should be explored. The principal with a large percentage of pupils living in a self-care or single-parent family may wish to tap into the various psychological and/or pediatric resources available in the community to help staff anticipate reactions and alleviate potential pressures on children and on themselves.

INFECTIOUS DISEASES

Over the last several years, the public has become more aware of HIV, hepatitis B, and other life-threatening diseases. The cases of rejection and controversy over students infected with HIV or hepatitis B have caused much emotion and often much pain. Parents have refused to send their children to school with HIV-infected students. Teachers have refused to have them in classes. Rules have changed on the athletic fields and courts regarding cuts and blood on uniforms.

Workshops for custodians, special education teachers, nurses, bus drivers, and many other classifications of employees are required. School districts are required to identify their at-risk employees for training and reporting purposes. Cleanup chemicals and materials are readily available, and all personnel should be strongly urged to protect themselves. The true story of a physician's graduation present of a box of latex gloves to his daughter, who had signed a contract as an elementary teacher, is testimony to his perception of the serious risk. The medical community is divided regarding the several ways HIV may be transmitted, but the school leader needs to accept responsibility for the safety of all in the school. Other diseases such as hepatitis B may be transmitted in the school setting, and precautionary measures will reduce the chances for contracting those diseases.

Less dangerous but potentially damaging diseases are transmitted in the school. Alert school personnel trained to observe the symptoms of measles and mumps can reduce the impact of the spread of those diseases. Since many children do not get regular health care such as immunizations, the risk appears to be increasing rather than diminishing.

Enlightened board policies need to be in place that give direction to all employees. The principal needs to be sensitive to the need for everyone—staff, students, and parents—to feel safe and to be safe.

A SOCIETAL MOSAIC OF CULTURES

One of the strengths of the United States is that it embraces peoples from other countries. These immigrants have brought heritages of culture, skills, language, arts, and viewpoints out of which the country has woven a rich and beautiful fabric, the envy of the world. Principals can make a positive difference in diverse communities by leading the school to celebrate the contributions and histories of the groups represented in the school population. A positive approach is important because sadly these differences in our heritage have sometimes led to intolerance, possibly long-standing distrust, and even occasional outbursts of violence. Students come to the schools with some of the baggage of their parents and subcultures, and, occasionally, the distrust and violence walk the school halls. It is from this perspective that we address this topic here.

Some school systems have seen the majority of the school population shift from white to Asian, Hispanic, African American, or a mix of cultural backgrounds. School districts near large, international corporations or research facilities find a truly multicultural influx of children of scientists or executives associated with the companies. To further complicate the situation, these children are not likely to be in the system very long. A wide range of ethnic and religious backgrounds can be found in most school systems, but in some, the range is very wide. Language diversity in some schools means twenty or more languages in that one school.

Racial tensions can flare up in minutes, as the nation witnessed in Cincinnati in 2001, and as almost any urban principal can attest. Preparation and preventive measures are essential to continually improving relationships and understanding. The cultural mix of the country will continue to change as new people come to our shores and as different groups migrate even within a city.[35]

Various forms of racism occur far too frequently. It has not disappeared via busing, court-ordered desegregation, or other "cures" to this ever-present challenge. Whether racism is really new or simply reflects deeply ingrained attitudes that have not gone away, the everyday climate created by prejudice can affect the learning of students. Obviously, the principal has a major role in reducing and even eliminating racism on as broad a scale as possible, but particularly within the school. A first step would be to examine policies and practices that perpetuate a system that makes assumptions about students of a particular race or ethnic or socioeconomic group. Such practices may include tracking, vocational guidance, assignment of teachers, disciplinary practices, and even teaching strategies. Opportunities for faculty to examine such practices in an open, nonthreatening setting may be helpful. Providing ideas about ways to improve students' self-images regarding potentials and opportunities may help offset other negative influences outside the school.

Schools are faced with the challenge of understanding the educational implications of each particular cultural perspective as well as offering visions of the possibilities that exist for all the students.

---

[35] Beverly D. Tatum, "Examining Racial and Cultural Thinking," *Educational Leadership* 57 (May 2000): 54–57.

There is a danger in simply dispensing information about groups in that doing so can create stereotypes, categories, or classifications into which any individual who is part of that group can be placed. Yet we know great variances exist within groups, so we should take care not to allow ourselves to classify an individual by simply labeling her or him as part of a group. For example, the practice of imposing expectations on students based on their particular group denies these individuals opportunities even when the expectations are intended to be positive or for "their" benefit. Such sets of expectations are an insidious form of "profiling." The individual who has a particular talent and interest somewhat different from the expectations of a group that has been prejudged to be excellent in mathematics or science could be viewed with disappointment by teachers if he or she does not do well according to the group label. It should be noted that similar practices are imposed on students from particular families. (See the discussion about handicapping in Chapter 11.)

The principal's responsibility also includes helping the student population be sensitive to the negative impact of labeling other students. Materials used in classrooms should give a balanced view of a field of endeavor. Overt acts rooted in racist beliefs or attitudes should be dealt with swiftly and, if possible, prevented.

Even in rural areas, which at first glance appear to be almost homogeneous, the school has an obligation to prepare its students to work and live with those who may be different in terms of race or culture. It would be a rare small town that provided career opportunities for all the students of its schools. Many will be moving miles or continents away; therefore, the school would be doing the students a disservice not to prepare them for dealing successfully with a mosaic of peoples and cultures.

Ⓢ U M M A R Y

The school opens its doors each day to people who face challenges that are sometimes difficult to comprehend. Teachers meet the children of pain, fear, drug damage, and hunger. Some youth have seen or experienced acts that no one should see or experience. It may be that the best the leader can do for some students is to provide a safe place where they can trust someone. The reward may be watching a student cross a stage at commencement time, knowing some of the challenges he or she has overcome.

Ⓕ OR FURTHER THOUGHT

Violence
1. Can we justify having police constantly on patrol in our schools? Discuss.

2. An educator stated, "School crime should be handled by the police, school discipline by the school." Is this too simplistic a concept? What do we do about the gray areas in between?

3. What violence prevention plan is in place in your school? What are the major components and who is responsible for each?

Gangs and Hate Groups

4. How can schools effectively show (not tell) potential gang members alternative routes to respect, status, and the "good life"?

5. How well informed are teachers and staff regarding recognition of gang activity?

6. Are there active hate groups in your community? What spinoff is noticeable in your school?

The Occult

7. How well informed are teachers and staff regarding recognition of occult involvement?

8. What differences are there in dealing with a student who may be involved with occult activity and one who may be involved in gang activity?

Child Abuse

9. What staff development components should be instituted in your school to help faculty distinguish between accidents and physical abuse?

10. Is the prevention of child abuse just one more thing the schools are being asked to do that is not within their proper role?

11. If the abused become tomorrow's abusers, what can the school do to break the cycle?

Substance Abuse

12. How do the written policies and procedures in your school compare with those suggested by the state and/or state and national professional organizations?

13. What unintended messages might the students be receiving as a result of the prevention program in your district?

14. How can the school offset the progression to harder drugs or liquor when the opposite messages of "real adults" (sophistication, appeal, etc.) come from so many sources?

Teenage Pregnancy and Sex Education

15. What effect do teen mothers have on the school and other students? Does their presence encourage promiscuity? Does it reflect on the quality of the school?

16. Is sexual activity of students outside the school really any of the school's business?

17. By "pandering" to the teen mother or mother-to-be, is the school contributing to increasing irresponsible behavior?

18. What should be done about the young father?
19. Is it unreasonable and unfair to expect the school to serve as an arbitrator among contending value systems?

Children on Their Own

20. What agencies in your district should the school link with to assist with the problem of children who must care for themselves before and/or after school hours?
21. How can a case be made that the additional expenses for the use of the school building beyond regular school hours are a good investment for the community in addressing this problem?
22. Should the school make special provisions for communicating with the single parents or guardians of latchkey children?

Infectious Diseases

23. What specific regulations are in effect in your school regarding the handling of infectious materials?
24. What are the relationships between the school and various community groups regarding educating youth about the transmission of infectious diseases? What steps might be taken to improve those relationships?
25. What staff development programs are in place regarding dealing with emergencies in relation to infectious diseases?

A Societal Mosaic of Cultures

26. What means are available to the nearly culturally homogeneous school to infuse realism into the school's efforts to help students become multiculturally aware?
27. How can a school enrich experiences for students regarding other cultures without creating the appearance of leaving others out? Is this even an important concern?
28. Is it possible that some group(s) may try to use the school to limit the rights of others under the guise of tolerance while creating an atmosphere of intolerance in so doing? How might this situation be avoided?

SELECTED READINGS

Dunne-Maxim, Karen, and Maureen Underwood. "Keeping Afloat in Suicide's Wake." *School Administrator* 48 (May/June 1991): 20–21, 23–25.

Elliott, Delbert S., Beatrix A. Hamburg, and Kirk R. Williams, eds. *Violence in American Schools.* New York: Cambridge University Press, 1998.

Fine, Gary Alan, and Jeffrey Victor. "Satanic Tourism." *Phi Delta Kappan* 76 (September 1994): 70–72.

Goldstein, A. P. *Delinquent Gangs: A Psychological Perspective.* Champaign, IL: Research Press, 1991.

Helge, Doris. *Child Sexual Abuse in America: A Report of a National Study.* Bellingham: Rural Development Institute, Western Washington University, 1992.

Hoffman, Allan M. *Schools, Violence and Society.* Westport, CT: Greenwood, 1996.

Katz, Jack. *Seductions of Crime: Moral and Sensual Attractions in Doing Evil.* New York: Basic Books, 1988.

McCarthy, Martha M., and L. Dean Webb. "Legal Principles in Preventing and Responding to School Violence." *NASSP Bulletin* 84 (March 2000): 32–45.

Monohan, Kathleen. "Crocodile Talk: Attributes of Incestuously Abused and Nonabused Sisters." *Child Abuse and Neglect: The International Journal* 21 (January 1997): 19–34.

Riley, Kevin W. *Street Gangs and the Schools: A Blueprint for Intervention.* Bloomington, IN: Phi Delta Kappa, 1991.

Tower, Cynthia C. *Child Abuse and Neglect.* Washington, DC: National Education Association, 1984.

CHAPTER 16

School-Centered Problems

o categorize problems as being school centered is not to imply that the school is the cause of the problems but rather that the problems are evident in the school and must be dealt with in the school. Society helps create the problems and therefore should be asked to participate appropriately in their solutions. Nevertheless, the school must take the initiative and responsibility in seeking solutions whether or not the school is able to obtain help from the general community.

SCHOOL DISCIPLINE

Discipline does not begin with metal detectors or canine locker patrols. For many years, discipline has ranked as one of the most serious problems facing our public schools, according to the annual Gallup Polls of Public Attitudes toward Education.[1] Teachers frequently cite discipline or the lack of it as one of their biggest problems and their reason for leaving the profession. Discipline is a major concern of the beginning teacher and most often used by administrators to explain a teacher's lack of success. Establishing and maintaining a safe and orderly environment is an important part of the principal's leadership function. A passive role regarding discipline invites problems; it is not found in effective schools.

Occasionally, school personnel are assaulted with demands by the community for order in the schools; there are exclamations of dismay or editorials in the newspapers about the sad state of discipline. Considering that hundreds of young persons, excitable and less than completely self-controlled, are together for hours, in a relatively crowded environment, the potential for problems is enormous. Consider also that these youth come from a society where aggravated assaults occur every

---

[1] See the annual issues of *Phi Delta Kappan* (usually the September issue) that report on these polls.

minute and scenes of violence can be seen at any time by turning on the television, even on children's cartoon programs. The schools find a student body enculturated by current negative and violent media of various forms.

School discipline is a problem. Issues emerge, however, when one asks certain questions: What is school discipline? Need it be punitive and authoritarian? How do you get it? Is it something an administrator and teacher get by hiring tough taskmasters? Does one obtain it by demanding obedience and order? Can a school have "good discipline" without the concerted efforts of all segments of the school community? Can an administrator operate the school as a model of democratic society and still have good discipline?[2] These are questions that will get as many different answers as these are people who are asked. The leadership dimension enters when one begins to articulate and assist the group, including students, to define what discipline is, what it is not, and the consequences of negative behaviors.

Two words that always emerge in discussions about school discipline are *order* and *respect*. Few would disagree that these two terms are key ingredients in keeping discipline, but many disagree on how order and respect are to be attained. Views run the gamut from strict authoritarianism to a definition of democracy that includes an almost anarchistic viewpoint—that self-discipline develops from within, by some type of osmotic contact with society.

The processes that create "good discipline" are generally the same processes important in "good teaching":

1. *Clear objectives known and understood by all*—The purpose of the school and clear behavior expectations for each class should be generally understood; vagueness predicts vague learning and unsettled behavior.
2. *An understanding of desirable behavior*—Desirable behavior must be modeled, taught, and learned. One cannot assume everyone knows and recognizes desirable behavior (there is a great variety in value systems).
3. *An environment of mutual respect*—Respect is not a one-way street. School personnel should respect each student as a fellow human facing life and its problems.

---

[2] One could get into a rather involved academic discussion over the relationship of discipline, violence, and vandalism. Certainly, a relationship exists. We are treating these as separate issues because while vandalism and school crime are discipline problems, they are abnormal and of such an extreme nature that they can and should be punishable through the regular laws of our society. The matter then is one of degree. In-school discipline is an everyday affair for every teacher and every school. It is an integral part of the teaching-learning process.

4. *Involvement*—Students should be actively involved in any learning process, including discipline (participation and sharing create personalization, understanding, and caring).

5. *Personal interest in students*—The school staff should be receptive to students' ideas and encourage their interaction with teachers and administrators (let them know someone cares).

6. *Modeling*—Teachers and administrators should serve as models of secure, well-ordered, sensitive, self-disciplined persons (modeling appears to be one of the best teaching-learning processes).

7. *Smooth transitions and operations*—Activities should flow in a smooth, logical sequence, illustrating careful planning and "with-it-ness" (disorganization causes frustration and confusion, leading to discipline problems).

8. *Real challenges as opposed to meaningless, repetitive routines*—Activities should be planned to stimulate interest, challenge, and encourage positive, productive thinking about the real world affecting the students.

9. *Overlapping relationships*—Efforts should be made to help students see the school as a whole and understand how the various parts (classes and activities) make up the whole in a clear, meaningful way.

10. *Accountability*—Students should understand they are accountable for their own behavior; there are rewards for positive behavior and well-understood penalties for undesirable behavior.

Good discipline is first attained through a teaching-learning process that encourages active participation and involvement of students as well as the entire school staff and, in most instances, the community. Students can be involved in setting and maintaining a standard of peaceful conduct, and they can learn alternatives to violent means to settle differences as well as their social responsibilities to each other.[3]

Meaning of Discipline

Strong evidence suggests that discipline has become a major school problem and a public issue because schools have dealt with it in a piecemeal, punitive fashion and consider it essentially an authoritarian process requiring "hands-on control." We contend that discipline should be considered one of the most meaningful learning experiences in the school. In the broadest sense, it involves learning to adjust and cope successfully

[3] Barbara M. Landau and Paul Gathercoal, "Creating Peaceful Classrooms: Judicious Discipline and Class Meetings," *Phi Delta Kappan* 81 (February 2000): 450–454.

with society and to relate positively with other people of various ages, intelligence, and backgrounds. It becomes the process through which a person discovers not only his or her rights and those of associates but also responsibilities for the proper functioning of the entire group. Through this process, respect for the human being is achieved regardless of race, color, sex, creed, intelligence, disability, or age; and valuable insights into the relationships of people and the consequences of positive and negative behavior are acquired. Discipline viewed in this sense is the process of helping students learn to live and work together productively and happily. As such, it becomes as important to the teaching-learning process as anything in the school curriculum. It becomes an imperative of learning, one so universal that it must be planned as a part of every activity of the school, day or night, in school or out. It warrants the constant cooperative consideration of all school personnel, especially the teachers, who are the key agents of the learning process. Discipline is one of the disciplines. It must be learned by every student and made a basic objective of every teacher and one of the broad objectives of the school. When this approach is taken, discipline will no longer be a major problem of our schools.

The fact that students are not divisible into learners of skills and facts versus learners of emotional behaviors must become a reality to all school personnel. We must treat the student (and each other) as a whole person, complete with feelings, a life before and after school that affects behavior, and reactions to things nonacademic that affect the academic.

The school is a real community—a social system, no matter who runs it or how well or poorly it operates. Students are placed in this community to live an important portion of their lives. When the professional educator places the entire emphasis on the cognitive process of learning subject matter, students may learn that subject but, at the same time and the same place, learn disruptive and irresponsible behavior from their peers. It is better to realize that learning takes place in every activity in the school, and responsible behavior is an important part of that learning process. Thus, each teacher, no matter what he or she teaches, must be considered a member of a professional educational team that has accepted collective leadership for developing and maintaining a climate that is positive and conducive to learning for all activities of the school, in class and out. Accepting this concept, they work together as a group to plan activities of both an experiential and a cognitive nature that encourage responsible individual and group behavior. Further, they plan ways to involve students in the process as an operating part of society, with parents and citizens as resources and participants.

Effective schools have attempted to develop a school climate that enhances discipline in the school, which requires the involvement of the total staff. Such a positive atmosphere is created through personalized contacts with students that exemplify courtesy, friendliness, respect, and humanness, to show both a model of behavior and a genuine concern for the individual. It is maintained with a great deal of visibility on the part of the principal and the faculty.

The goal of any school program should include self-discipline. A school populated with self-disciplined students and staff will have an environment conducive to learning. Horner et al. suggest three needs to be met to foster schoolwide discipline:

1. A culture in which expected student behaviors are clearly defined, taught, and supported
2. Rapid, efficient support for at-risk students
3. High-intensity support for high-intensity misbehaviors[4]

Profiling Students

Much has been written and said about authorities profiling certain groups. Schools could find themselves in a similar situation in identifying students who might be at risk to commit acts of violence or harassment in several forms. The U.S. Department of Education provides a list of characteristics of potentially violent students, as does the National School Safety Center. There is a wide divergence between these lists.[5] Given the disparity between these lists and certainly localized lists, schools are urged to approach profiling cautiously.

Accountability and Punishment

Every person must be accountable for his or her actions or lack of action. Life in its subtle way begins to make this clear at a relatively early age. Many persons will go to great extremes to avoid accountability, but if the rules are clear and reasonable and if, when the rules are broken, the penalty is just and fairly administered, the punishment generally is accepted in good faith. Weighing the consequences of unacceptable behavior against the rewards of acceptable behavior, each person makes a conscious decision as to a course of action.

Each social group, including the school, must determine the behavior necessary for the successful operation of that group. The more members of the group involved in determining what the proper behaviors and penalties for unacceptable behavior are, the more goodwill there will be in following the rules and accepting the consequences if members break them; everyone will recognize that the rules are for the good of the

---

[4] Robert H. Horner, George Sugai, and Howard F. Horner, "A School-wide Approach to Student Discipline," *School Administrator* 57 (February 2000): 20.

[5] Gil-Patricia Fey, J. Ron Nelson, and Maura L. Roberts, "The Perils of Profiling," *School Administrator* 57 (February 2000): 14. This source also notes several Websites for additional research.

group and therefore for the good of the individual. In other words, "we have rules and penalties because we care about the group and therefore we care about the individual." However, if the feeling prevails that rules are punitive and not group centered and that their enforcement implies the school does not care for the individual, then battle lines are drawn. It becomes the students against the teachers and administrators. Under these conditions, the more one can get away with unacceptable behavior and the more one can tolerate the punishment, the greater the hero he or she can become with his or her immediate peers.

One of the modes of punishment that appears to create special and often irrevocable alienation is suspension from school. This policy implies rejection and "not caring"; therefore, the student's common reaction is to fight back and in turn reject the school. Many incidents of vandalism and violence involve students who have been suspended in the past or are under suspension at the time of the incident. Too often suspensions (in the case of nondangerous behavior) result in more disciplinary problems rather than fewer.

The courts have also taken a careful look at suspension as a method of punishment. The number of court cases is multiplying in which suspension has been challenged as being contrary to the purposes of the school, as being unreasonable, or as violating the constitutional rights of the student. In the only exclusion case to be decided by the U.S. Supreme Court, the Court ruled that suspension is a serious event. The student to be suspended should be given the complete constitutional protection of the due process clause, and suspension may not be imposed "by any procedure the school chooses."[6]

Suspension is a negative approach. First, it is an overt act of rejection, encouraging retaliation. Second, when the student misbehaves because of difficulty with schoolwork (which is often the case), upon suspension he or she gets even further behind and often finds it impossible to catch up. One occasionally finds a school that punishes students for not coming to school by forbidding them to come to school. If there was a contest of wills, who won?

A more positive approach may be in-school restriction, in which certain privileges are withdrawn and the individual is isolated from the regular group as punishment. At the same time, he or she can be given special individual or group counseling to help improve behavior and keep up and even improve schoolwork during the isolation period. Saturday schools have been used effectively in some areas. Again, the students are not warehoused but given help to complete work required to keep pace with their peers.

Many counselors reject problem students because they wish to avoid the impression that counseling is part of the punishment to

---

[6] *Goss v. Lopez*, 419 U.S. 565, 576 (1975).

improve discipline. True, counselors should not be the disciplinarians of the school. However, the counselor is avoiding a most important responsibility if he or she does not help the problem student become more disciplined in behavior through proper counseling processes.

Strategies for Improving Discipline

Five hundred schools that were nominated as having good discipline were surveyed to determine characteristics that may be essential to a disciplined school. Thirteen characteristics were noted:

- Working with the principal is another staff member whose personal characteristics complement those of the principal.
- Emphasis is placed on the positive.
- The total environment is aimed toward good discipline.
- Faculty and staff have high expectations.
- Faculty and staff are student oriented.
- Causes of problems and their solutions are sought.
- Preventive rather than punitive actions are emphasized.
- Discipline programs are tailor made for the particular school.
- The principal is a key figure.
- The staff believe in students and spend a great deal of energy making their beliefs come true.
- Teachers handle routine problems.
- There are strong parent and community-agency ties.
- The schools are open to evaluation.[7]

The following is a condensed listing of activities that some schools have established to improve their orderly functioning; it is not intended to be a set of instructions delineating the steps necessary to eliminate discipline problems. All schools and communities are unique in that they have their own particular sets of conditions that should prompt them to develop their own strategies. However, these ideas could be adopted or adapted by the administrator within his or her own school system.

1. The school gets together as a community at frequent and regular intervals, in both large and small groups, to discuss and review the operation of the school as a community of students, teachers, and administrators.
2. A constitution and a bill of rights have been developed and approved for schools by the board of education that establish a basic legal framework for operation.

---

[7] The Phi Delta Kappa Commission on Discipline makes available a *Handbook for Developing Schools with Good Discipline* (Bloomington, IN: Author, 1982), from which these points are drawn.

3. A clearly written code of rights and responsibilities for the specific school is available to all students and parents, and it is frequently confirmed and updated. Successful sets of rules are usually simple and few and are easily stated by whatever level of student is being served.

4. Uniform and clear procedures have been established for enforcing the school code, with reasonable, established penalties for undesirable behavior. Teachers and other involved persons are informed about the disposition of each case.

5. Students, parents, teachers, and administrators have worked together to draw up the code and keep it up to date, with processes established for continual input.

6. The general morale of the school is assessed frequently to determine where special effort needs to be made to realize improvement.

7. The principal and assistants are visible and available throughout the school, actively involved in classroom observation, frequently walking in and out of class and extracurricular activities. They are friendly, open, and supportive of both students and teachers.

8. Special efforts are made to increase student involvement in the ongoing activities of the school. For example, some schools have found it workable to have a separate set of cheerleaders for each sport, a number of special performance groups, or different "service groups" for school activities, with each group composed of students not in the other similar groups.

9. Special positive-type reinforcement programs have been developed to enhance school spirit, school pride and loyalty, and the feeling of belonging; reinforce positive attitudes; and boost the esprit de corps.

10. A special effort is made to solicit parents' help in creating responsible behavior in the school and to communicate with them about school efforts to improve behavior.

11. Teachers work with the principal as a unified professional team to monitor and enforce the school code, at the same time involving students in appropriate, meaningful ways.

12. The faculty accepts responsibility, along with the principal, for discipline and order in the entire school enterprise. As teachers, they make their presence known as models and as friendly mentors but, beyond that, as persons of authority and responsibility who are seriously concerned that the business of the school goes on in an orderly fashion.

13. Workshops, seminars, and professional in-service efforts have been established for teachers and administrators so that they

keep up to date on discipline as a basic part of student learning and on the humanizing aspect of the school.

14. Punishment, when necessary, is handled uniformly, fairly, and quickly. The consequences, from least severe to most severe, need to be thought through prior to the anticipated negative behavior.

15. Out-of-school suspension is used as a means of discipline only when the student is considered to be dangerous and incorrigible. In place of the usual suspension, a more positive form of punishment is used, such as in-school restriction, where the student is isolated and loses privileges but at the same time is given special individual or group counseling to improve behavior as well as help to keep up and even improve school-work during isolation.[8]

16. Teacher aides are provided in larger schools to serve as building monitors during the school day (at least one male and one female). They should receive special in-service training. They may be assigned to the principal's office but should work closely with the teachers and act as teaching guides and mentors rather than as a police patrol.

17. Central administration and the board of education support the school discipline effort and provide the necessary resources to make it effectively operational.

18. The school building and grounds have been studied so that problem areas are identified; the school's class, recess, and activity schedules have been planned so that frustrating situations that spawn discipline problems, such as crowding and pushing, are eliminated.

19. Custodians are involved with students and teachers as part of a school committee responsible for encouraging and maintaining an environment that elicits pride. In addition, they are provided time and resources so that repairs are made swiftly and graffiti is erased immediately.

20. Local police are frequently involved in working positively with students in seminars and assembly sessions on drug abuse, crime prevention, vandalism, and other appropriate topics.

21. Committees of students, teachers, and parents are established singly and collectively to present suggestions to the principal on such topics as school safety, student rights, schedules, and buildings.

---

[8] The principal must pay particular attention to the in-school or out-of-school suspension or expulsion of a student designated as "disabled" in that such a status change may constitute a placement change, with all the procedures attendant to that shift; see Chapter 11.

22. Problems are identified early via continual monitoring and discussions. If a trouble-prone student is identified by several staff members, a meeting may be held to develop strategies for that individual.

Adviser-advisee programs have proven effective in many middle schools. Some schools have adjusted assignments to include all support personnel as well as teachers and administrators. Additional adjustments may be made to take advantage of special talents or in some cases to avoid special weaknesses in dealing with particular problems. An adviser-advisee program can fail if initial and continual training is not provided. Without proper preparation, confusion about adviser roles and program purposes can result and in turn cause adverse effects upon students.

Discipline does not just happen. It has to be planned, worked for, and on occasion guarded. The results of a successful, disciplined school are well worth the efforts and the frustrations encountered along the way.

School Uniforms

School uniforms, long present in some private and parochial schools, have been tried as a partial solution to discipline problems in some public schools. Arguments for school uniforms include avoiding gang colors, fostering a more serious academic atmosphere, and reducing obvious differences in economic status as a result of the clothing worn by students. Caruso cites the following as pro-uniform arguments: increased attendance, increased self-esteem, heightened esprit de corps, decreased clothing costs, improved behavior, and school recognition. He further notes the arguments against uniforms as an infringement of First Amendments rights, and a potential economic hardship. Another argument for uniforms is based on better academic achievement, but often that is not supported by data.[9] Evans observes that most uniform programs are in elementary schools, where the problems to be solved do not exist to a great degree, and that economic distinctions are not leveled in areas such as participation in extracurricular activities and expensive prom dresses.[10] The decision to have school uniforms is not an easy one and is certainly one in which wide involvement of the community is essential.

---

[9] Peter Caruso, "Individuality vs. Conformity: The Issue behind School Uniforms," *NASSP Bulletin* 80 (September 1996): 83–88.

[10] Dennis L. Evans, "School Uniforms: An Unfashionable Dissent," *Phi Delta Kappan* 78 (October 1996): 139.

Hazing

Hazing takes many forms and is aimed at a wide range of victims, including underclassmen, new members of sports teams, and ethnic groups (recently Asian Americans have been targeted). Some hazing goes far beyond having to wear some kind of clothing that identifies a student as a "freshman" or a member of some other group. High school students have reported having to eat disgusting things, abuse alcohol, and perform humiliating acts to be accepted as part of athletic, art, music, or theater clubs. In some instances, aspiring athletes were subjected to sexual abuse. Too often students do not report the abuse because they want to be part of the group or team or because of threatened consequences. Bushweller suggests the following as important to curb hazing, particularly as related to sports teams:

1. Have an anti-hazing policy that defines hazing and identifies unacceptable behavior.
2. React immediately and aggressively if hazing occurs.
3. Educate all teachers, coaches, and staff.
4. Have adult supervision in places where hazing can occur (e.g., locker rooms).
5. Pay attention to small clues.[11]

GENDER ISSUES

The school community is a microcosm of our society in general, and as such, it reflects perspectives about the "proper" role of boys and girls in class, in subjects to be taken, in sports, and in the work world for which they are preparing. Gender bias is not just talk—it is in every school and every community, where the rights must be operationalized. A true educational leader must accept the responsibility of knowing and understanding not only people's rights as enunciated by the U.S. Constitution and laws but also the loss of potential that occurs because of stereotyping and the failure to create productive learning environments for all.

Gender bias frequently begins with gender-role stereotyping in the very early years: the assumption is that because people share a gender, they also share common abilities, interests, values, and roles. Not only does stereotyping restrict the achievement of individual potential for both sexes, but also it frustrates those individuals who do not conform to traditional norms. One step toward equality of education regardless of gender is the completion of an in-depth examination of the school. This approach should expose both the overt and the hidden curricula of

---

[11] Kevin Bushweller, "Brutal Rituals, Dangerous Rites," *American School Board Journal* 187 (August 2000): 21. Further information is available at www. stophazing.org/laws.html.

gender-based biases that are part of most formal education and stereo-typed attitudes, practices, and materials, as well as the general school environment.

Title IX

According to Title IX of the Education Amendments of 1972, "No person . . . shall, on the basis of sex, be excluded from participation in, be denied the benefits of, or be subjected to discrimination under any education program or activity receiving federal financial assistance."[12] To be in compliance with this law, by July 21, 1976, all schools receiving federal assistance were required to have

- Completed a detailed self-evaluation,
- Taken and recorded any steps necessary to eliminate sex discrimination,
- Adopted and published a grievance procedure to resolve student and employee complaints of sex discrimination, and
- Appointed a Title IX coordinator.

Title IX provisions also prohibit discrimination in admission to certain kinds of institutions and in the treatment of admitted students, which includes housing, courses or other educational activities, counseling, financial aid, student health and insurance benefits, marital or parental status, and athletics. For employees of covered institutions, the regulation prohibits sex discrimination in all aspects of employment, recruitment, and hiring.

An enlightened consideration of Title IX is that it is a plan for assuring that the constitutional rights of all children and youth are implemented in schools. Although it may not be legally necessary for a private institution to comply specifically with Title IX, it has the moral responsibility of developing a plan of its own that complies with the constitutional rights of human beings in general.

Gender, Curriculum, and Instruction

Title IX compliance represents only one aspect of eliminating gender bias in education. The Title IX regulation does not require educators to use particular textbooks or curriculum materials, so the principal and staff must systematically examine the materials in use as well as those to be purchased. The following questions may be helpful for the examination:

1. Are both sexes shown in a wide variety of roles or only in traditional, stereotyped roles?

---

[12] *Peer Title IX Regulation Summary* (Washington, DC: Government Printing Office, 1972), 1.

2. Do the members of both sexes respect each other as equals?
3. Are males and females shown as having a wide range of emotions and responses? Of choices?
4. Are the lifestyles depicted realistic?
5. How many women have been included in the standard texts as compared with men? (Select books that will include representative women in the curriculum.)
6. Are there subtle forms of bias, such as white males in power relationships and women in subservient roles or subject to different standards of success? For example, are women rewarded for their good looks and culinary skills, whereas men succeed on the basis of their intelligence and fortitude?
7. Has the use of gender-biased language been questioned?
8. Do photographs, cartoons, and quotations represent an appropriate balance between the sexes?
9. Given the experiments, though controversial, with same-sex classes in science, mathematics, and other areas, what different structuring for academic classes has been provided? What positive/negative effects on achievement have been determined?

Staff Development

The issue of nonsexist curriculum extends beyond the selection of materials. Staff development should be undertaken to help the entire staff function in a nondiscriminatory fashion, including

- Heightening awareness of one's own prejudices and sexist behaviors;
- Providing teaching techniques to enable each person to overcome discriminatory behaviors;
- Giving training in developing nonsexist materials and using traditional resources in nonsexist ways;
- Dispensing general information concerning nonsexist resources, research findings, and so on; and
- Encouraging the staff to learn more about the contributions of women to our society.

Ongoing research and our own experience indicate that elementary teachers frequently treat boys and girls differently in everyday classroom interaction, often without knowing that they do so. Observations of secondary classrooms often reveal teachers unconsciously showing differences in dealing with males versus females. Primary school teachers tend to

- Talk more to boys, ask them higher-order questions, and urge them to try harder;

- Give boys specific verbal instructions about tasks but show girls how to do the tasks or do the tasks for them;
- Talk to boys regardless of their location in the classroom; and
- Praise boys for the intellectual quality of their work and criticize them for lack of form and neatness, but not do the same for girls.

The way children are grouped for instruction can contribute to positive or negative experiences. Using mixed-sex groups for instruction can improve boys' perceptions of themselves as leaders and problem solvers. This outcome may not result for girls, however. In fact, some girls do not choose to participate in the mixed-sex instructional groups. We must be careful, therefore, not to create new stereotypes as we seek to eradicate some of the old ones.

SEXUAL HARASSMENT IN SCHOOLS

Given the alleged misconduct of various lawmakers or officeholders, most readers are familiar with sexual harassment issues in the workplace but may not make the transfer to the potential for sexual harassment in the schools. One of the first scenarios that may come to mind is the teacher who makes unwanted advances to a student. The principal needs to be sensitive to other issues as well. For example, teachers may harass other teachers with off-color stories, innuendo, or direct attempts to embarrass or make an indecent proposal. Certainly, such unwanted behavior should not be tolerated. Also, students are increasingly harassing students. Results of a survey of 1,632 eighth through eleventh graders indicates "85 percent of girls and 76 percent of boys report they have been sexually harassed."[13]

The specter of staff sexually abusing students, verbally or physically, casts a long shadow on the school's walls. False accusations are a possibility, and a staff member's reputation and professional life are at stake. Note, though, that Shakeshaft and Cohan investigated 225 cases of students reporting sexual abuse by teachers or professional staff and found that only 7.5 percent of the accusations turned out to be false.[14]

Policies and procedures need to be in place and understood by all school personnel. A policy not to touch a student under any circumstances is a sterile approach and somewhat impractical; consider separating students in a fight that could result in injury to the students.[15] Poli-

[13] As reported in the *Detroit Free Press*, 2 June 1993, 6A.
[14] Carol Shakeshaft and Audrey Cohan, "Sexual Abuse of Students by School Personnel," *Phi Delta Kappan* 76 (March 1995): 518.
[15] Perry A. Zirkel and Ivan B. Gluckman, "Sexual Misconduct by Staff Members," *Principal* (March 1994): 63.

cies should provide for formal and informal complaint procedures, documentation of the complaints, specified routing of the complaints, investigation procedures including disposition of the accused staff member while the investigation is ongoing, and victim support.[16] How to deal with such incidents is not to be left until the situation arises. The principal needs to be very familiar with the policies and procedures before the event, since correct action must be taken immediately and a member of the media likely will be the first telephone call after the event becomes known.

Parents are not idly standing by and letting harassment continue, nor are they letting the schools ignore the problem. An example is the case of *Davis v. Monroe County Board of Education*, 119 S. Ct. 1661 (1999), in which a student was harassed over a long period of time and reported the action to her parent and to school officials, who took little effective action to prevent further consequences. The U.S. Supreme Court, in a 5–14 vote, implied that a school could be held liable for student-on-student sexual harassment, particularly if the school exhibited deliberate indifference to the situation.

MAKING THE GRADE IN A STANDARDS ASSESSMENT/TESTING ENVIRONMENT

If the nation faces a crisis, whether it is social or economic, the schools often are put into the spotlight as the culprit or the savior, and occasionally both. Often the principal is put between a questioning or demanding public and teachers who are trying to educate students beyond the scope of required achievement tests. Recently, an outbreak of student/parent boycotts against mandated testing has highlighted the amount of time, expense, and focus given to scoring well on required tests. Large numbers of students in affluent communities have been absent on mandated test days. At the same time, several states have funding mechanisms in place that would in effect punish the schools for lower scores on the mandated tests.

The pressure increases as states mandate the inclusion of special needs students in the testing program. The principal is obligated to help formulate reasonable accommodations for the special needs students that do not invalidate the testing situation. As noted in Chapters 12 and 13, the power tests partially based on time constraints cause problems for many students.[17] The timing of the tests, often in the spring semester, and the lengthy turn-around time to get the results make it difficult to adjust

---

[16] See Jeffrey T. Sultanik, "How to Conduct an Investigation of Sexual Harassment or Retaliation," *Your School and the Law* (November 1993).

[17] For an insightful discussion of this problem, see Frank Smith, "Just a Matter of Time," *Phi Delta Kappan* 82 (April 2001): 573–576.

instruction to meet deficiencies. The question arises as to whether the assessments provide meaningful information to inform instruction and curriculum or serve only to foster public opinion that the schools are being held accountable.

It is truly unfair to blame schools for a constellation of social or economic factors beyond their immediate control. Knowing this, the first reaction of some educators to negative headlines is defensiveness. Administrators and teachers must realize that seeking to instill work-world competencies is not an idea that will eventually go away, regardless of business views that the reason we are not globally competitive is the lack of highly skilled workers.[18]

Getting at the problem from a business perspective naturally precipitates a look at the "bottom line" of what these potential workers and leaders know. At first, test scores appeared to give the answers. Schools must deal with front-page stories comparing neighboring schools' test scores with the local school's. Today the standards movement is the driving force behind assessment. The Improving America's Schools Act (IASA) requires states to develop standards by which the success of schools are to be assessed. Grading on the curve is passé. Specific, high standards are the rulers by which student performance is to be measured.[19] Schools are facing testing using not only norm-referenced tests, but also performance tests indicating relative status regarding the agreed-upon standards (see Chapters 12 and 13).

The real issue is not whether schools are meeting standards or preparing competitive workers. The real issue is that the public has a legitimate right to be assured that the schools they have established, as "people's schools," are properly meeting the needs of children and society. Its roots are found deep in our way of life, with our tradition of public education in the United States. A free public system of education was established at great effort and expense so that every child would have an opportunity to develop into a productive, self-reliant citizen. To the public, the simple tools or needs of children are the basics: reading, writing, and arithmetic. The simple means of determining whether children possess these tools is to test. The public, beginning with the very first public school movement in the seventeenth century, has intended and expected that children would obtain basic skills for learning. They intended and expected that schools would be accountable for their efforts. From the very beginning of U.S. education, testing has been a common procedure for determining acquisition of the basics and establishing accountabil-

---

[18] See David C. Berliner and Bruce J. Biddle, *The Manufactured Crisis* (Reading, MA: Addison-Wesley, 1995).
[19] Dale Carlson and Adrienne Bailey, "The New Title I Assessment," *School Administrator* 53 (December 1996): 18–23.

ity—from grade to grade, from elementary school to high school, from high school to college.

True, there are many more basics and educational imperatives than reading, writing, and arithmetic. True, these basics may be harder to defend and may mean many things to many people. True, for a full life, each child needs varying physical, emotional, aesthetic, intellectual, and moral enrichments well beyond what we consider to be basic. Norm-referenced testing is only one of many types of assessment; many aspects of the cognitive, and especially the affective, we cannot truly test.

The standards movement does bring with it an additional approach to assessing progress. The problem is to keep school purposes and assessment and testing in perspective—this is where educators' efforts should be directed, not toward fighting assessment itself, for it does represent a public interest and concern about education. The true educational leader will agree that competencies and testing have an important place in the curriculum and then work with the public to help place them in proper perspective. The leader will show the public that formal paper-and-pencil testing is only one of many processes of assessment and that there are alternative ways to determine students' growth and achievement, assuring the public at the same time that schools stand ready to be accountable for their efforts.

The principal in the individual school can do little one way or another to change the state legislation relative to the standards established, except as he or she operates in professional organizations or exerts leadership through the community's sphere of influence. The principal does, however, have an exceptional opportunity to develop with teachers professional approaches that interpret and implement the deep-seated viewpoint regarding accountability of public schools. The discussion could begin by debating the pros and cons of the following statements and addressing the following questions:

1. Every course or subject in the school should have an important, measurable impact on both the cognitive and the affective learning of a student.
2. Every course or subject should have written, measurable objectives that relate to standards and competencies accepted by the state and/or by professional associations in the field (e.g., National Council of Teachers of Mathematics).
3. Every teacher should accept responsibility for measuring the degree of progress toward the standards by each student.
4. Every teacher should accept responsibility for diagnosing problems students have with achieving objectives and for prescribing corrective actions.
5. No matter what subject and grade level, every teacher has a responsibility to help children obtain and improve the basic

tools of learning, especially the commonly accepted three R's: reading, writing, and arithmetic.

6. Every course and subject taught in the school should have specific, built-in teaching and learning processes that will improve the competency of students in the so-called basics.
7. If the assessments do not match our curriculum, does this mean that the school's curriculum is inappropriate or that the assessments are inappropriate?
8. What should be the teachers' roles at various levels regarding the skills they consider essential for helping students achieve success at the next level?
9. How do we square assessment and norm-referenced testing with equal educational opportunity for all? Is the answer not more academic selectivity? If not, how do we handle this question?
10. An opportunity to learn something predicts a student's achievement score. Does everybody have an equal opportunity to learn reading, writing, and arithmetic? And does each level of the school establish processes to build on these skills?
11. How much should parents and community members be involved with what the schools should teach and what is important?
12. Given the pressure to maintain or improve the school's scores on mandated achievement tests, what can be done ethically to meet the demands to include all students in the assessments?

The principal can help offset some of the tensions and frustrations by working with teachers and parents to view the accountability issues reasonably. We have observed the pressures that result in primary grade children crying, high schoolers being absent, teachers abandoning the planned curriculum to focus on tests, and even teachers providing inappropriate "accommodations" for some students. (Remember Miss Pinkston in Chapter 13?)

These are fundamentally professional issues relating to the elements of accountability. They are important professional concerns, to be discussed profoundly and with the intent of arriving at some solutions that can be implemented locally.

COLLECTIVE BARGAINING AND THE PRINCIPAL

Collectively negotiated agreements regarding wages, salary, fringe benefits, and, in some instances, certain working conditions, such as hours and length of contract, are a fact of life in most school districts. The history of collective action by employees can be traced back at least as far as

TABLE 16.1

Actions paving the way for collective bargaining in the public and private sectors

1932	Norris–LaGuardia Act	Recognized workers' right to organize; prohibited companies from coercing workers to sign that they would not join a union; limited courts from restricting union activities via injunctions
1932	Wagner Act National Labor Relations Act	Guaranteed workers' right to organize to bargain collectively with employers; specified unfair labor practices by employers; established the National Labor Relations Board
1946	Teacher Strike—Norwalk, Conn.	
1947	Taft-Hartley Act Labor-Management Relations Act	Outlawed closed shop; specified unfair practices by labor; restricted use of labor funds and accounting thereof; protected individuals outside and within unions
1959	Landrum-Griffin Act Labor-Management Reporting and Disclosure Act	Amended Taft-Hartley Act; guaranteed freedom of speech in meetings; established elections and dues guidelines
1961	New York City teachers won collective bargaining rights.	
1962	Executive Order 10988	Gave federal employees right to unionize and to bargain collectively
1968	Executive Order 11491	Established Federal Labor Relations Council

the guilds in medieval Europe. Recently, legislation has been passed at the federal and state levels to permit, and in some cases require, collective bargaining in the public sector. Table 16.1 provides a brief overview of actions paving the way for and often controlling the activity of collective bargaining.

Principals have opted out of teacher bargaining units at the local level or have been pushed out by the language in state laws providing for collective bargaining for educational personnel. The principals, then, had to be nudged into being part of the management team. The collective bargaining process has often become a spectator sport for principals, who watch as their role is shaped, eroded, and from time to time ignored as the players—teachers and board—agree on tightly written documents. When a principal is not in a separate bargaining unit, he or she should be part of the administrative bargaining team by either providing input or being a participant. Such an arrangement is almost necessary if the principal's management prerogatives are not to be eroded beyond repair. An example of serious erosion is the medium-sized district in which principals may not enter a classroom to evaluate without the teacher's permission. Principals should actively pursue their direct involvement in the negotiations process as partially fulfilling their responsibility as leaders of the schools.

The majority of states have permissive or mandatory laws regarding collective negotiations for educational personnel either at the local level or at more than one level, including state employees. Some states recognize educators' right to strike, but only under specified conditions. Many states declare that strikes are illegal but unfortunately close their eyes to work stoppages that do occur. In certain areas, the toleration of work stoppages may be part of the culture. Teacher work stoppages, in defiance of state law to the contrary, may convey unwanted and unwarranted messages to the public and the pupils. The better part of wisdom may be to enact permissive legislation, stating specific and limited conditions under which work stoppages may be legal, but enforce the law when work stoppages occur that do not meet the stated conditions.

In the event of a work stoppage, the principal is ordinarily in the position of keeping the school open, at least until directed otherwise or conditions are deemed unsafe. Preplanning is essential.

Strike Plan

Ordinarily, a strike plan exists for each district and each building within the district. If such a plan does not exist, one should be formed, and all appropriate personnel should become thoroughly familiar with it, including their particular parts in implementing it. Board members, the central office staff, persons assigned to communications center operations, and building administrators will have specific roles and duties to perform. The following points may provide pertinent considerations for developing a strike contingency plan:

1. Each building administrator must avoid discussions of the strike situation with striking or nonstriking employees.
2. Building administrators must not recruit parent volunteers to supervise classrooms so that programs can continue during a strike.
3. Cafeteria personnel must provide normal services throughout the first day.

4. Building administrators must daily provide students with current and accurate information about the strike situation.
5. Each building administrator must inform officials of all community groups scheduled to use school facilities that the building will not be available for use until the strike has ended.
6. Building administrators must terminate all student activities outside the school building.
7. Building administrators must provide an in-service program for nonstriking employees to build the understanding and skills needed to ensure effective performance during a strike.
8. Building administrators must telephone each employee not reporting for work to determine whether the individual is officially on strike. The composite report must immediately be sent to the communications center staff.
9. Each nonstriking employee who does not report for work must be contacted daily to determine whether the employee intends to report for work the following school day. A composite report must be sent to the communications center staff.
10. Building administrators must conduct a daily meeting for substitutes to discuss problem students and build morale.
11. Building administrators must require that all nonstriking teachers develop and submit lesson plans for the following day.

The building administrator is well advised to take time to go over the details of a strike plan long before it is necessary to use it. Last-minute scrambling to find out how to do things (changing locks, safeguarding confidential records, maintaining heating/ventilating systems, etc.) not only will be unnerving but also could add unneeded fuel to the strikers' fire.

Contract Management

The principal is ordinarily involved informally in resolving questions about how the contract is to be implemented. These are fairly common occurrences, though apparently brief.

In the time utilization study described earlier, one of the least time-consuming tasks was administering the master contract. This positive finding indicates that principals and teachers are sophisticated enough to handle work on such an agreement, which also probably suggests that the language of the agreement is clear and reasonable. The principal can do several things if problems arise:

1. Know the specifics of the contract and what the language means.

2. Understand the roles of all levels of management and personnel in the bargaining unit regarding contract management.
3. Develop skills essential to handling grievances.
4. Analyze the language and its effect on the progress of the school toward its important goals, and make input for change.
5. Clearly understand the principal's position as a member of management.

Knowing the Specifics

There is no substitute for carefully reading and analyzing the contract and translating every part of the agreement into principal-behavior terms. Just as ignorance of the law is no excuse for speeding, ignorance of the meaning of a contract provision will not deter a grievance. Knowing the meaning of the contract language will assist the principal in using the flexibility that is provided to facilitate the school's work. The contract may serve as an excuse for not taking action that is needed, even though a careful reading would show that there may be ways to get the job done.

The principal should also know which practices have been permitted as the result of an administrator's interpretation (or misinterpretation) of the contract. This is a large chore for the new principal unless he or she has been in the system for quite some time. A careful look at the inclusion of past practices in the contract language may be in order, not only for awareness of the provision but also with an eye toward changing it or further refining the terms.

Understanding Management Roles

Though on occasion it may seem so, no principal is an island, particularly in administering within contract provisions. The personnel officer, the superintendent, and the assistant superintendents all have specific roles and concerns regarding proper administration within contract provisions. Each has specific contributions to make, and each can be helpful to the principal as decisions are made and new ideas are tried. Clearly understanding the duties of other administrators will help clarify the principal's role in the whole process, particularly in grievance situations.

The role of the bargaining unit representative in the building is one that, if not understood, can be a continual irritant. But if it is understood in perspective, the representative can be an important source of help. Involving the building representative of the union in discussions of proposed decisions is a way of gaining support for those decisions, as well as testing ideas that might not be palatable to the staff. Providing early warning to the building representative that a staff member seems unsatisfactory and may be dismissed is especially important.

Evidence suggests that in schools with professionally active union building representatives, teachers feel more involved in the essential decision-making process of the school. It would seem that the union building representative can be a key force in shaping the school as a professional organization, following professional standards and a collegial rather than a hierarchical structure. Much depends on how options are exercised. Schools will become more bureaucratized if unions are absolutely rule dependent and militant for militancy's sake. Schools can become more professional and democratic if they use their increased autonomy to improve professional practice through using theory and research on educational solutions and to make professional diagnoses and prescriptions.

Decentralization of decision making regarding curricula, time, and sometimes budget and personnel usually requires a suspension of contract language to operate the programs locally. As districts move toward districtwide adoption of site-based management, or charter schools, contract language may be changed or suspended. Nevertheless, grievances do occur when there are perceived violations of a contract.

Developing Grievance Skills

It is sometimes difficult to convince board members and the superintendent that a grievance procedure can be a useful process and not something to be feared. It can become a mechanism that is good for the health of the school system as well as for its individual members.

A grievance has come to generally mean (1) a claim based on an event or condition that affects the welfare or conditions of a teacher or group of teachers, (2) a dispute arising over the interpretation or application of the provisions of the contract, or (3) an alleged violation of the contract. The purpose of a grievance procedure is to solve problems as close to their origin as possible. Thus, in a high school, for example, most grievances can or should be solved at the departmental level or, if that fails, with the principal. Grievances in the elementary school may often be quickly settled by the union building representative and the principal. In a large school system, hundreds of grievances are settled rather quietly, with little or no publicity outside of the school system.

The principal obviously plays a key role in any grievance that reaches his or her office and then remains involved in those cases that move up the organizational ladder to the superintendent, the board of education, and arbitration, if necessary.

Certain skills are important in resolving grievances. Possibly the most critical is not a skill as much as a perspective or an attitude. One could view a grievance as a battle in a war of wills or a skirmish to test the strength of resolve. Under some adverse conditions, it may be so;

however, in most instances, it is not. The grievance procedure is a formalized way for an employee to communicate a disagreement, as we mentioned before. With the latter as a perspective, it opens the way to more positive communication between employee and management.

Listening Skills. The principal needs to demonstrate excellent listening skills if a grievance occurs. The excitement of the occasion may cause "static" because the real problem may not surface without probing, with one's own words, to find out what messages the aggrieved person is sending. The exchange of interpretations about what was said may help clarify the actual problem for both parties.

Recording Skills. Often a form, designed to record the grievance process, is used, but this is not sufficient to record the progress of the interactions toward a resolution. If tape recording the session is permissible, the recording problem is solved. In lieu of a tape recording, the principal should make careful notes as the interactions occur. As the points become clear, it is important that both parties agree about the issues in question. Carefully and accurately kept records of the interactions will prove helpful if the situation is not resolved at the building level.

Assessing Procedures. If the complaint/grievance procedures are to become a vehicle for communication, they should be finely tuned on a continuous basis to keep them fair, simple, and timely.

In Perspective

Collective bargaining has affected the principal's role, but so can the principal influence the outcome of collective bargaining. With shared decision making becoming more common and more inclusive, the principal can help shift the process toward considerations of what is good for students and society as well as those things that are personally good or convenient for teachers. Administering a well-written collectively bargained contract may be easy, encouraging an administrator to equate no contract problems with good leadership. Such intellectual atrophy is dangerous in a time when knowledge, technology, and global conditions are changing so rapidly that the schools must run ever faster even to stay in the same place. The opportunity to challenge the school community even via the bargaining process should not be overlooked.

CRISIS MANAGEMENT

Schools face unexpected crises, some of which can become media circuses with negative results for the school and often the principal. Faculty or student deaths, suicides, alleged sexual abuse, acts of violence, and natural disasters, to name a few, can create a crisis. It is not a matter of IF a crisis will occur; it is a matter of WHEN and WHAT the nature of the crisis will be.

Crisis management procedures should be established long before a situation occurs. The principal can help alleviate the effects of a crisis by preparing teachers and staff through discussions and training sessions and clarifying procedures for certain situations. Invariably, there are gaps in a building or district crisis management plan. The principal will need to work with district personnel and community personnel to refine procedures. An inventory of communication resources (telephones, two-way radios, closed circuit TV, etc.) needs to be made to assure that persons needing information during a crisis situation can be reached to assure the safety of all concerned.

Crisis teams should be identified. Response teams need information regarding their specific roles and how to access assistance. The team's composition will vary according to the kind of situation being faced. After-crisis counseling or care teams may consist of school personnel and community persons qualified for the roles needed. Obviously, these team members need to be pre-identified and have some prior training. Assembling such a team during a crisis period can produce some negative results.

Responsibility for who will deal with the media should be fixed. Ordinarily, this spokesperson will be a central office person, but in the midst of a crisis, the principal or a teacher is often before a camera and microphone. Staff development should be provided for all school personnel to familiarize them with policies and procedures.

The person dealing with the media should have a message to convey, not just be a reactor. Public and media questions should be anticipated as much as possible and answers provided. The media relations person should take control of the questioning. A "No comment" reply is not the best response. If you do not have the information, say so. Assume that recorders and cameras are on at all times and that there is really no such thing as "off the record." It is usually best if the principal can be free to take care of the most pressing matters during a crisis.[20]

SUMMARY

The school is only part of a multifaceted culture that brings to the school a wide range of problems and perspectives about how the school should handle those problems. This chapter touches on discipline, gender bias,

---

[20] See Les Davis, "Swimming with the Sharks," *School Business Affairs* 62 (September 1996): 23–27; John Dudley, "Amidst Crisis Be Prepared for Tough Questions," *School Administrator* (February 1996): 38–39. See also Theodore J. Kowalski, *Public Relations in Schools* (Columbus, OH: Merrill/Prentice Hall, 2000).

sexual harassment, expectations about assessment and testing, the principal's role in collective bargaining, and crisis management—which are only a few, given the spectrum of problems within the school walls. Successfully dealing with just these, however, will help maintain an environment in which students can learn without disruption, equally, and in a collaborative setting.

FOR FURTHER THOUGHT

School Discipline

1. Do you believe that the student behavior in schools is a mirror image of the society in which they exist? If so, should not the schools' approach to discipline reflect that society?
2. Is student behavior better or worse than it was twenty years ago? Present solid evidence for your answer.
3. The faculty of a school troubled with discipline problems have asserted, "We are not police officers! It is not our job to monitor the halls, lavatories, lunchrooms, and athletic events. We will not do it!" Do you agree with them? What could or should you do as principal in this situation?
4. What forms of power should a principal use to work with teachers in improving the climate of a school with major discipline problems? Assume the teachers have a strong professional union and a history of effective collective bargaining.
5. Is involving students in developing discipline a form of letting the fox watch over the chicken coop?

Gender Issues

6. At what point should the school ignore the mores of the community regarding gender bias? Same-sex classes? Sports?
7. Some have asserted that gender stereotyping can be found in every phase of school operation: textbooks, curriculum, social activities, recreation, and even school discipline. Much of this stereotyping affects females negatively, but some also affects males negatively. What is the research evidence in this regard? How do we deal with it?
8. Prepare an outline of a presentation you have agreed to make to a very conservative group regarding changes you wish to make in the school to eliminate gender bias.
9. How could screening texts for gender bias be a form of censorship by the professionals?
10. Review your school's existing policies regarding sexual harassment. Identify specific areas that are unclear regarding proper action, or topics that may be missing.

Living in an Accountability Environment

11. Debate: The emphasis on the acquisition of skills for economic competitiveness and on competency testing is discriminatory.
12. If a course or subject does not have known, accepted, and measurable objectives, can we really justify offering it in school?
13. With the emphasis on inclusion of special needs students, schools need to provide appropriate accommodations. What are some dangers involved?

Collective Bargaining

14. In what ways might the maturing of the collective bargaining process be likened to certain stages of human development?
15. What kinds of things are negotiable in your state? Are they discussible?
16. In collective bargaining, in what ways would it be important to distinguish between the principal as a person and the position?
17. Strong unionism might be called the result of inadequate administrative leadership. Discuss.
18. Should principals have their own collective bargaining unit? How would this affect the administrative team concept? What has been the impact in those school districts where principals have had their own collective bargaining unit?

Crisis Management

19. Does your school have a crisis management plan? What parts of the plan are unclear to you?
20. Who is to deal with the media during and regarding a crisis?
21. What staff development programs are in place to assist teachers and staff regarding crisis situations?

⬤ELECTED READINGS

Caruso, Peter. "Individuality vs. Conformity: The Issue behind School Uniforms." *NASSP Bulletin* 80 (September 1996): 83–88.

Center for Employment Relations and the Law. *The Impact of Teacher Collective Bargaining on School-Site Management in Florida.* Tallahassee: Florida State University, 1984.

Davis, Les. "Swimming with the Sharks." *School Business Affairs* 62 (September 1996): 23–27.

Fey, Gil-Patricia, J. Ron Nelson, and Maura L. Roberts. "The Perils of Profiling," *School Administrator* 57 (February 2000): 12–14.

Kessler, Rachael. *The Soul of Education.* Alexandria, VA: Association for Supervision and Curriculum Development, 2000.

Lieberman, Myron. "Teacher Unions and Educational Quality: Folklore by Finn."
Phi Delta Kappan 66 (January 1985): 341–343.

National Association of Elementary School Principals. *Developing a Discipline Code in Your School.* Reston, VA: Author, December 1983.

Shakeshaft, Carol, and Audrey Cohan. "Sexual Abuse of Students by School Personnel." *Phi Delta Kappan* 76 (March 1995): 518.

Management of Supporting Services

*W*e are firm advocates of organizational and operational patterns that relieve principals of much of the direct responsibility for routine management detail, which thereby allows them to focus on instructional and educational leadership as their major responsibility. We realize executives cannot abdicate responsibility for housekeeping details. Nonetheless, operational and staffing patterns can be established that relieve much of the daily concern for these tasks without sacrificing efficiency or adding prohibitive costs to the system. Much can be accomplished when principals are willing and able to delegate responsibility properly. In addition, central administration needs to accept with strong conviction that this delegation is necessary and appropriate. Principals should not feel guilty about delegation, nor should they attend every meeting related to business management activities, sign every paper, or personally brief the staff on every new housekeeping development. We believe that the principal's management technique in business matters should be "management by exception"; that is, routine matters should be handled by others who are responsible to the principal, and only special and exceptional matters should be referred to the principal.

By saying this, we do not mean to downgrade the importance of supporting services to school operation. We simply do not want principals to become housekeeping mechanics! The deployment of supporting services so that they give the instructional staff resources when needed is an important act of educational leadership and therefore an important part of the principal's task.

The chapters that follow discuss office, business, and facility management.

CHAPTER 17

The School Office: Information and Communications Center

*T*he school office is an essential center of information, communications, resource allocation, and control. In addition, the office is a production center, a data generation center, an information exchange center, and a public relations nerve center.

How the school office is managed communicates many messages about the principal and about the school in general. An efficient and effective school office is important to the realization of established educational goals. It is in the school's best interest that the principal strive to develop a strong office staff that understands and is dedicated to the school's goals.

The public really knows the school through the conduct of its office, perhaps even more than through contact with the teachers. Likewise, faculty members quickly sense attitudes that seem to emanate from the way the school office operates. If supply needs or heavy demands on the computer or printing facilities are anticipated and provision is made to reduce the problems that could arise, the principal's credibility is enhanced. If the secretary courteously answers the endless stream of questions and yet seems willing to go the extra step to be helpful, the public is more ready to listen to the school's message. Of course, care should be taken that these means do not become ends. One could easily fall into the trap of "If it isn't broken, don't fix it." Today's world requires keeping up with not only technology but also the concept of service to the educational programs of the school.

The management of an office includes (1) organization, (2) personnel, (3) facilities, (4) policies and procedures, (5) information, (6) communications, and (7) control. These parts need to be in proper balance to function effectively. Careful analyses of each office operation and the pre-planning of routines are important to consistent efficiency. Just as important is planning for the unknown, the emergencies, the new demands that may come from almost any direction. Of course, not all or even any of the unknown can be anticipated, but some coping plans can be thought out that may make an important difference in the welfare of the citizens in the school.

How each operation supports or affects other operations should be systematically reviewed so that the inevitable add-ons or timing changes do not adversely affect the overall effectiveness of the office. Annual job description reviews are helpful in this regard.[1]

A COMMUNICATIONS CENTER TO AND FROM THE DISTRICT AND COMMUNITY

The school office receives and sends a variety of communications via mail; telephone; modem; fax; interoffice memorandum; face-to-face contact with parents, teachers, and students; and many other means. It is important that the communication received is accurately understood and, if it is to be sent on to another person(s), that the message is conveyed accurately. The reverse is also true—the communication sent should be designed to convey the intended message accurately and effectively. Simply saying some words, putting them on paper, or sending them via electronic mail does not ensure communication of the intended message.

Occasionally, frequent communication is confused with good communication. Frequency is not as important as clarity of the purpose and clarity of the message. This is not to say that repetition is not a good practice for some topics, particularly new ideas and concepts. The receivers should have as much information as possible about why the communication is directed to them so that they will more freely accept it and try to understand it.

Communication must also be semantically in tune with the intended receivers. Since the five hundred most used words in the English language each have approximately twenty-eight separate meanings (a total of about fourteen thousand), the sender needs to be sensitive to misinterpretation of meaning. However, words are not the only vehicles of communication. Tone of voice, gestures, visual symbols, and many other elements convey messages to receivers. Given the increasing language diversity in many schools, great care must be taken not to exclude

---

[1] The reader may wish to review Chapters 3, 12, and 13 of Thelbert L. Drake and William H. Roe, *School Business Management: Supporting Instructional Effectiveness* (Boston: Allyn & Bacon, 1994).

one group or another by not considering their receptive communication needs.

SCHOOL-COMMUNITY COMMUNICATIONS

The several communities that the school serves make various inputs into the school system and individual school. (See Figure 3.1.) In turn, they expect certain communications from the school. Report cards, presentations at local meetings, announcements of upcoming events, and letters to individuals are communication media from school to community. Daily class assignments, special class events, and other information are expected. Both students and parents look forward to a weekly note about the student's progress and assignments for the week. On-line communications with parents can convey pertinent information as well as save time for everyone.[2] The quality of these communications conveys as much as the messages they attempt to get across. Relational word-processing programs have provided the office and teachers with tools to produce professional-looking materials (school or class newsletters) with minimal effort. The principal will wish to see that the office staff and faculty check written communications for accuracy of information, correct grammar and spelling, proper format, and clear duplication when needed.

Even with site-managed schools, the school district will have definite policies and procedures regarding the release of information to the public through the various media and school-produced materials. The principal should become thoroughly familiar with the school district's policies and current practices regarding communication with the public and the general plan, if any, for the school's public relations program.

All communication, including teacher initiated, needs to fit within policy guidelines so that awkward and sometimes damaging situations can be avoided. As noted earlier, a proper balance of time, effort, and expense on the possibilities available via computer-generated communications is needed. Without doubt, a blizzard of paper can increase costs rapidly. A readable, accurate, and useful communication related to enhancing student learning can provide positive dividends. The purpose of communication is to influence, which implies more in-depth thought about the communication than merely throwing out the information for whatever it is worth to the readers or listeners.

Communications programs via telephone call-in lines or e-mail can provide information on makeup work, continued homework assignments, and announcements of upcoming events. Usually, these are run

---

[2] Jeffrey Branzburg, "Talking to Parents Online," *Technology and Learning* 21 (April 2001): 54–56.

on dedicated telephone lines and computer driven, and the messages are teacher initiated. The principal's leadership is important in helping the technology tool become effective in that a commitment of the faculty is essential.

Internal Communications

As noted in earlier chapters, effective decision making requires information that is accurate and as complete as possible. Computers enhance data generation and analyses, and they can be particularly helpful in communicating to district or site personnel via e-mail, generating daily or even hourly updates on changes. An example of the latter would be the teacher-provided report to the office regarding attendance.

Internal communications should be routinized, clear, and concise but complete. Each communication should have a very distinct purpose, or it should be postponed or eliminated. It is desirable to routinize certain communications so that the faculty and staff can expect to receive a communication at a specific time each day (or on Monday, Wednesday, and Friday, or some other workable arrangement) in a familiar format so that minimum searching is required for needed information. The order of items presented should be the same each time (e.g., schedule changes, meeting announcements and agendas, professional information, personals).

Mail and Messages

The handling of mail and messages requires precise zero-error procedures to prevent misplacement, tardiness, or loss. Mail and messages should be assigned to a specific workstation for processing. Routine school mail should be opened, sorted out for priority, and directed to the proper destination with routing slips. Time and date stamps should be used on all incoming mail and messages for future chronological reference. Correspondence that should be directed to the principal's specific attention may be screened and prioritized by the school secretary, to include underlining or notation of pertinent information and appending of related correspondence or file documentation. Some principals have found it helpful to have a secretary sort materials into color-coded folders.

The School Website

To provide information about the school, programs, special events, and other communications, schools are finding a Website on the Internet to be useful. Entrepreneurs will help create a home page on the Internet, but most schools have the expertise needed among the faculty, staff, and students. In addition to increasing information access to the public, creating a Web presence can be a project that helps bring the school community together and makes an important statement to the school community about the importance of using technology. The principal will need to consider at least the following questions:

1. What are the specific purposes for the site?
2. What are the expenses for access and continuing charges?
3. How much will the design cost?
4. What community/state resources might be available to defray costs?
5. Who will administer the site?
6. How will it be updated and maintained?
7. Who will be able to have pages (e.g., teachers, grade levels, teams)?

Developing a Website is an opportunity, but it is also an undertaking of considerable time and potential expense. As the list of questions suggests, planning is important to creating a useful tool for communicating with anyone who might visit the site, whether that visitor is from the local community or not.[3]

INFORMATION SERVICES

Information is useless unless it is accurate, current, provided in meaningful form, accessible, and relevant to the decisions that need to be made. Much information now being collected in schools does not meet these criteria. Indeed, too much of it meets only the criterion of accuracy. A lot of it is kept in the event that it might prove useful someday to the school or another government agency.

Information is not an end in itself in the school setting. It is merely a means to provide a service to the decision-making process. Neither the information nor the system that generates, stores, or manipulates it is sacred. The information-gathering and -analyzing processes must be viewed as modified tools. The process should not limit decisions because it yields only certain kinds of data.

The information service should include an up-to-date, easily accessible reference shelf. This shelf should include pertinent state department of education bulletins, school board policy guides, administrative regulations, personnel policies, collective bargaining agreements, the budget and related financial documents, operational memos and handbooks,

---

[3] Several additional considerations are noted in Laurel O'Brien, "Home Away from Home," *Association Management* 48 (February 1996): 81–85, 186.

school calendars, data on all other local schools and personnel, local laws and ordinances important to education, and information on governmental and social agencies. The ability to access state department of education databases, networks, and bulletin boards is a must. Appropriately enough, part of the process of building the expert power we described in Chapter 6, on leadership, is developed through the perception that the principal is a quick and authentic source of information on almost anything regarding government and education. A good secretary can do much to enhance this perception by serving as a key information source and researcher for the principal's office.

A relational database program for student management, scheduling, library management, and fiscal accounting may be very helpful. The many programs and services now available can provide the principal with a wealth of information that can be designed for a specific school and used to assist in decision making. Data on the school's attendance area—pupils, teachers, and staff; the physical properties of the school, building, equipment, and supplies; and all attendant information about them—can be available to the principal as needed. Teacher data interpretation teams will need to be able to access material pertinent to the problem(s) they are working on.

Accurate, up-to-date information files on career and higher education opportunities are essential to the counseling program. Computer-accessible information on CDs, the Internet, or laser disks is helpful to students as they explore a variety of options.

Some Prior Questions

The answers to questions like the following will assist in planning what information should be included in the office:

1. What is needed to answer routine operating questions and generate required reports?
2. Who needs to use the information? Equally important, who should not have access to the information?
3. In what format is the information best stored, retrieved, and analyzed?
4. Is the information a duplication of other sources? Why?
5. How flexible is the system?
6. Is it consistently budgeted for operation and updating?

As with almost any facet of educational management, the principle of planning for planning applies. The principal will find it helpful to work out complete answers to questions like the foregoing, and he or she is cautioned not to try to develop a complete set of either questions or answers without beginning to involve some people who can generate the information, help analyze it, and use it.

OFFICE TECHNOLOGY

Building a useful information system linked with the central offices and the state department of education as well as other information sources around the globe is basic to operation in the twenty-first century. The information system can be helpful in answering questions that occur as the principal considers alternatives, particularly in districts where the budget is decentralized to the schools. Although the information system may be used to answer "What if . . . ?" questions at the district level, it can also help answer building-level questions, such as those dealing with schedules, personnel dollar decisions, pupil placement problems, building maintenance, and renovation. Linkages to state information systems can be useful and should be available. Budget, attendance, and enrollment changes are but a few of the reports that are, or soon will be, transmitted from the building or central district office via modem. State department of education bulletin boards and curricular help information files are available to schools via computer networks. Students, faculty, and administrators should be able to tap into material databases to get information needed for research and decisions.

The time saved by careful planning can be applied toward more direct service to the educational program. As the value of information increases, even the same amount of time spent on the collection and organization of information can yield a much higher return.

Rodriguez suggests getting someone on staff, at the central office or building level, who has the skills to make a total high-speed communications system work.[4] If possible, fiber optics should be used, at least systemwide. Newer developments with utilities and media companies may make this possible more readily, but budgets must be available. Oliver warns that when a technology plan is being developed, the operation "cannot be subject to erratic, up-and-down budgeting."[5] Implementing an effective technology-based information system that will be useful to all learners and decision makers requires long-term dollar and personnel commitment. To view it as a "frill" defeats its usefulness over time and sends a negative message to learners and the community.

School information, especially information shared by users such as counselors, teachers, and principal, needs to be secure so that only authorized users can access or change the data. Computers can be very helpful with attendance, finances, lunch payments, and so on but can be a source of embarrassment and even legal disputes if accessed by unauthorized

---

[4] Jesse Rodriguez, "Building an Adaptive Information System," *School Administrator* 54 (April 1997): 22–25.
[5] James Oliver, "Ten Must-Ask Questions When Developing a Technology Plan," *School Administrator* 54 (April 1997): 29.

persons. Young and Wodarz provide a checklist helpful to the principal in assessing the security of the office technology.[6]

THE SCHOOL SECRETARY

The readers' experiences with the many offices with which they come in contact by mail, by telephone, and in person are enough to remind them of the importance of the secretarial help in an office. A courteous word, pleasant manner, and apparent willingness to help can do much for the effectiveness of any office. Conveying the confidence that everything is under control and that whatever the request may be it will be competently handled is one of the greatest contributions the secretary can make. Many principals will give credit to a competent secretary for their own success.

An Important First Contact

The secretary is often the "voice" of the school to many parents and agency personnel. His or her work represents the school in written form. Accurate reports give the recipients of those reports an impression of the school. The secretary is usually the first person a teacher, student, parent, or any other person meets when contacting the principal. A very common cause of poor morale among both teachers and students is the negative way they are treated by the principal's office staff. Office staff should never create the impression that they are "door guards" or "gatekeepers" for access to the principal. However, a tactful receptionist becomes very skillful in carefully questioning the caller to determine whether something needs the principal's immediate personal attention or whether some other person can handle the problem.

Secretaries should not be burdened with having to communicate policies about what work they are supposed to do and for whom (e.g., typing or duplicating for teachers) or who is responsible for what tasks in the office. Those policies are made by the principal, who should make them clear to everyone.

Nothing implies poor management faster than having a receptionist say, "I don't know where he is" or "I don't know when she will be in." A sincere businesslike response must be made, such as "Mr. Jones is in conference," or "Mrs. Smith is at lunch," or "He's meeting with students." This should be followed by an offer to assist, such as "She will be back in the office at two. May I give her a message?" or "Shall I ask him

---

[6] Roger L. Young and Nan Wodarz, "Technology Security: A Checklist Approach to Assessment," *School Business Affairs* 66 (February 2000): 23–30.

to call you back?" or "Is there someone else who may be able to help you?"

These guidelines may help the principal avoid creating or reinforcing problems:

1. A clear ordering of priorities for work is important, which the principal can change as emergencies arise.
2. The services of the office and the responsibilities of the office worker should be made known to the teachers.
3. Office procedures should be periodically reviewed with the total staff.
4. Office directives to the professional staff should come from the principal, not the secretary.
5. Schoolwide decisions should not be made by the secretary. Plans should be worked out to cover unexpected situations if the principal is not in the school. On other than routine office work, the secretary should have someone to refer to if a new situation occurs.
6. Membership should be provided for the secretary in a school secretaries' subscription service or, if available, a school secretaries' association.

Continuing Training and Development

It is recognized that the central office of the school system will probably have a plan for the in-service training of office staff. After becoming familiar with this training program plan, the principal should assess training needs in his or her own office. Most principals inherit their office staff, and the secretaries see principals come and go. Yet the principal should not assume that all is as it should be in all the operational aspects of the office. If one is to assume that every operation can be made better, then opportunities to grow should be provided as well as the freedom to make changes.

Despite the importance of the office staff giving proper attention to the details essential to the school's effective operation and making a positive impression on the community, the least amount of money and time is usually spent on the in-service opportunities for them. If no systematic plan is available for this important investment in the human resources of the school, the principal should press for such a plan and, if necessary, pilot a demonstration program. The principal can encourage office personnel to participate in a local secretaries' association, if available, or help them work toward certification in a program such as that available through the National Association of Educational Office Professionals.[7]

---

[7] See www.naeop.org for additional details.

Evaluating the Office Staff

The responsibilities and tasks for each position in the office should be included in a job description. The job description provides the beginning for an evaluation process that addresses the level at which the person is fulfilling the job. Given the number of persons the secretary works with, there is ample opportunity to generate feedback from teachers, parents, students, and noninstructional personnel. The job description needs to be reviewed each year so that it reflects what is expected of the person in the job. (See also Chapter 13.)

WORK ANALYSIS

It may be important to assess the workloads and activities of the office workers to determine whether their time and energy are being used effectively. Complaints about interruptions, unavailable materials, and so on may indicate to the principal that steps should be taken not only to alleviate the stated problems but also to increase the efficiency of the office staff. Clerks or secretaries may be duplicating tasks, or the priorities of one may prevent others from completing their tasks.

The office staff can keep a simple log of tasks and time spent over one or two weeks. These can be tabulated and summarized by worker, day of the week, type of task, or any combination of these. The results should be helpful to the principal in asking questions about the office's operation.

If the principal is not sure how much work should be expected from a worker performing certain tasks, he or she may wish to discuss the matter with the business manager or business education personnel or review various guides that provide work standards.

OFFICE ENVIRONMENT

The principal should give special thought to the office environment, its layout, and its design. The behavioral science of people's relationships to their physical environment is known as *ergonomics;* it seeks to adapt the working conditions to suit the task of the worker. For example, sharp-edged desks and tables located in heavily trafficked parts of the office are ergonomically unsound because they present unnecessary hazards. But beyond this, workstations should be well defined and as self-sufficient as possible. They should be grouped in terms of work flow from station to station. Related tasks should be clustered both physically and according to personnel. Placing the files, equipment, and data concerned with related tasks will save time and energy for the person doing the work.

Traffic routes can be established by carefully placing furniture so as to channel people efficiently, discourage indiscriminate sojourns into the work area, and reduce nonproductive conversation. Special consideration should be given to providing a pleasant area for visitors to wait, secure spaces for cash handling and confidential records, and isolation for noisy business machines.[8]

Physical Surroundings

Joseph J. Jones entered the office, approached the China-Wall-like counter, and waited for the receptionist to cross the room from her desk. The printer and the photocopier seemed to be engaged in a staccato fugue, with the hum from the window air conditioner providing a bagpipe-sounding accompaniment. He told the receptionist that he had come for his 2:30 appointment with the principal but had to repeat his name since the ringing telephone added its voice to the orchestration. The principal's door was closed.

The receptionist asked him to wait because the principal was engaged in a telephone conversation, and she nodded toward two chairs tucked away behind the door and next to the teachers' mail holes and work pick-up baskets. The teachers certainly seemed to be friendly, but then close quarters always make for congenial conversation.

An intercom buzzer sounded, and within seconds the receptionist appeared from behind the great wall and told him that the principal was free. The principal's door was open, and he welcomed Mr. Jones warmly and asked him to make himself comfortable. He closed the door as he followed Mr. Jones into the room, commenting that it was necessary to keep the door closed to keep out the din from all those machines. Mr. Jones was surprised that he was aware of it.

The physical environment is important to persons working in it and to those who visit. The affective impact of the environment can unconsciously, and sometimes consciously, help or hinder the tasks at hand. In the case of Mr. Jones, noise was affecting his impressions. An average noise level between forty and fifty decibels is reasonable. Keeping noise at a reasonable level seems to be productive. Sound-absorbent materials and strategically placed objects can at least manage to reduce the noise level. Carpeting and drapes are very helpful. Soft material backings at strategic points can reduce noise (e.g., on a file cabinet next to a typewriter, near a computer/printer and/or copier area).

One should take care not to convey the idea that the focus of attention is on mechanical matters. If the "hard" area is what most people see first, they may come away with the impression of a high-tech control center or, at worst, a student yearbook office. A softness in both the outer

---

[8] The principal should also be aware of his or her personal appearance. One should take time to observe what sort of clothing helps convey a "can do" image. The same can be said of other personnel who represent the school in the office area or in the hallways.

office and the principal's office may convey not only a more gracious atmosphere but also one conducive to the sharing of important ideas. Lighting that is task specific may be better than the overall flickering fluorescent lights.

Accessibility to the office is important. The office is not just for adults but also for students. Secondary students may not encounter a size problem with the counter or furniture but may not feel the office area is a place where their concerns or needs are of any interest. The manner in which they are greeted or answered conveys clear messages, ranging from "How can we help you as part of this large learning family?" to "Why are you bothering us in our very important business?"

A PROCEDURES MANUAL

Many of the tasks of the school office are routine in procedure, process, time, or all of these. Purchasing procedures, attendance figures, routine maintenance requests, and many more are tasks for which proper procedures are designated by the central administration. These procedures usually are sent to the buildings in memorandum form, indicating changes, additions, and so on. On occasion, the central administration office will prepare a procedures manual for business-related procedures. If it has not, the principal may wish to inquire about the feasibility of developing such a manual.

A loose-leaf binder–type manual can be of great help to the secretary and other office workers. It can be divided and subdivided into as many categories as needed for quick reference (e.g., attendance, accounts, purchasing, emergency-medical, communications format). Copies of forms can be inserted, with proper distribution designated. As procedures and forms change, they can easily be replaced. If the principal wishes to add details or categories unique to the building, he or she can do so easily. All manuals and forms should be at the ready on disk so that needed changes can be made quickly.

The advantages are obvious: (1) compiling such a manual often clarifies many procedures, (2) new personnel have a reference from which to work, (3) a procedure is established for keeping information up to date, and (4) a manual can aid in relieving the principal from having to react to procedural administrivia.

Included in the manual should be an office master calendar providing a checklist of routine duties and deadlines. As certain dates are fixed (e.g., budget requests deadlines, program memoranda), they can be logged in so that all office workers are aware of time demands. Some principals have found a reminder on their computer calendars helpful.

SUMMARY

The school office is vital to an organization's well-being. It is the communications link, an information bank, and the processor of incoming and outgoing contacts. The office personnel, environment, and procedures communicate to people who come in contact with them. The communications products of the school office, and the information it collects, analyzes, and disseminates, do much to enlist internal and external support for the school. Important as it is, however, the office, as well as its operations, must remain a means rather than an end in itself.

FOR FURTHER THOUGHT

1. How can the school office influence the teaching-learning environment? Cite specific instances.
2. If you were a newcomer to the community, what words might describe the atmosphere conveyed to you on your first visit to your school's office? What specific changes might be helpful?
3. Examine the workloads of an office staff. What tasks have been reduced or eliminated by the effective use of technology? How many tasks are add-ons to an already reasonable workload?
4. Are there important differences in the principal's personnel administration practices when dealing with teachers as contrasted with clerical and nonprofessional personnel? Be specific. Should this be so?
5. Though a great deal of thought may be spent on the image of the principal conveyed by the office, how might a good image be destroyed by personal grooming and attire? Communication style?
6. Discuss how a principal can free office staff to improve processes and yet at the same time be responsible for the effective operation of the office.
7. Map out a work-flow traffic pattern for the school office, using the effective placing of furniture and machines. Have fellow students critically analyze your efforts.
8. Describe the information system available to teachers in your school. How is the building linked to other information services? For safety in an emergency, can the office notify everyone quickly, particularly if the intercom system is not appropriate?

SELECTED READINGS

Drake, Thelbert L., and William H. Roe. *School Business Management: Supporting Instructional Effectiveness.* Boston: Allyn & Bacon, 1994.

Mais, Charles. "Are Your Computers Communicating?" *School Business Affairs* 58 (May 1992): 22–25.

O'Brien, Laurel. "Home Away from Home." *Association Management* 48 (February 1996): 81–85, 186.

Oliver, James. "Ten Must-Ask Questions When Developing a Technology Plan." *School Administrator* 54 (April 1997): 26–29.

Young, Roger L., and Nan Wodarz. "Technology Security: A Checklist Approach to Assessment." *School Business Affairs* 66 (February 2000): 23–30.

Business-Related Management of a School

*D*ecentralized decision making, charter schools, and full-service schools are examples of more business-related functions being placed at the building level. Not only does the principal have responsibility for the traditional business functions of accountability, purchase requisitions, and materials management, but also these are expanded in scope, and in some instances, personnel budgets and/or energy management are part of the building administrator's responsibility. While no clear pattern has yet emerged regarding which business functions are delegated to the building level, the principal may find that a full array of them are part of his or her responsibility. Some districts may even include energy use, which can be a large budget item. (This topic is discussed in more detail in Chapter 19.) Other functions that may be within the principal's responsibility are maintenance, purchasing, and budget reallocation as well as receiving and accounting for extracurricular funds generated within the school. Such funds can total over $100,000 in a large high school.

The demand for accurate accounting for, and efficient responses to, the business-related matters of a school is justifiable. The principal needs to state clearly his or her expectations about how business matters will be handled. If these areas are operating smoothly, the principal can enjoy the credibility necessary to be effective in other areas.

It is easy to displace the most important goal of the school—effective student learning—with the here and now report due tomorrow. Although surprise demands can occur at any time, if barely squeaking by each deadline with near-panic efforts becomes a way of life, the system is not working well. If the principal is continually busy and seemingly unable to move into areas outside managing business and office affairs (or monitoring the cafeteria), the system may be a problem.

On the other hand, could it be that the principal chooses to spend an inordinate amount of time accounting for lunch money? The same may be asked of any of the business-related functions of the principal. While some may concentrate on an efficiently run accounting system, others may be proud of their ability to keep the supplies inventory at optimal level, right to the last sheet of paper used on the last day of school.

The principal, as the leader of an organization, will ensure that all of the staff—teachers, business office personnel, maintenance and operations personnel—see a connectedness among all the parts of the school and their own roles as contributing to the common purpose of improving student learning. This view of the leader as one who establishes and maintains the connections among the components of the process may appear to be in contrast to the manager-leader who designs job descriptions and then inspects to see that the jobs are done. If the business functions are treated that way, then there is a contrast. Efficient processes must be established and responsibilities placed for implementing the processes, but it is also important that the job holders have a sense of responsibility for the whole enterprise. A portion of the monitoring responsibility for continually improving the unit's performance may be shared by those doing the jobs. Indeed, if given sufficient training and resources, the job holders may be able to move toward excellence more rapidly than if limited by the "do-inspect" form of supervision. Accountability must be built into the system; otherwise, an employee can slide by with little or no evidence of improvement. Accountability for accuracy (and honesty) is essential. An internal control process should be in place to assure proper procedures.[1]

The principal's function, then, is to articulate what has to be done for what reasons and to provide a process so that people can see whether the jobs are being done. Management of business matters may be "by exception," with the principal dealing with only special situations.

This is not to imply that one should operate on the "If it works, don't fix it" rule. A well-conceived review of each operation and its effects on other operations should be at least an annual process. The central office business staff may be able to provide this service to the site-managed school. It may see some savings and efficiencies in cooperative efforts such as team maintenance and some operations functions such as carpet cleaning, vacation cleaning schedules, and so forth.

---

[1] Rita Dunn, "The Missing Factor in Accountability: Improving Internal Control Practices for School Financial Management," *Connections* 3 (April 18, 2001), at www.nassp.org/connections.

FINANCIAL RESPONSIBILITIES

An overall understanding of school finance and the local tax structure is important because local taxpayers often have questions about the impact of proposed changes on their tax bill. Teachers, too, occasionally need help in answering these questions.

We are not suggesting the principal needs to be a financial expert or accountant. But we do believe a practicing school administrator must be knowledgeable enough to keep on top of the school's budgeting and accounting process and to speak and understand the language. The principal should be able to participate on equal terms with central administrators when decisions that depend on the allocation of funds are being made.

Given the growing trend of allocating funds and greater budget decision-making power to individual schools under the site-based or site-managed philosophy of management (or a variety of similar terms), the principal will find it important to understand the rationale behind each allocation. If a lump-sum allocation is given on a per-pupil or per-program basis, what is the impact on the instructional program as enrollments change? Are utilities included? At what level are vacancies funded? Can one get experienced people? If personnel economies are realized, does the school have the remainder to use as it sees fit? Can new jobs be created with shifts in personnel or budget reallocation?

In the growth of education, finance has been a shaping and often governing factor. It is no idle statement to say, "Power follows the purse." A person who knows and understands finance has an advantage in dealing with other administrators, business managers, and comptrollers who may be only too willing to allow "money power" to accumulate in their office. We have dealt with some superintendents, business managers, and accountants who create the impression that finance is beyond the comprehension of any ordinary human being. Of course, these are the exceptions rather than the rule. They try to maintain control and power through the ambiguous discussion of funding and, when questioned, create the impression they are grappling with some mystic, elusive, unexplainable "they." The matter is not that complicated. An elementary knowledge of accounting and budgeting procedures, plus some simple study of the state's school finance procedures, the school's classifications system for accounting, and the school district's budget over the past five years, will provide the principal the fiscal basics to be a leader in any school system.

Money—or the lack of it—will govern the way an organization is managed and the way it succeeds. An educational activity may be encouraged by increasing its revenue, or it may be discouraged or enfeebled by denying it financial support. Thus, finance can become an instrument of control at the district or building level. From this circumstance, we discover the need for a fundamental identity between school policy and planning and school finance. Left unfettered and uncontrolled, finance can lead the way to destruction. Properly controlled and used as a tool for education, money can serve as the lifeblood for a growing and flourishing school. Thus, budgeting—the device for translating the educational plan into a financial plan—has become a more important administrative process each year. If handled properly, it is an important educational leadership activity and not a routine management detail.[2]

THE BUDGET

Some facetiously have called budgeting "worrying before you spend, instead of afterward." We define *educational budget* as the translation of educational needs into a financial plan that is interpreted to the public in such a way that when formally adopted, it expresses the kind of educational program the community is willing to support, financially and morally, for a given period.

Business and industry consider the budget an instrument of control. Making frequent comparisons between budget figures and actual performance enables management to control activities so that all efforts are coordinated toward the achievement of objectives. However, this is a rather restricted view of budgeting. A budget should be basically an instrument of planning and only incidentally one of control. It reflects the organizational pattern by breaking down the total plan into its sectional and departmental components, which allows costs to be more easily estimated. It then forces a coordination of these elements by reassembling costs so that a comparison may be made with total revenues. This process requires a kind of orderly planning that otherwise might never take place. Budgeting, then, forces the principal and faculty to plan together on what needs to be done, how it will be done, and by whom.

The benefits of budgeting may be listed as follows:

1. Establishes a plan of action for given periods in the long and short term
2. Requires an appraisal of past activities in relation to planned activities
3. Necessitates the development of specific goals and objectives
4. Necessitates the establishment of work plans to achieve goals and objectives
5. Provides security for the administration by assuring the financing and approval of a year's course of action
6. Necessitates foreseeing expenditures and estimating revenues

---

[2] For a more in-depth discussion, see Thelbert L. Drake and William H. Roe, *School Business Management: Supporting Instructional Effectiveness* (Boston: Allyn & Bacon, 1994).

7. Requires orderly planning and coordination throughout the organization
8. Establishes a system of management controls
9. Provides an orderly process of expansion in both personnel and facilities
10. Serves as a public information device

BUDGETING

Decades ago Bartizal suggested that budgets be developed at the local school level.[3] Some school-based management models, which have a community board of directors for individual buildings, have been successful, and some have been displays of misunderstood power gone wrong. The parent or school advisory board may go far beyond advice and attempt to operate the school as a policy-administrative board.

One of the most difficult tasks the principal faces is providing for the knowledgeable, positive participation of staff in the budget-making process. The quiet looks exchanged between teachers as the topic of budget is raised speak loudly. The specter of reams of requisitions with the business office's reject stamp haunts the teacher who may have spent long, extra hours poring over catalogs and received, after all, only the colored chalk. Worse yet is the nightmare of the teacher who carefully matched program needs to supply and laboratory equipment needs and did not receive any hint as to why he or she received only the beakers. For the principal to tolerate such a situation makes faculty participation in budgeting a farce.

Fortunately, with effective work regarding budgeting realities and with a committed group of teachers, a representative task force can be formed that can bring a number of perspectives to the budget situation and result in good programmatic decisions.

There are several approaches to budgeting, but seldom is one "pure" approach found in a school or school district. Each place develops its own adaptations, but the core of the process is usually one of three: (1) planning, programming budgeting system (PPBS), (2) zero-based budgeting (ZBB), or (3) incremental budgeting.

Planning, Programming Budgeting. To exert educational leadership, the principal must have an impact on the allocation of resources to the school's programs. The advent of program budgeting in its various forms provides an important means for the principal to effect progress toward achieving the school's objectives.

---

[3] J. R. Bartizal, *Budget Principles and Procedures* (Upper Saddle River, NJ: Prentice Hall, 1942), 1.

Much literature is available concerning planning, programming budgeting systems. Although the concept had its formal beginnings as far back as 1949, it gained momentum in the mid-1960s through governmental agencies, particularly the Department of Defense. Since that time, several states, cities, and institutions have adopted some form of PPBS.

These developments have brought even more pressure on persons responsible for programs, pressure to delineate their objectives in clear, precise terms. These systems are truly *systems* because no activity (e.g., budgeting) is considered in isolation. Rather, the total program—from objectives to output, including its relationships to other programs—is considered.

A number of school districts have found formal PPBS processes too cumbersome and difficult for boards of education and legislatures that normally deal with the traditional incremental-type budgets. Therefore, many schools require program budgets for specific schools and programs and then, in their total systemwide budgets, convert or provide standard crosswalks from the program budget to the traditional budget. The traditional budget then is used by central administration to summarize the costs based on standard classifications, and the program budget is a tool to explain costs more specifically and programmatically.

Establishing Priorities. Few, if any, school situations have unlimited budgets; therefore, as the process of relating needs to goals and objectives progresses, certain priorities are established. The principal is the key in this process because he or she must not only aid in relating each component of one school to the others but also keep the inputs from the school's central office and the community in balance with the "in-house" priority setting. The principal must be aware of the projected budget, including those increases that will cause the most resistance.

Once the list of needs is completed, it may be advantageous to have faculty and staff assist in establishing priorities. Suspected budget limits should not dictate what program needs are articulated. Yet it is important that a high-priority program not suffer at the expense of a lower-priority program's demands for some expensive materials or equipment.

Initiating the System. The machinery for faculty and staff involvement will vary from school to school. While one principal will find the department head structure most efficient and effective, another will find a small committee best. Regardless of the means, the faculty must be involved in the budgeting process in a way directly related to their functions, thereby positively affecting their responsiveness to the total financial processes of the school. The processes represented will involve short- and long-range planning and choices among alternative plans of action to best utilize available resources.

The human element is crucial. The principal has the responsibility to work with the staff regarding every process of the system that directly affects them. Clarifying the process does much to alleviate fears that can easily arise among faculty.

There is a particular need to be specific regarding the evaluation procedures. The principal has a dual responsibility of effecting a systemwide evaluation program and of being sure the faculty have proper input into the evaluation process. The partial solution to both these responsibilities lies in the development of objectives. If the objectives are stated properly, the evaluations of the programs are delineated. An objective that has no criterion to determine whether it has been reached is really not an objective. The principal should not be willing to accept inappropriate or unclear, nonspecific objectives. The principal then holds the programs accountable in relation to the resources used.

Zero-Based Budgeting. Zero-based budgeting (ZBB) requires annual justification for the continuation of each program. Ordinarily, budgets for each program are proposed at survival, maintenance, and improvement levels. Priorities regarding the programs and the funding levels may be established by the individual school and/or the central administration.

The ZBB approach can be time intensive. It requires continual analysis of program priorities, and at least theoretically, the highest priority programs are funded, which may result in some instability if the decisions are made by an ever-changing and volatile group.

Incremental Budgeting. Probably the most commonly used budgeting process is the traditional, or incremental, approach to budgeting. The starting point is last year's dollar amounts, and determinations are made regarding the distribution of new dollars to the various areas. The tendency for obsolete, nonproductive programs to continue without services review is a disadvantage to the incremental budget. Across-the-board increases to all programs may result in serious underfunding of critical programs and reduce their effectiveness for students.

EXTERNAL SOURCES OF REVENUE

Funds are available to schools from the federal government, states, governmental agencies, and private foundations. Resources from private foundations often are underutilized or untapped by schools. Research and grants offices in some universities and some state departments of education may help the entrepreneurial principal locate useful sources. The principal can encourage and assist teachers to apply for grants to help with special units or teaching innovations. One teacher in a small elementary school has received grants ranging from $5,000 to $25,000 for projects incorporating real community situations in the teaching of mathematics and other projects.

Some schools and/or districts have established externally controlled foundations that raise and distribute money for helping the schools realize their goals. Care should be taken that such a foundation is not used as a rationale for not supporting the school adequately through tax or other traditional revenues. One practical reason is that the foundation optimally will raise only $100 per child, and usually far less.[4] Given the limitations of annual available funds, it would be in order to focus on needs beyond the digital camera or new music stands.

Other sources of revenue could include user fees, booster clubs, shared facilities with other service agencies, fees from leasing facilities, and fund-raisers.[5] The same cautions noted earlier apply to all these potential sources of revenue, especially the booster clubs and fund-raisers. The principal might wish to work closely with the district business manager to explore these and other alternative sources of revenue.

Technology. There is a continuous scramble to maintain currency in technology. Many newer programs will not run on hardware just five years old. Older equipment often cannot be repaired because of unavailable parts or incompatible parts. There are sources to help with keeping equipment current such as technology-rich environments or corporations that wish to take advantage of the Tax Relief Act of 1997. Executive Order 12999 urges federal agencies to give preference to schools in donating educationally useful equipment.[6] Schools should not plan on harvesting used technology equipment to keep current and operable.

When building a budget for a school or district, the total cost of ownership of technology must be included; otherwise, what investments are made will soon be providing no learning/instructional returns. It is estimated that 30 percent of a school's technology budget should be allocated for staff development. Support services are essential but often not budgeted adequately. In short, the technology budget is an ongoing, continuous item involving more than acquiring a few processors, monitors, and keyboards.[7]

---

[4] Carol Merz and Sheldon S. Frankel, "School Foundations: Local Control or Equity Circumvented," *School Administrator* 54 (January 1997): 30.

[5] John C. Pijanowski and David H. Monk, "Alternative School Revenue Sources," *School Business Affairs* 62 (July 1996): 4–10.

[6] B. J. Wise, "Technology at Silver Ridge: An Update," *Principal* 79 (February 2000): 51. See also www.computers.fed.gov/doe/school/12999htm.

[7] Sara Fitzgerald, "Budgeting for Technology's 'Hidden' Costs," *School Business Affairs* 66 (February 2000): 4–7.

REPORTING AND ACCOUNTING FOR SCHOOL FUNDS

A budget is the spending plan for the school or school system. This plan supports the instructional programs of the school, which means that the accounting function is an instructional support system designed to see that the spending is done according to plan. The principal will find some apathy and possibly some negative reactions to the school's accounting necessities. If the faculty is genuinely involved in the budgeting, these reactions are minimized.

Computer accounting systems are used by most schools and school systems so that the time for reporting and analyzing accounts is minimized. The processes for receiving and expending monies must be understood by everyone who is part of the process because the automated systems can be only as accurate as the information provided them. False expectations concerning time saved should not be encouraged at the input point of the system. The initial work of recording information is necessary and takes time, but it is time well spent. The slightest hint of questionable practices with even the smallest fund will bear this out.

Petty Cash Fund

Often schools are discouraged from having cash on hand, yet it is common practice to have a small amount of cash available to make change or purchase small items that might be needed quickly and for which it would be counterproductive to go through the regular requisition procedure. Petty cash should not be used to thwart or circumvent established purchasing procedures; instead, it is a convenient accommodation to facilitate immediate, efficient acquisition of low-cost goods and services. Only the initial amount of money and the additions or deductions to it are included in this account. The petty cash fund may be in the form of actual cash on hand, and it may also include a small bank account.

The cash on hand plus the amount in the bank and all entries in the petty cash book, or on vouchers, should equal the original amount in the fund. The book or voucher should have entries showing

- A serialized number of entry or voucher,
- The person making payment,
- The amount of money,
- The account to be charged,
- The purpose of expenditure, and
- The signature of the person receiving money.

Other information may be dictated by the central accounting office to ensure compatibility with the central accounting system.

Purchases should be kept to a minimum. The cash on hand should also be kept to a minimum and always locked when unattended. Records of receipts and expenditures should be kept separately from the actual cash box or drawer.

Student Activity Funds

Student activity funds deserve special consideration because they are so often neglected and poorly managed, particularly monies derived from extra class fees, athletic contests, plays, concerts, sales, and special programs of all kinds. From these sources, many thousands of dollars may be handled each year, even in a small school; in the large school system, the figure easily reaches six digits.

The question has sometimes arisen whether this money is really public money and therefore under control of the board. In too many instances, boards have paid little attention to these funds and left their management unsupervised.

Generally speaking, monies collected as a part of school activities must be considered public money, and, therefore, "the proceeds of these activities belong to the board of school directors and must be accounted for in the same manner that other funds of the school district are accounted for."[8] As far as the courts are concerned, the fund is public in nature if it is produced through public facilities by public employees as a part of public services for which they are employed.[9] In essence, boards of education in all school districts are required to identify and control the funds of any school-approved and -administered student organization or school service agency.

While these funds are without question under the jurisdiction of the board of education, they may be handled in a manner slightly different from that in which ordinary school funds are handled. An effort should be made to keep these funds as close as possible to the students, providing learning situations for them and imparting to them a personal concern and feeling of responsibility for the proper control of money.

The centralized fund accounting system, in which a specific person, often known as the activity fund manager, does the accounting of activity funds for all schools of the district, has proven to be a success. The centralization process assures standardized procedures and security, and at the same time, it facilitates reporting, aids in postauditing, and provides uniform data for planning and administrative purposes. In districts

---

[8] *In re German Township School Directors*, 46 S. and C. 562 (Comm. Pleas Ct., Fayette Co. Pa. 1942).
[9] *Petition of Auditors of Hatfield Township School District*, 161 Pa. Super. 388, 54 A.2d 833 (1947).

with large schools and a great deal of money, the individual school will have a treasurer to account for fund activity.

Whether student treasurers or faculty or office workers are used, the following general guidelines will aid in developing a plan for properly handling monies received:

1. All money received should be acknowledged by issuing a type of receipt to the person from whom the money is received. This may be a formal receipt or simply a numbered ticket.
2. A deposit slip should be made out and all money deposited immediately.
3. A receipt should be issued to the person making the deposit.
4. The amount deposited should be recorded in a proper book or ledger, under the appropriate fund.
5. The person responsible for the fund should receive a regular (monthly, e.g.) status report of the fund.

It may be beneficial to have a set of student "books" if a student treasurer is used. The advantage of having dual records to check is obvious, as are the instructional advantages for the students.

Sample forms and entries may be found in publications from the Association of School Business Officials or texts in school business management. States ordinarily have guidelines for student activity or extracurricular funds. It would probably be most appropriate to review procedures and forms with the central office business manager.

Expenditures from the activity funds should be handled in at least the following steps:

1. A requisition/purchase order should be initiated by the person in charge of the activity fund.
2. Approval of the central comptroller in the school (usually the principal or representative) should be obtained.
3. All payments should be by check.
4. The expenditure should be recorded in the proper books or ledgers, under the appropriate fund.

Merchandising Activities

Some activities of the school have more than the cash receipts and expenditures to account for. Supplies of various kinds must be inventoried on a regular basis and reconciled with the fund accounting system to give a clear and accurate picture of certain student activities. Concessions at athletic events and school stores are examples.

Fund-raising via sales of candy, cookies, school mementos, and so forth can yield many dollars and many headaches. Natale notes three concerns regarding fund-raisers: safety, equity, and propriety.[10] In the first instance, safety of the students is a major concern. Selling and delivering goods door to door can have some disastrous results, as in Oklahoma where a student was killed while going door to door on a fundraiser. Obviously, these kinds of activities need to be carefully monitored. Other negative fallout on the school can occur when nonstudents pose as legitimate representatives of a school fund-raiser and instead collect money for themselves. Pascopella provides considerations for fundraising on the Web.[11]

Corporate Lures. A newer trend among large corporations is to use the schools to capture future customers via exclusive contracts for vending machines, technology hardware or software, or athletic events sponsorship. The offer of free computers if the school will agree to use them just four hours a day is hard to resist. A lucrative contract for exclusive rights for soft drink vending machines might provide some needed "extras." Hardy points out that carefully developed policies are needed to help the schools protect the students and themselves in a very competitive business environment.[12]

The principal should make every effort to clarify the decision process to both students and faculty so that misunderstandings are avoided. The same is true of the accounting procedures, which can have a negative connotation for students, much as the auditing function can for the principal if either or both parties misunderstand their roles.

Nonstudent Funds

Tradition has left some school offices with the task of accounting for funds collected and expended by nonstudent groups and organizations, such as the PTA, booster clubs, and so on. If the principal is in the happy situation of not having such funds, he or she should jealously guard this happiness. Often these nonstudent funds have supplemented or even maintained certain functions that should have been the responsibility of the community as a whole to support. Continuation of such relationships does not encourage the schools and community to shoulder the responsibility as they should. Rather, it may have the opposite effect.

The new principal would be in a most awkward position to try to disavow responsibility for accounting for and handling these nonstudent

---

[10] Jo Anna Natale, "When Fund-Raisers Go for the Gold, Do Schools Get the Shaft?" *Executive Educator* 12 (June 1990): 17–19.

[11] Angella Pascopella, "Fundraising on the Web," *Curriculum Administration* 37 (May, 2001): 58–59.

[12] Lawrence Hardy, "The Lure of School Marketing," *School Business Affairs* 66 (May 2000): 21.

funds if a tradition has been established. An educative process is much more productive.

Sandri suggests the following procedures to help prevent mishandling or fraudulent practices with nonschool funds: (1) bond the organization's officers, (2) reconcile monthly bank statements, (3) require two signatures on checks, (4) require two people to be present when cash is counted, (5) require those who turn over funds to the treasurer to audit the monthly bank deposits, and (6) require an annual audit.[13]

The principal's effort in working toward sound money procedures—even with school-related organizations such as study groups, boosters, and PTAs—may avoid embarrassments later. In response to both the rhetoric and the realities of poorly managed and poorly funded schools, parent groups have become involved in providing financial support as well as instructional support. The problem of the central administration or the rest of the community sitting back to let this happen over a long period of time may be similar to their counting on the PTA to furnish media equipment. The principal faces a situation in which, on the one hand, parent involvement is desirable and, on the other hand, it could lead to reinforcing inadequate support from the community at large. An open, candid approach with the school's supporters seems to be an appropriate response to the problem.

MANAGING SUPPLIES AND EQUIPMENT

In the general management process, a nationally recognized distinction is made between items of supply and pieces of equipment. *Items of supply* include paper, pencils, computer disks, and so on. They are generally inexpensive items that are consumed with use. It is normally more feasible and even less costly to replace supplies with new items rather than setting up a complicated system of control, retrieval, and repair. Supplies as expendable items are generally accounted for at the building and departmental levels, and if they are inventoried, it is to determine replacements rather than to control. *Pieces of equipment* are considered to be nonexpendable; that is, their use does not deplete them. Equipment includes desks, chairs, photocopiers, and computer hardware. It represents an investment of money that makes it feasible and advisable to capitalize the item and control it and, if broken after use, to repair it rather than replace it. Pieces of equipment are normally integrated into a comprehensive systemwide inventory control process.

Supply management as a total process deals with the purchasing, receiving, storing, and distribution of and accountability for supplies

---

[13] Edward R. Sandri, "Preventing Fund-Raising Fraud," *Executive Educator* 14 (February 1992): 39–41.

used in the operation and maintenance of a school. The way this management process is carried out is important; it can create among the public an impression of waste and dishonesty or thrift and integrity.

Many improved methods and techniques have been developed in the area of supply management over the past few years. Large-city schools are almost compelled by the immensity of their task to maintain a complicated central warehouse that operates daily. Small schools have begun to look with favor on the centrally administered, decentralized storage method. This plan combines the advantages of both the centralized and the decentralized methods of storage. At the same time, it provides adequate control by placing definite responsibility on specific people and by establishing a system of records that follows the flow of supplies from the planning and purchasing stage to the expendable stage.

In the end, it must be understood that systems are carried out by people. Thus, when developing procedures, administrators must give major consideration to the human element. When complicated reporting and follow-up procedures are required, more may be lost through poor morale and the cost of personnel services than the savings warrant. The real challenge to management is to create in all personnel an appreciation of the proper use of supplies and equipment.

Certain decisions will already have been made at the systemwide level concerning the storage and distribution of supplies. Large school systems will use a centralized warehousing system, with an infinite number of variations on the theme. Smaller school systems will probably use some form of centrally administered but decentralized storage supply management. Some districts have found cooperative purchasing, warehousing, and distribution to be effective. The principal does have the responsibility to know how the system operates, what delivery schedules are available, and so on. He or she also should be alert to any improvements that would be feasible in better supporting the instructional program.

Once the supplies and equipment reach the school, the principal must determine the best way to store, distribute, and account for the supplies and equipment. Equipment must also be maintained.

ACQUISITION

This aspect of supplies and equipment management is closely tied to the school's budgeting and purchasing processes. The principal should be familiar with the purchasing procedures of the system and the practices in the school. The idea of "those who share, care" also applies to the purchasing of instructional supplies and equipment. The faculty easily can feel as if they are not part of the purchasing cycle, particularly in giving feedback regarding quality to responsible officials. A sensitive principal can alleviate this problem and at the same time upgrade the quality of the supplies and equipment in the building as related to use and effectiveness. For instance, Product A may be judged by an off-site purchasing agent to be superior to Product B, but if the users almost always select Product B, then B is "better."

Certain details of the acquisition process may become the responsibility of the individual school if the supplies and equipment are delivered to the school directly by or from the vendor. In this case, the principal should see that the following steps are taken when receiving shipments:

1. Check the outside of the cartons or crates for damage as a result of shipping.
2. Note any damage, on the bill of lading, before signing for the shipment.
3. Check the contents to confirm that they are the same and in the same amount as those that were ordered and billed.
4. Notify the central office of the shipment, with instructions to pay for it if all is in order. The process for doing this varies from system to system but usually consists of forwarding a copy of the vendor's invoice and a local form.
5. Process the shipment for storage and distribution. In the case of textbooks or equipment, this usually means stamping or stenciling the school name and assigning a coded, serialized number to each item. In the case of expensive equipment, this coded number can be etched on the equipment at various points and the number and equipment description registered with local or state police to aid in recovery if the equipment is stolen.
6. Record the acquisition of supplies or equipment in the appropriate inventory book, card, or computer file. A record of the warranty and where repairs are to be made should be entered at the time of acquisition, for easy retrieval.

A perpetual inventory system should be maintained so that at any point in time the amount and location of supplies, materials, and equipment can be determined.

A hypercard application may be useful to locate equipment and specialized facilities, even room assignments. A periodic check of this inventory should be made. Checks may be necessary for selected supply items each month, and for others toward the end of each semester. At least once per year all items of supply and equipment should be inventoried.

STORAGE

Storage space seems to be a perpetual problem. It may be necessary to send nearly all supplies directly to the rooms in which they will be used.

Supplies Requisition Someday School		
Teacher		**Date**
Quantity	**Unit**	**Item**
		Newsprint, 9×12
		Newsprint, 18×24
	Ream	Newsprint, lined 9×12
	Dozen	Pencils, #2
	Roll	Cello tape
	Box	Staples

FIGURE 18.1
Supplies requisition: Someday School

This approach has obvious disadvantages, including the fact that few rooms have adequate storage space. In addition, the possibility of the mismanagement of the supplies is much greater. The pack rat in each of us has an opportunity to develop into a full-blown hoarder. It is desirable to make some provision for central storage space. The principal must then decide whether to have open or closed storage.

Open storage has at least the following advantages: standard supplies are available on very short notice; the need to hoard private caches of supplies is reduced, thus making perpetual inventory figures more real; and office paperwork and personnel time are reduced. Disadvantages of open storage include the possibility of a questionable inventory as a result of haste and added time to a teacher's already busy day. Occasionally, it is tempting to send pupils to gather supplies and deliver them.

Closed storage solves nearly all of the foregoing disadvantages. It also ties the diminishing levels of supplies more closely to those involved in the acquisition function. Closed storage can actually save the teachers time. A simple checklist of available supplies can be distributed to the faculty (see Figure 18.1). If all rooms are computer connected to the office, then e-mail communication could be used. A distribution schedule can be set up using custodial or, in some instances, student personnel so that the teachers know that supplies requisitioned by a particular time will be delivered after a specified time interval—for example, in twenty-four hours, in half a day, or by 10 A.M. the next day.

INVENTORIES

A perpetual inventory system is recommended. A simple balance sheet or a card for each item can provide an instant status report of frequently used supplies. A periodic check of the balances will provide information for requisitioning supplies, and if plotted over the year, it will give the office a means for anticipating next year's needs.

The principal will be evaluating the administrative processes of the office, and the management of supplies and equipment is no exception. The checklist in Figure 18.2 may be helpful in assessing the supplies and equipment acquisition and accounting process.

Adequacy	Yes	No	Comments
1. Supplies are appropriate to all instructional areas.			
2. Quantities of supplies will last for the year.			
3. Supplies are standardized for the district.			
4. Equipment is appropriate for all instructional areas.			
5. Equipment is in working order.			
6. Supplies and equipment are allotted on the same basis for all schools.			
7. Supplies are delivered on time without delaying the instructional process.			
8. Storage facilities are adequate.			
Maintenance/Replacement			
1. Equipment is on a regular maintenance schedule that is followed.			
2. Equipment is on a replacement schedule.			
3. Equipment repairs cause minimal down time.			
4. Inventory is centrally controlled.			
5. Teachers and staff know how to refer problems.			

continued

FIGURE 18.2
An equipment and supplies checklist

Acquisition	Yes	No	Comments
1. Emergency acquisitions are possible.			
2. Selection process includes users.			
3. Computer and paper trails are complete in the building and central office.			
4. Warranty and repair information is readily available on each piece.			
5. District supply/equipment catalogs are available to faculty and staff.			
Utilization			
1. All instructional areas have access.			
2. Faculty know how to use the equipment.			
3. Faculty know policies related to use.			
4. Users know the allotment process.			

FIGURE 18.2 (*continued*)

As in most management functions, the time spent on supply and equipment management can easily outweigh its relative worth if the principal does not guard against such a situation occurring. If he or she can enlist the aid of each staff member in properly evaluating and using supplies and equipment, a good portion of the task is done.

Ⓢ U M M A R Y

Handling the business affairs of a school well provides a credibility to internal and external publics so that other less visible or measurable results can be achieved. Careful attention to details, adherence to fiscal and personal integrity, and genuine efforts toward more efficient business practices that can enhance more effective learning are important if the school is to continue to improve. Balancing the business aspects with the learning and instructional aspects of the school is an important task for the principal.

Ⓕ OR FURTHER THOUGHT

1. How can budget building become a dynamic educational leadership process? How can it become a hindrance to educational improvement? Does either necessarily cost any more?
2. What policies are in place for your school or district to safeguard students and the schools from exclusive marketing contracts?

3. Survey a number of site-based management schools and find out how many patterns of (a) budget allocation and (b) faculty participation in the budget process there are.
4. What is the difference between accounting and accountability?
5. Debate: All activity funds, regardless of source, should revert to the general activity fund at the close of the fiscal year and be rebudgeted.
6. Should student organizations be encouraged to make money? Discuss pros and cons.
7. Distinguish between a zero-based budget and an incremental budget. What are the advantages and disadvantages of each?
8. Devise a plan so that administration of the activity fund can be a learning and responsibility experience for students and still be properly supervised by the board of education.
9. In your district, how are foundation funds used?
10. What safeguards might the central administrators create to discourage principals from emphasizing the business manager role?
11. Discuss the possibilities and pitfalls of a community of parents and patrons becoming a financial "booster club" for the school's needs.

ⓈELECTED READINGS

Drake, Thelbert L., and William H. Roe. *School Business Management: Supporting Instructional Effectiveness.* Boston: Allyn & Bacon, 1994.

Dunn, Rita. "The Missing Factor in Accountability: Improving Internal Control Practices for School Financial Management." *Connections* 3 (April 18, 2001). Accessible at www.nassp.org/connections.

Hardy, Lawrence. "The Lure of School Marketing." *School Business Affairs* 66 (May 2000): 17–21.

Natale, Jo Anna. "When Fund-Raisers Go for the Gold, Do Schools Get the Shaft?" *Executive Educator* 12 (June 1990): 17–19.

Odden, Allan. "Raising Performance Levels without Increasing Funding." *School Business Affairs* 63 (June 1997): 4–12.

Pijanowski, John C., and David H. Monk. "Alternative School Revenue Sources." *School Business Affairs* 62 (July 1996): 4–10.

Sandri, Edward R. "Preventing Fund-Raising Fraud." *Executive Educator* 14 (February 1992): 39–41.

CHAPTER 19

Facilities Management

*T*he principal has a key role in the planning and operation of the school facility. The school facility itself is a communications medium. Its appearance, design, and even the freedom in its use communicate much to pupils, staff, and the community at large, and to visitors, prospective new businesses, and neighboring communities. Yet school buildings are aging into becoming obstructive rather than facilitative to effective learning and instruction. Uline notes that "[f]or too many communities, the definition of 'decent' facilities remains narrow and miserly."[1] Part of the problem may be the way school districts communicate the needs of learners and teachers and how not adequately meeting those needs affects the learning outcomes. "We speak about the value of education and the need to reconceive schools, but the message is often incoherent and inarticulate and so too are the architectural outcomes."[2] Stevenson bluntly states that "[b]etter physical conditions produce better student outcomes."[3] There are strong cases to be made to renovate or build new facilities that enhance rather than inhibit learning. The principal can be helpful in articulating in language clear to all members of the community exactly how learning is affected by the current and proposed facilities.

FACILITIES EVALUATION

The principal will receive a great deal of input regarding the effectiveness of the building from faculty, students, and maintenance staff. If the building is frequently used by community groups, they, too, will have

---

[1] Cynthia L. Uline, "Decent Facilities and Learning: Thirman A. Milner Elementary School and Beyond," *Teachers College Record* 102 (February 2000): 457.
[2] Ibid.
[3] Kenneth Stevenson, "School Physical Environment and Structure: Their Relationship to Student Outcomes," *School Business Affairs* 67 (February 2001): 44.

suggestions. These suggestions are accompanied by expectations that the principal will do something about them, if no more than to route them to decision-making levels at which changes can be effected. To limit "facility evaluation" to such input places the principal in a reactive role. It is much better to provide a formal evaluation program that can incorporate suggestions from community groups.

In larger school districts, a continual evaluation of existing facilities is often conducted by a facilities planner or a unit of the business administrator's office. Ordinarily, these evaluations are concerned with the safety, maintenance, and energy use of the building and grounds and the facilities' pupil capacities. Questions to be answered include at least the following:

1. Are minimal health standards physically provided for in first aid care facilities, food service areas, restrooms, showers, lockers, heating, air circulation, and construction materials?
2. Are safety standards observed for these areas as well as within all shops, gymnasiums, outdoor areas, and disaster shelter areas?
3. Are the lighting, thermal, and sonic levels healthful and comfortable?
4. Are the components of communication equipment (telephones, two-way radios, pagers, etc.) in working order so emergency messages can be sent and received quickly?
5. Is security equipment updated and fully operable?
6. Is the building maintained so that health and safety standards are met and the building and grounds are pleasant?
7. Is the energy use efficient, given the weather conditions in the location?

The primary focus of the facility evaluation will be on the facility's educational adequacy. Specific evaluation questions must be set in the context of the school's overall mission in meeting the needs of the community and society at large. The answers to the questions need to be framed so that they fit into the systemwide planning process and policy development. Examples of some such questions follow:

1. Are the rooms or spaces available for changing instructional patterns throughout the instructional day? Are they adequate for the anticipated groupings and activities?
2. Is there access to and functional provisions for individuals with disabilities?
3. Are there nonfunctional areas either within the building or on the grounds? The principal may wish to be alert to dysfunctional areas, such as recessed entranceways, stairwells, and the

like, that might encourage vandalism or provide opportunities for violence.

4. Does the design provide for flexibility as new instructional modes are used? For instance, can all the rooms "talk" to a set of databases on and off site as well as to each other? Is fiber-optic wiring or wireless access equipment in place and operable?

5. Are space relationships such that student and faculty time can be used efficiently?

6. Do instructional or noninstructional activities in one area negatively affect instruction in another area?

7. Are equipment and spaces on an appropriate scale for the users? For example, the average classroom today is 900 square feet in area. Tanner sees 25 percent of all U.S. schools as overcrowded, partly because we have not considered social distance in calculating the minimum size of a classroom. He suggests 1,029 square feet for 20 elementary students and 1,344 square feet for 20 secondary students.[4]

8. Are there adequate and secure storage areas close to use areas? (Drama programs and computer work areas are often vulnerable to outgrowing secure storage space.)

9. Are electrical and plumbing services available where needed?

As mentioned previously, in the evaluation of a facility, the principal will be focusing on the relationship between the building and the educational programs that building is to serve. Once the process of establishing the priorities is completed and the staff to be involved in the evaluation understand the process as it applies to them, the mechanics of the evaluation (i.e., completing the forms or surveys, or group processes) can be carried out efficiently.

The communication of the results of the evaluation should follow a previously agreed-on form and distribution schedule. As with the evaluation of a new facility, misinterpretation of the results can offset the gains of a careful evaluation.

Look for Alternative Uses

Most facilities are not overly endowed with storage space, free space, or underutilized space, particularly given the closing of some schools and changes in modes of instructional delivery. Yet possibilities for additional uses do exist in most buildings. Corridors present opportunities for displaying student work. Simple wooden strips can provide almost limitless

---

[4] C. Kenneth Tanner, "The Classroom: Size versus Density," *School Business Affairs* 66 (December 2000): 22.

tack-board space. If regulations discourage the use of wood, screens of fireproof, porous tile can serve the same purpose and add an interesting dimension to often dismal, drab hallways. Local fire and safety regulations must be checked before changes are made.

The site can be used exclusively for recess, noontime activities, and structured physical education classes, or it can become part of nearly every class offered in the school. Science, art, history, literature, and mathematics can each become very involved in the miniature environment of a school site. Using the site as a springboard to related activities provides almost unlimited possibilities. For example, a group exploring measuring to determine area could become quickly involved in the history of surveying, the practicalities of boundaries, deeds, municipal government, and so on.

If the school is fortunate enough to have easy access to a natural area as part of the school site or at a nearby location, it can be converted to a great science/nature area by students, teachers, and community participants. Such an area can enhance several programs as well as provide a resource to the community in general.[5]

Community and Interagency Uses

The use of the building by community groups and agencies is, of course, controlled by board of education policy and administrative procedures. If procedures are not clear, the principal should make every effort to clarify and improve them where needed. The following may serve as a checklist for the principal, or preferably the services coordinator, who faces requests from community groups as attempts are made to involve the community more through extending the use of the available facilities:

1. What written policies are available regarding the use of the school buildings?
2. Who gives final approval? What routing is specified?
3. What steps are necessary to initiate requests? What forms?
4. How are charges determined?
5. What arrangements must be made for custodial services?
6. What community services should be notified (e.g., police, security patrol)? What are the appropriate procedures for this?
7. How much time should be allowed for each step and for the total request-approval process?
8. What measures should be taken with the faculty regarding the use of the building by community groups?

---

[5] C. Kenneth Tanner, "Into the Woods, Wetlands and Prairies," *Educational Leadership* 58 (April 2001): 64–67.

9. If the buildings can be scheduled by someone other than the principal, services coordinator, or administrative assistant, what safeguards exist to avoid scheduling conflicts?

Given the interest in continuing education and developing new skills to use time and resources wisely, increased utilization of the school building by the community makes good economic and public relations sense. The emergence of collaborative ventures like full-service schools (see Chapter 3) affects planning and scheduling. Use by religious clubs or groups can cause controversy, whether the use is granted or denied. Careful thought is needed in formulating policy regarding the use of public facilities by private groups.[6] The principal's sensitivity to the interests and needs of the people surrounding the building can lead to cooperation among the continuing education, recreation, and social agencies in using the building more fully. While an awareness of private enterprises is essential, the creative use of the buildings in a school system might bring opportunities to people who could not otherwise have them.

RELATIONSHIPS AND RESPONSIBILITIES REGARDING CUSTODIAL STAFF

An important consideration is the relationship of the school principal to the custodians in the building, the director of the school plant, and/or the supervisor of custodians. Invariably, one of the contributing factors in any troubled area is a lack of clear-cut understanding of the administrative relationships of these three positions. This area of school operation should not be a mystery. The relationships can be easily understood and spelled out, but mutual understanding, respect, and cooperation will need to be developed and maintained over time.

The principal may find himself or herself in a traditional situation, one in which he or she is responsible for all activities and functions carried on in the building. Strictly interpreted, this would give the principal immediate direction and supervision over all custodial employees in the building. The question then arises: Why should someone such as the principal, who knows little or nothing about custodial work, direct it? On the other hand, if the community, a site advisory board, and the central administration hold the principal primarily or exclusively responsible for educational leadership, an assistant (such as a services coordinator) will be primarily responsible for seeing that the maintenance and operations functions for the building are done satisfactorily.

---

[6] Ralph D. Mawdsley and Charles J. Russo, "Religious Groups and the Use of Public School Facilities," *School Business Affairs* 67 (February 2001): 45–50.

A supervisor for custodial services may be given responsibility for and authority over the operational functions throughout the district—except direct administration of the custodian in a building. Thus, the supervisor can determine what work should be done, establish standards of how it should be done by developing schedules, furnish the where-withal to do the work by providing supplies and equipment, and even see that it is done properly by inspecting and reporting through appropriate channels.

Several aids, in the form of task/time charts, are available to the principal and/or supervisor to help assess job performance and monitor the accomplishment of maintenance tasks. A loose-leaf book of scheduled daily, weekly, or monthly tasks can be compiled to help monitor the work. With such a tool, the services coordinator or principal should be able to pinpoint what task is being done at what location at almost any time of day.

In the traditional situation, the principal could still be considered the immediate administrator; otherwise, a services coordinator or a centrally assigned supervisor would perform this function for the specific building. Further clarification of relationships may be made by spelling out some of the duties of the supervisor of the school plant operation.[7]

When a principal's services coordinator or a central office person is responsible for the custodial services in the building, this means that that individual

- Is administratively or managerially responsible for the custodial personnel in the building;
- Determines, in cooperation with the supervisor, the personnel needed on long-term and emergency bases;
- Confers with the custodian on workload and work schedule;
- Inspects the building, compares schedules with accomplishments, and suggests improvements;
- Directs that emergency deviation from schedules be made and that out-of-routine chores be accomplished;
- Interviews and approves custodians assigned to the building;
- Recommends disciplinary action and correction; and
- Evaluates the custodians' work in line with the latter's contribution to the total objectives of the school (this function would, in most instances, be the principal's responsibility).

The principal may wish to explore with the central administration the possibilities of contracting for certain custodial services. Not only are there the advantages of not providing fringe benefits, avoiding hiring-

---

[7] For additional detail regarding custodial job expectations, see *Custodial Staffing Guidelines for Educational Institutions*, ed. Jack C. Dudley (Alexandria, VA: Association of Physical Plant Administrators, 1992).

firing problems, and not offering training programs for special needs, but contracting often makes enforcing performance standards easier.

By accepting the responsibility of an administrator, the principal or coordinator becomes responsible for each custodian's welfare and also for general performance on the job. The custodian cannot be left to himself or herself, and the work cannot be considered beneath the dignity of the principal's concern. Above all, the custodian must be accepted as part of the team assembled to render an important service to education.

ENERGY CONSERVATION

Given the recent rolling blackouts, the restricted output from energy companies, and the price instability of energy, schools simply can no longer afford to ignore energy conservation. Given tax limitations, it is probably unlikely that additional local revenues will be generated for supporting energy-wasting practices and facilities; therefore, the dollars will come from some other budget line. Regardless of energy source, energy consumption and cost can be reduced with the use of simple conservation and measures that foster constant awareness and monitoring of use. Such savings might be particularly important to a single building budget if a lump sum including utilities costs has been allocated to the building site administrator.

An example of the multiple benefits to be gained by examining present practices is that of a Massachusetts school that retrofitted exterior lighting with low-energy-use sodium lights. The new lights provided more light for security and maintenance activities, and the savings in energy costs—and a reduction in vandalism—paid for the changeover in fifteen months.

Energy audits have shown how to reduce energy costs by as much as 50 percent. Annual school calendars may need to be made with very cold or hot days in mind as well as snow days. Some districts have changed to four-day weeks to help in the use of energy, maintenance, and transportation.

BARRIER-FREE DESIGN

If schools are to provide opportunities for all to achieve in the least restrictive environment, administrators must develop a sensitivity to the facility's barriers to people with disabilities. Too often the physical aspects of initial access and movement are all that are considered. That is, are ramps available, and are the doors wide enough?

Although these things are essential, the principal should be assisting the total school in viewing a barrier-free environment more broadly.

For instance, once inside the classroom or general instructional space, is the student limited to certain types of instruction? Are the materials in a personalized learning center accessible? Can the student go to and use the media center, computer lab, or recreation area?

Would it be possible that the school could be minimally adequate for the disabled student but practically preclude an adult with disabilities from working in the building? Would the building's design effectively deter a parent in a wheelchair from visiting the school? If the school is used by adults for continuing education, cultural, and/or recreation activities, are only able-bodied persons privileged to participate?

The student or teacher with a broken leg, sprained ankle, or other accident-related temporary disability will also benefit from the barrier-free building and site. But other emergency situations should be considered. If rapid evacuation of the building or quick movement to shelter areas is necessary, not only is barrier-free design essential, but also a well-rehearsed plan for the movement of disabled students and staff is critical.

Many frustrations and even dangers arise when people with disabilities try to use many of the facilities the nondisabled use almost effortlessly. Imagine settling into a wheelchair for a short trip. Now try to get a drink at the water fountain. Attend a meeting and see how close to the table you can sit. Write a note at your desk. Little things mean a lot. Other problems that may not occur to the nondisabled might include the height of fire alarms and telephones, or a grill-like covering on a floor, or the width of doors. For further detail, refer to the sources in the Selected Readings, your own state guidelines, and the Americans with Disabilities Act.

RENOVATION AND/OR ADDITIONS

Educational facilities in many locations are in poor repair and do not facilitate technology applications needed for today's students. The U.S. General Accounting Office has estimated that $116 billion is needed to restore buildings to good condition and adapt them to needed learning and teaching technologies.[8] School renovations have gone far beyond painting, cleaning, and repairing to making major upgrades of the infrastructure to accommodate technology, teaching teams, community involvement, and child care.

Some questions need to be answered affirmatively before spending funds to renovate a building:

---

[8] Don I. Tharpe, "The Unique Problems of Inner City and Urban Districts," *School Business Affairs* 63 (April 1997): 29.

1. Will the renovated building be needed for at least 75 percent of its useful life?
2. Is the redistribution of pupils to nearby schools impractical?
3. Do the long-range plans cite needs for a renovated facility?
4. Do the structure and site lend themselves to meeting minimum standards prescribed by local and state regulations?
5. Will the changed building be adaptable to curricular or organizational changes (e.g., changes in technology) ten or fifteen years from now?
6. What is the cost of renovation over time as compared with the useful life of new construction?

The principal obviously plays a key role in bringing concerns to the attention of the central administration or in planning with it to provide facilities that really facilitate educational programs. Needs must be stated in terms of programmatic documentation rather than in a series of inconvenience complaints.

RELOCATABLES

It is estimated that over one-third of school districts use relocatable (portable) classrooms.[9] Temporary structures can accommodate sudden changes in enrollments, relocation needs resulting from natural disasters, and a number of other challenges. However, relocatable buildings should never be viewed as a substitute for planned, "permanent" structures or as a cheaper way out of traditional buildings. When traditional construction is not practical in the short run, temporary structures can serve useful purposes. Fleming cites four criteria when considering relocatables: Can the classroom be delivered on time? Do the vendors have creditable construction experience? Does the relocatable fit into a long-range plan? What are the costs?[10] In most situations, the cost of a relocatable classroom should be about half or less the cost of conventional construction. Therein, of course, lies the temptation toward permanency.

PLANNING A NEW FACILITY

Planning a new facility affords unlimited opportunities for the principal to show leadership ability. The planning process is a chance to make significant contributions to the education of generations, not a chore or an

[9] C. Kenneth Tanner, "The Classroom: Size versus Density," *School Business Affairs* 66 (December 2000): 22.
[10] James A. Fleming, "The Saga of Relocatable Classrooms," *School Administrator* 54 (June 1997): 14.

added burden. Few situations provide a greater chance for in-depth involvement with faculty and parents than focusing on issues central to what education is all about. Planning a new facility or a major renovation demands the clarification of the school's goals and objectives and the identification of the means by which those objectives are to be reached, not only for the year the building is completed but also for years thereafter. Given the rapid changes in needs and teaching technologies, therein lies a challenge.

All parts of the education community should be interacting with each other to seek optimal solutions. The board of education, the community, the central administration, the building administrator, teachers, parents, pupils, and university specialists should be involved. Indeed, it is the duty of the principal to see that he or she and the staff are involved. Although complete development of the planning process is not within the scope of this chapter, the principal should be conversant with it and ever ready to influence it. Therefore, a brief description of the process follows.

The Planning Process

Planning a building does not begin with the idea that a new building may be needed. The professional staff of the school system must consider continual planning an integral responsibility of the school itself. Planning must be planned for. It entails two phases: (1) systemwide, long-range, continual planning and evaluation and (2) the specific planning for a specific facility.

Long-Range Planning. The principal and staff need to be part of districtwide, long-range planning that encompasses all facilities as much as they are part of planning for a specific facility with which they are to be working. The principal should be involved in the following steps:

- Continual appraisal of existing facilities in regard to educational adequacy
- Awareness of new curricular and organizational patterns on the horizon that will impact existing facilities
- Awareness of emerging instructional technologies
- Continual assessment of population shifts in the attendance area and the enrollment implications of those shifts
- Awareness of new housing planned within the attendance area boundaries
- Awareness of changes in land usage within the attendance area boundaries
- Maintenance of meaningful communication with the attendance area citizens

Much has been written about the long-range planning for school facilities. The Selected Readings at the end of this chapter will help the principal who wishes to pursue the matter in depth.

Planning a Specific Facility. The principal is involved in at least five planning steps: educational planning; schematic design; equipping; orienting staff, students, and community; and continual evaluation.

Educational Planning. The expression of the planned educational program for a specific facility should be written in the form of educational specifications. Contrary to popular belief, the architect does not, and should not, develop the educational specifications. This is the responsibility of the school's professional staff. The educators, knowing about environmental factors important to teachers and learning and about the human input important to the total process, are the persons who must develop the educational specifications. The principal must insist on being involved and on having teachers involved also.

Yet the principal must be aware of certain pitfalls of being involved and involving the faculty. When teachers are asked to assist in the preparation of educational specifications, they are too often left to work completely on their own on the requirements for grades or subjects of their own particular interest. They dream great dreams, they develop exciting ideas, and then when they submit their report, it is tossed out as unrealistic. This is both disheartening and unfair. Prior to their involvement, the principal must see that the faculty are properly oriented to their task. This may be as simple as checking to see that the person responsible for the overall planning has made provisions for adequate and realistic orientation. The following guidelines might be helpful to prepare the faculty:

1. Provide information regarding the overall charge to the building planners.
2. Supply information regarding the procedures for review and approval, to minimize misunderstandings.
3. State the realistic limitations in terms of time, space, and financial considerations.
4. Offer helpful readings to stimulate ideas and more precise thinking. If possible, provide field trips to instructionally innovative schools and facilities seeking to achieve excellence.[11]

---

[11] For supplemental reading, see the Selected Readings. In addition, a number of organizations, such as the American Association of School Administrators, the Educational Facilities Laboratory (New York), several leading architectural firms, and the Council of Educational Facility Planners, publish stimulating materials.

Contents of Educational Specifications. Educational specifications describe who and how many will be involved in what kinds of learning situations and activities, during what times, and in what kind of relationships to other activities, both instructional and noninstructional. Such descriptions will require that space relationships, major pieces of equipment and furniture, and special environmental needs be included.

The school's goals and objectives are not static and will not remain the same tomorrow as they are today. Change occurs at an ever-increasing rate, to the point where our society has been described as "turbulent." The planning group is being asked to plan a structure that will be with the community for the next forty, fifty, or more years. What will be the goals, objectives, and means of reaching those objectives in 2060 A.D.? Will the core of the school be a media production center, with several studios for recording and for live programs? Will students need access connectors for their laptops? Should not all interior space be easily changed? Will there even be such things as "classes," in terms of a fixed number of students with a teacher assigned to a single space for a year? Will groups of students be engaged in service learning in the community, tapping national information sources and preparing electronically assisted reports? Castaldi states that the task is to "plan a building that is so flexible and adaptable that it can accommodate the unanticipated needs of future educational practices."[12]

Technology. As discussed in the previous chapter, budgeting for technology is essential to maintain currency. In planning for a new facility, or even finding space in an old or renovated facility, one must look as far into the future as possible, especially concerning technology. Rooms set aside as computer laboratories may be obsolete. Schools are now going "wireless" to provide access to the Internet and to portable tools for producing writing, reports, presentations, and so on. Instead of two wires connected to each computer, wireless-enabled laptops give students and teachers access wherever they are on campus. Cost comparisons favor wireless networks over the traditional arrangements.[13] In one sense, the computer laboratory can go to the students, along with the support person, rather than the students going to a remote laboratory. The rooms that were used as computer laboratories can now be converted to other uses or that new space planned to serve multiple purposes.

The principal must not be trapped into planning a facility to serve today's children using today's methods only. He or she must help plan for turbulence, for the unknown and the unforeseeable. With such a perspective set, the program anticipated for the next few years can be described.

---

[12] Basil Castaldi, *Educational Facilities* (Boston: Allyn & Bacon, 1994), 161.
[13] Sylvia Charp, "Wireless Networks," *T.H.E. Journal* 28 (January 2001): 12–14.

Space Relationships. Too often the educator tends to attempt the architect's job of making specific drawings. Rather than drawing details, or even specific shapes, it is best to express space relationships between clusters of activity by using circlelike designations, with some means of identifying the hierarchy of necessity for relationships.[14]

Occasionally, the relationships between certain indoor-based activities and the outdoors, or the site, are overlooked. The ones usually thought of first are the physical education and sports activities. However, many other activities should be considered when planning the site and relationships between the indoor and outdoor areas. Elementary through high school science should be incorporating the outdoors. The outdoors holds a wealth of material for the mathematics and social studies classes. In short, the site itself should be considered as learning space and planned accordingly. It should not be considered merely as a place to play ball or line up pupils during fire drills.

Orientation to the New Facility. The following points may serve as guidelines and idea stimulators for the principal helping plan the orientation:

1. Faculty members should know all the physical features of the building.
2. Faculty members should be able to explain, programmatically, why their particular area was designed as it was.
3. The faculty should be aware of the true economies in the building, such as energy conservation, time and space usage, low-maintenance materials, low-cost conversion to multiple uses, and so forth. Although some initial costs may have been greater as a result of some of these items, the long-range expenditures will be less.
4. Students should be made an integral part of the orientation. The fact that students will be the taxpayers of tomorrow is no small consideration. In addition, the orientation process gives students the opportunities to develop leadership among their peers, work with adults from the community and staff, and strengthen student organization ties with the total educational system.
5. Scouts, study groups, club members, community recreation participants, library users, and others who will be using the building should learn about the facilities available and the rationale for each of the aforementioned points.

---

[14] For examples of ways to express these space relationships, see the most current *Guide for Planning Educational Facilities* (Columbus, OH: Council of Educational Facility Planners) or Castaldi's *Educational Facilities,* cited in note 12.

6. The community in general should be made aware of the projected use of the building, its costs, and how it will help achieve the community's purposes. Faculty, staff, students, and, where possible, parents should be involved in the community orientation process.

Evaluating the New Facility. The evaluation of a new facility is a necessary part of the total planning process. Such evaluative feedback to both the central administrative office and the architect via that office should be accepted as routine responsibility. The principal's role will focus mainly on the program adequacy of the new facility.

Various evaluation forms may be found in the literature; however, it will be desirable for the principal and staff to tailor the evaluation to their own programs. This process should clearly state the program objectives and their implications for the learning environment and include the scoring procedures, or weights, applied to specific features of the environment. For example, if a high-priority program objective is to increase students' communication skills, the scoring weights assigned to provision of individual study stations might be quite different from that which a faculty might assign to the same facilities serving a program with an objective of developing individual research skills.

Evaluation of a facility is sensitive. The principal must work with the staff and central administration in such a way that misinformation and misinterpretation are minimized.

SUMMARY

The school building is often an expression of the community regarding itself and the value it places on education. Over time, it can also be an expression of the principal's values in the way it is maintained, used, and valued by students and staff. A key thought is that the term *facility* implies just that—the building should facilitate positive learning. The principal's challenge is, in the face of rapid changes, to seize quickly expanding opportunities to keep the building as a facilitating tool.

FOR FURTHER THOUGHT

1. "Form follows function" is an oft-quoted sentence used in connection with solutions to architectural problems. Does this adage apply to designing a school that proposes to educate in, and for, an ever-changing society in which the "functions" are unknown? Discuss.
2. Examine schools built in the 1940s, 1960s, and 1990s. Which features in these buildings reflect changes in educational practices?

3. Discuss how "opening up" an environment might cause greater restrictiveness.
4. Sometimes the way certain spaces are used becomes an unbendable tradition. How might the problem be avoided?
5. In a wheelchair, tour a school building built in the 1950s.
6. In your school, what process is used to monitor maintenance tasks?
7. Survey several districts to see which instruments are used in evaluating the educational effectiveness of buildings.
8. How might you anticipate the next set of teaching technologies and restructured patterns to facilitate learning?

ⓈELECTED READINGS

Castaldi, Basil. *Educational Facilities.* Boston: Allyn & Bacon, 1994.

DeJong, William S. "Building Change into New Buildings." *School Administrator* 54 (June 1997): 10–13.

Drake, Thelbert L., and William H. Roe. *School Business Management: Supporting Instructional Effectiveness.* Boston: Allyn & Bacon, 1994.

Guide for Planning Educational Facilities. Columbus, OH: Council of Educational Facility Planners, 1985.

Stevenson, Kenneth. "School Physical Environment and Structure: Their Relationship to Student Outcomes." *School Business Affairs* 67 (February 2001): 40–44.

Tharpe, Don I. "The Unique Problems of Inner City and Urban Districts." *School Business Affairs* 63 (April 1997): 29–36.

Uline, Cynthia L. "Decent Facilities and Learning: Thirman A. Milner Elementary School and Beyond." *Teachers College Record* 102 (February 2000): 442–460.

Conclusion

Reflections

*W*hat an exciting time to be principal of a school—a time of great expectations; a time when one can access (and be accessed by) instantly an infosphere of data and opinions; and a time when schools are the focus of attention. Opportunities abound to lead students and adults to a shared vision of academic excellence in a framework of responsible, caring behavior. But it requires a strong, grounded person to deal with the inevitable bumps in the road that has occasional blind curves and goes uphill from time to time.

Many voices clamor to be heard in the din of demands and opinions—voices that call on the schools to turn out economic competitors; voices that stridently deride bigotry but that would deny the right to believe or practice belief in an equally bigoted manner; voices that want the schools to return to the simple things that maybe never existed. All these and many other voices may be seeking to make the school in their own images. The school can become splintered into fragmented curricula so that the easiest thing for the members of the school to do is live in their own small worlds, do what they can, and hope it all comes out right in the end. After all, one person really cannot take responsibility for the whole thing, right? And so once again the school becomes a jousting area where various scholarly, political, or economic groups try to gain dominance over each other.

Peering around the corner of time toward the not-so-distant future, we may see our life spans extending to 120 years, worldwide information systems being tapped as we move from location to location, and communication systems spanning the spectrum of sight and sound and transcending former language barriers. Robotics will enable us to manufacture flawless products, clean and protect our dwellings, prepare our meals, and whisk us from place to place when we wish. Widespread hunger may exist only in electronic memories if we can find ways to eliminate people's inhumanity to people.

As we are caught up in the sweep of these possibilities, to our minds comes the image of a human-made Garden of Eden (sans snake) where we float, fly, and ride around in artistic, architecturally imposing malls and parks, popping pills for sustenance, rejuvenation, and revelation. All the while, automated industries are grinding out every possible gadget to relieve us of the necessity of doing anything physical for ourselves.

Have schools by default let advertising and entertainment media create these images of "beauty" and material things to emulate or accumulate as ultimate ends to be achieved? Should we be going beyond the material means toward a vision of how we should be relating to each other and the world in which we live? Or is it best to focus on improving test scores to ensure the school will still operate and our jobs are still there? What humans are doing to themselves and what they are doing to their environment in this ever-increasing taste for materialism as an end in itself should give us pause. Homelessness, hunger, and disease are not limited to foreign countries. Those conditions exist in our cities and towns and countryside. Even the outbreak of war or the senseless acts on September 11, 2001 are the result of the failure of human wisdom.

EXPECTATIONS AND MYTHS

A clear understanding of what is expected in a particular role such as the principalship can be comforting. All one has to do to be successful is to do those things expected of us and do them correctly: in short, do things right. Two problems arise, however. Different groups (e.g., business owners, parents, teachers, students) have different sets of expectations for the principal. The lack of congruency among those sets of expectations poses some serious problems for the would-be leader. How can she or he do all those things right?

One expectation is in the form of a myth—that education, as the consumer defines it, can solve societal and economic problems and lead the recipients of that education to the good life. This is just not true! More responsibility has been thrust on our schools than they should have accepted; more results have been expected than they could possibly have produced; and in too many cases, schools have assumed more than they should. An approach to dispelling this myth is to admit that the schools cannot function as a surrogate conscience for society, nor should society impose on schools the task of correcting, on their own, all of society's ills.

Educators do not need to believe that they alone should lead the way to the good life, that individual dreams can be realized simply by going to school and successfully completing the work. Regarded objectively, this is a most arrogant point of view. On the other hand, in the face of the great problems facing our society, the educator needs to say to the people about the schools, "We are one of the great and important social institutions of our nation. Let's work in partnership to identify important goals of our society, and then let's work hand in hand in reaching them." Certainly, in today's complicated society, much more should be done in networking social agencies so that a greater concentration of force can be exerted on needed improvements.

DREAMS DENIED?

Many pioneer educators dedicated their lives to the crusade against ignorance, poverty, and social injustice and strove mightily for an educational system with an extended role in social improvement. Many parents denied themselves to send their children to schools so those children could realize their dreams and the dreams of the parents. Education was seen as the answer. These dreams need not be abandoned, but it is time for the educational leader to become more realistic about how they are to be accomplished.

Although the educator has essential control over schooling, he or she has but nominal control over the extensive learning going on outside the school. Schools interact with students only 9 percent of their lives up to high school graduation. With over 90 percent of a student's life being outside school, good teachers may hope to guide the total learning experience but actually have little or no control over it. Both educators and the public at large should understand this.

Second, many problems are major by-products of our society. Schools should not shoulder complete responsibility for their assessment or solution, nor accept blame for their existence, but they also should not be guilty of reinforcing the problems. A few such societal by-products are racial and religious prejudice, drugs, violence, diseases, child neglect and abuse, and teenage pregnancy. However, the school can and should take appropriate leadership in alerting and working with the local and state community, which should be seeking solutions. In addition, the school must develop specific procedures for dealing with these problems when they emerge in the school itself.

Third, the public school, as an impartial social agency, must be attentive to the wishes of all the people but responsive ordinarily to the majority, while sensitive to the minority. It cannot hope to please all people and therefore will always be subject to criticism. The school principal is the one who experiences the brunt of this criticism on a face-to-face basis. Criticism must be accepted as "a cross to bear," understanding that healthy diversity is a part of the American way and to be expected in a successful democracy. Principals must know how to deal with criticism and diverse opinions gracefully, how to judge and assess them, and particularly how to utilize criticism to stimulate improvements in the school specifically and in society generally.

Fourth, the American public school is rooted in the history of U.S. civilization, and at any given moment, it necessarily operates as part of the accumulated heritage of this society. Life is not static: society changes; values undergo a revolution; communication technology and transportation shrink the world, causing our society to become intertwined politically and economically with other societies. New roles and functions of the school may chart a different course.

The new education leader must look beyond the school and into the complex, interacting components of society for the creation of the contributing, responsible citizen. The educator's dreams and visions must be shared with the public when rearticulating in a realistic way more specific purposes to be served by our schools. These dreams and visions may include how other social agencies can relate with the school in filling the obvious "voids" of society. Unless shared and mutually accepted visions are formed, the public school will remain misunderstood—a creature of additive reforms occasioned by periodic shifts in public preference, and the perpetual scapegoat for unrealized hopes.

CHANGES ARE NEEDED

Many changes will be necessary. We need to focus on the learner, what is being learned, and what needs to be learned to function in an information age and a global economy. Our organizations need to be more flexible so they can respond to real needs quickly and move on to create new visions of excellence. We need to put into practice structurally and procedurally what we say we believe. We say that we believe teachers should have professional autonomy to meet the diverse educational needs in the classrooms. Instead, we assign time and space and create tests and evaluations that reduce or almost eliminate autonomy of practice, if not of spirit as well. We say we believe students are all different from each other, yet we structure their time, space, and information resources as if they were all the same. We could be accused of reducing the players, teachers and students, to robotlike creatures, reactive and soulless.

The truth may hurt, but we do not teach as well as we know how or establish school environments that provide the best kinds of learning situations. We still teach the textbook and subject matter to classes and groups instead of teaching children. We still operate schools as if all teachers are the same and all children learn the same things at the same rate in the same way. We still teach as if the school is the only place children can learn and they can learn only from adults.

In other words, the thinking educator knows that many areas need improvement in our schools. Now the time is such that we no longer can make excuses, for we have a social environment conducive to change, and our future demands it.

Despite some of the clamor by people on either end of the liberal-conservative continuum, we do not need alternatives to schools as much as we need a variety of alternative forms of schooling within the present educational community. We need to form task teams of teachers, specialists, and community members to study, analyze, and implement solutions. These teams would be temporary and problem focused, and then new teams would be formed to meet new challenges.

It is time for school systems to incorporate diversity, flexibility, and a variety of options and learning places in the school and community so that each pupil can find learning strategies that suit him or her best and can move forward with success in terms of his or her own talents and interests.

ⓈUMMARY

Even with advances in life-extending procedures, cloned body parts, almost instant worldwide news available twenty-four hours a day, and the technology to communicate with each other globally, we find thousands, even millions, of people following leaders committed to hate and destruction, as evidenced on September 11, 2001. Within our own country, we find those who advocate hate and who openly suggest killing one another. We have created a technologically sophisticated society, but we have difficulty creating a caring, responsible one.

The ideological environment is changing also—in intensity if not in new ideas. We often hear and read language in the public sector that refers to spiritual values and experiences. Could this be considered a symptom of an emotional need, a reality search, or disappointment with the ability of material things to satisfy? The progress of art may be a commentary on a search for reality for universals. The title of a Gauguin painting, *What, Whence, Whither?* may express this feeling, much as Picasso's abstractions strive for some universal, apart from forms as we see them. Advertisements to the general public emphasize a self-centeredness. At the same time, a number of religious groups are springing up and rapidly gaining large followings of people who appear to want to be told what to do. It is frighteningly clear how leaders can mesmerize willing followers.

Materials, texts, whole curricula have been written on very specific value systems and/or theological bases. Struggles have occurred between "the state" and individuals and groups of individuals who insist on separate schooling. Will the schools as we now have them become competitors in the marketplace of values and ideas or possibly even be forced to look as if each were made in the federal education foundry, from the same mold?

In a world of diminishing nonrenewable resources, are morals relevant? Is the teaching of morality something to be left to chance? Indeed, is it proper at all to say what is moral or immoral? Or does such a question evade the responsibility to search one's own mind to determine for oneself what morality is or should be? If the principal and teachers are to help improve the quality of life for each person in the school, can they do so without clarifying what their own values are and what they believe? We think not! We believe a principal must go beyond the maintenance of an organization, beyond even leadership in techniques and organization, to face the question of who he or she is, and even why he or she is. Then, and possibly only then, can the principal aid other persons in answering similar questions about themselves. Only then will the principal be able to grasp reality and begin to shape it, adapt to it, and be able to tell which of various actions is appropriate. The leadership that engages in helping a community to consensus about what is right, what needs to be learned, is certainly engaged in moral activity.

What a great time to lead a group of people and the next generation toward responsible and moral solutions to these problems and those that will arise in the future.

⒡OR FURTHER THOUGHT

1. How have the ideas of acquiring wealth, materialism, and success as measured by money influenced the development of education? Has the idea of might makes right also had an effect, and if so, what?
2. Is cooperation natural to humans, or is competition, based on the law of the survival of the fittest, the motivating force? Do schools reinforce either?
3. Do school leaders have any responsible obligation to influence legislation that affects schools?
4. What difference does it make that there is a widening generation gap? After all, the schools should simply be concerned with their students, right?
5. What are the principal areas of misunderstanding, misinformation, and distortion about public education? What are some effective means of clarification?
6. Analyze and discuss the following statement: Uniformity rather than individuality is the major order of the day in too many schools.
7. Debate: Dare the principal take the lead in building a new social order?

8. Are there any identifiable common goals of our society? What is the school's responsibility in helping achieve these goals?

9. Given that some of our problems are worldwide in scope, is worldwide education in order? Are worldwide regulations necessary? What do these issues mean to the school principal?

10. Discuss: Principals must accept criticism as "their cross to bear," understanding that healthy diverse opinions are part of the American way.

Court Cases

Name	Reference	Date
Adams v. Campbell City	511 U.S. 1242	10th Cir. 1975
Arnold v. Carpenter	459 F.2d 939	7th Cir. 1972
Barbin v. State of Louisiana	506 So. 2d 888	La. App. 1987
Bauer v. Minidoka School District No. 331	778 P.2d 336	S. Cty, Idaho, 1989
Bethel School District No. 403 v. Fraser	478 U.S. 675	1986
Board of Education, Island Trees Union Free School District No. 16 v. Pico	457 U.S. 853	1982
Board of Education of Hendrick Hudson School Dist. v. Rowley	458 U.S. 176	1982
Board of Education of Westside Community Schools v. Mergens	110 S. Ct. 2356, 110 L. Ed. 191; 58 USLW 4720	1990
Bott v. Board of Education	392 N.Y.S.2d 274	1977
Bown v. Gwinnett County School District	112 F.3d 1464	11th Cir. 1997
Brown v. Board of Education	347 U.S. 483	1954

Name	Reference	Date
Bystrom v. Fridley High School	822 F.2d 747	8th Cir. 1986
Cedar Rapids v. Garret F.	526 U.S. 66, 119 S. Ct. 992	1999
Ceniceros v. Board of Trustees	66 F.3d 1535	9th Cir. 1995
Clark v. Arizona Interscholastic Association	886 F.2d 1191	U.S. App. 1989
Corporation of Presiding Bishop of Church of Christ of Latter-Day Saints v. Amos	483 U.S. 327	1987
Debra P. v. Turlington	644 F.2d 397	5th Cir. 1981
Denno v. School Board of Volusia County	182 F.3d 780	11th Cir. 1999
Desselle v. Guillary	407 So. 2d 74	La. App. 1982
Dixon v. Alabama State Board of Education	294 F.2d 150	5th Cir. 1961
Dixon v. Alabama State Board of Education	cert. denied, 368 U.S. 930	1961
Doe v. Bolton	694 F. Supp 440	N.D. Ill. 1988
Doe v. Duncanville Independent School District	994 F.2d 160	5th Cir. 1993
Doe v. Koger	480 F. Supp. 225	D.C. Ind. 1979
Doe v. Renfrow	635 F.2d 582	7th Cir. 1980
Doe v. Renfrow	cert. denied, 451 U.S. 1022	1981
Engel v. Vitale	370 U.S. 421	1962
Epperson v. Arkansas	393 U.S. 97	1968
Everson v. Board of Education	330 U.S. 1	1947
Fleischfresser v. Directors of School District	15 F.2d 680	7th Cir. 1994
Force v. Pierre City School District	570 F. Supp. 1020	W.D. Mo. 1983
Gary v. Menche	626 So. 2d 901	La. App. 1993
Goss v. Lopez	419 U.S. 565	1975
Hall v. Board of School Commissioners	656 F.2d 999	5th Cir. 1981

Name	Reference	Date
Hall v. Board of School Commissioners	modified, 707 F.2d 464	5th Cir. 1983
Harlow v. Fitzgerald	457 U.S. 800	1982
Harris v. Joint School District	41 F.3d 447	9th Cir. 1994
Hazelwood School District v. Kuhlmeier	484 U.S. 260	1988
Hines v. Caston School Corporation	651 N.E.2d 330	Ind. App. 1995
Honig v. Doe	484 U.S. 305	1988
Horton v. Goose Creek Independent School District	693 F.2d 524	CATex 1982
Horton v. Goose Creek Independent School District	cert. denied, 103 S.Ct. 3536, 463 U.S. 1207, 22 Cal. 3d 508	1983
Hoyem v. Manhattan Beach City School District	585 P.2d 851	1978
Immediato v. Rye Neck School District	73 F.3d 454	U.S. App. 2d Cir. 1996
In re German Township School Directors	Common Pleas., Fayette Co., Pa. 46 S. and C. 562	1942
In re Rogers	234 N.Y.S.2d 172	1962
Indiana High School Athletic Association v. Raillce	329 N.E.2d 66	Ind. App. 1975
Ingraham v. Wright	430 U.S. 651	1977
Jager v. Douglas County School District	862 F.2d 824	11th Cir. 1989
Jeglin v. San Jacinto Unified School District	827 F. Supp. 1459	CD Cal. 1993
Jones v. Clear Creek Independent School District	977 F.2d 963	5th Cir. 1993
Katzman v. Cumberland Valley School District	479 A.2d 671	Pa. Commonwealth, 1984
Keyishian v. Board of Regents	385 U.S. 589	1967

Name	Reference	Date
L v. Independent School District No. 314	289 N.W.2d 112	Minn. 1979
Lanner v. Wimmer	662 F.2d 1349	10th Cir. 1981
Lee v. Weisman	112 S. Ct. 1249	505 U.S. 577, 1992
Lemon v. Kurtzman	403 U.S. 602	1971
Lucia v. Duggan	303 F.Supp. 112	D. Mass. 1969
McCollum v. Board of Education School District, No. 71	333 U.S. 203	1948
McLaughlin v. Tilendis	253 N.E.2d, 68 S.Ct. 461, 92 L.Ed. 649	1969
Mozert v. Hawkins County Board of Education	827 F.2d 1058	6th Cir. 1987
Mozert v. Hawkins County Board of Education	cert. denied, 484 U.S. 106	1988
New Jersey v. T.L.O.	469 U.S. 325	1985
Oberti v. Board of Education	995 F.2d 1204	3d Cir. 1993
O'Connor v. Board of Education	645 F.2d 578	7th Cir. 1981
In re: Patrick Y.	354 Md. 113, 729 A.2d 404	1999
Petition of Auditors of Hatfield Township	161 Pa. Super. 388, 54 A.2d 833	1947
Pickering v. Board of Education	291 U.S. 563	1968
Rich v. Kentucky County Day Inc.	793 S.W.2d 832	Ky. App. 1990
Rodriguez v. Board of Education	480 N.Y. S.2d 901	1984
Roemer v. Maryland Public Works Board	426 U.S. 736	1974
Roman v. Eskew	333 N.E.2d 138	Ind. App. 1975
S-1 v. Turlington	635 F.2d 342	5th Cir. 1981
S-1 v. Turlington	cert. denied, 454 U.S. 1230	1981
Sacramento City Unified School District v. Rachel H.	14 F.3d 1398	9th Cir. 1994

Name	Reference	Date
San Antonio v. Rodriguez	cert. denied, 454 U.S. 1230	1973
School Board of Nassau County v. Arline	679 F. Supp. 833	U.S. Dist. 1987
School District of Abingdon Township v. Schempp and Murray v. Curlett	480 U.S. 273	1963
Scott v. Board of Education of City of New York	597 N.Y. 2d 385	App. Div. 1993
Sherman v. Community Consolidated School District	8 F.3d 1160	7th Cir. 1993
Smith v. Archbishop of St. Louis	632 S.W.2d. 516	Mo. App. 1982
Smith v. Board of School Commissioners of Mobile County	827 F.2d 684	11th Cir. 1987
Smith v. School City of Hobart	811 F . Supp. 391	U.S. Dist. N.D. Ind. 1993
Special School District of St. Louis County v. Miener	498 F. Supp. 944, 673 F.2d 969	U.S. Dist. 1983
Special School District of St. Louis County v. Miener	cert. denied, 459 U.S. 916	1982
Steirer v. Bethlehem Area School District	987 F.2d 989	3d Cir. 1993
Steirer v. Bethlehem Area School District	cert. denied, 510 U.S. 824	1993
Stephanie v. Nebraska School Activities Association	684 F. Supp. 626	D. Neb. 1988
Stevenson v. Davenport Community School District	110 F.3d 1303	8th Cir. 1997
Stuart v. Nappi	443 F. Supp. 1235	D. Conn. 1978
Tinker v. Des Moines Independent Community School District	393 U.S. 503	1969

Name	Reference	Date
Veronica School District 47 J v. Acton	515 U.S. 646 115 S. Ct. 2386	1985
Virgil v. School Board of Columbia County, Florida	862 F.2d 1517	11th Cir. 1989
Wallace v. Jaffree	472 U.S. 38	1985
West Virginia State Board of Education v. Barnette	319 U.S. 624	1943
Wood v. Strickland	420 U.S. 308	1985
Wytrwal v. Saco School Board	70 F.3d 165	U.S. App. 1995
Yellow Springs v. Ohio Athletic Association	647 F.2d 651	6th Cir. 1981
Zorach v. Clauson	343 U.S. 306	1952

Glossary

Accommodations   Adjustments for students with disabilities that allow them to fully participate in testing situations along with nondisabled peers.

Alternative schools   Schools that deemphasize the usual structure and formality of traditional schools and stress flexibility and openness to educate students not coping in the traditional setting.

Assessment   A systematic process of determining the extent to which standards or objectives have been met.

Balanced calendar   Ordinarily spreads the legal number of school days per year over the full calendar year with breaks between quarters.

Balkanized   A situation in which an entity (e.g., school, profession) fragments into competing and sometimes hostile groups.

Barrier-free design   The planning for complete access to all facilities by disabled persons.

Benchmark   Progress indicator of students' level of achievement of standard or objective.

Block schedule   A schedule that provides longer periods or blocks of time (often ninety minutes) within the school day, and one that frequently schedules subjects on alternate days.

Buckley amendment   A statute that provides protection for the privacy of students and their parents in connection with school records.

Budget   A spending plan over a specific amount of time designed to meet educational needs.

Charter school   An independent public school of choice that is freed from many of the rules of the school district to meet the specific needs of a group of students. Though freed from some rules, it is held accountable for results.

Collaboration   The process of two or more agencies (e.g., the school and community health services) working together in a shared decision-making venture to meet some mutually identified needs.

Common law   Derives from English common law passed on for generations and has come to be recognized as basic law. These "laws" prevail in the absence of other laws until they are overturned by more recent court decisions or legislative acts.

Community   A group of people conscious of a collective identity through common physical, geographic, cognitive, and/or affective relationships, needs and goals.

Constitutional tort   The genesis is found in the Civil Rights Act of 1871. It provides for the liability of a person acting under the aegis of the state who violates another's civil rights.

Content standards   Statements of what should be learned in various content (subject) areas, usually formulated by professional organizations associated with the subject (e.g., the National Council of Teachers of Mathematics).

Coprincipalship   An arrangement in which two or more persons share principalship duties as team equals.

Corporal punishment   The use of physical force as a means of enforcing discipline or punishing behavior.

Crisis team   A preselected group of people who apply their expertise (e.g., counseling) for those suffering from trauma (e.g., a suicide in the school).

Cyberfair   The exchange of displays of student projects from cooperating schools (even worldwide) via the Internet.

Decentralization   Key decisions are made at the operating level—in most cases, at the school building level.

Digital children   A term describing today's children, who understand and utilize technology as a matter of course of everyday life.

Disability   An objectively measurable impairment or dysfunction limiting or prohibiting performance.

Educational specifications   Descriptions of who will be involved in what kinds of learning/teaching activities and the relationships among those activities within the proposed structure.

Eight Year Study   A cooperative study between colleges and universities and thirty secondary schools that encouraged the schools to reconstruct their curricula to serve the needs of all youth regardless of whether they were going to college.

Equal Access Act   A law that makes it unlawful to deny equal access or fair opportunity or to discriminate against any student-initiated, noncurricular group of the basis of religion, politics, or philosophy.

Evaluation   The reflective process of gathering, analyzing, and valuing data/information to make decisions for action.

Flexible schedule   A schedule usually consisting of short time modules so that variable time modules can be allocated to different subjects or activities as opposed to rigid and equal time modules for every subject or activity.

Fourteenth Amendment   Prohibits states or individuals from depriving any person of life, liberty, or property without due process of law.

Full-service school   A school that attempts to integrate a number of programs such as health care, mental health service, parent education, and preschool or after-school care within or associated with the school. Usually houses collaborative ventures with many community service agencies.

Goal displacement   A situation in which original goals are abandoned in favor of matters perceived as more pressing.

Handicap   An arbitrarily imposed relative position in a particular society.

Hawthorne effect   A phenomenon observed in studies conducted at the Western Electric Company (in the late 1930s) in which workers would increase their production when they perceived that experimental changes (e.g., better lighting) were positive and that the company was interested in them. Associated with the early human relations movement.

Home schooling   The situation in which parents or someone they designate teaches their children in the home rather than the children attending a public or private school.

Improving America's Schools Act   An act requiring states to develop standards by which the success of schools are to be assessed.

In loco parentis   The school stands in place of the parent.

Individualized Education Plan (IEP)   A required plan to educate a student with a disability.

Infosphere   A term attempting to describe the accessible, rich data/information resources surrounding us.

In-service education   Employee training usually on an administratively selected topic related to building or district needs, and often a stand-alone event.

Interstate School Leaders Licensure Consortium (ISLLC)   A consortium of states articulating standards for the licensure of school administrators.

Lancaster Plan An organization of instruction whereby the older and more talented students in the upper grades tutor students in the lower grades.

Lemon test A tripartite test used by the courts since 1971 to determine the relationship between government and religion as related to the First Amendment.

Magnet schools Schools designed to meet the needs of students with special talents or interests (e.g., music, art, science.) Usually have much wider attendance areas than traditional schools.

Multiage grouping Grouping students within age spans of two to three years rather, for example, than just six-year-olds together in one grade arrangement.

National Policy Board for Educational Administration An association formed by ten professional organizations to formulate standards of knowledge and skills required for school administrators.

Net generation The generation of students who are knowledgeable about technology, particularly the Internet, and who use it with ease.

Objectives Short-range aims of a program, often with specific time frames. They usually set out specific steps toward achieving goals.

Organization A system of relationships among persons to achieve specific goals, having membership criteria, assigned responsibilities, and resources to accomplish goals.

Organizational culture Observable artifacts and consistent behaviors of people in an organization resulting from shared assumptions about realities, relationships, and purposes.

Performance standards Definitions of levels of learning considered to be satisfactory when students can demonstrate and apply what they have learned.

Postmodernism A view that uncertainty and indeterminacy are ever present; thus, there are only the results of discourse as opposed to facts or truths.

Quality circle A formal decision-making process to identify problems, determine possible solutions, and formulate recommendations to the administration.

Reality-oriented learning Learning opportunities structured around real-life problems and situations, occasionally involving work or intern experiences.

Regular education initiative Sometimes referred to as the inclusion law, it requires students with disabilities to be educated with their nondisabled peers.

Released time A situation in which students are released from school during regular school hours to attend religious instruction.

Reliability A test instrument is consistently valid.

Relocatable Sometimes referred to as a "portable classroom," a temporary classroom or office that can be moved to or from a site as needed.

Satan Deluder Act The Massachusetts Law of 1642 requiring colonists to educate their children so they could read the Bible and thus defeat Satan. Considered one of the earliest compulsory education laws.

Save harmless Educators may be indemnified for monetary losses for damage claims as long as their tortious acts occurred within the scope of their employment.

School choice The opportunity for parents to choose which public school within a district their children will attend, regardless of attendance area boundaries.

Service learning Planned, coordinated programs in which students are involved in experiences in the community and at the same time meet needs of those served.

Services coordinator A person with business and management skills hired to assist the principal so that the principal may devote more time to instructional leadership.

Site-based decision making The delegation of authority to the individual school to make decisions ordinarily reserved to central administration (e.g., budget allocation, personnel decisions).

Situational leadership The view that as situations change such as the maturity of the followers' skills or commitment to the organization's goals; emergence of a crisis threatening to destroy the organization, to be effective the leader's behavior must also change.

Sputnik A basketball-sized Russian satellite launched in 1957 that marked the beginning of space exploration and technology as well as focused national attention on education.

Stakeholders Those persons who have an interest or concern regarding the activities of a school as participants or affected observers.

Student activity funds Monies raised by student organizations, athletic events, fees, drama presentations, or similar activities not part of the regular budget.

Supervision of instruction The process whereby the principal works cooperatively with teachers to improve teaching and learning.

Theory Systematically organized information with a series of assumptions or hypotheses devised to help analyze, predict, or otherwise explain observed phenomena.

Theory X   Postulates that people dislike work and need direct control or they will avoid it.

Theory Y   Postulates that people can find work satisfying and will work well if committed to organizational goals.

Theory Z   Postulates that workers who are involved in decision making will develop loyalty and will be effective producers. Sometimes called Japanese management.

360-degree supervision   The collection of feedback about a person's job performance from multiple sources surrounding the individual.

Title IX   A federal law stating "[n]o person . . . shall, on the basis of sex, be excluded from participation in, or be denied the benefits of, or be subject to discrimination under any education program or activity receiving federal funds."

Tort   A civil wrong, not involving a breach of contract, for which damages may be recovered in a court of law.

Tracking   Placing students into a particular learning group (e.g., college bound, vocational), based upon their perceived abilities.

Transformational leadership   A process that leads others to higher levels of motivation, performance, and commitment to the organization's goals, even to the sacrifice of self-interests.

Validity   The test instrument measures what it is intended to measure.

Virtual high school   Access to courses, sometimes leading to a diploma, via The internet. Most virtual high schools at this time are state sponsored and have statewide access.

Weberian bureaucracy   A hierarchical structure, top-down authority, with control exercised through written rules and regulations. Work is divided into specializations.

WICCA   A movement or religion described as polytheistic, having paganlike practices, revering the earth or natural world.

Work-based learning   A school-organized and -supervised experience in the world of work, which would assist the student in the transition from school to a career.

Index